S0-BZI-746

PEARSON CUSTOM LIBRARY

LATIN

LAT 101/102
University of Rhode Island

PEARSON

Cover Art: "Ancient Mosaic" courtesy of Syagci/iStockphoto; Naphtalina, "Antique Book" courtesy of Naphtalina/iStockphoto; "in the name of Christ" courtesy of tempurasLightbulb/iStockphoto. Additional images courtesy of Corbis.

Copyright © 2014 by Pearson Learning Solutions

All rights reserved.

Permission in writing must be obtained from the publisher before any part of this work may be reproduced or transmitted in any form or by any means, electronic or mechanical, including photocopying and recording, or by any information storage or retrieval system.

Additional copyright information is included, where applicable, as a footnote at the beginning of each chapter.

Please visit our website at *www.pearsonlearningsolutions.com.*

Attention Bookstores: For permission to return any unsold stock, contact us at *pe-uscustomreturns@pearson.com.*

Pearson Learning Solutions, 501 Boylston Street, Suite 900, Boston, MA 02116
A Pearson Education Company
www.pearsoned.com

Printed in the United States of America.
V092

ISBN 10: 1-269-69482-0
ISBN 13: 978-1-269-69482-7

PEARSON
mylatinlab™ *Salve!*

Part of the **award-winning** MyLanguageLabs suite of online learning and assessment systems for basic language courses, MyLatinLab brings together—in one convenient, easily navigable site—a wide array of language-learning tools and resources, including an interactive version of the student text, an online Student Activities Manual, and all materials from the audio program. Chapter tests, tutorials, and English grammar readiness checks personalize instruction to meet the unique needs of individual students. Instructors can use the system to make assignments, set grading parameters, listen to student-created audio recordings, and provide feedback on student work. MyLatinLab can be packaged with the text at a substantial savings. For more information, visit us online at http://mylanguagelabs.com/books.html

A GUIDE TO IN-TEXT ICON

 Text Audio Program | This icon indicates that recorded material to accompany this text is available in MyLatinLab, on audio CD, or the Companion Website.

Note to Students:

Your text has been customized to fit your course exactly. For this reason, you'll notice that your book includes two sets of page numbers. The Table of Contents and Index of your custom book refer to the sequential page numbers that are located in the bottom corner of each page. The second set of page numbers are the original page numbers of the parent text(s) from which your custom text is derived; use these page numbers when referencing MyLatinLab or other in-text references in your text.

Table of Contents

Chapter 1. Intrōductiō
Kenneth Kitchell/Thomas Sienkcwicz

1

Chapter 2. In Tabernā
Kenneth Kitchell/Thomas Sienkewicz

17

Chapter 3. Negōtium Bonum
Kenneth Kitchell/Thomas Sienkewicz

29

Chapter 4. Intrat Hermēs
Kenneth Kitchell/Thomas Sienkewicz

43

Chapter 5. In Forum
Kenneth Kitchell/Thomas Sienkewicz

59

Chapter 6. In Lūdō Chīrōnis
Kenneth Kitchell/Thomas Sienkewicz

73

Chapter 7. Post Lūdum
Kenneth Kitchell/Thomas Sienkewicz

89

Chapter 8. Eāmus Domum
Kenneth Kitchell/Thomas Sienkewicz

107

Chapter 9. Per Viās Rōmānās
Kenneth Kitchell/Thomas Sienkewicz

119

Chapter 10. Quantī Id Constat?
Kenneth Kitchell/Thomas Sienkewicz

129

Chapter 11. Domum
Kenneth Kitchell/Thomas Sienkewicz

143

Chapter 12. In Domō Magnā
Kenneth Kitchell/Thomas Sienkewicz

157

Chapter 13. Māter et Fīlia
Kenneth Kitchell/Thomas Sienkewicz

173

Chapter 14. Dē Perseō
Kenneth Kitchell/Thomas Sienkewicz
187

Chapter 15. Frāter et Soror
Kenneth Kitchell/Thomas Sienkewicz
201

Chapter 16. In Cēnā
Kenneth Kitchell/Thomas Sienkewicz
215

Chapter 17. Dē Amōre et Lūdīs
Kenneth Kitchell/Thomas Sienkewicz
229

Chapter 18. Fugitīvus
Kenneth Kitchell/Thomas Sienkewicz
241

Chapter 19. Vēnātiō
Kenneth Kitchell/Thomas Sienkewicz
255

Chapter 20. Nōn Perseus sed Herculēs!
Kenneth Kitchell/Thomas Sienkewicz
271

Chapter 21. Speculum Aēneum
Kenneth Kitchell/Thomas Sienkewicz
285

Chapter 22. Harēna Pūrgātur
Kenneth Kitchell/Thomas Sienkewicz
301

Chapter 23. Consilia
Kenneth Kitchell/Thomas Sienkewicz
317

Chapter 24. In Theātrō
Kenneth Kitchell/Thomas Sienkewicz
335

Chapter 25. Parātūs Magnī
Kenneth Kitchell/Thomas Sienkewicz
351

Chapter 26. Epulae Rēgum
Kenneth Kitchell/Thomas Sienkewicz
367

Chapter 27. Duo Dōna
Kenneth Kitchell/Thomas Sienkewicz
385

Chapter 28. Labōrēs Herculis
Kenneth Kitchell/Thomas Sienkewicz
399

Chapter 29. Avus Cārus
Kenneth Kitchell/Thomas Sienkewicz
417

Chapter 30. Rēs Agendae
Kenneth Kitchell/Thomas Sienkewicz
433

Chapter 31. Fīat
Kenneth Kitchell/Thomas Sienkewicz
451

Chapter 32. Mementō Morī
Kenneth Kitchell/Thomas Sienkewicz
467

Chapter 33. Post Mortem
Kenneth Kitchell/Thomas Sienkewicz   485

Chapter 34. Patrōnus et Cliēns
Kenneth Kitchell/Thomas Sienkewicz   499

Appendix
Kenneth Kitchell/Thomas Sienkewicz   517

Verba Omnia
Kenneth Kitchell/Thomas Sienkewicz   543

Verba Discenda
Kenneth Kitchell/Thomas Sienkewicz   573

Maps
Kenneth Kitchell/Thomas Sienkewicz   589

Index   595

1

Augustus

Intrōductiō

Some Advice from a Roman Emperor

As you begin your study of Latin, consider this proverb, which was a favorite of the emperor Augustus:

> *FESTĪNĀ LENTĒ* Make haste slowly!

This seeming contradiction (we call this an oxymoron) offers some good advice. You certainly want to move ahead quickly in your study of Latin, but not so fast that you do not learn well as you go along.

Notice how the proverb is written all in capital letters with long marks (macrons) over some vowels. We will explain later in this chapter why this was done.

Antequam Legis

Drāmatis Persōnae

As you learn Latin in this book, you will read a story in Latin about two fictional families who live in Rome in the year 9 B.C. One of these families is upper class. The other is lower class. In this *drāmatis persōnae* (characters in the drama) are some brief introductions of the most important characters you will encounter. Others will be introduced as they appear.

GRAMMATICA
Writing Latin
The Latin Alphabet
Pronouncing Latin
Parts of Speech

ORBIS TERRĀRUM RŌMĀNUS
Iūdaea et Arcus Titī

MŌRĒS RŌMĀNĪ
Inscriptiōnēs Rōmānae

LATĪNA HODIERNA
English Loan Words

ANGULUS GRAMMATICUS
The Birth of "W" and "J"

> Meet the members of the Familia Valeriae and the Familia Servilii.

From *Disce! An Introductory Latin Course, volume 1*, First Edition. Francesco Bonavita. Copyright © 2011 by Pearson Education, Inc. Published by Pearson Prentice Hall. All rights reserved.

Familia Valeria (the lower-class family)

Plōtia (*aet.* 59) = **Valerius** (†)

C. Licinius († 14 B.C.) = **Valeria** (*aet.* 40)

M. Aelius (*aet.* 25) = **Licinia** (*aet.* 18)

C. Licinius C.f. (*aet.* 20) [*Leg. XVIII trans Rhēnum*]

M. Aelius M.f. (*infans*) ("**Maximus**")

Key:	†	=	deceased
	aet.	=	*aetātis* (age)
	C.	=	Gaius
	M.	=	Marcus
	C.f.	=	*Gaiī fīlius* (son of Gaius)
	M.f.	=	*Marcī fīlius* (son of Marcus)

Valeria, a 40-year-old widow of the farmer Licinius from Verona. Unable to run the farm alone and with her son in the army, she moved to Rome from Verona after the death of Licinius a few years ago. In Rome she now runs a snack shop stand near the Forum. Valeria put all the money she had into the shop, and as a result, she and her family live in a less respectable part of town called the Subura.

C. Licinius C.f., the son of Valeria and her late husband. While technically the legal head of the family, Licinius is in the army on the German border and has left his mother in charge of the family.

Licinia, Valeria's 18-year-old, married daughter, who works with Valeria at the snack shop stand. Licinia is pregnant.

Aelius, Licinia's husband. He works as a blacksmith in his own small shop near their apartment in the Subura.

Flāvia, a German slave girl who works in the shop and helps around the house.

Sōcratēs, Licinius' pet monkey. Licinius left the monkey with his mother when he enlisted. Socrates now "works" in Valeria's shop as entertainment for her customers.

Familia Servīliī (the upper-class family)

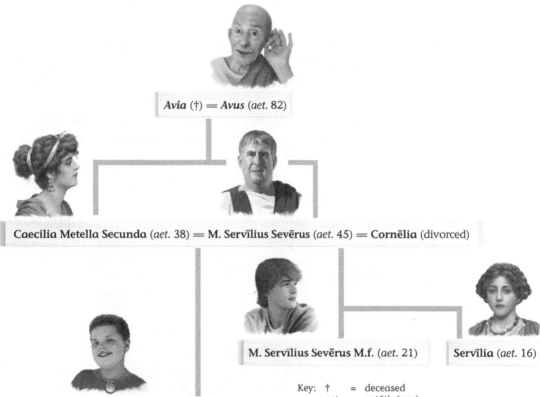

Avia (†) ═ *Avus* (aet. 82)

Caecilia Metella Secunda (*aet.* 38) ═ **M. Servīlius Sevērus** (*aet.* 45) ═ **Cornēlia** (divorced)

M. Servīlius Sevērus M.f. (*aet.* 21)   **Servīlia** (*aet.* 16)

L. Servīlius Noniānus (*aet.* 10)

Key: †   =   deceased
      aet.   =   *aetātis* (age)
      avia   =   grandmother
      avus   =   grandfather
      M.   =   Marcus
      L.   =   Lucius
      M.f.   =   *Marcī fīlius* (son of Marcus)

M. Servilius Severus, actually existed. He was consul in 3 A.D. At the time of this story he is 45 years old and is running for the office of praetor. Servilius had two children by his first wife, Cornelia, from whom he is now divorced: a 21-year-old son also named M. Servilius Severus and a 16-year-old daughter named Servilia.

M. Servilius Severus M.f., the 21-year-old son of Servilius. Marcus is preparing to study rhetoric in Greece before beginning his political career.

Servilia, Marcus' 16-year-old sister. She is anticipating marriage in the near future.

Caecilia Metella Secunda, present wife of Servilius.

L. Servilius Nonianus, the 10-year-old son of Servilius and Caecilia Metella. Known better as Lucius, he attends a school run by the grammarian Chiron and has a *paedagogus* (slave assigned to his education) named Hermes.

POSTQUAM LĒGISTĪ

1. How does the composition of the Licinia and Servilia families compare to that of modern American families and especially to your own family?
2. What kinds of lives do the characters in their twenties lead? How does this compare to the lives of you and your friends from high school?

Grammatica A

Writing Latin

A Roman living in the year 9 B.C. would have written the emperor Augustus' favorite proverb, *Festīnā lentē,* all in capital letters with little or no space between the words. It would have looked something like this:

FESTINALENTE

By the time that the moveable-type printing press was invented by Johannes Gutenberg (c.1450), small letters and real spacing between words had been introduced. So the earliest books printed in Latin used a font much like the one used in this book. This means that the capital letters we use in this book are the same ones the Romans used, but the small letters are different. Reading Latin as it is written in this book is easy for us, but it would not have been easy for an ancient Roman, any more than

READINGENGLISHINTHISFORMATISEASYFORUS.

Below at left is a page from a sixth-century manuscript of a letter by Pliny the Younger now in the Pierpont Morgan Library in New York. Notice how all the letters are capitalized and run together with no punctuation or spaces between the words.

At right is a transcription of the first lines at the top of the manuscript page (Book 3, iii):

EPISTVLARVM

·C·PLINIVS· CALVISIO SVO SALVTEM

NESCIOANVLLVMIVCVNDIVSTEMPVS

EXEGERIMQVAMQVONVPERAPVDSPV
RINNAMFVIADEOQVIDEMVTNEMINEM
MAGISINSENECTVTESIMODOSENESCE
REDATVMESTAEMVLARIVELIMNIHIL
ESTENIMILLOVITAEGENEREDISTIN
CTIVS

Cōdex Latīnus

EPISTVLARVM

·C·PLINIVS · CALVISIO SVO SALVTEM

NESCIO AN VLLVM IVCVNDIVS TEMPVS
EXEGERIM QVAM QVO NVPER APVD SPV
RINNAM FVI ADEO QVIDEM VT NEMINEM
MAGIS IN SENECTVTE SI MODO SENESCE
RE DATVM EST AEMVLARI VELIM NIHIL
EST ENIM ILLO VITAE GENERE DISTIN
CTIVS

and here is how these lines would be written today:

Epistulārum
C. Plinius Calvisiō suō salūtem.
Nesciō, an ullum iucundius tempus exēgerim, quam quō nuper apud Spurinnam fuī, adeō quidem, ut nēminem magis in senectūte, si modo senēnescere datum est, aemulārī velim; nihil est enim illō vītae genere distinctius.

Which version is easier for you to read? Which one would be easier for an ancient Roman?

The Latin Alphabet

English has 24 letters that are ultimately derived from the Latin alphabet.

A B C D E F G H I K L M N O P Q R S T U V X Y Z
a b c d e f g h i k l m n o p q r s t u v x y z

The letter V was also used for U. The small letters came later.

Pronouncing Latin

It is important to remember that we have no recordings of ancient Romans speaking Latin, so our modern pronunciations of Latin words are approximations. We know that there were many variations of pronunciation across the Roman Empire. The same is true for English of course. Just ask people from London, Boston, and Brooklyn to say "horse" or "murder."

Moreover, Latin was a living language spoken across the Mediterranean and Europe for millennia. Different pronunciations arose in various geographical areas and historical periods.

There are two major pronunciation systems in use today. The "classical" Latin pronunciation represents our best reconstruction of what the Latin of authors like Cicero and Caesar sounded like. The system called "ecclesiastical," "church," or "medieval" was more influenced by the sound of Italian. We use classical pronunciation in this book, but you will often hear church Latin sung in concert halls.

Remember always that you only get better by trying and that your ear needs to hear the language to help your brain understand it. So the only rule is to keep trying and model yourself on the pronunciation of your teacher and the online drills.

General Rules for Pronouncing Latin

There are two important keys to pronouncing Latin:

- There are no silent letters. Even final e's are pronounced. Latin is essentially WYSIWYG (What you see is what you get!).
- Unlike English, Latin is quite consistent in the sound a letter represents. This is especially true of vowels. Once you get used to a few rules and patterns, you can easily predict the pronunciation of a Latin word.

Consonants

Though the majority of Latin consonants are pronounced much as they are in English, the sounds of the letters are not always identical in the two languages. Note the following differences:

C   C is always hard, sounding like a K. *Cicerō* is pronounced "Kickero."

G   G is always hard, as in "great." It is never soft, as in "gem."

J/I   There is no J in classical Latin. The letter I took its place. The consonant "I" is pronounced like the Y in "yes."

R   The R was slightly rolled in Latin as it is in many modern languages.

S   Almost always a pure S sound, as in "guess." Try not to make it a Z as in "rays."

V   V is pronounced like the English letter W. Thus, the Latin *vector* is pronounced "wector" and *vortex* is pronounced "wortex."

W   There is no W in Latin.

X   Between vowels, X is pronounced as it is in English. Sometimes it begins a word (usually a Greek loan word). In this case, pronounce it like "KS."

Notā Bene: Pronounce every consonant. You pronounce *committō* (I commit) as *com-mit-tō*, with the first two syllables beginning **and** ending with a consonant.

Consonant Blends

GN   This is **not** pronounced as if in two words (e.g. "big nosed"). It is a nasal blend. Try to make it sound a bit like the "gn" in the Italian "lasagna."

QU   As in English, rather like the "kw" sound in "quiet."

CH   Latin CH is pronounced like the "ch" in "choir" or "chiropractor," **not** like the CH in the English word "church." Most Latin words with "ch" come from Greek letter "chi."

PH   Although many Latin students and teachers pronounce this like an "f," technically this combination of letters is pronounced like "p" followed by a breath. Most Latin words with PH come from the Greek letter "phi."

TH   Although many Latin students and teachers pronounce this like the "th" in "the," technically this combination of letters is pronounced like "t" followed by a breath. Most Latin words with TH come from the Greek letter "theta."

EXERCEĀMUS!

 1-1   **Pronouncing the Latin G**

Many Latin words come into English largely unchanged in spelling. These are called Latin loan words. We need to pay attention, however, to the Latin pronunciation of these words. For example, we use the Latin hard "g" in the word "gladiator." Sometimes, however, we change the Latin hard "g" to a soft one. Try pronouncing the g in each of the following words like the g in "girl." That is how the Romans pronounced it!

genius (spirit)	*agenda* (the things that must be done)
rigidus (stiff)	*magicus* (magical)

 1-2   **Pronouncing the Latin C**

The same applies to the letter C which, like the Romans, we pronounce hard in words like "campus" and "clamor." Frequently, however, we make the "c" soft in words we borrowed from the Romans. So try pronouncing a hard "c" in each of the following Latin words.

circus (racecourse)	*Cerēs* (goddess of grain)
censor (judge)	*biceps* (two-headed)
facile (easy)	*speciēs* (type)

Vowels

The same five vowels exist in Latin and English:

a   e   i   o   u

In Latin, vowels have two pronunciations depending upon whether they are long or short. In *DISCE!* a long mark (macron) is placed over long vowels to help you recognize them: ā, ē, ī, ō, ū. Romans did not use or need these macrons, but you should pay attention to these marks—they can be as important to meaning as the difference in English between the sounds of "meet" and "met" or "read" and "read" (past tense).

Here is a chart showing how vowels are pronounced in Latin:

SHORT VOWELS		LONG VOWELS	
Vowel	**English Example**	**Vowel**	**English Example**
a	ahead	ā	father
e	bet	ē	may
i	bin	ī	see
o	off	ō	role
u	put	ū	mood

Y   Extremely rare in Latin, this letter was introduced to spell words borrowed from Greek, like *peristӯlium* (a court surrounded by columns). The sound of "y" was equivalent to that of Greek upsilon, a sharp "u" sound made by combining the sounds "ee" and "u" together. Unlike English, it is always a vowel in Latin.

EXERCEĀMUS!

 1-3 **Pronouncing Latin Vowels**

Now apply the guidelines for the pronunciation of Latin vowels to these words from Exercises 1-1 and 1-2.

HINT: Don't forget to pronounce the g and c the classical Latin way!

genius	*agenda*
rigidus	*magicus*
facile	*circus*
Cerēs	*censor*
biceps	*speciēs*

Diphthongs

In addition to these simple or single vowels, Latin also combines two vowels to create a single sound. These double vowels are called diphthongs. Diphthongs are always long.

Here is a chart of Latin diphthongs:

DIPHTHONG	EXAMPLE
ae	**ai**sle
au	**ou**t
ei	**ei**ght
eu	**ey-oo**
oe	t**oi**l
ui	Ph**ooey**!

EXERCEĀMUS!

 1-4   **Pronunciation: Vowels and Diphthongs**

Use the key to pronounce the Latin words written in bold.

HINT: Always stress the first syllable in a two-syllable word.

Vowel	English Example	Latin Word	English Meaning
a	ahead	*at*	but
		capax	spacious
e	bet	*et*	and
		ede	eat
i	bin	*in*	in
		is	he
o	off	*odor*	scent
		dolor	sorrow
u	put	*ut*	in order to, that
		ulcus	ulcer
ā	father	*āla*	wing
		amās	you love
ē	may	*Lēthē*	river of forgetfulness
		nē	indeed
ī	see	*quī*	who
		sīc	thus
ō	rotate	*dōs*	talent
		ōrō	I pray
ū	mood	*ūsūs*	use
		frūx	crops
ae	**ai**sle	*aes*	bronze
		faex	sediment
au	**ou**t	*aut*	or
		pauper	poor
ei	n**eigh**	*ei*	alas!
		eia	wow!
eu	**ey-oo**	*seu*	or if
		neuter	neither
oe	t**oi**l	*Oedipūs*	Oedipus
ui	ph**ooey**!	*cui*	to whom

Syllables

Now that you know how to pronounce Latin consonants, vowels, and diphthongs, let's talk a little more about pronouncing whole words. Here are a few simple rules to remember:

1. There is a syllable for every vowel or diphthong

> *rabiēs* (ra·bi·es)   3 syllables
>
> *vacuum* (va·cu·um)   3 syllables

2. A consonant between two vowels is pronounced with the second vowel.

> *rabiēs* (ra·bi·es not rab·i·es)

3. When two or more consonants are between two vowels, only the last consonant is pronounced with the second vowel.

spectātor (spec·ta·tor)   consortium (con·sor·ti·um)

Stress

Word stress is important in English. Consider these sentences:

> I **refuse** to pick up the **refuse**.
> He cannot **conduct** the orchestra because of his previous **conduct**.
> Why do you **project** such negative vibes about my **project**?

In Latin stress is regular and predictable. The stress lands only on one of three syllables. Grammarians give them formal names. The technical terms are Latin-based. Let's look at *Rōmānī*, the Latin word for Romans.

	RŌ	MĀ	NĪ
Formal name	**antepenult**	**penult**	**ultima**
Latin meaning	before the next to last	next to last	last
Disce! nickname	S3 (syllable 3)	S2 (syllable 2)	S1 (syllable 1)

Rules for Stress

The following rules for syllable stress in Latin are simplified and omit the obvious (e.g., a one-syllable word takes the stress on the first syllable!), but they will get you started. Exceptions will be introduced when they are important.

1. The stressed syllable can never go further back than **S3**.
   Thus: Ō·ce·a·nī is impossible. The stress is Ō·**CE**·a·nī

2. Always stress the first syllable of a two-syllable word.

3. For words of three or more syllables,
   - if **S2** is short, the stress tends to fall back to **S3**,
   - if **S2** is long, it attracts the stress.

A syllable can be long two ways. It is long if:

1. it contains a long vowel, as in *fě·mi·NĀ·rum*

2. it comes before a double consonant like the *e* followed by *nd* in *a·GEN·da*

(There are exceptions to this, but you needn't worry about them right now.)

Latin Stress—Examples

	S3/ANTEPENULT	S2/PENULT	S1/ULTIMA
one-syllable word			*AT* *IN*
two-syllable word		*ACtor* *CAMpus* *FIat*	
three syllables or more, S2/penult long		*aGENda* *reGĀLia* *imiTĀtor*	
three syllables or more, S2/penult short	*FAcile* *HAbitat* *IAnitor*		

Grammatica B

Parts of Speech

Latin has the eight parts of speech similar to ours:

Verb (*verbum*, word): expresses an action or state of being. Here are some Latin verbs and their English equivalents. The English words in parentheses are derived from the Latin words and are called **derivatives**.

dūcit	leads (induce)	*dīcit*	says (dictate)
ambulat	walks (perambulate)	*respondet*	replies (respond)

Noun (*nōmen*, name): the name of a person, place, or thing.

fēmina	woman (femininity)	*taberna*	shop (tavern)
vir	man (virility)	*Forum*	forum

All of the nouns listed can serve as the subject of the Latin verbs we listed above, like this:

Fēmina ambulat.   The woman walks./A woman walks.

Adjective (*adiectum*, added to): describes a person, place, or thing.

bona fēmina	a good woman	*taberna parāta*	a prepared shop
magnus vir	a large man	*Forum meum*	my Forum

Notice that the endings on the adjectives change.

Pronoun (*prōnōmen*, instead of a noun): takes the place of a noun.

ego	I	*tū*	you
mē	me	*nōs*	we

Adverb (*adverbum*, to the verb): modifies a verb, an adjective, or another adverb.

valdē	very	*nōn*	not
nunc	now	*mox*	soon

Preposition (*praepositum*, placed before): expresses direction or relation.

in	in, on	*ē, ex*	out of
ad	to, toward	*sub*	under

Conjunction (*coniunctum*, joined together): connects two words, phrases, or sentences together.

et	and	*sed*	but

Interjection (*interiectum*, thrown between): an expression of surprise or emphasis.

Ō!	Oh! Hey!	*Heu!*	Alas!

Notā Bene: Unlike English, Latin has no words for "the" or "a," so you can translate any Latin noun the ways we translate *fēmina* here:

> *fēmina* woman, the woman, a woman

Orbis Terrārum Rōmānus

Iūdaea et Arcus Titī

Although most of the action in the narrative of *Disce!* takes place in the city of Rome, the city was the capital of a wide empire spanning east to west from Syria to Spain and north to south from the Danube to the Sahara. In order to illustrate this connection between Rome and her empire, we offer the Arch of Titus in the Roman Forum and its ties with Rome's Jewish Wars in the first century A.D.

Arcus Titī

Judaea became a Roman province in 6 A.D., but the territory had been under Roman control for decades before that date. The Jews revolted against Roman rule from 66 to 72 A.D. Jerusalem fell in 70 A.D. and the Jewish temple was destroyed. The Jews were defeated at Masada in 72 A.D. by the general Titus, son of the emperor Vespasian. Titus erected a triumphal arch in the Roman Forum to commemorate his victory in 80 A.D. Decoration on the arch includes the Roman army carrying plunder from Jerusalem.

Triumphus Titī

A series of coins were issued to celebrate the suppression of the revolt in Judaea in 70–71 A.D. In the coin at right a female figure representing captured Judaea sits under a palm tree while a Roman stands victorious at left with the inscription *Iūdaea Capta* ("Judaea Captured"). The abbreviation S.C. stands for "by the Decree of the Senate.

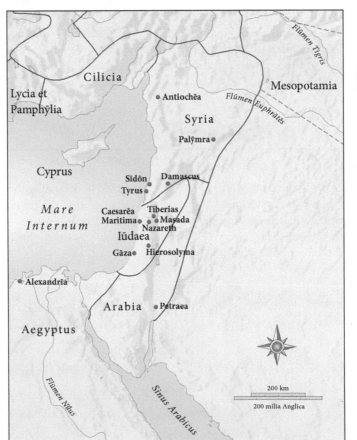

Iūdaea capta

Iūdaea

Gemma

Senātus Populusque Rōmānus is often abbreviated in inscriptions as **S.P.Q.R.** This abbreviation is still widely used in modern Rome.

Mōrēs Rōmānī

Inscriptiōnēs Rōmānae

Romans often carved writing onto buildings and other stone objects. Such writing is called an **inscription**. You can see such an inscription on the façade of the Arch of Titus. Notice how the inscription is written all in capital letters with no division between the words and no macrons. Here is a transcription of the inscription.

Inscriptiō Arcūs Titī

SENATVS
POPVLVSQVEROMANVS
DIVOTITODIVIVESPASIANIF
VESPASIANOAVGVSTO

Now here is the inscription written with word divisions and with the one abbreviation in the inscription expanded and underlined:

SENATVS
POPVLVSQVE · ROMANVS
DIVO · TITO · DIVI · VESPASIANI · <u>FILIO</u>
VESPASIANO · AVGVSTO

And here is how this inscription reads in English:

The Senate
And the Roman People
To the Divine Titus Vespasian Augustus
Son of the Divine Vespasian

Arcus Americānus in Eborāco Novō

The emperor Vespasian reigned 69–79 A.D. His son Titus reigned 79–81 A.D. The Romans often called their emperors divine after they died. Abbreviations are very common in Latin inscriptions, but the only abbreviation in this one is F[ILIO] "to the son"). Also notice the V's in *POPVLUS, ROMANVS,* and *AVGVSTVS,* which are usually transcribed as U's.

Gemma

Washington Square Arch in New York City, erected in 1889 to celebrate the 100th anniversary of George Washington's inauguration as President. The arch is modeled on Roman triumphal arches like the Arch of Titus. Another, more recent, U.S. example is The Millennnium Gate, dedicated in Atlanta, Georgia, in 2008.

Latīna Hodierna

English Loan Words

Many of the Latin words in the exercises should look familiar to you because they are actually English words borrowed from Latin. Remember that the pronunciation and stress of these words is not necessarily the same in Latin and English. This is also true for the meanings of these words. Here are a few examples of English loan words that have meanings different from the parent Latin word.

LATIN WORD	LATIN MEANING	ENGLISH MEANING
arēna	sand	enclosed area for competition
habitat	he lives	place where an animal or plant lives
minister	servant	a member of the clergy; a government official
rabiēs	madness	a disease of the nervous system
serum	whey, watery part of milk	clear part of blood used for medicinal purposes
trivia	places where three roads meet	commonplace or unimportant facts

QUID PUTĀS?

1. Compare the English proverb "Haste makes waste" to the Latin *Festīnā lentē*. Which proverb do you prefer and why?
2. Why do you think the English word "arena" comes from the Latin word for sand?
3. Why and where might you find Latin inscriptions on modern American buildings? Look for inscriptions on some of your campus buildings. Are any of them in Latin? If so, find out what they mean.

Use this *Verba Ūtenda* for the exercises that follow.

Gemma

Verba Ūtenda and *Verba Discenda:* Words marked in **bold** in the *Verba Ūtenda* (words to be used) become *Verba Discenda* (words to be learned) in that chapter. So

nōmen, nōminis n. name

is becoming a *Verbum Discendum* in this chapter. Right now the form *nōmen* makes sense to you but *nōminis* does not, but we always list *Verba Discenda* the way they are found in a Latin dictionary. We will explain the second form soon. The n. stands for neuter gender, which will also be explained later.

 VERBA ŪTENDA

ambulat walks	*fēmina* woman	*respondet* responds
clāmat shouts	*fīlia* daughter	*stat* stands
currit runs	*fīlius* son	**tibi your, to you**
dat gives	**mihi my, to me**	*vendit* sells
dīcit speaks	**nōmen, -inis n. name**	*vir* man
dūcit leads	**quid what?**	
est is	*quis* who?	

EXERCEĀMUS!

1-5 Colloquāmur

Practice the following dialogue with other people in your class.

Dialogue: *Quid est nōmen tibi?*   What is your name?

　　　　 Mihi nōmen est _____.   My name is _____ .

1-6 Colloquāmur

(To be done after Exercise 1-5.)
Point at student A and ask student B, *Quis est?* (Who is this?). Student B responds *John est.* Then student B points to student C and asks, *Quis est?* etc.

1-7 Scrībāmus

Make ten simple Latin sentences by taking a noun from column A and linking it with a verb in column B. Be sure to make at least one sentence with each verb. In order to do this, you will have to use the nouns in column A more than once. Follow the model below.

A	**B**
fēmina (woman)	*currit* (runs)
vir (man)	*ambulat* (walks)
fīlia (daughter)	*dīcit* (speaks)
fīlius (son)	*respondet* (responds)
	est (is)
	dat (gives)
	clāmat (shouts)
	stat (stands)
	vendit (sells)
➙ *Fēmina currit.*	*dūcit* (leads)

1-8 Translation

Now translate each of the Latin sentences you made in Exercise 1-7 into English. Follow the model.

→ *Fēmina currit.* "The woman runs."

1-9 Verba Discenda

Use your knowledge of English to determine the part of speech of each of the *Verba Discenda*. Follow the model.

🔊 VERBA DISCENDA

***est* is**	***nōmen, nōminis* n. name**	***tibi* to you, your**
***mihi* to me, my**	[nomenclature, nominate]	
	***quid* what?** [quid pro quo]	

Verbum	Part of Speech
mihi	→ to me (pronoun)
nōmen	
est	
quid	
tibi	

Gemma

Verba Discenda: Notice the English words "nomenclature" and "nominate" in brackets after *nōmen.* These words are derived from the Latin word. Recognizing the relationship between such derivatives and their Latin parents not only helps you learn the Latin word but also increases your English vocabulary.

Angulus Grammaticus

The Birth of "W" and "J"

The letter V originally stood for both for the consonant W and for the vowel U. It is now common practice to write Latin with the consonant V and the vowel U, but the Latin word *vacuus* (empty) was originally written as *VACVVS* or *vacvvs*. Only after the fall of the Roman Empire was the letter U used to distinguish the vowel from the consonant. Occasionally the Latin letter V became a W in English. Here are some examples:

Latin Word	Latin Meaning	English Word
vallum	rampart, palisade	wall
vastus	waste, deserted	waste
vīnum	wine	wine

Similarly, the letter I originally stood for both the consonant J and the vowel I. Occasionally in Latin texts, J is used as a consonant along with I as a vowel. Look at how this affects the change from Latin words to English words.

Latin	English
iniūria	injury
iānitor	janitor
iūnior	junior

Photo Credits

page 1 iStockphoto; **page 12** Shutterstock; **page 1 (top)** Mary Evans Picture Library/Alamy Images; **page 11 (top)** Victor Martinez/Photo by Victor Martinez, used with permission; **page 11 (middle)** Victor Martinez/Photo by Victor Martinez, used with permission; **page 11 (bottom)** Clipart.com; **page 12 (top)** Victor Martinez/Photo by Victor Martinez, used with permission; **page 12 (bottom)** Mikael Damkier/Shutterstock

In Tabernā

In tabernā

GRAMMATICA
The Present Tense (3rd Person)
Principal Parts
Latin Derivatives in English
The Concept of "Person" and Personal
    Endings
Simple Greetings and Imperatives

MŌRĒS RŌMĀNĪ
Nōmina Rōmāna

LATĪNA HODIERNA
Salutatorians and Valedictorians

ORBIS TERRĀRUM RŌMĀNUS
The *Argīlētum*

ANGULUS GRAMMATICUS
Tense and Aspect

Lectiō Prīma

Antequam Legis

The Family of Valeria

The three women in this *lectiō* form the core of one of the families who appear in the narrative of *Disce!* Valeria, the mother, runs the shop. Her daughter, Licinia, helps her in the shop. Licinius, husband of Valeria and father of Licinia, died a few years before in Verona. Valeria could not run their farm alone and therefore sold it and moved to Rome to make her way as best she could, running a snack shop near the Forum. You will learn more about shops like these in the *Mōrēs Rōmānī* section in Chapter 3. The third woman is Flavia, a German slave girl who helps run the shop. Notice that her dress is different from that of free women. You will learn more about the family and its other members as the story progresses.

As you read *Lectiō Prīma,* pay attention to the verbs. There are three of them: *est* (is), *sunt* (are), and *vendit* (sells).

EXERCEĀMUS!

2-1   Subjects and Verbs

As you read, notice that verbs are marked in **bold** and their subjects are marked in ***bold italics***. List all the subjects line by line in the subject column and all the verbs in the verb column. Then translate the subjects and verbs together. Follow the model.

Line	Subject	Verb	Translation
→ 1	fēminae	sunt	the women are

Now use the subjects to determine why some verbs end in *-t* and others end in *-nt*.

> **LECTIŌNĒS:**
> TRĒS FĒMINAE
> and
> MERĪDIĒS
>
> We meet Valeria and her daughter Licinia who run a snack shop near the Roman Forum.

15

From *Disce! An Introductory Latin Course, volume 1*, First Edition. Francesco Bonavita. Copyright © 2011 by Pearson Education, Inc. Published by Pearson Prentice Hall. All rights reserved.

🔊 TRĒS FĒMINAE

In pictūrā trēs *fēminae* **sunt**. *Fēmina* ad sinistram Valeria **est**.
Valeria Ītala **est**. *Fēmina* prope Valeriam Licinia **est**. *Valeria*
est māter. *Licinia* filia **est**. Tertia *fēmina* in pictūrā Flāvia **est**.
Flāvia Germānica **est**. *Flāvia* ancilla **est** et *Valeria* domina
5 **est**. In tabernā *Valeria* pōtum et cibum **vendit**.

In pictūrā trēs fēminae sunt.

🔊 VERBA ŪTENDA

ad sinistram to the left	*fēmina, -ae* f. **woman**	*māter* mother	*taberna, -ae* f. **snack shop**
ancilla maid servant	*filia* daughter	*pictūrā* picture	*tertia* third
cibum food	*Germānica* German	*pōtum* (n.) drink	*trēs* three
domina mistress	*in* **in, on, into**	*prope* near	*vendit* (she) sells
et **and**	*Ītala* Italian	*sunt* **(they) are**	

POSTQUAM LĒGISTĪ

1. What is the relationship between Valeria and Licinia?
2. What is the relationship between Valeria and Flavia?
3. What is the nationality of Valeria? What is Flavia's nationality?
4. What does Valeria sell in her shop?

Grammatica A

The Present Tense (3rd Person)

What did you learn from *Exercise 2-1*? In the following sentences, observe the change in verb endings.

Vir **est**.	He **is** a man.	singular verb
Virī **sunt**.	They **are** men.	plural verb
Fēmina **vendit**.	The woman **is selling**.	singular verb
Fēminae **vendunt**.	The women **are selling**.	plural verb

The endings of these verbs indicate that the subject is singular or plural.

- *-nt* indicates a plural subject, "they"
- *-t* indicates a singular subject, "he," "she," or "it"
- This concept is called the **number** of a verb.

Latin Verb Ending	Number	English Translation
-t	singular	he/she/it
-nt	plural	they

Principal Parts

Every Latin verb form consists of endings added to a **stem**. These stems are made from one of the four **principal parts** of every Latin verb.

English has principal parts as well. You have certainly spent a lot of time memorizing things like "sing, sang, sung" or "go, went, gone." English also uses them to form our tenses (e.g., I am going, I have gone). You can read more about English and Latin principal parts in the *Angulus Grammaticus* in Chapter 5.

Most Latin verbs have four principal parts. All four principal parts are given for *Verba Discenda*, but for now, we will focus only on the first two principal parts. Here are the first two principal parts of three verbs from this chapter.

- The 1st principal part is the 1st person singular of the present tense (i.e., I run, I see).
- The 2nd principal part is the infinitive (i.e., to run, to see).

1ST PRINCIPAL PART	TRANSLATION	2ND PRINCIPAL PART	TRANSLATION
ambulō	I walk	*ambulāre*	to walk
videō	I see	*vidēre*	to see
vendō	I sell	*vendere*	to sell

Here is how the 3rd person singular and plural are formed for these verbs:

SINGULAR		PLURAL	
ambulat	he/she/it walks	*ambulant*	they walk
videt	he/she/it sees	*vident*	they see
vendit	he/she/it sells	*vendunt*	they sell

Notā Bene:

- The Latin verb *vendit* can be translated three different ways: he/she/it sells, he/she/it is selling, he/she/it does sell.
- Latin verbs have a variety of vowels before the endings (*ambulat*, *videt*, *vendit*, *vendunt*). For now, simply use the *-t* or *-nt* ending to decide how to translate a given form, using "he, she, it" or "they."

EXERCEĀMUS!

2-2 **Principal Parts**

Here are the first two principal parts of the *Verba Discenda* for this chapter.

> *ambulō, ambulāre* **walk**
> *bibō, bibere* **drink**
> *dō, dare* **give**
> *veniō, venīre* **come**

Use this information to complete the following chart.

1ST PRINCIPAL PART	TRANSLATION	2ND PRINCIPAL PART	TRANSLATION
ambulō	I walk		
		bibere	
	I give		
			to come

Lectiō Secunda

Antequam Legis

Latin Derivatives in English

How many English words did you recognize in *Lectiō Prīma*? Here are some you might have found: feminine from *fēmina*; tavern from *taberna*; and maternal from *māter*. Finding English derivatives of Latin words is a good practice as you learn to read Latin. But you need to be cautious. Just looking like one particular Latin word does not necessarily mean that an English word is derived from it. You need to compare the meanings of the Latin and English words to make sure. When necessary, you should consult a dictionary. Look for more derivatives as you read *Lectiō Secunda,* in which you meet some of Valeria's customers.

Continue to pay attention to verb endings and watch for the plural -*nt* (they) versus the singular -*t* (he/she/it).

Also observe the way characters greet each other in this reading with the words *salvē*, and *valē*, and you will learn how to say "hello" and "goodbye" in Latin.

EXERCEĀMUS!

2-3 **Recognizing Derivatives**

Before you read *Lectiō Secunda*, use an English dictionary to determine whether either or both of the two English words are derivatives of the Latin word. All of these Latin words are marked in the reading.

Line	Latin Word	Meaning	Possible English Derivatives	
1	*merīdiēs*	noon	**mer**ry	**meri**dian
1	*sōl*	sun	**sol**arium	**sol**itary
1	*altus*	high	**alt**er	**alt**itude
1	*caelō*	sky	**cel**ebrant	**cel**estial
1	*urbe*	city	**urb**an	**turb**an
2	*multī*	many	**multi**plex	**multi**lateral
2	*viīs*	roads	**vi**aduct	**vi**tal
3	*populī*	people	**popul**ace	**popul**ar
3	*ambulant*	walk	**ambu**scade	**ambu**latory
4	*ūnus*	one	**un**favorable	**un**ique
4	*vir*	man	**vir**gin	**vir**ile
4	*venit*	comes	con**ven**tion	**ven**ial
5	*placet*	pleases	com**plac**ent	**plac**ard
6	*aquam*	water	**aqu**atic	**aqu**iline

MERĪDIĒS

Merīdiēs est et **sōl altus** in **caelō** est. In **urbe** Rōmā **multī** Rōmānī in **viīs** sunt. Diēs aestuōsus est et multī **populī**, dum **ambulant**, bibunt.

    Ūnus vir ad tabernam **venit** et "Salvē, Valeria," in-
5 quit. "Dā mihi calidum, sī **placet**."

    Alius venit et **aquam** poscit.

    Tertius venit. Valdē iēiūnus est et "Salvē," inquit, "dā mihi pānem et fīcōs, sī tibi placet." Valeria cibum dat. "Gratiās, domina," vir inquit, "Valē!"
10   "Valēte," Valeria respondet.

In urbe Rōmā multī Rōmānī in viīs sunt.

VERBA ŪTENDA

ad to, toward
aestuōsus hot
alius another
altus, -a, -um high
ambulō, ambulāre, ambulāvī, ambulātum walk
aqua, -ae f. water
bibō, bibere, bibī drink
caelō sky
calidum a hot drink

cibus, -ī m. food
dā mihi give (to) me
diēs day
dō, dare, dedī, datum give
domina ma'am
dum while
fīcōs figs
gratiās! Thanks!
iēiūnus hungry
inquit he says
merīdiēs midday, noon

multus, -a, um much, many
pānem bread
populī people
poscō, poscere to ask for
respondeō, respondēre reply
Rōmānī Romans
salvē hi, hello
sī (tibi) placet please ("if it pleases you")

sōl sun
sunt (they) are
tertius third
ūnus one
urbe city
valdē very
valē, valēte goodbye
veniō, venīre, vēnī, ventum come
viīs roads
vir, virī m. man

POSTQUAM LĒGISTĪ

1. What time of day is it?
2. What is the weather like?
3. What are some of the things Valeria's customers order from her?
4. How many customers does Valeria serve?

Grammatica B

The Concept of "Person" and Personal Endings

English verbs change to conform to their subject. Consider these examples:

- **Tom has** five dollars, but **I have** ten. Between us, **we have** fifteen.
- **Sally sees** the glass as half full, but **I see** it as half empty.

The English verb changes

by **number** (i.e., singular or plural) ⟶   he has, they have

by **person** (i.e., by the subject) ⟶   I have, you have

Gemma

inquit: This word is used to indicate that someone is speaking. Notice how it always comes after or even in between what the person says. You will only see this verb in the 3rd person singular (*inquit* he/she/it says) or the 3rd person plural (*inquiunt* they say).

Gemma

altus, -a, -um; multus, -a, -um: Both of these *Verba Discenda* are adjectives. The *-us, -a, -um* endings indicate different gender forms of these adjectives (masculine, feminine, neuter).

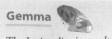

Gemma

The Latin adjective *multus* means "much" in the singular and "many" in the plural: *multum pānem* much bread *multī virī* many men

What is "person"?

	Singular	Plural
1st person = the one(s) speaking	I	we
2nd person = the one(s) spoken to	you	you (all)
3rd person = the one(s) spoken about	he/she/it	they

In Latin, the endings on the verb's stem indicate person and number. These endings are called **personal endings** because they show the "person" of the subject:

English Pronoun	Person	Number	Latin Personal Ending
he, she, it	3rd	singular	*-t*
they	3rd	plural	*-nt*

EXERCEĀMUS!

2-4 **Verb Analysis**

Fill in the grid following the pattern of the first examples. Don't worry about what these verbs mean. Just focus on the personal endings.

	NUMBER (SINGULAR, PLURAL)	ENGLISH PRONOUN (HE/SHE/IT, THEY)
videt	singular	he/she/it
vident	plural	they
significant		
est		
sunt		
adveniunt		
advenit		
dant		

Simple Greetings and Imperatives

Notice how Valeria greets her customer with the word *Salvē*. As a customer leaves, he says *Valē*. Valeria says goodbye to her customers with the word *Valēte*. In Latin, the greetings "Hello" and "Goodbye" are actually commands meaning "Be well." Latin distinguishes between a command to one person (singular) and to more than one person (plural).

	Singular	Plural
Hello	*Salvē*	*Salvēte*
Goodbye	*Valē*	*Valēte*

Notā Bene: *-ē* is used to address one person and *-ēte* is used to address more than one person. This form of the verb is called an imperative.

MŌRĒS RŌMĀNĪ

Nōmina Rōmāna

You have already seen how Romans used abbreviations (*contractiōnēs*) in the inscription on the Arch of Titus. Abbreviating is also common in Roman names. Do you remember from

Chapter 1 how *fīlius*, the Latin word for "son" is abbreviated "F" on the Arch of Titus and in the family charts of the characters in our narrative? Well, the Romans used abbreviations in a wide variety of written contexts.

There is only a small set of possible male first names (*praenōmina*), for example, and these were almost always abbreviated when written. Here are some of the more common ones:

Praenōmina

Twelve Common Men's First Names

A.	*Aulus*	P.	*Pūblius*
App.	*Appius*	Q.	*Quintus*
C.	*Gāius*	S.	*Sextus*
Cn.	*Gnaeus*	Ser.	*Servius*
L.	*Lūcius*	T.	*Titus*
M.	*Marcus*	Ti(b).	*Tiberius*

In addition to one of these *praenōmina*, or first names, a Roman male also could have

- a *nōmen*, i.e., a *gēns* (tribe or clan) name
- a *cognōmen*, a third name that could
  mark a family branch of a *gēns*
  indicate that a son was born after the death of his father (*Postumus*)
  show that the man had been adopted (via a name ending in *-iānus*)

Very illustrious Romans could have more than one *cognōmen* but less illustrious men often had fewer. Here are some examples:

Praenōmen	Nōmen	Cognōmen	Cognōmen	Cognōmen
M.	Tullius	Cicerō		
C.	Iulius	Caesar		
C.	Iulius	Caesar	Octaviānus	Augustus
M.	Servīlius	Sevērus		
M.	Aelius			

Servilius' son, also known as M. Servilius Severus, could add M.f. (*Marcī fīlius*) to distinguish himself from his father. Note how a lower-class Roman like Aelius often had no *cognōmen*, whereas emperors like Augustus could accumulate multiple *cognōmina*.

- Augustus was born C. Octavius.
- After his adoption by Julius Caesar he became C. Iulius Caesar Octaviānus.
- After he became emperor he took the *cognōmen* Augustus ("revered") and was often called by that name.

Roman women had far fewer options. All the daughters in a family simply bore the name of their father's *gens* or clan. So Servilius' daughter is Servilia, and Licinia bears the name of her father, Licinius. If there were more than one daughter in the family, they were often distinguished by formal nicknames like *Māior* (the Elder) and *Minor* (the Younger). If there were more daughters, they might be known as *Tertia* (the Third), *Quarta* (the Fourth), etc. These names were not abbreviated. For example, if Julius Caesar had had two daughters, the first would have been known as *Julia Māior* and her younger sister would have been *Julia Minor*. A Roman woman kept this birth name even after she was married.

When Romans sent letters, they also used abbreviations. Very often a Roman began a letter with the abbreviation S.D., which stands for the expression *salūtem dīcit/dīcunt* (he/she/it sends greetings or they send greetings). Notice how letter writers refer to themselves in the third person.

Gemma

The Latin abbreviation S.D. is sometimes used today in college diplomas in a formulaic way: "The college sends greetings to…"

Here is how the statesman Cicero addressed letters to his friend Atticus:

> CICERO ATTICO SAL.
> CICERO ATTICO S.D.
> CICERO SAL. DIC. ATTICO

All of these expressions stand for:

> CICERO ATTICO SALVTEM DICIT   Cicero sends greetings to Atticus.

Here is how Julius Caesar addressed a letter to Cicero and how Cicero replied. The abbreviation *imp.* stands for *imperātor* or "general."

> CAESAR IMP. S.D. CICERONI IMP.
> CICERO IMP. S.D. CAESARI IMP.

Another important abbreviation in letter writing is S.V.V., which stands for *Si valeās, valeō*. (If you are well, I am well.)

Latīna Hodierna

Salutatorians and Valedictorians

Did your high school graduation have a salutatorian and a valedictorian? The salutatorian is the one who says *Salvē* or "Hello" at the beginning of the ceremony and the valedictorian is the one who says *Valē* or "Goodbye." Here are some related English words. Remember that the essential idea is "Be well!" If you don't know the meaning of one of these English words, look it up!

Salvē!	*Valē!*
salutatorian	valedictorian
salutatory	valedictory
salutation	valediction
salutary	valetudinarian
salute	valetudinary

Orbis Terrārum Rōmānus

The *Argīlētum*

Valeria's *taberna* is imagined to be in an excellent location on a street called the Argiletum just off the Roman Forum, the chief political and commercial center of the city and the empire. The Argiletum is marked in red on the map on the next page. As you can see in the photographs at the left, the Argiletum leading out of the Forum essentially disappeared in the Imperial period and is not visible today.

Argīlētum ē Forō hodiē

Argīlētum ad Forum hodiē

Argīlētum ē Forō ad Subūram

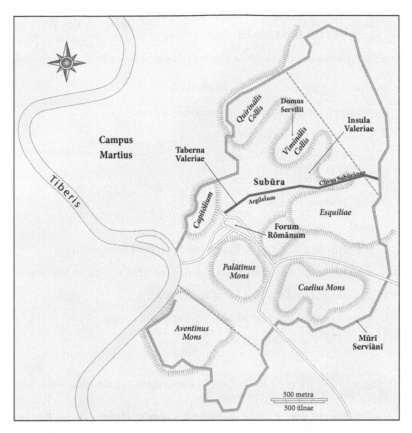

QUID PUTĀS?

1. How does the Roman use of abbreviations in letter writing compare to modern practice, especially in text messaging?
2. What does their elaborate system of naming males tell you about Romans and their society?
3. Use the Roman system of naming women to rename a visible today.woman in your family. For example, your mother would be known by her father's family name.
4. What observations about the role of women in Roman society can you make based on the way Roman women were named?

EXERCEĀMUS!

2-5 Colloquāmur

Use the following Latin phrases to say hello and goodbye to people in your class:

Salvē, magister.	Valē, magister.	(if your teacher is male)
Salvē, magistra.	Valē, magistra.	(if your teacher is female)
Salvē, discipule.	Valē, discipule.	(a male student)'
Salvē, discipula.	Valē, discipula.	(a female student)
Salvēte, discipulī.	Valēte, discipulī.	(more than one student)

🔊 VERBA ŪTENDA

discipula student (female)　　*discipulus* student (male)　　*magistra* teacher (female)　　*magister* teacher (male)

Verba Discenda

Find the Latin word in the *Verba Discenda* that best fits each of the statements. Follow the model.

→ one of your female classmates: *discipula*

1. word used to indicate when a person is speaking:

2. a place where you can buy a snack:

3. used to describe Mt. Vesuvius:

4. connects two words together:

5. the opposite of a *vir*:

6. used to address your teacher:

7. the verb used to get from Valeria's shop to the Forum on foot:

8. the verb used to describe what Valeria's customers come to her shop to do:

9. a word used to describe a lot of something:

10. a word used to describe what Valeria's customers eat:

11. a drink served at Valeria's shop:

🔊 **VERBA DISCENDA**

ad to, toward, for
altus, -a, -um high [altitude]
ambulō, ambulāre, ambulāvī, ambulātum walk [ambulatory, perambulation]
aqua, -ae f. water [aqueous, aquatic]
bibō, bibere, bibī drink [imbibe]
cibus, -ī m. food
discipula, -ae f. student (female) [disciple]

discipulus, -ī m. student (male)
dō, dare, dedī, datum give [data]
et and
fēmina, -ae f. woman [feminine]
in in, on, into
inquit, inquiunt say(s)
magister, -trī m. teacher (male)
magistra, -ae f. teacher (female) [magisterial, magistrate]

multus, -a, -um much, many [multitude]
sum, esse, fuī be (see *est* and *sunt*) [essence]
sunt (they) are
taberna, -ae f. snack shop
veniō, venīre, vēnī, ventum come [advent, prevention]
vir, virī m. man [virile, virility]

Angulus Grammaticus

Tense and Aspect

In English, **tense** primarily refers to the time of the action: past, present, or future. So far we have only talked about the present tense in Latin. You will, of course, be introduced to other tenses as we move along. But you should think about more than time when you talk about tense in Latin. You should also think about what is called **aspect**, i.e., the kind of action of the verb. In English we indicate aspect by adding helping verbs. Here are some examples:

he sells	simple action
he is selling	continuous action
he does sell	emphatic action

One way to distinguish a simple action from a continuous action is to think in terms of a photograph and a video of the same event. "He sells" is the photographic shot of an action, whereas "he is selling" is a video.

All three types of aspect are indicated by the Latin present tense, so the Latin word *vendit* can be translated in three different aspects:

he sells

he is selling

he does sell

Now try translating *vendunt* into English in three different aspects.

Although Latin is very subtle in many ways, English is more nuanced in its use of aspect. There can be a big difference in aspect in English present tense. Consider this little dialogue about Bill, the automobile salesman.

- **He sells** cars, doesn't he?
- Yes, **he does sell** cars.
- In fact, **he is selling** them right now.

In Latin, all three words in bold would be the same—*vendit*. Context will help you decide which aspect to use when you translate into English from Latin.

Photo Credits

page 15 (top) Private Collection/The Bridgeman Art Library; **page 19** Clipart.com; **page 22 (top)** Victor Martinez/Photo by Victor Martinez, used with permission; **page 22 (bottom)** Victor Martinez/Photo by Victor Martinez, used with permission

Negōtium Bonum

From *Disce! An Introductory Latin Course, volume 1*, First Edition. Francesco Bonavita. Copyright © 2011 by Pearson Education, Inc. Published by Pearson Prentice Hall. All rights reserved.

Taberna in Herculaneō

GRAMMATICA

The Concept of Case

The Nominative Case

The Accusative Case

Nominative and Accusative Endings

The 1st and 2nd Declensions

The Predicate Nominative

Word Order in Latin

MŌRĒS RŌMĀNĪ

The *Taberna* or *Thermopōlium*

LATĪNA HODIERNA

Taberna and Tavern

ORBIS TERRĀRUM RŌMĀNUS

Forum Rōmānum

ANGULUS GRAMMATICUS

Inflection vs. Word Order

> **LECTIŌNĒS:**
> MULTA PECŪNIA
> and
> MĒ ADIUVĀTE!
>
> Valeria and her daughter Licinia tend to the business of the snack shop.

3

Negōtium Bonum

Lectiō Prīma

Antequam Legis

Subjects and Objects

In this *lectiō*, Valeria continues to serve her customers. You should be able to read this narrative fairly easily even though it uses some noun endings you have not yet studied. These endings indicate the **subject** and the **object** of a sentence.

The **subject** of a verb is the one who performs the action (or simply "is," if there is no action):

John hit the wall.

John is in a world of pain.

The **direct object** receives the action of a verb:

John hit **the wall**.

EXERCEĀMUS!

3-1 **Subjects and Objects**

Before you read *Lectiō Prīma*, make a line-by-line list of the subjects (marked in **bold**) and the objects (marked in ***bold italics***). Find the verb that goes with each subject. Then try to put the three words together into an English sentence. Follow the models.

Line	Subject	Object	Verb	Translation
→ 1	Valeria	cibum	dat	Valeria gives food.
→ 1	Valeria	pōtum	dat	Valeria gives drink.

🔊 MULTA PECŪNIA

Valeria *cibum* et *pōtum* dat et ūnus vir "Grātiās," inquit "domina." **Aliī** *nihil* dīcunt sed sōlum edunt et bibunt. **Virī** *pecūniam* dant et "Valē," inquiunt "Valeria." "Valēte!" Valeria respondet. Tunc virī ad Forum ambulant.

5 Subitō, **multī virī** simul ad tabernam adveniunt et *fēminās* vident. Et *cibum* et *pōtum* simul poscunt. **Valeria** *virōs* videt et "Salvēte!" inquit. Valeria et Licinia et ancilla Flāvia strēnuē labōrant sed domina laeta est, quod **multī virī** **multam pecūniam** significant. Hodiē negōtium bonum est.

Valeria cibum et pōtum dat.

🔊 VERBA ŪTENDA

adveniunt come to	*hodiē* today	***respondeō, respondēre,***	*subitō* suddenly
aliī others	*labōrō, labōrāre* work	***respondī, responsum***	*tū* you (sing.)
cibum food	*laeta* happy	**reply, answer**	***tunc* then**
dīcō, dīcere say	*negōtium* business	***Salvē!/Salvēte!* Hello! Hi!**	*ūnus* one
domina mistress, ma'am	*nihil* nothing	*sed* but	***valeō, valēre, valuī, valītum***
edō, edere eat	***nōn* not**	*significō, significāre* mean,	**be well *Valē!/Valēte!***
et... et... both... and...	***pecūnia, -ae* f. money**	signify	**Farewell! Goodbye!**
Forum, -ī n. Forum, the city	*poscō, poscere* ask for	*simul* all at once, together	***videō, vidēre, vīdī, vīsum***
center	*pōtum* (a) drink	***sōlum* only**	**see, perceive**
grātiās thanks	***quod* because**	*strēnuē* hard	***vīnum, -ī* n. wine**

POSTQUAM LĒGISTĪ

Answer the questions in both Latin and English.
1. What does Valeria give the men?
2. What do the men give Valeria?
3. Where are the men going?
4. Why is Valeria happy?

Gemma

Et cibum et pōtum simul poscunt: When there are two *et*'s joining words in a sentence, the first *et* means **both** and the second **and**.

Grammatica A

The Concept of Case

With the vocabulary you know, you probably have no problem translating sentences like these:

*Ūnus **vir** ad tabernam advenit.*	One man comes to the shop.
*Multī **virī** ad tabernam adveniunt.*	Many men come to the shop.
*Subitō, Valeria ūnum **virum** videt.*	Suddenly, Valeria sees one man.
*Subitō, Valeria multōs **virōs** videt.*	Suddenly, Valeria sees many men.

These differing forms of the word *vir* demonstrate a crucial part of Latin grammar—the concept of **case**.

- The **case** of a word (nouns, adjectives, pronouns) indicates the **function** that word plays in the sentence (subject, direct object, showing possession, etc.). Words have a **case ending** that indicates this function.
- The **case endings** also vary by number (singular and plural).
- There are five major cases in Latin and we will learn them one at a time. In this chapter, you will learn the **nominative** and the **accusative** cases.

The Nominative Case

The **nominative case** is used for the **subject** of the sentence—that is, the person, place, or thing that is **being** or is **doing** an action.

The **woman** is working hard.	*Fēmina strēnuē labōrat.*
The **man** comes up to the shop.	*Vir ad tabernam advenit.*
The **man** is **happy**.	*Vir laetus est.*

In the last example, notice that the adjective *laetus* is nominative because it refers to the man, who is the subject of the sentence. This is an important concept to which we will return shortly.

The Accusative Case

The **accusative case** is used for the **direct object** of the verb. A **direct object** is a noun or pronoun that receives the direct action of a transitive verb.

The man sees the **woman**.	*Vir **fēminam** videt.*
The woman sees the **man**.	*Fēmina **virum** videt.*

A **transitive verb** is one that takes a direct object. The quick rule of thumb is that if you can do it to something else, then it is **transitive**. If the verb does not do something directly to something else, then it is **intransitive** (e.g., to exist or to seem).

Nominative and Accusative Endings

The following chart shows the nominative and accusative endings of some nouns you have learned so far. Note how the endings (in **bold**) change to indicate their case.

CASE	SINGULAR	PLURAL
Nominative	fēmina	fēmin**ae**
Accusative	fēmin**am**	fēmin**ās**
Nominative	taberna	tabern**ae**
Accusative	tabern**am**	tabern**ās**
Nominative	vir	vir**ī**
Accusative	vir**um**	vir**ōs**
Nominative	discipul**us**	discipul**ī**
Accusative	discipul**um**	discipul**ōs**

The 1ˢᵗ and 2ⁿᵈ Declensions

You probably noticed patterns in the endings you just learned. For example, all the accusative singulars end in *-m* and the accusative plurals in *-s*. But note *-ās* vs. *-ōs*. So the patterns are not exact matches. Still, they do tend to come in groups. We call these groups **declensions**, that is, groups of nouns that use the same endings.

English nouns also occur in certain groups that act alike with some degree of regularity. Most nouns make their plural by adding a simple **-s**, sometimes with vowel changes before the **-s**.

SINGULAR	PLURAL
house	houses
bed	beds
dog	dogs
party	parties

Others do not form the plural this way, and there are several groups of nouns that more or less act the same way.

SINGULAR	PLURAL
mouse	mice
louse	lice
goose	geese
tooth	teeth
man	men
woman	women
child	children

As you know from speaking English, the number of ways to make plurals seems infinite. It is a great problem for non-native speakers. Latin is, in fact, much tidier than English in this regard.

Most inflected languages are like this and sort their nouns into groups that tend to follow the same patterns. In Latin, there are five declensions and the majority of nouns occur in the first three. In this chapter, we have used mostly 1ˢᵗ and 2ⁿᵈ declension nouns:

	1ˢᵀ DECLENSION		2ⁿᴰ DECLENSION		
	Singular				
Nominative	fēmina	-a	discipulus	vir	-us
Accusative	fēminam	-am	discipulum	virum	-um
	Plural				
Nominative	fēminae	-ae	discipulī	virī	-ī
Accusative	fēminās	-ās	discipulōs	virōs	-ōs

Gemma

If it helps, you can think of the accusative singular ending as the same in English and Latin: *fēminam* and *virum* vs. "whom" and "him."

Nota Bene:

- The accusative singular ending for many Latin nouns, regardless of declension, is -**m** (*fēmina**m***, viru**m**).
- There are six major cases in Latin, singular and plural.
- Latin nouns, adjectives, and pronouns have case.
- There are five declensions of Latin nouns.
- Three of these declensions are used for Latin adjectives.
- There is some flexibility in the nominative singular as shown by *vir* and *discipulus*.

EXERCEĀMUS!

3-2   Nominative and Accusative

Use the chart of case endings to help you determine the case and number of the words marked in bold in each of the following sentences. Follow the model.

	CASE	NUMBER
→ **Fēmina** labōrat.	*nominative*	*singular*
1. **Fēminae** pōtum dant.		
2. **Virī** veniunt.		
3. **Vir** respondet.		
4. Fēmina **virum** videt.		
5. Vir **fēminās** videt.		
6. Virī **discipulum** vident.		
7. **Magistrī** respondent.		
8. Discipulae **pecūniam** vident.		
9. Fēmina multōs **virōs** videt.		
10. **Discipulī** respondent.		
11. Magistra **fēminam** videt.		

Lectiō Secunda

Antequam Legis

Things get quite busy in Valeria's shop as more and more customers appear. *Lectiō Secunda* also gives you practice with **word order**, **direct objects**, and **predicates**. A predicate nominative is a noun or an adjective linked to the subject by an intransitive verb. Remember: transitive verbs take direct objects, intransitive verbs do not.

*Vir **fēminam** videt.*
The man sees the woman.

Videt is a transitive verb and takes a **direct object**, *fēminam*.

*Vir **laetus** est sed fēmina nōn **laeta** est.*
The man is happy, but the woman is not happy.

Est is an intransitive verb and does not take a direct object. Both *laetus* and *laeta* are **predicate nominatives**.

*Valeria **fēmina** est.*
Valeria is a woman.

A noun can also be a predicate nominative.

In *Lectiō Secunda* the transitive verbs that have objects are in **bold** and the intransitive verbs are in ***bold italics***.

Word Order

In English, word order is everything. John Bogart, a former editor of the *New York Sun* reportedly said that if the headline reads "Dog bites man," it isn't news, but if the headline reads "Man bites dog," then you have yourself a news story. This is the power of word order in English—it controls meaning. But in Latin the endings rule.

In English our word order is fixed. We usually place the subject first, then the verb, and then the direct object.

Subject	**Verb**	**Object**
The man	sees	the woman.

In Latin the preferred word order is:

Subject	**Object**	**Verb**
Vir	*fēminam*	*videt.*

BUT: This sentence is also possible, is good Latin, and means the same thing:

Object	**Subject**	**Verb**
Fēminam	*vir*	*videt.*

Moreover, you have the endings to help you figure out which is which. As you read *Lectiō Secunda* pay attention to the word order of the Latin sentence.

EXERCEĀMUS!

3-3 **Skimming the Lectiō**

Find the answers to these questions before you read *Lectiō Secunda*. Give the answer in both Latin and English. Follow the model.

→ Whom does Valeria see in line 1? *multōs virōs* (many men)

1. What does Valeria ask Licinia to put in the cup in line 1?

2. What falls on the floor in line 3?

3. What do the men give Valeria in line 4?

4. What is Valeria's mood in line 5?

5. As you translate *Lectiō Secunda*, sort the Latin verbs below into "Transitive" and "Intransitive" groups. For each transitive verb, list the direct object. For each intransitive verb list the two words being linked. Follow the model.

Transitive		**Intransitive**
→ videt	*virōs*	→ est *Valeria* and *laeta*

adiuvāte
implē
dā
capit
sunt
habent
dant
est

🔊 MĒ ADIUVĀTE!

Valeria multōs virōs **videt** et clāmat: "Mē **adiuvāte!** Licinia, **implē** pōculum vīnō et **dā** mihi pānem. Ubi *est* Flāvia? Flāvia! **Dā** mihi fīcōs!" Flāvia fīcōs **capit**, sed quīnque fīcī ad terram cadunt. Valeria nōn laeta *est*, sed nihil **dīcit**. Nunc virī laetī **sunt** quod cibum et pōtum **habent**. Pecūniam **dant** et ad Forum ambulant. 5 "Valēte!" Valeria clāmat. "Et tū, valē!" virī respondent. Valeria valdē laeta *est* quod multam pecūniam **habet**. Ubi negōtium bonum *est*, Valeria semper laeta est!

Dā mihi fīcōs!

🔊 VERBA ŪTENDA

adiuvāte! help!	*Forum, -ī* n. Forum, the city	*nunc* now	*terra* the ground
bonus, -a, -um	center	*pecūnia, -ae* f. money	***tū*** you (sing.)
good	*habet* has	*pānem* bread	*ubi* when
cadunt fall	*implē* fill!	*pōculum* cup	*valdē* very
capiō, capere, cēpī,	***laetus, -a, -um*** happy	*quīnque* five	***videō, vidēre, vīdī, vīsum***
captum take	***mē*** me	***quod*** because	**see, perceive**
clāmat shouts	*negōtium* business	***sed*** but	*vīnō* with wine
fīcī / fīcōs figs	***nihil*** nothing	***semper*** always	

Gemma

bonus, -a, -um good
laetus, -a, um happy: These are the first adjectives to become *Verba Discenda*. The *-us, -a, -um* endings tell you how to form different genders (masculine, feminine, neuter).

POSTQUAM LĒGISTĪ

Find the Latin words that answer each of the following questions. Then answer the question in English.

1. Why does Valeria call to Licinia and Flavia?
2. What accident occurs in this reading?
3. How does Valeria react to the accident?
4. Why are Valeria's customers happy?
5. Why is Valeria happy?
6. Where do the customers go after they leave the shop? How do they get there?

Grammatica B

The Predicate Nominative

Compare these two Latin sentences:

> *Flāvia fīcōs capit.*
> *Valeria nōn laeta est.*

In the first sentence *capit* is a transitive verb that takes a **direct object** in the accusative case (*fīcōs*). But not all verbs take direct objects. Some verbs, like "is" and "are" link things together. Since they are saying that A = B, this means that, in Latin, the nouns joined by words like *est* and *sunt* are in the nominative case. For example,

> *Valeria fēmina est.*   Valeria is a woman.

In this sentence, both *Valeria* and *fēmina* are nominative case. That is because in this sentence the subject *Valeria* is linked with the word *fēmina* by the verb "is" and thus lies in the part of the sentence called the **predicate**. That is why this construction is called the **predicate nominative**.

The *est* acts like an equals sign. Therefore, the predicate nominative is also in the same number as the subject.

> *Valeria fēmina est.*
> *Valeria et Flavia fēminae sunt.*

So **transitive** verbs take **direct objects** in the accusative case, whereas some **intransitive** verbs (like "is") take **predicate nominatives**.

Word Order in Latin

Now let's look more closely at the word order of some of the sentences you read in *Lectiō Secunda* and make some more observations about Latin word order. Remember that these are just tendencies and that Latin word order is more flexible than English word order.

Personal verbs, i.e., verbs with personal endings, tend to be placed at the end of a sense unit or sentence in Latin:

> *Flāvia ficōs **capit**, sed quīnque ficī ad terram **cadunt**.*

The **subject**, if expressed, usually comes first.

> ***Flāvia** ficōs capit.*
> ***Valeria** nōn laeta est.*

The **direct object** most often comes between the subject and the verb.

> *Flāvia **ficōs** capit.*
> *Nunc virī **cibum** et **pōtum** habent.*

The **predicate nominative** comes between the subject and the verb.

> *Valeria valdē **laeta** est.*
> *Valeria semper **laeta** est!*

Orders or **imperatives**, however, come at the beginning or early in the sentence:

> ***Implē** pōculum vīnō et **dā** mihi pānem.*

EXERCEĀMUS!

3-4 **Translation**

Practice your grasp of endings (and Latin word order) by translating the following sentences. Let the endings be your guide, not your sense of English word order.

1. Vir fēminam videt.
2. Vir laetus est.
3. Laetī sunt virī.
4. Fēmina virum videt.
5. Fēminam virī vident.
6. Virī fēminās vident.
7. Vir fēminās videt.
8. Virum fēminae vident.
9. Fēminae virōs vident.
10. Fēmina laeta est.
11. Fēminae laetae sunt.

Mōrēs Rōmānī

The *Taberna* or *Thermopōlium*

Snack shops like Valeria's were a common feature of any Roman city or town. The Latin word for this type of eatery was *taberna*, but a form of the Greek word *thermopōlium* ("hot shop") is also found. Many examples of these shops can be seen today at the archaeological excavations at Pompeii, Herculaneum, and Ostia. These shops were often open to the street and had stone counters into which earthenware jars were set. The jars would keep food and

drink warm. Customers could walk up to the counter from the street to place an order. Sometimes, however, customers would have to step inside to find the food counter. Especially popular at a *taberna* was *calidum*, a hot spiced wine. Foods were mostly snack foods that could be eaten in the customers' hands, such as eggs, fruit, cheese, or meat.

Ancient Romans liked to conduct business in the street so much that the emperor Domitian (A.D. 81–96) passed an edict forbidding the use of the public thoroughfare for business purposes. This led the 1st-century A.D. poet Martial to comment in one of his poems:

Nunc Rōma est, magna taberna fuit.

Martial VII. 61.10

Taberna antīqua Pompēiīs

VERBA ŪTENDA

fuit was   *magna* big

Latīna Hodierna

Taberna and Tavern

The Romans borrowed the word *thermopōlium* (hot shop) from Greek, but the Latin word *taberna* (shop) has lived on in modern languages. Look what happens to *taberna* in these languages:

Latin	**taberna**
Italian	taverna
Spanish	taverna
French	taverne
English	tavern

Orbis Terrārum Rōmānus

Forum Rōmānum

Valeria's shop is very close to the *Forum Rōmānum*. Located in a valley between the Capitoline and Palatine hills, the Forum was the heart of the ancient city and consisted of an unplanned mix of buildings and monuments built over a long period of time on land that was once a swamp. Originally the central market of the city, the Forum became the religious, political, and legal center of Rome. During the reign of Augustus, Rome's first emperor, there was a great deal of construction in the Forum. Many of the buildings visible in the Forum today date from this period.

Cūria Iūlia

Three important Forum landmarks are very near the Via Argiletum and Valeria's shop:

- The ***Cūria Iūlia*** or the **Roman Senate House**, the traditional meeting place of the Roman Senate. The construction of this building, which still stands today, was begun by Julius Caesar to replace one that had burned down. The building was finished by Augustus and dedicated in 27 B.C.

- The ***Rostra***, was a platform just to the right and in front of the Curia, where speakers addressed the people. The platform is called *Rostra*, which means "beaks" in Latin, because of the bronze ship prows that were placed there after a Roman naval victory in 260 B.C. The *Rostra* was rebuilt according to the plans of Julius Caesar and finished by Octavian, the future emperor Augustus in 42 B.C. Mark Antony gave his funeral speech about Caesar from the unfinished *Rostra*.

- The ***Basilica Paullī*** was originally built in 179 B.C. by M. Aemilius Lepidus and M. Fulvius Nobilior. This large law court was reconstructed in the late 1st century B.C. when some shops were built into the front façade. The basilica burned in a fire in 14 B.C., shortly before the time in which our story is set, and was rebuilt by Augustus. It is commonly known by a later name, Basilica Aemilia.

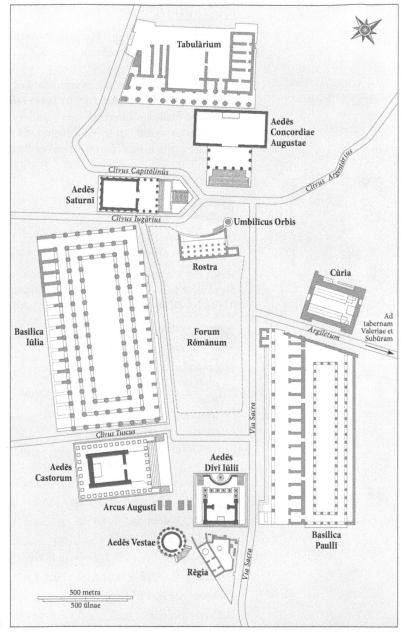

Forum Rōmānum

Rostra hodiē

Rostra Rōmāna

Basilica Paullī hodiē

QUID PUTĀS?

1. What do you think the poet Martial was suggesting about Rome's past when he described the former city as just a big shop? What does he mean when he says that now the city is "Rome"?
2. What would the modern equivalent of Valeria's snack shop be?
3. Compare the meaning of the Latin *taberna* with its English derivative "tavern." How are these facilities different?
4. To what buildings in Washington, D.C., or in your state capital could you compare the Curia, the Rostra, and the Basilica Paulli?

EXERCEĀMUS!

3-5 Scrībāmus

What follows is a version of the story with some blanks in it. Fill in the blanks with one of the Latin words provided in the *Verba Ūtenda*.

HINT: Pay attention to the number of the subject of the sentence, and remember that a singular subject takes a singular verb and a plural subject takes a plural verb. Not every word in the *Verba Ūtenda* is used but some can be used more than once.

> **◄))VERBA ŪTENDA**
>
> | | | | |
> |---|---|---|---|
> | ambulant | clāmant | habent | poscunt |
> | ambulat | clāmat | habet | respondent |
> | bibit | dant | inquit | respondet |
> | bibunt | dat | inquiunt | vident |
> | capit | edit | labōrant | videt |
> | capiunt | edunt | labōrat | |

Fēminae cibum et pōtum dant. Valeria cibum _____ et Licinia et Flāvia pōtum _____. Ūnus vir "Gratiās," inquit "domina." Tunc edit et bibit. Aliī virī "Grātiās," _____, "domina." Tunc virī _____ et _____. Ūnus vir pecūniam _____ et "Valē," inquit "Valeria." Aliī virī pecūniam _____ et "Valē," _____ "Valeria," "Valēte!" Valeria respondet. "Valēte!" Licinia et Flāvia _____. Tunc ad Forum virī _____. Subitō, multī virī simul ad tabernam veniunt. Licinia et Flāvia virōs vident. Valeria virōs _____ et "Salvēte!" dīcit. Virī fēminās _____ et cibum et pōtum simul _____. Licinia et ancilla Flāvia strēnuē _____. Valeria strēnuē _____. Nunc virī laetī sunt quod cibum et pōtum _____. Virī pecūniam _____ et ad Forum _____. "Valēte!" Valeria clāmat. "Et tū, valē!" virī _____. Valeria valdē laeta est quod multam pecūniam _____.

3-6 Colloquāmur

Use the narrative you created in Exercise 3-5 to tell the story to a classmate.

3-7 Verba Discenda

List the verbs from the *Verba Discenda* in one column, the nouns and pronouns in a second, and the adjectives in a third. Follow the model.

Verbs	Nouns, Pronouns	Adjectives
→ capiō	pecūnia	bonus, -a, -um

🔊 VERBA DISCENDA

bonus, -a, -um **good** [bona fide]	*pecūnia, -ae* f. **money** [impecunious, pecuniary]	*Salvē!, Salvēte!* **Hello, Hi, Be well!**	*valeō, valēre, valuī, valītum* **be strong, be well**; *Valē!, Valēte!* **Farewell, Goodbye, Be well!** [valedictorian]
capiō, capere, cēpī, captum **take** [capture, captive]	*quod* **because**	*sed* **but**	
laetus, -a, -um **happy**	*respondeō, respondēre, respondī, respōnsum* **reply, answer** [respondent, responsive]	*sōlum* **only** [solitary]	*videō, vidēre, vīdī, vīsum* **see, perceive** [invisible, video game]
mē **me**		*semper* **always**	
nihil **nothing** [nihilism]		*tū* **you (sing.)**	
nōn **not**		*tunc* **then**	*vīnum, -ī* n. **wine**
nunc **now**			

Angulus Grammaticus

Inflection vs. Word Order

Latin is an inflected language. **Inflection** is the modification of a word to indicate grammatical information, such as gender, tense, number, or person. As you have seen, the endings on a Latin verb change to indicate 3rd person singular (*videt*) and 3rd person plural (*vident*), and the endings of a Latin noun change to distinguish subject (*fēmina*) from object (*fēminam*). Although Modern English does not inflect as much as Latin does, here are some important examples: "I see" vs. "he see**s**," "ask" and "ask**ed**," and "horse" vs. "horse**s**." Instead of inflection, English uses word order to indicate subject and object. This was not always the case. Old English was also inflected.

Compare the Modern English and Old English sentences

The **father** loved his son.	*Sé **fæder** lufode pone sunu.*
	*Pone sunu lufode sé **fæder**.*
	*Lufode sé **fæder** pone sunu.*
The son loved his **father**.	*Sé sunu lufode pone **fæder**.*
	*Pone **fæder** lufode sé sunu.*
	*Lufode pone **fæder** sé sunu.*

Notice how changing the order of "father" and "son" completely changes the meaning of the Modern English sentence, whereas in Old English, subject and object are not distinguished by word order but by inflection. Thus *sé fæder* (father) or *sé sunu* (son) are subjects and *pone fæder* (father) and *pone sunu* (son) are objects, no matter where they appear in the sentence.

Latin is more like Old English than Modern English. The same sentences can be written in Latin like this:

The **father** loved his son.	*Pater filium amāvit.*
	*Fīlium **pater** amāvit.*
The son loved his **father**.	*Fīlius **patrem** amāvit.*
	***Patrem** fīlius amāvit.*

So remember, in Latin the **endings** make the **meanings**.

Photo Credits

page 26 (top) Thomas J. Sienkewicz/Photo by Thomas J. Sienkewicz, used with permission; **page 32** Clipart.com; **page 34 (top)** Photos.com; **page 34 (bottom)** Victor Martinez/Photo by Victor Martinez, used with permission; **page 35 (bottom left)** Marek Klimek/Fotolia, LLC— Royalty Free; **page 35 (bottom middle)** Victor Martinez/Photo by Victor Martinez, used with permission; **page 35 (bottom right)** Thomas J.Sienkewicz/Photo by Thomas J. Sienkewicz, used with permission

Intrat Hermēs

From *Disce! An Introductory Latin Course, volume 1*, First Edition. Francesco Bonavita. Copyright © 2011 by Pearson Education, Inc. Published by Pearson Prentice Hall. All rights reserved.

4

Intrat Hermēs

Lectiō Prīma

Antequam Legis

Meet Hermes, the *Paedagōgus* of Lucius Servilius

In this chapter we meet **Hermes**, a slave of M. Servilius Severus, the ambitious head of a fairly well-to-do family living on the Viminal Hill. Servilius' younger son, Lucius, age ten, attends school in a shop (a common practice) near Valeria's snack shop. He is brought to and from school every day by Hermes, his *paedagōgus*. The Latin word *paedagōgus* is borrowed directly from Greek and means "one who leads a child." A *paedagōgus* was a slave, often a Greek, who predictably formed a bond with the young boy and took a major role in his education.

The Genitive Case

We introduce a new case called the **genitive case** in this chapter. Here are some Latin nouns in the genitive case with their English equivalents.

fēminae	of the woman, the woman's
fēminārum	of the women, the women's
virī	of the man, the man's
virōrum	of the men, the men's

Each **genitive** in the story is marked in **bold**. For now, when you see a genitive, simply translate it with "of" or use the apostrophe form.

Paedagōgus

GRAMMATICA
The Genitive Case
Dictionary Entry for Nouns
-ne and -que
Personal Endings
The Present Stem
The 1st and 2nd Persons
Asking Yes/No Questions

MŌRĒS RŌMĀNĪ
Wine in Ancient Rome

ORBIS TERRĀRUM RŌMĀNUS
Urbs Roma

LATĪNA HODIERNA
The Hills of Rome Today

ANGULUS GRAMMATICUS
Enclitics and Word Stress

LECTIŌNĒS:
HERMĒS PAEDAGŌGUS
and
HERMĒS IN TABERNĀ
Hermes, the *paedagōgus* for the Servilius family, comes to pick up his young charge. He stops at the shop of Valeria for a drink while he waits.

EXERCEĀMUS!

4-1   Finding Genitives

Make a line-by-line list of all the genitive words (marked in **bold**) in *Lectiō Prīma*. Then translate each word both with "of" and with an apostrophe to show possession. Follow the model.

Line	Genitive	"Of" Translation	Apostrophe Translation
→ 1	Valeriae	of Valeria	Valeria's

Gemma

The Latin word *schola* comes from the Greek word *scholē*, which means "leisure." It came to mean "school" because in antiquity only people of leisure could attend school. The Latin word *ludus* means both "school" and "game."

HERMĒS PAEDAGŌGUS

Postrīdiē Valeria, Licinia, et Flāvia iterum in **Valeriae** tabernā sunt. Hodiē, sīcut herī, aestuōsus est. Multī populī in Forō ambulant et ad tabernās veniunt. Nunc Hermēs quoque ad **Valeriae** tabernam venit.

Hermēs paedagōgus **Lūciī** est. Lūcius filius **Servīliī** est. Cotīdiē māne
5 Lūcius ad lūdum **magistrī** venit. Chīrōn magister **lūdī** est. Cotīdiē māne Hermēs Lūcium ad scholam **magistrī** dūcit et tunc, merīdiē, Lūcium domum ad prandium dūcit. Tunc ad lūdum reveniunt. Sērius Hermēs Lūcium domum rursus dūcit.

Nunc Hermēs dūcere Lūcium domum parātus est. Venit ad **Valeriae**
10 tabernam et eam salūtat.

Hermēs paedagōgus

VERBA ŪTENDA

aestuōsus hot
Chīrōn Chiron, Lucius' teacher. The centaur Chiron was the tutor of both Achilles and Hercules.
cotīdiē daily, every day
***domus, -ī* f. home, house
domum home, to a house**

***dūcō, dūcere, dūxī, ductum* lead**
eam her
***fīlius, -ī* m. son**
herī yesterday
Hermēs m. Hermes, Lucius' *paedagōgus* or tutor. He shares his name with the Greek messenger god.
***hodiē* today**

in Forō in the Forum
***iterum* again, for a second time**
***lūdus, -ī* m. school, game**
***māne* early in the morning**
merīdiē at noon
paedagōgus a slave assigned to a young boy, a tutor
parātus prepared
populī people

postrīdiē the next day
prandium lunch
quoque also
rursus again
***salūtō, salūtāre, salūtāvī, salūtātum* greet**
scholam school
sērius later
sīcut just as, like
venit, veniunt come(s)

POSTQUAM LĒGISTĪ

1. How does the weather in this story compare to the weather in the previous story?
2. How many times a day does Hermes take Lucius to school? At what times?
3. Why is Chiron a good name for a teacher?
4. Why is Hermes a good name for a *paedagōgus*?

Gemma

domum: Note that neither Latin nor English uses a preposition to say "go home."

Grammatica A

The Genitive Case

Use the following chart to see the genitive endings, singular and plural. Compare the endings of the genitive with those of the nominative and accusative.

	1ST DECLENSION		2ND DECLENSION			
Singular						
Nominative	-a	fēmina	-us, -er, -ir	discipulus	magister	vir
Genitive	**-ae**	**fēminae**	**-ī**	**discipulī**	**magistrī**	**virī**
Accusative	-am	fēminam	-um	discipulum	magistrum	virum
Plural						
Nominative	-ae	fēminae	-ī	discipulī	magistrī	virī
Genitive	**-ārum**	**fēminārum**	**-ōrum**	**discipulōrum**	**magistrōrum**	**virōrum**
Accusative	-ās	fēminās	-ōs	discipulōs	magistrōs	virōs

Notā Bene:

- Whenever we show you a new case or ending, we will include the ones you already know to provide context.
- To identify the stem of a noun, drop the -ī on the genitive singular. This is especially important for words like *magister, magistrī,* in which the e in the nominative singular drops out in all the other case forms. More on this later.
- *Fēminae* and *virī* can, by form, be either nominative plural or genitive singular. A nominative plural is followed by a plural verb, but a genitive is linked to a nearby noun. What is the case of the word in bold in each of the following sentences?

  Fēminae *ad Forum ambulant.*
  Fēminae *taberna cibum et pōtum habet.*
  Paedagōgī *in Forō sunt.*
  Paedagōgī *pōtum vīnum est.*

- Translate the genitive as "of" or use an appropriate form of the apostrophe. Be careful to follow proper English usage:

  Valeriae of Valeria, Valeria's
  fēminae of the woman, the woman's
  fēminārum of the women, the women's

  Servīliī of Servilius, Servilius'
  virī of the man, the man's
  virōrum of the men, the men's

Notice how the genitive case indicates **possession**. Other uses of the genitive case will be introduced later.

EXERCEĀMUS!

4-2 **Translation**

Find the Latin phrase that best translates each English phrase.

1. Valeria's snack shop:
   a. *Valeriae taberna*
   b. *Valeriam taberna*
   c. *Valeriam tabernae*

2. the money of the man:
   a. *vir pecūnia*
   b. *virī pecūnia*
   c. *virōrum pecūnia*

3. the name of the mistress:
   a. *domina nōmen*
   b. *dominam nōmen*
   c. *dominae nōmen*

4. the men's daughters:
   a. *vir filiae*
   b. *virōrum filiae*
   c. *virī filiae*

5. the daughters' maid servants:
   a. *filiārum ancillae*
   b. *filiae ancillae*
   c. *filiās ancillae*

Dictionary Entry for Nouns

Now that you know about the genitive case, you can understand the dictionary entry for nouns.

- The nominative form is the main entry in your dictionary.
- The second form is genitive, usually abbreviated. The genitive tells you what declension a noun belongs to, so *-ae* means 1st declension and *-ī* means 2nd.
- The third item is gender: m. = masculine; f. = feminine, and n. = neuter.
- The last item is the meaning of the word.
- Drop the genitive ending to get the stem of a noun. So the stem of the 1st declension noun is *discipulae* is *discipul-* and the stem of the 2nd declension noun *discipul-* is also *discipul-*.

Thus, when you see the entry for *discipulus* in your dictionary, here is how to interpret it:

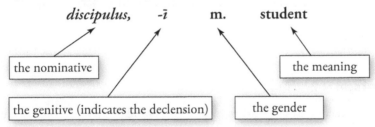

From now on, we will always give you the full dictionary entry for 1st and 2nd declension nouns in the *Verba Ūtenda*.

4-3   Dictionary Entries

Your turn. Take this dictionary form and identify its parts.

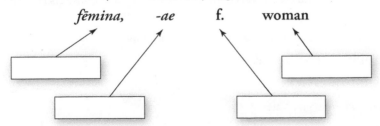

Lectiō Secunda

Antequam Legis

-ne and -que

Words with *-ne* attached at the end indicate that a question is being asked.

- *cupis* you want
- *cupisne* do you want?

Attaching *-que* at the end of a word is another way to say **and** in Latin.

- *vīnum aqua**que*** = *vīnum **et** aqua*

Personal Endings

You already know the verb endings *-t* (he, she, it) and *-nt* (they). In this reading you will see the Latin verb endings used for the English subjects I, we, and you. Here is how it works:

SINGULAR		PLURAL	
-ō	I	-mus	we
-s	you	-tis	you (all)
-t	he/she/it	-nt	they

Thus: *ambulās* you walk   *ambulāmus* we walk

As you read *Lectiō Secunda* use this chart and the context to help determine how these endings work.

EXERCEĀMUS!

4-4 **Personal Endings**

Before you read, make a list of all the verbs marked in **bold** in *Lectiō Secunda*. Underline the personal ending. Then translate the verb into English. Follow the model. Use the chart of personal endings to help you.

Line	Verb	Translation
→ 1	ambula<u>t</u>	he, she, it walks

4-5 **Skimming the *Lectiō***

Skim *Lectiō Secunda* to find the answers to these questions. Give the answers in both Latin and English.

1. Whom does Hermes see when he enters the snack shop?

2. How is business for Valeria today?

3. What does Hermes order?

4. What does Hermes give Valeria?

5. What does he put on the table?

HERMĒS IN TABERNĀ

Ad Valeriae tabernam Hermēs **ambulat**. Paedagōgus Valeriam **videt salūtat**que. "Salvē, Valeria!"

"Et tū, salvē," Valeria **inquit**. "Quid **agis** hodiē?"

"**Valeō**. Et tū? Quid tū et Licinia **agitis**? Et quid **agit** familia tua?"

"Bene! Omnēs **valēmus**. Et negōtium bonum est hodiē. Multī populī cibum pōtumque **cupiunt**. Iēiūnusne **es**?

5 Sitiensne **es**? **Cupis**ne aut cibum aut pōtum?"

Hermēs sitiens est et pōtum **poscit**. "Bibere **cupiō**," **inquit**, "dā mihi vīnum aquamque, sī **placet**."

Valeria vīnum aquamque in pōculō **pōnit**. Hermēs vīnumque aquamque **bibit** et laetus **est**. Rōmānī frequenter et vīnum et aquam in pōculō singulō **bibunt**, et in tabernā vīnum semper calidum **est**. Hermēs pecūniam **dat** et saccum in mensā **pōnit**.

VERBA ŪTENDA

agō, agere, ēgī, actum lead, drive

aut or; **aut... aut** either... or

bene well

calidum hot

cibum food

cupiō, cupere, cupīvī / cupiī, cupitum wish, want to

et and, also, even; **et... et** both... and

familia, -ae f. family

frequenter frequently

iēiūnus hungry

in tabernā in the tavern

mensā table

multī many

-ne asks a yes/no question

negōtium business

omnēs everyone

paedagōgus a slave assigned to a young boy, a tutor

pōculō cup

pōnō, pōnere, posuī, positum put

populī people

poscit asks for, orders

pōtum a drink

-que and; **-que... -que** both... and

Quid agis? How are you?; Quid agit familia tua? How is your family doing?

quoque also

saccus money sack

salūtō, salūtāre, salūtāvī, salūtātum greet, say **Salvē**

sī if

sī placet "if it pleases," "please"

singulō one, a single

sitiens thirsty

tua your

POSTQUAM LĒGISTĪ

1. What do Hermes and Valeria talk about right after they greet each other?
2. Why does Valeria say business is good?
3. In what way is the Roman custom of wine drinking different from typical practice today?
4. In what way is Hermes careless in this *lectiō*?

Grammatica B

The Present Stem

The Latin verbs *ambulat* and *respondet* consist of a **present stem** plus a personal ending.

VERB	PRESENT STEM	PERSONAL ENDING
ambulat	ambulā-	-t
respondet	respondē-	-t

Gemma

Compare *et... et* and *que... que*. They both mean *both... and* but their position is different:

> *vīnum**que** aquam**que***
> ***et** vīnum **et** aquam*

Gemma

Quid agis? Sometimes expressions cannot be translated literally from one language to another. This is a good example. Literally it means "What are you doing?" but it is equivalent of "How are you doing?" in English. Such expressions are called **idioms**.

You can usually determine the stem of a verb, at least for now, by dropping the personal ending from the end of the verb. Note that the stem of verbs like *ambulō* ends in *ā* and the stem of verbs like *respondeō* ends in *ē,* but these vowels can be long or short in the full form of the verb (*ambulās* vs. *ambulat*).

The 1st and 2nd Persons

In the previous chapter, you saw verbs in the present tense ending in *-t* (he, she, it) and *-nt* (they). You learned that these are the **3rd person** endings for the verb in Latin, but there are two more persons. Here is a summary of how person works in English:

		Singular Pronoun	Plural Pronoun
the speaker	1st person	I	we
the one spoken to	2nd person	you	you
the one spoken about	3rd person	he, she, it	they

In English we make minimal change to the actual verb and use personal pronouns to indicate the subject of the verb.

	Singular	Plural
1st person	I walk	we walk
2nd person	you walk	you walk
3rd person	he, she, it walk**s**	they walk

The English verb form only changes in the third person singular ("walks" instead of "walk"). Latin, being inflected, has a whole set of **personal endings**, and they are attached to the stem of the verb to indicate the person of the subject.

Here is a summary of how "person" works in Latin:

		Singular	Plural
the speaker	1st person	*-ō* (or *-m*)	*-mus*
the one spoken to	2nd person	*-s*	*-tis*
the one spoken about	3rd person	*-t*	*-nt*

Thus:

Person	Singular		Plural	
1st	ambul**ō**	I walk	ambulā**mus**	we walk
2nd	ambulā**s**	you walk	ambulā**tis**	you walk
3rd	ambula**t**	he, she, it walks	ambula**nt**	they walk
1st	responde**ō**	I respond	respondē**mus**	we respond
2nd	respondē**s**	you respond	respondē**tis**	you respond
3rd	responde**t**	he, she, it responds	responde**nt**	they respond

Notā Bene:
- Latin verbs consist of a stem plus a personal ending.
- The vowel between the stem and the personal ending changes according to the verb's conjugation or grouping.
- Latin always distinguishes between "you" singular and "you" plural, whereas English generally uses "you" to refer to either one or more than one person. But compare our American dialectical plurals: "y'all" (southern), "youse" (northern), and "yinz" (southern Pennsylvanian and Appalachian).
- English shows gender in the third person singular (he, she, it) but Latin does not.
- The first person singular of a verb like *ambulō* is the only one of these forms for which you cannot obtain the present stem by dropping the personal ending. This is because *ambulā + -ō → ambulo.* (If you want, you can remember it this way: "O's eat A's!")
- Although you will not encounter 1ˢᵗ person singular verbs ending in *-m* until later, here is a memnonic you can use to remember the personal endings:

MOST (*-m -o, -s, -t*)   MUST (*-mus*)   ISN'T (*-tis, -nt*)

EXERCEĀMUS!

4-6 Conjugation

Use the foms for *ambulō* and *respondeō* as models to fill in the charts for *salūtō* and *valeō.*

PERSON	SINGULAR		PLURAL	
1ˢᵗ	*salūtō*	I greet		
2ⁿᵈ				
3ʳᵈ			*salūtant*	they greet
1ˢᵗ	*valeō*	I am well		
2ⁿᵈ				
3ʳᵈ			*valent*	they are well

Asking Yes/No Questions

To ask a yes/no question in English we usually put the verb first and the subject second and add a question mark. Sometimes we add "do/does."

He is prepared to run.	Is he prepared to run?
You are hungry.	Are you hungry?
He wants wine.	Does he want wine?

To ask a yes/no question in Latin, add *-ne* to the first word in the sentence.

Currere parātus est.	*Est**ne** parātus currere?*
He is prepared to run.	Is he prepared to run?
Iēiūnus es.	*Es**ne** iēiūnus?*
You are hungry.	Are you hungry?
Vīnum cupit.	*Vīnum**ne** cupit?*
He wants wine.	Does he want wine?

Sitiens es.	*Sitiensne es?*
You are thirsty.	Are you thirsty?
Cupis aliquid bibere aut edere.	*Cupisne aliquid bibere aut edere?*
You want something to eat or drink.	Do you want something to eat or drink?

Notā Bene: *-ne* is not used when another interrogative word appears in the sentence.

Quid tibi nōmen est?	What is your name?
Ubi es?	Where are you?

Mōrēs Rōmānī

Wine in Ancient Rome

Prēlum antīquum Pompeiīs

Although grapes for wine had been grown north of Rome in Etruria and in Greek southern Italy for centuries, the cultivation of wine grapes and the consumption of wine did not become popular in Rome until the second century B.C. The earliest written work on wine in Rome was translated from Punic shortly after the end of the Third Punic War in 146 B.C. The first Roman to write about the topic was Cato the Elder in a work called *Dē Agrī Cultūrā* (*On Agriculture*). One of the most important documents on Roman wine production and use appears in Book XIV of *Historia Nātūrālis* (*Natural History*) by Pliny the Elder (23–79 A.D).

Vine cultivation in Rome spread quickly, and by the middle of the second century B.C., Rome was a major producer of wine grapes. In fact, in 154 B.C. the Roman Senate prohibited the cultivation of vines north of the Alps to preserve the market for Roman producers. Wine was cultivated on large estates worked by slaves. By the first century A.D., wine consumption in Rome was so high that wines were imported from provinces in Spain and France.

Romans especially liked sweet wines produced from very ripe grapes. *Mulsum,* a wine drink heavily flavored with honey, was especially popular among the lower classes. *Lōra,* a drink made from grape skins soaked in water and fermented, was often served to slaves.

Many Roman authors discuss multiple types of wine but especially praised a wine called Falernian, produced from grapes grown on Mount Falernus south of Rome.

Some of the finest Italian wines were produced in antiquity on the slopes of Mt. Vesuvius. The picture at left shows Bacchus, the god of wine, dressed in grapes and standing on the slope of the mountain, which is covered by grape vines. Evidence for wine production in this area includes the wine press (*prēlum, -ī* n.) depicted in the picture.

Latin continues to have a presence in modern wine-making: *Est! Est!! Est!!!* is a white wine produced in Montefiascone, north of Rome near Lake Bolsena. The name of the wine is attributed to a German bishop named Johann Fugger, who was going to Rome for the coronation of Henry V in the year 1125. Fugger sent a servant ahead of him to mark the inns with the best wine with *Est* (for *Vīnum bonum est*). At one inn in Montefiascone the servant apparently liked the wine so much that he wrote *Est! Est!! Est!!!*

The Romans had a lot to say about drinking wine. With the help of the *Verba Ūtenda,* you can understand what they said.

One of the earliest Roman writers to refer to wine is the 2nd-century B.C. playwright Plautus, who said:

Vesuvius et Bacchus

> *Magnum hoc vitium in vīnō est. Vīnum pedēs captat prīmum;*
> *Vīnum luctātor dolōsus est.*
>
> Pseudolus (act V, 1, 5)

A Roman proverb quoted by Pliny the Elder, reads:

In vīnō vēritās (est).

Doc Holliday also quoted this proverb in Latin in the 1993 film *Tombstone*.

In poem I.7 of his *Carmina* (*Odes*), the poet Horace (65–27 B.C.) said:

Nunc vīnō pellite cūrās.

In Petronius' *Satyricon 34* (1st century A.D.), a character named Trimalchio said:

Vīta vīnum est.

Finally, in his discourse *Dē Īrā* (*On Anger*, 2.19) the philosopher Seneca the Younger (c. 4 B.C.–65 A.D.) said:

Vīnum incendit īram.

🔊 VERBA ŪTENDA

captat (he, she, it) seizes	*luctātor* wrestler	*vīta* life
cūra, -ae f. care, concern	*pedēs* feet	*vīnō* with wine
dolōsus clever, crafty	*Pellite!* Banish!	*vīnum* despite the *-um*
hoc this	Drive away!	ending, this word is
incendit sets fire to, burns	*prīmum* first	nominative
īra, -ae f. anger	*vēritās* truth	*vitium* vice

Gemma

Cavē! (Beware!) The stem of *vīta* (life) is *vīt-* and the stem of *vitium* (vice) is *viti-*. That final *-i-* can make all the difference in Latin between "life" and "vice." The macron in *vīta* certainly helps, but how can the declension endings also be useful here?

Orbis Terrārum Rōmānus

Urbs Rōma

The major geographical landmarks of the city of Rome are the Tiber River (*Tiberis, -is* m.), which runs through the city, the *Campus Martius* (Field of Mars), and the following seven hills:

Capitoline (*Capitōlīnus Collis, Capitōlīnī Collis* m.; also *Capitōlium, -iī* n.)

Palatine (*Palātīnus Mons, Palātīnī Montis* m.; *Palātium, -iī* n.)

Esquiline (*Esquiliae, -ārum* f. pl.)

Caelian (*Caelius Mons, Caeliī Montis* m.)

Viminal (*Vīminālis Collis, Vīminālis Collis* m.)

Quirinal (*Quirīnālis Collis, Quirīnālis Collis* m.)

Aventine (*Aventīnus Mons, Aventīnī Montis* m.; *Aventīnum, -ī* n.)

Septem collēs Rōmae

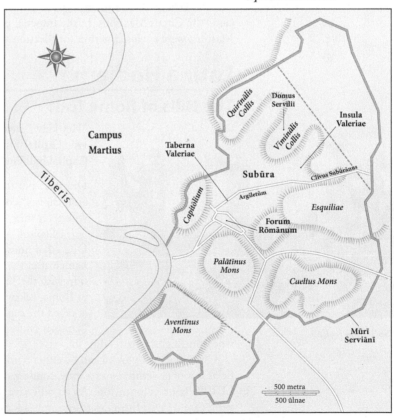

Dē Forō Rōmānō ad Capitōlium hodiē

Forum Rōmānum et Palātium hodiē

The Roman Forum is located in the valley between the Palatine and the Capitoline. It was on the Palatine Hill that the founders of Rome, Romulus and Remus, were said to have been nursed as infants by a she-wolf. On the Capitoline Hill were located the chief temples of the city, especially the Temple of Jupiter Capitolinus (*Capitōlium, -iī* n.), the most important temple in the city. Victorious generals led their triumphal processions along the Via Sacra through the Forum up to the *Capitōlium*. The route of the Via Sacra runs between two more hills, the Esquiline and the Caelian. The Viminal and the Quirinal Hills lie to the north of the Esquiline. The Velia is the projection of the Esquiline toward the Palatine. The seventh hill, the Aventine, lies to the south of the Palatine. In the valley between the Palatine and the Aventine was the Forum Boarium, an important market area, and the open space that eventually became the Circus Maximus. In the Imperial period, all seven of these hills, but not the Campus Martius, were enclosed within fortification walls.

Latīna Hodierna

The Hills of Rome Today

Capitōlium hodiē

"Hey kids, I have a **capitol** idea! Let's go to the nation's **capitol**, and visit **Capital** Hill where we can see all the Greek **capitols** on the **Capital** building!"

Did you spot the spelling errors in that sentence? Both "capital" and "capitol" come from Latin. Once you know their origins, you will never misspell them again.

"Capitol," in English, refers to the building in Washington, D.C., that houses the Congress. It stands on Capitol Hill and it is named after the *Capitōlium* in Rome, implying a clever identification with the Temple of Capitoline Jupiter on the Capitoline Hill in Rome. Likewise, the building in which a state legislature meets is called the capitol (lower case). These uses, and the Capitol Reef National Museum in Utah, are the only common forms of the words in English that end in -ol.

"Capital" with an -al can be either a noun or an adjective. As a noun it can mean: the official seat of government of a state, country, or the like; wealth, as in "capital funds"; CAPITAL LETTER; or column top. As an adjective "capital" means "chief" or "excellent." Both -al words are derived from *caput, -itis* n. head, main part.

So now you know that the paragraph at the beginning of this section *should* have read: "Hey kids, I have a **capital** idea! Let's go to the nation's **capital**, and visit **Capitol** Hill where we can see all the Greek **capitals** on the **Capitol** building!"

The city of Richmond, Virginia, is built on seven hills. The state capitol is located (naturally) on Capitol Hill.

Several of Rome's hills have taken on special meaning in some modern languages. For example, because Augustus and later emperors built elaborate homes on the Palatine hill, *Palātium* is the source of the word for "palace."

The president of modern Italy lives in a palace on the Quirinal Hill, so "Quirinale" in Italian means "the presidential palace." In English and French, "Quirinal" can also refer to the palace of the Italian president.

Now look at some other derivations:

Capitōlium Americānum

LATIN	ENGLISH	FRENCH	ITALIAN	SPANISH
Capitōlīnus	Capitoline	Capitole	Campidoglio Monte Capitolio	Capitolio
Capitōlium	Capitol	Capitole	Campidoglio	Capitolio
caput, capitis	capital	capitale	capitale	capital
Palātium	palace	palace	palazzo	palacio

QUID PUTĀS?

1. Why do you think *schola* and *lūdus*, two Latin words for "school," both originally referred to leisure and games?
2. Compare the Roman statements about wine to modern attitudes toward wine. Which of the Roman statements best express your own attitude toward wine. Why?
3. How have modern wine drinking tastes changed from Roman times?
4. Why do you think that the U.S. Capitol building has such close linguistic ties with the Capitoline Hill in Rome?

EXERCEĀMUS!

4-7 Scrībāmus

Answer each of these questions in Latin. Use complete sentences. You may use *ita* or *sīc* (yes) and *nōn* (no/not) in your answers as well. Follow the model.

HINT: All of these sentences are based on the quotations about wine in the *Mōrēs Rōmānī* section.

➤ Estne vēritās in vīnō? *Ita, vēritās in vīnō est!*

1. Estne magnum vitium in vīnō?

2. Captatne vīnum prīmum pedēs?

3. Estne vīnum luctātor?

4. Pellitne vīnum cūrās?

5. Vītane vīnum est?

6. Incenditne vīnum īram?

4-8 Colloquāmur

As you ask a classmate the following questions, use one of the words suggested in parentheses. Then have your classmate respond as she or he thinks fit. Follow the pattern in the model and experiment with word order.

⟶ Estne vēritās (in aquā, in cibō, in pōculō)?

Student #1   *Estne vēritās in aquā?*

Student #2   *Nōn, vēritās in aquā nōn est.*   or

               Nōn, vēritās nōn in aquā est.   or

               Ita, vēritās in aquā est.   or

               Sīc, in aquā vēritās est.

1. Valeriane (cibum, pecūniam, pōtum) in pōculō pōnit?

2. Vītane (vīnum, aqua, saccus, negōtium) est?

3. Hermēsne (aquam, Valeriam, pōculum) in mensā pōnit?

4. Cupiuntne omnēs (pecūniam, negōtium bonum, vīnum calidum)?

4-9 Verba Discenda

For each of the following English words, list the *Verbum Discendum* that is its source. Be sure to include the meaning of the Latin word. Then use the meaning of the Latin word to define the English word. Follow the model.

HINT: If you need help, use an English dictionary.

⟶ reactivate: *agō, agere, ēgī, actum* do, drive; to make to do again

1. depopulate   6. salutation

2. beneficiary   7. affiliation

3. introduction   8. iteration

4. deposition   9. domicile

5. ludicrous   10. cupidinous

🔊 VERBA DISCENDA

agō, agere, ēgī, actum **act, do, lead, drive** [agile, active]

aut **or; aut... aut either... or**

bene **well** [benefactor]

cupiō, cupere, cupīvī / cupiī, cupītum **wish, want to** [Cupid, cupidity]

domus, -ī f. **home, house** *domum* **home, to a house** [domicile]

dūcō, dūcere, dūxī, ductum **lead** [duct, induct]

et **and, also, even; et... et both... and**

familia, -ae f. **family** [familiarity]

fīlius, -ī m. **son** [filial]

hodiē **today**

iterum **again** [reiterate]

lūdus, -ī m. **school, game** [ludicrous]

māne **early in the morning**

-ne asks a yes/no question

pōnō, pōnere, posuī, positum **put, place** [position]

populus, -ī m. **people** [popularity]

-que **and; -que... -que both... and**

Quid agis? Quid agitis? **How are you?**

salūtō, salūtāre, salūtāvī, salūtātum **greet** [salutation, salutatorian]

Angulus Grammaticus

Enclitics and Word Stress

Did you notice anything unusual about *-ne* and *-que*, two words introduced in this chapter? They are not really independent words. Rather the hyphen tells you that they are always attached to another word. This type of linguistic element is called an **enclitic**. Technically, an enclitic is an element that has no stress or accent of its own and is tightly bound to the word that precedes it.

One question that arises with enclitics in Latin is the issue of pronunciation and stress. Though everyone agrees that enclitics like *-ne* and *-que* are never stressed themselves, there is debate as to how they affect the accent of the words to which they are attached.

Early Roman grammarians claimed that the enclitic was a sort of "accent magnet" and always attracted the accent to the syllable before the enclitic, whether that syllable was long or short. This would yield forms like:

acTORque
imitāTORque

This approach is the one most commonly used in classrooms today. But some later grammarians tend to believe that in the time of Augustus, the enclitic affected stress little or not at all and that the word was subject to the normal rules of stress. This would yield forms such as:

ACtorque
imiTÁtorque

Final certainty is not possible. As in English, there were probably variants even in antiquity. In various parts of America you might hear either version of this sentence:

"Don't forget your umbr**EL**la because if you catch
cold and die, we have no ins**UR**ance."

or

"Don't forget your **UM**brella because if you catch
cold and die, we have no **IN**surance."

How do you pronounce this sentence?

Photo Credits

page 38 (top) Lessing Archive/Art Resource/Art Resource, N.Y.; **page 46 (top)** Fotografica Foglia/Art Resource, N.Y. Fotografica Foglia/Scala/Art Resource, NY; **page 46 (bottom)** Vanni/Art Resource, N.Y.; **page 48 (top left)** Victor Martinez/Photo by Victor Martinez, used with permission; **page 48 (top right)** Victor Martinez/Photo by Victor Martinez, used with permission; **page 48 (bottom)** Clearview/Alamy Images; **page 49** Photos.com

In Forō

From *Disce! An Introductory Latin Course, volume 1*, First Edition. Francesco Bonavita. Copyright © 2011 by Pearson Education, Inc. Published by Pearson Prentice Hall. All rights reserved.

Forum Rōmānum

5

In Forō

GRAMMATICA

Asking Questions: *Num* and *Nōnne*

Prepositions

The Concept of Conjugation

More Principal Parts

MŌRĒS RŌMĀNĪ

Marmor et Templa Rōmāna

ORBIS TERRĀRUM RŌMĀNUS

Mausōlēum Augustī

LATĪNA HODIERNA

Animālia Rōmāna

ANGULUS GRAMMATICUS

Principal Parts in English and Latin

LECTIŌNĒS:
SĪMIA SŌCRATĒS
and
SĪMIA SAGAX

While at Valeria's snack shop, Hermes teases Socrates, the shop's pet monkey. Socrates snatches Hermes' money bag, and the angry *paedagōgus* chases the monkey through the Roman Forum.

Lectiō Prīma

Antequam Legis

Socrates the Monkey

While Hermes is at Valeria's *taberna*, he makes the mistake of teasing Socrates, the pet monkey in Valeria's shop. As you can see in the relief from Ostia in the *lectiō*, monkeys were often found in such shops. In this scene, two untied monkeys sit on the counter of a food store. (The rabbits are undoubtedly not pets, but are rather for sale.) Keeping pets in stores to attract customers is a phenomenon common to this day.

As you read about Hermes and the monkey, look out for more ways to ask questions in Latin.

Asking Questions with *Num* and *Nōnne*

Read this sentence aloud: "He wants to eat chicken."

Now read this sentence aloud: "He wants to eat chicken?"

Notice that we can tell that a spoken sentence is a question from the tone of voice, but a written question requires a punctuation mark. Spanish wisely puts an inverted question mark at the beginning of a question.

¿Dónde está el pollo?

Like Spanish, Latin puts its question indicators at the beginning of the sentence. There are three such Latin words, and each expects a different kind of answer:

Habēsne sīmiam?	a yes/no question	Do you have a monkey?
Nōnne sīmiam habēs?	expects a "yes" answer	You do have a monkey, don't you?
Num sīmiam habēs?	expects a "no" answer	You don't have a monkey, do you?

EXERCEĀMUS!

5-1 Asking Questions

Translate the following questions, using the chart as a guide.

1. Valeriane tabernam habet?
   Num Valeria tabernam habet?
   Nōnne Valeria tabernam habet?

2. Sīmiaene nōmen Sōcratēs?
   Nōnne sīmiae nōmen Sōcratēs?
   Num sīmiae nōmen Sōcratēs?

3. Nōnne Rōmānī vīnum bibunt?
   Rōmānīne vīnum bibunt?
   Num Rōmānī vīnum bibunt?

Gemma

Is the monkey Socrates male or female? *Sīmia, -ae* is 1st declension where most words are feminine. But some words are "common" gender, i.e., masculine or feminine.

Now watch for *-ne*, *nōnne*, and *num*, marked in **bold**, in *Lectiō Prīma*.

🔊 SĪMIA SŌCRATĒS

Subitō Hermēs sīmiam in tabernā videt. Nōmen sīmiae Sōcratēs est et in Valeriae tabernā cōtīdiē sedet et lūdit.

Hermēs rīdet. "Salvē, sīmia!" paedagōgus
5 inquit. "Quid agis? Habēs**ne** nōmen?"

Sīmia nihil respondet sed "Nōmen sīmiae," inquit Valeria, "Sōcratēs est." Sīcut Sōcratēs philosophus, sīmia habet nāsum plānum, ergō nōmen Sōcratēs est.

"Hermēs "Cupis**ne**," inquit vīnum, Sōcratēs?" et pōculum ostendit.

10 "**Num** vīnum," Licinia, Valeriae fīlia, clāmat, "eī das?!"

Error est. Sīmiae nōn vīnum amant, sed semper iocōs amant et Sōcratēs subitō saccum paedagōgī rapit.

"Ecce!" Hermēs clāmat. "Sīmia saccum meum habet. **Num**, sīmia, pecūniam meam cupis? **Nōnne** vīnum cupis? Dabis**ne** mihi saccum?"

Subitō Hermēs ad sīmiam salit, sed eum nōn capit. Sīmiae valdē celerēs sunt. Sōcratēs ē tabernā currit.

Sīmiae in tabernā Rōmānā

🔊 VERBA ŪTENDA

ad (+ acc.) to, toward
amō, amāre, amāvī, amātum love
clāmō (1) shout
celerēs fast, swift
cotīdiē daily
currō, currere, cucurrī, cursum run
dabisne? will you give?
ē / ex (+ abl.) out of, from
Ecce! Look!
eī to him

ergō therefore
error mistake, error
eum him
fīlia, -ae f. daughter
habeō, habēre, habuī, habitum have, hold
in (+ abl.) in, on, at; (+ acc.) into, against
iocus, -ī m. joke
lūdō, lūdere play
meus, -a, -um my
nāsus, -ī m. nose

nōnne asks a question expecting a yes answer
num asks a question expecting a no answer
ostendō, ostendere show
philosophus, -ī m. philosopher
plānum flat
pōculum, -ī n. cup
poscō, poscere, poposcī ask for, demand, request
Quid agis? How are you doing?

rapiō, rapere seize
rīdeō, rīdēre laugh
saccus, -ī m. money sack
saliō, salīre leap
sedeō, sedēre sit
sīcut just like
sīmia, -ae f. monkey
Sōcratēs, -is m. Socrates, a Greek philosopher
subitō suddenly
valdē very

Sōcratēs philosophus nāsum plānum habet.

Answer the first four questions in both Latin and English. Answer question 5 in English.

1. Why is the monkey called Socrates?
2. What mistake does Hermes make?
3. What does the monkey take from Hermes?
4. How does Hermes react?
5. What do you think is going to happen next?

Grammatica A

Asking Questions: *Num* and *Nōnne*

You have learned that to ask a yes/no question in Latin, you add the enclitic -*ne* to the first word in the sentence. Here are a few examples:

Currere parātus est.	*Est**ne** currere parātus?*
He is prepared to run.	Is he prepared to run?
Iēiūnus es.	*Es**ne** iēiūnus?* or *Iēiūnus**ne** es?*
You are hungry.	Are you hungry?

The person asking these questions is looking for simple yes/no information and is not anticipating a particular response.

It is possible, however, to ask the same questions in expectation of a particular answer. For example:

You are hungry, aren't you?	(expects the answer "yes" or "certainly")
You aren't hungry, are you?	(expects the answer "no" or "not at all")

Here is how Latin asks the same questions:

Nōnne iēiūnus es?	(expects the answer *ita* or *ita vērō*)
Num iēiūnus es?	(expects the answer *nōn* or *nōn vērō*)

EXERCEĀMUS!

5-2 **Answering Questions**

Use *Lectiō Prīma* to answer the following questions by saying either *ita*/(*sīc*) (yes) or *nōn* (no) and repeating the verb. Follow the models.

→ Q: Videt**ne** Hermēs sīmiam in tabernā?
   A: Ita, videt.

→ Q: **Num** sedet Sōcratēs in tabernā Valeriae cotīdiē?
   A: Nōn sedet.

1. **Num** sīmiae vīnum amant?
2. **Nōnne** rapit Sōcratēs saccum paedagōgī?
3. **Nōnne** amant sīmiae iōcōs semper?
4. Currit**ne** Sōcratēs ē tabernā?
5. **Num** sīmiae nōmen Hermēs est?
6. Capit**ne** Hermēs sīmiam?

Lectiō Secunda

Antequam Legis

Prepositions

In this *lectiō* Hermes chases Socrates through the Forum. The map will help you trace their route. **Prepositions** are parts of speech used with nouns or pronouns to express direction (in, on, around, through, under), the source of an action (by, on account of, etc.), or relationship (about, concerning, etc.). In English, the preposition does not affect the appearance of the noun or pronoun but in Latin it does. Note the following examples:

into the shop	*in tabernam*
in the shop	*in tabernā*
out of the shop	*ē tabernā*
through the shop	*per tabernam*

As these examples show, prepositions in Latin are used with either the **accusative case** or the **ablative case**. You are already familiar with the accusative. You will meet the ablative in the next chapter.

EXERCEĀMUS!

5-3 Prepositional Phrases

Before you read *Lectiō Secunda*, make a line-by-line list of 10 of the prepositions marked in **bold**. Then find the object of each preposition and decide whether the object is in the accusative or ablative case. Then translate the prepositional phrase. Follow the model.

HINT: You can recognize prepositions in the vocabulary because they are followed by **+ abl.** or **+ acc.** in the *Verba Ūtenda* to tell you which case they take.

REMEMBER: If it's not accusative, it's ablative!

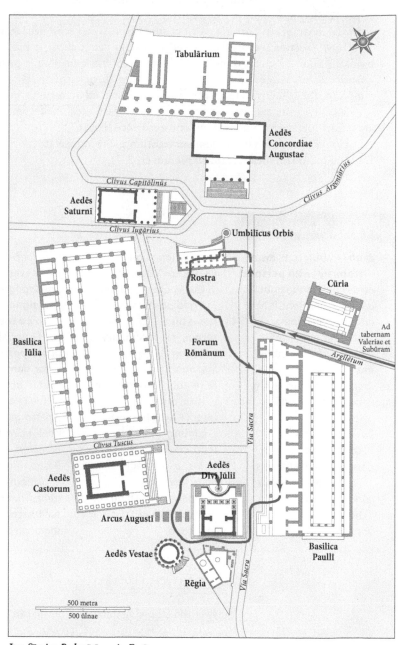

Iter Sīmiae Pedagōgique in Forō

Line	Preposition	Object	Case	Translation
→ 1	ad	Forum	acc.	to the Forum

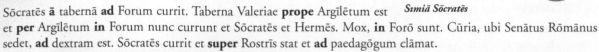

 SĪMIA SAGAX

Sīmiā Sōcratēs

Sōcratēs **ā** tabernā **ad** Forum currit. Taberna Valeriae **prope** Argīlētum est et **per** Argīlētum **in** Forum nunc currunt et Sōcratēs et Hermēs. Mox, **in** Forō sunt. Cūria, ubi Senātus Rōmānus sedet, **ad** dextram est. Sōcratēs currit et **super** Rostrīs stat et **ad** paedagōgum clāmat.

Tunc Sōcratēs **trans** Forum et **ad** Basilicam Paullī currit et basilicam intrat. **Per** basilicam currit et tunc **ē**
5 basilicā rumpit. Sōcratēs nunc **in** Viā Sacrā est. Sīmia latēre vult et **post** Dīvī Iūliī templum quiescit. Sed nōn diū quiescit, nam Hermēs advenit. Sōcratēs iterum currit et nunc stat medius **inter** Vestae templum et Castorum templum. Paedagōgus, valdē īrātus, sīmiam videt et **ad** eum currit.

Sōcratēs fessus est, sed adhūc saccum tenet. Sed, ecce! Paedagōgus valdē īrātus iam adest! Sōcratēs territus **ad** āram Dīvī Iūliī currit. Salit in āram et magnā vōce clāmat.

10 Hermēs **prope** āram stat. Sīmiam territum **in** ārā videt et rīdet. "Sīmia sagax es, Sōcratēs. **In** ārā sacrā salvus es! Dā mihi pecūniam meam et omne bonum est."

 VERBA ŪTENDA

ā, ab (+ abl.) **from, away from; by (with persons)**
ad dextram to the right
adest he is present, is here
adhūc to this point, still, yet
adveniō, advenīre come
āra, -ae f. altar
Argīlētum the Argiletum, (a street leading into the Roman Forum)
basilica, -ae f. basilica, courthouse
Castorum of the Castors, i.e., Castor and Pollux
cūria, -ae f. curia, senate house
dā! give! (command)

diū for a long time
dīvus Iūlius "divine Julius" (Julius Caesar was made a god posthumously)
fessus tired
forum, -ī n. **forum, city center**
iam now
in (+ abl.) **in, on;** (+ acc.) **into, onto**
inter (+ acc.) **between, among**
intrō, intrāre enter
īrātus, -a, -um angry
lateō, latēre hide
magnā vōce in a loud voice
medius midway
mox soon

nam for, because
omne everything
paedagōgus, -ī m. **a slave assigned to a young boy, a tutor**
per (+ acc.) **through**
poscō, poscere, poposcī ask **for, demand, request**
post (+ acc.) **behind, after**
prope (+ acc.) **near**
quiescō, quiescere rest
rīdeō, rīdēre laugh
Rōmānus, -a, -um Roman
Rostra, -ōrum n. pl. speaker's platform
rumpō, rumpere burst
sacra sacred, holy
sagax wise

saliō, salīre leap
sedeō, sedēre, sēdī, sessum sit
senātus senate
sīmia, -ae f. **monkey**
stō, stāre, stetī, stātum stand
super (+ acc. or abl.) **over, on top of**
templum temple
territus afraid, scared
trans (+ acc.) **across**
tunc then
ubi **where, when**
via, -ae f. **road, way**
valdē very
Vesta, -ae f. Vesta, goddess of the hearth
vult he wishes, wants

POSTQUAM LĒGISTĪ

Answer the following questions in English.

1. Where does Socrates run when he leaves Valeria's snack shop?
2. What is the Curia used for?
3. Which building does Socrates enter?
4. What does Socrates want to do once he gets to the Via Sacra?
5. Between which two temples does Socrates stand?
6. Where does the chase end?
7. Why does Hermes tell Socrates he is a wise monkey?

Grammatica B

Prepositions

Here are several prepositional phrases you saw in the reading:

per Argīlētum	through the Argiletum
ad āram Dīvī Iūliī	to the altar of Divine Julius
trans Forum	across the Forum
ad Forum	to the Forum
post Dīvī Iūliī templum	behind the temple of Divine Julius
ad Basilicam Paullī	to the Basilica Paulli

Notice how all of these prepositions are followed by nouns in the accusative case. These words are called the **objects of the prepositions**. The preposition plus its object is called a **prepositional phrase**.

Not all objects of prepositions are accusative. Some are ablative, a case you will learn in the next chapter. Here are some ablative objects of prepositions you have already seen.

ā tabernā	away from the snack shop
ē tabernā	out of the snack shop
in tabernā	in the snack shop
in ārā	on the altar
super Rostrīs	on top of the Rostra

Notā Bene: *ā* and *ē* tend to be used before consonants, *ab* and *ex* before vowels.

The Concept of Conjugation

You have noticed that verbs have a variety of vowels before their personal endings. Which vowel to use with which verb depends on that verb's **conjugation**. Latin verbs are grouped into four categories or **conjugations** depending upon which vowel appears before the *-re* of the infinitive.

CONJUGATION	INFINITIVE	STEM	VOWEL SIGN
1st	*ambulāre*	*ambulā-*	stem ends in *-ā*
2nd	*respondēre*	*respondē-*	stem ends in *-ē*
3rd	*vendere*	*vende-*	stem ends in *-e*
4th	*venīre*	*venī-*	stem ends in *-ī*

In your dictionary, each verb is listed with its four **principal parts**, and these, too, help you create various tenses and forms of the verb. For now we are focusing on 1st and 2nd conjugation verbs.

More Principal Parts

You will find a Latin verb listed in the dictionary under its 1ˢᵗ person singular form, generally followed by three other forms. These four forms are called principal parts (PP). Here is what you will find for the verb *salūtō*:

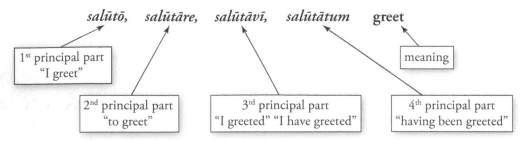

salūtō, salūtāre, salūtāvī, salūtātum **greet**

1ˢᵗ principal part "I greet"

2ⁿᵈ principal part "to greet"

3ʳᵈ principal part "I greeted" "I have greeted"

meaning

4ᵗʰ principal part "having been greeted"

Notā Bene: The pattern of principal parts for 1ˢᵗ conjugation verbs like *salūtō* is so predictable that, from now on, we will only list them in *Verba Discenda* like this: *salūtō* (1).

EXERCEĀMUS!

5-4 **Dictionary Entries**

Your turn. Take this dictionary form and identify its parts.

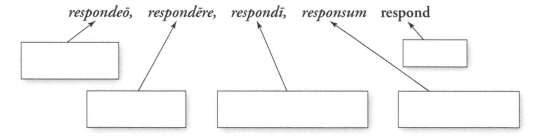

respondeō, respondēre, respondī, responsum **respond**

Mōrēs Rōmānī

Marmor et Templa Rōmāna

The Romans themselves justly boasted of their impressive forum and its history. They often noted with pride that the area filled with majestic buildings in the time of Augustus was once only swampland. Here the poet Ovid (43 B.C.–17 A.D.) describes the site:

hōc ubi nunc fora sunt, palūdēs ūdae tenuēre

Fasti vi.401

The Emperor Augustus himself boasted about his own building projects. He said:

(Urbem) marmoream relinquō, quam laternciam accēpī

Suetonius *Dīv Aug* 28

🔊 VERBA ŪTENDA

accēpī I accepted, received	*palūdēs* swamps	*tenuēre* (they) held
hōc here	*quam* which	*ūdus, -a, -um* wet
latericiam made of brick	*relinquō, relinquere*	*urbem* city
marmoream made of marble	leave	

Caesar Augustus Dīvus Iūlius

Ironically, the marble veneer has generally been removed from the surviving monuments of the Augustan Age, and only their brick infrastructure remains, as you can see on the tomb of Augustus in Rome today. We often have to use our imagination to appreciate how the monuments originally appeared.

Many of these Augustan monuments are temples. The Romans considered these buildings to be homes for the cult statues of the gods, not buildings in which large congregations could worship. The typical Roman temple (*templum, -ī* n.; also *aedēs, aedis* f.) was rectangular. It was fronted by a tall staircase leading to a collonaded portico. Though the columns of a Greek temple commonly ran around all four sides of the building, the columns on a Roman temple were usually only in front. Inside were the cult statue of the deity and other sacred objects.

Aedēs Vestae et Aedēs Castorum hodiē

Aedēs Castorum, the Temple of Castor and Pollux, follows this design. Originally built after the Battle of Lake Regillus in 496 B.C., a Roman victory where the twin gods (also known as *Geminī*) were thought to play a major role in Roman victory, the temple burned down in 14 B.C. Its reconstruction was not finished until 6 A.D. when it was rededicated by the Emperor Tiberius. So when Hermes chases Socrates through the Forum, the new temple is still under construction (as is the Basilica Paulli).

Aedēs Vestae, the Temple of Vesta (Roman goddess of the hearth), is unusual in that its design is circular instead of rectangular. Here the Vestal Virgins, the priestesses of Vesta, always kept a fire burning on the public hearth of the city. The temple was built in the 3rd century B.C. and was rebuilt after the famous fire of 64 A.D. during the reign of Nero. This is one of the few buildings in the Forum that Augustus did not construct or rebuild.

Aedēs Dīvī Iūliī hodiē

Aedēs Dīvī Iūliī was built on the site where Julius Caesar's body was cremated after his assassination on the Ides of March in 44 B.C. The temple was dedicated to the deified Caesar by Augustus on August 18, 29 B.C. On one side of the Roman coin depicted at left, Julius Caesar is celebrated as divine. Note the comet with eight rays, one with a tail, which is said to have been seen in 44 B.C. after his death. The other side of the coin shows the image of Augustus. As long as Socrates sat on the altar in front of this temple, he was protected by the ancient law of suppliants, which said that anyone being chased could seek sanctuary or protection from pursuers by taking refuge at such a religious spot.

Āra Dīvī Iūliī hodiē

Forum Rōmānum dē Palātīnō

Orbis Terrārum Rōmānus

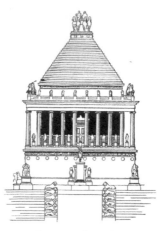

Exemplar Mausōlēī Halicarnassī

Mausōlēum Augustī

Augustus started building his own mausoleum in Rome in 28 B.C., three years after he defeated Mark Antony and Cleopatra at the Battle of Actium. In planning this tomb, Augustus certainly had in mind monuments like the Mausoleum of Halicarnassus, built in 353 B.C. and one of the Seven Wonders of the Ancient World. Only the foundations of Mausolus' tomb remain today, but ancient descriptions provide some idea of its appearance. Mausolus' tomb was so famous that "mausoleum" became the name for any tomb. Compare its design with the Masonic House of the Temple of Scottish Rite in Washington, D.C.

Inside Augustus' mausoleum were the cinerary urns of the emperor and his family. This fragmentary inscription from the Mausoleum commemorates Augustus' sister Octavia:

OCTAVIA . C . F | SOROR | AVGV

And here is a fuller version of the text with the abbreviations explained in brackets and the possible missing text supplied in parentheses.

OCTAVIA . C[AII]. F[ILIA] | SOROR | AVGV(STI . CAESARIS)

Can you translate this on your own?

Mausōlēum Augustī hodiē

Imitātiō Mausōlēī Halicarnassī

Latīna Hodierna

Animālia Rōmāna

English has borrowed many Latin words for animals. Here are just a few examples:

Latin	Animal	English
sīmia, **sīmi**ae	monkey	**simi**an
canis, **can**is	dog	**can**ine
fēlēs, **fēl**is	cat	**fel**ine
bōs, **bov**is	bull, cow	**bov**ine
piscis, **pisc**is	fish	**pisc**ine
serpens, **serpent**is	snake, serpent	**serpent**ine

Notice how the English word is often derived from the genitive (rather than nominative) form of the Latin word. The general rule is that the stem of a Latin word is determined by dropping the ending on the genitive singular form of the Latin word. So the stem of *sīmia* is *sīmi-* from *sīmiae* and the stem of *serpens* is *serpent-* from *serpentis*.

QUID PUTĀS?

1. Compare the design of Roman temples described in *Mōrēs Rōmānī* with a place of worship with which you are familiar.
2. Are there any modern parallels to the right of sanctuary that prevents Hermes from seizing Socrates on the Altar of Divine Julius?
3. Using the *Latīna Hodierna* as a guide, can you find any more English words based on the Latin word for an animal followed by the suffix **-ine**?

EXERCEĀMUS!

5-5   Scrībāmus

Answer the following questions with complete Latin sentences based on the *Lectiōnēs* in this chapter. The result will be a paragraph about *Lectiō Prīma*. We have started the narrative for you.

→ Does Socrates sit in Valeria's snack shop every day?
Sōcratēs in tabernā Valeriae cotīdiē sedet.

1. Does the monkey love wine?

2. Does Socrates snatch the *paedagōgus's* wallet?

3. Do monkeys always love jokes?

4. Does Socrates run from the snack shop?

5. Where does Socrates run?

6. Does Hermes catch the monkey?

5-6   Colloquāmur

Practice asking and answering the questions in Exercise 5-5 with other members of your class, but change each sentence a bit before you ask it. For example:

→ Q: Does the monkey like money?
A: Ita, sīmia pecūniam amat.

5-7   Verba Discenda

Draw a simple house (*casa, -ae* f). Then, pick out all the prepositions from the *Verba Discenda* and illustrate each one with the house you have drawn. Thus, *in casam* would have an arrow going into the house.

🔊 **VERBA DISCENDA**

ā, ab (+ abl.) away from
ad (+ acc.) to, toward
clāmō (1) shout
currō, currere, cucurrī, cursum run [curriculum, cursor]
ē / ex (+ abl.) out of, from
forum, -ī n. forum, city center
habeō, habēre, habuī, habitum have, hold [habit]

in (+ abl.) in, on, at; (+ acc.) into, onto
inter (+ acc.) between, among [intermediary]
meus, -a, -um my
nōnne asks a question expecting a yes answer
num asks a question expecting a no answer

paedagōgus, -ī m. a slave assigned to a young boy, a tutor [pedagogy]
per (+ acc.) through
poscō, poscere, poposcī ask for, demand, request
post (+ acc.) after, behind
prope (+ acc.) near [propinquity]
sedeō, sedēre, sēdī, sessum sit [sedentary]

sīmia, -ae m. monkey [simian]
stō, stāre, stetī, stātum stand [stationary, station]
trans (+ acc.) across [transfer]
ubi where, when [ubiquitous, ubiquity]
via, -ae f. road, way [viaduct]
vult (s)he wishes, wants

Angulus Grammaticus

Principal Parts in English and Latin

Though most Latin verbs have four principal parts, English verbs typically have only three.

Base	Past	Past Participle
walk	walked	walked

What are these principal parts? These are the words you need to use the verb in all its forms. Here are examples of forms you can make from each principal part:

Base	Past	Past Participle
I walk	I (have) walked	(having) walked
walking		

Many English verbs are fairly regular and form their principal parts, on the **-ed** model.

dance	danced	danced
work	worked	worked
tie	tied	tied
try	tried	tried

But we are all aware of the number of irregular verbs English has.

go	went	gone
bring	brought	brought
lie	lay	lain
lay	laid	laid

What others can you think of?

So how does a person learning English learn such forms? By trial and error and by memorization. We have all heard a child say, "Yesterday we goed to the zoo." You will have to do the same as you learn Latin. There are some general patterns that can help.

1st conjugation verbs are generally so regular that we can write their principal parts in shorthand in your vocabulary lists.

Thus, *ambulō* (1) stands for

| *ambulō* | *ambulāre* | *ambulāvī* | *ambulātum* |

Notā Bene: This is how we list 1st conjugation verbs in *Disce!* So *temptō* (1) means "this is a regular 1st conjugation verb."

2nd conjugation verbs have a few more patterns to their principal parts:

videō	*vidēre*	*vīdī*	*vīsum*
teneō	*tenēre*	*tenuī*	*tentum*

3rd conjugation verbs have the most variation of all, but a few patterns can help you with the 3rd PP. Notice verbs like:

dūcō	*dūcere*	*duxī*	*ductum*
regō	*regere*	*rexī*	*rectum*
mittō	*mittere*	*mīsī*	*missum*

Such verbs form the perfect stem (here, the 3rd PP) by adding an *-s* to the stem.

$$\text{dūc} + \text{s} \longrightarrow \text{dux-}$$
$$\text{rēg} + \text{s} \longrightarrow \text{rex-}$$
$$\text{mitt} + \text{s} \longrightarrow \text{mīs-}$$

Some verbs reduplicate (repeat) the first consonant of their stem.

currō	*currere*	*cucurrī*	*cursum*
cadō	*cadere*	*cecidī*	*casum*

But in many instances, you simply have to memorize the stem. It is important! It is often the only thing that differentiates a form:

dūcit	she leads	*dūxit*	she led
fugit	he flees	*fūgit*	he fled

4th conjugation verbs have a large group that parallels the 1st conjugation format.

dormiō	*dormīre*	*dormīvi*	*dormītum*

Others act rather like third conjugation verbs.

veniō	*venīre*	*vēnī*	*ventum*

Again, pay attention!

equus venit	the horse is coming
equus vēnit	the horse has come

Photo Credits

page 52 (top) Victor Martinez/Photo by Victor Martinez, used with permission; **page 53** Erich Lessing/Art Resource/Art Resource, N.Y.; **page 56** Clipart.com; **page 58** Kalkriese Museum/akgimages/The Image Works/The Image Works; **page 59 (top)** Victor Martinez/Photo by Victor Martinez, used with permission; **page 59 (top middle)** Thomas J. Sienkewicz/Photo by Thomas J. Sienkewicz, used with permission; **page 59 (bottom left)** Victor Martinez/Photo by Victor Martinez, used with permission; **page 59 (bottom right)** Victor Martinez/Photo by Victor Martinez, used with permission; **page 60 (top)** Clipart.com; **page 60 (bottom left)** Hunter Nielson/Photo by Hunter Nielson, with permission; **page 60 (bottom right)** Julia Sienkewicz/Photo by Julia Sienkewicz, with permission

In Lūdō Chīrōnis

From *Disce! An Introductory Latin Course, volume 1*, First Edition. Francesco Bonavita. Copyright © 2011 by Pearson Education, Inc. Published by Pearson Prentice Hall. All rights reserved.

Ludī magister cum discipulīs

GRAMMATICA

The Ablative Case

Translating the Ablative

Prepositions and Case

The Verb *Sum*

The Infinitive

The Imperative

Mood

MŌRĒS RŌMĀNĪ

Magistrī Rōmānī

LATĪNA HODIERNA

Latin Words in American Education

ORBIS TERRĀRUM RŌMĀNUS

Hispānia

ANGULUS GRAMMATICUS

Ablatives with and without Prepositions

> **LECTIŌNĒS:**
> MAGISTER CHĪRŌN
> and
> CHĪRŌN ĪRĀTUS
>
> Hermes returns from the Forum to the school (*lūdus*) run by the freedman Chiron. He watches events at the school for a while and then begins the journey home with Lucius.

6

In Lūdō Chīrōnis

Lectiō Prīma

Antequam Legis

In this chapter we meet Chiron, Lucius' *magister* (teacher). He is a *lībertīnus* (freedman), a slave who has been freed. Some freedmen became very wealthy and influential in Rome, but a teacher was seen as a lower-class worker. Like Hermes, Chiron bears a name his master thought was funny. Chiron was the centaur who tutored the heroes Achilles and Hercules.

The Verb *Sum*

The verb **to be** is irregular both in English and in Latin. These forms are in *italics* in *Lectiō Prīma*.

sum	I am	*sumus*	we are
es	you are	*estis*	you are
est	he, she, it is	*sunt*	they are
		esse	to be

The Ablative Case

You have seen the ablative case already in previous readings, but now we introduce it formally. Here are a few facts:

- If the ablative is used with a preposition, simply translate the word according to the meaning of the preposition: e.g., **ē** *lūdō* **out of** the school, **sub** *tabulā* **under** the table.
- If the ablative is alone, remember the acronym **BWIOF**. This stands for:

By With In On From

When you see an ablative alone, substitute whichever of the BWIOF prepositions sounds the best. It is that simple.

EXERCEĀMUS!

6-1 Ablative Case

The ablatives in *Lectiō Prīma* are marked in **bold**. List their line number, indicate if they are used with a preposition and translate the ablative with the preposition or with BWIOF. Follow the models.

Line	Ablative	Preposition?	Translation
→ 1	tabernā	*in*	at the snack shop
→ 2	vīnō	no	with wine

🔊 MAGISTER CHĪRŌN

In **tabernā** Valeria Liciniaque īrātae *sunt* sed Hermēs nōn īrātus *est*. Sīmia territus sub **mensā** sē abdit. Licinia pōculum **vīnō** implet et aquam addit. Pōculum in **mensā** ponit et Hermēs vīnum cum **aquā** bibit. (Sīmia sub **mensā** semper est.)

"Domina," inquit Hermēs, "Nōn īrātus *sum*. Habeō saccum meum et omnem
5   pecūniam meam. Sine **culpā** es et sīmiae *sunt* sīmiae."

Respondet Valeria: "Benignus *es*, amīce. Hodie vīnum tuum sine **pretiō** *est*. Accipe pecūniam tuam!"

Paedagōgus cum **fēminīs** breviter confert et tunc ad lūdum magistrī Chīrōnis ambulat. Chīrōn lībertīnus et Hispānus *est*. Prō **lūdō** magistrī, decem puerī et duae
10   puellae in **terrā** sedent. Magister Chīrōn prō **discipulīs** stat, sed nōn docet. Omnēs puerī et puellae tabulās et stilōs habent, sed nōn scrībunt **stilīs** in **tabulīs**. Spectant Lūcium et magistrum. Sōlus Lūcius tabulam et stilum nōn habet. Chīrōn tabulam et stilum Lūciī tenet et tabulam inspectat. In **tabulā** pictūram videt et pictūra pulchra nōn *est*. Pictūra *est* figūra virī. In **pictūrā** vir nāsum longum et sōlum trēs capillōs longōs habet.

15   Chīrōn prō **puerō** stat. Valdē īrātus *est*. "Puer," inquit, "quis *est* in **pictūrā**? Num in **pictūrā tuā** *sum*?"

"Nōn in **pictūrā** *es*, magister. **Nūllō modō** caput tuum *est*! Tū omnīnō calvus es et ille vir trēs capillōs habet!"

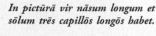
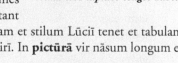

In pictūrā vir nāsum longum et sōlum trēs capillōs longōs habet.

🔊 VERBA ŪTENDA

abdō, abdere hide
accipiō, accipere take
addō, addere add
amīcus, -ī m. friend
benignus, -a, -um kind
calvus, -a, -um bald
capillus, -ī m. hair
caput head
cogitō (1) think
conferō, conferre talk together
culpa, -ae f. blame, fault
cum (+ abl.) with
decem ten
doceō, docēre teach

domina ma'am
duae two
figūra, -ae f. shape
Hispānus, -a, -um Spanish
iam now, already
ille that
impleō, implēre fill
inspectō (1) look at
īrātus, -a, -um angry
libertīnus, -ī m. freedman
longus, -a, -um long
mensa, -ae f. table
nāsum, -ī n. nose
nūllō modō in no way
omnem all

omnīnō completely
pictūra, -ae f. picture
pretium, -iī price, cost
prō (+ abl.) in front of, before
pulchra pretty
puella, -ae f. girl
puer, -ī m. boy
quis? who?
saccus, -ī m. money bag
scrībō, scrībere, scrīpsī, scrīptum write
sē himself
sedeō, sedēre sit
sine (+ abl.) without

stilus, -ī m. stilus, pen
sōlum only
spectō (1) look at
sub (+ abl.) under, from under; (+ acc.) under
tabula, -ae f. slate, tablet
teneō, tenēre, tenuī, tentum hold
terra, -ae f. land, ground
territus afraid
trēs, tria three
tuus, -a, -um your (sing.)
valdē very

1. How does Hermes explain and justify Socrates' behavior? Do you agree with him?
2. How do the women try to make amends to Hermes for what Socrates did?
3. How does Chiron's classroom compare to modern schoolrooms?
4. Do you think the reply Lucius gives to Chiron's questions at the end of the reading will make the schoolmaster angry or happy? Why?
5. What does Lucius' reply to Chiron tell you about Lucius' personality?

Grammatica A

The Ablative Case

Here are the endings of the **ablative case** for the first two declensions.

	1ST DECLENSION		2ND DECLENSION		
Singular					
Nominative	-a	fēmina	-us, -er, -ir	discipulus	magister	vir
Genitive	-ae	fēminae	-ī	discipulī	magistrī	virī
Accusative	-am	fēminam	-um	discipulum	magistrum	virum
Ablative	**-ā**	**fēminā**	**-ō**	**discipulō**	**magistrō**	**virō**
Plural					
Nominative	-ae	fēminae	-ī	discipulī	magistrī	virī
Genitive	-ārum	fēminārum	-ōrum	discipulōrum	magistrōrum	virōrum
Accusative	-ās	fēminās	-ōs	discipulōs	magistrōs	virōs
Ablative	**-īs**	**fēminīs**	**-īs**	**discipulīs**	**magistrīs**	**virīs**

Notā Bene:
- The ablative singular form in both declensions has a long vowel (-*ā* or -*ō*).
- The ablative plural form is the same in both declensions (-*īs*).
- Add the ablative ending to the stem of the noun. The stem is the genitive singular minus the ending, so *magistrō*.

Translating the Ablative

You probably have no trouble translating the following phrases because of the prepositions that precede them. All the words in **bold italics** are in the **ablative case**.

in tabernā	*in terrā*	*in pictūrā*	*prō puerīs*
in the shop	on the ground	in the picture	before the boys

Did you also notice these ablative phrases, which have no preposition in Latin?

*Licinia pōculum **vīnō** implet.*	Licinia fills the cup **with wine**.
*Discipulī nōn scrībunt **stilīs** in tabulīs.*	The students are not writing **with stiluses** on their tablets.

In both of these sentences, the English preposition is understood with the Latin ablative.

Notā Bene:
- Translate the preposition if there is one. If not, supply one using BWIOF.
- Most uses of the ablative have grammatical names:
  If Valeria fills the cup with wine (*vīnō*) or the boys write with styluses (*stilīs*), this is called an **ablative of means**.
  If Valeria is shouting with Joy or Chiron is acting with anger, this is an **ablative of manner**.
  More information on these constructions can be found in the *Angulus Grammaticus*.

Prepositions and Case

In Chapter 5, we introduced prepositions that took the accusative case. Now look at some prepositional phrases that take the ablative case:

***cum** fēminīs*	with the women	***in** tabernā*	in the snack shop
***dē** amīcīs*	concerning friends	***in** tabulā*	on the tablet
***ē** lūdō*	out of the school	***sub** mensā*	under the table

Now study these accusative prepositional phrases:

per Argīlētum	through the Argiletum
ad āram Dīvī Iūliī	to the altar of Divine Julius
trans Forum	across the Forum

Do you see any patterns here?

Hints:
- If the prepositional phrase expresses "motion toward," the object is generally accusative.
- If the prepositional phrase expresses location (e.g., in, on), the object is generally ablative.
- If the phrase expresses motion away from (e.g., out of, away from, down from), the object is generally ablative.
- When you learn a Latin preposition, it is important to learn in what case its object is placed.

Here is a list of prepositions by case:

Ablative **Location / Motion Away From**	**Accusative** **Motion Toward / Position in a Series**
ā, ab from, away	*ad* to, toward
cum with	*inter* between
dē from, down from	*per* through, across
ē, ex out of, from	*in* into
in in, on	*post* after, behind
prō in front of	*sub* under
sine without	*super* over
sub under	*trans* through, across
super over	

Notā Bene:

- Some prepositions can take either the accusative or the ablative, depending on whether they are showing location or movement toward:

Super Rostrīs stat.	He stands on top of the Rostra.
Super Rostra currit.	He runs over the top of the Rostra.

- The preposition *in* can be translated three different ways in English, depending on context:

  in + accusative = into:
  In *basilicam currit.* He runs **into** the basilica.
  in + ablative = in, on
  In *basilicā est.* He is **in** the basilica.
  Saccum **in** *mensā pōnit.* He puts his money bag **on** the table.

  Consider the *taberna* in the following sentences:

Sīmia in tabernam currit.	The monkey runs **into** the snack shop.
Sīmia in tabernā sedet.	The monkey is sitting **in** the snack shop.
	The monkey is sitting **on** the snack shop.

The Verb *Sum*

Notice that although the verb *sum* is irregular, it actually uses the personal endings you already know, except in the 1st person singular:

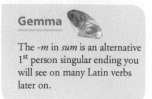

Gemma

The *-m* in *sum* is an alternative 1st person singular ending you will see on many Latin verbs later on.

	SINGULAR	PLURAL
1st person	su**m**	su**mus**
2nd person	e**s**	es**tis**
3rd person	es**t**	su**nt**
Infinitive	esse	

Now you can understand why that mnemonic for personal endings begins with *m-*:

MOST MUST ISN'T

Notā Bene:
- The stem of this verb is irregular. Sometimes it appears as *su-* (*sum, sumus, sunt*) and sometimes as *es-* (*es, est, estis*).
- The personal endings are the same as those used for other verbs like *ambulō* except in the 1st person singular, where *-m* is used instead of *-ō*.
- The infinitive *esse* does not end in *-re* (as in *ambulāre*).

EXERCEĀMUS!

6-2 Agreement

Use the English prompts provided in parentheses to write the correct Latin form of *sum* needed to complete each sentence. Follow the model.

→ In lūdō laeta (you sing.) _____: *es*. You are happy in school.

1. In lūdō laetus (I)
2. In lūdō laetī (we)
3. In lūdō laetī (they)

4. In lūdō laetus (he)
5. In lūdō laetae (you pl.)

Lectiō Secunda

Antequam Legis

The Infinitive

In English infinitives are made by adding "to" in front of a verb: to give, to speak, etc. All the infinitives marked in **bold italics** in the *lectiō* end in *-re*.

The Imperative

Imperatives are used to give commands or orders. You have seen them already in forms like *Salvē!* or *Valēte!* Here are a few others:

Tabulae stilusque

Singular	Plural	Translation
Spectā!	*Spectāte!*	Look!
Sedē!	*Sedēte!*	Sit down!

In Latin most negative imperatives consist of two words: *Nōlī* or *Nōlīte* (Don't!) plus an infinitive.

Singular	Plural	Translation
Nōlī dare!	*Nōlīte dare!*	Don't give!
Nōlī adiuvāre!	*Nōlīte adiuvāre!*	Don't help!

In the *lectiō*, we have marked all the imperatives in **bold**.

EXERCEĀMUS!

6-3 Imperatives

As you read, make line-by-line lists of infinitives and imperatives and translate each into English. Remember that infinitives are marked in **bold italics** and imperatives in **bold**. Follow the models.

	Infinitives	Imperatives
→ Line 3		Observā!
→ Lines 4–5	verberāre	Nōlī verberāre

CHĪRŌN ĪRĀTUS

Omnēs puerī et puellae rīdent et, in viā, Hermēs quoque rīdet. Sōlus Chīrōn
nōn rīdet, sed virgam capit et ad Lūcium ruit. "Puer male! Numquam *discere*
vīs! Observā!" Lūcius valdē timet. Sedet sub virgā magistrī et tremit. Chīrōn
virgam altē tollit sed tunc Hermēs magnā vōce clāmat: "**Nōlī**, magister,

5 puerum *verberāre*! Bonus puer, sed animōsus, est."

Chīrōn paulisper cōgitat et virgam dēpōnit. Magistrī saepe discipulōs
virgā pulsant, et Chīrōn Lūcium *verberāre* vult, sed Chīrōn Servīlium, patrem Lūciī, *irrītāre* nōn vult. Servīlius vir potens Rōmae est.

Chīrōn in sellā sedet et "Discipulī," inquit "**Sedēte** et **scrībite** in tabulīs

10 vestrīs. **Este** quiētī et **nōlīte** sonum *facere*!"

Puerī puellaeque clāmant, "Nōnne sumus bonī discipulī, magister?" et
stilīs in tabulīs *scrībere* incipiunt. Sōlus sonus in lūdō est sonus stilōrum.
Chīrōn surgit et circum discipulōs *ambulāre* incipit. Pauca post mōmenta
nōn iam īrātus est. Prō puerīs et puellīs magister stat et "Discipulī," inquit.

15 "Domum **ite**! Fīnis studiōrum est. **Discite** trēs sententiās Publiliī Syrī et
revenīte crās!"

Hermēs ad Lūcium ambulat. "Puer," inquit, "ambulā mēcum! Iēiūnusne
es? Aliquid *edere* cupis?"

Puer "Rēctē dīcis," inquit, "iēiūnus sum. **Dūc** mē ad cibum!" Puer

20 paedagōgusque ad Valeriae tabernam eunt priusquam domum eunt.

Magister īrātus virgam altē tollit. Lūcius valdē timet.

VERBA ŪTENDA

aliquid something
altē high
animōsus, -a, -um spirited
circum (+ acc.) around
crās tomorrow
cupiō, cupere want
dēpōnō, dēpōnere lay down
discō, discere, didicī learn
dīcō, dīcere speak
Dūc! Lead!
edō, edere eat
Este! Be!
eunt they go
faciō, facere, fēcī, factum
   make, do
fīnis end
iēiūnus, -a, -um hungry
incipiō, incipere begin
inquam, inquit say
īrātus, -a, -um angry

īte! go!
irrītō (1) upset
malus, -a, -um bad
mēcum = cum mē, with me
mōmentum, -ī n. moment
nōn iam not any longer
numquam never
observō (1) pay attention (to)
omnēs all
paulisper for a little while
patrem father
pauca a few
potens powerful
priusquam before
prō (+ abl.) in front of,
   before
Publilius Syrus Publilius the
   Syrian, author of a book
   of proverbs.
puella, -ae f. girl

puer, -ī m. boy
pulsō (1) beat
quiētus -a, -um quiet
quoque also
rēctē rightly, correctly
reveniō, revenīre come
   back
rīdeō, rīdēre laugh
Rōmae at Rome
ruō, ruere rush
scrībō, scrībere, scrīpsī,
   scrīptum write
saepe often
sella, -ae f. chair
sentenia, -ae f. proverb,
   saying
sōlus, -a, -um only,
   alone
sonum, -ī n. sound
stilus, -ī m. pen

studium, -iī n. study,
   eagerness
sub (+ abl.) under,
   from under; (+ acc.)
   under
surgō, surgere get up
tabula, -ae f. slate,
   tablet
timeō, timēre fear
tollō, tollere raise
tremō, tremere
   tremble
trēs, tria three
valdē very, a lot
verberō (1) beat
vester, vestra, vestrum
   your (pl.)
virga, -ae f. rod
vīs you want
vōce voice

POSTQUAM LĒGISTĪ

1. Who is laughing and who is not at the beginning of this *lectiō*? What is the reason for this laughter? (HINT: Think back to *Lectiō Prīma*.)
2. What does Hermes not want Chiron to do to Lucius? Why?
3. How is Chiron's behavior different from the way a teacher would respond in a modern classroom?
4. Why does Chiron follow Hermes' advice?
5. Describe the atmosphere in the classroom after this incident.
6. What homework does Chiron assign?
7. Where do Hermes and Lucius go after school? Where do they stop on the way? Why?

Gemma

studium, -iī n. study, eagerness, zeal: Note the -iī ending in the genitive. This tells you that the stem of *studium* is *studi-* and that genitive singular is *studiī*.

Grammatica B

The Infinitive

The infinitive is generally described as a "verbal noun." That means it does certain things that both a verb and a noun do.

I love **to play ball.**	*Pilā lūdere* amō.
I want **to play ball.**	*Pilā lūdere* volō.
To play ball is good.	*Pilā lūdere* bonum est.

Gemma

pauca post mōmenta Notice this word order in line 14. Latin sometimes likes to put the preposition between its object and an adjective describing that object. English would never do this. So translate "few after moments" as "after a few moments."

These infinitives are surely verbs, but they also function as nouns. In the first sentence, for example, the infinitive is a direct object, no different in function than the direct object in the sentence "I love cookies." In the last example, the infinitive is the subject of the sentence.

The Imperative

The Romans had an impressive number of ways to give commands, as befits a martial people. The **imperative mood** is the simplest way to do this. Here are the simple formulae for making imperatives in Latin:

The **singular imperative** = the present stem (2nd principal part -*re*):

1st conjugation	*Vocā!* Call!
2nd conjugation	*Implē!* Fill!
3rd conjugation	*Scrībe!* Write!
4th conjugation	*Venī!* Come!

The **plural imperative** = present stem + **-te**:

1st conjugation	*Vocāte!* Call!
2nd conjugation	*Implēte!* Fill!
3rd conjugation	*Scrībite!* Write! (note: -*ete* ⟶ -*ite*)
4th conjugation	*Venīte!* Come!

A **negative imperative** = nōlī (sing.) or nōlīte (pl.) + infinitive:

Singular:	*nōlī* + infinitive	*Nōlī vocāre!*	Don't call!
Plural:	*nōlīte* + infinitive	*Nōlīte vocāre!*	Don't call!

REGULAR IMPERATIVE		1ST	2ND	3RD	4TH
Singular	Present Stem	*Vocā!*	*Implē!*	*Scrībe!*	*Venī!*
Plural	Present Stem + -te	*Vocāte!*	*Implēte!*	*Scrībite*	*Venīte*
NEGATIVE IMPERATIVE					
Singular	*nōlī* + infinitive	*Nōlī vocāre!*	*Nōlī implēre!*	*Nōlī scrībere!*	*Nōlī venīre!*
Plural	*nōlīte* + infinitive	*Nōlīte vocāre!*	*Nōlīte implēre!*	*Nōlīte scrībere!*	*Nōlīte venīre!*

Notā Bene:

- Latin imperatives always distinguish between singular and plural, while English does not. Is the phrase "Call the cops!" directed at one or many bystanders? In Latin *Vocā!* is used for one person and *Vocāte!* is for more than one.
- The imperative forms of *sum* are irregular:

Es! (singular)	Be!	*Este!* (plural)
Es sine culpā!	Be without worry!	*Este sine cūrā!*

- Other irregular imperatives include:

Dīc!	Speak!
Dūc!	Lead!
Fac!	Do it!
Fer!	Carry!

These verbs lack a vowel at the end. Remember: "*Dīc, dūc, fac,* and *fer,* lack the e that ought to be there."

Which of these irregular imperatives did you see in *Lectiō Secunda*?

Mood

When we think of "mood" in English, we are talking about states of mind. When we think of "mood" in Latin, it is a grammatical term, more akin to "mode" or "manner" than to "mood."

The verbs you have met in the earlier chapters are in the **indicative mood**. That is, they "indicate" a fact. *Ambulat* denotes a fact: he/she/it is walking. This mode is easy to understand and, for day-to-day purposes, can be said to be the mood that indicates a fact, while the **imperative mood** indicates a command or order.

EXERCEĀMUS!

6-4 **Imperatives**

Match each of the following Latin imperative phrases with the appropriate English command. Indicate whether the command is addressed to one person (singular) or more than one (plural). Follow the model.

Revenīte crās!	Venī hūc!	Observā!
Sedēte!	Dūc mē ad cibum!	Nōlīte sonum facere!

ENGLISH COMMAND	LATIN COMMAND	NUMBER
→ Pay attention!	Observā!	Singular
1. Come here!		
2. Return tomorrow!		
3. Sit!		
4. Lead me to the food!		
5. Don't make a sound!		

Mōrēs Rōmānī

Magistrī Rōmānī

Here is a description of a schoolteacher in an epigram written by the poet Martial. We have modified the epigram slightly to make it easier to read. This schoolteacher keeps the poet Martial and his neighbors awake with his pedagogical techniques. Keep in mind that Roman classrooms, like Chiron's, were usually out in the open.

> Ō scelerāte magister lūdī, caput tuum invīsum ā puerīs et puellīs est!
> Mane iam murmure saevō verberibusque tonās. Mītior clāmor in
> magnō amphitheātrō est, ubi turba victōrem applaudat. Tuī vīcīnī
> somnum—nōn tōtā nocte—rogāmus: nam vigilāre leve est, pervigilāre
> grave est. Discipulōs tuōs dīmitte. Quantum pecūniae, ō garrule, vīs
> accipere ut clāmēs, ut taceās?

Epigrams. IX:68

Gemma

There are two ways to refer to the dates surrounding the life of poet like Martial. 40–c.102–103 A.D.: *c.* stands for Latin *circa* (about) and means that we do not know the exact date of his death. Fl. 86–103 A.D.: *fl.* Stands for *floruit* and indicates that "he flourished," or was writing his poetry, around those dates.

🔊 VERBA ŪTENDA

ā puerīs et puellīs by boys and girls
accipiō, accipere accept, receive
applaudō (1) applaud
caput head (Martial means not only his head but his whole body)
clāmor cry, uproar
dīmittō, dīmittere send away
garrule chatterer, chatterbox
grave a serious thing, a big deal
iam already
invīsus, -a, -um hated
leve easy, no big deal (refers to *vigilāre*)
magnus, -a, -um great

mane in the morning
mītior softer
murmure with a murmur, growling (ablative)
nōndum not yet
pervigilō (1) be awake all night, be up all night
quantum pecūniae… A tricky phrase. "Are you willing to take as much money to do X as to do Y?" Martial is offering to buy off the noisy teacher.
rogō (1) ask for
scelerāte wicked (vocative masc. sing.) "O wicked person!"

saevō furious (describes *murmure*)
somnum, -ī. n. sleep
taceās you be quiet
tam so
tonō (1) thunder
tōtā nocte the whole night through
turba, -ae f. crowd
tuus, -a, -um your (sing.)
ut clāmēs to shout
ut taceās to be quiet
verberibus with blows (ablative)
victōrem a victorious fighter
vīcīnus, -ī m. neighbor
vigilō (1) wake up, be awake
vīs are you willing

Magister Chīron et Achilles discipulus

Education in ancient Rome was private rather than public. Children only went to school if their families could afford to pay tuition to a teacher like Chiron. Some education certainly took place in the home, where children could begin their studies with their parents or family slaves. A *lūdus* like Chiron's offered the earliest formal schooling beginning around the age of seven. Here, pupils (mostly boys and occasionally upper-class girls) learned to read, write, and count from a teacher called the *lūdī magister* or *litterātor*. Sometimes Greek was also taught in the *lūdus*. Much of the learning was by rote, and the instruction was often reinforced by physical punishment like the rod with which Chiron threatens Lucius in the story.

Once students had mastered the basics, some, at about the age of eleven, would move on to a *grammaticus*, who would instruct them in the literature of Rome and Greece. Many Romans, especially the upper-class ones, were bilingual and knew both Latin and Greek. About the age of sixteen, a select few might then move to a *rhētor* or rhetorician who would introduce them to the art of public speaking.

Gemma

centaurus, -ī m. centaur: Lucius' teacher Chiron is named after a centaur (half man and half horse), who served as the tutor of both Achilles and Heracles. He was known for his wisdom, patience, and moderation.

Latīna Hodierna

Latin Words in American Education

Many of the words we use in our schools and colleges come from Latin. Here are just a few. Notice how the meaning of the English word or phrase is often slightly different from the Latin word or phrase.

ENGLISH TERM	LATIN WORD OR PHRASE AND MEANING
college	*collēgium, -ī* n. corporation, brotherhood
campus	*campus, -ī* m. field
university	*ūniversitās, -tātis* f. community
dormitory	*dormītōrium, -ī* n. a place for sleeping
alma mater	*alma māter* foster mother
alumna; alumnus	*alumna, -ae* f. foster daughter; *alumnus, -ī* m. foster son
cum laude	*cum laude* with praise

Macaca sylvanus

Orbis Terrārum Rōmānus

Hispānia

The Romans spent more than two centuries trying to conquer Spain. This task was not completed until 19 B.C., under the reign of Augustus. After this the peninsula was divided into three provinces: *Hispānia Tarrconensis*, *Hispānia Baetica*, and *Lusitania*.

During the imperial period, the region was a major source of metals, grains and wine, and its inhabitants became increasingly Romanized. Latin became so well established as the language of the inhabitants that Latin survived the fall of the Roman Empire and evolved on the Iberian peninsula into the Romance languages Spanish and Portuguese.

Some famous Romans from the Iberian peninsula include: **Quintilian**, a famous rhetorician (c. 35–c. 100 A.D.); **Seneca the Elder**, rhetorician and scientist (c. 54 B.C.–c. 39 A.D.), author of model debate texts called *Suasōriae* and *Contrōversiae*; **Seneca the Younger**, nephew of the Elder Seneca, Stoic philosopher, tragedian and tutor of the emperor Nero (c. 4 B.C.–65 A.D.), born in Corduba; **Martial**, the poet (40–c.102–103 A.D.), born in Bilbilis; and the emperor **Trajan** (53–117 A.D.).

Several modern Spanish cities have Roman roots, including Mérida (Emerita Augusta); Córdoba (Corduba); Tarraco (Tarragona); and Barcelona (Barcino).

Hispānia Rōmāna

QUID PUTĀS?

1. Read through Martial's poem to determine what hours the school must have kept.
2. Compare the American educational system to Roman practice.
3. Do you think Chiron the schoolmaster is well named after the centaur Chiron? Why or why not?
4. Why was the schoolmaster in Martial's poem so disturbing to his neighbors? What solution does Martial propose to the problem? Can you think of a comparable situation today?
5. Explain how the *campus*, the Latin word for "field" acquires its modern English meaning. Can you apply the word "field" to any part of a college campus?
6. Compare the meaning of the Latin word *ūniversitās* to the meaning of its English derivative "university".
7. What evidence of the Roman occupation of the Iberian peninsula survives today?

EXERCEĀMUS!

6-5 Scrībāmus

Theātrum Rōmānum in Emeritā Augustā hodiē

Make each of the following singular imperatives negative. Then make the singular imperatives plural. Follow the model.

Singular	Negative	Plural	Negative
→ Ambulā!	Nōlī ambulāre!	Ambulāte!	Nōlīte ambulāre!
1. Venī!			
2. Stā!			
3. Sedē!			
4. Clāmā!			

6-6 Colloquāmur

Take turns addressing the command in Exercise 6-5 to one or more people in your class. If you wish, you can make this into a "Simon dīcit" type game.

6-7 Verba Discenda

Substitute the word in **bold** in each sentence with one derived from a *Verbum Discendum*. Follow the model.

Gemma

tuus and *vester.* Just as Latin distinguishes between "you" singular and "you" plural in verbs (*scrībis* vs. *scrībitis*), it does also with "your":

Scrībe in tabulā tuā!
Write on your tablet!

Scrībite in tabulīs vestrīs!
Write on your tablets!

→ Magellan **sailed around** the world. *circumnavigated*

1. When it comes to term papers, I tend to **put things off to tomorrow**.
2. Gandhi had many **student followers**.
3. Don't make him so **angry**!
4. The police will catch the **evil doer**.
5. The gila monster's bite is very **stubborn**.
6. I just ordered an **annual contract** to receive *Newsweek*.
7. Superman lives in the Fortress of **Aloneness**.
8. The professor kept his books in his **room for learning things**.

🔊 VERBA DISCENDA

circum (+ acc.) **around** [circumference]

crās tomorrow [procrastinate]

cum (+ abl.) **with**

discō, discere, didicī learn [discipline, discourse]

faciō, facere, fēcī, factum make, do [facile, factory, manufacture]

īrātus, -a, -um angry [irate]

malus, -a, -um bad [mal-odorous, malevolent]

prō (+ abl.) **in front of, before, for** [project]

puella, -ae f. girl

puer, -ī m. boy [puerile]

quis? who?

saepe often

scrībō, scrībere, scripsī, scriptum write [scribe, script]

sine (+ abl.) **without** [sincere]

sōlus, -a, -um only, alone [solitary, solitude]

studium, -iī n. study, eagerness, zeal [studious]

sub (+ abl.) **under, from under; (+ acc.) under** [subsurface]

teneō, tenēre, tenuī, tentum hold [tenacious]

trēs, tria three [trifold, trifecta]

tuus, -a, -um your (sing.)

vester, vestra, vestrum your (pl.)

Angulus Grammaticus

Ablatives with and without Prepositions

Earlier you saw ablative phrases in which the ablative case is used without a preposition and the English preposition **with** is understood.

Licinia ūnum pōculum vīnō implet.	Licinia fills one cup **with wine**.
Licinia alium pōculum aquā implet.	Licinia fills another cup **with water**.
Magistrī saepe discipulōs virgā pulsant.	Teachers often strike students **with a rod**.

These are examples of an ablative called **ablative of means**. The rule about the ablative of means is that the ablative case is used alone, without a preposition, to indicate the instrument or tool used to perform an action. One way to recognize an ablative of means is by asking whether it makes sense to translate the ablative with the phrase "by means of."

Licinia fills the cup by means of wine (*vīnō*) and by means of water (*aquā*).

In Latin these tools must be physical objects. If Lucius cries out "with joy," for example, Latin would use the prepositional phrase *cum gaudiō*. This is called an **ablative of manner**.

But note the following. If Lucius cries out "with great joy," then the preposition is optional in Latin and, if the preposition **is** used, it is placed between the adjective and the noun. So,

Lūcius **cum gaudiō** *clāmat.*	ablative of manner with preposition
Lūcius **magnō gaudiō** *clāmat.*	ablative of manner with adjective and without preposition
Lūcius **magnō cum gaudiō** *clāmat.*	ablative of manner with adjective and with preposition in special position

Now, when you graduate *summa cum laude*, you will know why the words are in that order!

Actions performed with or by people **always** use a preposition in Latin. One example is the **ablative of accompaniment**. For example, if Lucius cries out "with the boys," Latin would use the prepositional phrase *cum puerīs*. The ablative of accompaniment indicates a person who performs an action "along with" or "together with" the subject of the verb. So here Lucius cries out along with the boys.

Lūcius clāmat **cum puerīs**.	ablative of accompaniment

Can you figure out which ablatives are means, which are manner, and which are accompaniment in the following sentences?

Magistrī saepe discipulōs **virgā** *pulsant.*

Magistrī saepe discipulōs **cum īrā** *pulsant.*

Magistrī saepe discipulōs **magnā īrā** *pulsant.*

Magistrī saepe discipulōs **magnā cum īrā** *pulsant.*

Magistrī saepe discipulōs **cum virīs** *pulsant.*

Notā Bene:

- It is usually not important for translation purposes to distinguish means from manner or accompaniment, and you can easily translate the ablatives without prepositions if you remember **BWIOF**. But the categories have a long history in the study of Latin.

Photo Credits

page 64 (top) Bettmann/CORBIS—NY; **page 69** Clipart.com; **page 73** Clipart.com; **page 74** Creative Images/Creative Images/Getty Images, Inc.; **page 75 (bottom)** Jeronimo Alba/AlamyImages

Gemma

When the preposition *cum* is used with 1st person personal pronouns like *mē* or *tē*, the pronoun always comes first and the prepositional phrase is written as one word:

mēcum	with me
tēcum	with you

Note: In English a "vade mecum" (*Vāde mēcum!* "Go with me!") is an edition of a book small enough to be put in your pocket to take along on a trip.

Post Lūdum

From *Disce! An Introductory Latin Course, volume 1*, First Edition. Francesco Bonavita. Copyright © 2011 by Pearson Education, Inc. Published by Pearson Prentice Hall. All rights reserved.

Tabula stilusque
Picture Desk, Inc./Kobal Collection/Dagli Orti

GRAMMATICA

The Irregular Verbs *Volō, Nōlō,* and *Mālō*
The Irregular Verb *Possum*
Complementary Infinitives
The Irregular Verb *Eō*
Forming the Present Tense: All Four
   Conjugations
Using the Present Stem for the
   1st and 2nd Conjugations
Using the Short Present Stem for the
   3rd and 4th Conjugations
Summary of Imperatives

MŌRES RŌMĀNĪ

Slavery and the Manumission of Slaves

LATĪNA HODIERNA

Volō in English

ORBIS TERRĀRUM RŌMĀNUS

Syria

ANGULUS GRAMMATICUS

More Irregular Verbs in Latin and Modern
   Languages

> **LECTIŌNĒS:**
> DE LŪDŌ CHĪRŌNIS
> and
> CHĪRŌN IN LŪDŌ
> Hermes and Lucius stop for an after-
> school snack, while Chiron has doubts
> about being a teacher and seeks the
> solace of the tavern.

7

Post Lūdum

Lectiō Prīma

Antequam Legis

School is over. Hermes gives Lucius some mild advice about his behavior, while Chiron wonders whether he should even be a teacher. You will see many variations on wishing in this *lectiō,* because the Latin word for "wish" is an irregular verb.

Some Irregular Verbs

In this chapter we introduce you to four irregular but very common, verbs. Here are their principal parts and English meanings:

> *possum, posse, potuī* be able to, can
> *volō, velle, voluī* want to, wish to
> *nōlō, nōlle, nōluī* not want to, not wish to, be unwilling to
> *mālō, mālle, māluī* prefer to

You will recognize most of their endings—it is mostly their stems that are irregular.

EXERCEĀMUS!

7-1   Irregular Verb Forms

Before you read *Lectiō Prīma,* look for all of the irregular verb forms marked in **bold**. Make a list of them line by line. Then use the principal parts listed above and the personal endings you already know to determine a possible translation of each word. Follow the model.

Line	Irregular Verb	Personal Ending	Meaning
→4	*volunt*	-nt	they wish

DE LŪDŌ CHĪRŌNIS

Hermēs Lūcium ā lūdō ad tabernam dūcit. Dum ambulant, dē lūdī magistrō dīcunt.

Hermēs "Lūcī," rogat, "dīc mihi aliquid! Cūr puerī magistrum irrītāre **vọlunt**? Estne magister tam malus?"

5 Respondet puer: "Chīron nōn malus est, sed nōs dēlectāre nōn **potest**. Nōs puerī in lūdō male facere **nōlumus** sed aliquandō nōn aliter facere **possumus**!"

"Fortasse," inquit paedagōgus, "**nōn vultis**, sed nihilōminus male facitis. **Nōlī** male facere, puer. Tū et amīcī bonī esse **potestis**. Tū bonus 10 esse **potes**! **Nōlō** magistrum maestum vidēre. Chīron ōlim servus erat sīcut nunc ego servus sum. Esse benignior **potes**!"

Nunc puer paedagōgusque ad Valeriae tabernam adveniunt.

Valeria "Salvēte," clāmat.

Valeria "Puer," inquit, "aliquid bibere aut ēsse **vīs**? Puerī semper aliq-15 uid ēsse **possunt**! Sed sīcut dīcit Publilius Syrus, 'is quī habet quod **vult**, est vir quī **velle** quod satis est **potest**.'"

Lūcius rīdet et fīcōs duās pānemque poscit.

"Et tū, Hermēs. Quid tū et puer bibere **vultis**?"

"**Mālō** vīnum bibere, sī placet, sed puer aquam bibere debet."
20 "Licinia!" clāmat Valeria, "Fer pōculum vīnī et alium pōculum aquae!"

Licinia ūnum pōculum vīnō et alium pōculum aquā implet. Puerī apud familiam vīnum bibere **possunt**, sed nōn in viā vīnum bibere debent!

Hermēs et Lūcius bibunt. Puer sīmiam videt et paedagōgus fābulam dē saccō narrat. Lūcius rīdet et "Iam," 25 inquit, "Hermēs, dūc mē domum! Fessus sum!"

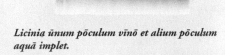

Licinia ūnum pōculum vīnō et alium pōculum aquā implet.

VERBA ŪTENDA

adveniō, advenīre come to
aliquandō sometimes
aliquid something
aliter otherwise
alium another
amīcus friend
apud familiam at home
benignior kinder
cūr why
***dē* (+ abl.) concerning, about, down from**
***dēbeō, dēbēre, dēbuī, dēbitum* owe, ought**
***dīcō, dīcere, dīxī, dictum* say, tell**

dēlectō (1) amuse
dum while
***duo, duae, duo* two**
***edō, ēsse / edere, ēdī, ēsum* eat**
***ego* I**
eō, īre, īvī / iī, itum go
erat was
fessus tired
fīcōs duās two figs
    [*Fīcōs* is feminine.]
fortasse perhaps
iam now
impleō, implēre fill
irrītō (1) annoy, bother

is quī habet … quod satis est potest "A person who has what he wants, is one who is able to want (only) what is enough."
maestus sad, gloomy
male facere to misbehave
***mālō, mālle, māluī* prefer**
malus bad
nihilōminus nevertheless
narrō (1) to tell about
***nōlō, nōlle, nōluī* not want to, be unwilling**

nōs we, us
ōlim once
pānem bread
***possum, posse, potuī* be able to, can**
***rīdeō, rīdēre, rīsī, rīsum* laugh**
rogō (1) ask
servus, -ī m. slave
***sī* if**
***sī placet!* Please!**
sīcut just as
tam so
***volō, velle, voluī* want to, be willing to**

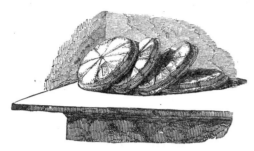

Pānem poscit

POSTQUAM LEGISTĪ

Try to answer these questions in Latin. The sentences can be short and you will find patterns for the answers in the *lectiō*. Follow the model.

→ What do Lucius and Hermes talk about as they walk from school?
Dē lūdō magistrī Chīrōnis dīcunt.

1. Why do the students act up in class?
2. What do Lucius and Hermes each drink at the snack shop?
3. Why don't they order the same thing?
4. What story does Hermes tell Lucius while they are in the snack shop?

Grammatica A

The Irregular Verbs *Volō*, *Nōlō*, and *Mālō*

	volō, velle, voluī		*nōlō, nōlle, nōluī*		*mālōm, mālle, māluī*	
Singular						
1st Person	*volō*	I want	*nōlō*	I do not want	*mālō*	I prefer
2nd Person	*vīs*	you want	*nōn vīs*	you do not want	*māvīs*	you prefer
3rd Person	*vult*	he/she/it wants	*nōn vult*	he/she/it does not want	*māvult*	he/she/it prefers
Plural						
1st Person	*volumus*	we want	*nōlumus*	we do not want	*mālumus*	we prefer
2nd Person	*vultis*	you want	*nōn vultis*	you do not want	*māvultis*	you prefer
3rd Person	*volunt*	they want	*nōlunt*	they do not want	*mālunt*	they prefer
Infinitive	*volle*	to want	*nōlle*	not to want	*mālle*	to prefer

Notā Bene:
- The personal endings are regular. It is the stem of the verb that changes.
- If you know *volō*, you can do *nōlō* and *mālō*.
- The forms of *nōlō* are basically *nōn* + *volō*, i.e., "I do not want." Sometimes they are contracted (as in *nōlumus*) and at other times not (*nōn vult*).
- You have already seen the imperative forms of *nōlō*: *nōlī* and *nōlīte*! (Do not wish to . . . ! Don't . . . !)
- The *ma-* of *mālō* is from the Latin *magis* meaning "more." Thus, the forms of *mālō* basically mean "to want more," that is, "to prefer." They are all contracted; e.g., **ma**(gis) + (vo)**lō** → *mālō*.

The Irregular Verb *Possum*

In many languages some very common verbs are irregular. This is especially true of the verb **to be** in both English and Latin.

Remember the conjugation of *sum*:

sum	I am	*sumus*	we are
es	you are	*estis*	you are
est	he/she/it is	*sunt*	they are
	esse	to be	

Now consider *possum* (I am able to, I can):

*pos**sum***	I can, I am able to	*pos**sumus***	we can, we are able to
potes	you can, you are able to	*potestis*	you can, you are able to
potest	he can, he is able to	*pos**sunt***	they can, they are able to
	posse	to be able to	

Notā Bene:
- The actual stem of *possum* is *pot-*. You can see this in words like *potēns* (powerful) or *potentia* (power) and in the English "potentate" or "potency."
- Put this stem in front of the normal form of *sum* to say "I am able." Notice what happens:

$$t + s \longrightarrow ss$$

$$potsum \longrightarrow possum$$
$$potsumus \longrightarrow possumus$$
$$potsunt \longrightarrow possunt$$

t + a vowel remains unchanged

$$potes, potest, potestis$$

Complementary Infinitives

Volō, nōlō, mālō, and *possum* are all usually followed by an infinitive, which completes the meaning of the verb. This infinitive is called a **complementary infinitive**.

*Cūr puerī magistrum **irrītāre volunt**?*
Why do the boys **want to annoy** the teacher?

*Puerī apud familiam vīnum **bibere possunt**.*
Boys **are able to drink** wine at home.
Boys **can drink** wine at home.

*Nōlō magistrum maestum **vidēre**.*
I **do not want to see** the teacher sad.

*Mālō vīnum **bibere**.*
I **prefer to drink** wine.

It will help you remember to look for these complementary infinitives if you get in the habit of translating these verbs like this:

volō	want **to**, wish **to**	*mālō*	prefer **to**
nōlō	not want **to**, not wish **to**	*possum*	be able **to**

Notā Bene:
- *Volō, nōlō,* and *mālō* can also be used with a direct object rather than an infinitive:

  Vīnum volō. Aquam nōlō. Vīnum mālō.
  I want wine. I don't want water. I prefer wine.

- *Possum* almost always needs an infinitive to complete its meaning.

  Vīnum bibere possum.
  I am able to drink wine.
  I can drink wine.

EXERCEĀMUS!

7-2 *Volō, nōlō, mālō,* and *possum*

Translate each of the following forms of *volō, nōlō, mālō,* and *possum*. Then change the form from singular to plural. Finally, translate the word you made. Follow the model. Check the verb chart in *Grammatica A* if you do not remember how to conjugate these irregular verbs.

Singular	**Plural**
→ *possum* I can, I am able	*possumus* we can, we are able

1. vīs
2. nōlō
3. māvis
4. potest
5. vult
6. nōn vult

Gemma

Possum generally has an infinitive in Latin, but in English translation it can lose the infinitive: *Ambulāre possumus.*
We are able to walk,
We can walk.
In medieval Latin, the infinitive *posse* came to mean "power, body of men." Through the legal phrase *posse comitatus*, the noun **posse** came into English to mean a group of deputized citizens.

Lectiō Secunda

Antequam Legis

While Lucius is on his way home, his discouraged teacher Chiron lingers at the school and tries unsuccessfully to get some work done. Eventually he goes to Valeria's snack shop and finds comfort in wine and amusement in Socrates. As you read this *lectiō*, look more closely at verbs of the 3rd and 4th conjugations and the irregular verb *eō*.

The Irregular Verb *Eō*

This too is an irregular verb. The principal parts are: *eō, īre, īvī/iī, itum*.

SINGULAR		PLURAL	
eō	I go	*īmus*	we go
īs	you go	*ītis*	you go
it	he/she/it goes	*eunt*	they go
Ī!	Go!	*Īte!*	Go!
īre		to go	

The verb *eō* is extremely common and is found in many compounds that are easy to figure out by just combining "go" with the meaning of the preposition used as a prefix: *transeō* (go across), *adeō* (go toward), *abeō, ineō,* etc. Watch for these as you read. Forms of this verb are in **bold italics** in the *lectiō* that follows.

The 3rd and 4th Conjugations

In this reading you will be introduced formally to 3rd and 4th conjugation verbs. They should be no problem. In *Lectiō Prīma*, for example, you have already seen such 3rd and 4th conjugation verbs as:

dūcit	he leads
poscit	he asks for
adveniunt	they arrive

Since the personal endings are the same for all four conjugations, just use what you know already and you should have little trouble understanding the 3rd and 4th conjugation verbs which are marked in **bold** in *Lectiō Secunda*.

EXERCEĀMUS!

7-3 **3rd and 4th Conjugation Verbs**

As you read, group the verbs in bold according to the vowels that link the stem to the personal endings. Thus, in line 1 *tollit* would go in the "i-group" and *legere* would go in the "e-group." Be sure to have a group for long "ī" as well as short "i."

e-group	i-group	ī-group	u-group	iu-group
→ legere	tollit			

🔊 CHĪRŌN IN LŪDŌ

Chīrōn sōlus in lūdō sedet. Propter discipulōs malōs nōn laetus est. Librum **tollit** et **legere** temptat, sed nōn potest. Librum in mēnsam rursus **ponit**. Sōlum dē discipulīs malīs putat. **Scrībere** nōn potest. Pecūniam numerāre temptat, sed nōn **succēdit**.

5   Chīrōn vītam suam dēplōrat et "Ēheu," inquit, "lībertīnus sum et nunc dominī servus nōn sum. Sed lūdī et discipulōrum malōrum servus sum. Cupiō docēre sed discipulī nōn **audiunt**, nōn **discunt** et nōn **discere cupiunt**!" Tunc Chīrōn ā lūdō **abit** et ad Valeriae tabernam **adit**. "Satis!" inquit, "Nunc est bibendum!" et rīdet.

Sīmia ūnam ē fīcīs ad magistrum portat.

10   Ubi Sōcratēs magistrum in tabernā videt, sīmia dē mēnsā **currit** et in bracchia Chīrōnis **salit**. Sōcratēs Chīrōnis bonus amīcus est.

   Chīrōn "Ō sīmia," inquit, "**Curris**ne ad mē? Tū saltem mē vidēre vīs. Discipulī mē aut vidēre aut **audīre** nōlunt et tē vidēre magis quam meōs discipulōs mālō!"

   Sīmia dē magistrō **salit** et ad mensam **currit**. In mensā quattuor fīcī sunt et Sōcratēs ūnam ē fīcīs **capit** et ad
15 magistrum portat. Chīrōn ficum **capit** et clāmat: "Amīce, **venī**. Da mihi reliquās fīcōs. **Ī**, sī tibi placet." Sīmia iterum ad mensam **adit** et aliās portat. "Bene, sīmia, **discis**!" Chīrōn rīdet et "Ecce, amīcī," inquit "sīmia bonus discipulus est. Poscō, et sīmia **it** et **facit**!" Omnēs prope tabernā **plaudunt** quod sīmia sagāx est. "Sīmia," Chīrōn inquit, "mē amat magis quam puerī. Fortasse nōn puerōrum, sed sīmiārum, magister esse dēbeō. Sed satis est! Nunc bibō!" Tunc Chīrōn tacitus vīnum **bibit** et ficōs **edit** dum omnēs **bibunt** et rīdent.

🔊 VERBA ŪTENDA

abeō, abīre, abīvī / abiī, abitum go away
adeō, adīre, adīvī / adiī, aditum go to
aliās "the other (figs)"
aliōrum other
amīcus, -ī m. friend
amō (1) love
audiō, audīre, audīvī / audiī, audītum hear, listen to
bibendum est "it's time to drink"
bracchia arms
dē (+ abl.) down from, concerning
dēbeō, dēbēre, dēbuī, dēbitum owe, ought
dīco, dīcere, dīxī, dictum say, tell

doceō, docēre teach
dēplōrō (1) lament
dum while
duo, duae, duo two
Ecce! Behold! Look!
edō, ēsse / edere, ēdī, ēsum eat
ēheu alas
eō, īre, iī / īvī, itum go
fīcus, -ī f. fig
fortasse perhaps
in (+ acc.) translate here as "onto"
imperō (1) command
legō, legere read
liber, librī m. book
lībertīnus, -ī m. freedman
magis more
mālō, mālle, māluī prefer
mēnsa, -ae f. counter, table

nōlō, nōlle, nōluī not want to, be unwilling
numerō (1) count
omnēs everyone
plaudō, plaudere clap
portō (1) carry
possum, posse, potuī be able to, can
propter (+ acc.) on account of
putō (1) think
quam than
quattuor four
reliquās the remaining
rīdeō, rīdēre, rīsī, rīsum laugh
rursus again
sagāx wise
saltem at least
saliō, salīre leap, jump

satis enough
servus, -ī m. slave, servant
sī if
sī tibi placet please
sīcut just as
succēdō, succēdere succeed
suam "his"
tacitus silently
tē you (direct object)
temptō (1) try
tollō, tollere lift, raise
ūnam ē fīcīs "one of the figs"
ūnus, -a, -um one
vīta, -ae f. life
volō, velle, voluī want to, be willing to

Gemma

Chiron makes a school teacher's joke. He is quoting a famous line from the poet Horace, who said *Nunc est bibendum!* "Now is the time to drink!" in his poem of jubilation over the defeat and death of Cleopatra in 30 B.C.

POSTQUAM LEGISTĪ

1. Why is Chiron unhappy? What does he do to try to distract himself without success?
2. So what does he do instead?
3. What finally cheers him up?
4. What advice would you give Chiron about his teaching techniques?

Grammatica B

The Irregular Verb *Eō*

Did you look for forms of the irregular verb *eō* in *Lectiō Secunda*? How many did you find? Besides *it* (he goes) and *Ī!* (Go!), did you notice words like *abit* (he goes away) and *adit* (he goes to), which contain forms of *eō*? These compound forms of *eō* are formed by adding directional prefixes like *ab-* and *ad-* to the verb. These two compounds become *Verba Discenda* in this chapter:

abeō, abīre, abīvī / abiī go away

adeō, adīre, adīvī / adiī go to

Compounding is easy:

	SINGULAR		PLURAL
abeō	I go away	*abīmus*	we go away
abīs	you go away	*abītis*	you go away
abit	he/she/it goes away	*abeunt*	they go away
abī!	Go away!	*abīte!*	Go away!
abīre	to go away		

What do you think these *eō* compounds mean?

exeō   subeō   intereō   transeō

Notā Bene:
- The stem of *eō* is usually *i-*, as in *īs, it,* and *īmus.*
- But the irregular forms use *e-*, as in *eō* and *eunt.*
- Look for more on compounding in the *Angulus Grammaticus* in *Chapter 10*.

Forming the Present Tense: All Four Conjugations

If you made the list requested in the *Antequam Legis*, it should look something like this:

E:	legere, discere
I:	tollit, discis, venit
Ī:	audīre, venī
U:	bibunt
IU:	audiunt

You have discovered all the vowels that are used in 3rd and 4th conjugation verbs to link the stems to personal endings!

When you are reading Latin, the change in linking vowels causes little or no problem. But if you try to speak or write Latin (as you are sometimes asked to do), you need to know how to find the stem and what vowel is used to link it to its personal ending. There are many "formulas" you can learn for making the present tense, but the one presented here allows for the fact that 1st and 2nd conjugations form their present tenses one way whereas 3rd and 4th conjugation verbs use a different formula. It also helps you form the next two tenses you will learn.

Using the Present Stem for the 1st and 2nd Conjugations

You already know the general rule for forming present tense of verbs in the 1st and 2nd conjugations:

Present Stem (2nd principal part – *-re*) +

ō	*mus*
s	*tis*
t	*nt*

1st Conjugation

vocō, vocāre ⟶ Present Stem: *vocā*

vocā + ō ⟶ *vocō*   *vocā + mus* ⟶ *vocāmus*

vocā + s ⟶ *vocās*   *vocā + tis* ⟶ *vocātis*

vocā + t ⟶ *vocat*   *vocā + nt* ⟶ *vocant*

2nd Conjugation

moneō, monēre ⟶ Present Stem: *monē*

monē + ō ⟶ *moneō*   *monē + mus* ⟶ *monēmus*

monē + s ⟶ *monēs*   *monē + tis* ⟶ *monētis*

monē + t ⟶ *monet*   *monē + nt* ⟶ *monent*

Using the Short Present Stem for the 3rd and 4th Conjugations

For 3rd and 4th conjugation verbs we use a different stem, called the Short Present Stem (SPS), which is found by removing the *-ō* from the 1st principal part:

dūcō, dūcere ⟶ SPS *duc-*

audiō, audīre ⟶ SPS *audi-*

To this SPS add the following pattern of vowels and personal endings to form the present tense of 3rd and 4th conjugation verbs:

SPS +

ō	*imus*
is	*itis*
it	*unt*

Thus

3rd Conjugation

dūcō → SPS *dūc-*

dūc + ō → *dūcō*   *dūc + imus* → *dūcimus*

dūc + is → *dūcis*   *dūc + itis* → *dūcitis*

dūcō + it → *dūcit*   *dūc + unt* → *dūcunt*

3rd Conjugation *-iō* Verbs

There is a special group of 3rd conjugation verbs called *-iō* verbs because their first principal part ends in *-iō* (*capiō, capere*) instead of *-ō* (*dūcō, dūcere*). You already know some of these verbs as *Verba Discenda:*

capiō, capere, cēpī, captum take

cupiō, cupere, cupīvī / cupiī, cupitum wish, want to

faciō, facere, fēcī, factum make, do

These 3rd conjugation *-iō* verbs work the same way as other 3rd conjugation verbs, but with one special rule: i + i → i. Thus, the correct 3rd person singular form of *capiō* is *capit*, not "capiit."

capiō → SPS *capi-*

capi + ō → *capiō*   *capi + imus* → *capimus*

capiō + is → *capis*   *capi + itis* → *capitis*

capi + it → *capit*   *capi + unt* → *capiunt*

4th Conjugation

4th conjugation verbs also follow the rule of i + i → i:

audiō → SPS *audī-*

audi + ō → *audiō*   *audi + imus* → *audīmus*

audiō + is → *audīs*   *audī + itis* → *audītis*

audī + it → *audit*   *audi + unt* → *audiunt*

And here is a summary of how 3rd, 3rd *-io*, and 4th conjugation verbs work. Notice how 3rd conjugation *-iō* verbs are sometimes like the regular 3rd conjugation verbs and sometimes like the 4th, but that the long marks of the 4th conjugation forms can be very helpful.

PERSON	3RD REGULAR		3RD -IŌ		4TH	
	Singular	Plural	Singular	Plural	Singular	Plural
1st	*dūcō*	*dūcimus*	*capiō*	*capimus*	*audiō*	*audīmus*
2nd	*dūcis*	*dūcitis*	*capis*	*capitis*	*audīs*	*audītis*
3rd	*dūcit*	*dūcunt*	*capit*	*capiunt*	*audit*	*audiunt*

Summary of Imperatives

And here is a summary of **imperatives**.

1st, 2nd, 4th conjugation	Singular imperative = Present Stem (2nd principal part – -re)
	Plural imperative = Present Stem + te

Vocā!	*Monē!*	*Audī!*
Vocāte!	*Monēte*	*Audīte!*

3rd conjugation	Singular imperative = Present Stem (2nd principal part – -re)
	Plural imperative = Short Present Stem (1st principal part – -ō) + -ite

Mitte!	*Mittite!*
Pone!	*Ponite!*

And remember: "*Dīc, dūc, fac,* and *fer* lack the -e that 'ought to' be there."

EXERCEĀMUS!

7-4 **3rd and 4th Conjugation Verbs**

Use the charts in *Grammatica B* to complete the following charts for *dīco, dīcere, dīxī, dictum* and *faciō, facere, fēcī, factum*. Be sure to watch out for irregular imperative forms! We have done some for you.

Person	3RD CONJUGATION		3RD CONJUGATION -IŌ	
	Singular			
1st	*dīcō*		*faciō*	
2nd				you do, you make
3rd			*facit*	
	Plural			
1st				
2nd				
3rd		they say		
Infinitive	*dīcere*			
Imperatives	*Dīc!*		*Fac!*	

Mōrēs Rōmānī

Slavery and the Manumission of Slaves

The relationships between the slave Flavia and her mistress Valeria and between the *paedagōgus* and Lucius illustrate the central role slavery played in ancient society and economy. Even a poor family like Valeria's would often own one or two slaves. These slaves would live in close quarters with their masters and, in fact, legally belonged to the *familia* of the master. In Latin the word *familia* includes not only parents, children, and other relatives, but also any slaves belonging to the *paterfamiliās*, or head of the family.

Pilleus lībertātis

A German woman like Flavia could have been born into slavery, or she could have been sold into slavery as a result of war. Unlike slavery in the American experience, Roman slavery was not racially based. Anyone could become a slave if they were in the wrong place at the wrong time.

Chiron is a *lībertīnus* or freedman. This means that he is a former slave who has managed to purchase his own freedom or who was freed by his master through the process of manumission, a formal legal process. The master and slave went before a judge to whom the master said *hunc hominem līberum volō* (I want this person to be free), while holding the slave with his hand. The master then let go (*ēmīsit ē manū*) of the slave who was then free. Note that the English word **manumission** describes the actual process of a Roman master releasing his slave. The newly freed slave then put on a special hat or cap of liberty (*pilleus, -eī* m.), seen at left on a coin issued by Brutus after the assassination of Julius Caesar in 44 B.C.

The two daggers represent the assassination of Julius Caesar. In the center of the coin is a *pilleus*, a cap of liberty, suggesting that Brutus brought liberty to Rome by assassinating Caesar. The letters below, EID • MAR are an abbreviation for ĪDIBUS MARTIĪS "on the Ides of March" (March 15th) referring to the date of the assassination.

The freed slave, now known as a *lībertīnus* or *lībertīna*, often took the *praenōmen* and *nōmen*, the names, of his or her former master. The master (*dominus*) became patron (*patrōnus, -ī* m.). Thus, when Cicero freed his secretary Tiro, he gave him the name Marcus Tullius Tīrō, who would legally append L. (for *lībertus*) after this name.

Lībertīnī could become wealthy and powerful members of Roman society. In fact, some of Rome's most important authors, including the playwrights Plautus and Terence, were once slaves.

Do you remember the homework assignment Chiron gave his pupils at the end of the last chapter? He told them to learn three *sententiae* of Publilius Syrus. *Sententiae* (The Sentences or Proverbs), a collection of Latin maxims, survives under the name of Publilius Syrus, who lived in the first century B.C. Syrus was born in Syria (hence *Syrus* "the Syrian") and came to Italy as a slave. Like Chiron, he was eventually freed and became a *lībertīnus*. He wrote mimes (*mīmus, -ī* m.), a popular, if somewhat lower class, farcical stage performance, which even Julius Caesar enjoyed. The mimes are lost, but a collection of his most famous sayings has survived, rather like the proverbs and maxims collected from the pen of "Poor Richard," Benjamin Franklin.

Here are some of his *Sententiae* featuring forms of the verb *volō*. You should be able to understand these with the help of the *Verba Ūtenda* provided.

> *Quod vult habet, quī velle quod satis est potest.*

(Valeria quotes a slightly simpler version of this *sententia* in *Lectiō Secunda*.)

> *Quod esse tacitum vīs, id nūllī dīxeris.*
> *Sī vīs beatus esse, cōgitā cogitā hoc prīmum: contemne contemnī.*
> *Imperium habēre vīs magnum? Imperā tibi!*

And here is one more famous maxim using a form of *volō*. This one is not by Publilius Syrus but by Publius Flavius Vegetius Renatus, whose work on military affairs, *Epitoma reī mīlitāris* (c. 400 A.D.), has been read by military tacticians into modern times.

> *Sī vīs pācem, parā bellum.*

Gemma

Parā Bellum: This short phrase by Vegetius has had significant impact in the modern world and illustrates the continuing use of Latin in our society. The famous German pistol that we know as the Luger was originally called the "Luger Parabellum" and derives its name from the second half of Vegetius' phrase.
The heavy metal group Metallica also uses the phrase (in English) in the lyrics of "Don't Tread on Me."

🔊 VERBA ŪTENDA

beātus happy	*contemnō, contemnere*	*imperō* (1) rule, command	*quī* he, who
bellum, -ī n. war	scorn	*nūllī* "to no one, to	*quod* that which
cōgitō (1) think	*dīxeris* "you will have said"	nobody"	*satis* enough
about	*id* it	*pācem* peace	*tacitus, -a, -um* silent,
contemnī "to be	*imperium, -iī* n. supreme	*parō* (1) prepare	secret
scorned"	command	*prīmum* first	*tibi* "yourself"

Latīna Hodierna

Volō in English

Latin is very helpful in building our English vocabulary, but you must be sure of the Latin word that lies at the root. Consider *volō, velle, voluī* "to wish" and *volō, -āre* "to fly." In English, their stems look alike, but which Latin verb provides the root of the following English words?

volatile   volition   volley

voluntary   volunteer

Notice how similarity in spelling is not a sure indicator that a specific English word is derived from a Latin word. You have to pay attention to meaning as well as spelling.

Nōlō appears in a variety of contexts in the modern world. Here is an example from art:

- **Noli me tangere.** "Don't touch me!" This refers to a type of painting based on the words of Jesus to Mary Magdalene after his resurrection (John 20:17). The 1511–1512 painting by the Italian artist Titian (Tiziano Vecellio), now in the National Gallery, London, is a good example.

We also find *nōlō* in the law.

- **Nolle prosequi.** "To be unwilling to continue." Used in law to refer to a plaintiff or prosecutor's decision not to pursue a case.

- **Nolo contendere.** "I do not wish to contest the charge." In criminal law, the accused has the option of making this plea instead of a declaration of guilt or innocence.

©National Gallery, London/Art Resource, NY

Nōlī mē tangere

Orbis Terrārum Rōmānus

Syria

Syria, the homeland of Publilius Syrus, was conquered by Pompey the Great in 64 B.C. and became a Roman province. With its strategic location on the border of the Parthian Empire, Syria was important militarily, and the governor of the province had several legions at his command in the first century A.D.

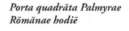

Porta quadrāta Palmyrae Rōmānae hodiē

Major trade routes to Arabia and to the east, especially the Silk Road to China, passed through the province, and in the early empire, made its capital, Antioch (*Antiochēa ad Orontem*, Antioch on the Orontes), the largest city in the East, except for Alexandria. Besides Antioch, important cities of Roman Syria included Damascus and Palmyra (in modern Syria), and Tyre and Sidon (in modern Lebanon).

Syria was also an important producer of wine and vegetables (especially onions), and manufacturer of linens and wools for clothing.

Julia Domna (died 217 A.D.), the wife of the emperor Septimius Severus and the mother of his successor Caracalla, was born in Syria.

Tyrus antīqua et hodierna

Ā Syria ad Sīnās

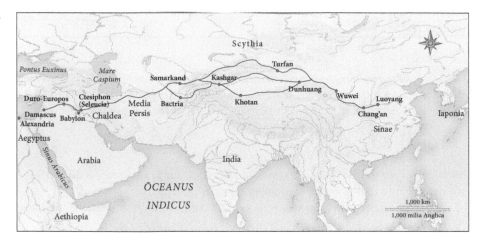

QUID PUTĀS?

1. Which of Publilius Syrus' *Sententiae* is most appealing to you? Why?
2. How would you describe the treatment of Flavia and Hermes as slaves?
3. How is the Roman practice of slavery similar to and different from slavery in the American experience?
4. How does the Roman practice of slavery affect your view of ancient Roman society?
5. Use the Roman practice of manumission of slaves to show how different the Roman institution of slavery was from the American experience.
6. Why would lawyers continue to use Latin expressions like *nolo contendere* in the modern world?

7. What cities could be compared to Antioch and Damascus as major trade crossroads in the modern world?

EXERCEĀMUS!

7-5 Scrībāmus

Refer to *Lectiō Prīma* to answer each of the following questions in Latin. Use either *ita / sic* or *nōn* and then give a complete-sentence answer. Follow the model.

→ Dūcitne Lūcius paedagōgum ad tabernam?

Nōn, paedagōgus Lūcium ad tabernam dūcit!

1. Estne Chīron Lūciī magister?
2. Vultne Hermēs magistrum maestum vidēre?
3. Eratne Chīron ōlim servus?
4. Estne Hermēs nunc lībertīnus?
5. Vultne Lūcius aliquid bibere?

7-6 Colloquāmur

Now practice asking and answering the questions in Exercise 7-5 with a classmate.

Rōmānī in Oriente

7-7 Verba Discenda

Refer to the *Verba Discenda* to answer the following questions.

1. What conjugation is *audiō* in?
2. What word means the opposite of *abeō*?
3. What numbers appear in this list?
4. Find a noun in this list. What does it mean?
5. What word means the opposite of *volō*?
6. Find a verb in the 2nd conjugation. How do you know?
7. What is the first principal part of *iī*?
8. The English word **adit** means a mine entrance. What verb is it from?
9. Find a verb in the 3rd conjugation.
10. Find a verb in the 4th conjugation.
11. What is the alternate form of *audīvī*?

🔊 VERBA DISCENDA

abeō, abīre, abīvī / abiī, abitum go away

adeō, adīre, adīvī / adiī, aditum go to

amīcus, -ī m. friend [amicable]

audiō, audīre, audīvī / audiī, audītum hear, listen to [audible, auditory]

dē (+ abl.) down from, concerning

dēbeō, dēbēre, dēbuī, dēbitum owe, ought, have to [debt, debit]

dīcō, dīcere, dīxī, dictum say, tell [dictator, dictation]

duo, duae, duo two [dual]

edō, ēsse / edere, ēdī, ēsum eat

ego I [egotism, egotistical]

eō, īre, īvī / iī, itum go

mālō, mālle, māluī prefer

nōlō, nōlle, nōluī not want to, be unwilling

possum, posse, potuī be able, can [potential]

rīdeō, rīdēre, rīsī, rīsum laugh [risible, ridiculous]

servus, -ī m. slave, servant [servitude]

sī if

sī tibi placet! please!

sīcut just as

ūnus, -a, -um one [unicycle]

volō, velle, voluī want to, be willing to [volition]

Angulus Grammaticus

More Irregular Verbs in Latin and Modern Languages

The Latin verb *edō, ēsse / edere, ēdī, ēsum* (to eat) is irregular in the present tense. Here is its conjugation, compared to the verb *sum, esse, fuī* (to be).

EDŌ TO EAT		SUM TO BE	
edō	I eat	*sum*	I am
ēs	you eat	*es*	you are
ēst	he/she/it eats	*est*	he/she/it is
edimus	we eat	*sumus*	we are
ēstis	you eat	*estis*	you are
edunt	they eat	*sunt*	they are
ēsse *edere*	to eat	*esse*	to be

Note that the infinitives *ēsse* "to eat" and *esse* "to be" as well as some other forms (marked in bold) have the same spelling but are pronounced differently. Later in its history, Latin developed a regular infinitive *edere* to replace *ēsse*. But the long marks can make a difference. Consider this old Latin schoolboy's joke:

Mea mater mala sus est.

Without long marks or punctuation, it can mean either "My mother is a bad pig" or "My mother, the pig is eating apples!" See if you can put in the required punctuation and long marks for each meaning.

Knowing how irregular verbs like *sum, esse* work in Latin can help you understand some modern languages better. Here are some examples:

LATIN	ENGLISH	FRENCH	ITALIAN	SPANISH
sum	I am	*je suis*	*sono*	*soy*
es	you are	*tu es*	*sei*	*eres*
est	he/she/it is	*il/elle est*	*é*	*es*
sumus	we are	*nous sommes*	*siamo*	*somos*
estis	you are	*vous êtes*	*siete*	*sois*
sunt	they are	*ils/elles sont*	*sono*	*son*
esse	to be	*être*	*essere*	*ser*

Notā Bene:
- Notice how the three Romance languages, French, Italian, and Spanish transform the Latin personal endings.
- Like Latin, Spanish and Italian do not need personal pronouns with the verb. French, like English, does.
- The French and Italian forms of the verb "to be" are descended directly from Latin *sum, esse*.

One of the challenges for English speakers in learning Spanish is that Spanish has two forms of the verb "to be": *ser*, which is used to indicate identity and quality, and *estar*, which is used to indicate health, location, and state. *Estar* is derived from the Latin verb *stō, stāre* (to stand).

LATIN	SPANISH
stō	*estoy*
stās	*estás*
stat	*está*
stāmus	*estamos*
stātis	*estáis*
stant	*están*
stāre	*estar*

Photo Credits

page 78 (top) Dagli Orti; **page 80** Clipart.com; **page 88** Clipart.com; **page 89 (top)** ©National Gallery, London/Art Resource, NY; **page 89 (middle)** JTB Photo Communications, Inc./Alamy Images; **page 89 (bottom)** Alan Keohane/Alamy Images Alan Keohane/Imagestate Media Partners Limited/Alamy

8

Eāmus Domum!

Lectiō Prīma

Antequam Legis

The Vocative Case

In Chapter 7 you learned about the imperative mood. Very often imperatives are accompanied by nouns indicating the person(s) or thing(s) being addressed. In English we often mark these nouns with interjections like "Hey, John" or "Oh, Melissa." Latin sometimes uses a similar interjection *Ō*, but always puts the one addressed into a case called the **vocative** (from *vocāre*, to call).

As you read this next episode, in which Lucius meets his older sister Servilia on his way home from school, look for the vocatives (marked in **bold**). Most vocative forms are the same as the nominative, but some have different endings.

EXERCEĀMUS!

8-1 Vocatives

As you read, put the vocatives (marked in **bold**) into two lists. The first list is for vocatives that look like a nominative form. The second list is for vocatives that do not look like a nominative.

Lectīca ornāta

GRAMMATICA
The Vocative Case
The Perfect Tense: 3rd Person
   Singular and Plural
The Perfect Stem
Tense
The 3rd Principal Part
Latin Time Expressions

MŌRĒS RŌMĀNĪ
Tempus Fugit

LATĪNA HODIERNA
Telling Time by the Romans

ORBIS TERRĀRUM RŌMĀNUS
Campus Martius

ANGULUS GRAMMATICUS
More on 2nd Declension Vocatives

LECTIŌNĒS:
IN LECTĪCĀ ORNĀTĀ
and
Ē TABERNĀ
While Lucius gets a ride home with his sister Servilia, Valeria and her daughter close up their shop for the day.

93

From *Disce! An Introductory Latin Course, volume 1,* First Edition. Francesco Bonavita. Copyright © 2011 by Pearson Education, Inc. Published by Pearson Prentice Hall. All rights reserved.

🔊 IN LECTĪCĀ ORNĀTĀ

Dum paedagōgus cum puerō ambulat, lectīcam ornātam in viā vident.
Lectīca familiae Servīliī est. Quattuor servī lectīcam portant et in lectīcā
sedet Servīlia, soror Lūciī et fīlia Servīliī. Prō lectīcā servus magnus ambulat
et hominēs ā viā āmovet. Post lectīcam ancilla Servīliae quoque ambulat.

5 Lūcius magnā vōce vocat: "**Servī**, sistite!" Servī lectīcam in terrā
pōnunt et sub arbore stant. Puer "Salvē," inquit, "**soror**! Quid agis?"

Servīlia Lūcium videt et perlaeta est. "**Lūcī**," inquit Servīlia, "Venī
hūc, et audī aliquid dē amīcō novō meō!" Servīlia sēdecim annōs nāta est
et marītum nōndum habet sed mox nūbere oportet. Lūcius decem annōs

10 nātus est.

"Intrā in lectīcam meam, ō **mī frāter**, et dum domum īmus, dē
novō amīcō meō audī!"

Lūcius nihil dē amīcīs puellārum cūrat, sed melius est in lectīcā
sedēre quam in viā ambulāre.

15 Ergō frāter respondet, "Bene, **Servīlia**, intrō" et in lectīcam intrat.

Nunc "**Mī paedagōge**," Lūcius inquit, "post lectīcam ambulā!" Subitō Servīlia clāmat; "Ō **servī**! Num fessī
estis? Nōlīte illīc stāre! Nōs portāte domum!"

Servī nōn laetī sunt quod nunc duōs et nōn ūnam portant, sed nihil dīcunt. Servī sagācēs semper nihil dīcunt.

Lectīcam ornātam in viā vident.

🔊 VERBA ŪTENDA

aliquid something	**fīlia, -ae f. daughter**	*mox* soon	*puella, -ae* f. girl
āmoveō, āmovēre move away	*frāter* brother	*nātus, -a, -um* See *annōs natus, -a est*	*quam* than
	hominēs people		*quattuor* four
ancilla, -ae f. female servant	*hūc* here, to this place	*nōndum* not yet	**quoque also**
	iam now, already	**novus, -a, -um new**	*sagācēs* wise
annōs nātus, -a est he/she is …years old	*illīc* there, over there	*nūbō, nūbere* marry	**sēdecim sixteen**
	intrō (1) enter	*oportet* (+ inf.) it is fitting that	**sistō, sistere, stetī / stitī, statum stop, stand still**
arbore tree	**inquam, inquit say**		
audiō, audīre hear	*lectīca, -ae* f. litter, sedan chair	*ornātus, -a, -um* decorated	*soror* sister
cūrō (1) care			*subitō* suddenly
decem ten	**magnus, -a, -um large, great, loud**	*perlaetus, -a, -um* very happy	**terra, -ae f. land**
dum while	*melius* better	*prō* (+ abl.) in front of	**vocō (1) call**
ergō therefore	*mī* my (vocative)	**portō (1) carry**	*vōce* voice
familia, -ae f. family			

POSTQUAM LĒGISTĪ

1. Describe how Lucius' sister Servilia travels through Rome. How would his sister travel today?
2. How old is Servilia? What are her plans and expectations for the immediate future?
3. What news does Servilia want to share with Lucius?
4. What does Lucius want to do?
5. In line 18 you read that the slaves carry *duōs et nōn ūnam*. To whom does *ūnam* refer? To whom does *duōs* refer? Note how Latin uses masculine gender to refer to male and female together.
6. Why are Servilia's slaves unhappy at the end of this story? What do they do about this? Why?

Grammatica A

The Vocative Case

Scan the list you made of vocative forms as you read *Lectiō Prīma*. Here are the rules for forming the vocative:

- Most vocative singulars and all vocative plurals are the same as their nominatives.
- The only exceptions are in the singular vocative of 2nd declension nouns ending in *-us* (re-read that—every word is important). And in such a case:

  The ending *-us* → *-e*

  Thus *amīcus* → *amīce!* or *paedagōgus* → *paedagōge!*

  The ending *-ius* → *-ī*

  Thus *fīlius* → *fīlī!* or *Lūcius* → *Lūcī!*

1ST DECLENSION			2ND DECLENSION			
Singular						
Nominative	-a	fēmina	-us, er, ir	vir	discipulus	fīlius
Genitive	-ae	fēminae	-ī	virī	discipulī	fīliī
Accusative	-am	fēminam	-um	virum	discipulum	filium
Ablative	-ā	fēminā	-ō	virō	discipulō	fīliō
Vocative	**-a**	**fēmina**	**-e**	**vir**	**discipule**	**fīlī**
Plural						
Nominative	-ae	fēminae	-ī	virī	discipulī	fīliī
Genitive	-ārum	fēminārum	-ōrum	virōrum	discipulōrum	fīliōrum
Accusative	-ās	fēminās	-ōs	virōs	discipulōs	fīliōs
Ablative	-īs	fēminīs	-īs	virīs	discipulīs	fīliīs
Vocative	**-ae**	**fēminae**	**-ī**	**virī**	**discipulī**	**fīliī**

Notā Bene:

- 2nd declension words that do not end in *-us* have a vocative that *is* identical with the nominative. *Ō vir! Ō magister!*
- Be careful of confusing forms. *Ō amīcī* can fool the casual reader. It is plural. And compare *Ō fīlī* (sing.) with *Ō fīliī* (pl.). Forms like these cause fewer problems if you get into the habit of reading aloud. The ear is less easily fooled than the eye.

EXERCEĀMUS!

8-2 **Vocative Fill-Ins**

Choose the correct vocative form to complete the sentence. Pay attention to singulars and plurals! Follow the model.

→ (Lūcius / Lūcī), intrā in lectīcam meam. *Lūcī*

1. Venī, ō (Licinia / Liciniae).
2. (Serve / Servī), nōlīte illīc stāre!
3. Ō (fēminae / fēmina), venīte.
4. (Servīlia / Servīliae), portā Sōcratem!
5. Ō (paedagōgum / paedagōge), intrā in lectīcam meam.

Lectiō Secunda

Antequam Legis

Latin Expressions of Time

The next reading presents expressions of time, several using the word *hōra, -ae* (f. hour). They are marked in ***bold italics***.

- When the phrase is accusative, the English word "for" generally is the best translation.
- When it is ablative, try "at" or, if appropriate, "during."

The Perfect Tense

In the next reading, as Valeria closes up shop for the day, we introduce you to the **perfect tense**. To help you spot the new tense, we have put all perfects in *Lēctiō Secunda* in **bold**. For now, simply translate them in one of two ways:

as a **simple past tense**:	*salūtāvit* he/she/it **greeted**
	salūtāvērunt they **greeted**
as a **compound past tense**:	*salūtāvit* he/she/it **has greeted**
	salūtāvērunt they **have greeted**

You will see only 3rd person forms right now. The personal endings of these forms will be familiar because the singular ends in *-t* and the plural ends in *-nt*, just as in the present tense!

EXERCEĀMUS!

8-3 **Scanning the Text**

Before you read, scan the *lectiō* to find the answers to the following questions.

1. What time does business in the Forum begin to slow down?
2. Why is Valeria tired?
3. Why is she happy?
4. What are Valeria, Licinia, and Flavia no longer able to do today?
5. Now that the time for work is over, what is it time for?

🔊 Ē TABERNĀ

Octāva hōra est. Paucī hominēs aut in Forō aut in viīs nunc adsunt. Senātōrēs et mercātōrēs negōtium reī pūblicae **ēgērunt** et omne negōtium ad fīnem **prōcessit**. Nōn iam tempus negōtiī est, sed tempus ōtiī. Multī hominēs ā Forō ad familiās suās nunc prōcēdere incipiunt.

5   In tabernā, Valeria quoque parum negōtiī agit quod hominēs absunt. Fessa est, quia māne **surrexit** et ad tabernam **vēnit**. *Multās horās* **labōrāvit**. Licinia et Flāvia quoque *multās horās* **labōrāvērunt**. Valeria multōs virōs in tabernā **salūtāvit**. Multī virī in tabernā **ēdērunt** et **bibērunt**. Valeria laeta est quod multī virī multam pecūniam **dedērunt**.

10   Sed nunc *octāvā hōrā*, sine populō in viā, Valeria nūllum negōtium in tabernā agere **potuit**. Tempus negōtiī **fīnīvit**.

Valeria filiam ancillamque magnā voce **vocāvit** et eīs **dīxit**. "Ō Licinia! Flāvia!" **clamāvit**, "Hūc venīte! Plūs negōtiī hodiē agere nōn possumus. Lābor iam **fīnīvit**. Tempus ōtiī est. Ergō, nōlīte illīc stāre! Eāmus domum!

Tempus negōtiī fīnīvit.

🔊 VERBA ŪTENDA

absum, abesse, āfuī be away, be absent

adsum, adesse, adfuī be present

ancilla, -ae f. female servant

aut…aut either…or

Eāmus! Let's go! (from *eō*)

ēgērunt "they did" (from *agō*)

eīs to them (i.e., Licinia and Flavia)

ergō therefore

fessus, -a, -um tired

fīlia, -ae f. daughter

fīnem end

fīniō, fīnīre, fīnīvī / fīniī, fīnītum finish

hūc here, to this place

hominēs people

hōra, -ae f. hour, time

iam now, already

illīc there

incipiō, incipere, incēpī begin

intrō (1) enter

lābor work

labōrō (1) work

magnus, -a, -um large, great, loud

mercātor merchant

negōtium, -iī n. business, task

nōn iam no longer

octāva hōra = eighth hour, about 2 P.M.

ōtium, ōtiī n. leisure, rest

parum (+ gen.) little

paucī few

plūs more

prōcēdō, prōcēdere, prōcessī proceed, advance

quia because

quoque also

reī pūblicae of the republic

senātōrēs senators

sine (+ abl.) without

suās their

surgō, surgere, surrexī to get up

tempus time

vōce voice

vocō (1) call

POSTQUAM LĒGISTĪ

1. Compare the time expressions *multās horās* in line 6 and *octāvā horā* in line 10. Note that one is in the accusative and one is in the ablative. How does Latin use case to indicate different kinds of time?
2. Does the timing of a Roman business day resemble any modern countries' commercial patterns?
3. What effect might the Italian climate have had on the Roman business day?
4. *Ōtium* means "leisure" and *negotium* is a compound (*nec* + *ōtium*) meaning "not leisure." What does this seem to say about Roman priorities?

Grammatica B

The Perfect Tense: 3rd Person Singular and Plural

Did you find *salūtāvit, surrexit, vēnit* and *fīnīvit* in this scene? Compare these perfect forms with the present.

Present	*salūtat*	she greets
Perfect	*salūtāvit*	she greeted
Present	*surgit*	she gets up
Perfect	*surrexit*	she got up
Present	*venit*	she comes
Perfect	*vēnit*	she came
Present	*Labor fīnit.*	Work ends.
Perfect	*Labor fīnīvit.*	Work has ended.

- For now, you will see only the 3rd person, singular and plural.
- The endings are: 3rd singular *-it* and 3rd plural *-ērunt*.
- Translate the perfect as a simple past or use the helping verb "has/have."

salūtāvit	she greeted	*salūtāvērunt*	they greeted
surrēxit	she has arisen	*surrēxērunt*	they have arisen
vēnit	she went	*vēnērunt*	they went
fīnīvit	it has ended	*fīnīvērunt*	they have ended

The Perfect Stem

The perfect stem (used to form three tenses) is found by dropping the -ī from the 3rd principal part.

1st PP	2nd PP	3rd PP	Perfect Stem
habitō	habitāre	habitāvī	habitāv-
videō	vidēre	vīdī	vīd-
dūcō	dūcere	dūxī	dūx-
veniō	venīre	vēnī	vēn-
sum	esse	fuī	fu-

Some stems are very close to each other and may seem hard for the eye to catch, such as *venit* (present, "he comes") vs. *vēnit* (perfect, "he came"). But for the Romans it was a matter of hearing the difference—*weh-nit* vs. *wey-nit*. It gave them no greater pause than this sentence gives you: "I love to **read**, so yesterday I **read** three books." Again, try reading aloud whenever you can.

Tense

A verb has tense as well as mood. The tense of a verb indicates the time of an action and the kind of action (simple or continuous). So far you have seen two tenses, **present** and **perfect**. For now, distinguish these two tenses in terms of time. The present tense indicates actions happening "now," whereas the perfect tense indicates actions that have happened in the past.

ambulat	he walks	now
ambulāvit	he walked	in the past

Later we will deal with other aspects of tense.

The 3rd Principal Part

The third form of a Latin verb listed in the dictionary is its 1st person singular perfect active form. This is called the third principal part. Here are examples for some verbs you have already learned.

1st Conjugation	*ambulō* I walk	*ambulāre* to walk	*ambulāvī* I walked
2nd Conjugation	*respondeō* I reply	*respondēre* to reply	*respondī* I replied
3rd Conjugation	*agō* I do	*agere* to do	*ēgī* I did
3rd Conjugation -iō	*capiō* I seize	*capere* to seize	*cēpī* I seized
4th Conjugation	*veniō* I come	*venīre* to come	*vēnī* I came
Irregular	*sum* I am	*esse* to be	*fuī* I was

Perfect stems vary widely, but there are some patterns:

PATTERN	PRESENT STEM	PERFECT STEM
add -v-	clāmā-	clāmāv-
add -u-	habē-	habu-
add -s-	dūc- scrīb-	dūx- scrips-
lengthen vowel	ven-	vēn-
reduplicate (double) initial sound	curr-	cucurr-
complete stem change	fer- ag-	tul- ēg-

EXERCEĀMUS!

8-4 | 3rd Principal Parts

Use the patterns described in the chart to identify the 1st principal part of each of the following *Verba Discenda*. Then describe the type of pattern change. Follow the model.

	1st PP	**Pattern**
→ vocāvī	*vocō*	add -v-
1. portāvī		
2. debuī		
3. dīxī		
4. ēdī		
5. didicī		
6. fuī		

Latin Time Expressions

Latin uses the accusative and the ablative cases to express time.

The **accusative case** is used to show how long an action lasted. This is called the **accusative of duration of time** or **accusative of extent of time** or, if you will, "the accusative of time how long." For example:

> *Multās hōrās labōrāvit.*　　She worked **(for) many hours**.

The **ablative case** is used to show when an action took place or the time during which the action took place. These are usually called the **ablative of time when** and the **ablative of time within which**.

> *Octāvā hōrā dormīvit.*　　**At the eighth hour** she was sleeping.
>
> *Nocte labōrāvit.*　　She worked **at night**.

The biggest challenge posed by these expressions for English speakers is supplying the right English preposition, since Latin uses none. As a rule, you know it is **accusative of time** if you can use either **for** or no preposition in your translation, as in:

> "She worked **for many hours** on the homework assignment."
> "She worked **many hours** on the assignment."

In either case the English words become *multās hōrās* in Latin.

It is an **ablative of time** expression if you use the prepositions **at**, **during**, or **in,** as in

"She finished the assignment **at noon**." ⟶ *merīdiē*

"She finished the assignment **during the night**." ⟶ *nocte*

"She went home **at the eighth hour**." ⟶ *octāvā hōrā*

These three time expressions in **bold** become ablative in Latin: it is the reader's job to choose the English preposition that works the best.

Mōrēs Rōmānī

Tempus Fugit

Sōlārium Rōmānum Pompēiīs

Several Roman expressions about time have passed the test of time and have become proverbial expressions today. Perhaps the most famous of these is *Tempus fugit*, which we know in English as "Time flies." This expression can be traced back to a line in Vergil's *Georgics* (III.284), written in the late first century B.C. Use the *Verba Ūtenda* to help you translate.

> *Sed fugit intereā* **fugit** *irreparābile* **tempus***.*

In one of his *Odes*, Vergil's friend Horace uses *aetās* instead of *tempus* as he offers a comment on time that you will recognize:

> *Dum loquimur, fūgerit invida*
> *Aetās:* **carpe diem***.*
> > *Carmina* I.11.7–8

A generation later, the poet Ovid wrote the following in *Metamorphoses* XV.233:

> *Tempus edax rērum*

Notice how Ovid uses *edax* (devouring) from *edō, ēsse* to describe time here as the "devourer of things."

Finally, in his first speech against Catiline in 65 B.C., the famous orator Cicero (106–43 B.C.) also used an expression about time that is often quoted today:

> *Ō tempora, ō mōrēs!*

Cicero here is lamenting the bad state of affairs in Rome, that a man like Catiline, who was plotting to overthrow the Roman government, would dare to show his face in the Roman Senate. This speech became so famous that any Roman at the end of the 1st century B.C. would know many phrases from it by heart. This particular phrase is also quoted today when people want to complain about the present and to compare it unfavorably with the "good old days."

🔊 VERBA ŪTENDA

aetās age, period of time	*edax* devouring (from *edō*); refers to *tempus*	*intereā* meanwhile	*loquimur* we speak
carpō, carpere seize, pluck, enjoy	*fūgerit* "will have fled"	*invida* envious (refers to *aetās*)	*mōrēs* customs, habits
diem day	*fugiō, fugere, fūgī* flee, run away	*irreparābile* unrecoverable, irreparable	*rērum* "of things"
dum while			*tempora* times
			tempus time

The Romans had no mechanical clocks, so telling time during the day was not an exact science. They did, however, have the sundial (*sōlārium, -iī* n.) and the water clock (*hōrologium, -iī* n.). The *hōrologium* was especially useful for telling time during the dark hours. It worked by calibrating the level of water flowing from one vessel into another.

The Romans divided daylight time into twelve equal *hōrae* or hours, rather than assigning a fixed amount of time for each hour. Nighttime was divided into four equal *vigiliae* or watches. Since there is more daylight in summer than in winter, a Roman *hōra* ended up being much longer in summer than it was in winter. Thus, if sunrise were at 6 A.M., then *prīmā hōrā*, "at the first hour," would be 6–7 A.M. *Secundā hōrā*, "at the second hour," was thus 7–8 A.M.

Latīna Hodierna

Telling Time by the Romans

Though our ability to tell time today is much more exact than the Roman method, Latin words are still used in the modern vocabulary for telling time.

Latin	English	French	Italian	Spanish
hōra	hour	heure	ora	hora
hour, season, time				
hōrologia water clock		l'horloge	l'orologio	
minutia	minute	minute	minuto	minuto
from a stem meaning "tiny"				
secunda	second	seconde	secondo	segundo
that following first				
diēs	day			día
day, daylight				
diurnus, -a, -um,		jour	giornata	
daily				

Business travelers often receive a *per diem* allowance. This is a set amount for daily expenses. The phrase literally means "through the day, daily."

Orbis Terrārum Rōmānus

Campus Martius

The Campus Martius (Field of Mars) was an open, flat area north and west of the Capitoline Hill. An early temple of Mars gave the area its name. Since it was located outside the *pomerium* (the official, religious boundary) of the city of Rome, the Campus Martius was used frequently for military gatherings and exercises. It was also the place where citizens gathered to vote in the *comitia centuriata* (a political assembly). In the Republican period, several important structures were erected there including the Circus Flaminius (221 B.C.) and the Theater of Pompey (52 B.C.), where Julius Caesar was assassinated.

In the Augustan period, the Campus Martius saw several major building projects, including the Mausoleum of Augustus, the Ara Pacis, the original Pantheon (built by Agrippa) and the *Solārium Augustī*, a huge horological park near his Mausoleum. Augustus dedicated this monument in 10 B.C. to celebrate the restoration of Egypt to Roman power (after the battle of Actium in 31 B.C.) He used an Egyptian obelisk as the arm of the sundial to mark not only the hours of the day but also the seasons of the year. This obelisk, now in the Piazza Montecitorio in Rome, appears in a photograph on page 102.

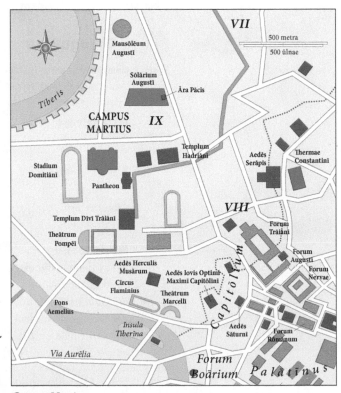

Campus Mārtius

Sōlārium (Hōrologium) Augustī in Campō Martiō

QUID PUTĀS?

1. "Time flies" is not an accurate translation of Vergil's *tempus fugit*. Can you give a better one based on what the verb *fugiō* really means? Which version do you like better and why?
2. Why does Vergil describe time as *irreparābile*? How is the literal meaning of the Latin word different from the English derivative "irreparable"?
3. Explain how each of the different possible meanings of the verb *carpō* adds new meaning to the phrase *Carpe diem*.
4. Where have you seen the phrase *Carpe diem* used today? Do you agree with this statement? Why or why not?
5. Compare the *sōlārium Augustī* illustrated in *Mōrēs Rōmānī* with the meaning of the English word "solarium." What do they have in common?
6. Compare the Campus Martius to a park or other open space in your home town. How are these spaces similar? How are they different?

EXERCEĀMUS!

8-5 Scrībāmus

Retell in the past tense the meeting between Socrates and Chiron that you read in the last chapter. In order to do this replace all the present tense verb forms (marked in bold in parentheses) with perfect ones. Follow the model.

Chīrōn ā lūdō ___*abīvit*___ (**abit**) et ad tabernam Valeriae _____ (**adit**). Ubi Sōcratēs magistrum in tabernā _____ (**videt**), sīmia dē mensā et in bracchia Chīrōnis _____ (**currit**). In mensā quattuor fīcī _____ (**sunt**) et Sōcratēs ūnum dē ficīs _____ (**capit**) et ad magistrum _____ (**portat**). Sīmia ficum _____ (**dat**) et magister _____ (**rīdet**). Chīrōn tacitus vīnum _____ (**bibit**) dum omnēs in tabernā _____ (**rīdent**).

8-6 Colloquāmur

With a classmate or your instructor, practice asking and answering the questions based on the pattern sentences. Be sure to use the vocative with your question and answer. Here is some vocabulary you can use:

Questions
Quid hoc est?
  (What is this?)
Ubi est . . . ?
  (Where is . . .)
Monstrā mihi . . .
  (Show me . . .)

Addressee
amīca (female friend)
amīce (male friend)
discipula (female student)
discipule (male student)
magister (male teacher)
magistra (female teacher)

Classroom Objects
charta (paper)
fenestra (window)
hōrologium (clock)
liber (book)
mensa (table, desk)
porta (door)
sella (chair)
stilus (pen or pencil)
tabula (notebook)

Words in Answers
hīc (here)
illīc (there)

→ **Q:** Amīce, quid hoc est?   **A:** Hoc est sella!

→ **Q:** Magistra, ubi est liber?   **A:** Liber hīc est.

8-7 Verba Discenda

Find the Latin word in the *Verba Discenda* that best answers each of the following questions.

→ Valeria would address Licinia with this word: *fīlia*

1. This noun can refer to the girl who accompanies Servilia:

2. This noun refers to Valeria, Licinia, and her husband as a group:

3. Servilia's age:

4. What is conducted in the Roman Forum:

5. There are twelve of these in a Roman day:

6. How Valeria and Licinia feel at the end of a hard day's work:

7. Use this verb to refer to an object that is no longer moving:

8. This noun is walked on:

VERBA DISCENDA

ancilla, -ae f. female servant [ancillary]
ergō therefore
familia, -ae f. family [familiar]
fessus, -a, -um tired
fīlia, -ae f. daughter [filial]
fīniō, fīnīre, fīnīvī / fīniī, fīnītum finish [infinity]

hōra, -ae f. hour, time [hour]
iam now, already
illīc there
intrō (1) enter [introduce]
magnus, -a, -um large, great, loud [magnitude]

negōtium, -iī n. business, task [negotiate]
novus, -a, -um new [novelty]
portō (1) carry [porter, portable]
praeter (+ acc.) along, beyond; except
quoque also

sēdecim sixteen
sistō, sistere, stetī / stitī, statum stand still [desist]
terra, -ae f. land [terrestrial]
vocō (1) call [vocative, vocation]

Angulus Grammaticus

More on 2ⁿᵈ Declension Vocatives

You know that the vocative case usually has the same endings as the nominative case and that ALL vocative plurals are identical to the nominative plural forms. The only significant exceptions occur in the 2ⁿᵈ declension singular. Here are the rules:

- If the nominative singular ends in -*r*, the vocative is the same as the nominative.

  puer   *Ō puer*

- If the nominative singular ends in -*us*, the vocative is -*e*.

  amīcus   *Ō amīce*

- If a nominative singular noun ends in -*ius*, the vocative is -*ī*.

  fīlius   *Ō fīlī*

- Rarely, if a nominative singular adjective ends in *-ius*, the vocative is *-ie*. There are not many of these.

  fīlius tertius   *Ō fīlī tertie*

- The vocative singular of *meus* is *mī*.

  meus amīcus   *Ō mī amīce*

Here is a chart summarizing how this works:

SINGULAR					
Nominative	vir	discipulus	filius	tertius	meus
Vocative	**vir**	**discipule**	**filī**	**tertie**	**mī**
PLURAL					
Nominative	virī	discipulī	filiī	tertiī	
Vocative	**virī**	**discipulī**	**filiī**	tertiī	

The interjection *Ō* is an easy way to recognize a vocative in a phrase, but it is not required. Just as, in English, we can say, "Hey, John, where are you?" or simply "John, where are you?" Latin says, *Ō Marce, ubi es?* or *Marce, ubi es?*

Photo Credits

page 93 (top) Victor Martinez/Photo by Victor Martinez, with permission; **page 100** Vincenzo Vergelli/iStockphoto.com Vincenzo Vergelli/Sundial/iStockphoto; **page 102** Photo by Daniel McCaffrey, with permission

9

Per Viās Rōmānās

Lectiō Prīma

Antequam Legis

Subūra

In this chapter, Valeria, Licinia, and Aurelia walk home through a lively Roman neighborhood called the Subura, which was located in the valley between the Viminal and Esquiline hills. The Subura was a lower-class area with lots of activity, both legal and illegal, taking place in the street. All sorts of businesses set up shop in the street, including barbers, as you will see, and there were all sorts of street vendors and performers, as in many modern American cities.

One of the topics of conversation on the street is an upcoming performance of a play called *Amphitryō* by Plautus, a 2nd-century B.C. author of comedies. Later in this book, you will "attend" this performance.

As you read about life in the Subura, watch for more verbs in the perfect tense. **Note:** The following story intentionally mixes the present and perfect tenses. Be sure of the tense before you translate.

Uses of the Genitive Case

This reading introduces you to two new uses for the genitive, the **genitive of description** and the **genitive of the whole**. We use a **genitive of description** in English in phrases like "a man of great wisdom." Latin can say the same thing: *vir magnae sapientiae.*

Latin uses a **genitive of the whole** in expressions indicating the part of a whole, as in the phrase *plūs negōtiī* "more of business" = "more business."

Per viam Pompēiānam

GRAMMATICA
The Genitive of Description
  and Genitive of the Whole
Possessive and Reflexive Adjectives

MŌRĒS RŌMĀNĪ
Fullōnica Rōmāna

LATĪNA HODIERNA
Latin in Modern Commerce

ORBIS TERRĀRUM RŌMĀNUS
Subūra

ANGULUS GRAMMATICUS
What Kind of Genitive Is That? Genitives
  with Nouns and Adjectives

LECTIŌNĒS:
AD SUBŪRAM
and
VIA OCCUPĀTA

Valeria and her daughter walk home to the Subura. Along the way they experience Roman street life.

105

From *Disce! An Introductory Latin Course, volume 1*, First Edition. Francesco Bonavita. Copyright © 2011 by Pearson Education, Inc. Published by Pearson Prentice Hall. All rights reserved.

Gemma

Another idiom: *Quid novī?*
Literally, "What of new?" We
would say "What's new?"

EXERCEĀMUS!

9-1 Translating Genitives

As you read *Lectiō Prīma*, make a list of the genitives marked in **bold** along with the word that is linked to this genitive. Then identify each of them as either a **genitive of possession**, a **genitive of description** or a **genitive of the whole**. Follow the models.

Line	Genitive	Type
→ 1	plūs negōtiī	of the whole
→ 1	tabernā Valeriae	possession

🔊 AD SUBŪRAM

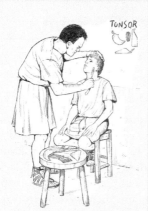

Plūs **negōtiī** nōn in Forō est. Multī hominēs ā Forō et ā tabernā **Valeriae** abīvērunt et ad familiās suās adīvērunt. Nunc, ergō, parum **negōtiī** in tabernā est. Labor **fēminārum fessārum** in tabernā finīvit.

Valeria Liciniaque tabernam clausērunt et per Argīlētum fēminae ambulāvērunt ad
5 Subūram, ubi **Valeriae** familia habitat. Dum ambulant, fēminae multa varia vīdērunt.

Dum Valeria et Licinia per viās eunt, hominēs multōs et variōs vīdērunt. Prīmum, **tonsōris** tabernam vīdērunt. Tonsor, vir **magnae statūrae**, prō tabernā suā stetit et virum **parvae statūrae** rāsit dum aliī virī circumstant et multa dē multīs dīcunt. In antīquitāte, sīcut hodiē, virī in tabernīs **tonsōrum** multa dīcunt!

10 "Quid **novī**, amīce?" ūnus **ē virīs** rogāvit.

Amīcus respondit: "Multī dē theātrō dīcunt." Alius addidit: "Mox in theātrō **Marcellī** *Amphitryō*, fābula **Plautī** erit."

Et tertius: "Quid dē rēbus **Augustī**?"

"St! Tacē, stulte!" monuit ūnus **ē virīs**. "Nōlī audēre talia verba dīcere! Fortasse aliquis **malī animī** nostra verba
15 audīre potest!" Nēmō **virōrum** magnā vōce dīcere voluit.

Tonsor virum rāsit

🔊 VERBA ŪTENDA

addō, addere, addidī add
aliquis someone
alius, -a, -um other, another
animus, -ī m. mind, spirit
antīquitāte antiquity
audeō, audēre, ausus sum dare
audiō, audīre, audīvī, audītum hear
circumstō, circumstāre, circumstetī stand around
claudō, claudere, clausī close, shut up
dum while
ē virīs of the men

ergō therefore
erit there will be
fābula, -ae f. play, story
fortasse perhaps
hominēs people
labor work
moneō, monēre, monuī warn
mox soon
multa dē multīs much about many things
multa varia many different things
nēmō no one, nobody
noster, nostra, nostrum our
nunc now

parum little
parvae small
plūs more
prīmum first, at first
prōnuntiō (1) pronounce, say
prō (+ abl.) before, in front of
rādō, rādere, rāsī shave
rēbus "the affairs"
rogō (1) ask
sīcut just as
st! shh! shush!
statūra, -ae f. stature
stulte! stupid!

suus, -a, -um his/her/its/their own
suā his (refers to the barber)
Subūra, -ae f. Subura, a neighborhood in Rome
taceō, tacēre, tacuī be silent
talia such
tertius a third (person)
theātrum, -ī n. theater; the Theater of Marcellus was new at the time
tonsōris "of a barber"
tonsōrum "of barbers"
varia various things
verba words

POSTQUAM LĒGISTĪ

Answer the following questions in Latin. You can easily find the material for your answer in the *lectiō*, but be sure your answers are in complete sentences. Follow the model.

→ Quid in viīs fēminae vīdērunt?
  Hominēs multōs et variōs vīdērunt.

1. Quid Valeria Liciniaque agunt?
2. Ubī Valeriae familia habitat?
3. Ubi virī multa dē multīs dīcunt?
4. Quid mox in theātrō erit?

Gemma

Compare the verbs *audēre* and *audīre*. If you remember that their stems are *audē-* (dare) and *audi-* (hear), you will be able to tell them apart.

Grammatica A

Genitive of Description and Genitive of the Whole

You have already seen the genitive used in phrases like *Servīliī fīlius* (Servilius' son), *Liciniae vir* (Licinia's husband), and *Valeriae taberna* (Valeria's shop) in which the genitive case was used to show **possession**. You see two other uses of the genitive in *Lectiō Prīma*: the **genitive of description** and the **genitive of the whole**, also known as the **partitive genitive**.

The **genitive of description** is used to describe the general characteristics of a person or a thing.

        vir magnae statūrae   a man of great stature

The **genitive of the whole** is used to indicate a part or portion of a larger whole.

        quid novī   "what of new" or "what's new"
        plūs negōtiī   "more of business" or "more business"

Now look over the list you created while you were reading the *lectiō*. Is there anything from Exercise 9-1 you need to put in a different category?

Notā Bene:

- Notice how the genitive of the whole can be translated into English without "of," as in "more business" instead of "more of business." In fact, English prefers it that way!
- In English we might say "many of the men" but Latin would rather say *multī virī* (many men).
- With numbers Latin prefers to use *ex* + the ablative instead of the genitive of the whole: *ūnus ē virīs* (one of the men)

EXERCEĀMUS!

9-2 **Translating Genitive Phrases**

Match the genitive phrase in column A with its English translation in column B.

A	B
_____ 1. domus magnī spatiī	A. a house of great space
_____ 2. fēminae magnae sapientiae	B. a man of evil mind
_____ 3. fēminae taberna	C. a tutor of few words
_____ 4. paedagōgus paucōrum verbōrum	D. boys of little ambition
_____ 5. plūs spatiī	E. more space
_____ 6. puerōs paucae industriae	F. none of the men
_____ 7. nēmō virōrum	G. the man's daughter
_____ 8. vīnum parvī pretiī	H. the woman's snack shop
_____ 9. vir malī animī	I. wine of small price (cheap wine)
_____ 10. virī fīlia	J. women of great wisdom

Hint: Use the vocabulary you know to identify the words you don't know.

Lectiō Secunda

Antequam Legis

Reflexive Adjectives

As you read *Lectiō Prīma*, did you notice how the barber stood *prō tabernā suā* (in front of his shop)? *Suā* is a form of the adjective *suus, -a, -um*, a word that has no fixed translation, but rather means "the subject's own". This word is used to show possession by the subject. You can translate it as "his (own)," "her (own)," "its (own)," or "their (own)," depending on the subject of the sentence. Nothing like it exists in English. Note the following phrases and their translations.

*Valeria fīliam **suam** amat.*	Valeria loves **her** (own) daughter.
*Aelius uxōrem **suam** amat.*	Aelius loves **his** (own) wife.
*Licinia virum **suum** amat.*	Licinia loves **her** (own) husband.
*Sīmia familiam **suam** amat.*	The monkey loves **its** (own) family.
*Aelius et Licinia familiam **suum** amant.*	Aelius and Licinia love **their** (own) family.

Watch for more forms of this adjective marked in **bold** as you read about all the people in the streets of the Subura.

EXERCEĀMUS!

9-3 **Translating Reflexive Adjectives**

As you read *Lectiō Secunda*, make a line-by-line list of all the forms of *suus, -a, -um*. Then identify the subject of the sentence in which the word is found. This subject will tell you whether to translate the word as **his**, **her**, **its**, or **their**.

Line	Form of *suus, -a, -um*	Subject	Translation
→ 3	suam	actōrēs	their

VIA OCCUPĀTA

Porrō fēminae ambulāvērunt et multōs aliōs hominēs vīdērunt.

Hīc in viā sunt musicī et saltātōrēs. Actōrēs magnī ingeniī quoque in viā fābulam **suam** agunt. Illīc, in tabernae angulō, nōnnūllī virī paucae industriae āleās iēcērunt. Virī paucae industriae et paucae pecūniae semper multam pecūniam ob-
5 tinēre spērant, sed saepe (aut semper!) pecūniam **suam** āmittunt.

In viā nōnnūllī puerī pilā lūdunt et ad lūdum amīcōs **suōs** vōcant. Puellae rīdent et dē **suīs** amīcīs narrant. Ūna puella cum amīcā **suā** ambulat et clārē canat.

Servī dominōs **suōs** in lectīcīs portant. Ūnus servus magnam arcam **suī** dominī portat. Nōnnūllī aliī conservum **suum** servant. Ancillae post dominārum **suārum** lectīcās ambulant. Alia **suae** dominae passerem in caveā portat.

10 Fēminae quoque sūtōrēs, unguentāriōs, laniōs, argentāriōs, librāriōs, et multōs aliōs vīdērunt. Illī virī magnae industriae sunt et tōtam per diem in officīnīs **suīs** labōrant.

In aliā viae parte fullōnica est. Fullōnica est taberna ubi fullō tunicās, togās, et omnia alia vestimenta ūrīnā pūrgat. Dum prope fullōnicam ambulant, fēminae nāsōs texērunt propter odōrem fortem ūrīnae ē fullōnicā. Fullō, vir natūrae laetae, eās salūtāvit, sed festīnāvērunt fēminae et mox insulam **suam** conspexērunt. Propter odōrem fullō vir paucōrum amīcōrum est.

Fēminae nāsōs texērunt

🔊 VERBA ŪTENDA

actōrēs actors
adiuvō (1) help
ālea, -ae f. die (singular of "dice")
alius, -a, -um other, another, aliī...aliī some...others
aliōs "other people"
amīca, -ae f. (girl) friend
āmittō, āmittere, āmīsī, āmissum lose
angulus, -ī m. corner
ante (+ acc.) ahead, before
arca, -ae f. chest
argentārius, -iī, m. banker
canō (1) sing
cavea, -ae f. cage
clārē clearly, loudly
conservus, -ī m. fellow slave
conspiciō, conspicere, conspexī, conspectum

catch sight of, look at, observe
diem day
dominus, -ī m. master
dum while, as long as
eās them (females)
fābula, -ae f. story, play
festīnō (1) hasten
fortem strong
fullō, -ōnis m. launderer
fullōnica, -ae f. laundry
hīc here, to this place
hominēs people
iaciō, iacere, iēcī to throw
illī they
illīc there
industria, -ae f. ambition
ingenium, -ī n. talent
insula, -ae f. island, apartment block

labōrō (1) work
lanius, -iī m. butcher
lectīca, -ae f. litter, sedan chair
librārius, -iī m. bookseller, book copier
mox soon
musicus, -ī m. musician
nasus, -ī m. nose
natūra, -ae f. nature, disposition
nōnnūllī, -ae, -a some, several
obtineō, obtinēre, obtinuī, obtentum hold, support, gain
occupāta busy
odōrem odor, scent
officīna, -ae f. (work)shop
omnia everything
parte part, piece

passerem sparrow
paucus, -a, -um few, little
pila, -ae f. ball
porrō further
propter (+ acc.) on account of
pūrgō (1) clean
rādō, rādere, rāsī shave
saltātōrēs dancers
spērō (1) hope
sūtōrēs cobblers, shoemakers
suus, -a, -um his/her/its/their own
tegō, tegere, tēxī cover
toga, -ae f. toga
tōtus, -a, -um entire, whole, all
tunica, -ae f. tunic
unguentārius, -iī m. perfume seller
ūrīna, -ae f. urine

POSTQUAM LĒGISTĪ

1. Where are the actors performing? What are the men doing in the corner of a shop?
2. What are the boys and girls doing in the street?
3. What are the various slaves doing?
4. What kinds of shops do Valeria and Licinia see?
5. Which shop do they dislike and why?
6. Describe the owner of this shop.
7. How does this street scene compare to a street in your hometown?

Grammatica B

Possessive and Reflexive Adjectives

"My" "your" "his" "her" "its" "our," and "their" are all examples of **possessive adjectives**. Can you see how these adjectives got their name? Here is an overview of Latin possessive adjectives. All of these words are *Verba Discenda*.

Hīc in viā sunt musicī et saltātōrēs.

PERSON	POSSESSIVE ADJECTIVES	TRANSLATION
Singular		
1st	**meus, -a, -um**	my
2nd	**tuus, -a, -um**	your
3rd	**suus, -a, -um** (reflexive)	his/her/its own
Plural		
1st	**noster, nostra, nostrum**	our
2nd	**vester, vestra, vestrum**	your
3rd	**suus, -a, -um** (reflexive)	their own

The 1st and 2nd person possessive adjectives are easy to translate.

Fēmina familiam **meam** *amat.*	The woman loves **my** family.
Fēmina familiam **nostram** *amat.*	The woman loves **our** family.
Fēmina familiam **tuam** *amat.*	The woman loves **your** family.
Fēmina familiam **vestram** *amat.*	The woman loves **your** family.

Suus, -a, -um, the 3rd person possessive, is more complicated because it is **reflexive**, that is, it must always refer back to (or "reflect") the subject of the sentence. In other words, *suus, -a, -um* means "the subject's own," and how we translate it depends on the subject. Notice how the translation of *suam* changes in each of the following sentences.

Vir familiam **suam** *amat.*	The man loves **his (own)** family.
Fēmina familiam **suam** *amat.*	The woman loves **her (own)** family.
Fēminae familiam **suam** *amant.*	The women love **their (own)** family.
Virī familiam **suam** *amant.*	The men love **their (own)** family.

In these sentences *suam* is a feminine singular adjective referring to *familiam*, but it is translated into English as "his own," "her own," or "their own" depending upon the subject of the sentence. In English translation the word "own" is optional.

Notā Bene: With body parts and personal artifacts like clothing, *suus, -a, -um* is not used; e.g., *Fēminae nāsōs texērunt propter odōrem fortem ūrīnae ē fullōnicā.* No *suōs* is needed here to tell you that the women cover their (own) noses!

EXERCEĀMUS!

9-4 **Translating Reflexive Adjectives**

Remember that the meaning of a reflexive adjective depends on the subject of the sentence, so the translation can change as the subject changes. Use the following sentences as models for translating the forms of *suus, -a, -um* accurately in this exercise.

→ Virī saepe pecūniam **suam** āmittunt.	Men often lose **their** money.
→ Vir saepe pecūniam **suam** āmittit.	The man often loses **his** money.
→ Fēminae saepe pecūniam **suam** āmittunt.	Women often lose **their** money.
→ Fēmina saepe pecūniam **suam** āmittit.	The woman often loses **her** money.

1. Actōrēs in viā fābulam suam agunt. Actor in viā fābulam suam agit. Fēminae in viā fābulam suam agunt. Flāvia in viā fābulam suam agit.	The actors perform their play in the street.
2. Puerī ad lūdum amīcōs suōs vōcant. Flāvia ad lūdum amīcōs suōs vōcat. Marcus ad lūdum amīcōs suōs vōcat.	The boys call their friends to the game.
3. Licinia cum amīcā suā ambulat. Lūcius cum amīcā suā ambulat. Puerī cum amīcīs suīs ambulant.	Licinia walks with her girlfriend.
4. Servus suī dominī magnam arcam portat. Servī suī dominī magnam arcam portant. Ancilla suī dominī magnam arcam portat.	The slave carries his master's chest.
5. Quisque in officīnā suā labōrat. Virī in officīnā suā labōrant. Fēmina in officīnā suā labōrat.	Each works in his own office.

Mōrēs Rōmānī

Fullōnica Rōmāna

A *fullōnica* or laundry was a place where clothes were cleaned. It was also sometimes a place to process cloth in other ways, like starching and dyeing. Such facilities were noted for the stench of sulphur and urine, both of which were used in the cleaning process. Such a laundry was probably not a very healthy place to work.

The simplest Roman laundry consisted of a one- or two-room establishment with work tables and one or two basins where clothes were soaked. They were then put in large terra cotta basins filled with detergents. Workers stomped on the clothes in these bowls to remove grease. The philosopher Seneca described this process as *saltus fullōnicus* or "the launderer's dance" (*Epistulae* 15.4). Urine, both animal and human, was used for bleaching. Some laundries were adjacent to public restrooms where urine was collected and piped into the laundry. Other laundries may simply have provided a large container outside the building to collect urine from passers-by. Burning sulphur was also used to clean the cloth. After the cleaning process, the cloth was soaked again in the basins in order to remove the cleaning agents. Then it was dried in the sun.

Here is a wall inscription from a laundry in Pompeii (CIL IV, 9131):

> *Fullōnēs ululamque canō nōn arma virumq(ue)*

The whole line is a pun on the first line of Vergil's *Aeneid*:
Arma virumque canō . . .

Dea Minerva cum būbōne

The owl (*būbō, būbōnis* m.) was the bird of the goddess Minerva, the patroness of craftsmen like fullers.

🔊 **VERBA ŪTENDA**

arma (pl.) arms	*canō* (1) sing about	*fullōnēs* fullers, launderers	*ulula, -ae* f. screech owl

Latīna Hodierna

Latin in Modern Commerce

The Roman Empire was based as much on commerce as it was on Roman military might. Roman traders and merchants plied their wares all around the empire and beyond. As a result, Latin remains an important presence in the vocabulary and the philosophy of commerce in the modern world.

LATIN WORD	ENGLISH DERIVATIVE
commercium, -iī n. trade, commerce	commerce
merx, mercis f. merchandise, goods, wares	mercantile, mercantilism
mercātor, -ōris m. merchant	merchant
vendō, vendere sell	vend, vendor
redemptiō, -iōnis f. buying up; bribing, ransoming captives; tax farming	redeem, redemption
redemptor, -ōris m. buyer, contractor, independent tax gatherer; savior	redemptor
crēditus, -a, -um trusted	credit
dēbitus, -a, -um owed	debit
contrahō, contrahere, contraxī, contractum form an agreement	contract

And don't forget this Latin phrase, which expresses a basic principal of modern capitalism:

Caveat emptor   "Let the buyer beware"

So the next time you make a major purchase, read the fine print and think about the Romans.

Orbis Terrārum Rōmānus

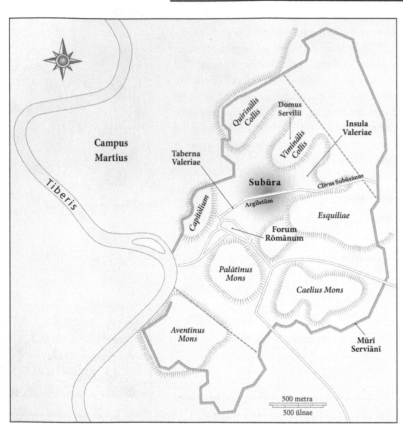

Subūra antīqua

Subūra

Valeria and her family live in the Subura (*Subūra, -ae* f.), a working-class neighborhood (*vīcus, -ī* m.) between the Viminal and Esquiline hills in Rome. Despite the Subura's reputation as a rough district in antiquity, the biographer Suetonius tells us, in his life of Julius Caesar (*Caes.* 46), that the future dictator grew up in this neighborhood. Many craftsmen worked in this part of the city, and there were many tenement houses (*insula, -ae* f.) here. The late 1st-century Roman satirist Juvenal described the neighborhood as *fervēns* ("teeming," XII.51). His contemporary Martial, who lived in Subura, called the area *clāmōsa* ("noisy," XII.18.2) and *sordida* ("filthy," V.22.5). The Argiletum (now known as Via Leonina and Via della Madonna dei Monti) was the main road from the Forum through the Subura. There are also references to a synagogue here in the 1st century B.C.

QUID PUTĀS?

1. What impressions of Rome do you get from the *lectiōnēs* in this chapter, especially the information about laundry techniques in *Mōrēs Rōmānī*?
2. Have you ever experienced a situation in which the expression *caveat emptor* would apply?
3. What does it suggest about Rome that there is still a neighborhood called "Suburra" there today?
4. Can you think of neighborhoods in modern large cities that are like the Subura? Why do people live there? How might this be the same for ancient Romans?

EXERCEĀMUS!

9-5 Scrībāmus

Look at the list of people and things Valeria and Licinia see on their walk through the Subura. Write a paragraph describing what they see. Keep it simple. All you need to do is link each phrase with *vident* (all the nouns are in the accusative case). For variety, you could also put some of the nouns in the nominative case and use the phrase *in viā est/sunt*. (Don't try to do this with nouns ending in *-em* or *-ēs*. These are 3rd declension nouns.) Occasionally link two phrases together with *et*. We have started the paragraph for you.

tonsōris tabernam
actōrēs
virōs paucae pecūniae
puerōrum pilam
puellārum pictūrās
sūtōrēs
insulam suam

dominōs suōs in lecticīs
dominī magnam arcam
passerem in caveā
unguentāriōs
laniōs

argentāriōs
librāriōs
virōs magnae industriae
fullōnicam
fullōnem natūrae laetae

Valeria et Licinia per viās eunt et populōs multōs et multa vident. Fēminae _____ vident. In viā sunt _____ . . . etc.

9-6 Colloquāmur

With a classmate, practice asking and answering questions based on the phrases in Exercise 9-5. In order to make it more challenging and fun, use the following list of people and items Valeria and Licinia do **not** see in the street. Mix these in with the phrases from 9-5, so the person you question has to think about the answer and reply *sīc* or *ita* (yes) or *nōn* (no). Follow the model. Use complete sentences.

sīmiam
Servīliam in lecticā
mē (in answer, use *tē* "you")
Chīrōnis discipulōs
Lūciī magistrum

Chīrōnis pictūram
multam pecūniam
domum tuam
paedagōgī saccum
poculum vīnī

Subūra hodierna

→ Videntne in viā Valeria et Licinia *sīmiam*?

Nōn. Sīmiam nōn vident.

9-7 Verba Discenda

Answer the following questions about the *Verba Discenda*.

1. Write out the 3ʳᵈ principal part of each verb (except *audeō*) in the *Verba Discenda*. Then translate this verb form into English.
2. Give the genitive singular of the two nouns in the *Verba Discenda*.
3. Find the two prepositions and indicate what case each takes.
4. Why do you think that the Romans used the word for "island" to refer to a block of apartments?
5. Give at least one additional English derivative for any five of the *Verba Discenda*.

Via in Subūrā hodierna

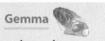

Gemma

audeō, audēre, ausus sum dare: The 3ʳᵈ principal part of this verb is a special form. You will not be asked to use it until later.

🔊 VERBA DISCENDA

alius, -a, -um **other, another** [alienate]
āmittō, āmittere, āmīsī, āmissum **lose**
audeō, audēre, ausus sum **dare** [audacious]
audiō, audīre, audīvī, audītum **hear** [auditory, audible]

conspiciō, conspicere, conspexī, conspectum **catch sight of, see, look at, observe** [conspicuous]
festīnō (1) **hasten**
fābula, -ae f. **story, play** [fable, fabulous]
insula, -ae f. **island, apartment block** [insulate, insulin]

labōrō (1) **work** [laborious, laboratory]
mox **soon**
nōnnūllī, -ae, -a **some, several**
noster, nostra, nostrum **our** [nostrum, pater noster]
obtineō, obtinēre, obtinuī, obtentum **hold, support, gain** [obtain]

paucus, -a, -um **few, little** [paucity]
prō (+ abl.) **before, in front of** [project]
propter (+ acc.) **on account of** [post hoc, propter hoc]
spērō (1) **hope**
suus, -a, -um **his/her/its/their own**

Angulus Grammaticus

What Kind of Genitive Is That?
Genitives with Nouns and Adjectives

At first glance, the Latin genitive seemed straightforward and easy to translate, didn't it? All you had to do was put an "of" in front of the word. But the phrase *Servīliī fīlius* is most readily translated into English as "Servilius' son." In fact, only the genitive of possession can be translated with an 's or s' into English, and this is one way to know you have a genitive of possession. Compare these genitive phrases:

Valeriae taberna (the shop of Valeria)	genitive of possession
virī paucae pecūniae (men of little money)	genitive of description
nēmō virōrum (no one of the men)	partitive genitive

Only the first of these can be translated with 's.

Some grammarians distinguish several other kinds of genitives:

- **Subjective genitive**, in which the noun in the genitive can be the subject of the action described. For example, *odor ūrīnae* means "the smell of urine." You could argue that this is a genitive of possession, but others might say that urine is the subject emitting the odor.

- **Objective genitive**, in which the noun in the genitive can be the object of the action described. For example, *amōr Valeriae* means "love for Valeria" rather than Valeria's love for someone else. A famous example of an objective genitive is the phrase *lacrimae rērum* (the tears of things) in Vergil's *Aeneid* (I.462), the better translation of which would be "here are things worth crying over."

- **Genitive with adjectives**, in which the noun in the genitive answers the question "how." This genitive is usually not translated with "of." For example, *sagāx lūdōrum* ("wise in games" or "wise in respect to games"), in which the genitive *lūdōrum* explains "how" the person is wise. This is a poetic expression you will not find very often.

These genitives are relatively rare, and you can usually get by with translating a genitive with "of."

Photo Credits

page 105 (top) Thinkstock; **page 109** Araldo de Luca/©Araldo de Luca/CORBIS; **page 111** Clipart.com; **page 113 (top)** Victor Martinez/Photo by Victor Martinez, with permission; **page 113 (bottom)** Victor Martinez/Photo by Victor Martinez, with permission

10

Quantī Id Constat?

Lectiō Prīma

Antequam Legis

In this story Valeria negotiates the cost of several items she wants to buy. In Latin you use the **genitive case to ask how much something costs** and the **ablative case to give the price**. Here are some examples:

Quantī constat?	How much does it cost?
Quattuor dēnāriīs constat.	It costs four denarii.

The Dative Case

In this *lectiō* all the words marked in **bold** are in the **dative case**. It is one of the easiest cases to learn and is best translated by using **to** or **for**.

Valeriae *sellam fabricāvī.*	I made a chair **for Valeria**.
Virō *pecūniam dedī.*	I gave money **to the man**.

EXERCEĀMUS

10-1 Dative Case

As you read *Lectiō Prīma*, group all the words in the dative case (marked in **bold**) by similar endings. You will have an *-ae* group, an *-ō* group, and an *-īs* group.

Exemplar īnsulae Rōmānae

GRAMMATICA
Genitive of Cost and Ablative of Price
The Dative Case
Indirect Objects
Dative with Compound Verbs
Dative with Adjectives
Neuter Nouns
A Word on Adjectives

MŌRĒS RŌMĀNĪ
Monēta Romāna

LATĪNA HODIERNA
Roman Money Today

ORBIS TERRĀRUM RŌMĀNUS
Aedēs in Capitōliō

ANGULUS GRAMMATICUS
Forming Compound Verbs

> **LECTIŌNĒS:**
> **ANTĪQUA ŌVA?**
> and
> **ASTROLOGUS**
>
> Before going home, Valeria and Licinia do some shopping and consult a soothsayer about the baby Licinia is carrying.

115

From *Disce! An Introductory Latin Course, volume 1*, First Edition. Francesco Bonavita. Copyright © 2011 by Pearson Education, Inc. Published by Pearson Prentice Hall. All rights reserved.

ANTĪQUA ŌVA?

Tunc fēminae **macellō** appropinquāvērunt. Ecce—hominēs animāliaque ubīque sunt!
Mūlī, equī, et asinī hīc et illīc astant et aliquis **mūlīs, equīs,** et **asinīs** faenum dat.
Post macellum, prope lanium, canēs ossa edunt. Fēminae odōrem piscium et car-
nis et stercoris sēnsērunt. Hominum et animālium vōcēs fortēs audīvērunt. Sed
5 fēminae emere aliqua **cēnae** bona voluērunt et cibum in mensīs inspexērunt.
Holera et ōva et pōma spectāvērunt et dē cēnā cōgitāvērunt.

"Salvē!" inquit venditor.

"Et tū, salvē," inquit Valeria, "Quantī ista holera mala constant? Idonea
equīs sunt!"

10 "Mala holera? Quid dīcis!? Nōn mala sunt sed bona. **Augustō** idōnea!
Hodiē māne in agrō meō haec holera fuērunt! **Cēnae** bona sunt! Tribus assibus
constant."

Illa "Nimium pecūniae rogās," inquit. Venditor et Valeria longē arguērunt et
dēmum Valeria **virō** duōs nummōs dedit et venditor **Valeriae** holera dedit.

15 "Et, sī placet," inquit, "quantī constat ūnum ōvum? Ūnum ex istīs antīquīs ōvīs?"
"Antīqua ōva? Antīqua??!! Haec ōva hodiē sub gallīnā meā fuērunt. Haec ōva **aliīs** praes-
tant! Sex bona ōva tribus assibus bonīs constant. Aut quattuor ōva duōbus assibus."

Valeria et venditor iterum arguērunt et, dēmum venditor **Valeriae** concessit. Valeria **virō** duōs nummōs dedit et
venditor **Valeriae** quīnque ōva dedit. Ita Valeria quīnque ōva duōbus assibus ēmit.

Quantī constat ūnum ōvum?

VERBA ŪTENDA

ager, agrī m. field
aliīs others (other eggs)
aliqua some (things)
aliquis someone
animālium "of animals"
antīquus, -a, -um old, ancient
appropinquō (1) (+ dat.) to approach, come near
arguō, arguere, arguī to argue
asinus, -ī m. donkey
assibus asses (an "as" is a small Roman coin, like a penny)
astō, astāre, astitī stand (up)
bona good things
canēs dogs
carnis "of meat"
cēna, -ae f. dinner
cōgitō (1) think
concēdō, concēdere, concessī (+ dat.) yield to

constō, constāre, constitī, constātum to cost
dēmum at last, finally
duōbus two
Ecce! Behold! Look!
equus, -ī m. horse
faenum, -ī n. hay
fortēs strong, loud
gallīna, -ae f. hen
haec these (eggs)
hīc here, in this place
holera vegetables (nominative and accusative plural)
hominum of men, of people
idōnea suitable, fit
illa she
illīc there
inspiciō, inspicere, inspexī, inspectum look closely at
ista those
ita so, thus; yes

lanius, -iī m. butcher, butcher shop
longē for a long time
macellum, -ī n. grocery shop
mūlus, -ī m. mule
nimium too much
nummus, -ī m. coin
odōrem odor
omnibus all
ossa bones
ōvum, -ī n. egg *ōva* = eggs (nominative and accusative plural)
parvus, -a, -um small
piscium "of fish"
pōmum, -ī n. apple; *pōma* apples (accusative plural)
praestō, praestāre, praestitī, praestātum (+ dat.) to be superior to; stand out from; surpass

prōcedō, prōcēdere, prōcessī, prōcessum to proceed
Quantī constat? How much does it cost?
quantus, -a, um how much
quattuor four
quinque five
rogō (1) ask (for)
sentiō, sentīre, sensī smell
sex six
sī placet please
spectō (1) look at
stercoris "of dung"
super (+ acc.) over
timeō, timēre, timuī fear, be afraid
tunc then
trēs, tribus three
ubīque everywhere
venditor merchant
vōcēs voices

POSTQUAM LĒGISTĪ

1. Describe the scene around the grocery store. How would it be different today?
2. How does the grocer respond when Valeria suggests the vegetables are not fresh? And what about his eggs?
3. What price does the grocer quote for eggs? How much does Valeria want to pay? How much does she pay in the end?
4. According to the grocer's first price quote, how much would two eggs cost? Three? Try to answer in Latin.

Haec ōva hodiē sub gallīnā meā fuērunt

Grammatica A

Genitive of Cost and Ablative of Price

In the *lectiō* Valeria asks:

> *Quantī ista holera constant?* How much do these vegetables cost?

and the merchant responds:

> *Tribus assibus constant.* They cost three asses.

Notice how the genitive case is used to indicate cost and the ablative to give the price. Here is how it works:

We say: "How much does that cost?" **Romans said:** "Of how much does it cost?"
                                                       Quantī constat?
                                                       Genitive of Cost

We say: "It costs five dollars." **Romans said:** "It costs at five denarii."
                                                       Quinque dēnariīs constat.
                                                       Ablative of Price

Rules: "Genitive of cost..........ablative of price"

                Cost = genitive. Price = ablative. Remember it!

Expressing price is easy because most numbers (like *quattuor*, *quīnque*, and *sex*) are indeclinable. Here are the ablative forms for the numbers 1, 2 and 3, which are declinable:

	M.	F.	N.
1	ūnō	ūnā	ūnō
2	duōbus	duābus	duōbus
3	tribus	tribus	tribus

(You will learn the other forms of these numbers later.)
So,

> ***Ūnō dēnāriō** constat.* It costs one denarius.
> ***Duōbus dēnāriīs** constat.* It costs two denarii.
> ***Tribus dēnāriīs** constat.* It costs three denarii.

The Dative Case

Here is a chart for the 1st and 2nd declensions with the dative case added. This completes your chart of case endings for the 1st and 2nd declensions!

	1ST DECLENSION		2ND DECLENSION			
Singular						
Nominative	-a	fēmina	-us, -er, -ir	discipulus	vir	fīlius
Genitive	-ae	fēminae	-ī	discipulī	virī	fīliī
Dative	**-ae**	**fēminae**	**-ō**	**discipulō**	**virō**	**fīliō**
Accusative	-am	fēminam	-um	discipulum	virum	fīlium
Ablative	-ā	fēminā	-ō	discipulō	virō	fīliō
Vocative	-a	fēmina	-e, -ī, -r	discipule	vir	fīlī
Plural						
Nominative	-ae	fēminae	-ī	discipulī	virī	fīliī
Genitive	-ārum	fēminārum	-ōrum	discipulōrum	virōrum	fīliōrum
Dative	**-īs**	**fēminīs**	**-īs**	**discipulīs**	**virīs**	**fīliīs**
Accusative	-ās	fēminās	-ōs	discipulōs	virōs	fīliōs
Ablative	-īs	fēminīs	-īs	discipulīs	virīs	fīliīs
Vocative	-ae	fēminae	-ī	discipulī	virī	fīliī

Gemma

Words like *fēminae* can be genitive singular, dative singular, or nominative plural. *Virī* and *virō* can each be two different cases. Don't worry. Usage and word order make it hard to confuse them in a sentence. This is part of the beauty of Latin, that there is so little room for confusion and still a relative economy of endings.

Notā Bene:

- In any given declension, the dative and ablative plurals are **always** identical.
- In the 2nd declension, the dative and ablative singular are also identical.

Indirect Objects

The dative case is used to indicate someone or something **indirectly affected** by an action or a situation. A major use of the dative is the **indirect object**, which is very frequently used with the English verb "give" and the Latin verb *dō, dare*. In fact, the word "**dat**ive" comes from *dō, dare, dedi, **dat**um*.

Compare these two sentences in which the accusative *sīmiam* is the direct object and the dative *fīliae* is the indirect object:

> *Valeria **Liciniae** sīmiam dedit.*
> *Valeria sīmiam **Liciniae** dedit.*

We can translate either sentence into English in two ways:

> Valeria gave the monkey **to Licinia**.
> Valeria gave **Licinia** the monkey.

Gemma

Mihi and *tibi* are two datives you have already seen. ***Mihi** sīmiam dedit.* He gave me a monkey. ***Tibi** sīmiam dedit.* He gave you a monkey.

Usually the indirect object comes before the direct object in Latin, but note that reversing the order of these objects does not change the meaning of the Latin sentence as long as the case endings remain the same. In English, however, reversing the order of the direct and indirect objects can change the meaning in unintended ways:

> Valeria gave **Licinia** a monkey.
> Valeria gave a monkey **Licinia**.

Which sentence doesn't work?

Dative with Compound Verbs

Latin is very fond of compound verbs, i.e., verbs that are prefixed with a preposition to change their meaning slightly. Many of these verbs take a dative where we would expect an accusative direct object in English. Watch for datives especially if the compound is formed with one of the following prepositions: *ad, ante, circum, con* (from *cum*), *in, inter, ob, post, prae, sub,* or *super*.

Here are the compound verbs you saw in *Lectiō Prīma*. Note the datives (marked in **bold**) in the phrases that accompany them.

- *ad* (to) + *propinquāre* (to draw near) ⟶ *appropinquāre* (to draw near to, approach)

Nunc fēminae **macellō** *appropinquāvērunt.*	Now the women approached the grocery store. Now the women drew near to the grocery store.

Notā Bene: Notice how "grocery store" is the object of the verb "approached" in English. But if you remember that *appropinquō* also means "draw near **to**," it is easier to understand the dative in Latin.

- *con* (very) + *cēdere* (to yield, give way) ⟶ *concēdere* (to yield to, give in to, to concede)

Venditor **Valeriae** *concessit.*	The grocer gave in to Valeria.

- *prae* (before) + *stāre* (to stand) ⟶ *praestāre* (to stand before, surpass)

Haec ōva **omnibus aliīs** *praestant!*	These eggs surpass all others!

- *ad* (to) + *esse* (to be) ⟶ *adesse* (to be present for, to be there for someone, to support, to help)

Fēminīs *adesse voluit.*	He wanted to help the women. He wanted to be there for the women.

Such verbs will have a notation in the vocabulary that reads "(+ dat)."
HINT: Pay attention to the way the preposition changes the spelling of the forms. More on this in *Angulus Grammaticus*.

Dative with Adjectives

The dative is also used with certain adjectives:

Augustō *idōneum*	fit **for Augustus**
bona **mihi**	good **to/for me**
via tūta **fēminīs**	a road safe **for women**

Note again that the English adjective also suggests the dative: "good **for**" and "safe **for**."

EXERCEĀMUS!

10-2 Datives

Find the dative in each sentence and translate it. Follow the model.

⟶ Venditor Valeriae holera dedit.   *Valeriae*   (to) Valeria

1. Valeria ōva tria familiae emit.
2. Fēminae emere aliqua cēnae bona voluērunt.
3. Valeria ūnum ōvum virīs emit.
4. Nunc fēminae macellō appropinquāvērunt.
5. Venditor mihi quattuor ōva dedit.
6. Valeria tibi duōs nummōs dedit.

Gemma

Chaldaea: Rome was filled with people who came from far and wide to make their fortune at the center of the known world. The astrologer is from Chaldea. Can you find Chaldea on the map? What country would it be called today?

Maximus hērōs Graecus Perseus

Lectiō Secunda

Antequam Legis

Neuter Nouns

You have already learned the following *Verba Discenda*:

> *forum, -ī* forum
> *ōvum, -ī* egg
> *vīnum, -ī* wine

It is time you learned why they have nominative singulars ending in *-um*. The *-um* ending tells you that these second declension nouns are neuter rather than masculine.

Watch for neuter nouns in *Lectiō Secunda*. They are marked in **bold**. Note that nominative and accusative plural neuter nouns end in *-a*; e.g., *fora*, *ōva*, and *vīna*. We will talk more about these neuter nouns after you read the *lectiō*.

EXERCEĀMUS!

10-3 **Neuter Nouns**

Make a line-by-line list of all the neuter nouns marked in **bold** in *Lectio Secunda*. Then determine the case from the context of the sentence. Remember that subjects need to agree with the main verb in number. So, for example, a neuter noun ending in *-a* is plural and cannot be the subject of a singular verb. Then give the meaning of the neuter word. Follow the model.

Line	Neuter Word	Number	Case	Reason	Meaning
→ 1	holera	plural	acc.	object of *ēmit*	vegetables

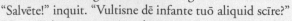

🔊 ASTROLOGUS

Valeria **holera** et **ōva** et **vīnum** ēmit. Tunc domum fēminae prōcessērunt.

Domus in insulā magnā fuit et sōlum duās cellās parvās continuit. In duābus cellīs quinque hominēs habitant—Valeria, Licinia, Aelius (Liciniae vir), Plōtia (Valeriae māter) et ancilla Flāvia—et mox infans!

5 Priusquam fēminae insulam suam intrāvērunt, **dēlūbrum** Iūnōnis Lūcīnae vīdērunt.

Valeria "Offerāmus aliquid deae," inquit. "Gravidae fēminae aliquid deae Iūnōnī dare dēbent." Ūnum **ōvum** in **dēlūbrō** prō infante futūrō relīquērunt. Iuxtā **dēlūbrum** astrologus Chaldaeus sēdit. Chaldaea terra antīqua in Mesopotamiā fuit et

10 multī Chaldaeī astrologī fuērunt. Astrologus fēminās salūtāvit:

"Salvēte!" inquit. "Vultisne dē infante tuō aliquid scīre?"

"Certē!" clāmāvērunt. Astrologō nummōs paucōs dedērunt et silenter stetērunt.

Astrologus **oleum** super aquam effūdit. **Oleum** lentē in aquam diffūdit et formās figūrāsque variās fēcit. Formās figūrāsque inspexit et diū nihil dīxit. Dēnique **praedictum** astrologus Liciniae dīxit:

15 "Ecce! Infans tuus puer est. **Fātum** bonum est. Sānus est hodiē et sānus crās erit. Puerī **fātum** iam omnibus virīs praestat. Fortis puer erit et **magna opera** faciet. Nōlī timēre, **omnia bona** sunt. Fīlius tam fortis quam pater suus erit. Tam fortis quam maximus hērōs Graecus Perseus erit!"

Oleum formās figūrāsque variās fēcit

🔊 VERBA ŪTENDA

aliquid something

astrologus, -ī m. astrologer

cella, -ae f. room

certē certainly

Chaldaeus, -a, -um Chaldaean, an inhabitant of Mesopotamia

contineō, continēre, continuī contain, hold

dea, -ae f. goddess

dēlūbrum, -ī n. shrine

diffundō, diffundere, diffūdī spread out

Ecce! Behold! Look!

erit "he will be"

diū for a long time

effundō, effundere, effūdī pour out

faciet "he will do"

fātum, -ī n. fate, destiny

figūra, -ae f. shape, figure

forma, -ae f. shape, form

fortis strong

futūrus, -a,-um future, coming

gravidus, -a, -um pregnant

habitō (1) live in

hērōs hero

holera vegetables

infans m./f. infant; *infante* (abl.)

inspiciō, inspicere, inspexī, inspectum look closely at

lūnō, lūnōnis f. Juno, queen of the gods; *lūnōnī* "to Juno"

iuxtā (+ acc.) near

lentē slowly

māter mother

maximus very great

Mesopotamia, -ae f. Mesopotamia, the land between the Tigris and Euphrates rivers

nummus, -ī m. coin

offerāmus "let us offer"

oleum, -ī n. oil

omnia everything

opera works, deeds

ōvum, -ī n. egg

parvus, -a, -um small

pater father

Perseus Perseus, Greek hero who decapitated Medusa

praedictum, -ī n. prophecy, prediction

praestō, praestāre, praestitī, praestātum (+ dat.) be superior to; stand out from; surpass

priusquam before

quam than

relīnquō, relīnquere, relīquī leave

sānus, -a, -um healthy

sciō, scīre, sciī / scīvī know

silenter silently

super (+ acc.) over

tam . . . quam as . . . as . . .

timeō, timēre, timuī fear, be afraid

varius, -a, -um mixed, varied

POSTQUAM LĒGISTĪ

1. Describe Valeria's home. What does this residence tell you about the family's social status?
2. Where do the women stop as they near their apartment house? Why?
3. Describe some of the religious practices which occur in this *lectiō*. Do they have any modern parallels?
4. What is the fate predicted for the child?
5. How do Licinia's efforts to learn about her child's future compare to the things parents do in various modern cultures?

Grammatica B

Neuter Nouns

Did you have any trouble understanding the following sentences in *Lectiō Prīma* and *Secunda*?

Quantī ista holera mala constant?	How much are these rotten vegetables?
Quantī constat ūnum ex istīs antīquīs ōvīs?	How much is one of these old eggs?

If you remember that Latin uses the genitive to ask about cost, you will recognize that *quantī* is a genitive and not a nominative plural. Then it is clear from the context and word order that *holera* is actually the subject even

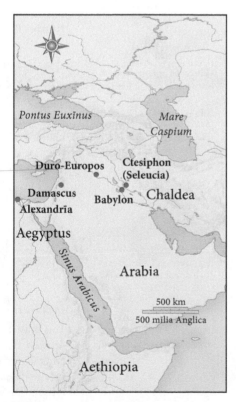

Chaldea

though it ends in *-a*. Since the verb ends in *-nt*, you also have a hint that *holera* is, in fact, neuter plural.

In the 2nd declension, neuter nouns have the same endings as masculine nouns, with three exceptions. Look at the chart first, find the exceptions, then learn the three "neuter rules" listed below.

1ST DECLENSION		2ND DECLENSION	
Singular			
	Feminine	**Masculine**	**Neuter**
Nominative	fēmina	discipulus	**vīnum** ←
Genitive	fēminae	discipulī	vīnī
Dative	fēminae	discipulō	vīnō
Accusative	fēminam	discipulum	vīnum
Ablative	fēminā	discipulō	vīnō
Plural			
Nominative	fēminae	discipulī	**vīna** ←
Genitive	fēminārum	discipulōrum	vīnōrum
Dative	fēminīs	discipulīs	vīnīs
Accusative	fēminās	discipulōs	**vīna** ←
Ablative	fēminīs	discipulīs	vīnīs

Gemma

There are some exceptions to the second part of the "Neuter Rules." One is *haec* (these things), as in *haec holera* (these vegetables here) in *Lectiō Prīma*. But the rule is still a good one.

Neuter Rules:

- The nominative and accusative of every neuter noun are identical.
- The nominative neuter singular always ends in *-um* in the 2nd declension.
- Neuter nominative and accusative plurals end in *-a*.

These rules are true not only in the 2nd declension but in other declensions you will learn later. In fact, *holera* is a 3rd declension noun, but you can recognize its case and number because it is neuter and all neuter nominative and accusative plurals end in *-a*, no matter what declension they are in.

Gemma

Remember: Not all "things" are neuter in Latin. *Mensa* (table) is feminine, for example, whereas *cibus* (food) is masculine.

grammatical gender ≠ natural gender

Notā Bene:

- If what seems to be the subject ends in *a* but the verb is plural, you probably have a neuter noun. Check to be sure.
- If a subject seems to end in *-um*, check to see if it is a 2nd declension neuter.
- There are no neuter nouns in the first declension.

A Word on Adjectives

You may have noticed that we have been listing adjectives with three forms, as in *magnus, -a, -um*. This is the standard dictionary entry for such words. These forms are used to help adjectives "agree" with their nouns. The *-us, -a, -um* endings for all adjectives are listed in the *Verba Ūtenda*. These three forms are masculine (*-us*), feminine (*-a*), and neuter (*-um*). These three classifications represent the **gender** of the adjectival form. Study the following chart.

GENDER	MASCULINE 2ND DECLENSION	FEMININE 1ST DECLENSION	NEUTER 2ND DECLENSION
Singular			
Nominative	magn**us**	magn**a**	magn**um**
Genitive	magn**ī**	magn**ae**	magn**ī**
Dative	magn**ō**	magn**ae**	magn**ō**
Accusative	magn**um**	magn**am**	magn**um**
Ablative	magn**ō**	magn**ā**	magn**ō**
Vocative	magn**e**	magn**a**	magn**um**
Plural			
Nominative	magn**ī**	magn**ae**	magn**a**
Genitive	magn**ōrum**	magn**ārum**	magn**ōrum**
Dative	magn**īs**	magn**īs**	magn**īs**
Accusative	magn**ōs**	magn**ās**	magn**a**
Ablative	magn**īs**	magn**īs**	magn**īs**
Vocative	magn**ī**	magn**ae**	magn**a**

EXERCEĀMUS!

10-4 Declining 2nd Declension Masculines and Neuters

Use *discipulus* (m.) and *vīnum* (n.) as guides to decline *servus* (m.) and *ōvum* (n.). Underline those masculine and neuter endings that are different from each other.

Mōrēs Rōmānī

Monēta Rōmāna

The Latin word for money is *pecūnia, -ae* (f.), and is actually related to *pecus* (cattle), since wealth was once measured in livestock. But because Roman coins were minted in the Temple of Juno Moneta on the Capitoline Hill in Rome, the Latin word for "coinage" is *monēta, -ae* (f.). Here is a list of major Roman coin denominations. To help put it into context, consider that a Roman legionary in the time of Augustus earned 225 *dēnāriī* a year. An *astrologus* like the one in the story earned much less.

NAME OF COIN	MATERIAL	VALUE
uncia	bronze	½ as
quadrans		¼ as
dupondius	bronze or copper	2 asses
sestertius	metal alloy	4 asses
dēnārius	silver alloy *argentum, -ī* n.	16 asses
aureus	gold *aurum, -ī* n.	400 asses

The emperor Vespasian (69–79 A.D.) was known for his caustic wit. Once, when his son Titus criticized him for introducing a tax on the urine collected in public toilets for use by fullers and others, the emperor is said to have held a coin up to Titus and to have asked him if he was offended by the odor. When Titus replied "no," Vespasian, suggesting to his son that any tax revenue was good revenue, said:

Atquī ē lōtiō est.
Suetonius, *Vesp.* 23

Vespasian's comment about money is better known today in this form:

Pecūnia nōn olet.

Did F. Scott Fitzgerald know his Suetonius? He may be referencing Vespasian's words in *The Great Gatsby* (1925) when he refers to cities "built . . . out of non-olfactory money."

Here is the inscription around the edge of the coin issued by the emperor Vespasian and depicted at left:

IMPCAESARVESPASIANAUGPMTRPPPCOSIII

Once the abbreviations are expanded, you see:

Imp(erātor) Caesar Vespāsiān(us) Aug(ustus) P(ontifex) M(aximus)
Tr(ibūniciā) P(otestāte) P(ater) P(atriae) Co(n)s(ul) III

Many of these imperial titles began with Augustus, the emperor at the time of our story, and were routinely held by later emperors. Each office carried not only a certain prestige, but also some actual power.

Monēta Vespāsiānī

🔊 VERBA ŪTENDA

atquī yet	*lōtium, -ī* n. urine	*potestāte* f. with the power, authority
consul m. consul	*maximus, -a, -um* chief	
imperātor m. commander, general	*oleō, olēre* smell, stink	*pontifex* m. priest
III = three times	*pater* m. father	*tribūnicius, -a, -um* m. belonging to a tribune
	patria, -ae f. country	

Latīna Hodierna

Roman Money Today

Look at how several Latin words dealing with money have become part of four modern languages:

LATIN	ENGLISH	FRENCH	SPANISH	ITALIAN
pecūnia, -ae (f.) money	impecunious (broke)	*impécunieux* (broke); *impécuniosité* (state of being broke)		
monēta, -ae (f.) coin	money	*la monnaie* (money, small change)	*la moneda* (money)	*la moneta* (money)
argentum, -ī (n.) silver	argent Argentina argentine	*l'argent* (money)		
dēnārius, -iī (n.)	denary (tenfold)		*el dinero* (money)	*il denaro* (money)

Orbis Terrārum Rōmānus

Aedēs in Capitōliō

Two important temples stood on the Arx (*arx, arcis* n. summit) of the Capitoline Hill. The one known as the Temple of Juno Moneta (*Aedēs Iūnōnis Monētae*) was built by L. Furius Camillus in 344 B.C. to fulfill a vow. By tradition, this was the spot where Juno's sacred geese warned the Romans of danger during a siege by the Gauls in 390 B.C. Juno's epithet *Monēta* (related to the verb *moneō*, warn) seems to refer to this event and to the goddess' protective role in Roman so-

Gemma

Note that *aedēs* is generally the Latin word for the house of a god. *Templum* is used for a larger religious precinct. In English we refer to both kinds of structures as "temples."

ciety. A workshop for minting coins built near this temple came to be known as the *Monēta* (the Mint), leading to the derivation of the English word "money." The remains of the Temple of Juno Moneta lie within and under the Church of Santa Maria in Aracolei (*Ara Coelī* "Altar of Heaven") on the Capitoline Hill. (See photo below.)

The coin below, depicting the goddess Juno, is a silver denarius issued in honor of Faustina, the wife of the emperor Septimius Severus (193–211 A.D.). On the obverse the head of the empress is surrounded by the words FAUSTINA AUGUSTA. On the reverse is an image of Juno standing with a peacock at her feet. Around the edge of the reverse is the word IUNO.

Capitōlium

The second temple was the Capitolium or Temple of Jupiter Optimus Maximus (*Aedēs Iovis Optimī Maximī Capitōlīnī*). Here Jupiter was worshipped together with the goddesses Juno and Minerva. For this reason, the temple is also called the Capitoline Triad. Each deity had a separate room in the temple. Traditionally, this temple is said to have been built in the 6th century B.C. by Tarquin the Proud, the last king of Rome. Excavations begun in 1998 in the Roman Garden inside the Palazzo dei Conservatori of the Capitoline Museums have uncovered some of the foundations of the Temple of Capitoline Jupiter.

Many cities throughout the Roman Empire had Capitolia in their fora.

Templum Iūnōnis Monētae hodiē

Iūno dea

QUID PUTĀS?

1. Explain to a friend what the emperor Vespasian meant when he said that "the money doesn't stink."
2. Look at what the Romans chose to put on their coins. Compare this with the American penny in order to get a sense of each society's numismatic propaganda. How are they alike or different?
3. Why would Christians have built a church dedicated to Mary the mother of Jesus on the site of the Temple of Juno Moneta?
4. What modern country or countries comprise the area of ancient Chaldea?

EXERCEĀMUS!

10-5 Scrībāmus

So far you have learned the numbers I–VI in Latin: *ūnum* (I); *duo* (II); *tria* (III); *quattuor* (IV); *quinque* (V); and *sex* (VI). Using the model below, create additional problems based on these numbers. (Be sure your answers don't go higher than six!)

→ *Ūnum et ūnum sunt: duo*

10-6 Colloquāmur

Each member of the class has six tokens. One person poses in Latin one of the mathematical problems in Exercise 10-5 to another member of the class. If the person responds correctly in Latin, the questioner gives the responder a token. If not, the responder gives the questioner a token. Change partners after each question. The first person to get ten tokens wins.

10-7 Verba Discenda

Use the meaning of the *Verba Discenda* to explain the meaning of each of the following English derivatives. If you need help, consult an English dictionary.

→ antiquarian   *someone who studies or deals with old artifacts, especially books*

1. ovary	5. sextuplet	9. parvovirus
2. processional	6. supernumerary	10. quaternary
3. quantify	7. timid	11. timidity
4. interrogatory	8. figuration	

🔊 VERBA DISCENDA

antīquus, -a, -um old, ancient [antique]
cōgitō (1) think [cogitation]
constō, constāre, constitī, constātum to cost
figūra, -ae f. shape, figure [configure]
hīc here, in this place
inspiciō, inspicere, inspexī, inspectum look closely at [inspect]

ōvum, -ī n. egg [ovulate]
parvus, -a, -um small [parvovirus]
praestō, prāestare, praestitī, praestātum be superior to; surpass
prōcēdō, prōcēdere, prōcessī, prōcessum to proceed [procession]
quam than
quantus, -a, -um how much [quantum physics]

quattuor four
quinque five [quinquennial]
rogō (1) ask (for) [interrogate]
sex six [sextet]
spectō (1) look at [spectator]
super (+ acc.) over [supernatural]
timeō, timēre, timuī fear, be afraid [timid]

Angulus Grammaticus

Forming Compound Verbs

Note the spelling changes that occur in compound verbs:

ad- + fuī = affuī
cum- + cēdō = concēdō
ob- + ferō = offerō

These changes are called **assimilation**. Typically the prepositional prefix changes to be more similar in sound to the verb form. Here are some rules for assimilation that apply to nouns, verbs, adjectives, etc.:

- **ad:** when added to a word beginning with a vowel, *ad-* remains the same; e.g., *adesse*.

When added to a word beginning with a consonant, the "d" usually changes to match the consonant at the beginning of the verb; e.g., *appropinquāre* and *affuī*.

- **cum:** usually becomes *con-* as a prefix; e.g., *concēdō*. But before a word beginning with "m," the "n" becomes "m"; *committō*

Note that English follows the Latin pattern here: "concede," "commit."

- **in:** before a vowel, is unchanged. Before other letters, such as "m," it becomes "m." e.g., *immittō*.
- **ob:** unchanged before a vowel, doubles before a consonant. Thus, *offerō*.

Knowing about compound verbs may save you many unnecessary trips to the dictionary. Note how the assimilation can change if the principal parts of the verb change:

***ad**sum, **ad**esse, **af**fuī*
***af**ferō, **af**ferre, **at**tulī, **al**lātum*

Also, you can determine the general meaning of the compound verb by combining the meaning of the verb with the meaning of the prepositional prefix.

***ad**sum = sum* (I am) + *ad* (to, at) = "I am at"

If you look this word up in the dictionary, it means "I am present."

***of**ferō = ferō* (I carry) + *ob* (for) = "I carry for" or "I bring before"

Photo Credits

page 115 (top) © Photos.com; **page 117** iFotosearch.com, LLC/Royalty Free; **page 120** Drawing by Julia A. Sienkewicz, with permission; **page 124** Clipart.com; **page 125 (bottom left)** Victor Martinez Photo by Victor Martinez, with permission; **page 125 (bottom right)** American Numismatic Society/American Numismatic Society of New York

Domum

From *Disce! An Introductory Latin Course, volume 1*, First Edition. Francesco Bonavita. Copyright © 2011 by Pearson Education, Inc. Published by Pearson Prentice Hall. All rights reserved.

Cavē canem.

GRAMMATICA
Three Kinds of Infinitive
More on the Perfect

MŌRĒS RŌMĀNĪ
Iūno Dea

LATĪNA HODIERNA
Vēnī, Vīdī, Vīcī

ORBIS TERRĀRUM RŌMĀNUS
Gallia Est Omnis Dīvīsa in Partēs Trēs?

ANGULUS GRAMMATICUS
The "Present Perfect" and the "Inchoate
   Suffix" -scō

LECTIŌNĒS:
LATRŌNĒS
and
QUID ACCIDIT HODIĒ?
The Valeria and Servilia families arrive
home.

128

11

Domum

Lectiō Prīma

Antequam Legis

In *Lectiō Prīma* Valeria and Licinia are mugged as they approach their *insula*. As you read about how the women escape from the muggers, you will learn more about infinitives.

Watch for Infinitives

Earlier you saw how Latin uses complementary infinitives with verbs like *possum* and *volō* in phrases such as:

Vīnum potāre possum.	I can drink wine. / I am able to drink wine.
Vīnum potāre volō.	I want to drink wine.

In this chapter, you will see other ways Latin uses infinitives, including:

Vīnum potāre dēbeō.	I ought to drink wine.
Vīnum potāre Marcum iubeō.	I order Marcus to drink wine.
Vīnum potāre bonum est.	Drinking wine is good.

In *Lectiō Prīma* words which introduce infinitives are marked in **bold** and the infinitives themselves are marked in ***bold italics***.

EXERCEĀMUS!

11-1 **Skimming for Comprehension**

Before you read the *lectiō,* scan it and try to find the answers to these questions. This will help you translate. We give you a line range within which to find your answer. Follow the model.

Lines 1–4

→ Why are Licinia and Valeria happy?
   Because of what the astrologer said about the baby

1. Why is Flavia happy?
2. Why is Socrates happy?

Lines 5–7

3. Whom do the ladies see as they approach their *insula*?

4. Where is he and what is he doing?

Lines 8–11

5. How does Socrates try to defend the women from the muggers?

6. How does Aelius do the same? With what?

Lines 12–16

7. What do the muggers see that scares them off?

Gemma

Grātiās ēgērunt: This phrase is an idiomatic use of the verb *agō, agere*. It literally means "to do thanks." If you want to say "thank you" in Latin, say *grātiās tibi agō* or *grātiās vōbis agō*. "I do you thanks."

Gemma

The Latin word *musculum* is the origin of the English word "muscle." Literally, in Latin it means "little mouse" (*mūs*).

🔊 LATRŌNĒS

Licinia et Valeria laetae fuērunt propter verba bona astrologī dē infante et grātiās maximās et deae et astrologō ēgērunt. Flāvia quoque laeta fuit quod nunc insula nōn longinqua fuit. Flāvia quoque fessa fuit quod saccum (et Sōcratem!) longē per viās *portāre* **dēbuit**. Et Sōcratēs laetus fuit quod iēiūnus fuit et cibus domī fuit.

Dum fēminae insulae suae appropinquāvērunt, Aeliī fabricam vīdērunt. Aelius prō fabricā suā stetit et labōrāvit. Licinia laeta virum suum *salūtāre* et virō suō omnia dē verbīs astrologī *narrāre* **voluit**.

Sed subitō trēs latrōnēs ex angiportō saluērunt. Saccum fēminārum *rapere* **voluērunt** et fēminae territae fuērunt. Trēs fēminae fortiter clāmāvērunt. Sōcratēs quoque clāmāvit et ad terram saluit. Sōcratēs etiam ūnum latrōnem momordit! Nunc latrō quoque fortiter clāmāvit!

Aelius vōcēs in viā audīvit. Fēminās vīdit et in latrōnēs magnā cum īrā cucurrit. Malleum magnum tenuit. Fēminīs *adesse* **voluit**. Aelius latrōnēs *currere* **vetuit**. Sed, dum virīs malīs appropinquat, latrōnēs et malleum et musculōs Aeliī vīdērunt. Aelium *pugnāre* **nōluērunt**. Aeliō *concēdere* **māluērunt** et celeriter sine saccō fūgērunt.

Sīc semper est. Viae Rōmānae, praesertim in Subūrā, fēminīs (atque virīs!) tūtae nōn sunt. *Vīvere* Rōmae valdē **difficile est**!

Aelius malleum magnum tenuit

🔊 VERBA ŪTENDA

adsum, adesse, afuī (+ dat.) to be present, be "there for" someone, be of assistance, help, aid

angiportum, -ī n. alley

angustiae, -ārum f. pl. trouble, difficulty

***appropinquō* (1) (+ dat.) approach, come near to**

atque and, and also, and even

celeriter quickly

concēdō, concēdere, concessī go away, withdraw

***dea, -ae* f. goddess**

difficile hard, difficult

domī at home

etiam and also, too

fabrica, -ae f. workshop

fortiter loudly

fugiō, fugere, fūgī flee

in (+ acc.) against

infante infant

īra, -ae, f. anger

iēiūnus, -a, -um hungry

latrō, latrōnis m. thief, robber

***longē* a long distance, far off**

longinquus, -a, -um far away

malleus, -ī m. hammer

maximus, -a, -um greatest

mordeō, mordēre, momordī bite

musculus, -ī m. muscle

narrō (1) tell, seek

omnia everything

portō (1) carry

praesertim especially

pugnō (1) fight

rapiō, rapere, rapuī snatch, seize

***Rōma, -ae* f. Rome;** *Rōmae* at Rome

***Rōmānus, -a, -um* Roman**

***saccus, -ī* m. wallet, sack, bag, pocketbook**

***saliō, salīre, saliī/saluī, saltum* leap, jump**

sīc **thus, in this way; yes**

subitō **suddenly**

teneō, tenēre, tenuī hold

territus, -a, -um scared, terrified

tūtus, -a, -um safe

***valdē* very, a lot**

***verbum, -ī* n. word**

vetō, vetāre, vetuī forbid

vīvō, vīvere, vīxī live

vōcēs voices

1. How does this scene compare with life in a modern American city?
2. Does this scene remind you of any episodes in movies you have seen? How?
3. Have you or someone you know ever been in a similar situation? How was the situation the same? How was it different?

Grammatica A

Three Kinds of Infinitive

Grammarians divide infinitives into three types: **complementary, subjective,** and **objective**. Here are some sentences with infinitives from the story you just read. The infinitives are in **bold**.

> *Licinia laeta virum suum* ***salūtāre*** *voluit.*
> *Aelius fēminīs* ***adesse*** *voluit.*
> *Flāvia saccum longē per viās* ***portāre*** *dēbuit.*

All of these sentences contain **complementary infinitives**. A complementary infinitive is used to complete the action of certain verbs, like *volō, nōlō, mālō, possum,* and *dēbeō*. Generally it is easy to recognize and translate complementary infinitives because these verbs work the same way in Latin and in English.

scrībere volō	I want to write.
scrībere nōlō	I do not want to write.
scrībere mālō	I prefer to write.
scrībere possum	I am able to write. I can write.
scrībere dēbeō	I ought to write.

Remember that, as a **verbal noun**, an infinitive is a verb that functions like a noun in the sentence. This will help you understand two other kinds of infinitive.

An **objective infinitive** is used as the direct object of certain verbs, like *cupiō* (I wish), *doceō* (I teach), *vetō* (I forbid) and *iubeō* (I order). Just as you can want an apple, you can want someone to do something. Consider these examples:

Valeria Flāviam saccum ***portāre*** *iussit.*	Valeria ordered Flavia to carry the sack.
Valeria Flāviam saccum ***portāre*** *cupit.*	Valeria wishes Flavia to carry the sack.
Valeria Flāviam saccum ***portāre*** *vetat.*	Valeria forbids Flavia to carry the sack.

Why all the accusatives? Even though you can easily translate the sentences above, you might ask why *Flāviam* and *saccum* are both accusative. Here are the basics.

- The object of the main verb (*iussit, cupit, vetat*) is actually the infinitive, *portāre*. The subject is ordering/wanting/forbidding the "carrying." Remember that an infinitive is a **verbal noun**.
- You know that the subject of a conjugated verb is nominative, but in Latin, the subject of an **infinitive** is always in the accusative case. That is why *Flāviam* is accusative in each sentence.
- But the "verbal" part of the infinitive can also take a direct object: that is, Flavia is carrying **something**. This too has to be in the accusative, and in these sentences, that word is *saccum*.
- In situations like this, where you have two accusatives in a row with an infinitive, the **first one is the subject** of the infinitive and the **second one is the object** of the infinitive. Word order makes a difference here! Compare these two sentences:

Flāviam sīmiam portāre iubeō.	I order Flavia to carry the monkey.
Sīmiam Flāviam portāre iubeō.	I order the monkey to carry Flavia.

Latin also sometimes uses an infinitive as the subject of a sentence. As you might guess, this is called the **subjective infinitive**. In such cases, the infinitive is commonly accompanied by a form of *est* and, as a verbal noun, is neuter singular. English more commonly uses a gerund ending in "-ing" to translate a Latin subjective infinitive.

*Pecūniam **rapere** malum est.*	To steal money is bad.
Errāre hūmānum est.	To err is human.

EXERCEĀMUS!

11-2 Infinitives

Find the infinitive in each of the following sentences and indicate whether it is complementary, subjective, or objective. HINT: Look for verbs like *volō* and *possum* for complementary infinitives, *est* for subjective infinitives, and *cupiō* for objective infinitives. Follow the model.

→ **Vīvere** Rōmae difficile est!   *Vīvere is a subjective infinitive because it is the subject of **est**.*

1. Latrōnēs saccum rapere volunt.

2. Latrōnēs Aelium pugnāre nōluērunt.

3. Amīcōs salūtāre bonum est!

4. Fēminae Sōcratem clāmāre cupīvērunt.

5. Licinia Aeliō verba astrologī narrāre cupīvit.

6. Licinia verba astrologī narrāre potest.

7. Verba astrologī narrāre difficile est.

8. Paedagōgus sīmiam fugere vetat.

Lectiō Secunda

Antequam Legis

Perfect Tense—All Persons

You already know the 3rd person perfect active endings: *-it* and *-ērunt,* as in *vēnit* and *vēnērunt*.

In *Lectiō Secunda* Lucius tells his mother what happened today at school and you are introduced to the remaining perfect active endings. Before you read, be sure to do Exercise 11-3, as it will teach you the other forms of the perfect tense.

EXERCEĀMUS!

11-3 Recognizing the 1st and 2nd Person Perfect Forms

This exercise is designed to let you discover the endings for the 1st (I, we) and 2nd (you, y'all) persons of the perfect tense. The following chart lists the stems of all the verbs in *Lectiō Secunda* with 1st or 2nd person perfect active endings. These words are marked in **bold** in the reading. Your job is to supply the endings from the readings and to use hints and context from the *lectiō* to translate the words in the correct person. Here are some clues to finding the endings in the text.

- All the endings you seek begin with the letter *-i*.
- When you see the pronoun *ego* you can expect a 1st person singular verb.
- The 1st person plural ending looks a lot like the 1st person plural present.
- Look for 2nd person verb endings with vocatives.

Fill out the following chart as you read.

PERFECT ACTIVE		
Person	Singular	Plural
1st person	audīv-	audīv-
	fodicāv-	rīs-
	vīd-	vīd-
2nd person	cucurr-	audīv-
	nōv-	vīd-
	vīd-	

Cavē!! Be very attentive to the tenses of the verbs in this reading. Lucius is a young lad and, like many younger speakers, he switches tenses at the drop of a hat, especially when he is excited.

QUID ACCIDIT HODIĒ?

Lūcius, Servīlia, et Hermēs ad domum Servīliī adveniunt. Canem familiae salūtant. Nōmen canī Albus est. (Nōmen iocōsum est quod Albus niger, nōn albus est.) Caecilia Metella et Marcus vōcēs Lūciī et Servīliae audiunt, ad ianuam adve-
5 niunt, et in ātriō stant.

Lūcius ē lectīcā surgit et in domum currit. "Marce! Mātercula!" clamat, "**audīvistis**ne dē sīmiā in Forō? Crēdite mihi—iocōsum fuit!!"

Māter respondet: "Fīlī, nōn **audīvī**. Quid accidit? Cūr
10 **cucurristī**? Cūr tam agitātus es?"

"Et ego nōn **audīvī**, mī frāter," addit Marcus, "Dīc mihi! Quid **vīdistī**?"

"In lūdō ego et aliī puerī sumus. Chīrōn librum legit—ut semper! Fessī sumus et amīcus meus, Iūlius, dormit (ut semper!). Sed
15 Chīrōn eum nōn videt. Neque magister dīcit "Cūr dormīs, Iūlī?" neque virgam tollit. Ego Iūliī latus **fodicāvī** et ille oculōs aperuit.

"Subitō clāmōrem magnam **audīvimus**. Ecce! Prīmum sīmiam **vīdī**. Tunc paedagōgum in viā **vīdimus**. Hermēs et sīmia cucurrērunt per viam. Paedagōgus permaximē clāmāvit
20 et post sīmiam cucurrit. Sīmia saccum paedagōgī habuit. Fortasse hunc sīmiam **nōvistī**? Valeriae sīmia est. Valeria tabernam illam iuxtā Forum habet. Hermēs, valdē īrātus, clāmāvit et sīmiam capere voluit. Paedagōgus sīmiae appropinquāvit sed eum nōn capere potuit. Dēnique sīmia in āram Dīvī
25 Iūliī saluit. **Rīsimus!** Marce māterque, sīmiam umquam **vīdistīs** in Forō? Sīmiam in ārā vidēre rīdiculōsum est!"

Caecilia in ātriō stat

🔊 VERBA ŪTENDA

accidō, accidere, accidī happen	*clāmōrem* shout	*iocōsus, -a, -um* funny	*Grammaticus* for explanation)
addō, addere, addidī add	*crēdō, crēdere, crēdidī* believe	*iuxtā* (+ acc.) near to	*oculus, -ī* m. eye
adveniō, advenīre, advēnī, adventum arrive at, come to	**cūr why**	*latus* side, ribs	*permaximē* very loudly
albus, -a, -um white	*dēnique* finally, at last	*legō, legere, lēgī* read	*prīmum* first, at first
aperiō, aperīre, aperuī open	*dormiō, dormīre, dormīvī* sleep	*liber, librī* m. book	**saccus, -ī m. wallet, sack, bag, pocketbook**
appropinquō (1) (+ dat.) approach come near to	*erat* "it was"	*māter* mother	**saliō, salīre, saliī/saluī, saltum leap, jump**
ātrium, -iī n. atrium, public greeting room of a Roman house	*eum* him	*mātercula, -ae* f. dear mother, mommy	**subitō suddenly**
canī "of the dog"	*fodicō* (1) poke; *latus fodicāre* poke in the ribs	*mī* my (vocative)	*surgō, surgere, surrēxī* get up, rise
	fortasse perhaps	*neque. . . neque* neither . . . nor	*umquam* at any time, ever
	frāter brother	*niger, nigra, nigrum* black	*ut* as
	hunc "this" (refers to *sīmiam*)	**noscō, noscere, nōvī, nōtum know, get to know;** *nōvisti* "you know" (See *Angulus*	**valdē very, a lot**
	ianua, -ae f. door		*virga, -ae* f. rod
	illam (adj.) that		

POSTQUAM LĒGISTĪ

1. What is the name of the dog of the Servilius family? Why is this name a joke? Do you know any pets with similarly funny names? Explain.
2. With what event does Lucius begin as he describes his day to his mother and brother?
3. What event is the highlight of his day? What did Lucius like about this event?

Grammatica B

More on the Perfect

The chart you filled in as you read *Lectiō Prīma* should have given you the following new endings (marked with an asterisk) for the **perfect tense**. You now know the full perfect. Note the perfect infinitive form, also.

	SINGULAR		PLURAL	
1st person*	vēn**ī**	I came	vēn**imus**	we came
2nd person*	vēn**istī**	you came	vēn**istis**	you all came
3rd person	vēn**it**	he/she/it came	vēn**ērunt**	they came
Infinitive	vēn**isse**	to have come		

Notā Bene:

- All the personal endings in the perfect active begin with *-i-* except the 3rd person plural, which begins with *-ē-*.

Gemma

- Note *ad domum* in line 1. *Domum* without a preposition means "home" as in "I am going home." Sometimes, as here, a preposition is used when the word *domus* just meant "house."
- Lucius calls his mother *mātercula* instead of *māter* as a term of endearment. Add *-culus, -a, -um* to a Latin word to make it smaller or dearer. You already saw this with *musculum* (little mouse).

- The present and perfect share some common endings. This means that, with some verbs, the only difference between a present and a perfect may be a long vowel. So a macron can make quite a difference:

  *Ille ignāvus hodiē **fugit** sīcut semper **fūgit**.*
  That coward is fleeing today just as he always has fled.

- Some verbs, like *accidō*, have identical present and perfect stems. These can be troublesome to translate, but let context help you.
- Don't worry about the perfect infinitive now. You will not see it used in Latin for many chapters. For now, just be aware of its existence.

Here are some more present and perfect forms that appear very similar to each other and require that you pay careful attention to the stems:

Present	vs.	Perfect
habēmus	vs.	*habuimus*
habet	vs.	*habuit*
videt	vs.	*vīdit*
dīcit	vs.	*dīxit*
venit	vs.	*vēnit*

EXERCEĀMUS!

11-4 Presents and Perfects

Match the Latin form in column A with the best translation from column B.

	A		B
_____	1. audīvimus	A.	he can
_____	2. audīmus	B.	he shouted
_____	3. vīdistis	C.	he shouts
_____	4. vidētis	D.	he wished
_____	5. cucurrit	E.	she could
_____	6. currit	F.	she ran
_____	7. clāmāvit	G.	she runs
_____	8. clāmat	H.	she wishes
_____	9. voluit	I.	we hear
_____	10. vult	J.	we heard
_____	11. potuit	K.	you have seen
_____	12. potest	L.	you see

Mōrēs Rōmānī

Iūno Dea

Iūnō Rēgīna

You met *Iūnō Monēta* in Chapter 10, but the Roman goddess Juno was best known as the wife of the sky god Jupiter and as queen of the gods. For this reason the Romans often depicted her wearing a crown and carrying a scepter as on the coin at left. Her sacred bird was the peacock. Many of the myths associated with her emphasized the jealousy she displayed toward her husband's numerous lovers, including Danae (mother of Perseus), Semele (mother of Dionysus), and especially Alcmena (mother of Hercules).

The goddess was also a major divine force of the Romans. Along with Jupiter and Minerva, Juno was one of the Capitoline Triad worshipped by the Romans on the Capitoline Hill.

For pregnant women like Licinia, Juno was most important as *Iūnō Lūcīna*, or "she who brings to light (*lux*)." In other words, Juno was the goddess of childbirth.

On March 1st the Romans celebrated the *Mātrōnālia*, the anniversary of the founding of Juno's temple on the Esquiline Hill. On this feast day, Roman wives were honored by their husbands with gifts. In *Lectiō Secunda* Licinia and Valeria visited a small roadside shrine dedicated to Juno Lucina, rather than a major temple. On the Roman coin to the right Juno is depicted as Lucina. You can read the last part of the word "Lucina" around the rim. The SC on either side of standing Juno mean "by decree of the Senate."

Iūnō Lūcīna

Latīna Hodierna

Vēnī, Vīdī, Vīcī

Now that you have seen all the forms of the perfect active you can better appreciate Julius Caesar's famous phrase *Vēnī, Vīdī, Vīcī*, which was used to describe his lightning victory over king Pharnaces II of Pontus in 47 B.C. at the battle of Zela in what is now Turkey. The brevity of the statement is telling. The lack of conjunctions (like *et*), the avoidance of detailed description, and the quick succession of verbs were intended to emphasize not only the speed of Caesar's victory but also his decisiveness. Also note the assonance of the phrase, i.e., the repetition of the sounds *v* and *ī*.

Caesar's use of the perfect tense is significant here and further demonstrates his boastfulness. Compare these possible variations of Caesar's statement:

I came. I saw. I conquered.

I have come. I have seen. I have conquered.

I did come. I did see. I did conquer.

When I came (to Pontus), I saw (the situation) and I conquered (Pharnaces).

Which of these four English translations do you think comes closest to expressing the simplicity of Caesar's three simple words?

Watch for Caecilia, the wife of Servilius, to use a variation of this famous phrase in the next chapter. This phrase quickly became proverbial, so it is no surprise that a woman like Caecilia would use it in everyday conversation.

Julius Caesar's phrase *Vēnī, Vīdī, Vīcī* has become part of our modern culture, and you will find it used in many unexpected places. For example, the token depicted below, from the 1975 Mardi Gras in New Orleans, is modeled on an ancient coin with Caesar's famous saying.

Several other sayings by Caesar are sometimes quoted in Latin today. Use the *Verba Ūtenda* to translate any unfamiliar phrases.

- *Ālea iacta est.* By tradition, Caesar said this as he crossed the Rubicon River and entered Italy with his army in 49 B.C. By law Caesar was not supposed to bring his army into Italy without the permission of the Senate. By saying *Ālea iacta est*, Caesar was suggesting that there was no turning back and war was inevitable.

- *Et tū Brute?* "Even you, Brutus?" According to the Greek historian Plutarch, Caesar actually spoke his dying words in Greek, not Latin. Brutus has been one of Caesar's closest friends, so Brutus' involvement in the assassination came as a great surprise to Caesar.

Gemma

In 1843, or so the story goes, a British general named Napier annexed an area of Pakistan that was then called Sinde (alternatively Sindh or Sind). With a flair for the theatrical, Napier dispatched the news of his victory to the British government in Latin: *Peccāvī!* This is translated as "I have sinned," and was a pun for "I have Sinde," that is," I have taken the area of Sinde."

Regrettably, the story appears to have been published first in the magazine Punch as a joke. But it does demonstrate the power of a good Latin-based education.

◄))) VERBA ŪTENDA

ālea, -ae f. die (singular of dice)
iactus, -a, -um thrown, cast

"Vēnī, Vīdī, Vīcī" hodiē

🔊 **VERBA ŪTENDA**

dīvīsus, -a, -um divided
Gallia omnis "all of Gaul,"
    the Roman province now
    known as France
partēs parts

- *Gallia est omnis dīvīsa in partēs trēs.* These are the famous first words in Caesar's *Dē Bellō Gallicō* (*On the Gallic War*). His succinct style is reflected in this short but memorable beginning.

The following two famous expressions associated with Caesar are not used in Latin:

- Once, when rumor had implicated his wife in a religious scandal that also involved adultery, Caesar divorced her even though she might be innocent. Caesar is supposed to have said that "Caesar's wife must be above suspicion." In other words, people associated with a person of prominence must avoid scandal.

- And then there is the famous "Beware of the Ides of March." Caesar was assassinated on the Ides of March (March 15th) in 44 B.C. The words are from Act I, Scene ii, of Shakespeare's *Julius Caesar*, where they were spoken, to no avail, to Caesar by a soothsayer.

Orbis Terrārum Rōmānus

Gallia Est Omnis Dīvīsa in Partēs Trēs?

For the Romans *Gallia* (the land of the Gauls) encompassed not only modern France, but also Belgium, parts of Switzerland, and even northern Italy. The Gauls had been a constant threat to Rome over many centuries. The Gauls invaded Rome around 390 B.C., and the Roman defenders on the Capitoline Hill were saved only by the honking of Juno's sacred geese. In the Second Punic War (218–201 B.C.) the Gauls in northern Italy sided with the Carthaginian invader, Hannibal. At one point there were three provinces of Gaul:

- *Gallia Cisalpīna* (Gaul on this side of the Alps)
- *Gallia Transalpīna* (Gaul on the other side of the Alps), what is now southern France
- *Gallia Narbōnensis*, named after the city of *Narbō* (modern Narbonne). Because the Romans often referred to this province simply as *Prōvincia Nostra* or simply *Prōvincia* (the Province), this region of France is known today as Provence.

It was as governor of *Gallia Narbōnensis* that Julius Caesar began the conquest of the rest of Gaul in 58 B.C. This long and brutal war ended only in 52 B.C. with the defeat of the Gallic chieftain, Vercingetorix, at the battle of Alesia. About one fourth of the inhabitants of Gaul died during Caesar's campaign and many more were enslaved. Over the next centuries, Gaul became fully Romanized, and the Celtic language was replaced by Latin (and eventually by its descendant, modern French).

Templum Nemausī

Aquaeductus Rōmānus hodiē

Gallia Antīqua

When Julius Caesar began his history of the wars in Gaul (*Dē Bellō Gallicō*) with the words *Gallia est omnis dīvīsa in partēs trēs,* he was talking about the non-Roman regions of *Gallia Transalpīna*. These were *Belgica* (approximately modern Belgium), *Aquitānia* (approximately the French region of Aquitaine) and *Celtica* (most of France).

In imperial times there were seven Gallic provinces:

- *Aquitānia*
- *Gallia Lugdunensis*, with a capital at *Lugdunum* (modern Lyon)
- *Belgica*
- *Gallia Narbōnensis*, with its major city *Massilia* (modern Marseille)
- and three small provinces around the Alps (*Alpēs, -ium* f.): *Alpēs Maritimae, Alpēs Penninae,* and *Alpēs Cottiae*

Paris, the capital of modern France, was only a minor town (*Lutetia*) in Roman times.

One of the best preserved Roman temples is in Nemausus (modern Nîmes). Built by Agrippa in 19–16 B.C., it is known today as the Maison Carrée. One of the best preserved Roman aqueducts was built in the 1st century A.D. to carry water to Nemausus. It is known today as the Pont du Gard. Both structures are depicted at the bottom of page 136.

QUID PUTĀS?

1. Use the Internet to find a 1942 statement of General Douglas MacArthur that is just as famous and just as pithy as *Vēnī, Vīdī, Vīcī.*
2. Why do you think Juno was called Lūcīna ("she who brings light") as goddess of childbirth?
3. Do you think that Caesar's statement that "Caesar's wife must be above suspicion" applies to prominent people today? Is the statement also sexist, implying that the men could get away with anything?
4. What do you think is the modern French attitude toward Julius Caesar and his conquest of Gaul? Why?

EXERCEĀMUS!

11-5 Scrībāmus

Retell the following episode from Chapter 6 in the perfect tense. In order to do this, you need to change the words marked in **bold** from present to perfect tense. You have already seen all of these words as *Verba Discenda*, so if you do not remember the perfect stem, look it up! If you are really ambitious, try adding a bit more to the story in your own words. We have started the retelling for you.

> Chīrōn īrātus prō Lūciō **stat**. Omnēs puerī et puellae **rident** et, in viā, Hermēs quoque **rīdet**. Sōlus Chīrōn nōn **rīdet**, sed virgam **capit** et Lūciō **appropinquat**. Lūcius **sedet** sub virgā magistrī et valdē **timet**. Chīrōn virgam altē **tollit** sed tunc Hermēs paedagōgus magnā vōce **clāmat**. Chīrōn paulīsper **cōgitat**. Chīrōn Lūcium verberāre **vult**, sed Chīrōn Servīlium, patrem Lūciī, irrītāre nōn **vult**.

> ⟶ *Chīrōn īrātus prō Lūciō **stetit**.*

11-6 Colloquāmur

Now ask your classmate a "Who?" question based on the narrative you rewrote for Exercise 11-5. In order to do this, simply replace a singular subject with *quis* or a plural subject with *quī*. Follow the model.

> ⟶ Chīrōn īrātus prō Lūciō **stetit**. ⟶ Quis prō Lūciō stetit?
> *Chīrōn prō Lūciō stetit.*

11-7 Verba Discenda

Find the following in the *Verba Discenda*: five verbs, seven adverbs, four nouns, one interjection, and one adjective.

🔊 VERBA DISCENDA

adveniō, advenīre, advēnī, adventum arrive at, come to [advent, adventure]

appropinquō (1) (+ dat.) approach, come near to [propinquity]

cūr why

dea, -ae f. goddess [deify]

Ecce! Behold! Look!

fortasse perhaps

longē far off, far, a long distance

noscō, noscere, nōvī, nōtum know, get to know [notation]

Rōma, -ae f. Rome

Rōmānus, -a, -um Roman

saccus, -ī m. wallet, sack, bag, pocketbook

saliō, salīre, saliī/saluī, saltum leap, jump [salient]

sīc thus, in this way; yes

subitō suddenly

tam so, so much (as)

tollō, tollere, sustulī, sublātum lift, raise

valdē very, a lot

verbum, -ī n. word [verbose]

Angulus Grammaticus

The "Present Perfect" and the "Inchoate Suffix" -scō

The normal use of the perfect tense is to indicate a single act that was finished some time in the past: "I painted the house," "We have gone there before," and the like. But in Latin, the perfect tense can also have a sense that the thing that was done has an effect on the present. Consider these sentences:

> I have come to save you!   (I am here to save you)
> I've learned *that* lesson!   (I'm too smart for that now)

This concept will be important for some grammatical concepts you will learn later on. For now, however, it affects your understanding of some very special verbs. The most common one that you have encountered is *nōvī*, which, though perfect tense, is always translated in the present.

> *Nōvistīne eum?*   *Ita, eum nōvī.*
> Do you know him?   Yes, I know him.

How did this happen? The full verb is *noscō, noscere, nōvī, nōtum* which, in the present tense, means "to come to know something." Thus, *nōvī*, the perfect of *noscō*, means "I have come to know something," and, if you have come to know something, then you do in fact know it.

There is another verb that is perfect tense in form, but is translated as a present tense:

ōdī is perfect in form but is translated in the present tense: "I hate"

In his famous poem #85, Catullus says *Ōdī et amō* (I hate and I love)—both at the same time—and thus captures the essence of many love affairs.

Note the *-sc-* in the 1st principal part of the verb *noscō*. This suffix is added to Latin verbs to show that the action is just starting or beginning. That is why *noscō* is translated as "begin to know, get to know." Verbs with this verbal suffix are sometimes called **inchoatives**, from the Latin verb *inchoō* (1) "to begin."

You will find this inchoate suffix in several English derivatives. See if you can figure out how each of the following Latin verbs indicates the beginning of an action. We have done the first one for you.

LATIN WORD	VERB MEANING	ENGLISH DERIVATIVE	"BEGINNING TO..."
adulēscō	grow up, mature	adolescent	beginning to grow, be an adult
crēscō	grow	crescent	
nāscor	be born	nascent	
quiēscō	be quiet	quiescent	

Noscō is a common verb and is found in a lot of Latin compound verbs:

agnoscō   to recognize
cognoscō   to get to know someone
ignoscō   to pardon, excuse (literally, "getting not to know any more;" i.e., "to forget")

Photo Credits

page 128 (top) Clipart.com; **page 134** American Numismatic Society/American Numismatic Society of New York; **page 135 (top)** American Numismatic Society/American Numismatic Society of New York; **page 135 (bottom left)** Photo by Kenneth Kitchell used with permission; **page 135 (bottom right)** Kenneth Kitchell/Photo by Kenneth Kitchell used with permission; **page 136 (left)** Thomas J. Sienkewicz/Photo by Thomas J. Sienkewicz used with permission; **page 136 (right)** Thomas Watkins/Photo by Thomas Watkins used with permission

In Domō Magnā

From *Disce! An Introductory Latin Course, volume 1*, First Edition. Francesco Bonavita. Copyright © 2011 by Pearson Education, Inc. Published by Pearson Prentice Hall. All rights reserved.

Ātrium

GRAMMATICA
Dative with Special Verbs
Impersonal Verbs and Expressions
Saying Please in Latin
Adverbs
Adjective Agreement

MŌRĒS RŌMĀNĪ
Domī Rōmānae

LATĪNA HODIERNA
The Vocabulary of a Roman House
    in English

ORBIS TERRĀRUM RŌMĀNUS
Pompēiī et Herculāneum

ANGULUS GRAMMATICUS
Natural vs. Grammatical Gender

LECTIŌNĒS:
HERMĒS ET SĪMIA
and
DOMUS SERVĪLIĪ

Lucius finishes telling his family about his day, and the Servilius family is described.

12

In Domō Magnā

Lectiō Prīma

Antequam Legis

At the Home of the Servilii

In this chapter you will visit the home of the wealthy and upwardly mobile Servilii, who share the events of their day. As you read, you should look for the following:

- new uses of the dative
- impersonal verbs
- adverbs

Dative with Special Verbs

Watch in the readings for **special verbs** like *noceō, nocēre* (to harm), which take dative rather than accusative objects. Don't worry right now about why these verbs take the dative rather than the accusative. You can easily understand what they mean; for example, in *Lectiō Prīma*, Hermes tells his family:

*Sīmiae **nocēre** nōn potuī.*   I was not able **to harm** the monkey.

The words marked in **bold** in *Lectiō Prīma* are special verbs, so just look for a dative object when you see one.

Impersonal Verbs and Expressions

"It is going to rain." Easily understood in English, but hard to define grammatically. What is the subject of the verb? "It." Such verbs are called **impersonal** because no "person" is the subject, just a sort of vague "it." Latin has the same construction. Consider these sentences in which the underlined infinitive is the subject of the impersonal verb.

Paedagōgum sīmiam <u>capere</u> oportet!	It is fitting for the tutor to catch the monkey.
	The tutor ought to catch the monkey.
Paedagōgō sīmiam <u>capere</u> necesse est!	It is necessary for the tutor to catch the monkey.
	The tutor has to catch the monkey.

All of the impersonal expressions in *Lectiō Prīma* are marked in **bold italics**. When you see them, remember to make the subject "it" and look for an infinitive to serve as the subject of the impersonal expression.

Adverbs

The part of speech introduced in this chapter is the **adverb**, a word that describes a verb, an adjective, or another adverb. Many English adverbs are made by adding **-ly** to an adjective.

Adjective	**Adverb**
angry	angri**ly**
timid	timid**ly**

Latin can make adverbs in a similar way, by adding *-ē* to an adjective's stem.

Adjective	**Adverb**
īrātus	*īrātē*
timidus	*timidē*

Watch for these and other adverbs ending in *-ē* (sometimes *-e*) as you read *Lectiō Prīma*.

EXERCEĀMUS!

12-1 Impersonal Expressions and Datives with Special Verbs

As you read *Lectiō Prīma*, make two line-by-line lists. In the first, list the *impersonal expressions* (marked in *bold italics*) and the infinitives that are their subjects. In the second, list the **special verbs** (marked in **bold**) and their dative objects. Finally, translate the two words together. Follow the model.

Impersonal Expressions

	Line	Verb	Infinitive Subject	Translation
→	1	placet	audīre	it is pleasing to hear

Special Verbs

	Line	Verb	Dative Direct Object	Translation
→	5	crēde	mihi	believe me

🔊 HERMĒS ET SĪMIA

Fābulam audīre dē sīmiā in Forō Marcō **placet**. Marcus rīdet et Hermem rogat, "Cūr tam valdē īrātus fuistī, ō paedagōge? Cūr tam strēnuē cucurristī?"

"Ah, domine," Marcō respondit, "Sīmia malus furtīvē saccum meum cēpit et ad Forum fūgit. Illa pecūnia patris tuī est et mihi saccum custōdīre **necesse est**. Nōn
5 sīmiīs pecūniam habēre **licet**! Hōc officium meum est. Sīmiam cēpī, sed mihi **crēde**—sīmiae nōn **nocuī**, sed **ignōvī**!"

"Quōmodo sīmiam capere potuistī?"

"Sīmiae **imperāvī** sed semper cucurrit. Tōtum per Forum longē cucurrimus, sed eum capere nōn potuī. Dēmum, sīmia fessus fuit et ad āram
10 Dīvī Iūliī cucurrit ubī sēdit, tremuit, et timidē clāmāvit. Eum tunc īrātē cēpī sed sīmiae **nocēre** nōn potuī. In illō locō sacrō et sīmiīs **parcere oportet**."

"Euge!!" Caecilia clāmāvit, "Bene factum!!! Sīmiam cēpistī. Vēnistī. Vīdistī. Vīcistī!"

15 "Ita vērō," Marcus inquit, "Nōn iam paedagōgus es, sed bestiārius! Ille sīmia malus in mūneribus in amphitheātrō pugnāre dēbet! Animal perīculōsum est!"

Paedagōgus Marcō respondit: "Sī tibi **placeat**, domine, nōlī mē irrīdēre! Territus fuī! Sī pecūniam patris tuī āmīsī…"

"Sed pecūniam nōn āmīsistī!" Caecilia confirmāvit. "Omnia salva sunt. Nunc cēnāre **necesse est**. Lūcī et Marce,
20 vōs cēnae parāte. Servīlia, tē mihi **adesse oportet**."

In illō locō sacrō et sīmiīs parcere oportet.

🔊 VERBA ŪTENDA

adsum, adesse, adfuī (+ dat.) be near, be present; be "there for" someone, be of assistance, help, aid
āmittō, āmittere, āmīsī lose
bestiārius, -iī m. animal fighter
***cēna, -ae* f. dinner**
***cēnō* (1) dine**
confirmō (1) reassure
crēdō, crēdere, crēdidī (+ dat) believe
custōdiō, custōdīre, custōdīvī / custōdiī guard, watch
dēmum at last
dominus, -ī m. master, lord
et here, "even"
euge! Good! Great!
eum him

factum "done"
***fugiō, fugere, fūgī, fugitum* flee**
furtīvē secretly
ignōscō, ignōscere, ignōvī (+ dat.) forgive, pardon
illa and *ille* that
imperō (1) (+ dat.) command
implōrō (1) plead, beg
īrātē angrily
irrīdeō, irrīdēre, irrīsī laugh at
ita yes
licet (+ dat.) it is permitted
locus, -ī m. place
longē far
mūneribus games
***necesse est* (+ dat. + inf.)** it is necessary to

nōs us
***noceō, nocēre, nocuī, nocitum* (+ dat.) harm, do injury to**
officium, -iī n. duty, task, job
omnia everything
***oportet, oportuit* (+ inf.)** one ought
***parcō, parcere, pepercī / parsī / parcuī, parsūrus* (+ dat.) spare, pardon, show mercy to**
***parō* (1) prepare, make ready**
perīculōsus, -a, -um dangerous
***placeō, placēre, placuit, placitum* (+ dat.)** please, be pleasing to;

***sī placet* (+ inf.) =** "please"; "it is pleasing to"
***pugnō* (1) fight**
quōmodo how
sacer, sacra, sacrum holy, sacred
salvus, -a, -um safe
strēnuē vigorously
timidus, -a, -um timid
tōtus, -a, -um the whole
tremō, tremere, tremuī tremble
tuus, -a, -um your
vērō indeed
***vincō, vincere, vīcī, victum* conquer**
vōs yourselves

POSTQUAM LĒGISTĪ

Answer these questions in both Latin and English. Follow the model.

→ Why does Marcus laugh at the beginning of the *lectiō?*
Fabūla Lūciī Marcō placet. Lucius' story pleases Marcus.

1. What part of his job does Hermes emphasize in the story about the monkey?

2. Why does Hermes say that he did not harm the monkey?

3. What words of Caecilia are a paraphrase of a famous saying by Julius Caesar? How are her words different from Caesar's?

4. What joke does Marcus make about Hermes and the monkey?

Gemma

In the phrase *et sīmiīs* (line 11) the word *et* does not mean "and." It means "even." Translate *et* in this way when two things are not being connected.

Grammatica A

Dative with Special Verbs

Read the following sentence from *Lectiō Prīma*:

In illō locō sacrō et **sīmiīs** *parcere oportet.*

In this sentence, **sīmiīs** is the dative object of the verb *parcere* (to spare). In English we simply consider "monkeys" to be the object of "spare." So we might expect Latin to use an accusative case, but it doesn't. Instead *sīmiīs* is in the dative case. The rule is that Latin has a number of verbs that take a dative object instead of an accusative one. These special verbs include the following *Verba Discenda:*

Gemma

Note that Latin indicates that, as a "student," you are supposed to be "eager" and "devoted" to your learning process!

noceō, nocēre, nocuī, nocitum (+ dat.)	harm, injure, do injury to
parcō, parcere, pepercī, parsūrus (+ dat.)	spare, show mercy toward
placeō, placēre, placuī, placitum (+ dat.)	please, be pleasing to
studeō, studēre, studuī (+ dat.)	be eager to, devote oneself to, study
respondeō, respondēre, respondī, responsum (+ dat.)	respond to, answer

Such verbs are always marked in the dictionary by (+ dat.). Notice how English translations of these verbs often include prepositions, indicating, for example, that the action is happening "to" or "toward" someone. So

Sīmiae parcere oportet.

can be translated two ways:

One ought to spare the monkey.
One ought to show mercy **toward** the monkey.

EXERCEĀMUS!

12-2 Translating More Than One Way

Retranslate each of the following sentences to include the word "to" or "toward." Follow the model. HINT: Use the translations provided in the list of special verbs that take the dative.

→ *Sīmiae parcit.*   He spares the monkey.
            He shows mercy **toward** the monkey.

1. *Cēna mihi placet.*	Dinner pleases me.
2. *Fīliō crēdō.*	I believe my son.
3. *Ancillīs ignoscimus.*	We pardon the maid servants.
4. *Servō imperāvit.*	He commanded the slave.
5. *Num amīcō nocēs?*	You are not harming your friend, are you?

Impersonal Verbs and Expressions

Impersonal verbs do not have "persons" as subjects. These verbs are often translated in English with "it," as in "it is necessary that," and they commonly have special constructions, especially infinitives, associated with them. In all of the following examples, the subject of the impersonal expression is the infinitive *facere.* Some use the dative to show the person affected by the verb, some do not. Compare the following:

IMPERSONAL EXPRESSION	EXAMPLE	TRANSLATION	NOTES
necesse est	*Discipulīs opus facere necesse est.*	The students have to do their work.	necessity implied, dative
oportet	*Discipulōs opus facere oportet.*	The students ought to do their work.	less forceful, no dative
placet	*Discipulīs opus facere placet.*	It is pleasing for the students to do their work.	dative
licet	*Discipulīs opus facere licet.*	The students are allowed to do their work.	dative

Notā Bene:

- The dative *discipulīs* tells you to whom it is pleasing, while the accusative *opus* is the direct object of the infinitive *facere.*
- Look for another impersonal verb, *decet* (it is fitting), in the next reading.

Saying Please in Latin

Did you notice the impersonal expression *sī tibi placeat* in *Lectiō Prīma*? Literally, it means "if it might be pleasing to you." This is a very polite way of saying "please" in Latin. Here are some other ways to say "please":

sī placet	if it is pleasing
sī tibi placet	if it is pleasing to you
sī placeat	if it might be pleasing (more polite)

If you are speaking to more than one person, use *vōbīs*:

sī vōbīs placet	if it is pleasing to (all of) you

Adverbs

Here are some of the adverbs used in *Lectiō Prīma*:

*Cūr tam **strēnuē** cucurristī?*	Why did you run so **vigorously**?
*Sīmia **timidē** clāmāvit.*	The monkey cried **timidly**.
*Eum tunc **īrātē** cēpī.*	Then I seized him **angrily**.

All of these adverbs were made by adding **-ē** to the stem of an adjective ending in *-us, -a, -um*.

īrātus, -a, -um angry	*īrātē* angri**ly**
strēnuus, -a, -um strong	*strēnuē* strong**ly**
timidus, -a, -um fearful, timid	*timidē* fearful**ly**, timid**ly**

Unlike adjectives, adverbs have no gender, number, or case, so the ending is always the same. Sometimes the stem changes in the process of making an adverb:

bonus, -a, -um good	*bene* well (from *bon-* + *-e*)
validus, -a, -um strong	*valdē* very (contracted from *val(i)dē*)

Gemma

Note that the final "e" in *bene* is short.

Lectiō Secunda

Antequam Legis

The family of Valeria does not have much money and lives in a small, crowded apartment. The Servilii, on the other hand, are patricians (members of established families) and live high on a hill in an expensive house, spacious enough for the entire household, which includes many slaves. In this *lectiō* you read about many of the people who live in this house.

Adjective Agreement

As you read, look closely at the **adjectives**. Adjectives agree with the nouns they modify in gender, number, and case (**GNC**). Often this means that they have the same endings (*multam pecūniam*) **but not always**! Sometimes an adjective has a different ending from the noun but still agrees with it in GNC. As you read *Lectiō Secunda*, look for the adjectives and nouns marked in **bold**. These are noun/adjective pairs that do not have identical endings but still agree. After you read, we will explain how adjective agreement works.

EXERCEĀMUS!

12-3 Adjective Agreement

Using the words marked in **bold** as a guide, answer the following questions as you scan *Lectiō Secunda*. Then translate each noun/adjective pair. Follow the model. HINT: Use the *Verba Ūtenda* if you do not know the meaning of a word.

→ Line 1	What word describes *domus*?	**magna**	the large house
1. Line 4	What word describes *avus*?		
2. Line 7	What word describes *uxor*?		
3. Line 7	Now find another word describing *uxor*.		
4. Line 10	What word describes *frāter*?		
5. Line 13	What word describes *parte*?		
6. Line 13	What word describes *domī*?		

DOMUS SERVĪLIĪ

Domus Servīliī valdē **magna** est quod Servīlius multam pecūniam habet. In Vīminālī multī Rōmānī aedificia magna fabricāvērunt. Hīc multae familiae in aedificiīs magnīs habitant. **Domus antīqua** Servīliī quoque magnum spatium habet et plūs quam quindecim conclāvia—et parva et magna—continet. Hīc habitant Servīlius, **cara uxor**, Caecilia Metella, et trēs līberī Servīliī. Pater Servīliī quoque hīc habitat, sed rārē ē cubiculō exit, quod **avus aeger** est
5   et octōgintā duōs annōs **nātus** est.

Servīlius pater familiās est. **Vir** quadrāgintā quīnque annōs **nātus** est. Caecilia Metella, Servīliī uxor, trīgintā octō annōs nāta est. Caecilia Servīliī **uxor secunda** est. Cornelia **uxor prīma** fuit, sed Servīlius Corneliam dīmīserat abhinc duodecim annōs.

Caecilia Metella māter Lūciī est. **Puer**, Chīrōnis discipulus, decem annōs **nātus** est.

10   Cornēlia māter Marcī et Servīliae est. Servīlia sēdecim annōs nāta est, sed nōndum virum habet. **Frāter** ūnum et vīgintī annōs **nātus** est et rhētoricae studet.

Domus quoque servōs multōs habet. Hermēs hīc habitat et, quamquam servus est, paedagōgō cubiculum proprium habēre decet. Aliī servī—ancillae, coquī, lectīcāriī, custōdēs, iānitor inter aliōs—in **aliā parte domī magnae** habitant ubi multī in cubiculō ūnō dormiunt.

VERBA ŪTENDA

abhinc duodecim annōs "twelve years ago"	***decem* ten**	*nōmine* "by name"	*rārus, -a, -um* rare
aedificium, -iī n. building	*dīmīserat* (he) had divorced	*nōndum* not yet	*secundus, -a, -um* second
***annus, -ī* m. year**	***duodecim* twelve**	***octō* eight**	***sēdecim* sixteen**
avus, -ī m. grandfather	*exit* leaves	*octōgintā* eighty	*spatium, -iī* n. space
cārus, -a, -um dear	*fabricō* (1) build	*parte* part	***studeō, studēre, studuī* (+ dat.) to devote oneself to, be eager for, to study**
Chīrōnis of Chiron	***habitō* (1) live in, inhabit**	*pater* m. father	
conclāvia rooms	*iānitor* doorkeeper	*pater familiās* m. head of the family	
contineō, continēre contain	*inter* (+ acc.) among	*plūs* more	*trīgintā* thirty
coquus, -ī m. cook	*lectīcārius, -iī* m. litter bearer	*prīmus, -a, -um* first	*uxor* f. wife
***cubiculum, -ī* n. bedroom**	*līberī, -ōrum* m. pl. children	*proprius, -a, -um* one's own	***vīgintī* twenty**
custōdēs guards	*māter* f. mother	*quadrāgintā* forty	*Vīminālis* the Viminal Hill
decet, decēre, decuit (+ dat.) it is fitting	*nam* for	*quamquam* although	*virum* husband
	***nātus, -a, -um* born, xx annōs; *nātus est* = is xx years old**	*quindecim* fifteen	

POSTQUAM LĒGISTĪ

Wherever possible, answer these questions in both Latin and English.

1. Describe the neighborhood in which the *familia Servīliī* live. How does it compare to your neighborhood?
2. Identify the people who live in this house. Would this be considered a large household today?
3. Describe the kinds of household slaves in the house. Compare these workers to the kind of staff in a wealthy house today. What would the modern equivalent of a *lectīcārius* be?

Grammatica B

Adjective Agreement

You probably had no trouble translating the title of this chapter, *In Domō Magnā*, even though endings of *domō* and *magnā* are not the same. In *Lectiō Secunda* you saw a variety of other examples of noun/adjective pairs which do not match in endings: *vir nātus, puer nātus, uxor prīma, pater nātus*, etc.

Adjectives must agree with the noun they describe in gender, number, and case. As shorthand, we say they "GNC" (pronounced "ga-nick"). Technically, this is called **grammatical agreement**. You have mostly seen noun/adjective pairs where the endings mirror each other, as in *fēmina bona* or *ōvum malum*. It would be nice if this were always the case, but it is not.

Nouns and adjectives belong to certain declensions and use the endings that are reserved for that declension. Adjectives like *bonus, bona, bonum* or *noster, nostra, nostrum* are sometimes called **2-1-2 adjectives**, because they use endings from those declensions. Adjectives cannot change the declension endings they use. 2-1-2 adjectives use 2nd declension endings for the masculine and neuter forms and 1st declension for the feminine.

So adjectives and nouns must GNC, but they do not necessarily have to have the same endings. Consider these pairs. *Sīmia* is 1st declension but can be either masculine or feminine. *Domus* is second declension but is feminine.

Notice how the endings do not match, but the words GNC. Can you continue the declension of both words into the plural?

Nom.	sīmia bonus	domus bona
Gen.	sīmiae bonī	domī bonae
Dat.	sīmiae bonō	domō bonae
Acc.	sīmiam bonum	domum bonam
Abl.	sīmiā bonō	domō bonā

For more on 1st declension masculine nouns see the *Angulus Grammaticus*.

In the reading you also saw pairs with non-identical endings like *uxor prīma* and *frāter nātus*. Here a 2-1-2 adjective is modifying a 3rd declension noun. You will learn these nouns in the next chapter.

Summary

- Nouns and adjectives must GNC.
- But they must use the endings from the declension to which they belong.

All you do is choose the appropriate ending from the 2-1-2 columns based on which GNC you need.

EXERCEĀMUS!

12-4   Adjective Agreement

The 2-1-2 adjectives are marked in **bold** in the following sentences. Identify the nouns they modify and use the 2-1-2 adjective to determine the gender, number, and case of these nouns. Follow the model. In some examples, the nouns are 3rd declension, but you should be able to figure them out from the adjectival endings.

	Noun	**Gender**	**Number**	**Case**
→ Hermēs **bonus** intrat.	Hermēs	m.	sing.	nom.

1. Domus **magna** Servīliī in colle Vīminālī est.
2. Caecilia Servīliī uxor **secunda** est.
3. Aliī servī in **aliā** parte domī habitant.
4. Chīrōn **īrātus** est.
5. In pictūrā vir **malus** nāsum longum habet.
6. Lūcius patrem **bonum** videt.
7. Hermēs sīmiae **malō** vīnum dat.
8. Fabūla dē sīmiā **malō** iocōsa est.
9. Nōmen sīmiae **malō** Sōcratēs est.
10. Familia sīmiae **malī** bona est.
11. Sīmiae **malī** pecūniam cēpērunt.

Mōrēs Rōmānī

Domī Rōmānae

The house of the Servilii is a more modest version of an upwardly-mobile Roman's residence, both in the city and throughout Italy. (The best examples survive in the city of Pompeii.) The façade of this building would have little ostentation. Indeed the house would look little different from storefronts, warehouses, and apartments in the same block. Romans put their money and effort into decorating the inside of the dwelling. Sometimes shops were built into the front wall of the house and rented out for income or used in a family business. Two such shops are at the front of the house of the Servilii.

The front door was large, heavy, and strongly bolted. A prosperous family like the Servilii would have a *iānitor*, a slave who guarded the door and controlled access to the home. Some of these "janitors" were even chained to the spot and not allowed to leave. Just inside the door was a passageway called the *vestibulum*, originally a place to hang one's cloak (*vestis*). The *vestibulum* is also sometimes called the *faucēs* (jaws) or *ostium* (mouth). This leads into the *ātrium*, the main public room of the house where guests were greeted. In the center of the atrium was the *impluvium*, a pool intended to catch water from the *compluvium*, a hole in the roof directly above the *impluvium*. The *compluvium* let in light and allowed the household to collect drinking water in a cistern. By the time of the first century B.C., however, most of the *impluvia* were merely decoration and the rainwater ran out through a channel into the street.

The rooms on either side of the *ātrium* often served as *cubicula* or bedrooms. Sometimes a small shrine to the household gods was located in the corner of the atrium, near the front door. The Servilii had such a shrine in their house, and as you will see later, exhibited the death masks of their ancestors in the *ātrium*. All of this was done partly out of piety and partly to remind visitors that the Servilii came from good stock.

Beyond the *ātrium* was the *tablīnum* or office where the head of the house conducted business. It often had screens that could be drawn to close it off from the *ātrium* (and from

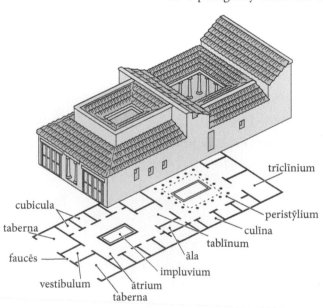

triclīnium
peristȳlium
culīna
tablīnum
cubicula
āla
taberna
faucēs
impluvium
vestibulum
ātrium
taberna

Domus Rōmāna

the *peristȳlium* behind). Two *alae* (wings) were small rooms flanking the *ātrium*. They may have been used to receive guests. The *peristȳlium* was a garden toward the back of the house. It usually had a colonnaded area along the outer perimeter and an unroofed area in the center, where the garden was located. A Roman family would spend much of its time in the peristyle, where only good friends would be welcome and where, in very hot weather, meals could even be served. Along the side of the peristyle are one or more *trīclīnia* or dining rooms. The *culīna* or kitchen was often located along the peristyle also.

Especially in city houses, there might also be a second story of rooms, and Servilia will put this area to good use during a party that you will read about.

Wealthy and ambitious Romans like Servilius acquired houses to advance their careers and reputations. Cicero, for example, owned a prominent house on the Palatine Hill. In his philosophical work *Dē Officiīs* (*On Duty*, I.138), however, Cicero preaches caution in this area.

> *Ornāta enim est dignitās domō, nōn ex domō tōta quaesīta, nec domō dominus,*
> *sed ā dominō domus honestāta est.*

In *Odēs* II.14 the poet Horace includes *domus et placens uxor* among the joys lost as we grow old and die.

In *Carmina* (*Poems*, XXIII.436) Apollinaris Sidonius, a 5th-century A.D. bishop and poet from Gaul, sings *ō dulcis domus, ō piī penātēs*, reminiscent of our "Home sweet home." In fact, *Dulce Dōmum* is the Latin title of Chapter 5 of Kenneth Graham's *Wind in the Willows*. Later on you will learn enough to understand that these words are actually rather bad Latin.

🔊 VERBA ŪTENDA

dignitās f. dignity (subject of *est*)	*ornāta* decorated	*quaesīta* sought
dulcis sweet	*penātēs* household gods	*tōta* entirely
honestāta honored	*pius, -a, -um* pious	*uxor* wife
	placens pleasing	

Latīna Hodierna

The Vocabulary of the Roman House in English

Did you notice how many terms related to a Roman house are used in English today? Sometimes the meanings are the same. Sometimes they have changed significantly.

LATIN WORD	MEANING	ENGLISH WORD	MEANING
domus	house	**dom**icile	place of residence
ātrium	greeting room	**atrium**	a large open area within a building
vestibulum	corridor leading from the front door into the atrium	**vestibul**e	entry area of a building
iānitor	slave guarding the front door	**janitor**	someone who cleans and maintains a large office or residential building
peristȳlium	a colonnaded courtyard	**peristyl**e	a colonnade
culīna	kitchen	**culina**ry	pertaining to food

Orbis Terrārum Rōmānus

Pompēii et Herculāneum

Our best knowledge of Roman houses and furnishings comes from the archaeological excavations at Pompeii and Herculaneum, two cities destroyed in the eruption of Mt. Vesuvius in 79 A.D. Preserved in the ash and lava of the volcanic eruption were not only many homes but also wall paintings and various household artifacts, including mosaics, sculpture, and even wooden bedframes, chairs, and chests.

But keep in mind that the houses in these two resort cities are not typical everyday dwellings.

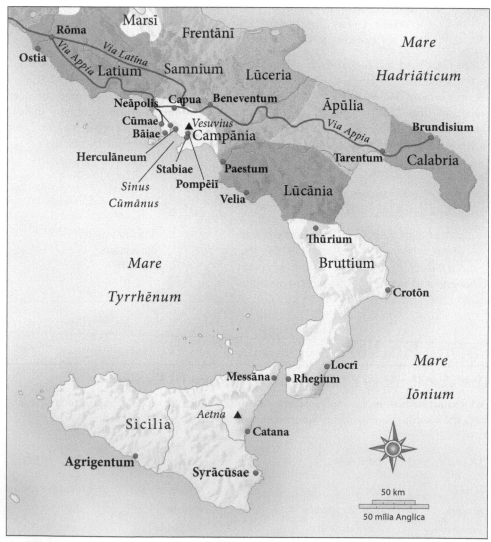

Sinus Cūmānus

Pompēiī et Vesuvius hodiē

Peristȳlium Pompēiīs

QUID PUTĀS?

1. Do you think that most Americans agree with Cicero that the reputation of the owner brings prominence to the house, not vice versa? What does Cicero's statement suggest about Roman attitudes toward home and career?
2. What do you think it would be like to live in a house like that of the Servilii? Would this architecture be practical in your hometown? Why or why not?
3. The architecture of a Roman house has been called "inward," since it presents a blank face to passersby. Why might the Romans have chosen to do this?
4. How might the architecture of a Roman house reflect the climate of the area?

EXERCEĀMUS!

12-5 Scrībāmus: Answering Questions—Perfect Tense

Use the *lectiōnēs* in this chapter to write a response in Latin for each of these questions, using the perfect tense. In your reply, you should respond *Ita/Sīc* or *Nōn*, followed by a complete sentence. Follow the model.

→ Fuitne Hermēs valdē īrātus?
Ita, valdē īrātus fuit.

1. Cucurrēruntne Hermēs et sīmia strēnuē?
2. Cēpitne sīmia Valeriae saccum furtīvē?
3. Cucurrēruntne Hermēs et sīmia tōtum per Forum longē?
4. Fuitne domus Servīliī valdē magna?
5. Habuitne Hermēs cubiculum proprium in domō Servīliā?
6. Fuitne Servīlia nāta decem annōs?
7. Habuitne Servīlia virum?
8. Habitāvitne Lūcius in aedificiō magnō in Vīminālī?

12-6 **Colloquāmur**

Ask a classmate any one of the questions in Exercise 12-5. The classmate should respond *Ita/Sīc* or *Nōn*, followed by a complete sentence.

12-7 **Verba Discenda**

Use the *Verba Discenda* to answer the following questions.

1. Give the first principal part of these verb forms: *fūgimus, studuit, vīcistis, dormīvit.*

2. Find the four numbers in the *Verba Discenda* and give their English equivalents. Remember that these numbers are indeclinable—this means that they do not show case or gender.

3. Make a list of the four *Verba Discenda* that are special verbs that take the dative. Then use the 1st principal part in a short Latin sentence illustrating this use of the dative. Finally, translate the Latin sentence into English.

4. Make a list of the three *Verba Discenda* that are impersonal verbs. Add an infinitive to this impersonal verb. Then translate this Latin phrase into English.

VERBA DISCENDA

annus, -ī m. year [annual]
cēna, -ae f. dinner
cēnō (1) dine
cubiculum, -ī n. bedroom [cubicle]
decem ten [December]
dormiō, dormīre, dormīvī / dormiī, dormītum sleep [dormant, dormitory]
duodecim twelve
fugiō, fugere, fūgī, fugitum flee [fugitive]

habitō (1) live in, inhabit [habitat]
nātus, -a, -um born, xx, *annōs; natus est* = is xx years old [natal]
necesse est (+ inf.) it is necessary to
noceō, nocēre, nocuī, nocitum (+ dat.) harm, do injury to [noxious, innocent]
octō eight [octave, October]

oportet, oportuit (+ inf.) one ought; it is necessary, proper to
parcō, parcere, pepercī / parsī / parcuī, parsūrus (+ dat.) spare, pardon, show mercy to
parō (1) prepare, make ready [preparation]
placet, placēre, placuit, placitum (+ dat.) please, be pleasing to;

placet (+ inf.) "it is pleasing to" [placebo]
pugnō (1) fight [pugnacious]
studeō, studēre, studuī (+ dat.) to devote oneself to, be eager for [studious]
vīgintī twenty
vincō, vincere, vīcī, victum conquer [invincible]

Gemma

parcō, parcere, pepercī / parsī, parsūrus: Note the unusual ending on the 4th principal part. This ending is used to indicate that a verb lacks certain verb forms. More on this later.

Angulus Grammaticus

Natural vs. Grammatical Gender

We have already talked about how gender in Latin is more grammatical than natural. So most 1st declension nouns are feminine and most 2nd declension nouns are masculine or neuter. But there are exceptions.

- The first declension has **some** masculine nouns.

The more common ones are sometimes called the **PAINS** words.

P	*poēta* (poet), *pīrāta* (pirate)
A	*agricola* (farmer)
I	*incola* (inhabitant)
N	*nauta* (sailor)
S	*scrība* (scribe)

Notice how most of these tend to be naturally masculine (at least from an ancient Roman point of view). Some can be either masculine or feminine:

advena, -ae	foreigner, stranger
convīva, -ae	dining partner, guest
sīmia, -ae	monkey

Such words are often said to have "common" gender.

- **The second declension has some feminine nouns** including *domus, -i* f. house. Also, most trees are feminine in Latin (they were associated with nymphs), and thus most second declension trees are feminine.

fraxinus, fraxinī	ash tree
mālus, mālī	apple tree
pīnus, pīnī	pine tree
ficus, ficī	fig tree

Now see how this works with agreement of adjectives:

agricola Rōmānus
poētae bonī
nautās territōs
mālus mala (= a bad apple tree! Note the macron.)

Gemma

Trees may be feminine but the gender of their fruit can vary. The figs Valeria sells are feminine but apples (*pōma* or *māla*) are neuter.

Photo Credits

page 140 (top) Pedicini/Index Ricerca Iconografica; **page 151 (top left)** Leigh Anne Lane/Photo by Leigh Anne Lane with permission; **page 151 (top right)** Leigh Anne Lane/Photo by Leigh Anne Lane used with permission

Māter et Fīlia

From *Disce! An Introductory Latin Course, volume 1*, First Edition. Francesco Bonavita. Copyright © 2011 by Pearson Education, Inc. Published by Pearson Prentice Hall. All rights reserved.

Māter et Fīlia
The J. Paul Getty Museum/Getty Villa Museum

GRAMMATICA
The 3ʳᵈ Declension
3ʳᵈ Declension Nouns and 2-1-2 Adjectives

MŌRĒS RŌMĀNĪ
Echoes of Catullus

LATĪNA HODIERNA
Latin in Modern Families

ORBIS TERRĀRUM RŌMĀNUS
Vērōna

ANGULUS GRAMMATICUS
How Multi-Faceted a Word *Quam* Is!

> **LECTIŌNĒS:**
> FESTĪNĀ LENTĒ!
> and
> NĒMŌ MĒ INTELLEGIT!
>
> Servilia tries to tell her mother about a young man she has seen.

154

13

Māter et Fīlia

Lectiō Prīma

Antequam Legis

Watching for a New Declension

In *Lectiō Prīma*, Servilia tries to tell her family about her day and, especially, about her feelings for a young man named Cordus, but she finds her brothers and mother unreceptive.

In this reading we want you to look out for nouns in a new declension. You have seen some of these words before, but now we will formally introduce the **3ʳᵈ declension** endings to you.

EXERCEĀMUS!

13-1 Recognizing 3ʳᵈ Declension Nouns

In *Lectiō Prīma* all the 3ʳᵈ declension nouns are marked in **bold**. As you read, make a line-by-line list of these words and indicate the case and number of each word, based on how the word is used in the sentence. You should be able to find at least one word used in each case and number (except the vocative plural). Follow the models.

	Line	Word	Case	Number
→	1	*māter*	vocative	singular
→	3	*frātrem*	accusative	singular

Once you finish this list, see if you can make a declension chart for *frāter*.

CASE	SINGULAR	PLURAL
Nominative		
Genitive		
Dative		
Accusative	frātrem	
Ablative		
Vocative	frāter (1)	

GAIUS
VALERIUS
CATULLUS

87 AC–54 AC

🔊 FESTĪNĀ LENTĒ!

"Sed, ō **māter** cāra," clāmāvit Servīlia, "dē meō amīcō novō nōndum dīximus! Hodiē amīcam meam Naeviam visitāvī et **frātrem** eius vīdī. **Nōmen frātrī** Quīntus Naevius Cordus est, et . . ."

5 "Festīnā lentē, fīlia!" respondet **māter**. "Dē amīcīs post cēnam dīcere possumus. Mox **pater** domum revenit et nōs parātae esse dēbēmus. Nunc est **tempus** quiescere et dē cēnā cōgitāre."

Lūcius "Heus! Moxne cēnāmus?" rogāvit. "Iēiūnus sum.
10 Paene mortuus sum quod multās hōrās nihil nōn ēdī! Dē amīcō **sorōris** . . ."

In culīnā frātrēs placentās petīvērunt.

Marcus manum super **ōs** Lūciī posuit et "Eho, frātercule, tacē," mōnuit. "**Soror** et **māter** occupātae sunt. Venī mēcum. Aliquid cibī in culīnā invenīre possumus. **Frāter** meus mortuus esse nōn dēbet!" Duo **frātrēs** abeunt et cibum quaerunt. Caecilia post **frātrēs** clāmāvit: "Tū, Lūcī, tē lavā! Sordidus es!"

15 In culīnā **frātrēs** placentās ā coquō petīvērunt. Coquus, **nōmine** Sicō, **frātribus** duōbus placentās dedit et rīsit: "Lūcī, grātiās **frātrī** tuō agere dēbēs! **Frātrēs** māiōrēs semper **custōdēs frātrum** minōrum sunt!"

🔊 VERBA ŪTENDA

aliquid some
amīca, -ae f. (female) friend, girlfriend
atque and, and also, and even
cārus, -a, -um dear, expensive
cēnō (1) dine
custōs, custōdis m. guardian, protector
coquus, -ī m. cook
culīna, -ae f. kitchen
eho! here you! hey! (often followed by *tū* or a vocative)
eius her, his

eum him
festīnō (1) hasten, hurry
frāter, frātris m. brother
frāterculus, -ī m. dear brother, little brother
grātiās agere to give thanks (to), to thank
heus! hey! you there! (to draw attention)
iēiūnus, -a, -um hungry
inveniō, invenīre, invēnī find, discover
lavō, lavāre, lāvī wash
lentē slowly
māior older

manum hand
māter, mātris f. mother
minōris younger (gen.)
mortuus, -a, -um dead
nōndum not yet
nōs we
occupātus, -a, -um busy
ōs, ōris n. mouth, face
paene almost
pater, patris m. father
placenta, -ae f. cake (Roman cakes looked more like pancakes)
quaerō, quaerere, quaesīvī / quaesiī seek, look for, ask for

quiescō, quiescere, quiēvī rest
reveniō, revenīre, revēnī come back, return
Sicō, Sicōnis m. Sico, a man's name
sordidus, -a, -um filthy
soror, sorōris f. sister
spīrō (1) breathe
taceō, tacēre, tacuī, tacitum be quiet, be silent
tē yourself
tempus, temporis n. time, season
visitō (1) visit

POSTQUAM LĒGISTĪ

Answer in Latin. The clues are in the *lectiō*.

1. What does Servilia want to talk about?
2. When does Caecilia say they will talk about Cordus?
3. What is Lucius worried about?
4. Why does Marcus tell Lucius to be quiet?
5. Where do the brothers go at the end of the *lectiō*?
6. Who is Sico?

Gemma

"*Nihil nōn ēdī*" cries the always hungry Lucius. In Latin double negatives are acceptable to show emphasis.

Grammatica A

The 3ʳᵈ Declension

Third declension words are marked by the genitive singular ending *-is*. Their nominative singular forms vary widely.

Finding the stem: Remember that the stem of a noun is identified by dropping the ending of the genitive singular. This is especially important in the 3ʳᵈ declension. Consider the range of stems in these 3ʳᵈ declension nouns:

Nominative	Genitive	Stem
homō	*hominis*	*homin-*
frāter	*frātris*	*frātr-*
nōmen	*nōminis*	*nōmin-*

Notā Bene: English words derived from 3ʳᵈ declension nouns often include the stem, not the nominative form: e.g., "hominid" from *homō, hominis*; "nominal" from *nōmen*, and "fratricide" from *frāter*. The rule is not universal, however, as you can see in "homicide," "fraternity," and "nomenclature."

Gender: All three genders appear in the 3ʳᵈ declension. There are no hard and fast rules about this, but here are some general tendencies:

- Sometimes the genders are logical to us, like the genders of *pater* (m.), *māter* (f.), *frāter* (m.), and *soror* (f.).

- Words that indicate ideas or concepts often end in *-tās* and *-tūdō* and are feminine: *antīquitās, antīquitātis* (antiquity), *lībertās, lībertātis* (freedom, liberty); *longitūdō, longitūdinis* (length), and *fortitūdō, fortitūdinis* (strength, bravery).

- But the majority of words in the 3ʳᵈ declension follow no easily discernable pattern. Just pay attention to the entry for the word in the vocabulary or dictionary.

Endings: Now see how the list you compiled of the 3ʳᵈ declension endings in Exercise 13-1 compares to this chart.

3ᴿᴰ DECLENSION		
Singular	**Feminine**	**Neuter**
Nominative	soror	nōmen
Genitive	sorōr**is**	nōmin**is**
Dative	sorōr**ī**	nōmin**ī**
Accusative	sorōr**em**	nōmen
Ablative	sorōr**e**	nōmin**e**
Vocative	soror	nōmen
Plural		
Nominative	sorōr**ēs**	nōmin**a**
Genitive	sorōr**um**	nōmin**um**
Dative	sorōr**ibus**	nōmin**ibus**
Accusative	sorōr**ēs**	nōmin**a**
Ablative	sorōr**ibus**	nōmin**ibus**
Vocative	sorōr**ēs**	nōmin**a**

Notā Bene: The following statements are generally true of all declensions:

- **For all nouns**

    Within a given declension, the dative and ablative plurals are identical.
    The genitive plurals end in *-um* (puellā**rum**, virō**rum**, frātr**um**).

- **For masculine and feminine nouns**

    The accusative singular ends in *-m* (puella**m**, viru**m**, frātre**m**).
    The accusative plural ends in *-s* (puellā**s**, virō**s**, frātrē**s**).

- **For neuter nouns**

    The accusative always is identical to its nominative, singular or plural.
    All neuter nominative and accusative plurals, end in *-a* (for**a**, nōmin**a**).

In general, these rules apply to pronouns and adjectives as well as nouns, with some exceptions that you will meet later.

EXERCEĀMUS!

`13-2` Substitutions: 3ʳᵈ Declension

Replace the underlined 1ˢᵗ or 2ⁿᵈ declension word with the correct form of the 3ʳᵈ declension word in parentheses. Follow the model.

→ Illa pēcūnia <u>fīliī</u> tuī est. (pater, patris m.)
Illa pēcūnia patris tuī est.

1. Mox <u>dominus</u> domum revenit. (pater, patris m.)
2. <u>Fēminae</u> emere cēnam voluērunt. (māter, mātris f.)
3. Hodiē <u>amīcam</u> meam Naeviam visitāvī. (soror, sorōris f.)
4. Vēnditor <u>Valeriae</u> holera dedit. (māter, mātris f.)
5. Nunc fēminae <u>virō</u> appropinquāvērunt. (homō, hominis m./f.)
6. <u>Fēminārum</u> vōcēs fortēs audīvīmus. (homō, hominis m./f.)
7. Virī dē <u>cēnā</u> cogitāvērunt. (tempus, temporis n.)
8. Dē <u>amīcīs</u> post cēnam dīcere possumus. (frāter, frātris m.)
9. Caput hominis ūnum <u>nāsum</u> habet. (ōs, ōris n.)

Lectiō Secunda

Antequam Legis

More on Adjective Agreement

Now that you are more familiar with 3ʳᵈ declension nouns, look for them modified by 2-1-2 adjectives in *Lectiō Secunda*. These noun adjective pairs are marked in **bold**. Think about what you learned in the last chapter about adjective agreement and see if you can see how it works with the 3ʳᵈ declension.

EXERCEĀMUS!

`13-3` GNC'ing with 3ʳᵈ Declension Nouns

Remember that adjectives GNC with nouns. So a 2-1-2 adjective agreeing with a 3rd declension noun does not use 3rd declension endings. It stays 2-1-2 and agrees with the noun in gender, number, and case. Before you read, make a line-by-line list of the noun/adjective pairs marked in **bold** in *Lectiō Secunda*. Determine the GNC for each pair. Then translate the two words into English. Follow the model.

	Line	Noun	Adjective	Gender	Number	Case	Translation
→	1	frātrēs	iēiūnī	m.	pl.	nominative	the hungry brothers

NĒMŌ MĒ INTELLEGIT!

Postquam **frātrēs iēiūnī** abiērunt, Servīlia dīxit. "**Māter cāra**," clāmāvit fīlia, "Sī tibi placeat, audī mē dē Cordō! Ego et Naevia in peristȳliō fuimus et Cordus intrāvit. Expalluī! Spīrāre nōn potuī! Sonitus magnus in **auribus meīs** fuit!! Dīcere nōn potuī! Et tunc Cordus . . ."

Caecilia "Pāx! Tacē, mea fīlia!" inquit. "Sērius! Sērius dē Cordō cum **patre tuō** dīcere tempus est! Nunc mē in
5 culīnam īre et cum Sicōne, coquō nostrō, dē cēnā dīcere oportet." Et abiit.

Servīlia, in ātriō sōla stetit et effūsē lacrimāvit. "Nēmō mē intellegit!" clāmāvit, "Nēmō dē vītā meā cūrat! Ō mī Corde! Quam fōrmōsus es! Quam pulcher! Quam **homō rōbustus** atque nōbilis! Quam vehementer tē amō!" Sīc dīxit et ad cubiculum suum cucurrit.

In cubiculō, Servīlia librum Catullī tollit et legit. Paulo post, Servīlia
10 susurrat et dīcit,

Cordus mihi pār deō esse vidētur
Cordus, sī fās est, superāre deōs vidētur,
Cordum dulciter rīdentem vīdī et omnēs sēnsūs
ā mē fūgērunt. Nam simul atque tē aspexī,
15 Corde, mihi superest **nūlla vōx** in **ōre meō**.
Audiō **nōmen tuum** et lingua mea torpet
et tenuis flamma per **corpus meum** movet!
Aurēs meae sonitū suō tintinnant!
Et nox oculōs meōs tegit!

20 Tum Servīlia sē super lectum iēcit et rursus effūsē lacrimāvit.

Servīlia librum Catullī legit.

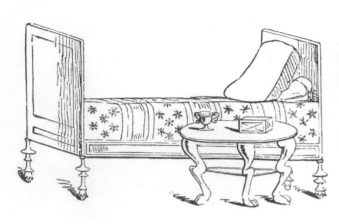

Lectus in cubiculō

Lectus antīquus

🔊 VERBA ŪTENDA

amō (1) love

aspiciō, aspicere, aspexī look at

ātrium, -iī n. atrium, public greeting room of a Roman house

auris, auris f. ear

cārus, -a, -um dear, expensive

coquus, -ī m. cook

corpus, corporis n. body

cubiculum, -ī n. bedroom

culīna, -ae f. kitchen

cūrō (1) care for

deus, -ī m. god

dulciter sweetly

effūsē a lot

expallescō, expallescere, expalluī turn very pale

fās est it is right

flamma, -ae, f. flame

formōsus, -a, -um handsome, pretty

frāter, frātris m. brother

homō, hominis m./f. person, human being, man

iaciō, -ere, iēcī throw

iēiūnus, -a, -um hungry

intellegō, intellegere, intellēxī, intellectum understand

lacrimō (1) cry, shed tears

lectus, -ī m. bed

lingua, -ae f. tongue

māter, mātris f. mother

moveō, movēre, mōvī move, affect

nēmō, nēminis m./f. nobody

nōbilis, -e noble

nox, noctis f. night

nullus, -a, -um no

ōs, ōris, n. mouth

pār equal

pater, patris m. father

pāx! quiet! enough!

peristȳlium, -iī n. peristyle, colonnaded garden

postquam after

pulcher, pulchra, pulchrum pretty, handsome

rōbustus, -a, -um strong

quam! how!

rīdentem laughing

rursus again

sē herself

sensūs senses (nom. pl.)

sērius later, too late

simul atque as soon as

sonitū suō with their own sound

spīrō (1) breathe

superō (1) surpass, conquer

supersum, superesse, superfuī be left

susurrō (1) whisper, mutter

taceō, tacēre, tacuī, tacitum be quiet, be silent

tegō, tegere, texī hide, cover

tempus, temporis n. time, season

tenuis thin (modifies flame)

tintin(n)ō (1) ring

torpeō, torpēre, torpuī grow numb

ut as

vidētur (he) seems

vīta, -ae f. life

vox, vōcis f. voice

POSTQUAM LĒGISTĪ

1. Do you think that Servilia is right that no one understands her? Why?
2. What physical effect does seeing Cordus have on Servilia?
3. What does Caecilia want Servilia to do instead of talking about Cordus?
4. Does Servilia do what her mother wants her to do?
5. Where does Servilia go at the end of the *lectiō*? Where would you go under similar circumstances?
6. What does Servilia mean when she says "night covers her eyes"?
7. Are Servilia's symptoms of love sickness ever found today?

Grammatica B

3rd Declension Nouns and 2-1-2 Adjectives

Do you remember **GNC** from the last chapter? Adjectives agree with their nouns in **G**ender, **N**umber, and **C**ase. You will be especially aware of this when you see adjectives from one declension modifying nouns from another, as you did in these pairs from the last reading:

> *frātrēs iēiūnī*   *māter cāra*   *auribus meīs*

In all three phrases, a 2-1-2 adjective is describing a 3rd declension noun. Notice how the noun/adjective combination can help you determine case and number. For example, *frātrēs* can be nominative or accusative plural, but *frātrēs iēiūnī* can only be nominative. The accusative would be *frātrēs iēiūnōs*. An adjective is often the difference between a right and a wrong translation!

Here is a declension chart to help demonstrate this fact to you.

NOUN-ADJECTIVE AGREEMENT			
Singular	**Feminine**	**Masculine**	**Neuter**
Nominative	māter mea	pater meus	nōmen meum
Genitive	mātris meae	patris meī	nōminis meī
Dative	mātrī meae	patrī meō	nōminī meō
Accusative	mātrem meam	patrem meum	nōmen meum
Ablative	mātre meā	patre meō	nōmine meō
Vocative	māter mea	pater mī	nōmen meum
Plural			
Nominative	mātrēs meae	patrēs meī	nōmina mea
Genitive	mātrum meārum	patrum meōrum	nōminum meōrum
Dative	mātribus meīs	patribus meīs	nōminibus meīs
Accusative	mātrēs meās	patrēs meōs	nōmina mea
Ablative	mātribus meīs	patribus meīs	nōminibus meīs
Vocative	mātrēs meae	patrēs meī	nōmina mea

Since the gender of a 3rd declension noun is often difficult to predict and requires memorization, it is helpful to learn a 3rd declension noun with a 2-1-2 adjective; i.e., if you learn *nōmen meum* you know right away that *nōmen* is neuter.

EXERCEĀMUS!

13-4 Adjective Agreement

Use the adjective to help you determine the GNC of the following phrases with 3rd declension nouns. Follow the model.

HINT: Those marked with an asterisk have two possibilities.

	Gender	Number	Case
→ *homō novus*	*masculine*	*singular*	*nominative*

1. mātris tuae
2. sorōrī tuae
3. fullōnēs Rōmānī
4. latrōnēs Rōmānōs
5. actōribus īrātīs*

6. tonsōrum bonōrum
7. nōmen longum*
8. frātrī parvō
9. operum perīculōsōrum
10. temporī necessāriō

11. pater fessus
12. opus perīculōsum*
13. vōce magnā
14. senātōrēs agitātī
15. opera perīculōsa*

Mōrēs Rōmānī

Echoes of Catullus

In *Lectiō Secunda* Servilia echoes the love poet Catullus, a contemporary of Caesar. She recites one of his most famous poems, specifically the one where Catullus describes the first time he laid eyes on Lesbia, his future lover.

Before you read, you might also want to think about your own experiences. If you have ever been in the presence of someone you love or with whom you are falling in love, how many of Catullus' symptoms did you experience? Catullus died about 45 years before the time of our story. Yet his description was perfect for Servilia, and aptly describes lovers today.

We have modified the original poem a bit to help you read it. We have also used combinations of boldfacing and italics to show you which words go together. With this help, in addition to the *Verba Ūtenda* below, you should be able to understand the poem.

> Ille (vir) mihi pār deō esse vidētur,
> ille, sī fās est, superāre deōs (vidētur),
> (ille) quī sedēns adversus, tē
> > identidem spectat et audit
>
> 5 *(tē)* dulciter **rīdentem,** quod **omnēs sēnsūs**
> ā *mē miserō* ēripit: nam simul atque, Lesbia,
> tē aspexī, mihi superest nihil
> > vōcis in ōre
>
> Sed lingua (mea) torpet, **tenuis flamma**
> 10 sub **artūs (meōs)** dēmānat, *sonitū suō*
> tintinant aurēs (meae), *geminā nocte*
> > oculī (meī) teguntur.

Catullus 51.1–12

🔊 VERBA ŪTENDA

adversus (+ acc.) opposite (*tē* is object)	*fās* right, proper	**ōs, ōris** n. mouth	*superō* (1) conquer
artūs limbs (acc.)	*flamma, -ae* f. flame	*pār* equal	*supersum, superesse, superfuī* be left
aspiciō, aspicere, aspexī, aspectum look at	*geminus, -a, um* twin;	*prius* formerly, in the past	*tenuis* thin
auris, auris f. ear	*identidem* again and again	*quod* a fact that, something which	*tintin(n)ō* (1) ring
dēmānō (1) flow out, spread out	*ille* he	*rīdentem* laughing	*torpeō, torpēre, torpuī* grow numb
deus, -ī m. god	*lingua, -ae* f. tongue	*sedēns* sitting	*vidētur* seems
dīvus, -a, -um divine	*lūmen, lūminis* n. light; "lights" = "eyes"	*sēnsūs* feelings (acc. pl.)	*vox, vōcis* f. voice; goes with *nihil;* "nothing of voice" = "no voice"
dulce sweetly	*mihi* to me	*simul atque* as soon as	
ēripiō, -ere, ēripuī snatch	*miser, misera, miserum* wretched	*sonitū suō* with their own sound	
et even	*nox, noctis* f. night	*spectō* (1) look at	

Catullus 51 is actually a loose translation of a famous poem by the Greek poet Sappho of Lesbos. In his poem, Catullus does not mention this. He assumes that his Latin readers will recognize and appreciate how he has used Sappho's poem. In today's world, what Catullus did might be considered plagiarism or stealing someone else's literary property. In the ancient world such imitation was the highest form of praise. For example, the Roman poet Vergil used Homer's *Iliad* and *Odyssey* as close models for his long epic poem, the *Aeneid*. In the *Divine Comedy* Italian national poet Dante Alighieri (1265–1321) borrowed from the *Aeneid* many scenes and characters (including Vergil himself). Several of Shakespeare's plays are retellings of plays of Plautus and the Roman playwrights Plautus and Terence themselves modeled their comedies on earlier Greek works. In their prologues, in fact, they often tell their audiences what Greek plays they are "translating."

Although we are much more cautious about copying the work of others today, the writings of the ancient Romans are certainly past the statute of limitations for modern copyright laws. So their works and sayings have often been used and reused, worked and reworked by modern authors. To take an ancient author's works and to imitate them or to incorporate parts of them into one's own work remains a very high compliment and lends the luster of classical erudition to the modern author!

Latīna Hodierna

Latin in Modern Families

Although English words for family members like "father," "mother," "brother," and "sister" are all native English words derived from Anglo-Saxon sources, Latin words related to the family are widely used in English.

We can begin with the word "family" itself, which comes from the Latin word *familia, -ae* f. Both the Latin and English words have a wide range of meanings. Consider:

familia, -ae f.

In English, a "family" can refer to a household of people living together. It can also refer to all the members of the "clan" that are related to each other. Biologically, it can refer to a grouping of organisms. But the Roman word is more legal than biological in meaning. A Roman could use this word to refer to a "household," to all individuals under the legal control of a *pater familias* (father of the family), including relatives and even slaves. Some Roman wives were never legally members of their husband's family, and many Roman children were members of a family by adoption rather than birth.

Now consider how words for specific family members come into English.

LATIN WORD	MEANING	ENGLISH DERIVATIVES
pater, patris m.	father	**pater**nal, **pater**nity, **pat**ricide
māter, mātris f.	mother	**mater**nal, **mater**nity, **mat**ricide
fīlius, -ī m.	son	a**fīli**ate, a**fīli**ation, **fīli**al,
fīlia, -ae f.	daughter	**fīli**ation
soror, sorōris f.	sister	**soror**al, **soror**ity, **soror**icide
frāter, frātris m.	brother	**frater**nal, **frater**nity, **frat**ricide
avunculus, -ī m.	mother's brother	**unc**le, **avuncul**ar
patruus, -ī m.	father's brother	
nepos, nepōtis m.	grandson, descendant	**nepot**ism, **nep**hew
neptis, neptis f.	granddaughter	

Note that Latin had separate words for mother's brother and father's brother. The relationship between a Roman and these men is indicated by the fact that *patruus* could also mean "a severe critic" in Latin whereas an *avunculus* was considered more loving and caring. *Nepos* means both "nephew" and "grandson" so Latin often simply said *fīlius/fīlia frātris* (brother's son/daughter) or *fīlius/fīlia sorōris* (sister's son/daughter).

Marriage was an important legal event in a woman's life. Before marriage, she was under the father's *patria potestās* (authority). After marriage, she often went under the authority of her husband and earned the status of *mātrōna*, i.e., a "married woman." There were certain political and religious activities that only married women could perform. Note that the English word "matron" has a much more limited use today.

Orbis Terrārum Rōmānus

Vērōna

The poet Catullus and the family of Valeria were all from Verona. Catullus was probably born in c. 84 B.C., when the city was part of the Roman province of *Gallia Cisalpīna* (which we visited in the *Orbis Terrārum Rōmānus* in Chapter 11). His father was said to have been a friend of Julius Caesar, who was governor of the province in 58–49 B.C. Catullus mentions Caesar, not always favorably, in some of his poems.

Vērōna in Galliā Cisalpīnā

Vērōna hodiē

Located at major crossroads in northern Italy, Verona was an important transportation center. The city became a Roman colony in 89 B.C. Residents of the city were granted Roman citizenship in 59 B.C. and ten years later the city was raised to the status of *mūnicipium* (a town subject to Rome but governed by its own laws).

By the time Valeria and her family left Verona for Rome, Augustus had changed the status of *Gallia Cisalpīna* from a province to a part of Italy.

An amphitheater, which could hold at least 20,000 spectators, was built in Verona in 70–80 A.D. This structure (now known as Arena di Verona) is one of the best preserved Roman amphitheaters and is still used today for opera performances.

C. Valerius Catullus

QUID PUTĀS?

1. How well do you think Catullus describes the emotion of being in love?
2. Do you think modern attitudes toward copying and plagiarism have changed from the ancient Roman view, or do today's poets and authors do much the same thing?
3. The English word "matron" comes from the Latin *mātrōna* (wife, matron). Would you call your mother or wife a matron? When would you use the word "matron" in English? How is the word used in England?
4. Relate the English word "nepotism" to the meaning of the Latin word *nepos, -ōtis* m. grandson.
5. List two modern literary works based directly on the work of an ancient Roman author.

EXERCEĀMUS!

13-5 Colloquāmur

Pick a partner. Take turns describing your family to each other. Use the following questions to get started. Follow the model. Don't worry about making mistakes. Just try to communicate! Additional vocabulary you may need:

grandfather	*avus, -ī* m.
grandmother	*avia, -ae* f.
stepbrother	*vītricī fīlius* (acc. *vītricī fīlium*)
stepfather	*vītricus, -ī* m.
stepmother	*noverca, -ae* f.
stepsister	*novercae fīlia*
twin	*geminus, -ī* m.

→ Habēsne frātrem in familiā tuā?   *Ita, trēs frātrēs habeō*!   *Frātrēs nōn habeō.*

1. Habēsne frātrem minōrem (younger)?
2. Habēsne frātrem māiōrem (older)?
3. Habēsne sorōrem in familiā tuā?
4. Habēsne sorōrem minōrem?
5. Habēsne sorōrem maiōrem?
6. Suntne geminī in familiā tuā?
7. Estne avus aut avia in familiā tuā?
8. Habēsne cubiculum tuum in domō?
9. Estne soror aut frāter in cubiculō tuō?

13-6 Scrībāmus

Write a short paragraph in Latin that describes your family. You can use phrases from the previous exercise and from the readings in this chapter. You could also refer back to the description of the Servilian family in *Lectiō Secunda* of Chapter 12. When you need to refer to numbers you do not know (but that you will learn soon) feel free simply to write the number as a number—use Roman numerals if you know how! We have begun a sample paragraph for you.

→ In meā familiā sumus ego, pater meus, māter mea, I (ūnus) frāter et III (trēs) sorōrēs. Meus frāter XIII annōs nātus est et mea soror VIII annōs nāta est. In familiā ūna avia et duo avī sunt. Mea māter trēs frātrēs sed sorōrem nōn habet . . .

13-7 Verba Discenda

Use an English dictionary, if necessary, to find at least one additional English derivative for ten of the *Verba Discenda*. See if you can use the meaning of the Latin word to define each English derivative.

Here is one to get you started:

amorous, from *amō* "pertaining to **love**"

Gemma

Why do you think Jules Verne named the main character in *Two Thousand Leagues Under the Sea* Captain Nemo?

🔊 VERBA DISCENDA

amīca, -ae f. friend, girlfriend [amicable]
amō (1) love [amity]
cārus, -a, -um dear, expensive
cūrō (1) care for [curative]
frāter, frātris m. brother [fraternal]
homō, hominis m./f. person, human being, man [hominid]

iēiūnus, -a, -um hungry [jejune]
intellegō, intellegere, intellexī, intellectum understand [intellect]
māter, mātris f. mother [maternal]
nēmō, nēminis m./f. nobody
ōs, ōris n. mouth, face [oral]
pater, patris m. father [paternal, paternity]

pulcher, pulchra, pulchrum pretty, handsome [pulchritude]
quam! how!
soror, sorōris f. sister [sorority]
taceō, tacēre, tacuī, tacitum be quiet, be silent [tacit]
tempus, temporis n. time, season [temporal]
vīta, -ae f. life [vital, vitality]

Angulus Grammaticus

How Multi-Faceted a Word *Quam* Is!

Quam is one of a number of Latin words that can have widely different meanings depending on context. In this chapter you have seen how *quam* is used in Latin to introduce the exclamation "How!" in phrases like the following:

Quam formōsus est!
Quam pulcher!
Quam nōbilis atque rōbustus!
Quam vehementer tē amō!

In all of these cases, *quam* is an adverb modifiying an adjective or an adverb to create expressions like "How handsome!" or "How strongly!"

Until now you have mostly seen *quam* used to mean "than" in expressions like:

> *Sīmia mē amat magis* **quam** *puer.*
> *Sedēre in lectīcā melius est* **quam** *ambulāre in viā.*

In this case, *quam* is used to express a comparison, i.e., to show that something is more "X" than something else.

Finally, you have seen *quam* used with *tam* to mean "as X as."

> *Puer tam fortis* **quam** *pater suus est.*

Later on, you will find out that *quam* can also mean "whom" or "which." It can also mean "as X as possible" with a superlative adjective or adverb, like *quam fortissimus* (as strong as possible) or *quam fortissimē* (as strongly as possible).

So, how can you know how to translate *quam* when you see it? Well, your best guide is to pay attention to *quam*'s surroundings. For example, if *quam* is at the beginning of a sentence ending in an exclamation point, it probably means "How!" If *quam* is used with a comparative like *magis* or *melius* it probably means "than."

English does the same sort of thing even more frequently than Latin does. For example, think of all the ways the word "iron" can be used in English. As a noun, the word "iron" can refer to an element, a household tool, and a golf club. And it can also be a verb meaning "to iron clothing" or "to iron out a problem." Or it can be an adjective as in the phrase "an iron rod." How do we know what "iron" means in English? The same way we do in Latin. By context!

Photo Credits

page 154 (top) Getty Villa Museum; **page 158 (bottom left)** Clipart.com; **page 158 (bottom right)** Nelson Eby/Photo by Nelson Eby used with permission; **page 163 (bottom)** Robert Hellenga/Photo by Robert Hellenga used with permission; **page 164** Susan Bonvallet/Photo by Susan Bonvallet used with permission

14

Dē Perseō

Acrisius, Danaēque Perseus Infansque et Arca
Attic red-figured hydria, attributed to the Gallatin
Painter, from Gela, ca. 490 B.C. H: 0.417 m, D: 0.27 m.
Francis Bartlett Fund. Courtesy, Museum of Fine Arts,
Boston

Lectiō Prīma

Antequam Legis

The astrologer told Licinia that her child would be a new Perseus, the Greek hero who decapitated the Gorgon Medusa and rescued the Ethiopian princess Andromeda from a sea monster. In this reading you will learn about Perseus' birth and his early adventures. Acrisius, king of the Argives, had heard that any son of his daughter, Danaë, would overthrow him. So he shut her up in a bronze chamber. But this was no impediment to Jupiter, who visited Danaë in the form of a golden rain shower. Danaë tried to keep hidden the resulting child, Perseus, but to no avail. Our story picks up when Acrisius is planning to do away with Perseus.

2nd Declension Nouns and Adjectives in *-er*

As you read the story of Perseus and his mother, watch out for 2nd declension words like *liber, librī* (book) and *ager, agrī* (field). They are 2nd declension words with nominative singulars in *-er* instead of *-us*. All the other endings are the same 2nd declension endings you already know. Look for more of these 2nd declension *-er* words (*puer* "boy" and *pulcher* "pretty") marked in **bold**.

Substantives

Also look in the *lectiō* for adjectives that stand by themselves and are not associated with any expressed noun. These words, which act as if they are nouns, are called **substantives**. In order to translate substantives, determine their gender and number and add "man/men," "woman/women," "one/ones/people," or "thing/things" accordingly. Thus, in *Lectiō Prīma* you have:

multa	= many things
omnia	= all things
parvus	= the small one
territōs	= the terrifed ones/people
quīdam	= certain people

We have marked all the substantives in the *lectiō* in ***bold italics***.

GRAMMATICA
2nd Declension Nouns in *-er*
2nd Declension Adjectives in *-er*
Substantives
3rd Declension i-Stems
Deceptive Pairs—Agreement Review

LATĪNA HODIERNA
Liberty and Libraries

MŌRĒS RŌMĀNĪ
Romans and Greek Myth

ORBIS TERRĀRUM RŌMĀNUS
Palātium

ANGULUS GRAMMATICUS
Latin Homonyms and Homophones

> **LECTIŌNĒS:**
> **PERSEUS INFANS**
> and
> **DANAĒ ET DICTYS**
>
> Here you read about Perseus, the Greek hero to whom Licinia's unborn child was compared in Chapter 10.

167

From *Disce! An Introductory Latin Course, volume 1*, First Edition. Francesco Bonavita. Copyright © 2011 by Pearson Education, Inc. Published by Pearson Prentice Hall. All rights reserved.

EXERCEĀMUS!

14-1 Derivatives

Before you read the story about Perseus, use the English words in parentheses to help you match the Latin word in column A with its meaning in column B. This will help with the vocabulary you will see in the chapter.

	A		B
_____	1. *arcā* (ark)	A.	sleep
_____	2. *dormit* (dormitory)	B.	afraid
_____	3. *inclūdunt* (enclose)	C.	mother
_____	4. *ligneam* (ligneous)	D.	storm
_____	5. *mare* (marine)	E.	wooden
_____	6. *māter* (maternal)	F.	greatest
_____	7. *maximus* (maximum)	G.	chest, box
_____	8. *narrant* (narrate)	H.	sea
_____	9. *tempestās* (tempest)	I.	tell
_____	10. *territōs* (terrified)	J.	shut in

Watch for these words in the following story about the Greek hero Perseus.

PERSEUS INFANS

Astrologus *bona* Liciniae dīxit: "Infans tuus tam fortis quam maximus hērōs Graecus Perseus erit!" Poētae Rōmānī *multa* dē Perseō in **librīs** narrant. Perseus fīlius Iovis, rēgis deōrum, fuit; avus eius, Acrisius nōmine, rex Argōrum in Graeciā fuit.

Acrisius **puerum** interficere cupit; servī Acrisiī igitur arcam ligneam faciunt. Perseum parvum capiunt et in arcā cum mātre **pulchrā** includunt. Tum arcam in mare coniciunt. Danaē, Perseī māter, magnopere territa est; enim
5 tempestās magna mare turbat. *Parvus* autem in mātris cārae brācchiīs dormit. Quid futūrum infanti est?

Iuppiter tamen *omnia* videt, et fīlium suum servāre cupit. Igitur mare tranquillum facit et arcam ad insulam Serīphum perdūcit. Postquam arca ad lītus advenit, Danaē infansque in harēnā quiescunt. Post breve tempus *quīdam* mātrem et infantem inveniunt et *territōs* per **agrōs** ad rēgis frātrem addūcunt. (Nōmen frātrī Dictys est.)

VERBA ŪTENDA

addūcō, addūcere, addūxī bring in, lead to
ager, agrī m. field
arca, -ae f. chest
Argī, Argōrum m. pl. the people of Argos, a city in Greece; Argives
autem however
avus, -ī m. grandfather
brāc(c)hium, -iī n. arm
brevis, breve short
coniciō, conicere, coniēcī hurl, cast
Danaē, Danaēs f., Danaë, Perseus' mother
deus, -ī m. god; dī (alternate nom. pl.)

Dictys, -yos m. Dictys, brother of the king of Seriphos
eius his
enim for
erit (he) will be
futūrum, -ī n. future
harēna, -ae f. sand
igitur therefore
inclūdō, inclūdere, inclūsī shut in, enclose
infans, infantis m./f. infant
insula, -ae f. translate as "island" here, referring to Seriphos
interficiō, interficere, interfēcī, interfectum kill

inveniō, invenīre, invēnī, inventum find, discover
Iuppiter, Iovis m. Jupiter, king of the gods
liber, librī m. book
ligneus, -a, -um wooden
lītus, lītoris n. shore
magnopere greatly
mare, maris n. sea
maximus, -a, -um very great
narrō (1) say, tell
omnia "all things," everything
perdūcō, perdūcere, perdūxī conduct, bring through
Perseus, -eī m. Perseus

poēta, -ae m. poet
Polydectes, -is m. Polydectes, king of Seriphos
postquam after
quīdam some men
quiescō, quiescere, quiēvī, quiētum rest
rex, rēgis m. king
servō (1) save, protect
tamen nevertheless
tempestās, tempestātis f. storm
territus -a, -um afraid
tranquillus, -a, -um still, peaceful
turbō (1) disturb

POSTQUAM LĒGISTĪ

Try to answer these questions in both Latin and English.

1. What is Perseus' relationship with each of the following: Jupiter, Acrisius, and Danaë?
2. How does Acrisius try to kill Perseus?
3. Why is Perseus not afraid?
4. Who finds Perseus and his mother? Who gives them sanctuary?
5. What happens to Perseus and Danaë at the end of *Lectiō Prīma*?

Gemma

Notice the unusual genitive endings for *Danaē* and *Dictys*. These names are Greek and retain Greek genitive endings in Latin.

Grammatica A

2nd Declension Nouns in *-er*

Some masculine words of the second declension have a nominative singular ending in *-er* instead of *-us*. These include the following *Verba Discenda*:

> *ager, agrī* m. field   *liber, librī* m. book   *puer, puerī* m. boy

Notā Bene:

- Sometimes the stem loses the "e" as in *liber, librī* and *ager, agrī*.
- Other stems retain the "e" as in *puer, puerī*.
- English derivatives can help you know whether the "e" stays or drops out: "library," "puerile," and "agriculture." You do not, after all, go to the liberary to read a book on "agericulture"!
- The other endings of the declension remain unchanged.
- The vocative is the same as the nominative.

	SINGULAR		PLURAL	
Nominative	liber	puer	librī	puerī
Genitive	librī	puerī	librōrum	puerōrum
Dative	librō	puerō	librīs	puerīs
Accusative	librum	puerum	librōs	puerōs
Ablative	librō	puerō	librīs	puerīs
Vocative	liber	puer	librī	puerī

2nd Declension Adjectives in *-er*

Some 2-1-2 adjectives work the same way. Consider these *Verba Discenda*:

> *līber, lībera, līberum* **free**
> *pulcher, pulchra, pulchrum* **pretty, handsome**

"What is going on with the stem of *pulcher*?" you may ask. Is it *pulcher* or *pulchr-*? It is the latter. But the stem of *līber* is *līber-*. **You find the stem of an adjective by dropping the ending from the nominative singular feminine form**. That is why vocabularies and lexicons give you the entire nominative singular as an entry. Thus:

pulcher, pulchra, pulchrum ⟶ stem *pulchr-*
līber, lībera, līberum ⟶ stem *līber-* (not to be confused with the short *-i* noun *libr-*, book)

Notā Bene:

- English helps once more. Consider: "If you doubt my spelling of **pulchr**itude, you are at **liber**ty to look it up in the **libr**ary!"
- *līberī, -ōrum* (m. pl. substantive) means "children"—the non-adults in the house who were "the free ones." The others, of course, were slaves.

Substantives

Look closely at the words in bold in these sentences:

*Poētae **multa** dē Perseō narrant.*	The poets tell **many things** about Perseus.
*Iuppiter **omnia** vīdit.*	Jupiter saw **all things**.
***Multa varia** vīdērunt.*	They saw **many different things**.
*Astrologī **multa** dē **multīs** dīcunt.*	Astrologers say **many things** (much) about **many things**.

All of the words in bold are examples of **substantives** or adjectives being used as nouns. Another way to explain this is to say that the adjective agrees with the gender, number, and case of a noun understood but not expressed. When we translate Latin substantives into English, we usually need to supply the understood noun. So in the sentence

*Virī circumstant et **multa** dīcunt.*

multa is neuter accusative plural with "things" understood.

Here are some other examples where the understood noun is very clear:

Bonus venit.	The good man is coming.
Bona venit.	The good woman is coming.
Bonum venit.	A good thing is coming.
Bonī veniunt.	Good men are coming.
Bonae veniunt.	Good women are coming.
Bona veniunt.	Good things are coming.

Sometimes you can only tell from context how to translate a substantive. For example, in the sentence

Virī dē bonīs dīcunt.

the substantive *bonīs* can be translated as "good men," "good women," or "good things" depending on the context and what went before.

Sometimes the verb helps you sort things out. Compare the following two sentences. The verb in each sentence tells us how to translate *mala* the way we do.

*Mala celeriter **advenit**.*	The bad woman is approaching quickly.
*Mala celeriter **adveniunt**.*	Bad things are approaching quickly.

Now let's see some substantives in action. Democritus was a fifth-century pre-Socratic philosopher who theorized that the essential elements of matter were indivisable elements called, in Greek, *atomī* (literally, "those things that cannot be cut"). Cicero uses a series of neuter plural accusative substantives in this description of the extent of Democritus' wisdom. These substantitives are all marked in **bold**:

Democritus lūminibus āmissīs **alba** discernere et **ātra** nōn poterat, at vērō **bona mala, aequa, inīqua, honesta, turpia, ūtilia, inūtilia, magna, parva** poterat.

Cicero. *Tusculan Disputations.* V.114

🔊 VERBA ŪTENDA

aequa "fair things"
alba "white things"
at = sed
ātra "black things" (from *āter, ātra, ātrum*)
bona "good things"
discernō, discernere distinguish

honesta "decent things"
inīqua "unfair things"
inūtilia "useless things"
lūminibus āmissīs "after he lost his lights (eyes)," i.e., when he became blind

magna "great things"
mala "bad things"
poterat he was able
turpia "vile things"
ūtilia "useful things"
vērō indeed, truly

EXERCEĀMUS!

14-2   Substantives

Choose the correct translation of the substantive underlined in each of the following sentences. Remember to translate a neuter as "thing/things," a feminine as "woman/women," and a masculine as "man/men."

1. <u>Multī</u> dē theātrō dīcunt. (many men, many things, many women)

2. Valeria <u>bona</u> videt. (a good woman, good things, a good thing)

3. Puerī <u>pauca</u> dē theātrō dīcunt. (few men, few things, few women)

4. Paedagōgus <u>multa</u> audit. (many women, many things, many men)

5. Dē <u>bonō</u> māter dīcit. (a good thing, a good woman, good men)

6. Marcus <u>pulchram</u> vidēre vult. (the pretty woman, the pretty women, pretty things)

Lectiō Secunda

Antequam Legis

In *Lectiō Secunda* Danaë retells in the perfect tense the story told in the present tense in *Lectiō Prīma*. This will give you practice working with both tenses. Also note that *Lectiō Prīma* was in the 3rd person whereas *Lectiō Secunda* is mostly in the 1st person.

This reading also introduces you to a special group of 3rd declension words called **i-stems** because an *-i-* is sometimes added to or substituted for the regular 3rd declension ending. Such words are marked in **bold** in *Lectiō Secunda*. See if you can use what you know about the 3rd declension and the context to determine how they are used.

EXERCEĀMUS!

14-3   Recognizing 3rd Declension i-Stems

Before you read *Lectiō Secunda* make a line-by-line list of all the words marked in bold. These are all 3rd declension i-stems. Indicate the case, number, and meaning of each word. Follow the model. Can you identify the ending that has an *-i-* added?

Line	Word	Case	Number	Meaning
→ 7	*mare*	accusative	singular	sea

🔊 DANAĒ ET DICTYS

Poētae multa alia dē Perseō in librīs narrant:

Dictys, ubi fēminam infantemque vīdit, "Quis es?" inquit. "Et unde tū et puer tuus vēnistis?" Danaē respondit et frātrī rēgis suam fābulam dīxit: "Nōmen mihi Danaē est. Fīlia lībera rēgis Acrisiī sum. Unā **nocte** Iuppiter
5 ad mē in nimbō aureō vēnit et decem post **mēnsēs** fīlium deī, Perseum nōmine, peperī. Pater meus, avus infantis, eum interficere voluit. Ergō nōs in arcā posuit et in **mare** iēcit. Sed tūtī hūc vēnimus. Virī tuī nōs invēnērunt et per agrōs apud tē addūxērunt. Simul atque tē vīdī, tē benignum esse invēnī. Cupimus, fīlius meus et ego, domum tūtam. Concēde nōbīs, quaesō, nōmen
10 hospitum et nōn **hostium**. Nōn **hostēs** sed hospitēs sumus. Parce nōbīs et concēde nōbīs **ignem** et aquam. In insulā tuā concēde **sēdem** tūtam."

Ubi Dictys mātrem et parvum benignē excēpit, Danaē respondit: "Mihi fīliōque **sēdem** tūtam in **fīnibus** tuīs dedistī. Hoc dōnum libenter accipiō." Sīc Danaē laeta prō tantō beneficiō hominī bonō et deīs grātiās ēgit. Ergō
15 māter fīliusque multōs annōs ibi habitāvērunt et multōs annōs Perseus cum mātre cārā vītam beātam ēgit.

Perseus et Danaē

🔊 VERBA ŪTENDA

accipiō, accipere, accēpī accept, receive
adducō, adducere, addūxī lead to
ager, agrī m. field
alia other "things"
apud tē "to your house"
aureus, -a, -um golden
avus, -ī m. grandfather
beātus, -a, -um blessed, happy
benignē kindly
benignus, -a, -um kind
beneficium, -iī n. favor, benefit

concēdō, concēdere, concessī grant
cum when
deus, -ī m. god; **dī** (alternate nom. pl.)
dōnum, -ī n. gift
eram "I was"
eum him
excipiō, excipere, excēpī receive
fīnis, fīnis m. end; pl. country, territory
grātiās agere to thank
hoc this
hospes, hospitis m./f. guest, stranger

hostis, hostis m./f. stranger, foreigner, enemy; pl. the enemy
hūc to this place
iaciō, iacere, iēcī throw
ibi there
ignis, ignis m. fire
infans, infantis m./f. infant
interficiō, interficere, interfēcī, interfectum kill
inveniō, invenīre, invēnī, inventum find, discover
libenter freely, willingly
liber, librī m. book
līber, lībera, līberum free
mare, maris n. sea
mensis, mensis f. month

nimbus, -ī m. cloud
nōbīs to us
nox, noctis f. night
pariō, parere, peperī give birth to
poēta, -ae m. poet
posteā afterward, then
quaesō, -ere, quaesivī / quaesiī ask, beg
rex, rēgis m. king
sēdēs, sēdis f. seat, home, residence
simul atque as soon as
tantus, -a, -um so great a
territus -a, -um afraid
tūtus, -a, -um safe
unde from where

POSTQUAM LĒGISTĪ

Try to answer these questions in both Latin and English.

1. What questions does Dictys ask when he sees Danaë?
2. What new details does Danaë add to the story you read in *Lectiō Prīma* about what happened in Argos?

3. Why does Danaë mention *hostēs* in line 10?

4. What do you think happens next in the story?

Grammatica B

3rd Declension i-Stems

You have just seen how there is a special group of 2nd declension nouns with nominative singulars ending in *-er*. In the 3rd declension there is a special group of nouns that are notable for the presence of an *-i* in certain endings. These are called **3rd declension i-stems**. You saw several of these words in *Lectiō Secunda*. All of them are *Verba Discenda*.

> *fīnis, fīnis* **m. end**
> *hostis, hostis* **m./f. enemy**
> *mare, maris* **n. sea**
> *nox, noctis* **f. night**
> *sēdēs, sēdis* **f. seat, home**

As the following chart shows, i-stems differ in only a few spots from the "regular" 3rd declension endings. We have marked the different endings with an asterisk.

	3RD REGULAR	MASC./FEM. I-STEM	NEUTER I-STEM
		Singular	
Nominative	homō	ignis	mare
Genitive	homin**is**	ign**is**	mar**is**
Dative	homin**ī**	ign**ī**	mar**ī**
Accusative	homin**em**	ign**em**	mare
Ablative	homin**e**	ign**e** or ign**ī***	mar**ī***
		Plural	
Nominative	homin**ēs**	ign**ēs** or ign**īs***	mar**ia***
Genitive	homin**um**	ign**ium***	mar**ium***
Dative	homin**ibus**	ign**ibus**	mar**ibus**
Accusative	homin**ēs**	ign**ēs** or ign**īs***	mar**ia***
Ablative	homin**ibus**	ign**ibus**	mar**ibus**

Generally you do not need to know which nouns are i-stems, as long as you recognize *-ium* as an alternative genitive plural ending and *-ī* and *-ia* an alternative neuter endings. But here are some rules to determine whether a 3rd declension noun is an i-stem:

Masculine and Feminine

1. **Parisyllabic rule:** if the nominative ends in *-is* or *-ēs* and the genitive singular has the same number of syllables as the nominative:

> *aedēs, aedis* f. building, temple
> *hostis, hostis* m./f. enemy
> *mensis, mensis*, f. month

Gemma

decem post mensēs: You may have noticed that the story says Danaë gave birth in her tenth month. Biology has not changed over the millennia, but counting has.

The Romans practiced "inclusive" counting. Whereas we say that 0–9 is 9 months, the Romans included both the first and the last month in their count and thus made the total ten.

Gemma

ignem et aquam: "Fire and water" were two life necessities that the Romans used to symbolize communal sharing. When a Roman was sent into exile, the expression used was *aquā et ignī interdīcere* "to forbid fire and water (to someone)." So Danaë is asking the king to welcome her and her son into the community of Seriphos.

2. **Double consonant rule:** if the stem of the noun ends in two consonants:

mens, mentis f. mind
mons, montis m. mountain
nox, noctis f. night

3. **Neuters:** If the neuter nominative singular ends in *-e*, *-al*, or *-ar*:

animal, -ālis n. animal
exemplar, -āris n. example
mare, maris n. sea

Notā Bene:

- There are notable exceptions to the rules. For example, *canis, canis* m./f. "dog", *infans, infantis* m./f., and *iuvenis, -is* "youth, young man" should act like i-stems but do not.
- The ablative singular of masculine and feminine i-stems varies between *-e* and *-ī*. Be on the lookout for either. Neuter *-i* stems almost always have the *-ī*. Thus, *animalī*.
- Some older words in the language had an *-i* in every case ending. Sometimes these are called "pure" i-stems. Thus you will encounter forms like *Tiberim* (accusative singular for the river Tiber) and *tussīs* (nom./acc. pl.) "cough." In context, these will not cause much of a problem.

Summary

- I-stems are only found in the 3rd declension.
- I-stem endings only differ from regular 3rd declension endings in the following instances:

All genders	i-stems ⟶ gen. pl.	*-ium*
Masc. and fem.	abl. sing.	sometimes *-ī*
	nom./acc. pl.	sometimes *-īs*
Neuter i-stems ⟶	abl. sing	*-ī* (almost always)
	nom./acc. pl	*-ia*

EXERCEĀMUS!

14-4 **i-Stems**

Make the nominative and genitive plural forms of each of the following i-stem nouns.
HINT: Remember how the special *-ium* and *-ia* endings are used.

1. hostis, hostis m./f.
2. nox, noctis f.
3. sēdēs, sēdis f.
4. mare, maris n.
5. animal, animālis n.
6. mons, montis m.
7. ignis, ignis m.
8. aedēs, aedis f.

Deceptive Pairs—Agreement Review

Now consider the following phrases from the *lectiōnēs*:

tempestās magna	a great storm
pater meus	my father
hominī bonō	to the good man

Notice that in each case the adjective does not have the same ending as the word it modifies. Nevertheless, the adjective agrees (GNCs) with its noun in gender, number, and case. Thus

tempestās magna	feminine singular nominative
pater meus	masculine singular nominative
hominī bonō	masculine singular dative

Latīna Hodierna

Liberty and Libraries

English has two words that mean basically the same thing: "freedom" (an Anglo-Saxon–based word) and "liberty," which finds its origin in the Latin adjective *līber* (free). In Latin, the equivalent of "liberty" is *lībertās, lībertātis* f.

Compare these cognates of *lībertās, lībertātis* f. in some Romance languages:

liberté	French
libertad	Spanish
libertà	Italian
liberdade	Portuguese

Now consider how many other English words are related to the Latin word *līber*.

liberal	liberate	libertarian
liberalism	liberation	libertine
liberality	Liberia	libertinism
liberalize		

Can you see the "freedom" in each of those words?

Now consider why the words "library" and "librarian" were not included in that list. This is because these two words are derived from *liber, librī* m. (book) rather than *līber, lībera, līberum* (free). It is easy to distinguish them if you remember that *libr-* is the Latin stem for "book" whereas *līber-* is the Latin stem for "free."

Finally, look at these Latin words dealing with books:

librārius, -a, -um related to books
librārius, -iī m. someone who copies books (keep in mind that all ancient
          books were "manuscripts," i.e., they were written by hand)
librārium, -iī n. a bookcase
taberna librāria a book store
bibliothēca, -ae f. a book collection, a library (a Latin word borrowing from
          the Greek, meaning "book repository")

Notice how both English and Romance languages have borrowed from these Latin words. (But note that Latin borrowed *bibliothēca* from Greek.)

Latin	*librārium, -iī* n. a bookcase	*bibliothēca, -ae* f. a library
English	library	bibliotheca (a book collection)
French	librairie (bookstore)	bibliothèque
Italian	libreria (bookstore or bookcase)	biblioteca
Spanish	librería (bookstore or bookcase)	biblioteca

Librī

Mōrēs Rōmānī

Romans and Greek Myth

Although Perseus was a Greek hero, he was well known by Romans who liked to hear his story or see it depicted in art. The Roman poet Ovid, for example, described the hero's adventures, including his conception by Zeus in a shower of gold, in the *Metamorphoses* (*Changes of Shape*). All of the stories in this poem deal with humans and gods changing their shape. The disguise Zeus used in his encounter with Danaë is an example of such a metamorphosis.

The Romans were fond of linking tales about Greek heroes with their own legends. For example, they could easily compare Acrisius' attempt to kill his grandson with a similar effort by king Numitor to dispose of his daughter's twin sons, Romulus and Remus, who eventually founded the city of Rome. Both grandfathers set their grandsons adrift on water, Perseus in the chest and Romulus and Remus in a reed basket on the bank of the Tiber River, where they were nursed by a she-wolf and discovered by a shepherd named Faustulus. The nursing wolf became an important symbol of Rome, and images of Romulus, Remus, and the she-wolf are proudly displayed in Rome to this day.

Here is a simplified version of the story of Romulus and Remus as told by the historian Livy in book one of *Ab Urbe Conditā* (*From the Founding of the City*):

Lupa in Capitōliō

Sed fāta statuērunt, ut opīnor, orīginem tantae urbis et principium maximī imperiī. Vestālis geminum partum ēdidit et Martem incertae stirpis patrem nuncupāvit. Sed nec dī nec hominēs aut ipsam aut stirpem ā crūdēlitāte rēgis, patris suī, vindicāvērunt. Rex iussit fēminam in custōdiam darī et puerōs in aquam pōnī. Servī puerum in alveō in aquā exposuērunt, sed tenuis aqua alveum in siccō destituit. Tunc lupa sitiens ē montibus quī circā erant ad vāgītum puerōrum vēnit et infantibus mammās dedit. Magister pecoris—cui Faustulus nōmen erat—lupam puerōs linguā lambentem invēnit. Faustulus puerōs ad stabula portāvit et Larentiae uxōrī dedit. Faustulus et Larentia puerōs ut suōs ēdūxērunt.

🔊 VERBA ŪTENDA

alveus, -eī m. tub, basin
circā round about
crūdēlitās, -tātis f. cruelty
cui to whom
custōdia, -ae f. custody
darī to be given
destituō, destituere, destituī leave
deus, -ī m. god; dī (alternate nom. pl.)
ēdō, ēdere, ēdidī beget
ēdūcō, ēdūcere, ēdūxī rear, raise
erant were

expositus, -a, -um exposed
fātum, -ī n. fate
geminus, -a, -um twin
imperium, -iī n. rule, empire
incertus, -a, -um uncertain, illegitimate
infans, infantis m./f. infant
inveniō, invenīre, invēnī, inventum find, discover
ipsam herself
iubeō, iubēre, iussī order
lambentem licking
lingua, -ae f. tongue
lupa, -ae f. she-wolf

mamma, -ae f. breast
Mars, Martis m. Mars, god of war
maximus, -a, -um greatest
mons, montis m. mountain
nuncupō (1) name
opīnor I believe; the subject is Livy
orīgō, -ginis f. origin
partum birth
pecus, pecoris n. herd
principium, -iī n. beginning
quī which
rex, rēgis m. king

siccum, -ī n. dry land
sitiens thirsty
stabulum, -ī n. stable
statuō, statuere, statuī decree
stirps, stirpis f. offspring, children
tantus -a, -um so great
tenuis mild
urbs, urbis f. city (Rome)
ut as
uxor, uxōris f. wife
vāgītum crying
Vestālis, Vestālis f. Vestal virgin
vindicō (1) protect

Orbis Terrārum Rōmānus

Palātium

The story of Romulus and Remus is especially associated with the Palatine Hill (*Palātium, -iī* n.), which you already know is one of the most important of the seven hills of Rome. In fact, it was on this hill that the emperors built their palaces. Even more important in Roman history and tradition is the association of the Palatine with Romulus and Remus, and thus with the early history of Rome and Roman religion. The life-sized bronze statue of a she-wolf (depicted above), now in the Capitoline Museum in Rome, has traditionally been dated to the 5th century B.C. while the bronze figures of the infants Romulus and Remus were added in the Renaissance.

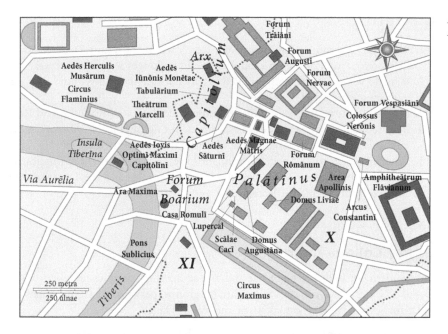

Potesne invenīre Casa Romulī in Palātiō?

The Romans revered the *Casa Romulī* ("Hut of Romulus") on the Palatine Hill. Ancient sources tell us that this hut, considered a sacred shrine, was rebuilt in a traditional oval shape every time the old one was destroyed by fire or fell into permanent disrepair. Several Iron Age (8th century B.C.) circular houses have been found near this spot.

By tradition the Lupercal (*Lupercal, -ālis* n.) or the cave of the she-wolf who nursed Romulus and Remus, was also located on the Palatine Hill, but no physical evidence for this shrine was known until 2007, when archaeologists uncovered, deep in the hill, a vaulted structure decorated with marble, mosaics, and shells, which may have been the sacred place.

Every February at the Lupercal on the Palatine, the Romans celebrated the Lupercalia (*Lupercālia, -ōrum* n. pl.), a religious festival directed by Luperci (*Lupercus, -ī* m.), or priests dressed in goatskins, who sacrificed goats on an altar at the Lupercal, smeared goat's blood on their foreheads, cut thongs from the skins of the sacrificed animals, and then, running naked around the Palatine Hill, struck female by-standers with the straps. Women struck by the straps were believed to be granted fertility and an easy childbirth. Animal sacrifice, by the way, was an important feature of Roman ritual. The association of Lupercal with fertility is carried down in the celebration of Valentine's Day at the same time of year today.

① Forum Rōmānum   ② Palātium

Forum Rōmānum (ā sinistrā) et Palātium (ā dextrā)

Domus antīquissima Palātiī

QUID PUTĀS?

1. What do you think is the point of Cicero's statement about Democritus? What could Democritus still know even though he could no longer see with his eyes?
2. Why do you think the Romans liked to tell Greek myths? Why would they want to model their own stories on Greek ones?
3. How is the story of Moses similar to those of Perseus or of Romulus and Remus?
4. If someone from France or Spain asked you, in English, for the "library" in the mall, what might they actually be looking for? How did they make their error?
5. What places in the United States might have been given the same national respect and state-sponsored preservation that the Hut of Romulus and the Lupercal on the Palatine enjoyed from the ancient Romans?

EXERCEĀMUS!

14-5 Colloquāmur

One student volunteers to be Danaë and to read her story to other members of the class. After Danaë tells her story, you should prepare (in groups, perhaps) to ask her follow-up questions in Latin. Several students can alternate the role of Danaë.

Here is Danaë's script. (Dont' worry about the bold boldfacing right now.)

> Fīlia rēgis Acrisiī **sum**. Unā nocte in torō **eram**, cum Iuppiter ad mē in nimbō aureō vēnit. In uterō meō deī fīlium **tulī** et decem post mēnsēs puerum pulchrum, Perseum nōmine, **peperī**, sed infantem **celāvī** quod avus infantis eum interficere voluit. Sed in arcā ligneā hūc **vēnimus**. Domum tūtam **cupīvī**. Cum fīliō meō multōs annōs ibi **habitāvī**.

Here is one sample follow-up question.

⟶ Quid nōmen patrī est?

14-6 Scrībāmus

Now rewrite the script from Exercise 14-5 to retell this narrative as if you are talking **about** Danaë to Polydectes. In other words,

- Change all the 1st person verbs marked in **boldface** into 3rd person.
- Change all the 1st person pronouns and adjectives to 3rd person.
- HINT: "her" (direct object) = *eam*; "her" (adjective) = *suus, -a, -um*.

Here is a sample sentence to use as a model:

⟶ In uterō **meō** deī fīlium **tulī** et decem post mēnsēs puerum pulchrum, Perseum nōmine, **peperī** . . .

becomes

⟶ In uterō **suō** deī fīlium **tulit** et decem post mēnsēs puerum pulchrum, Perseum nōmine, **peperit** . . .

14-7 Verba Discenda

Most of these *Verba Discenda* are nouns. Make three columns and list each noun (nominative and genitive) by declension. Mark 2nd declension -*er* nouns and 3rd declension i-stems with asterisks. Follow the model.

1st Declension	2nd Declension	3rd Declension
⟶	ager, agrī*	

🔊 VERBA DISCENDA

ager, agrī m. field
[agriculture]

brāc(c)hium, -iī n. arm
[brachiation]

deus, -ī m. god; **dī** (nom. pl.) [deify]

fīnis, fīnis m. end; pl. country, territory
[finite, infinite]

futūrum, -ī n. future
[future]

hostis, hostis m./f. stranger, foreigner, enemy; pl. the enemy [hostile]

infans, infantis m./f. infant
[infantile]

interficiō, interficere, interfēcī, interfectum kill

inveniō, invenīre, invēnī, inventum find, discover [invention]

liber, librī m. book
[library]

līber, lībera, līberum free
[liberty]

mare, maris n. sea [marine]

mensis, mensis m. month
[menstruation]

narrō (1) say, tell
[narration]

nox, noctis f. night
[nocturnal]

poēta, -ae m. poet
[poetic]

quiescō, quiescere, quiēvī, quiētum rest
[quiescent]

rex, rēgis m. king
[regal]

sēdēs, sēdis f. seat, home, residence

territus, -a, -um afraid

tūtus, -a, -um safe

Angulus Grammaticus

Latin Homonyms and Homophones

Homonyms are words that have the same spelling and different meanings, like "refuse" (n.) / "refuse" (v.). **Homophones** are words that have the same sound but different meanings, like "to" / "two" / "too." Here are two pairs of Latin homonyms. Which pair are also homophones?

> *liber līber*   the free book   *līberī līberī*   the free children

Now compare these Latin homophones, distinguished only by gender:

> *mālus, -ī m.*   pole, ship's mast   *mālus, -ī f.*   apple tree

which also share this homonym:

> *malus, -a, -um*   bad

So consider these pairs where the gender of the adjective indicates the meaning of the noun:

> *mālus mala*   *mālus malus*
> the bad apple tree   the bad mast

To make matters worse, you can add the verb *mālō* (I prefer) as another homonym, and create the following Latin oddity, probably the work of bored schoolboys (who took a bit of liberty with formal grammar rules):

> *Mālō mālō mālō mālō.*
> I prefer (to be in) an apple tree than to be on a bad mast.

Benjamin Britten interpreted the last *malō* slightly differently when he wrote his libretto for the 1954 opera *The Turn of the Screw:*

> Malo: I would rather be
> Malo: in an apple-tree
> Malo: than a naughty boy
> Malo: in adversity.

What other translations are possible, if you write it as the Romans would, without long marks?

Photo Credits

page 167 (top) Attic red-figured hydria, attributed to the Gallatin Painter, from Gela, ca. 490 B.C. H: 0.417 m, D: 0.27 m. Francis Bartlett Fund. Courtesy, Museum of Fine Arts, Boston **page 172** Erich Lessing/Art Resource, N.Y.; **page 175** Elnur/Fotolia, LLC—Royalty Free; **page 176** Photos.com; **page 177 (bottom left)** Thomas J. Sienkewicz/Photo by Thomas J. Sienkewicz used with permission; **page 177 (bottom right)** SF Photo/Shutterstock

Frāter et Soror

From *Disce! An Introductory Latin Course, volume 1*, First Edition. Francesco Bonavita. Copyright © 2011 by Pearson Education, Inc. Published by Pearson Prentice Hall. All rights reserved.

Iuvenis Rōmāna
Picture Desk, Inc./Kobal Collection/Dagli Orti (A)

GRAMMATICA
3rd Declension Adjectives
Types of 3rd Declension Adjectives
3rd Declension Adjectives:
    Agreement and Substantives
3rd Declension Adverbs

MŌRĒS RŌMĀNĪ
Mōs Māiōrum

LATĪNA HODIERNA
Virtūtēs Rōmānae Hodiē

ORBIS TERRĀRUM RŌMĀNUS
Ītalia Cicerōnis

ANGULUS GRAMMATICUS
Much, Many, Each, and Every

LECTIŌNĒS:
LACRIMAE IN CUBICULŌ
and
CORDUS

Marcus and Servilia talk about her
infatuation with Naevius Cordus.

15

Frāter et Soror

Lectiō Prīma

Antequam Legis

The *lectiōnēs* in this chapter continue the family conversations in the house of Servilius. In *Lectiō Prīma* Marcus has a private conversation with his sister Servilia.

3rd Declension Adjectives

In this chapter you are introduced formally to 3rd declension adjectives. You have seen some of these adjectives before. For example, in Chapter 7 Hermes used the 3rd declension adjective *omnis* (each, every; all):

> *Habeō saccum meum et **omnem** pecūniam meam.*

The astrologer used the 3rd declension adjective *fortis* (brave, strong) to describe the hero Perseus in Chapter 10:

> ***fortis** quam maximus hērōs Graecus Perseus erit!*

And Servilia used *nōbilis* (noble, notable) to describe Cordus in Chapter 13:

> *Quam homō rōbustus atque **nōbilis!***

Notice how all three adjectives have the same nominative ending (*-is*) as 3rd declension i-stem nouns like *fīnis* and *hostis*. This is because **3rd declension adjectives use i-stem endings.** Watch for these adjectives as you read *Lectiō Prīma*.

EXERCEĀMUS!

15-1 **Pre-Reading Vocabulary**

For each of the 3rd declension adjectives in column A find an English meaning and derivative in column B. Watch for some of these adjectives marked in **bold** in *Lectiō Prīma*.

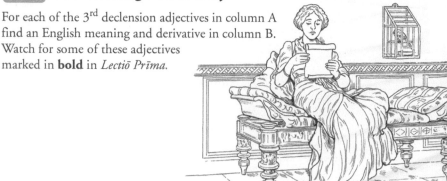

	A		B
___	1. *celer*	a.	clever, smart (an **intelligent** idea)
___	2. *crūdēlis*	b.	exalted (a **nobl**e goal)
___	3. *difficilis*	c.	each, all (an **omni**bus tax bill)
___	4. *facilis*	d.	easy (a **facile** argument)
___	5. *fortis*	e.	harsh (the **cruel** fact)
___	6. *gravis*	f.	heavy, serious (a **grav**e situation)
___	7. *intellegens*	g.	not easy, hard (a **diffic**ult task)
___	8. *nōbilis*	h.	powerful (a **pot**ent medication)
___	9. *omnis*	i.	strong (**fort**itude)
___	10. *potens*	j.	swift (an ac**celer**ant for fire)
___	11. *tristis*	k.	unhappy, sad (Chopin's *Valse **Triste***)

🔊 LACRIMAE IN CUBICULŌ

Dum ambulat in peristȳliō, librum legit.

Servīlia **tristis** et īrāta in cubiculō suō sedet. Marcus sorōrem suam audit et in cubiculum intrat. Marcus quoque **tristis** est quod Servīliae lacrimās vīdet et sorōrem suam valdē amat. Servīliae appropinquat et "Cūr lacrimās, soror?" rogat, "Quōmodo tē adiuvāre possum?"

"Nēmō mē," respondet Servīlia, "adiuvāre potest. Vīta tam **crūdēlis** est! Amō iuvenem
5 formōsum et **intellegentem**, Naevium Cordum nōmine, et nēmō nec dē Cordō nec dē mē cūrat!"

"Vēra nōn dīcis, soror. Ego multum cūrō. Dīc mihi **omnia** dē iuvene. Hic Cordus—nōnne frāter **māior** amīcae tuae, Naeviae, est?"

"Rectē dīcis. Hodiē Cordum in domō meae amīcae Naeviae vīdī. Adulescentem in peristȳliō vīdī et corpus **forte** et formam **nōbilem** habuit. Dum ambulat, librum lēgit et verba **potentia** ōrātiōnis Cicerōnis, optimī ōrātōris, prōnun-
10 tiāvit. Cum clāmāvit 'Quam diū etiam furor iste tuus nōs ēlūdet?' cor meum palpitāvit. Vox Cordī praeclāra et **gravis** est et iuvenis quoque praeclārus est!"

"Et ego Cordum nōvī," inquit Marcus, "amīcus meus est. Ego et Cordus artī **difficilī** rhētoricae studēmus. Et vēra dīcis—adulescens bonus est et in studiō rhētoricō perītus. In gymnasiō quoque **fortis** et **celer** est."

🔊 VERBA ŪTENDA

adiuvō, adiuvāre, adiūvī help
adulescens, -entis m./f. youth
ars, artis f. art, skill
celer, celeris, celere fast, swift
cor, cordis n. heart
corpus, corporis n. body
crūdēlis, crūdēle harsh, cruel
cum when
difficilis, difficile hard, difficult
diū long, for a long time
ēlūdet "will mock"
etiam also, even
forma, -ae f. beauty

formōsus, -a, -um handsome
fortis, forte strong, brave
furor, furōris m. fury, rage
gravis, grave heavy, serious
gymnasium, -iī n. gymnasium, open area for training
hic this
intellegens, intellegentis smart, intelligent
iste tuus "that ___ of yours"
iuvenis, iuvenis m./f. youth
lacrima, -ae f. tear
lacrimō (1) cry, shed tears

legō, legere, lēgī, lectum read, gather, choose
māior, māius greater, larger, older; m. pl. ancestors, elders
multum a lot
nec and not; nec...nec... neither. . .nor. . .
nōbilis, nōbile notable, noble
omnis, omne each, every; pl. all
optimus, -a, -um best
ōrātiō, -iōnis f. speech
ōrātor, -ōris m. speaker, orator

palpitō (1) beat, throb
peristȳlium, -iī n. peristyle
perītus, -a, -um experienced, skillful
potens, potentis powerful
praeclārus, -a, -um very clear, noble, excellent
prōnuntiō (1) recite, report
quōmodo how
rhētoricus, -a, -um rhetorical
tristis, triste sad
vox, vōcis f. voice

POSTQUAM LĒGISTĪ

Try to answer these questions in both Latin and English.

1. Describe Servilia's feelings as the *lectiō* begins. Why does she feel this way?
2. Why does Marcus come to talk to her?
3. What does this suggest to you about their relationship as brother and sister? How does this compare to brother-sister relationships you have known?
4. Servilia tries to explain her feelings to her brother. Summarize what she says.
5. Does Marcus agree with what her sister says? Why or why not?
6. Where did Servilia see Cordus and what was he doing?
7. Would an American girl typically admire a boy for doing what Cordus was doing?
8. How does Marcus know Cordus? What is his opinion of him?

Grammatica A

3rd Declension Adjectives

Latin has two major groups of adjectives:

1. 2-1-2 adjectives using endings of the 1st and 2nd declension, like:

   bonus, -a, -um   *līber, lībera, līberum*   *pulcher, pulchra, pulchrum*

2. 3rd declension adjectives using endings of the 3rd declension

   celer, celeris, celere   *fortis, forte*   *potens*

Third declension adjectives are declined like 3rd declension i-stem nouns with one exception. Try to spot it in the following chart, where we have put all the i-stem endings in **bold**. Locate the one place where the adjective differs from the pattern in the nouns.

	3RD DECLENSION			
	i-Stem Nouns		**Adjectives**	
Gender	Masc./Fem.	Neuter	Masc./Fem.	Neuter
		Singular		
Nominative	hostis	mare	fortis	forte
Genitive	hostis	maris	fortis	fortis
Dative	hostī	marī	fortī	fortī
Accusative	hostem	mare	fortem	forte
Ablative	hoste	marī	fortī/e	fortī
Vocative	hostis	mare	fortis	forte
		Plural		
Nominative	hostēs	mar**ia**	fortēs	fort**ia**
Genitive	host**ium**	mar**ium**	fort**ium**	fort**ium**
Dative	hostibus	maribus	fortibus	fortibus
Accusative	hostēs	mar**ia**	fortēs	fort**ia**
Ablative	hostibus	maribus	fortibus	fortibus
Vocative	hostēs	mar**ia**	fortēs	fort**ia**

Notā Bene:

i-Stem Similarities

- Genitive plurals end in *-ium*
- Neuter nominative and accusative plurals end in *-ia*
- **BUT** ablative singulars can end in *-ī* for all genders (not just neuter). Note that some authors use an *-e* ending here as well.
- The dative and ablative singular of 3rd declension adjectives are identical, but you have seen the same ending serve two cases before (e.g., all dative and ablative plurals), and you know that context and the endings of the nouns and adjectives can help you sort it out:

> *Ego et Cordus **fēminae potentī** appropinquāmus.*

The word *potentī* could be dative or ablative, but the ending on the 1st declension noun tells you that it must be dative.

The 3rd declension adjectives appear in your vocabularies and dictionaries in one of three ways. Note how each of the following would be listed in a dictionary:

celer, celeris, celere	adj.	swift, quick
fortis, forte	adj.	strong
potens, potentis	adj.	powerful

Types of 3rd Declension Adjectives

Celer is a **three termination adjective**, so named because it has three distinct endings in the nominative singular—masculine, feminine, and neuter. In adjectives like this, the masculine and feminine have identical endings everywhere **but** in the nominative singular. Remember that the stem of an adjective comes from dropping the ending from the nominative feminine singular: *celer* ➔ *celer-*. Thus:

> *Virum **celerem** videō.*
> *Fēminam **celerem** videō.*
> *Animal **celere** videō.*

Celer is the only three termination adjective you will learn right now.

Fortis, forte is a **two termination adjective**. In such words, the first form is masculine and feminine and the third form is neuter. You get the stem from the first form in such an instance: *fortis* ➔ *fort-*. Thus:

> *Virum **fortem** videō.*
> *Fēminam **fortem** videō.*
> *Animal **forte** videō.*

Potens, potentis is a **one termination adjective**. In this case, the first form listed in a dictionary is masculine, feminine, and neuter nominative singular. The second form is genitive singular and is used to determine the stem of the adjective: *potentis* ➔ *potent-*. Thus:

> *Virum **potentem** videō.*
> *Fēminam **potentem** videō.*
> *Animal **potens** videō.*

This sort of adjective can be a bit confusing if you do not remember the neuter rule that the neuter nominative = the neuter accusative. But context generally helps.

Gemma

The English word "bus" is a shortened, "clipped" form of the Latin word *omnibus* (for all people, for all things). So a bus was originally a vehicle to carry "everyone." In government, the word *omnibus* is used to refer to a law that covers a variety of issues.

Here are several common **two termination** 3rd declension adjectives. The ones marked in **bold** are *Verba Discenda* in this chapter.

crūdēlis, crūdēle cruel	*gravis, grave* heavy, serious
***difficilis, difficile* not easy, harsh, difficult**	*nōbilis, nōbile* dignified, noble
dulcis, dulce sweet	***omnis, omne* each, every (sing.); all (plural)**
facilis, facile easy	***tristis, triste* sad**

Common **one-termination** 3rd declension adjectives include the following:

dīves, dīvitis rich, wealthy   *fēlix, fēlīcis* happy, fortunate   ***intellegens, intellegentis* clever, smart**

EXERCEĀMUS!

15-2 3rd Declension Adjectives

Identify all the possible GNCs for each of the following 3rd declension adjective forms. Note: Some words have more than one possibility. This is an important exercise because as you read along in Latin, your brain often has to decide between such options on the fly. Follow the model. Then give the meanings.

	Adjective	Gender	Number	Case	Meaning
→	intellegens	MFN	singular	nominative (MFN) accusative (N)	intelligent

1. omnēs
2. difficilia
3. tristibus
4. nōbilium

Lectiō Secunda

Antequam Legis

As you continue reading the conversation between Marcus and Servilia about Cordus in *Lectiō Secunda*, consider the following features of 3rd declension adjectives.

GNC'ing and Agreement

Now that you have learned a bit about 3rd declension adjectives, pay attention in the next reading to their **GNC**, i.e., to their agreement in gender, number, and case, especially with nouns in the 1st and 2nd declensions. Consider the phrase *Servīlia miserābilis* (miserable Servilia) in line 1 of *Lectiō Secunda*. Note how the 3rd declension adjective *miserābilis* agrees with the 1st declension noun *Servīlia*. All 3rd declension adjectives are marked in **bold** in this *lectiō*.

Substantives

Also look in *Lectiō Secunda* for some of 3rd declension adjectives used as substantives, like *omnia* (all things, everything). These are **<u>bold and underlined</u>** in the *lectiā*

Adverbs

Finally, look for **adverbs** formed from 3rd declension adjectives marked in ***bold italics*** in this reading. HINT: They end in *-iter* or *-ter* as in *fortiter* (strongly) from *fortis*.

EXERCEĀMUS!

15-3 More on 3rd Declension Adjectives

As you read, create a list based on the one below that shows nouns modified by 3rd declension adjectives marked in **bold** in *Lectiō Secunda*. Follow the models.

Gemma

Notice the form *filiābus* in this reading. The Romans used this irregular dative (and ablative) plural form of *filia* to distinquish "daughter" from "son" in legal documents.

	Line	Noun/Adjective	GNC	Translation
→	1	Servīlia miserābilis	fem. nom. s.	miserable Servilia
→	1	frātrem māiōrem	masc. acc. s.	older brother

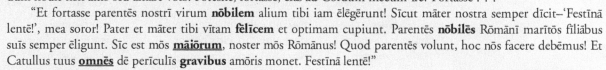

 CORDUS

Nunc Servīlia **miserābilis** frātrem **māiōrem** dē Cordō interrogat: "Et nōnne pater Cordī Naeviaeque vir **dīves potens**que est?"

"Vērē, dīcis," respondet Marcus. "Pater Augustī amīcus est et Cordus in domō imperātōris mox laborāre cupit. Quid Cordus tibi dīxit?"

5   Servīlia "Nōlī **nūgās** dīcere!" inquit. "Sōlum procul Cordum vīdī et audīvī. Cordum bene noscere cupiō sed hoc *faciliter* facere nōn possum!"

Frāter respondet: "Nōnne semper legis carmina poētae bonī et **intellegentis** Catullī? In carminibus Catullī multa verba apta dē amōre et **dulcī** et **trīstī** sunt! Sī Cordum nōn nōvistī, sī eum sōlum vīdistī, quōmodo eum amāre potes?"

10   "Sed Cordum noscere cupiō! Adulescens **fortis** et pulcher est! Fortasse Cordum hodiē nōn amō sed amāre volō! Potesne, fortasse, crās ad Cordum mēcum īre? Fortasse . . ."

"Et fortasse parentēs nostrī virum **nōbilem** alium tibi iam ēlēgērunt! Sīcut māter nostra semper dīcit–'Festīnā lentē!', mea soror! Pater et māter tibi vītam **fēlīcem** et optimam cupiunt. Parentēs **nōbilēs** Rōmānī marītōs filiābus suīs semper ēligunt. Sīc est mōs **māiōrum**, noster mōs Rōmānus! Quod parentēs volunt, hoc nōs facere debēmus! Et

15 Catullus tuus **omnēs** dē perīculīs **gravibus** amōris monet. Festīnā lentē!"

"Sed **difficile** est!" Servīlia clāmat *miserābiliter.*

Marcus **tristis** "Ita, vērō," inquit. "Sērius, post cēnam, patrī dē Cordō tuō dīcam. Crēde mihi, nōs **omnēs**—ego, māter, pater, Lūcius—vērē tē **fēlīcem** esse cupimus."

Lūcius, quī post iānuam stetit et **omnia** audīvit, "Sed ego," inquit, "ego cibum cupiō. Cēna parāta est. Eāmus

20 *celeriter!*"

Nōnne semper legis carmina Catullī?

 VERBA ŪTENDA

adulescens, -entis m./f. youth
amor, amōris m. love
aptus, -a, -um fit, suitable
carmen, carminis n. poem
celer, celeris, celere fast, swift
celeriter swiftly, quickly
crēdō, crēdere, crēdidī (+ dat.) believe, trust
dīcam "I will speak"
difficilis, difficile hard, difficult
dīves, dīvitis rich
dulcis, dulce sweet
eāmus "let's go!"
ēligō, ēligere, ēlēgī pick out, choose

faciliter easily
fēlix, fēlīcis happy
fortis, forte strong, brave
gravis, grave heavy, serious
hoc this
iānua, -ae f. door
intellegens, intellegentis smart, intelligent
interrogō (1) ask, question
ita so, thus; yes
legō, legere, lēgī, lectum gather, choose; read
lentē slowly
māior, māius greater, larger, older; m. pl. ancestors, elders
marītus, -ī m. husband
mēcum with me

miserābilis, miserābile miserable
miserābiliter miserably
mōs, mōris m. custom; pl. character; mōs māiōrum the custom of our ancestors.
nec and not; nec . . . nec . . . neither . . . nor . . .
nōbilis, nōbile notable, noble
nūgae, -ārum f. pl. trifle, nonsense
omnis, omne each, every; pl. all
optimus, -a, -um best
parātus, -a, -um ready, prepared

parens, parentis m./f. parent
perīculum -ī n. danger
potens, potentis powerful
princeps, -cipis m. head, leader, chief. One of Augustus' titles.
procul from far away
quī who
quod that which
quōmodo how
sērius later
tristis, triste sad
vērē truly
vērō indeed
vērus, -a, -um true

POSTQUAM LĒGISTĪ

Answer these questions in both Latin and English if the question is followed by (L). Otherwise, just respond in English.

1. What information do you learn about Cordus and his family in this *lectiō* (L)?
2. Why does Marcus tell Servilia about the poet Catullus?
3. Describe Servilia's relationship with Cordus at this point. Have the two met, spoken, etc.?
4. What do you learn about Roman customs regarding engagement and marriage in this reading? Who makes the decisions?
5. Why is Marcus sad in line 17? (L)
6. Where was Lucius and what does he want? (L)

Grammatica B

3rd Declension Adjectives: Agreement and Substantives

In previous chapters we have talked about adjective agreement (**GNC**), especially in terms of noun/adjective combinations in which the endings agree but are not the same. For example, *bonus puer, magnus poēta,* and *magna māter.* 3rd declension adjectives work the same way and create phrases like *fortis puer, celer poēta,* and *fēlix māter.* Here are some examples you saw in *Lectiō Secunda*:

*homō **dīves***	masculine nominative singular	"rich person"
(*dē*) *amōre **dulcī***	masculine ablative singular	"about sweet love"
nōbilēs *marītōs*	masculine accusative plural	"noble husbands"

Notice how GNC works in all these phrases.

Here is how *fortis, forte* works with 1st and 2nd declension nouns:

	1ST DECLENSION		2ND DECLENSION			
Gender	**Feminine**		**Masculine**		**Neuter**	
Singular						
Nominative	fēmina	fortis	discipulus	fortis	vīnum	forte
Genitive	fēminae	fortis	discipulī	fortis	vīnī	fortis
Dative	fēminae	fortī	discipulō	fortī	vīnō	fortī
Accusative	fēminam	fortem	discipulum	fortem	vīnum	forte
Ablative	fēminā	fortī	discipulō	fortī	vīnō	fortī
Vocative	fēmina	fortis	discipule	fortis	vīnum	forte
Plural						
Nominative	fēminae	fortēs	discipulī	fortēs	vīna	fortia
Genitive	fēminārum	fortium	discipulōrum	fortium	vīnōrum	fortium
Dative	fēminīs	fortibus	discipulīs	fortibus	vīnīs	fortibus
Accusative	fēminās	fortēs	discipulōs	fortēs	vīna	fortia
Ablative	fēminīs	fortibus	discipulīs	fortibus	vīnīs	fortibus
Vocative	fēminae	fortēs	discipulī	fortēs	vīna	fortia

Like 2-1-2 adjectives, 3rd declension adjectives can also serve as **substantives**. The two examples in the reading were *omnia* (all things, everything) and *māiōrum* (of those older, of elders, ancestors).

Here are some examples from *Lectiō Secunda*

*Catullus **omnēs** admonet.*	*omnēs* = all people, everyone
*Lūcius **omnia** audīvit.*	*omnia* = all things, everything

3rd Declension Adverbs

Most 3rd declension adjectives form adverbs by adding *-iter* or *-ter* to the stem. These adverbs are easy to recognize. You don't need to worry too much about when Latin adds *-iter* and when it adds *-ter*, but here are some simple guidelines:

- Most 3rd declension adjectives form adverbs with *-iter*; e.g., *facil**iter***
- Some 3rd declension adjectives add *-ter*; e.g., *audac**ter***
- If the stem already ends in *-t*, just add *-er*; e.g., *potent**er*** or *intellegent**er***

Here are some phrases from *Lectiō Secunda* with adverbs formed from 3rd declension adjectives:

*Hoc **faciliter** facere nōn possum.*	I cannot do this **easily**.
*Servīlia clāmat **miserābiliter**.*	Servilia shouts **miserably**.
*Eāmus **celeriter**!*	Let's go **quickly**!

EXERCEĀMUS!

15-4 3rd Declension Adverbs

Fill in the blanks to identify the stem of each adjective. Then form the adverb and indicate its meaning. Do the best you can, since the rules for forming these adverbs are fairly flexible. Follow the models.

Adjective	Stem	Adverb	Meaning
→ facilis, facile	facil-	facil**iter**	easi**ly**
→ intellegens, intellegentis	intellegent-	intellegent**er**	clever**ly**

1. fortis, forte

2. gravis, grave

3. potens, potentis

4. dulcis, dulce

5. celer, celeris, celere

Mōrēs Rōmānī

Mōs Māiōrum

Mōs māiōrum ("the custom of our ancestors") was the unwritten code of behavior by which Romans were taught to live. It emphasized tradition, respect for authority, both divine and civic, and obedience to one's elders. Good Romans were expected to place their own needs second to the needs of family and the state. They were expected to show *disciplīna* (an ordered life), *industria* (diligence) *frūgālitās* (economy), *gravitās* (seriousness), *officium* (a sense of obligation), and *virtūs* (manliness, excellence, virtue).

Above all, they were to have *pietās* (dutifulness) to their fathers (*patrēs*), to their *patria* (fatherland), and to their gods, especially to Jupiter, whose very name contains a root meaning "father" (*-piter*). A common example for *pietās* was Aeneas, the Trojan hero who escaped from burning Troy with his elderly father Anchises on his shoulders and with the household gods of Troy in Anchises' arms. He appears on the silver denarius depicted at right. This coin was issued by Julius Caesar from an African mint in 47–46 B.C. On the obverve is the image of the goddess Venus, Caesar's maternal ancestor. On the reverse is an image of Venus' son Aeneas with his father Archises.

Aenēās et Pater

VERBA ŪTENDA

abūtēre (+abl.) you will abuse
audācia, -ae f. daring
effrēnātus, -a, -um unbridled
ēlūdet will escape
etiam also, too, even now
finis, -is m. end
furor, -ōris m. fury, rage
iactābit will hurl, throw
iste, ista, istud that _____ of yours
patientia, -ae f. patience
quam diū for how long
quem ad finem to what end?
quōusque how long
tandem at last, at length, finally

Both Marcus and Servilia were raised on the *mōs māiōrum* and are aware of its obligations. For Servilia this means that she will have to accept the husband chosen for her by her father, even if she likes Cordus better.

The speech Servilia hears Cordus reciting as part of his rhetorical training is Cicero's first speech against Catiline (*In Catilīnam*). There were four of these speeches, which Cicero gave in the Senate in 63 B.C. while he was consul. Servilia's grandfather (whom you will meet later in the story) would have been in his prime during this period.

In these speeches Cicero describes the plot of Catiline and his followers to overthrow the Roman government. He begins the first speech against Catiline with a series of three blistering questions addressed directly to Catiline, who was present in the senate when this speech was given.

Pay attention to the verbs in the future tense (which are glossed in the *Verba Ūtenda*). We will learn the future in the next chapter.

> *Quōusque tandem abūtēre, Catilīna, patientiā nostrā? Quam diū etiam furor iste tuus nōs ēlūdet? Quem ad finem sē effrēnāta iactābit audācia?*

Cicero does not really expect Catiline to answer these questions. Rather he uses them for dramatic effect upon his audience. These kinds of questions are called **rhetorical questions** and must have produced quite a response in the senate house. Notice how the *furor* and *audācia* which Cicero associates with Catiline contrast with traditional Roman virtues.

This speech was well known and admired even in Cicero's lifetime and was long practiced by young men studying rhetoric.

Latīna Hodierna

Virtūtēs Rōmānae Hodiē

"Duty, Honor, Country" is the motto of the U.S. Military Academy at West Point. This motto also appears on the academy's coat of arms. In many ways these words celebrate the same ideals honored in the Roman concept of *mōs māiōrum*. Indeed, the Puritan virtues that were the foundational principles of American society were similar to Roman ones. Now look at these Roman virtues and the English derivatives. Notice how the meanings of the Latin words and of their English derivatives are not always the same.

LATIN WORD	ENGLISH MEANING	DERIVATIVES
virtūs, virtūtis f.	manliness, excellence, worth	virtue virtuous
disciplīna, -ae f.	training, education, an ordered life based upon such training	discipline disciplinary
frūgālitās, -tātis f.	economy	frugal frugality
gravitās, -tātis f.	weight, heaviness, seriousness, authority	grave gravity
industria, -ae f.	diligence, hard work	industry industrious
officium, -iī n.	duty, obligation, service, business	office officious officiousness
pietās, pietātis f.	dutifulness	piety pious

Orbis Terrārum Rōmānus

Ītalia Cicerōnis

For Cicero, home was Rome, and there was no place he would rather have been. When he served as governor of Cicilia (in modern Turkey) or when he was sent into exile, he was miserable and could not wait to return to the city. But Cicero had strong connections with several places outside the city:

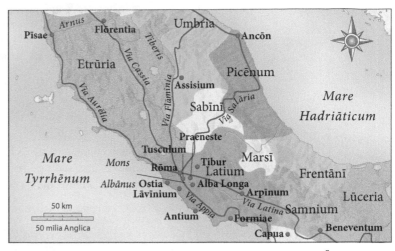

Ītalia Cicerōnis

Arpinum (*Arpīnum, -ī* n.; modern Arpino), his birthplace in the Alban Hills of Latium in central Italy. Arpinum was originally a Volscian and Samnite settlement, but its residents were granted Roman citizenship in 188 B.C. Cicero kept his family estate in Arpinum and visited it occasionally. The city also boasted as native sons C. Marius (Julius Caesar's uncle) and M. Vipsanius Agrippa (Augustus' advisor and son-in-law). You will meet Agrippa later in the narrative.

Tusculum (*Tusculum, -ī* n.), an ancient town of Latium. Tusculum accepted Roman control in 381 B.C, and its citizens were granted Roman suffrage in the same year. Marcus Porcius Cato (Cato the Elder) was born here in 234 B.C. The city was considered a health spa and was a popular place for wealthy Romans to own villas. Cicero owned a favorite villa here where he wrote a famous philosophical treatise called *Tusculānae Disputātiōnēs* (*Tusculan Disputations*).

Formiae (*Formiae, -iārum* f. pl.; modern Formia). Cicero owned a seaside villa in this popular resort town on the Appian Way in Latium. It was here that he was killed by Marc Antony's troops in 43 B.C. A structure called the tomb of Cicero is shown to tourists to this day.

Arpīnum

QUID PUTĀS?

1. What speeches in American history would be as famous as Cicero's speeches about Catiline were in ancient Rome? What lines can you recite from memory?
2. Give an example of a rhetorical question you might address to a friend.
3. How many of the traditional Roman virtues do you think are admired in modern American society? How many are actually followed?

EXERCEĀMUS!

15-5 Scrībāmus

Transform each of the following Latin sentences into questions by putting the verb at the beginning of the sentence and adding *-ne*. Then answer the question with either *sīc/ita* or *nōn* and a complete sentence. Follow the model.

→ Servīlia fēlix in cubiculō suō sedet.

   Quaestiō: Sedetne Servīlia fēlix in cubiculō suō?
   Responsum: Nōn, Servīlia nōn fēlix est.

1. Tristis Servīliae vīta est.
   Quaestiō:
   Responsum:

2. Cordus pater Marcī est.
   Quaestiō:
   Responsum:

3. Servīlia Cordum in domō suā vīdit.
   Quaestiō:
   Responsum:

4. Vōx Cordī crūdēlis fuit!
   Quaestiō:
   Responsum:

15-6 Colloquāmur

Now ask another member of your class one of the questions you made in Exercise 15-5. Your classmate will respond with an appropriate response from the same exercise. Follow the model.

→ Sedetne Servīlia fēlix in cubiculō suō?
   Nōn. Servīlia nōn fēlix est.

15-7 Verba Discenda Count Down!

Use the *Verba Discenda* to find the information required.

Decem. Find ten adjectives in this list.
Novem. Find nine 3ʳᵈ declension adjectives.
Octo. Find an additional English derivative for any eight different words on this list.
Septem. Find seven neuter nominative singular adjective forms.
Sex. Find six two-termination 3ʳᵈ declension adjectives.
Quinque. Find five nouns.
Quattuor. Find four 3ʳᵈ declension nouns.
Tria. Find three adjectives that could describe a hero.
Duo. Find two one-termination 3ʳᵈ declension adjectives.
Ūnum. Find one three-termination 3ʳᵈ declension adjective.

🔊 VERBA DISCENDA

adulescens, -entis m./f. youth [adolescent]

amor, amōris m. love [amorous]

celer, celeris, celere fast, swift [accelerate]

corpus, corporis n. body [incorporate]

cum when

difficilis, difficile hard, difficult [difficulty]

fortis, forte strong, brave [fortitude]

gravis, grave heavy, serious [gravity]

intellegens, intellegentis smart, intelligent [intelligentsia]

iuvenis, iuvenis m./f. youth [juvenile]

legō, legere, lēgī, lectum gather, choose; read [legible, lecture]

māior, māius greater, larger, older; m. pl. ancestors, elders [majority]

mōs, mōris m. custom; pl. character [mores]

nec and not; nec . . . nec . . . neither . . . nor . . .

nōbilis, nōbile notable, noble [nobility]

omnis, omne each, every; pl. all [omnipotent]

potens, potentis powerful [potential]

tristis, triste sad

vērē truly

vērus, -a, -um true [verify]

vox, vōcis f. voice [vocal]

Angulus Grammaticus

Much, Many, Each, and Every

Sometimes you will see dictionary entries like this:

> *multus,-a, -um* much; (pl.) many
> *omnis, omne* each, every; (pl.) all

This means that the word has one translation in the singular and another in the plural. So when you see these adjectives in a sentence you need to think a bit more before you translate them. Pay attention especially to the number of the noun, which determines how the adjective is translated. Here are some examples:

omnis puer	every boy	*omnēs puerī*	all (the) boys
multum vīnum	much wine	*multa vīna*	many wines

Notā Bene: In English derivatives, "mult(i)-" commonly means "many" and "omn(i)-" can mean "every" or "all." Here are some examples:

multidisciplinary "having many areas of study"
multiethnic "having many ethnic groups"
multifaceted "many-sided"
multilingual "having many languages"
multipolar "having many centers of power"
multivalent "having many meanings or values"

omnidirectional "moving in all directions" or "moving in every direction"
omnipotent "having all powers" or "having every power"
omnipresent "being present in all places" or "being present in every place"
omniscient "knowing all things" or "knowing everything"
omnivorous "eating all things" or "eating everything"

Photo Credits

page 180 (top) Dagli Orti (A); **page 187** American Numismatic Society/American Numismatic Society of New York; **page 189 (bottom)** Rupert Hansen/Alamy Images

In Cēnā

From *Disce! An Introductory Latin Course, volume 1*, First Edition. Francesco Bonavita. Copyright © 2011 by Pearson Education, Inc. Published by Pearson Prentice Hall. All rights reserv

Cēna Rōmāna

GRAMMATICA

The Future Tense

The Future of *Sum, Eō,* and Other Irregular Verbs

MŌRĒS RŌMĀNĪ

Rhetoric and Oratory

LATĪNA HODIERNA

Latin in the New World

ORBIS TERRĀRUM RŌMĀNUS

Latium

ANGULUS GRAMMATICUS

Reading Backward in Latin

LECTIŌNĒS:
IN TRĪCLĪNIŌ
and
PATER ET FĪLIA

At dinner the family discuss their day. The boys talk about school. Servilia tells her father about Cordus. Her father responds with some news his daughter does not want to hear.

192

16

In Cēnā

Lectiō Prīma

Antequam Legis

The family of Servilius is now sitting down for dinner and discussing their day. Lucius and Marcus both talk about events at school, and their father looks toward their future careers. As you read, pay attention to how the Romans ate their meals. It is rather different from our customs.

Looking Into the Future

In this chapter we introduce you to the **future tense**. It is easy to recognize, but like the present tense, the future tense of the 1st and 2nd conjugations is formed differently than the 3rd and 4th conjugations.

Future				
1st and 2nd Conjugations	Present Stem +		-bō	-bimus
			-bis	-bitis
			-bit	-bunt
3rd and 4th Conjugations	Short Present Stem +		-am	-ēmus
			-ēs	-ētis
			-et	-ent

Remember:	Present Stem	= 2nd principal part, drop *-re*
	Short Present Stem	= 1st principal part, drop *-ō*

Translate the future just like the English future, by using the helping verb "will."

216

EXERCEĀMUS!

16-1 **Future Tense**

We have put all the future tenses in *Lectiō Prīma* in **bold**. Before you read, make a list of these forms and use the preceding rule to indicate whether each is a 1st/2nd conjugation future or a 3rd/4th conjugation verb. Then identify the actual conjugation it is (you may have to check your vocabulary for this). Follow the models.

Line	Verb	Type	Conjugation
→ 4	portābunt	1st/2nd	1st
→ 6	scrībēs	3rd/4th	3rd

Gemma

Did you notice the Latin verb *exspectō* (1)? Despite the English "expect," the Latin spelling is correct. Latin tends to keep an "s" after an "x," where English drops it.

IN TRĪCLĪNIŌ

In trīclīniō tōta familia recumbit et cēnam exspectat. Servīlius et Marcus et Lūcius in lectīs recumbunt. Et Caecilia et Servīlia in sellīs sedent. (Fēminīs in lectīs recumbere nōn decet.) Mox aliī servī cibum vīnumque ad mensās **portābunt** et aliī post lectōs **stābunt** et familiam **adiuvābunt**.

Servīlius pōculum in mensā ponit.

5   Lūcius parentibus multum dē sīmiā nārrat et omnēs rīdent. Pater "Eugae, Lūcī!" inquit. "Fābulās bene nārrās. Fortasse, sīcut Horātius noster, fābulās aut saturās aliquandō **scrībēs** et, praeclārus poēta, fāmam et glōriam **capiēs!**" Caecilia rīdet et "Fīlius noster" inquit, "praeclārus iam est! Lucius tantum cibum quantum Herculēs dēvorat! Mox familia nullum cibum in culīnā **habēbit!**"

Marcus dē Valgiō Rufō rhētore suō dīcit et "Valgius Rufus," inquit, "nōbīs nimium labōris rursus hodiē dedit.
10   suāsōriam scrībere dēbuimus—*Caesar dēlīberat an Antōniō clēmentiam offerre necesse sit.* Heu mē! Difficile est bonam suāsōriam scrībere et nihil Valgiō placet! Ars rhētorica difficilis est! Crās rursus nimium labōris **habēbimus!**"

Servīlius pōculum in mensā ponit. Rīdet et "Marce," inquit, "labor strēnuus numquam nēminem necāvit. Scrībere ōrātiōnēs bonās difficile est, sed quoque necesse est! Mox ōrātiōnēs multās **habēbis**—et in Forō et in Senātū—et eō tempore disciplīna Valgiī tibi **placēbit**. Ōrātiōnēs bonae tē hominem fortūnātum atque praeclārum in
15   Senātū **facient**. Tunc tū et amīcī tuī Valgiō grātiās maximās **agētis!**"

VERBA ŪTENDA

adiuvō, adiuvāre, adiūvī,
* adiūtum* help
aliī servī . . . aliī some
  slaves . . . other
  (slaves)
aliquandō someday
an whether
ars, artis f. art, skill
atque and, and also
clēmentia, -ae f. mercy,
  clemency
decet it is fitting
dēlīberō (1) debate,
  deliberate
dēvorō (1) devour,
  consume

disciplīna, -ae f. instruction,
  knowledge
eugae! terrific! bravo!
exspectō (1) await, wait for
fortūnātus, -a, -um lucky,
  fortunate
Heu mē! Oh, my!
labor, labōris, m. work,
  labor
lectus, -ī m. dining couch
mensa, -ae f. table
multum a lot, much
necō (1) kill, slay
nimium too much
numquam never
offerō, offerre, obtulī offer

ōrātiō, ōrātiōnis f. speech
ōrātiōnem habēre to
  deliver a speech
parens, parentis m./f.
  parent
praeclārus, -a, -um very
  clear, famous, noble,
  excellent, beautiful
quantum See *tantum.*
recumbō, recumbere,
  recubuī recline, lie down
rhētor, rhētoris m.
  teacher of rhetoric
  (public speaking)
rhētoricus, -a, -um
  rhetorical

rursus again
satura, -ae f. satire
sella, -ae f. chair, seat
senātū senate (ablative
  sing.)
sit "might be"
strēnuus, -a, -um hard,
  strenuous
suāsōria, -ae f. persuasive
  speech
tantum . . . quantum as
  much . . . as
tōtus, -a, -um whole,
  entire
trīclīnium, -iī n. dining
  room

POSTQUAM LĒGISTĪ

Answer these questions in both Latin and English if the question is followed by (L). Otherwise, just respond in English.

1. List the Latin words that tell you what kinds of furniture the family uses to dine.
2. Who else is in the room, and what they are doing?
3. What does Lucius talk about? How do his parents respond? (L)
4. What does Marcus talk about? (L)
5. Why does Servilius laugh after Marcus finishes talking?
6. What plans does Servilius have for his two sons?
7. How does this family meal compare to a meal in your house?
8. Are there any rules for dining today that are based on gender, similar to those of Rome?

Grammatica A

The Future Tense

The future tense is quite regular in English. All we need to do is put "will" between pronoun and verb and we are in the future.

he will work   they will drive   it will happen

1st and 2nd Conjugation Future

To form the future: present stem (2nd principle part minus the *-re*) + *-bō, -bis, -bit, -bimus, -bitis, -bunt*.

FUTURE	
vocā**bō**	I **will** call
vocā**bis**	you **will** call
vocā**bit**	he/she/it **will** call
vocā**bimus**	we **will** call
vocā**bitis**	you **will** call
vocā**bunt**	they **will** call

Notā Bene:

- The future uses the same personal endings as the present in the 1st and 2nd conjugations: *-ō, -s, -t, -mus, -tis, -nt*.
- Note the vowel pattern before the personal endings in the future: (*ō, i, i, i, i, u*). You have already seen that pattern in the present tense of 3rd and 4th conjugation verbs.

3rd Conjugation Future

To form the future: short present stem (1st principal part minus the *-ō*) + *-am, -ēs, -et, -ēmus, -ētis, -ent*.

FUTURE	
scrībam	I **will** write
scrībēs	you **will** write
scrībet	he/she/it **will** write
scrībēmus	we **will** write
scrībētis	you **will** write
scrībent	they **will** write

3rd -io and 4th Conjugation Future

To form the future: short present stem (1st principal part minus the *-ō*) + *-am, -ēs, -et, -ēmus, -ētis, -ent.*

FUTURE			
capiam	I **will** seize	audiam	I **will** hear
capiēs	you **will** seize	audiēs	you **will** hear
capiet	he/she/it **will** seize	audiet	he/she/it **will** hear
capiēmus	we **will** seize	audiēmus	we **will** hear
capiētis	you **will** seize	audiētis	you **will** hear
capient	they **will** seize	audient	they **will** hear

Notā Bene:

- The 3rd *-io* future is formed exactly like the 4th conjugation future.
- Note the *-m* ending in the first person singular future and remember:

    MOST MUST ISN'T!

Possible Sources of Confusion

The *-e* in verb endings can be confusing. If you do not know that *vidēmus* comes from a 2nd conjugation verb, you might think that it is a 3rd conjugation future. So if you were to come upon a verb you did not know, as in a form like *merētis*, you would not know if it were from a 2nd conjugation verb *mereō, -ēre* or a 3rd conjugation verb *merō, -ere*. You might even guess it means "to earn" (which it does) but you would not know whether to translate it "you earn" or "you will earn."

The verb is, in fact, 2nd conjugation, once more showing the economy of Latin endings, but there is little confusion as long as you know the conjugation. So here is your new mantra: **When in doubt, look it up!**

EXERCEĀMUS!

16-2 **Present vs. Future**

Indicate whether each of the following verbs is present or future.

1. habent

2. habēbimus

3. dūcitis

4. dūcam

5. ambulābimus

6. ambulat

7. capiet

8. capīmus

9. vocābō

10. dīcent

Gemma

Iullus Antonius (45–2 B.C.), the son of Marc Antony and his third wife Fulvia, was raised by Octavia, Antony's fourth wife and sister of Octavius, the future Augustus. He later married his stepsister, the daughter of Octavia, and was eventually forced to commit suicide because of a scandalous affair with Julia, Augustus' daughter. His engagement to Servilia in our story is pure fiction.

Lectiō Secunda

Antequam Legis

Finally Servilia has an opportunity to tell her parents about Cordus but her father has some unexpected news for her. He has already chosen a husband for her and his name is Iullus Antonius.

Iullus Antonius

Iullus Antonius, the man chosen as Servilia's spouse by her father, is a historical figure, although we have taken certain liberties with the course of his life. He would have been just the sort of husband Servilius would seek for his daughter, since he was the son of Marc Antony and was connected closely by marriage with the family of Augustus. In fact, his story is indicative of the way marriages became political during this period.

The Future of *Sum* and *Eō*

In this *lectiō* you are introduced to the future forms of the irregular verbs *sum* and *eō*. The future of *sum* uses personal endings you are familiar with:

erō	I will be	*erimus*	we will be
eris	you will be	*eritis*	you will be
erit	he/she/it will be	*erunt*	they will be

Once you know this you also know the future of *possum*. If you remember that its stem is *pot-*, you will easily understand its future forms like *poterō* (*pot+erō*).

The future of *eō* is also easily recognized:

ībō	I will go	*ībimus*	we will go
ībis	you will go	*ībitis*	you will go
ībit	he/she/it will go	*ībunt*	they will go

Remember that *eō* is found in many compounds. So you should be on the lookout for forms like *adībis*.

The futures of all these verbs are marked in **bold** in the *lectiō*.

EXERCEĀMUS!

16-3 **Pre-Reading Questions**

These are questions to answer as you read this *lectiō* for the first time. If you keep these questions in mind, they will help you translate more quickly and accurately.

Line 9: What is the object of *nārrāvit*?

Line 13: What is the subject of *ambulābunt*?

Line 15: What word requires *parentibus* to be in the dative case?

Line 18: *Lēgī* can mean "I read" or "I chose." Which makes better sense here?

Line 21: To whom does *virō* refer?

🔊 PATER ET FĪLIA

Pater "Et tū, Servīlia," inquit. "Quid agit apud amīcam tuam Naeviam? Nōnne Fortūna Naeviae et familiae omnī favet?"

Servīlia "Omnis familia bene agit," inquit. "Nūper Naevia et māter adiērunt ad templum Fortūnae Prīmigeniae et familiam Praenestīnam
5 visitāvērunt. Hodiē mihi multa narrāvit dē templō praeclārō in monte et dē tessellātīs Nīlōticīs in templō. **Poterimusne** aliquandō illūc iter facere?"

Servīlius "Fortasse, fīlia," inquit. "mox cum matre **adībis**."

Tunc Servīlia parentibus omnia dē Cordō narrāvit. Diū dīxit et, tandem, "Crās, cum Marcō, rursus ad Naeviam **ībō**! Cordus et ego in hortōs
10 Maecēnātis **ībimus** et circumambulābimus. Nōlīte anxiī esse, mī parentēs, ancillae meae **aderunt** et nōbīscum ambulābunt!! Omnia salva **erunt**, pater, nam Marcus quoque nōbīscum **erit**."

Pater! Nōlī frontem contrahere!

Fīliae verba parentibus nūllō modō placent et diū Servīlius et Caecilia nihil dīcunt. Silentium tōtum trīclīnium tenet. Tandem pater, haud laetus, "Ecce mē, fīliola," inquit. "cum Cordō īre in hortōs Maecēnātis nōn **poteris**. Cum
15 Cordō nōn **ībis**. Rē vērā, cum Cordō numquam **eris**. Iam marītum tibi lēgī. Bonus vir est, dē familiā nōbilī, et mox apud Augustum labōrāre **poterit**."

Servīlia "Ēheu! Quid dīcis?" susurrāvit. "Sed quis marītus meus **erit**?"

"Nōmen," pater respondit, "virō Iullus Antōnius est et fīlius Marcī Antōniī et Fulviae est. Ego et Iullus Antōnius multa prō rē pūblicā efficere **poterimus**! Iam amīcī sumus, sed post nuptiās affīnēs **erimus**! Iullus Antōnius marītus
20 tuus **erit**. Mox **eris** mātrōna! Et fortasse nepōtēs **erunt**. . . ."

Pater multum magis dīcit sed fīlia nōn audit . . .

Intrā sē puella "Nōn," inquit "Iullī sed Cordī uxor **erō**! Sed, quōmodo **poterō**?"

🔊 VERBA ŪTENDA

adsum, adesse, affuī be present
affīnēs related by marriage
aliquandō sometime, some day
anxius, -a, -um uneasy, anxious
apud (+ acc.) at the house of, with, at _____'s
circumambulō (1) walk around
diū for a long time
ēheu! alas! oh no!
faveō, favēre, fāvī (+ dat.) favor
fīliola, -ae f. dear daughter

fortūna, -ae f. fortune, luck, chance
haud by no means
hortus, -ī m. garden
illūc (to) there
intrā sē to herself
Maecēnās, Maecēnātis m. G. Clinius Maecenas (70–8 B.C.)
magis more, rather
marītus, -ī m. husband
mātrōna, -ae f. married woman
mons, montis m. mountain
multum a lot, much

nepōs, nepōtis m. grandchild
Nīlōticus, -a, -um of the Nile (river)
nōbīscum with us
nūllus, -a, -um not any, non
nūper recently, not long ago
nūptiae, -ārum f. pl. marriage
parens, parentis m./f. parent
praeclārus, -a, -um very clear, famous, noble, excellent, beautiful
Praenestīnus, -a, -um of Praeneste, a town in Latium
prīmigenius, -a, -um original

quōmodo how
rēs pūblica, reī pūblicae f. republic
rē vērā in fact
rursus again
salvus, -a, -um alright, safe, well
silentium, -(i)ī n. silence
susurrō (1) whisper
tandem at last, finally
tessellāta, -ōrum n. mosaic
tōtus, -a, -um whole, entire
trīclīnium, -iī n. dining room
uxor, uxōris f. wife
vīsitō (1) visit

Gemma

Maecenas was a close adviser to Augustus, especially on cultural matters. He built the gardens Servilia mentions in the *lectiō* out of his wealth. He will die soon after the events described in this narrative, in 8 B.C.

POSTQUAM LĒGISTĪ

Answer these questions in both Latin and English if the question is followed by (L). Otherwise, just respond in English.

1. What trip did Naevia and her mother recently make? What did they see there? (L)
2. What does Servilia ask her parents about this trip? What is the answer? (L)
3. Why does Servilia think her parents are anxious about her plans to see Cordus? How does she try to reassure them? Would modern American parents have similar concerns?
4. Why is Servilius not happy? What news does he have for his daughter? How does he try to make her happier about this news? (L)
5. What does this conversation between Servilia and her parents tell you about the relationship between Roman parents and their daughters?
6. Why do you think Caecilia is not a more active participant in this conversation?

Grammatica B

The Future of *Sum, Eō*, and Other Irregular Verbs

Compare the present and future forms of *sum*:

SUM			
Present		**Future**	
sum	I am	*erō*	I will be
es	you are	*eris*	you will be
est	he/she/it is	*erit*	he/she/it will be
sumus	we are	*erimus*	we will be
estis	you are	*eritis*	you will be
sunt	they are	*erunt*	they will be

Once you know the future of *sum* you can make the future of compounds like *adsum* (I am present): *aderō* (I will be present). You can also use the future of *sum* to make the future of *possum*. Just add these forms to the stem *pot-*:

pot**erō**	I will be able	pot**erimus**	we will be able
pot**eris**	you will be able	pot**eritis**	you will be able
pot**erit**	he/she/it will be able	pot**erunt**	they will be able

The irregular verbs *volō, nōlō,* and *mālō* are quite regular in the future with 3rd conjugation future endings:

volam	nōlam	mālam
volēs	nōlēs	mālēs
volet	nōlet	mālet
volēmus	nōlēmus	mālēmus
volētis	nōlētis	mālētis
volent	nōlent	mālent

How would you translate these words?

The verb *eō, īre, īvī/iī* (go) is an exception. Although its infinitive shows that it is a 4th conjugation verb, it uses the 1st and 2nd conjugation *-bō, -bis* endings:

ībō	I will go	*ībimus*	we will go
ībis	you will go	*ībitis*	you will go
ībit	he/she/it will go	*ībunt*	they will go

EXERCEĀMUS!

16-4 Irregular Verb Review

Select the form of *sum, eō, volō, nōlō,* or *mālō* that best represents the underlined English words in the sentence. Be careful of tense!

_____   1. <u>I will be</u> there at 5 P.M.   A. abīmus
_____   2. Where <u>is he going</u>?   B. aderunt
_____   3. <u>Will he be able</u> to help us?   C. erō
_____   4. Trust me, <u>you will not want</u> to see that movie.   D. es
_____   5. Charlie? <u>He was</u> here, but he left.   E. fuit
_____   6. He scratched our car, but <u>we preferred</u> not to prosecute.   F. ībis
_____   7. <u>Will you be going</u> to see the new movie?   G. it
_____   8. <u>You are</u> so right!   H. māluimus
_____   9. Tell me, <u>will they be present</u> too?   I. nōn volēs
_____   10. <u>We will leave</u> at 6 A.M.   J. poterit

Mōrēs Rōmānī

Rhetoric and Oratory

The importance of public speaking in Roman society is illustrated by the impact of Cicero's speeches against Catiline, discussed in the previous chapter. Young Roman men from prominent or ambitious families were expected to follow their study of literature under a *grammaticus* with an intense rhetorical education under a *rhētor*. This education consisted of declamation and practice in public speaking, such as Cordus' recitation of Cicero that Servilia overhears, as well as speech writing. In *Lectiō Prīma* Marcus refers to these written exercises, which are often called either *suāsōriae* (persuasive speeches) or *contrōversiae* (fictional law cases and legal arguments). Following his time with the *rhētor*, a young man from a wealthy family might go off to southern Italy or Greece to study under a master rhetorician or philosopher. Marcus is about to make such a journey.

Marcus' rhetoric teacher, Valgius Rufus, is based on a real person of that name. A close friend of Horace, Augustus, and his "minister of culture" Maecenas, Rufus wrote poetry but also may have written some works on rhetoric. We have made him a *rhētor* for the sake of the plot.

Rufus asks Marcus to write a *suāsōria* addressed to Julius Caesar on the necessity of clemency. This sort of historical topic was very popular in Greek and Roman rhetorical schools. Some examples of both *suāsōriae* and *contrōversiae* survive in the works of that name by the Spaniard Seneca the Elder (54 B.C.–39 A.D.). Here are some topics for *suāsōriae* mentioned by Seneca. (We have simplified the Latin for you. The *Verba Ūtenda* will also help.)

> *Dēliberat Alexander an Ōceanum nāviget.*
> *Trēcentī Laconēs contrā Xerxen missī dēliberant an fugiant.*
> *Dēliberat Agamemnōn an Īphigenīam immolet.*
> *Dēliberat Cicerō an Antōnium dēprecētur.*

Such themes from mythology, Greek history, and current Roman events were very popular in schools of rhetoric.

🔊 **VERBA ŪTENDA**

Agamemnōn, -nonis m. Agamemnon, king of Mycenae; note the Greek nom. sing.
Alexander, -ī m. Alexander (the Great), king of Macedonia
an whether
contrā (+ acc.) against
dēlīberō (1) deliberate, debate
dēprecētur (+ dat.) "he should seek pardon from"
fugiant "they should flee"
immolet "he should sacrifice"
Īphigenīa, -ae f. Iphigenia, daughter of Agamemnon
Lacō, Laconis m. Laconian, Spartan
missus, -a, -um sent
nāviget "he should sail"
trēcentī 300
Xerxen Xerxes, king of Persia; note the Greek acc. sing.

Latīna Hodierna

Latin in the New World

We can never understimate the lasting influence of Latin. When the Spaniards came to the New World, they brought with them the Latin language and Roman culture, Here, for example, is some advice on table manners written in the margin of a text of Ovid's *Tristia* published in Mexico in 1577. You might imagine Caecilia giving her sons much the same advice as they sit down to the family's evening meal. (We have simplified and shortened the passage.)

Beginning in line 3, each line contains an imperative. Can you find the verb in the future tense?

Ad Iuventūtem

> Nēmō quī haec documenta spernit, cibum capiet:
> Dum mensae accumbitis:
> Vultum hilarem habē!
> Sāl cultellō cape!
> 5 Rixās et murmur fuge!
> Membrīs rectīs sedē.
> Mappam mundam tenē.
> Nōlī scalpere!
> Aliīs partem oblatōrum da!
> 10 Modicum (sī crēbrō) bibe
> Grātiās deō semper age!

🔊 VERBA ŪTENDA

accumbō, accumbere, accubuī
(+ dat.) recline at table
aliīs to others
crēbrō frequently
cultellus, -ī m. knife
documentum, -ī n. instruction, warning
fuge! avoid!
Grātiās age! "Give thanks!"
haec these
hilaris, hilare cheerful
iuventūs, -tūtis f. youth

mappa, -ae f.
table napkin
membrum, -ī n. limbs
(arms and legs)
modicum moderately
mundus, -a, -um clean
murmur, murmuris
n. whispering,
murmuring
oblāta, -ōrum n. pl. "that
which has been served"
pars, partis f. part, piece

quī who
quid what
rectus, -a, -um straight
rixa, -ae f. violent
quarrel
sāl, salis m./n. salt
scalpō, scalpere
scratch
spernō, spernere, sprēvī
reject, scorn
vultum m. face

Orbis Terrārum Rōmānus

Latium

The region around Rome was called Latium (*Latium, -ī* n., modern Lazio), i.e., the land of the Latins or the Latin-speaking people. Originally the region consisted of a number of independent towns that organized in the seventh century B.C. into the Latin League, under the leadership of the town of Alba Longa. Rome was not originally part of this league, which was

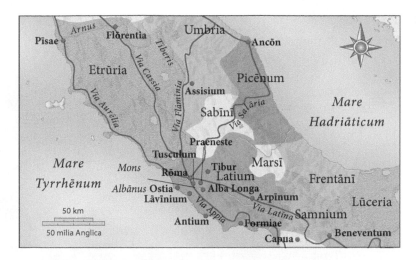

Latium Antīquum

intended as a defensive coalition against powerful Etruscan cities in Etruria and other non-Latin peoples. It took Rome several centuries to bring Latium fully under its control, and in 90 B.C., by the *Lex Iulia*, all the Latin peoples gained full Roman citizenship.

The towns of Arpinum, Tusculum, and Formiae described in the last chapter are all in Latium. Another prominent town is Praeneste (modern Palestrina), located about 23 miles east of Rome. In the imperial period, Praeneste became a fashionable resort town and was especially known for its oracle and imposing temple of *Fortūna Prīmigenia* (Original Fortune) which Servilia's friend Naevia and her mother recently visited.

Tessellāta Nīlōtica Praenestīna

Picture Desk, Inc./Kobal Collection/Dagli Orti (A)

Praeneste hodiē

QUID PUTĀS?

1. If *suāsōriae* and *contrōversiae* were written today what might some of the topics be?
2. What does the career of Iullus Antonius tell you about this period in Roman history? Can you compare his career to that of any famous Americans?
3. How do the table manners described in the poem from Mexico compare to the manners you were taught as a child?
4. How would you describe Rome's relationship with the cities of Latium?

EXERCEĀMUS!

16-5 Scrībāmus

To practice your new knowledge of the future of regular and irregular verbs, we return to the story of Valeria and the thieves from Chapter 11. Replace all the words marked in **bold** with appropriate future forms. Follow the model.

→ Licinia et Valeria ab Iūnōne deā beneficia **petent** . . .

Licinia et Valeria ab Iūnōne deā beneficia **petīvērunt** et grātiās maximās astrologō **ēgērunt**. Fēminae laetae **fuērunt** propter verba bona dē īnfante. Flāvia quoque laeta **fuit** quod nunc īnsula nōn longinqua est. Flāvia fessa **fuit** quod saccum (et Sōcratem!) longē per viās portāre dēbuit. Et Sōcratēs laetus **fuit** quod iēiūnus est et cibus domī **fuit**.

Subitō trēs latrōnēs ex angiportō **saluērunt**. Saccum rapere **voluērunt** et fēminae perterritae **fuērunt**. Fēminae fortiter **clāmāvērunt**.

Aelius vōcēs in viā **audīvit**. Fēminās in angustiīs **vīdit** et in latrōnēs magnā cum īrā **cucurrit**. Malleum magnum **tenuit**. Latrōnēs et malleum et musculōs Aeliī **vīdērunt**. Aelium pugnāre **nōluērunt**. Aeliō concēdere **māluērunt** et celeriter sine saccō **fūgērunt**.

16-6   Colloquāmur

Now use the narrative in Exercise 16-5 to ask and answer questions with a classmate using perfect or future tense verbs randomly. See how many answers you can make, using interrogative words like *-ne, quid, quis,* etc. Follow the models.

Based on line 1, you could ask

→ *Quid Licinia et Valeria ab Iūnōne deā petivērunt?*
→ *Quid Licinia et Valeria ab Iūnōne deā petent?*

The appropriate responses would be

→ *Licinia et Valeria ab Iūnōne deā beneficia petivērunt.*
→ *Licinia et Valeria ab Iūnōne deā beneficia petent.*

16-7   Verba Discenda

Use the *Verba Discenda* to find the following:

1. the 3rd principal part of *exspectō*

2. a preposition that takes the accusative

3. a 2nd declension noun

4. the feminine equivalent of *praeclārus*

5. a 3rd declension noun that is both masculine and feminine

6. an interjection

7. the genitive singular of *labor*

8. a 1st declension noun

🔊 VERBA DISCENDA

adiuvō, adiuvāre, adiūvī,
  adiūtum **help**
  [adjutant]
apud **(+ acc.) at the**
  house of, with,
  at _____'s
ars, artis **f. art, skill**
  [artistic]
diū **for a long time**
ēheu! **alas! oh no!**
exspectō **(1) await, wait**
  for [expectation]

haud **by no means**
labor, labōris
  m. work, labor [laborious]
magis **more, rather**
  [magiscule]
marītus, -ī **m. husband**
  [marital]
mensa, -ae **f. table**
multum **a lot, much**
nimium **too much**
ōrātiō, ōrātiōnis
  f. speech [oration]

parens, parentis **m./f.**
  parent [parental]
praeclārus, -a, -um **very**
  clear, famous, noble,
  excellent, beautiful
rhētor, rhētoris **m.**
  teacher of rhetoric
  (public speaking)
  [rhetorician]
rhētoricus, -a, -um
  rhetorical
rursus **again**

Angulus Grammaticus

Reading Backward in Latin

When you learn Latin, you are, in a way, rewiring your brain to process word elements in an order that is the reverse of English.

In English we have phrases like: "she will work" and "we will have." The pronoun comes first, then the "will," which tells us the tense we are dealing with, and finally, we get to the sense of the verb.

Pronoun	Tense	Meaning
she	will	work

But where is it written that this is the only way a language can work? The Latin verb reads from front to back. For example,

Verb Meaning	Tense	Pronoun
labōrā	*bi*	*t*
work	will	he/she/it
habē	*bi*	*mus*
have	will	we
disc	*ē*	*tis*
learn	will	you

This is true not just for the future but for other verb tenses as well. Here are some examples from the perfect:

labōrāv	*it*
worked	he/she/it
habu	*imus*
had	we
didic	*istis*
learned	you

So the Latin verbs are rather like Yoda-speak. Just don't translate this way!

Photo Credits

page 192 (top) ANCIENT ART & ARCHITECTURE/© ANCIENT ART & ARCHITECTURE/Danita Delimont.com; **page 201 (bottom)** Dagli Orti (A); **page 202** Hunter Nielson/Photo by Hunter Nielson used with permission

17

Dē Amōre et Lūdīs

Lesbia Passerque

Lectiō Prīma

Antequam Legis

This *lectiō* shows us a distraught Servilia in her room, consoling herself with her pet sparrow named Lesbia.

Present Participles

In this chapter you are introduced to a new verb form called the **participle**. A participle is a **verbal adjective**. In English we make present participles by adding **-ing** to a verb. So "work" becomes "working." In the sentences

The man **working** in the kitchen is old.   I saw the man **working**.

the word "working" is a participle describing the man. Here are the same sentences in Latin:

*Vir **labōrāns** in culīnā senex est.*   *Virum **labōrantem** vīdī.*

For now, as you read, do the following:

- Translate any participle (in **bold**) with the verb form ending in "-ing."
- Watch for the case endings and just translate them accordingly.
- Ask who is performing the action of the participle, i.e., "who is —ing?"

All the participles are marked in **bold** in the *lectiō*.

EXERCEĀMUS!

17-1 **Participles**

Find the words that ten participles marked in **bold** in the *lectiō* modify (GNC). With the help of this word and what you already know about case endings, identify the case and number of each participle. Then translate the word together with its participle. Follow the model.

Line	Participle	Word	Case	Number	English Translation
→ 1	lacrimāns	Servīlia	nom.	sing.	Servīlia

GRAMMATICA
Forming the Present Participle
Using Participles
Special Adjectives: UNUS NAUTA
Is, Ea, Id
Demonstrative Pronouns and Adjectives

MŌRĒS RŌMĀNĪ
Roman Attitudes Toward Animals

LATĪNA HODIERNA
Opposites in Latin and English

ORBIS TERRĀRUM RŌMĀNUS
Prōvinciae Āfricānae

ANGULUS GRAMMATICUS
Gender

LECTIŌNĒS:
SERVĪLIA MAESTA
and
DĒ MŪNERIBUS
After a difficult conversation with her parents, Servilia consoles herself by petting Lesbia, her pet sparrow. Meanwhile her brothers look forward to tomorrow's games in the amphitheater.

205

From *Disce! An Introductory Latin Course, volume 1*, First Edition. Francesco Bonavita. Copyright © 2011 by Pearson Education, Inc. Published by Pearson Prentice Hall. All rights reserved.

SERVĪLIA MAESTA

Post cēnam Servīlia sōla in cubiculō **lacrimāns** sedet. Puella, sōlāciolum suī dolōris **petēns**, passerem **sedentem** in gremiō tenet. Passer lūdit et puella tristis lacrimat. Nōmen passerī Lesbia est. Lesbia praeclāra est quod poēta Catullus
5 eam amāvit et, sīcut omnēs poetae **amantēs**, dē eā multa carmina amātōria scrīpsit. Lesbia quoque passerem habuit et Catullus carmen fāmōsum dē morte illīus passeris scrīpsit. Omnēs amantēs carmina Catullī legere dēbent!

Servīlia, hoc carmen in mente **habēns**, passerī
10 **pīpiantī** plōrāvit: "Quid facere necesse est, dēliciae meae? Quōmodo vītam meam dūcam cum hōc virō ignōtō? Iullus Antonius vetus est! Plūs quam trīgintā quinque annōs nātus est! In domō istīus senis numquam habitābō! Cor meum virō senī numquam dabō! Cor meum Naeviō adulescentī iam dedī! Nūllī aliī virō cor numquam meum dabō. Fortasse neutrī cor meum dabō et neuter mē in mātrimōnium dūcet! Fortasse ego **habitāns** sōla numquam nūbam!
15 "Ōh, quid facere necesse est, dēliciae meae? Nōn istum Iullum nōvī! Iullum in viā **ambulantem** numquam vīdī! Numquam vōcem Iullī **dīcentis** audīvī. Vae mē! Nōlō tālem ignōtum nūbere. Cordum nūbere volō! Eum in peristyliō **ambulantem** vīdī! Vōcem Cordī **dīcentis** audīvī. Cūr pater illī ignōtō mē dat? Cūr parentēs meī Cordum **ignōrantēs** mē nōn auscultant? Nōn Iullum sed alterum amō! Vae mē! Tōta vīta mea miserābilis erit."

Passer **circumsiliēns** et **pīpiāns** nihil puellae **lacrimantī** dīcit. Servīlia passerī prīmum digitum dat et avis digi-
20 tum puellae **lacrimantis** rostrō mordet. Avis sīc cūrās tristēs puellae levat. Servīlia, etiam misera, rīdet per lacrimās **cadentēs** et "Passer," inquit puella, "amīcus meus fidēlis es."

Puella passerem in gremiō tenet.

VERBA ŪTENDA

alter, altera, alterum the other (of two)
amātōrius, -a -um amatory, love
auscultō (1) listen to
avis, avis f. bird
cadō, cadere, cecidī fall
carmen, carminis n. song, poem
circumsiliō, circumsilīre, circumsiluī leap around, hop
cor, cordis n. heart
cūra, -ae f. care, concern
dēliciae, -ārum f. pl. delight, pet
digitus, -ī m. finger (see *prīmum*)

dolor, dolōris n. pain, grief; *suī dolōris* is gen., but translate "for her sorrow."
dūcere in mātrimōnium marry
etiam still, and also, even now
fidēlis, -e faithful
gremium, -iī n. lap
hoc/hōc this
ignōrō (1) be ignorant of
ignōtus, -a, -um unknown
ille, illa, illud he, she, it; they; that, those; *illīus* of that; *illī* to that
is, ea, id he, she, it; they
iste, ista, istud that one (derogatory); *istīus* of that

lacrimō (1) cry, shed tears
levō (1) lift, lighten
maestus, -a, -um sad
mens, mentis f. mind
miser, misera, miserum wretched, miserable
miserābilis, -e miserable
mordeō, mordēre, momordī bite
neuter, neutra, neutrum neither; *neutrī* "to neither"
nūbō, nūbere, nupsī marry
nūllus, -a, -um no, not any, none; *nūllī aliī* to no other
numquam never
ōh oh! (used to express surprise, joy, pain, etc.)

passer, passeris m. sparrow
petō, petere, petīvī/petiī seek, look for
pīpiō (1) chirp
plōrō (1) weep, cry
plūs more
prīmum digitum the tip of her finger
quōmodo how
rostrum, -ī n. beak
senex, senis m. old man
sōlāciolum, -ī n. relief, comfort
tālis, -e such
tōtus, -a, -um whole, all
trīgintā thirty
vae woe! (in pain or dread)
vetus, veteris old

POSTQUAM LĒGISTĪ

Answer in English or Latin (L) as directed.

1. (L) Where and when does *Lectiō Prīma* take place?
2. (L) What is Servilia doing as the *lectiō* begins?
3. What is the name of Servilia's pet bird? Why does it have this name?
4. Why is Servilia upset?
5. How do Servilia's situation and feelings compare to those of a modern American teenage girl in similar circumstances?
6. Why does Servilia laugh at the end of the *lectiō*?

Grammatica A

Forming the Present Participle

As verbal adjectives, participles have grammatical features of both parts of speech.

- **As verbs,** they express actions, can take objects, and have tense and voice.
- **As adjectives**, they agree with nouns in gender, number, and case (GNC).

The participles you are learning right now are **present** tense and are translated by adding -ing to the verb; e.g., *vōcans* (calling). There are also participles in other tenses you will learn later.

Here are the complete forms of the present active participle *vocāns*:

SINGULAR		CASE	PLURAL	
Masculine/ Feminine	**Neuter**		**Masculine/ Feminine**	**Neuter**
vocāns	vocāns	Nominative	vocantēs	vocantia
vocantis	vocantis	Genitive	vocantium	vocantium
vocantī	vocantī	Dative	vocantibus	vocantibus
vocantem	vocāns	Accusative	vocantēs	vocantia
vocantī / vocante	vocantī / vocante	Ablative	vocantibus	vocantibus

Reminder: The neuter differs from the masculine/feminine forms in only a few places. Find them.

Notā Bene:

- Present participles generally use the same endings as 3rd declension adjectives.
- The ablative singular normally ends in -*ntī*. You will learn later when the -*nte* ending is used.

Forming participles from other conjugations is just a matter of getting the connecting vowel(s) right:

1st Conjugation	2nd Conjugation	3rd Conjugation	3rd -*iō* Conjugation	4th Conjugation
vocāns	*habēns*	*dūcēns*	*capiēns*	*audiēns*
calling	having	leading	taking	hearing

While you were doing Exercise 17-1, you probably noticed that most of the participles were marked by -*ēns*/-*ent*-. The -*e*- is of limited help in determining the conjugation of the participle. The only sure way to confirm the conjugation is to look up the verb in a dictionary.

EXERCEĀMUS!

17-2 Identifying Participles

Use the declension of *vocāns* to identify the correct case and number of each of the following participles.

1. dūcentis: a. genitive singular; b. genitive plural; c. accusative plural; d. ablative plural

2. audientem: a. nominative singular; b. genitive singular; c. dative singular; d. accusative singular

3. capientēs: a. accusative singular; b. genitive plural; c. nominative plural; d. ablative plural

4. habentibus: a. nominative singular; b. genitive plural; c. accusative plural; d. dative plural

5. ambulantium: a. ablative plural; b. accusative singular; c. genitive plural; d. nominative singular

6. dūcentī: a. accusative singular; b. ablative singular; c. nominative singular; d. genitive singular

7. audiēns: a. nominative singular; b. nominative plural; c. ablative singular; d. genitive singular

8. capientibus: a. accusative singular; b. genitive plural; c. nominative plural; d. ablative plural

Using Participles

Participles as Substantives

As adjectives, participles describe people and things and therefore have gender, number, and case. So, as you noticed when you did Exercise 17-1, whenever you see a participle in a Latin sentence you must ask yourself what this participle is describing or modifying.

Sometimes, however, participles have no noun to describe but are **substantives**, i.e., they are adjectives acting like nouns.

Here is an example of a participle used as a substantive, from *Lectiō Prīma:*

> Omnēs **amantēs** carmina Catullī legere dēbent.
> All those loving ought to read the poems of Catullus.
> All people loving ought to read the poems of Catullus.
> All people who are in love ought to read the poems of Catullus.
> All lovers ought to read the poems of Catullus.

Notice how many ways we can translate **amantēs** into English to show that it is plural. Here are a few more examples based on sentences from *Lectiō Prīma.*

Post cēnam in cubiculō **lacrimāns** sedet.	**lacrimāns** = the person crying
Post cēnam sōla in cubiculō **lacrimāns** sedet.	**lacrimāns** = the crying girl
In vīā **ambulantem** numquam vīdī.	**ambulantem** = a person walking
In vīā **ambulantēs** numquam vīdī.	**ambulantēs** = people walking

How many other ways can you translate these participles into English?

Relative Time in Participles

The tense of a participle does not show real time, but relative time. This means that the participle has no time of its own but rather shows a relationship with the time of the main verb. This takes some consideration to understand, and you will learn a lot more about relative time as you continue your study of Latin. The **present participle** indicates that the "time" of the participle is the **same time as the main verb**.

Compare these sentences:

Servīliam lacrimantem videō.	I see Servilia crying.
Servīliam lacrimantem vīdī.	I saw Servilia crying.
Servīliam lacrimantem vidēbō.	I will see Servilia crying.

In each case, the present participle indicates that the crying is, was, or will be simultaneous with the main verb.

EXERCEĀMUS!

17-3 Translating Participles

Translate these sentences, which show various cases of the participle. Three are substantives. The participles are underlined.

1. Passer puellae <u>lacrimantis</u> in gremiō sedet.
2. Nōmen <u>lacrimantī</u> Servīlia est.
3. Marcus sorōrem <u>lacrimantem</u> valdē amat.
4. Cor <u>amantis</u> saepe triste est.
5. Catullus <u>amantēs</u> bene intellegit.

Lectiō Secunda

Antequam Legis

In this *lectiō* Marcus and Lucius talk about the upcoming gladiatorial games. As you read about these games, watch for examples of a special group of adjectives and pronouns.

-īus/-ī Adjectives

Consider the following sentences from *Lectiō Prīma:*

> *In domō **istīus** senis numquam habitābō!* (line 12)
> ***Nūllī aliī** virō cor umquam meum dabō!* (line 13)
> *Fortasse **neutrī** cor meum dabō.* (line 13)

These words marked in bold are part of a group of adjectives and pronouns that have normal 2-1-2 adjective endings, **except in two places**:

- m./f./n. gen. sing. *-īus*   *nūllīus, neutrīus, istīus, alīus*
- m./f./n. dative sing. *-ī*   *nūllī, neutrī, istī, aliī*

You should have no trouble translating these words, once you recognize their special genitive and dative singular endings. Watch for more of these words in *Lectiō Secunda*, where they are marked in **bold**.

EXERCEĀMUS!

17-4 *-īus/-ī* Adjectives

Find ten *-ius/-ī* adjectives marked in **bold** in *Lectiō Secunda*. List the number, case, and meaning of each word. Remember that *-ius* is genitive singular and *-ī* is dative singular. Follow the models.

	Line	*-ius/-ī* Adjective	Number	Case	Meaning
→	1	aliā	sing.	abl.	other
→	2	ipse	sing.	nom.	himself

DĒ MŪNERIBUS

Sedentēs in **aliā** parte domī Servīlius, Marcus et Lūcius dē mūneribus dīcunt. Crās Imperātor Augustus **ipse** magna mūnera in amphitheātrō dabit.

"Marce et Lūcī, spectābitisne mūnera?" Servīlius rogat.

5 "Certē, pater," respondet Marcus. "Haec mūnera magnifica erunt! Sed quid vidēbimus in amphitheātrō sedentēs?"

"Vidēbitis," respondet pater, "gladiātōrēs cum **aliīs** gladiātōribus pugnantēs. **Aliī** gladiīs pugnābunt, **aliī** tridentibus et rētibus. In **ūnā** pugnā duō gladiātōrēs pugnābunt—**ūnus** gladiō et **alter** tridente 10 pugnābit. Fortasse **neuter** vīvus ex amphitheātrō exībit."

Lūcius rogat: "Eruntne animālia in mūneribus? Quālia animālia?"

Pater "Sīc, fīlī," inquit. "**Nōnnūllī** gladiātōrēs et multī damnātī cum animālibus exōticīs **tōtīus** Āfricae pugnābunt. Vidēbitis leōnēs et panthērās et elephantēs. Et harēnam cruentam quoque vidēbitis—cruōrem et 15 animālium et hominum!"

"Euax! Quandō," poscit Lūcius, "ad amphitheātrum ībimus?"

"Māne," respondet **alter** frāter, "īre dēbēbimus, sī **ulla** animālia vidēre poterimus. Multī māne surgentēs ad amphitheātrum venient et **illī** advenientēs māne optimum prospectum habēbunt." Sed tū, pater, ībisne nōbīscum?"

Servīlius "Nōn vōbīscum," inquit, "īre possum. Crās **nūlla** mūnera vidēbō quod multa negōtia mihi erunt. Sed 20 **illa** mūnera nōn **ūnīus** diēī sed trium diērum sunt et fortasse sērius ea vidēbō.

Leō ferox damnātum in harēnā interficit.

VERBA ŪTENDA

Āfrica, -ae f. the Roman province of Africa (modern Tunisia and Algeria)
aliī . . . aliī some . . . others . . .
alter, altera, alterum the other (of two)
amphitheātrum, -ī n. amphitheater
animal, -ālis n. animal
certē certainly
cruentus, -a, -um bloody
cruor, cruōris m. gore, blood
damnātus condemned criminal
diēs, diēī m. day

ea them
elephās, -antis m. elephant
euax! hurray!
exōticus, -a, -um strange, exotic
ferox, ferōcis, fierce
gladiātor, -ōris m. gladiator
gladius, -iī m. sword
haec these
harēna, -ae f. sand
ille, illa, illud he, she, it; they; that, those
imperātor, -tōris m. emperor
ipse, ipsa, ipsum he, she, it; they; himself, herself,

itself, themselves (emphatic)
is, ea, id he, she, it, they
leō, leōnis m. lion
magnificus, -a, -um noble, elegant, magnificent
mūnus, -eris, n. function, duty; gift; pl. games, public shows, spectacles
neuter, neutra, neutrum neither
nōbīscum with us
nōnnūllī some, several
nūllus, -a, -um no, not any, none
optimus, -a, -um best

panthēra, -ae f. leopard
pars, partis f. part, piece
prospectum m. view
pugna, -ae f. fight
quālis, quāle? what kind of? what sort of?
quandō when
rēte, rētis n. net
sērius later, too late
surgō, surgere, surrēxī rise, get up
tōtus, -a, -um whole, all
tridens, tridentis m. trident
ūllus, -a, -um any
vīvus, -a, -um living
vōbīs dat./abl. you (all);
vōbīscum "with you"

POSTQUAM LĒGISTĪ

Answer in English or Latin (L) as directed.

1. What characters are holding a conversation in *Lectiō Secunda*? Where are they?
2. What kinds of gladiatorial contests are mentioned in this conversation?

3. When will these gladiatorial contests take place? Who is sponsoring them?
4. (L) Answer Lucius' questions in lines 11-12: *Eruntne animālia in mūneribus? Quālia animālia?*
5. At what other times in European or American history have condemned criminals been a source of sport or entertainment for the general public?
6. (L) Why is Servilius unable to go to these games?
7. How does this form of entertainment compare to those in the United States today?

Grammatica B

Special Adjectives: UNUS NAUTA

A number of Latin 2-1-2 adjectives have *-īus* genitive singular endings and *-ī* dative singular endings. The phrase UNUS NAUTA forms an acronym to help you remember most of these words.

> *Ūllus, -a, -um* any
> *Nūllus, -a, -um* no, none
> *Ūnus, -a, -um* one
> *Sōlus, -a, -um* alone, only
>
> *Neuter, neutra, neutrum* neither
> *Alter, altera, alterum* the other (of two)
> *Uter, utra, utrum* either, which (of two)
> *Tōtus, -a, -um* whole, entire
> *Alius, -a, -ud* another, other

Notā Bene:

- Most of these adjectives have masculine singulars ending in *-us*, but *uter* and *neuter* have *-er* endings and have stems like *pulcher, pulchra, pulchrum; alter* has a stem like *līber, lībera, līberum.*
- The rest of the endings for these words are regular.

Here is the full declension of *sōlus* with the unusual endings in **bold**.

	SINGULAR		CASE	PLURAL		
Masculine	**Feminine**	**Neuter**		**Masculine**	**Feminine**	**Neuter**
sōlus	sōla	sōlum	Nominative	sōlī	sōlae	sōla
sōlīus	**sōlīus**	**sōlīus**	Genitive	sōlōrum	sōlārum	sōlōrum
sōlī	**sōlī**	**sōlī**	Dative	sōlīs	sōlīs	sōlīs
sōlum	sōlam	sōlum	Accusative	sōlōs	sōlās	sōla
sōlō	sōlā	sōlō	Ablative	sōlīs	sōlīs	sōlīs

The endings of these words can cause some confusion. For example, *ūllī* can be masculine nominative plural or dative singular, any gender. But often the accompanying words will help you identify what GNC the pair represents.

ūllī fēminae	dative singular (*ūllī* cannot be masculine here because it is GNC'ing with a feminine word)
ūllī virī	nominative plural (**virī** can be genitive singular or nominative plural, but **ūllī** can only be nominative plural)
ūllīus virī	genitive singular
ūllī virō	dative singular

Gemma

Note *trium* "of three" in this reading. The number "three" is a two-termination adjective in the 3rd declension:

trēs	*tria*
trium	*trium*
tribus	*tribus*
trēs	*tria*
tribus	*tribus*

Gemma

Criminals were often condemned (*damnātī*) to die in the arena in ancient Rome.

Gemma

UNUS NAUTA is also a great way to remember that, although *nauta* is in the 1st declension, it is nevertheless masculine.

Is, Ea, Id

These pronouns are declined similarly to the UNUS NAUTA words. They are most common-ly used as **3rd person personal pronouns**, i.e., to indicate "he," "she," "it," and "they." You al-ready learned some forms of *is, ea, id*. Now look at the entire declension and take special note of the genitive and dative singular forms in **bold**.

SINGULAR			CASE	PLURAL		
Masculine	**Feminine**	**Neuter**		**Masculine**	**Feminine**	**Neuter**
is	ea	id	Nominative	eī	eae	ea
eius	**eius**	**eius**	Genitive	eōrum	eārum	eōrum
eī	**eī**	**eī**	Dative	eīs	eīs	eīs
eum	eam	id	Accusative	eōs	eās	ea
eō	eā	eō	Ablative	eīs	eīs	eīs

Notā Bene:

- The plural forms are entirely regular 2-1-2 adjectives, with the stem *e-*.
- Note *eius* vs. *sōlīus*, i.e., the short rather than long *-i-*.
- Unlike the English "they," the forms of *is, ea, id* can distinguish the gender in the 3rd person plural:

Vocant.	They call.
Eī vocant.	They (men) call.
Eae vocant.	They (women) call.

Demonstrative Pronouns and Adjectives

Three demonstrative pronouns and adjectives also have the same endings as the UNUS NAUTA words and *is, ea, id*. **Demonstratives** are words used to point out (*demonstrō, demon-strāre*) or emphasize the nouns to which they refer. Some English demonstratives are "this," "that," "these," and "those."

Your job is just to remember what they mean and not to forget the endings you already know, especially *-īus* in the genitive singular and *-ī* in the dative singular.

ipse, ipsa, ipsum	one's self (emphatic)
iste, ista, istud	that man (of yours), that woman, that thing
ille, illa, illud	that man, that woman, that thing

Notā Bene:

- *Iste* is generally not well intentioned. So *iste amīcus tuus* often means "that so-and-so friend of yours."
- *Ipse* is translated depending on what it modifies or refers to. Compare:

*Fēmina **ipsa** id fēcit.*	The woman **herself** did it.
*Ego **ipse** id fēcī.*	I **myself** did it.
*Nōs **ipsī** id fēcimus.*	We **ourselves** did it.

- The forms of *ille* can be either pronouns or adjectives. Compare:

ille	he	*ille vir*	that man
illa	she	*illa fēmina*	that woman
illud	it	*illud carmen*	that song

17-5 GNC'ing

Identify the GNCs of these word pairs. Then translate the pairs accordingly.

1. alīus puellae
2. neutrō homine
3. nūllī hominī
4. sōlōrum animālium

5. ūllae sorōrēs
6. aliī ancillae
7. virī ipsīus
8. iste adulescens

9. tōtā familiā
10. illīus fēminae

Mōrēs Rōmānī

Roman Attitudes Toward Animals

Romans had a more practical view of animals than we do today. For the most part, domesticated animals were kept for specific purposes. They provided food (sheep, goats); labor (oxen, horses, mules); raw material (wax, horn, pelts, fibers); and entertainment (the exotic animals at the games). Dogs were kept for guarding or hunting. Cats were ratters, and you will soon meet a cat that earns its keep in the Subura. Socrates the pet monkey served as entertainment for the customers at Licinia's *taberna* and is modeled on actual depictions of such animals in Roman life.

The animals Romans kept also varied according to their social status, wealth, and living accommodations. Dogs were commonly employed in the city as watchdogs, but in the country they would guard herds and flocks. Other dogs were used for hunting. A lap dog indicated that the owner could afford an animal that served no useful purpose. This definition of a "pet" fits Servilia's sparrow nicely.

Here is a simplified version of Catullus 2, the poem about Lesbia's sparrow. This poem served as an inspiration for the scene with Servilia and her pet sparrow. See how many echoes of this poem you can find in *Lectiō Prīma*.

> Passer, dēliciae meae puellae,
> quīcum lūdere solet
> quem in sinū tenēre solet
> cui prīmum digitum dare appetentī solet
> 5 et cui acrīs morsūs incitāre solet,
> cum libet dēsīderiō meō iocārī,
> et sōlāciolum suī dolōris invenīre
> ut tum ardor gravis acquiescat:
> tēcum lūdere sīcut ipsa
> 10 et cūrās tristēs animī levāre possem!

🔊 VERBA ŪTENDA

acquiescō (1) quiet down, subside
acer, acris, acre sharp; *acrīs = acrēs*
aliquid something
animus, -ī m. mind
appetō, appetere, appetīvī / appetiī seek, grasp for
ardor, ardōris m. fire, flame
cui to whom

cūra, ae f. worry, concern, care, anxiety
dēliciae, -ārum f. pl. delight, favorite, pet
dēsīderium, -iī n. desire, wish
digitus, -ī m. finger
dolor, dolōris m. pain, grief
incitō (1) incite; spur on
iocārī to joke
***ipse, ipsa, ipsum* he, she, it; they; himself, herself,**

itself, themselves (emphatic)
levō (1) lift, lighten
libet imp. (+ dat.) it is pleasing (to someone)
lūdō, lūdere, lūsī play, tease
morsūs bites, nibbles (acc. pl.)
passer, passeris m. sparrow
possem "I wish I were able"
prīmum digitum fingertip

quem whom
quīcum with whom
quid = aliquid some
sinū lap
sōlāciolum, -ī n. relief, comfort
soleō, solēre be accustomed (to)
tum then
ut so that, in order that

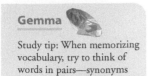

Gemma

Study tip: When memorizing vocabulary, try to think of words in pairs—synonyms and antonyms work very well.

Latīna Hodierna

Opposites in Latin and English

Thinking in terms of opposites not only helps you learn Latin vocabulary but will increase your English vocabulary. Here are some examples:

magnus, -a, -um	large	**magn**ify, **magn**ificent
parvus, -a, -um	small	**parv**ovirus
longus, -a, -um	long	**long**itude, e**long**ate, pro**long**
brevis, -e	short	**brief**, **brev**ity, **brev**iary
immānis, immāne	huge, vast	**immen**se
exiguus, -a, -um	scanty, very small	**exigu**ous, **exigu**ity
celer, celeris, celere	swift, fast	**celer**ity, ac**celer**ate, de**celer**ate
tardus, -a, -um	slow	**tard**y, **tard**iness

Orbis Terrārum Rōmānus

Prōvinciae Āfricānae

The Romans used the word *Āfrica* to refer in general to the entire continent as far as it was known to them; however, the word most commonly referred to the province located in what is now modern Tunisia and Algeria, bordering on the Mediterranean. This area came under Roman control after 146 B.C. with the final defeat of Carthage in the Third Punic War.

By the time of Augustus, both Numidia and Mauritania had also come under direct Roman control and the original province became known as *Āfrica prōconsulāris* (Proconsular Africa), *Āfrica Vetus* (Old Africa), or *Āfrica Propria* (Africa Proper). The entire region became

Prōvinciae Āfricānae

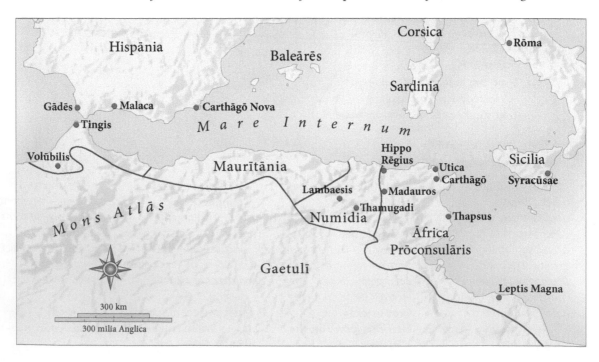

very urbanized with important cities like Carthage, Leptis Magna, Thapsus, and Utica. During the Empire, the entire Mediterranean coast of Africa was an important agricultural and commercial region as well as an important source for wild beasts for the games in the arena. Many army veterans were also settled in colonies at Thamugadi (modern Timgad, Algeria) and Lambaesis (also in Algeria).

Some important Romans from the provinces of Africa included:

Basilica Septimiī Sevērī Leptis Magnae

- **Apuleius** (ca. 123/125–ca. 180 A.D.), the author of *Metamorphōsēs* (*The Metamorphoses*) or *Aureus Asinus* (*The Golden Ass*), was born in Madaurus (now M'Daourouch, Algeria) in Numidia.

- **Septimius Sevērus** (145–211 A.D.), emperor from 193 until 211, was born in Leptis Magna (now in Libya). As emperor he beautified and enriched his hometown. The remains of the Severan basilica in Leptis Magna illustrate the magnificence of his gifts.

- **Augustine** (354–430 A.D.), was a major theologian and Father of the Christian Church. He was born in Hippo Regius, where he later served as bishop. He was also the author of an autobiography called *Confessiōnēs* (*The Confessions*).

QUID PUTĀS?

1. How do you think Roman attitudes toward animals compare to modern American attitudes?
2. How do the boundaries of the Roman provinces in African compare to national boundaries today?
3. Servilia takes solace in the poetry of Catullus. Where might a modern American go for similar comfort today?
4. Use Latin to explain the relationship between the English words "immense" and "exiguous."

EXERCEĀMUS!

17-6 Scrībāmus

Use the *lectiōnēs* to answer the following questions in Latin. Base your answers on the story (not on the Catullus poem) and answer in complete Latin sentences. Follow the model.

→ Quis sōlāciolum suī dolōris petēns rīdet?
   Servīlia, sōlāciolum petēns, rīdet.

1. Quis passerem sedentem in gremiō tenet?

2. Quis Iullum ambulantem in viā numquam vīdit?

3. Quis circumsiliēns et pīpiāns nihil dīcit?

4. Quis circumsilientī passerī dīcit?

5. Quis digitum puellae lacrimantis mordet?

17-7 Colloquāmur

Use the questions and answers in Exercise 17-6 to practice asking and answering questions with a classmate.

Gemma

Since *neuter, neutra, neutrum* = **neither**, "neuter" gender is "neither" masculine nor feminine!

17-8 Verba Discenda

Use the *Verba Discenda* to answer the questions below.

1. List the UNUS NAUTA words included in this *Verba Discenda*. What do they mean?

2. Find at least three words directly related to the Roman games. What do they mean?

3. What is the 3rd principal part of *lacrimō*?

4. What Latin word is the plural equivalent of *tibi*?

5. Which Latin pronoun in the *Verba Discenda* would you use to refer to someone you do not like?

6. *Passerēs, leōnēs, panthērae,* and *elephantēs* are examples of this *Verbum Discendum*.

🔊 VERBA DISCENDA

alter, altera, alterum the other (of two) [alteration]

amphitheātrum, -ī n. amphitheater

animal, -ālis n. animal

carmen, carminis n. song, poem

cor, cordis n. heart [cordial]

etiam still, and also, even now

gladiātor, -ōris m. gladiator

gladius, -iī m. sword [gladiola]

ille, illa, illud he, she, it; they; that, those

ipse, ipsa, ipsum he, she, it; they; himself, herself, itself, themselves (emphatic)

is, ea, id he, she, it; they [id]

iste, ista, istud that one (derogatory)

lacrimō (1) cry, shed tears [lacrimose]

mūnus, -eris, n. function, duty; gift; pl. games, public shows, spectacles [munificence]

neuter, neutra, neutrum neither [neutral]

nūllus, -a, -um no, not any, none [nullify]

numquam never

quōmodo how

sērius later, too late

tōtus, -a, -um whole, all [totality]

ūllus, -a, -um any

vōbīs dat./abl. you (all)

Angulus Grammaticus

Gender

English, like Latin, knows about grammatical gender. What do we mean by that? Well, in English we can show gender by means of pronouns like "he," "she," and "it" and with words like "his," "her," and "its." Sometimes we can distinguish male and female by changing suffixes; for example, "-ess" in "seamster"/"seamstress," "poet"/"poetess," "master"/"mistress".

English has also borrowed from Latin another suffix that can make English nouns feminine instead of masculine: "-trix," as in "mediator"/"mediatrix," "aviator"/"aviatrix," and "testator"/"testatrix". But these gender indicators began dying out in English as gender equality became more and more important in American society.

Latin, on the other hand, uses the concept of gender more rigorously, since every noun bears a **grammatical gender**. So words like *pecūnia* (money), *virtūs* (virtue, manliness), and *mālus* (apple tree) are always feminine, while *mālus* (ship's mast), *lūdus* (game, school), *amor* (love), and *annus* (year) are always masculine. This makes little sense to an English speaker for whom all these words are things and therefore neuter. Modern European languages like French, Spanish, Italian, and German, however, employ gender in much the same way that Latin does. So studying Latin can help you understand how those languages work.

Photo Credits

page 205 (top) Poynter, Sir Edward John (1836–1919)/Christie's Images/The Bridgeman Art Library; **page 215** Martin Beddall/Alamy Images

18

Fugitīvus!

Lectiō Prīma

Antequam Legis

Here we get to see a glimpse of life inside an *insula*. We meet Mendax the beggar, his cat Felix, and an unexpected visitor. Amid all this you will also meet the **imperfect tense**.

The Imperfect Tense

The imperfect tense of regular verbs:

- has the tense marker *-ba-* before the normal personal endings. Thus: *-bam, -bās, -bat, -bāmus, -bātis, -bant.*

- Translate it by using the English "used to" or "was/were 'verb'ing". Thus, *vocābāmus* is translated "we used to call" or "we were calling."

The imperfect tense of *sum* and *possum*:

- Do you remember that the stem of *sum* for the future was *er-* as in *erō, eris, erit*, etc.?

- The imperfect of *sum* uses the same *er-* stem but with a different vowel pattern: *eram, erās, erat*, etc. Translate as a simple "was/were" or "used to be."

- The imperfect of *possum,* whose stem is *pot-* is easy: *poteram, poterās, poterat*, etc. Translate as "was/were able" or "could."

  That is all you need to know in order to translate the next section. To help you, all the imperfect tense verbs are in **bold** in the *Lectiō Prīma.*

Pistrīnum Pompeiīs

GRAMMATICA
Forming the Imperfect Tense
Aspect of the Imperfect and Perfect
Interrogative and Relative Pronouns
   and Adjectives
Using Interrogatives and Relatives

MŌRĒS RŌMĀNĪ
Roman Slavery

LATĪNA HODIERNA
Slaves, Slavs, and Serfs

ORBIS TERRĀRUM RŌMĀNUS
Ostia

ANGULUS GRAMMATICUS
Building Your Latin Vocabulary

LECTIŌNĒS:
MENDAX
and
TENĒ MĒ QUIA FŪGĪ

Valeria and her family arrive home and chat with Mendax, the beggar who lives in their *insula.* Their conversation is interrupted by the arrival of a runaway slave.

217

From *Disce! An Introductory Latin Course, volume 1*, First Edition. Francesco Bonavita. Copyright © 2011 by Pearson Education, Inc. Published by Pearson Prentice Hall. All rights reserved.

Fēlix Fēlēs Murēs Multōs Capit.

EXERCEĀMUS!

18-1 **Identifying Imperfects**

Before you read *Lectiō Prīma*, make a line-by-line list of all the imperfect verbs (marked in **bold**). Determine their person and number. Then use the *Verba Ūtenda* to translate them. Follow the model.

Line	Verb	Person	Number	English Translation
→ 2	adveniēbant	3ʳᵈ	plural	they were arriving at

MENDAX

Dum Marcus et Lūcius in Vīminālī dē mūneribus dīcunt, in Subūrā Licinia, Valeria, et Flāvia ad insulam suam **adveniēbant**. Multī habitantēs in insulā egēnī sunt et nūllam pecūniam habent. Ūnus ex eīs Mendax est.
Ōlim, cum in pistrīnō **labōrābat**, nōmen eī "Quintus" **erat** sed labor
5 strēnuus **erat** et mox Quintus, aegrescēns, nōn **labōrābat**. Rōmam **veniēbat** sed aeger labōrem invenīre nōn **poterat**.

Ut Mendāx dīcit: "Egēnus **eram** et famem magnam **habēbam**. Ergō, pecūniam ab hominibus in viā ambulantibus poscere **incipiēbam**. Quid aliud facere **poteram**?"

10 Mox Quintus nōmen novum **habēbat**—Mendax. Cūr? Quod mendīcus est vir pecūniam ab aliīs poscēns et tālēs hominēs rārō vērum dīcunt.

Mendax prō paucīs nummīs nōn cellam propriam sed parvum spatium sub scālīs habēre **poterat**. Hoc spatium parvum et fētidum, sed siccum est, et hīc nōn sōlum Mendax sed etiam fēlēs sua, Fēlix nōmine,
15 trēs annōs habitant. Fēlix illud nōmen habet quod Mendax eam aegram et paene mortuam in viā invēnit. Omnēs Fēlīcem amant quod iam dūdum mūrēs multōs in insulā capit—et in Subūrā multī mūrēs sunt!

Valeria in insulam intrāns Mendācem salūtat. "Salvē, Mendax," inquit Valeria, "quid tū et Fēlix agitis? Quid fortūnae hodiē **capiēbātis**?"

20 "Bonum nōbīs est," respondet Mendax. "Hodiē ego multōs nummōs et Fēlix quinque mūrēs cēpimus. Mea fēlēs fortis in amphitheātrō pugnāre dēbet!"

Subitō, vir territus in insulam rūpit. Sē ad terram iēcit et, "Mē adiuvāte!!" clāmāvit.

Valeria et aliī attonitī sunt quod homō territus servus est. Collāre in collō habet et collāre inscriptiōnem habet. Prīmae magnae litterae sunt "TMQF" et hae litterae significant "Tenē mē quia fūgī." Ecce, servus fugiēns!

Hīc habitat Familia Valeriae—omnēs in duābus cellīs!

Ōlim Mendax in pistrīnō labōrābat.

Gemma

The fact that the slave is wearing a collar bearing the inscription TMQF means that had run away before.

🔊 VERBA ŪTENDA

aeger, aegra, aegrum sick
aegrescō, aegrescere
  grow sick
attonitus, -a, -um
  astonished
cella, -ae f. room
collāre, collāris n. collar
collum, -ī n. neck
dūdum See *iam.*
egēnus, -a, -um destitute,
  poverty stricken
famēs, -is f. hunger
fēlēs, fēlis f. cat
**fēlix, fēlīcis lucky,
  fortunate**
fētidus, -a, -um foul
  smelling
hae these
iaciō, iacere, iēcī hurl,
  throw

iam dūdum for a long time
  now (used with
  present tense)
**incipiō, incipere, incēpī,
  inceptum begin**
inscriptiō, -iōnis f.
  inscription
intrō (1) enter
littera, -ae f. letter of the
  alphabet
mendax, mendācis
  untruthful; *Mendax* "Liar"
mendīcus, -ī m. beggar
mortuus, -a, -um dead
mūs, mūris m. mouse
nōn sōlum ... sed etiam
  not only ... but also
nummus, -ī m. coin
ōlim once, formerly
paene almost

pistrīnum, -ī n. mill
prīmus, -a, -um first
proprius, -a, -um one's own
quia since
rārō rarely
Rōmam "to Rome"
rumpō, rumpere, rūpī burst,
  break open
scālae, -ārum f. pl. stairs,
  staircase
siccus, -a, -um dry
significō (1) mean
spatium, -iī n. space
strēnuus, -a, -um hard,
  strenuous
tālis, tāle such, of such a
  sort
vērus, -a, um true; *vērum* is a
  substantive, so translate
  here as "the truth"

POSTQUAM LĒGISTĪ

1. What was the beggar Mendax's original name? Where did he work formerly?
2. How did he become a beggar? And how did he get the name *Mendax*?
3. Why do the residents of this apartment building like Felix?
4. Who appears suddenly at the end of the story? How is his identity known?

Grammatica A

Forming the Imperfect Tense

The imperfect tense is the third and last tense in what is called the **present system**, which also includes the present and future tenses. The following chart shows you how to form the imperfect.

FORMING THE IMPERFECT			
1st / 2nd Conjugations		3rd / 4th Conjugations	
Present Stem + (2nd principal part – *-re*)		**Short Present Stem** + (1st principal part – *-ō*)	
-bam	-bāmus	-ēbam	-ēbāmus
-bās	-bātis	-ēbās	-ēbātis
-bat	-bant	-ēbat	-ēbant

Thus:

IMPERFECT ENDINGS	1ST CONJUGATION	2ND CONJUGATION	3RD CONJUGATION	3RD-iō CONJUGATION	4TH CONJUGATION
-bam	vocā**bam**	monē**bam**	dūcē**bam**	capiē**bam**	audiē**bam**
-bās	vocā**bās**	monē**bās**	dūcē**bās**	capiē**bās**	audiē**bās**
-bat	vocā**bat**	monē**bat**	dūcē**bat**	capiē**bat**	audiē**bat**
-bāmus	vocā**bāmus**	monē**bāmus**	dūcē**bāmus**	capiē**bāmus**	audiē**bāmus**
-bātis	vocā**bātis**	monē**bātis**	dūcē**bātis**	capiē**bātis**	audiē**bātis**
-bant	vocā**bant**	monē**bant**	dūcē**bant**	capiē**bant**	audiē**bant**

Notā Bene:

- 3rd -io and 4th conjugation verbs have *-ie-* before *-ba-*.
- *Sum* and *possum* use familiar endings but have an irregular stem for the imperfect:

SUM	POSSUM
eram	poteram
erās	poterās
erat	poterat
erāmus	poterāmus
erātis	poterātis
erant	poterant

Aspect of the Imperfect and Perfect

Why does Latin need both an imperfect and a perfect tense? The answer is something grammarians call **aspect**. The perfect tense indicates that the action of the verb is simple, i.e., it happened only once in the past. (Think of a photograph.) The imperfect tense indicates that the action of the verb is a continuing action in the past. (Think of a video recording.) Consider this English sentence:

> We were watching television when the lights went out.

"We were watching television" is the equivalent of the Latin imperfect. It shows that the action continued in the past for a period of time. "The lights went out" is the equivalent of the Latin perfect. It indicates that the action happened only once.

Note: Latin and English tenses do not always match on a one-to-one basis. For example, Latin uses the **present tense** to indicate a continuous action that started in the past but continues in the present, in an expression like:

> *Hīc Mendax et fēlēs sua, Fēlix nōmine, trēs annōs **habitant**.*
> Here Mendax and his cat, Felix by name, have lived for three years.

In this case English prefers the perfect tense (have lived) while Latin uses the present tense (*habitant*). Likewise, whereas English says "While we were walking …" Latin says *Dum ambulāmus…* literally, "While we walk." This is always the case, even if the surrounding verbs are in the past tenses.

Compare this example of **continuous time with the conjunction *dum*** in a sentence from *Lectiō Prīma*:

> ***Dum*** *Marcus et Lūcius dē mūneribus **dīcunt**, in Subūrā Licinia, Valeria, et Flāvia ad insulam suam adveniēbant.*
> While Marcus and Lucius were talking about the games, in the Subura Licinia, Valeria, and Flavia were arriving at their apartment house.

18-2 Tense Substitution

Change each of the following present tense verbs to the imperfect without changing person and number. Then translate both verbs. Follow the model.

	Present	Translation	Imperfect	Translation
→	dīcunt	they say	dīcēbant	they were saying

1. habitant	6. venītis	11. intrāmus
2. advenis	7. potest	12. estis
3. habent	8. incipiunt	13. amātis
4. est	9. possumus	14. capit
5. labōrō	10. invenit	

Lectiō Secunda

Antequam Legis

The inhabitants of the *insula* are in a bind. Helping a runaway slave was a serious crime and their instincts fight with their sense of self-preservation. As they do so, they use a lot of what Latin students have called "all those Q-words."

Interrogative and Relative Pronouns and Adjectives

The "Q-words" tend to look alike and be used in several ways. In English they are the "W-words" as in "who, what, which" and their various forms.

Here is what you need to know to read the following passage:

- *Quī, quae, quod* can mean "who," "which," or even "that."
- *Quis, quid?* are always interrogative and mean "who?" or "what?"
- *Cuius, quōrum, quārum* can mean "whose," of "whom," or "of which."
- Some forms, like *quō* and *quārum,* use 2-1-2 declension endings.
- Other forms, like *cuius* and *cui,* have genitive and dative singular endings like those in *is* and *ille.*

As you read the *lectiō* use these hints to translate the "Q-words." But keep your eyes peeled. Sometimes the "Q-word" is used alone and sometimes it modifies a noun. At other times it asks a question.

18-3 Identifying Relative and Interrogative Pronouns

As you read *Lectiō Secunda* make a line-by-line list of all Q-words marked in **bold**. Use the endings and the guidelines above to identify the case and number of each. Then translate the word into English. Use a question mark where appropriate. Follow the model.

Line	Pronoun	Case	Number	Translation
→ 1	quis	nom.	sing.	who?

TENĒ MĒ QUIA FŪGĪ

Servus, tremēns, oculōs ad terram tenēbat. Valeria eum rogāvit, "**Quis** es, aut, rectius, **cuius** es? **Cui** labōrās? Ā **quō** fūgistī? Ad **quem** locum fugis?"

Servus nihil dīxit, sed digitō trementī collāre monstrāvit. Valeria litterās **quae** in collārī erant lēgit: "TMQF. Revocā mē dominō meō Publiō Nonniō Zēthō, Ostiēnsī. Praemium accipiēs."

5 Brevī tempore silentium erat. Perīculōsum est servō fugientī auxilium dare. Cīvēs Rōmānī servīs **quī** fūgērunt nūllum auxilium dare dēbent.

Sed Valeria alma servō iterum dīxit: "Publiī Nonnī es. Hoc sciō. Sed **quis** est ille Publius Nonnius? **Quem** aut **quid** quaeris?"

Vox servī trementis dēbilis erat: "Zēthus pistor est et Ostiae pistrīnum habet. In pistrīnō
10 istō ego labōrābam dōnec dominus meus, iste Zēthus, uxōrem meam **quā**cum labōrābam āmīsit. Dominus crūdēlis est et ergō fūgī."

Mendax et Valeria cicātrīcēs, **quae** in dorsō servī sunt, aspexērunt. Valeria servum adiuvāre volēbat, sed nōn audēbat. Cibum, **quem** in macellō ēmit, eī dedit, et maesta, nihil dīcēns, ad cellās suās ascendit. Flāvia, **quae** ipsa serva est, quoque maesta erat sed nihil agere aut dīcere potu-
15 it. Illa quoque ascendit.

Nunc Mendax, quia omnēs pistōrēs ōdit, servum adiuvāre volēbat. Sed quōmodo?

Subitō vōcem virī clāmantis in viā audīvērunt: "Quaerō servum **quī** herī ā mē fūgit. Aliquisne eum vīdit?"

Mendax servum sub pannīs fētidīs, **quī** prō lectō sunt, abdit. Rōmānus obēsus **quī**
20 fustem in manū tenēbat, in insulam rumpēbat.

Servus tremēns oculōs ad terram tenēbat

VERBA ŪTENDA

abdō, abdere, abdidī hide
aliquis, aliquid someone, something
almus, -a, -um nourishing, kind, dear
ascendō, ascendere, ascendī climb
aspiciō, aspicere, aspexī look at
auxilium, -ī n. help, aid
brevis, breve short
cella, -ae f. room
cicātrīx, cicātrīcis f. scar
cīvis, cīvis m./f. citizen
crūdēlis, crūdēle cruel
dēbilis, dēbile weak
difficultās, -tātis f. difficulty
digitus, -ī m. finger

dominus, -ī m. master
dōnec until
emō, emere, ēmī, emptum buy
fētidus, -a, -um filthy
fugitīvus, -ī m. runaway, fugitive
fustis, fustis m. staff, club
hoc "this (thing)"
lectus, -ī m. couch, bed
littera, -ae f. letter of the alphabet
locus, -ī m. place
macellum, -ī n. market
maestus, -a, -um sad, gloomy
monstrō (1) point out, show

nōn sōlum ... sed etiam ... not only ... but also ...
obēsus, -a, -um fat
oculus, -ī m. eye
ōdī, ōdisse hate
Ostia, -ae f. Ostia, the harbor of Rome; *Ostiae* " at Ostia"
Ostiēnsis, -e pertaining to Ostia, Rome's port, Ostian
pannus, -ī m. cloth, garment, rag
perīculōsus, -a, -um dangerous
pistor, pistōris m. miller
pistrīnum, -ī n. mill, bakery
praemium, -iī n. reward

prō lectō sunt "served as his bed"
quaerō, quaerere, quaesīvī / quaesiī, quaesītum ask, seek, look for
quī, quae, quod who, which
quia since, because
quis, quid who? what?
rectius "more correctly"
revocō (1) bring back, return
rumpō, rumpere, rūpī burst, break open
silentium, -iī n. silence
tremō, tremere, tremuī tremble
uxor, uxōris f. wife

POSTQUAM LĒGISTĪ

1. What is written on the slave's collar?
2. Where did the slave work?
3. (L) Why did he run away?
4. What does Valeria give the slave? Why doesn't she help him more?
5. Why does Mendax help the slave? Where does he hide him?
6. Who do you think the fat Roman is and what does he want?

Gemma

***Ostiae* = in Ostia**: Note how Latin expresses location in a city with a special ending (*-ae*) and no preposition. You have seen this already with *Rōmae* "at Rome." This is called the **locative** case. You will learn more about it later.

Grammatica B

Relative and Interrogative Pronouns and Adjectives

First of all, what do we mean by interrogatives and relatives?

- A **relative pronoun** connects or relates two pieces of information about the same person. "I know the person **who** ate your cake." That is it "relates" one part of a sentence to another.
- An **interrogative pronoun** asks a question; for example, "**Who** ate my piece of cake?"
- An **interrogative adjective** modifies a noun and asks "which?" as in "which person did that?"
- Notice that, in English, the interrogative and relative words are exactly the same.

Here are some examples of interrogative and relative pronouns in English:

Interrogative Pronouns

	SINGULAR		PLURAL	
CASE	Masc./Fem. Who	Neuter Which	Masc./Fem. Who	Neuter Which
Nominative	**quī/quis**	**quod/quid**	quī	quae
Genitive	cuius	cuius	quōrum	quōrum
Dative	cui	cui	quibus	quibus
Accusative	quem	**quod/quid**	quōs	quae
Ablative	quō	quō	quibus	quibus

Gemma

quācum: *"with whom"*: Note that the preposition *cum* follows the ablatives *quō, quā,* and *quibus*: *quōcum, quācum, quibuscum*

Relative Pronouns and Interrogative Adjectives

	SINGULAR			PLURAL		
CASE	Masculine Who	Feminine Who	Neuter Which	Masculine Who	Feminine Who	Neuter Which
Nominative	quī	quae	quod	quī	quae	quae
Genitive	cuius	cuius	cuius	quōrum	quārum	quōrum
Dative	cui	cui	cui	quibus	quibus	quibus
Accusative	quem	quam	quod	quōs	quās	quae
Ablative	quō	quā	quō	quibus	quibus	quibus

Gemma

You may have already seen some of these Latin interrogative and relative pronouns in English in phrases like:

- cui bono (*cui bonō*) "to what good?"
- quid pro quo (*quid prō quō*) "what for what?"
- sine qua non (*sine quā nōn*) "without which not"

We have given you the literal translations of the Latin phrases. What do they mean in English?

Notā Bene:

- The neuter plural nominative and accusative do not end in "-*a*."
- The genitive and dative singular endings remind you of the *UNUS NAUTA* declension.
- So … what four GNC's can the form *quae* be?
- You might want to compare the two charts and circle the forms that are different from one chart to the other. You will see that there are very few.
- Relative pronouns and interrogative adjectives are the same in Latin but not in English.

Relative Pronoun	**Interrogative Adjectives**
Quaerō servum **qui** *ā mē fugīt.*	**Qui** *servus ā mē fūgit?*
I seek the slave **who** fled from me.	**Which** slave fled from me?

- Don't worry about the Latin forms that look alike. Context will always make it clear whether the word is a relative or an interrogative.
- There is nothing here you have not seen before. It is just an amalgam of endings from different declension patterns.

EXERCEĀMUS!

18-4 **Forms of *Quī, Quae, Quod***

Answer the following questions.

1. Find the forms in the chart that are the same as the 1st and 2nd declensions.

2. Find the forms that look like 3ʳᵈ declension endings.

3. Find the forms that use UNUS NAUTA endings that were first introduced to you in *is, ea, id* and *ille, illa, illud*.

Using Interrogatives and Relatives

Interrogatives

You can usually recognize an interrogative because of the question mark at the end of the sentence.

Quis *es?*	Who are you?
Cuius *es?*	Whose (slave) are you?
Cui *labōrās?*	For whom do you work?
Ad **quem** *locum fugis?*	To what place are you fleeing?

Relatives

A relative pronoun "relates" one part of a sentence to another. It is used to avoid choppy sentences. Consider this English.

Licinia works in the snack shop. Licinia is Valeria's daughter.
Licinia, **who** is Valeria's daughter, works in the snack shop.

Notā Bene:

- Two sentences have been made into one, with the second sentence becoming a **relative clause** introduced by the word "who."
- In the second sentence, "who" refers back to Licinia but it also is the subject of the clause set off by commas.
- The relative pronoun can be in any case but still refer back to the same noun. Consider:

Licinia, whose husband is Aelius, works in the snack shop. (genitive)
Licinia, to whom I gave a present, is Valeria's daughter. (dative)
Licinia, with whom I walked home, has a jealous husband. (ablative)

The concepts are the same in Latin as in English, but, of course, there are endings to consider. A relative pronoun has **gender**, **number**, and **case (GNC)**. Here are two important rule:

- A relative pronoun takes its **gender and number from the antecedent**.
- But it takes its **case from the function it performs in its own clause**.

Let's try this in English first.

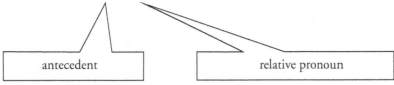

- The **who** refers to "slave," so it must be masculine and singular.
- But in the clause **who** is the nominative subject of "fled."
- So the Latin form for **who** would be masculine, singular, nominative: *quī*.

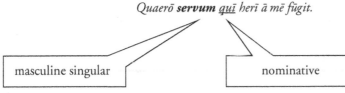

Determining the gender and number is always fairly simple, but sometimes it is difficult to determine the case of a relative pronoun. To determine the case, break the long sentence into two short ones.

I seek the slave <u>who</u> ran away from me yesterday.
I seek a slave.
The slave ran away from me yesterday.

Notā Bene: Interrogatives don't have antecedents. They simply ask a question.

Relative: *Quaerō servum <u>quī</u> herī ā mē fūgit.* (antecedent is *servum*)
I seek the slave who fled from me yesterday.

Interrogative: *Quis herī ā mē fūgit?* (antecedent is unknown)
Who fled from me yesterday?
Quī servus herī ā mē fūgit?
What slave fled from me yesterday?

Summary and Simplification

WHEN YOU SEE	CASE	TRANSLATE
quī, quae, quod	nominative	who/which/that
cuius, quōrum, quārum	genitive	whose/of whom/of which
cui, quibus	dative	to whom/to which
quem, quam, quōs, quās, quae	accusative	whom/which
quō, quā, quibus	ablative	BWIOF whom/which

18-5　GNC'ing Relative Pronouns

What would be the GNC of the underlined relative pronoun if the sentence were in Latin? Follow the model.

→ Valeria, <u>whom</u> I saw yesterday, owns the snack shop.
　　fem. s. (refers to Valeria), acc. (direct object of clause)

1. Aelius, <u>whose</u> wife is Licinia, is a very strong man.

2. Servilia, <u>for whom</u> a husband has been chosen, is very unhappy.

3. Lucius, <u>who</u> is always hungry, wants to see the games.

4. The cat, <u>who</u> catches many mice, is named Felix. (*fēlēs, fēlis* f. cat)

5. The mice, <u>which</u> Felix catches, don't much care for him. (*mūs, mūris* m. mouse)

18-6　Forming Relative Pronouns

Now go back and, using the declension chart of *quī, quae, quod*, determine what the relative pronoun would be in Latin for the sentences in Exercise 18-5.

→ fem. acc. s. → *quam*

Mōrēs Rōmānī

Roman Slavery

Slavery was always part of Roman life, and few in antiquity questioned its cruelty or inhumanity. As the Roman Empire grew, especially following the conquest of Greece and Carthage in the second century B.C., many slaves flooded into Italy. A good number of these were captives

Kirk Douglas, Spartacus Americānus

of war. Slavery was a major factor in the growth of large rural estates called *lātifundia* owned by wealthy Romans who lived in the city and left the management of these estates to managers (who were often themselves slaves or former slaves).

The possibility of runaway slaves was a major concern for Roman society and law. Romans were expected to return runaway slaves to their masters, and it was illegal to assist a runaway. To discourage flight, slaves were sometimes branded or collared with identifying tags like the one on the fugitive in the story.

Slave revolts occasionally occurred and were brutally suppressed. The most famous of these was led by Spartacus, a Thracian gladiator slave whose brilliant successes against the superior Roman army made him a folk hero. Perhaps you have seen Kirk Douglas starring as Spartacus in Stanley Kubrick's 1960 film or a more modern television series on Spartacus. Behind all the romanticism of these portrayals stands a real historical figure and the brutal reality of Roman slavery. Spartacus died in battle, and 6,600 of his followers were crucified along the Appian Way from Rome to Brundisium after their defeat by the Roman general M. Licinius Crassus in 71 B.C.

Slaves were considered property, not people. In a farming manual entitled *Dē Rē Rusticā* (*On Country Matters*) Marcus Terentius Varro (116–27 B.C.) considers slaves no more than *instrūmentī genus vōcāle* (a talking sort of tool). Here is Varro's quote in context, modified just a bit to help you read it. (Note all the relative pronouns marked in **bold**! Can you find their antecedents?)

Dē fundī quattuor partibus, **quae** cum solō haerent, et dē alterīs quattuor, **quae** extrā fundum sunt et ad cultūram pertinent, dīxī. Nunc dīcam, dē rēbus **quibus** agrōs colunt. Hās rēs aliī dīvidunt in duās partēs, in hominēs et instrumenta hominum, sine **quibus** colere nōn possunt; aliī in trēs partēs, in-
5 strūmentī genus vōcāle et sēmivōcāle et mūtum—vōcāle, in **quō** sunt servī; et semivōcāle, in **quō** sunt bovēs; et mūtum, in **quō** sunt plaustra.

Dē Rē Rusticā 1.17.1

🔊 VERBA ŪTENDA

ager, agrī m. field
aliī ... aliī ... some ... others ...
bōs, bovis m./f. bull, cow
colō, colere, coluī look after, care for
cultūra, -ae f. agriculture
extrā (+ acc.) beyond, outside of
fundus, -ī m. farm

genus, generis n. type
haerent are connected with
instrūmentum, -ī n. tool
mūtus, -a, -um speechless, mute
pars, partis f. part
pertineō, pertinēre, pertinuī belong to

plaustrum, -ī n. wagon
dē rēbus quibus "about those things by means of which"
sēmi- prefix, "half"
solum, solī n. earth, soil
vōcālis, vōcāle speaking, vocal

Latīna Hodierna

Slaves, Slavs, and Serfs

Would you see any connection between the words "slave," "Slav," and "serf"? They are actually connected through the Latin word *servus, -ī* m. slave. In medieval times, so many people of Slavic background came to be enslaved that *sclavus*, a Latin word for "Slav," came to be used for "slave." At the same time, the meaning of the word *servus* shifted to mean someone bound to the land or a "serf." Here is how these two words come into some modern languages.

	SERVUS (SLAVE)	*SCLAVUS (SLAV)*
Italian	servo della gleba	schiavo/a
Spanish	siervo	esclavo
French	serf	esclave
English	serf	slave

Orbis Terrārum Rōmānus

Ostia

The fugitive slave escaped from his master in Ostia the port of Rome. Ostia is located about sixteen miles east of the capital city, at the mouth (*ōs, ōris* n.) of the river Tiber (*Tiberis, Tiberis* m.). This area was an important source of salt, which Romans exported from earliest times, and was Rome's first colony (*colōnia, -ae* f.).

Ostia was a major source of imported essentials and luxuries for Rome. Large ships could not sail up the Tiber, so cargoes had to be unloaded at Ostia and stored in large warehouses until the merchandise could be taken in smaller sail or tow boats up the river to Rome.

In the mid first century A.D. the emperor Claudius built a major new harbor for Ostia a few miles north of the city. This harbor was expanded by later emperors, especially by Trajan in the early second century.

Ostiā Rōmam

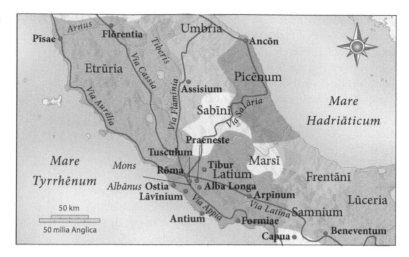

Horrea Ostiae

Insula Ostiae

The area around Ostia silted up over the centuries and the ancient city, which has been excavated by archaeologists, is no longer on the sea. Its warehouses (*horrea, -ōrum* n. pl) and large *insulae* or apartment houses (like the one Valeria and her family live in) are important evidence for similar architecture that did not survive in Rome.

QUID PUTĀS?

1. Varro lists three categories of things without which fields cannot be taken care of. Can you list these three categories and one example from each?
2. What effect do you think slavery had on Roman society?
3. In what ways do you think the institution of slavery was similar and different in American and Roman societies?
4. Do you think that ancient Romans would have romanticized the story of Spartacus the way Hollywood has? Why or why not?
5. To which American cities could you compare Ostia? How?

EXERCEĀMUS!

18-7 Scrībāmus

Use *Lectiō Secunda* to answer each of the following questions in Latin. Follow the model.

→ Quid servus in collō habet? *Collāre habet.*

1. Quis tremēns oculōs ad terram tenēbat?
2. Cuius est fugitīvus?
3. Quid Valeria in servī collārī lēgit?
4. Quōcum fugitīvus in pistrīnō labōrābat?
5. Quis est Publius Zēthus?
6. Quem Publius Zēthus āmīsit?
7. Quid Mendax et Valeria in dorsō fugitīvī aspiciunt?
8. Cui Valeria cibum dat?
9. Quid Rōmānus obēsus quaerit?
10. Sub quibus Mendax celeriter servum abdit?

18-8 Colloquāmur

This exercise is like a spelling bee. All the students in the class stand up and the teacher asks each student one of the questions from Exercise 18-7. Students responding correctly in Latin remain standing for the next round. Students responding incorrectly sit down and do not continue to the next round. The teacher continues to ask questions until only one student remains standing and is the victor.

HINT: Students may prepare more questions to use prior to the activity. Use the questions randomly and the same questions can be used more than once.

18-9 Verba Discenda

Use the *Verba Discenda* to answer the questions that follow. All of the answers are in the *Verba Discenda*.

1. What is the nominative neuter singular form of *crūdēlis*?
2. Give an English expression employing a form of the word *almus, -a, -um*. It is mostly associated with colleges and universities. What does it mean in common usage? How is it translated literally?
3. Which form of *maestus, -a, -um* would be used with *uxor*?
4. If the pen- in the English word "peninsula" comes from *paene*, what does "peninsula" literally mean?
5. What is the feminine form of *aliquis, aliquid*?
6. What is the neuter nominative singular form of *fēlix*?
7. What is the alternate form for *quaesiī*?

VERBA DISCENDA

aliquis, aliquid someone, something	**dominus, -ī m. lord, master** [dominate, dominion]	**begin** [incipient, inception]	**quaerō, quaerere, quaesīvī / quaesiī, quaesītum ask, seek, look for** [question]
almus, -a, -um nourishing, kind, dear [alma mater]	**emō, emere, ēmī, emptum buy**	**lectus, -ī m. couch, bed**	
brevis, breve short [brevity]	**fēlix, fēlīcis lucky, fortunate** [felicity]	**maestus, -a, -um sad**	**quī, quae, quod who, which**
cella, -ae f. room [cell]	**incipiō, incipere, incēpī, inceptum**	**nōn sōlum . . . sed etiam . . . not only . . . but also . . .**	**quia since**
crūdēlis, crūdēle cruel		**paene almost** [peninsula]	**quis, quid who? what?**
		prīmus, -a, -um first [primary]	**uxor, uxōris f. wife** [uxorious]

Angulus Grammaticus

Building Your Latin Vocabulary

You can increase your Latin (and English) vocabulary by paying attention to the way Latin uses prefixes and suffixes to form words. Look at some examples in the following charts. Combine the meaning of the stem with the meaning of the suffixes (and prefixes) to determine the general meaning of the word. For example,

dictātor   "one who speaks"

Look the word up in a Latin dictionary for more precise meanings. Do you recognize any English words in this list?

dict- say

PREFIX	STEM	SUFFIX	LATIN WORD	
	dict- say	-or "one"	**dict**ātor, -ōris m.	one who speaks
	dict- say	-iō "the act of"	**dict**iō, -iōnis f.	act of speaking
contrā "against"	**dict-** say	-iō "the act of"	contrā**dict**iō, -iōnis f.	act of speaking against

fac- make, do

PREFIX	STEM	SUFFIX	LATIN WORD	
	fac- make, do	-ilis "able to"	**fac**ilis	able to do
dis- "not"	**fac-** make, do	-ilis "able to"	dif**fic**ilis	not able to do
	fac- make, do	-iō "the act of"	**fac**tiō, -iōnis f.	act of doing

pot- be able

PREFIX	STEM	SUFFIX	LATIN WORD	
	pot- be able	-ens "-ing"	**pot**ens	being able
in- "not"	**pot-** be able	-ens "-ing"	im**pot**ens	not being able
	pot- be able	-ia "state of"	**pot**entia, -ae f.	state of being able
in- "not"	**pot-** be able	-ia "state of"	im**pot**entia	state of not being able
	pot- be able	-tās "the act of"	**pot**estās, -tātis f.	act of being able

pōt- drink

PREFIX	STEM	SUFFIX	LATIN WORD	
	pōt- drink	-or "one who"	**pōt**or	one who drinks
	pōt- drink	-rix "she who"	**pōt**rix	she who drinks
	pōt- drink	-iō "act of"	**pōt**ātiō, pōtātiōnis f.	act of drinking
	pōt- drink	-iō "act of"	**pōt**iō, pōtiōnis f.	act of drinking, a drink

Photo Credits

page 217 (top) Thomas J.Sienkewicz/Photo by Thomas J. Sienkewicz used with permission; **page 218 (top)** Juniors Bildarchiv/F240/Alamy Images; **page 218 (middle)** Russell Barnett © Dorling Kindersley; **page 218 (bottom)** Thomas J. Sienkewicz/Photo by Thomas J. Sienkewicz used with permission; **page 226 Photos** 12/Alamy Images; **page 228 (bottom left)** Thomas J. Sienkewicz/Photo by Thomas J. Sienkewicz used with permission; **page 228 (bottom right)** SCALA/Art Resource, N.Y.

19

Vēnātiō

Opus Mūlō nōn Virō Aptum
Wikipedia Commons/Foto Musei Vaticani

Lectiō Prīma

Antequam Legis

Work in a Mill

In this *lectiō* the runaway slave describes his work in the bakery/mill. His job was to turn enormously heavy millstones around all day long, pushing on a beam that was inserted into the square hole. Life in a mill was one of the worst fates a slave could endure, and slaves were often sent to work there as punishment.

The Pluperfect Tense

As you read the story, you will learn the **pluperfect tense**. This tense, represented in English by the helping verb "had," indicates a completed action that preceded another action in the past; for example, "I had seen" or "you had run."

For now, when you see a form with the endings marked in **bold** below, translate the verb using the helping verb "had."

-*eram*	-*erāmus*
-*erās*	-*erātis*
-*erat*	-*erant*

Note that these endings are identical to the imperfect forms of the verb *sum, esse.*

mans**erat**	**he had** remained
labōrāv**erāmus**	**we had** worked

GRAMMATICA

The Pluperfect Tense
The Demonstrative *hic, haec, hoc*
Forming Comparatives in Latin
Using Comparatives in Latin
Translating Comparatives

MŌRĒS RŌMĀNĪ

Mūnera Rōmāna

LATĪNA HODIERNA

Latin Comparative Adjectives in English

ORBIS TERRĀRUM RŌMĀNUS

Amphitheātrum Flāviānum

ANGULUS GRAMMATICUS

"This Here" Deictic Enclitic -*c(e)*

LECTIŌNĒS:
IN NOCTEM
and
MŪNERA

Mendax sends the owner of the fugitive slave off on the wrong track. The next morning the games begin.

231

From *Disce! An Introductory Latin Course, volume 1*, First Edition. Francesco Bonavita. Copyright © 2011 by Pearson Education, Inc. Published by Pearson Prentice Hall. All rights reserved.

Hic, haec, hoc

Other words to look for in this *lectiō* are forms of *hic, haec, hoc* (this/these). This demonstrative pronoun/adjective is the counterpart to *ille, illa, illud* (that/those) and it, too, is one of the words with a genitive in *-ius*. Pay attention to the forms, marked in ***bold italics*** in the *lectiō*. Note especially the following substantives where the adjective is used as a noun:

- Dative singular forms: *huic* (to this man/woman/thing)
- Accusative singular forms: *hunc, hanc, hoc* (this man/woman/thing)
- Neuter nominative and accusative plural forms: *haec* (these things)

EXERCEĀMUS!

19-1 *Hic, haec, hoc*

Create a line-by-line list of all the phrases with *hic, haec, hoc* in *Lectiō Prīma*. Before you read, use the phrases to help you identify the GNC of the *hic, haec, hoc* forms. When in doubt, check out the context of the phrase in the *lectiō*. Watch out for substantives. Follow the model.

⟶ hunc servum (line 3): *masc. sing. acc.*

IN NOCTEM

Zēthus in insulam irrūpit et Mendācī appropinquāvit. "Cīvis," inquit, "quaerō servum quī herī ā mē fūgit. Num ***hunc*** servum vīdistī?"

Mendax rīdēns, "Nēminem," inquit, "in ***hāc*** insulā
5 vīdī. Fortasse ***hic*** servus in cloācā sē abdidit aut fortasse in Forum ad āram Caesaris fūgit. ***Hoc*** sōlum certē dīcere possum—nōn adest."

P. Nonius Zēthus

Zēthus circumspectāvit et locum in quō servus latēbat inspectāvit, sed pannōs fētidōs tangere nōluit. Fustem quatiēns et fortiter clāmāns abiit.

10 Servus territus quī sub pannīs quiētus **manserat** diūtius mansit et tunc exiit. "Abestne Zēthus?" rogāvit.

"Ita, vērō" respondit Mendax, "abest. Nunc dīc mihi dē ***hāc*** difficultāte tuā."

"Ut scīs, nōs in pistrīnō ***huius*** Zēthī multōs annōs **labōrāverāmus** cum subitō dominus uxōrem āmīsit. Uxor pānem in furnō torrēbat et ego molās cotīdiē prōpellēbam—opus mūlō nōn virō aptum."

Mendax quī quoque in pistrīnō **labōrāverat** cachinnāvit et ***huic*** servō exclāmāvit: "Rectē dīxistī, amīce. ***Hī***
15 Rōmānī quibus labōrāvistis vōs servōs 'animālia loquentia' aut 'instrūmenta vōcālia' nōminant. Tū et uxor, laetīne **fuerātis?**"

Servus dīxit: "Aliquid pecūniae **servāverāmus** quā lībertātem nostram emere spērābāmus. Sed dominus nōbīs dīxit: 'Aliud pistrīnum in Calabriā habeō, sed pānis illīus pistrīnī malus est. Uxōrem tuam quae pānem optimum torret ad illum pistrīnum crās mittam.'"

20 "Abhinc quattuor diēs uxor mea abiit et quattuor diēs miser sum. Sine uxōre meā, servus ***huius*** malī dominī nōn erō! Propter ***haec***, herī ab ***hōc*** malō dominō fūgī. Perīculōsum est, sed uxōrem quam valdē amō invenīre necesse est. Ōlim antehāc **fūgeram** et ergō mihi ***hoc*** collāre dominus **dederat.** Et nunc iterum fugitīvus sum. Grātiās tibi permaximās agō, sed nunc abeō. Uxōrem meam invenīre dēbeō."

Tālia dīcēns in noctem abiit.

VERBA ŪTENDA

abdō, abdere, abdidī,
*   abditum* hide, conceal
abhinc ago
absum, abesse, āfuī be
*   absent, gone*
adsum, adesse, adfuī be
*   near, be present here,*
*   be there for, help*
antehāc before this time
aptus, -a, -um fit, suitable
āra, -ae f. altar
cachinnō (1) laugh
*   loudly*
Calabria, -ae f. region in the
*   heel of Italy*
certē certainly
circumspectō (1) look
*   around*
cīvis, cīvis m./f. citizen
cloāca, -ae f. sewer
collāre, collāris n. collar

cotīdiē daily
cum when
difficultās, -ātis f.
*   difficulty*
diūtius (comparative) for a
*   bit longer*
exeō, exīre, exiī go out
fētidus, -a, -um filthy
fugitīvus, -ī m. fugitive
furnus, -ī m. oven,
*   bakehouse*
fustis, fustis m. club, stick
grātia, -ae f. grace; favor;
*   pl. thanks; grātiās*
*   agere* to thank
*   someone*
herī yesterday
hic, haec, hoc this
inspectō (1) look
*   closely at*
instrūmentum, -ī n. tool

irrumpō, irrumpere, irrūpī
*   burst*
ita so, thus; yes
lībertās, -tātis f. freedom
locus, -ī m. place
loquentia "talking"
maneō, manēre, mansī stay,
*   remain*
miser, misera, miserum
*   wretched, miserable*
mittō, mittere, mīsī send
molae, -ārum f. pl. mill
mūlus, -ī m. mule
nōbīs to us
nōminō (1) name
nōs we, us
ōlim once, formerly
optimus, -a, -um best
opus, operis n. work
pānis, pānis m. bread
pannus, -ī m. cloth, rags

perīculōsus, -a, -um
*   dangerous*
permaximus, -a, -um very
*   great*
pistrīnum, -ī n. bakery
prōpellō, prōpellere,
*   prōpulī* drive, push
*   forward*
quatiō, -ere, quassī shake,
*   wave about*
quiētus, -a, -um quiet
servō (1) save
spērō (1) hope
tālis, tāle such
tangō, tangere, tetigī
*   touch*
torreō, torrēre, torruī
*   bake*
ut as
vōcālis, -e speaking

POSTQUAM LĒGISTĪ

Answer these questions in English. If the question is followed by (L), also answer in Latin.

1. Where does Mendax suggest the runaway slave is hiding? Where is he really hiding? (L)
2. Why does Mendax laugh when he learns that the runaway slave worked in a mill? (L)
3. What plans did the runaway slave and his wife have?
4. Why was the wife sent to Calabria? (L)

Grammatica A

The Pluperfect Tense

The pluperfect tense is the second member of the perfect system you have met. The first was the perfect tense. Here are the "formulas" for forming these two tenses:

Gemma

P. Nonius Zethus was a real baker and priest of Augustus in Ostia. A marble block intended to hold the cinerary urns of Nonius, a fellow freedwoman and his wife, is illustrated in *Lectiō Prīma*. Here is a transcription of the inscription on the front:

P. NONIUS ZETHUS
AUG(USTALIS)
FECIT SIBI ET
NONIAE HILARAE
CONLIBERTAE
NONIAE P. L(IBERTAE)
PELAGIAE CONIUGI
P. NONIUS HERACLIO

Perfect	◆ Perfect Stem		-ī	-imus
	Perfect stem = 3rd principal part minus the -ī	+	-istī	-istis
			-it	-ērunt
Pluperfect	◆ Perfect Stem		-eram	-erāmus
		+	-erās	-erātis
			-erat	-erant

Here is the conjugation of *vocō* in the perfect and pluperfect. Notice how easy it is to form the pluperfect from the perfect by using endings identical to the imperfect of *sum*.

PERFECT		PLUPERFECT	
vocāvī	I have called	vocā**veram**	I had called
vocāvistī	you have called	vocā**verās**	you had called
vocāvit	he/she/it has called	vocā**verat**	he/she/it had called
vocāvimus	we have called	vocā**verāmus**	we had called
vocāvistis	you have called	vocā**verātis**	you had called
vocāvērunt	they have called	vocā**verant**	they had called

Notā Bene:

- The plu- in "pluperfect" comes from the Latin word *plūs* "more." So the tense is literally "more than perfect."
- The **pluperfect** is sometimes called the "past perfect" because it refers to a time prior to the perfect.

Marcus dormīvit postquam cēnāverat.
Marcus **slept** after he **had dined**.

EXERCEĀMUS!

19-2 Using the Pluperfect

Take each pair of Latin sentences and combine them into one sentence beginning with *postquam* (after). Put the sentence with the verb marked in **bold** after *postquam*, and put that verb into the pluperfect tense. Follow the model.

→ Zēthus ex insulā **abiit**. Servus in noctem fūgit.
Postquam Zēthus ex insulā abierat, servus in noctem fūgit.

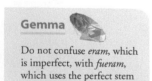

Gemma

Do not confuse *eram*, which is imperfect, with *fueram*, which uses the perfect stem and is pluperfect.

1. Publius Zēthus in insulam **rūpit**. Zēthus Mendācī appropinquāvit.

2. Servus ā Zēthō **fūgit**. Zēthus fugitīvum quaesīvit.

3. Mendax fugitīvum in pannīs fētidīs **abdidit**. Zēthus locum in quō servus latēbat inspectāvit.

4. Zēthus fustem quatiēns et fortiter clāmāns **abiit**. Servus ē pannīs exiit.

5. Servus et uxor in pistrīnō Zēthī multōs annōs **labōrābant**. Dominus uxōrem āmīsit.

6. Servus et uxor aliquid pecūniae **servāvērunt**. Dominus uxōrem ad alterum pistrīnum mīsit.

7. Dominus servō collāre **dedit**. Servus ab hōc malō dominō fūgit.

8. Fugitīvus Mendācī grātiās **ēgit**. In noctem abiit.

The Demonstrative *hic, haec, hoc*

Here is the full declension of *hic, haec, hoc* (this, these):

	MASCULINE	FEMININE	NEUTER
Singular			
Nominative	hic	haec	hoc
Genitive	huius	huius	huius
Dative	huic	huic	huic
Accusative	hunc	hanc	hoc
Ablative	hōc	hāc	hōc
Plural			
Nominative	hī	hae	haec
Genitive	hōrum	hārum	hōrum
Dative	hīs	hīs	hīs
Accusative	hōs	hās	haec
Ablative	hīs	hīs	hīs

All the singular forms of this word are translated "this" in English. All the plurals are "these." *Hic, haec, hoc* refers to someone or something close by or recently mentioned whereas *ille, illa, illud* (that, those) refers to someone or something farther away or mentioned earlier.

Notā Bene:

- Note the *-ius* ending in the genitive singular. Where have you seen this ending before?
- The ending *-c* means "here" and follows familiar endings: *hui-* like *cui* (dative singular) and the ablative singular 2-1-2 endings *-ō, -ā, -ō; hum + c → hunc* and *ham + c → hanc*.
- Compare *hoc* and *hōc*. How does the macron change the meaning of this word?
- All the plural forms except the neuter nominative and accusative have regular 2-1-2 endings.
- The feminine nominative singular and the neuter nominative and accusative plural forms also have the *-c* (here) ending. Note that *haec* can thus mean "this woman," "these things" (subject), or "these things" (object).

Hic, haec, hoc is used as a demonstrative (pointing out) adjective, so remember that it GNCs:

hic vir	this man	*haec fēmina*	this woman	*hoc dōnum*	this gift
hī virī	these men	*hae fēminae*	these women	*haec dōna*	these gifts

Lectiō Secunda

Antequam Legis

In this *lectiō* we get a glimpse of the world of the Roman gladiatorial games. You will practice the pluperfect a bit more and learn how to express comparisons in Latin.

Comparisons

"More," "better," "less," "happier …" All these words are what grammarians call **comparatives**, and they all seem to require the word "than." "X is bigger *than* Y." "A is happier *than* B." Note that the simplest way to make a comparative in English is to add **-er** to the adjective. Sometimes, English uses "more" instead, for example, "more beautiful," "more careful."

The words marked in **bold** in *Lectiō Secunda* are comparatives. The ones that are regular add some form of the ending *-ior* to the basic stem of the adjective. Thus, you will have no trouble in seeing that *longior* means "longer/taller" and *brevior* "shorter."

Other words are irregular (e.g., *melior* "better") and will have to be looked up and/or memorized. Most languages, including English, tend to have some irregular comparatives. Think of "good, better, best," for example.

Whether regular or irregular, all comparatives use the endings of regular 3rd declension nouns, so there is nothing new to learn!

You have already seen how *quam* is used in Latin to mean "than," but "than" can also be expressed in Latin in another way. We have put all the "than" expressions in *italics* in *Lectiō Secunda*. Try to figure out from context the other way that the Romans expressed "than."

EXERCEĀMUS!

19-3 Translating Comparatives

All of the words in column A are comparative adjectives marked in **bold** in *Lectiō Secunda*. Use the reading and English derivatives to match each adjective with its English meaning in column B.

	A		B
_____	1. difficiliōra	A.	better
_____	2. ferociōra	B.	bigger
_____	3. iuvenior	C.	fiercer
_____	4. māior	D.	harder
_____	5. meliōra	E.	higher
_____	6. minor	F.	more
_____	7. pēiora	G.	smaller
_____	8. plūs	H.	worse
_____	9. superiōre	I.	younger

Gemma

Rōmam = "to Rome": Notice that the "ad" you would expect is not here. That is normal in Latin with the names of cities.

MŪNERA

Amphitheātrum plēnum hominibus est quod hodiē Imperātor mūnera magna populīs Rōmānīs dat. In variīs locīs aliī alia agunt.

Hīc, ēditor lūdōrum et Fabius, vir quī animālia Rōmam mūneribus portāvit, in ūnā parte amphitheātrī stant. Ēditor "Fabī," inquit, "anteā, multa bona animālia Rōmam ab Āfricā
5 portāvistī, sed haec animālia quae nūper tulistī **meliōra** atque **ferociōra** *quam* illa omnia alia animālia sunt!"

Illīc, in aliō locō filiī Servīliī colloquuntur. "Lūcī," Marcus rogat, "timēsne mūnera et animālia ferōcia?"

"Nūllō modō!" respondet Lūcius īrātus. "Ōlim, ubi **iuvenior** et **minor** eram, strepitum et cruōrem timēbam, sed nunc aetāte **māior** sum et nōn iam timeō. **Plūs** sanguinis et cruōris **melius** est!"

10 In parte **superiōre** amphitheātrī nōnnūllī spectātōrēs dē mūneribus dīcunt.

Ūnus rogat: "Vīdistīne mūnera quae ōlim Pompeius Magnus dedit? Haec mūnera certē bona erunt, sed illa **meliōra** erant."

Alibī paucī gladiātōrēs pauca verba dīcunt sed **plūrēs** silentium tenent. Ūnus gladiātor "Ille Thrax" intrā sē inquit "multō **māior** *aliīs* est. Contrā hunc pugnāre nōn volō!" Et Thrax: "Ille gladiātor quī prope mūrum stat" intrā sē inquit "ille
15 multō **minor** *mē* est. Contrā hunc pugnāre volō. Fortasse in fīne mūnerum vīvus erō!" Sīc omnēs stant, aliī alia cōgitantēs.

Duō aliī gladiātōrēs quī amīcī sunt inter sē dīcunt. Ūnus "Haec," inquit, "animālia in Urbe nunc **difficiliōra** et **māiōra** sunt *quam* illa **pēiōra** animālia quae tunc in prōvinciīs pugnābāmus."

In aliō locō ūnus bestiārius vestem Herculis trahēns sōlus et maestus stat. Hodiē contrā multōs leōnēs pugnābit sīcut ōlim Herculēs contrā leōnem pugnāvit. Nōn gladiō sed fuste pugnābit, sīcut Herculēs. Hodiē hic bestiārius certē
20 in terrā iacēbit.

Vēnātor et Leō Pugnantēs in Arēnā

🔊 VERBA ŪTENDA

aetās, aetātis f. age, period

Āfrica, -ae f. the Roman province of Africa (modern Tunisia)

alibī elswhere, in other places

aliī alia agunt "Some were doing some things while others were doing others."

anteā previously

atque and, and also

bestiārius, -iī m. animal fighter

certē certainly

colloquuntur "(they) are speaking"

contrā (+ acc.) against, opposite (to)

cruor, cruōris m. gore, blood

cum when

ēditor, -ōris m. organizer; *ēditor ludōrum* public official in charge of the games

ferōx, ferōcis fierce

fustis, fustis m. staff, club

gerō, gerere, gessī, bear, carry, wear

hic, haec, hoc this

hīc here

iaceō, iacēre, iacuī lie

illīc there

imperātor, imperātōris m. general, commander, emperor

intrā sē "to himself"

iuvenis young; *iuvenior,* younger

leō, leōnis m. lion

locus, -ī m. place

maestus, -a, -um sad

māior, māius greater, larger, older; m. pl. ancestors, elders

melior, melius better

minor, minus smaller

mīrābilis, mīrābile amazing, wonderous

modus, -ī m. way, manner

mūrus, -ī m. wall

nōn iam no longer

nūper recently

ōlim once, formerly

pars, partis f. part, piece

pēior, pēius worse

plēnus, -a, -um (+ abl.) full of, filled with

plūrēs, plūra more (in number)

plūs more (in amount)

prior, prius former

priusquam before

Rōmam "to Rome"

sanguis, sanguinis m. blood

silentium, -iī n. silence

spectātor, -ōris m. spectator

strepitum m. noise

superior, superius higher

Thrax, Thrācis m. Thracian; a fighter with lighter armor, including a helmet and greaves on both legs

urbs, urbis f. city, esp. the city of Rome

varius, -a, -um varied, mixed

vestis, vestis f. garments, clothing

vīvus, -a, -um living

POSTQUAM LĒGISTĪ

Answer these questions in both Latin and English if the question is followed by (L). Otherwise, just respond in English.

1. What job does the *ēditor lūdōrum* do and what does he think about the animals acquired for today's games?
2. How has Lucius' attitude toward the games changed over the years?
3. What did people think about the games sponsored by Pompey the Great? (L)
4. What weapon does the bestiarius dressed like Hercules carry? What will he fight in the arena? (L)
5. What would your reaction be if you witnessed such games today? Why?

Grammatica B

Forming Comparatives in Latin

Most regular comparative adjectives are formed by adding *-ior* (masc. and fem.) and *-ius* (neuter) to the stem, followed by regular 3rd declension endings. It does not matter whether the simple (positive) form of the adjective uses 2-1-2 or 3rd declension endings. Here is how it works:

vērus, -a, -um   *vēr-* + *-ior, -ius* = *vērior, -ius* truer, rather true, fairly true

pulcher, pulchra, pulchrum   *pulchr-* + *-ior, -ius* = *pulchrior, -ius* more beautiful

fortis, forte   *fort-* + *-ior, -ius* = *fortior, -ius* braver

Now see how the other forms are made. Comparative adjectives are two-termination 3rd declension adjectives.

	MASCULINE / FEMININE	NEUTER	MASCULINE / FEMININE	NEUTER
Singular				
Nominative	pulchrior	pulchrius	fortior	fortius
Genitive	pulchriōris	pulchriōris	fortiōris	fortiōris
Dative	pulchriōrī	pulchriōrī	fortiōrī	fortiōrī
Accusative	pulchriōrem	pulchrius	fortiōrem	fortius
Ablative	pulchriōre	pulchriōre	fortiōre	fortiōre
Plural				
Nominative	pulchriōrēs	pulchriōra	fortiōrēs	fortiōra
Genitive	pulchriōrum	pulchriōrum	fortiōrum	fortiōrum
Dative	pulchriōribus	pulchriōribus	fortiōribus	fortiōribus
Accusative	pulchriōrēs	pulchriōra	fortiōrēs	fortiōra
Ablative	pulchriōribus	pulchriōribus	fortiōribus	fortiōribus

Notā Bene:

- Comparative adjectives use regular 3rd declension, not i-stem, endings. Thus, you find the genitive plural *fortiōrum* (not *fortiōrium*) and neuter nominative and accusative plural *fortiōra* (not *fortiōria*).
- The neuter nominative and accusative singular forms are the only ones not formed from the *-ior* stem. To create these forms, drop the *-or* and add *-us*, as in *pulchrius* and *fortius*.

Some Latin adjectives form their comparatives by changing their stems. This happens in English too:

good	better
bad	worse

Latin does the same thing with these words:

bonus, -a, -um	***melior, melius***	better
malus, -a, -um	***pēior, pēius***	worse

The following adjectives have regular comparatives in English but irregular ones in Latin. Remember that the words marked in bold are *Verba Discenda*.

magnus, -a, -um	***māior, māius***	greater, older
multus, -a, -um	**(no masc./fem.), *plūs***	more (in amount)
multī, -ae, -a	***plūrēs, plūra***	more (in number)
parvus, -a, -um	***minor, minus***	smaller, younger

The Latin **comparative adverb** is identical in form to the neuter nominative comparative adjective. Compare these sentences:

***Melius** vīnum videō.*	I see a better wine.
***Melius** nunc videō.*	I see better now.

In the first sentence *melius* is an adjective modifying *vīnum*. In the second it is an adverb describing the verbal action. How can you tell the difference between a comparative adjective and a comparative adverb? If there is no singular neuter noun in the sentence, try the adverb first. In other words, let context be your guide, just as in English, where the two uses of "better" rarely confuse us.

Using Comparatives in Latin

Typically, a comparative is comparing two people or things. If both elements are expressed, they are joined in Latin by the word *quam* and in English by the word "than":

Hic **melior quam** *ille est.*	This person is **better than** that one.
Haec **intelligentior quam** *hic est.*	This woman is **more intelligent than** this man.
Haec **celerius quam** *hic currit.*	She runs **faster than** he does.

When you read *Lectiō Secunda*, did you notice the other way that Latin can express a comparison? Here are some examples:

Ille Thrax multō **māior aliīs** *est.*	That Thracian is much bigger than the others.
Ille multō **minor mē** *est.*	That guy is much smaller than I am.

In these sentences Latin has used the ablative case instead of *quam*. This is called the **ablative of comparison**.

Translating Comparatives

If comparatives can be translated "more," "rather," and "too," how do you know which to choose? If no explicit comparison is being made in the sentence, it may make more sense to translate the comparative as a simple (positive) adjective with "rather" or "too."

> *Haec* **melior** *est.* "She is better." or "She is rather good." or "She is too good."
> *Hic* **intelligentior** *est.* "He is more intelligent." or "He is rather intelligent." or "He is too intelligent."

In general, pick the translation that makes the best sense in context! It is useful to know that, in order of frequency, the translations are: "more," then "rather," and finally "too."

Gemma

Notice the use of *multō* with comparative adjectives: *multō māior* = much older Literally this means "older by much" in Latin. *Multō* is in the ablative case and this use of the ablative is called **ablative of degree of difference**.

EXERCEĀMUS!

19-4 Comparatives

Choose the word in parentheses with which the comparative adjective in bold agrees in GNC. Then translate the sentence two ways, if the sentence allows it. Follow the model.

> → Haec (bursae, animālia, virī) **meliōra** sunt.
>
> *Haec animālia meliōra sunt.*
> These animals are rather good.
> These animals are better.

1. (Fēminae, virīs, animālia) **meliōrēs** sunt.

2. (Fēmina, virōs, animālia) **ferōciōra** invēnērunt?

3. (Puer, Animal, Puellae) **pēior** est.

4. (Gladiī, Forum, Insula) **mīrābiliōrēs** sunt.

5. (Mūnera, Puella, Gladiātōrēs) **grandiōra** quam illa vīderāmus!

6. **Plūrēs** (spectātōrēs, animālia, gladiātōribus) mūnera vident.

Gemma

Avĕ, imperātor. Moritūrī tē salūtant! Hail, Emperor! (Those about to die salute you).

There is no evidence that gladiators regularly addressed the emperor in this way at the beginning of games, but it has become a fixture in Hollywood, even showing up in the title of a fairly forgettable 1937 movie entitled "We Who Are About to Die," which was a prison escape film!

Mōrēs Rōmānī

Mūnera Rōmāna

Mūnera, or games like the ones described in this chapter, were a regular feature of Roman life from early times. The earliest ones were probably funeral games held in honor of important men.

Over time, games became more and more elaborate and were organized around religious festivals and other public occasions. *Aedīlēs,* elected magistrates in charge of public works, were responsible for these games, which they were expected to pay for out of their own pockets. Ambitious politicians like Julius Caesar went deeply into debt as aediles to organize very expensive games in order to curry favor with the public.

These games often included gladiators, or fighters with a *gladius* (sword). Most gladiators were prisoners of war, slaves, or indentured free citizens. Some were even condemned criminals. There were different kinds of gladiators, distinguished by their weaponry and armor.

- **Samnīs, Samnītis** m. Samnite. A heavily armed and armored fighter, equipped with helmet (*galea, -ae* f.), oblong shield (*scūtum, -ī* n.), sword (*gladius, -iī* m.), wide leather belt (*balteus, -ī* m.), and metal greave (*ocrea, -ae* f.) on one leg only.

- **Mirmillō, -ōnis** m. Mirmillo. Armed like a Samnite, but with a special, fish-shaped helmet.

- **Rētiārius, -iī** m. Netter. This fighter was protected only with a shoulder guard (on his left side). For attacking, he carried a trident and a net and was often pitted against a Samnite or a Mirmillo.

- **Thrax, Thrācis** n. Thracian. A fighter with lighter armor, including a helmet and greaves on both legs. With a bare torso and an arm guard (*manica, -ae* f.) on his right arm, he carried a small shield (*parmula, -ae* f.) in one hand and a short sword (*sīca, -ae* f.) in the other.

In addition to these gladiators, other performers in the games included the animal fighter (*bestiārius, iī* m.) and hunter (*vēnātor, -ōris* m.), both of whom specialized in battling exotic animals like elephants, lions, bears, and leopards.

Roman spectators especially enjoyed unusual pairings of contestants, not only human vs. human, but even human vs. wild animal. Despite its many historical inaccuracies, Ridley Scott's film *Gladiator* (2000) captures the exotic and bloody nature of such contests.

Gemma

The Latin expression *pollicem vertere* (to turn the thumb) may actually have referred to turning the thumb toward the chest, not downward, to call for death as shown in a famous painting by Jean-Léon Gérôme depicted below and in many a Hollywood film.

Gladiators were the sports superstars of ancient Rome and were often celebrated out of the arena. Here is an excerpt from a poem by Martial (V, 24), in which the many great qualities of a gladiator named Hermes are listed. There is no main verb in this poem. In each line, understand Hermes as the subject of *est* (Hermes is . . .). See the *Verba Ūtenda* and you should be able to translate this fairly easily.

> Hermēs Martia saeculī voluptās,
> Hermēs omnibus ērudītus armīs,
> Hermēs et gladiātor et magister,
> Hermēs, vincere nec ferīre doctus,
> Hermēs cūra laborque lūdiārum.

Notice Hermes' great reputation among the women. This was apparently not unusual. Here are two pieces of graffiti from the walls of Pompeii to illustrate this appeal:

> Suspīrium puellārum Celadus Thrax.

> *Corpus Inscriptiōnum Latīnārum* (C.I.L.) IV, 4397

> Crescens rētiārius pupārum nocturnārum

> C.I.L. 4. 4356

Pollice Verso, *pictūra (1872) ā Jean-Léon Gérôme (1824–1904)*

🔊 VERBA ŪTENDA

arma, armōrum n. pl. arms, weapons
Avē! Hail!
cūra, ae f. worry, concern, care, anxiety
doctus, -a, -um learned

ērudītus, -a, -um skilled
feriō, ferīre hit, kill, slay
lūdia, -ae f. a gladiator's girl, "girl of the *lūdus*," a sort of groupie!

Martius, -a, -um of Mars, martial
nocturnus, -a, -um nocturnal, of the night
pūpa, -ae f. doll, girl

rētiārius, -ī m. netter
saeculum, -ī n. age, era
suspīrium, -ī n. sigh, heartthrob

Latīna Hodierna

Latin Comparative Adjectives in English

Latin comparatives have resulted in a number of English derivatives. Knowing the meaning of the Latin word makes it easier to understand what these English words mean:

Latin Comparative	English Meaning	Derivative
melior, melius	better	ameliorate
pēior, pēius	worse	pejorative
māior, māius	greater, older	majority
(no masc./fem.), *plūs*	more (in amount)	plus
plūrēs, plūra	more (in number)	plurality
minor, minus	smaller, younger	minus, minority
posterior, posterius	later; inferior	posterior
priōr, prius	former	priority
superior, superius	higher	superiority

Notā Bene:

- Remember the birth of "J" illustrated in words like "pejorative" and "majority."
- In mathematics the words *plūs* (+) and *minus* (-) are used to refer to arithmetic functions.

Lawyers, for example, talk about arguments a fortiori (from the stronger), in which one claim is proven or supported by another stronger argument. For example, one can argue a fortiori that, if it is illegal to steal $10, then it is also illegal to steal $50.

Philosophers talk about a priori (from the former) and a posteriori (from the later) proofs or knowledge. For example, we know a priori that all Romans spoke Latin but we know a posteriori that some Romans also spoke Greek. Note the *-ī* alternate ending for the ablative singular.

The motto of the International Olympic Committee consists of three comparative Latin adverbs:

Citius! Altius! Fortius! "Faster! Higher! Stronger!"

Watch for a character to use the Olympic motto in an upcoming *lectiō*.

The motto of the State of New York is the comparative adjective *Excelsior!* (Higher!).

Finally, don't forget the following expression inscribed on the Great Seal of the United States of America (to the right):

Ē plūribus ūnum "Out of many, one"

Can you find this expression on the detail of a dollar bill at right? Although we have used the traditional translation of this expression, "many" does not accurately translate *plūribus*, does it? This is another good reason to study Latin!

Ē Plūribus Ūnum

Orbis Terrārum Rōmānus

Amphitheātrum Flāviānum

The earliest gladiatorial contests were informal affairs fought in temporary facilities in open areas like the Roman Forum. The first stone amphitheater was built in Rome in 29 B.C. and was destroyed in the great fire in 64 A.D. during the reign of Nero.

Work on a new stone amphitheater began in 70–72 A.D. under the reign of Vespasian, but the building was not completed until 80 A.D., under Titus, with spectacular games commemorated in the poetry of Martial. The original name of this building was the Flavian Amphitheater (*Amphitheātrum Flāviānum*).

This amphitheater was the largest such structure ever built by the Romans. Because of its size and because of the Colossus, a giant statue of Nero located nearby, the amphitheater eventually became known as the Colosseum, the name by which we know it today.

The structure, a masterpiece of Roman engineering, was built of concrete and stone with a marble façade. The amphitheater was capable of holding about 50,000 spectators and had awnings that could be drawn to protect these crowds from the elements. So the Colosseum was in many ways comparable to one of our modern domed stadiums.

Adjacent to the Flavian Amphitheater and connected via an underground passage way was the *Lūdus Magnus*, a gladiatorial school with its own practice arena in the same elliptical shape as that of the amphitheater.

The Colosseum remained intact and was used for games and entertainment until the medieval period. Unfortunately, in subsequent years the building was used as a quarry for building materials.

Amphitheātrum Flāviānum, Lūdus Magnus et Colossus Nerōnis

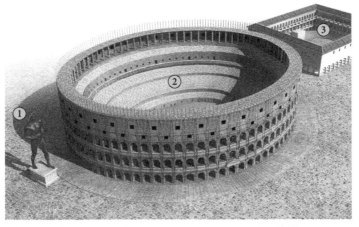

① **Colossus Nerōnis**   ② **Amphiteātrum Flāviānun**   ③ **Lūdus Magnus**

Amphitheātrum Flāviānum Hodiē

Lūdus Magnus et Amphitheātrum Flāviānum

QUID PUTĀS?

1. Compare the gladiator Hermes described by Martial to a modern American athlete. Be sure to explain why you chose that particular athlete.

2. Why do you think the Romans had so many different types of gladiators?

3. In a contest between a retiarius and a Samnite, which do you think would have the advantage and why?

4. What modern building or monument would have a reputation comparable to that of the Colosseum in Rome? Why?

5. Why do you think the expression "e pluribus unum" was chosen as the motto of the United States? Why do you think that the Founding Fathers chose to say this in Latin instead of English?

(1) Forum Rōmānum   (2) Amphitheātrum Flāviānum

Amphitheātrum Flāviānum et Forum Rōmānum dē Caelō

EXERCEĀMUS!

19-5 Scrībāmus

Retell events from *Lectiō Prīma* in the present tense by changing the form of every verb marked in **bold** in the following sentences. HINT: You may have to consult the *Verb Ūtenda* following *Lectiō Prīma* for help with principal parts.

1. Zēthus in insulam **rūpit** et Mendācī **appropinquāvit**.

2. Zēthus **circumspectāvit** et locum, in quō servus **latēbat**, **inspectāvit**, sed pannōs fētidōs tangere **nōluit**.

3. Fustem quatiēns et fortiter clāmāns **abiit**.

4. Servus sub pannīs diūtius **mansit** et tunc **exiit**.

5. Mendax dē difficultāte servī audīre **voluit**.

6. Tunc servus dē difficultātibus suīs **dīxit**.

7. In pistrīnō huius Zēthī cum uxōre **labōrāveram**.

8. Uxor pānem in furnō **torrēbat** et ego molās cotīdiē **prōpellēbam.**

9. Talia dīcēns, servus in noctem **abiit**.

19-6 Colloquāmur

For this class exercise you will need some items found in any classroom. Here are some suggestions: two writing utensils (*stilus, -ī* n.), two books (*liber, librī* m.), two sheets of paper (*charta, -ae* f.), two wristwatches (*hōrologium, -iī* n.), and two coins (*nummus, -ī* m.). Pile these objects in two groups in different parts of the classroom. Then make commands following the models.

Point to the book in the far pile and say to one classmate

→ *Da mihi, sī tibi placet,* ***illum librum***.

Now point to the book in the pile near you and say to more than one classmate

→ *Date mihi, sī vōbīs placet,* ***hunc librum***.

Continue asking for other objects using similar patterns.

19-7   Verba Discenda

Use the *Verba Discenda* to form the comparative adjective for each Latin adjective listed below. Then give the meaning of each and an English derivative for the comparative form. Follow the model.

Adjective	Meaning	Comparative	Meaning	Derivative
→ *bonus, -a, -um*	good	melior, melius	better	ameliorate

1. *malus, -a, -um*; 2. *multus, -a, um*; 3. *multī, -ae, -a*; 4. *parvus, -a, -um*; 5. *superus, -a, -um*

VERBA DISCENDA

abdo, abdere, abdidī, abditum **hide, conceal**

absum, abesse, āfuī **be absent, gone**

adsum, adesse, adfuī **be near, be present or here, be there for, help**

āra, -ae f. **altar**

contrā (+ acc.) **against, facing** [contradict]

gratia, -ae f. **grace; favor; pl. thanks;** *gratiās agere* **to thank someone**

herī **yesterday**

hic, haec, hoc **this** [ad hoc]

inspectō (1) **look closely at** [inspector]

locus, -ī m. **place** [locality]

māior, māius **greater, larger, older; m. pl. ancestors, elders**

melior, melius **better** [amelioration]

minor, minus **smaller** [minority]

ōlim **once, formerly**

pars, partis f. **part, piece** [partition]

pēior, pēius **worse** [pejorative]

plūrēs, plūra **more (in number)** [plurality]

plūs **more (in amount)**

prior, prius **former** [priority]

priusquam **before**

superior, superius **higher** [superiority]

Angulus Grammaticus

"This Here" Deictic Enclitic -c(e)

The forms of *hic, haec, hoc* make more sense if you know that Latin can add a *-c(e)* at the end of a word to mean "here" or "there." The technical term for this is a **deictic enclitic**, i.e., a word ending that points out or shows something, especially direction. In earlier Latin authors like Plautus, there are forms like *illīc* (that man there) and *illaec* (that woman there). This type of expression is not that far from some dialectical forms of American English where we can still hear "this here one" and "that one yonder."

The genitive singular of *hic, haec, hoc* is *huius*, but, occasionally, Romans used *huiusce,* as in the expression *huiusce modī* (of this type here). The *-c(e)* was not regularly used with *huius*, but now look back at the declension of *hic, haec, hoc* and point out the forms where this *-c(e)* was always used.

The *-c(e)* is visible is in other Latin words, such as *Ecce!* (Look here!), and is useful for understanding the following Latin adverbs:

hīc	at this place here	*illīc*	at that place over there
hūc	to this place here	*illūc*	to that place over there
hinc	from this place here	*illinc*	from that place over there
hāc	by this path here	*illāc*	by that path over there

Now compare these adverbs with those formed from *iste, ista, istud:*

illīc	at that place over there	*istīc*	at that place of yours, where you are
illūc	to that place over there	*istūc*	to that place of yours, to where you are
illinc	from that place over there	*istinc*	from that place of yours, from where you are
illāc	by that path over there	*istāc*	by that path of yours

By comparison, adverbs formed from *is, ea, id* do not have this deictic emphasis:

ibi	there	*eō*	to that place	*eā*	that way, by that path

If you can recognize the fine distinctions in meaning among all these words, you know you are really beginning to think like a Roman.

Photo Credits

page 231 (top) Wikipedia Commons/Foto Musei Vaticani; **page 232** Wikipedia Commons/Foto Musei Vaticani; **page 236** Thomas J. Sienkewicz; **page 240** Photos.com; **page 241** Photos.com; **page 242 (bottom left)** Victor Martinez/Photo by Victor Martinez used with permission; **page 242 (bottom right)** Thomas J. Sienkewicz/Photo by Thomas J. Sienkewicz used with permission; **page 243** SF Photo/Shutterstock

20

Nōn Perseus sed Herculēs!

Herculēs Infans cum Serpente

Lectiō Prīma

Antequam Legis

In *Lectiō Prīma* Aelius and Licinia talk together about their unborn child. Their decision to compare him to the hero Hercules instead of Perseus leads Aelius to tell his wife the story of baby Hercules and the snakes.

Hercules

Hercules was the son of Jupiter and Alcmena, a mortal Greek woman, who was already pregnant by her mortal husband, Amphitryon, when Jupiter visited her. You will hear about all these events again soon, when the two families attend a play of Plautus based on this story. Alcmena bore twins, Hercules (son of Jupiter) and his mortal half brother, Iphicles (son of Amphitryon). Juno, Jupiter's sister and jealous wife, was furious and tried to eliminate Hercules. This is the point in the story where *Lectiō Prīma* starts.

Superlatives

In Chapter 19 you learned about comparatives (e.g., bigger, better). There is a third degree of adjective, called the **superlative**. In English we form these by using the word "most" or by adding "-est" to the adjective, but there are irregular forms as well.

POSITIVE	COMPARATIVE	SUPERLATIVE
angry	angrier more angry	angriest most angry
tall	taller	tallest
good	better	best
bad	worse	worst
many	more	most

Most Latin superlatives end in *-issimus, -a, -um*. But be sure to do Exercise 20-1 as you read.

GRAMMATICA
Superlative Adjectives and Adverbs
The Future Perfect Tense
More on Adverbs and Conjunctions

MŌRĒS RŌMĀNĪ
Herculēs Rōmānus

LATĪNA HODIERNA
Herculēs Hodiē

ORBIS TERRĀRUM RŌMĀNUS
Herculēs Rōmae

ANGULUS GRAMMATICUS
The Future Perfect and Sequence of Tenses

> **LECTIŌNĒS:**
> **NOSTER NŌVUS HERCULĒS**
> and
> **SCELUS HERCULIS**
>
> Aelius and Licinia worry about the future of their unborn child and decide to compare him to the hero Hercules instead of Perseus. Aelius tells his wife stories about Hercules' childhood and great deeds.

245

From *Disce! An Introductory Latin Course, volume 1*, First Edition. Francesco Bonavita. Copyright © 2011 by Pearson Education, Inc. Published by Pearson Prentice Hall. All rights reserved.

Notā Bene:

- Superlatives can also be translated as "very," e.g., *Vir fortissimus* can indicate a "very brave man." A *fēmina fortissima* could be "a most brave woman!"
- **Superlative adverbs** are formed by dropping the 2-1-2 adjective ending and adding *-ē*.

facillimus, -a, -um easiest ⟶ *facillimē* most/very easily

EXERCEĀMUS!

20-1 Classifying Superlatives

As you read, look for superlative adjectives and adverbs marked in **bold**. Put them into the following four groups according to how they are formed: *-issimus, -a, -um*; *-illimus, -a, -um*; *-rimus, -a, -um*; and all the others (with special or irregular forms). Follow the model.

⟶ *perterritissima*   *-issimus, -a, -um*   *-illimus, -a, -um*   *-rimus, -a, -um*   irregular

🔊 NOSTER NŌVUS HERCULĒS

Ūnā nocte Aelius et Licinia sedent et dē verbīs astrologī multa dīcunt. Licinia "Vērumne est?" inquit, "Eritne puer noster hērōs sicut Perseus? Sed quae facta magna hic puer facere poterit? Āh, Aelī, **perterritissima** sum. Et tū? Quid ac-
5 cidet? Eritne necesse fīliō nostrō monstra **difficillima** oppugnāre?"

Aelius lēniter rīdet et mulierem mulcet. "Nōlī," inquit, "timēre, Licinia. Astrologī nōn semper vēra dīcunt. Fīlius nōn Perseus nōvus nōbīs erit, sed nōvus Herculēs, hērōs
10 māior erit! Nulla perīcula eī nocēbunt! Per totum orbem terrārum ībit et **maxima** monstra necābit sicut Herculēs ipse necābat sed nec perīculum nec vulnera habēbit. Deī ipsī fīliolum nostrum et nōs cōnservābunt! Ecce! Audī fābulam **clārissimam** dē Hercule:

Herculēs dē Forō Boāriō

15 "Herculēs, Alcmēnae fīlius, ōlim in Graeciā habitābat. Hic omnium hominum **optimus** hērōs erat. At Iūnō, rēgīna deōrum, Alcmēnam ōderat et Herculem īnfantem necāre voluit. Mīsit igitur duōs serpentēs **ferōcissimās** et **saevissimās** quae mediā nocte in cubiculum Alcmēnae
20 vēnērunt, ubi Herculēs cum frātre suō dormiēbat. Nec autem in cūnīs nec in lectīs, sed in scūtō **maximō** cubābant. Serpentēs **celerrimī** appropinquantēs scūtum movēbant; itaque puerī ē somnō excitātī sunt.

"Iphiclēs, frāter Herculis, **fortissimē** exclāmāvit; sed
25 Herculēs ipse, **fortissimus** puer, haudquāquam timēbat. **Minimīs** manibus serpentēs ferōcēs statim prehendit, et **facillimē** colla eārum magnā vī compressit. Tālī modō puer serpentēs necāvit. Alcmēna autem, **miserrima** māter puerōrum, **horrendissimum** clāmōrem audīverat, et marītum suum ē somnō excitāverat. Ille **celerrimē** gladium suum rapuit et tum ad puerōs properābat, sed ubi ad locum vēnit, rem **mīrābilissimam** vīdit, Herculēs enim rīdēbat
30 et serpentēs mortuās mōnstrābat."

🔊 VERBA ŪTENDA

accidō, accidere, accidī
   happen
Alcmēna, -ae f. Alcmena,
   mother of Hercules
***at* but, and yet**
***autem* however**
***clāmor, clāmōris* m. shout**
clārus, -a, -um famous
collum, -ī n. neck
comprimō, comprimere,
   compressī press, squeeze
   together
conservō (1) preserve, keep
   safe
cubō (1) sleep, lie
cūnae, cūnārum f. pl. cradle
***enim* for, because**
excitō (1) awaken, excite,
   raise; *excitātī sunt* "were
   awakened"
exclāmō (1) call out
***facilis, facile* easy**

***factum, -ī* n. deed**
fāma, -ae* f. fame, rumor,
   report
ferox, ferōcis fierce, savage
fīliolus, -ī m. little son
   (affectionate)
Graecia, -ae f. Greece
haudquāquam by no means
Herculēs, Herculis m.
   Hercules
hērōs, hērōis m. hero
horrendus, -a, -um horrible,
   terrible
***igitur* therefore**
***itaque* therefore**
lūnō, lūnōnis f. Juno, queen
   of the gods
lēniter gently
manibus "with his hands"
***maximus, -a, -um* greatest**
medius, -a, -um the middle of
***minimus, -a, -um* smallest**

mīrābilis, mīrābile
   astonishing, amazing
mittō, mittere, mīsī,
   ***missum* send**
modus, -ī m. way, manner
monstrō (1) show
monstrum, -ī n. monster
mortuus, -a, -um dead
moveō, movēre, mōvī
   move
mulceō, mulcēre, mulsī
   soothe, stroke
mulier, mulieris f. woman,
   wife
necō (1) kill, slay
nōbīs to us; *nōs* us
nox, noctis f. night
ōdī, ōdisse hate
oppugnō (1) attack
***optimus, -a, -um* best**
orbis, orbis* m. circle, ring;
   ***orbis terrārum* circle of**

   the lands, i.e., "the
   world"
***perīculum, -ī* n. danger**
perterritus, -a, -um very
   frightened
prehendō, prehendere, pre-
   hendī seize, take hold of
properō (1) hasten
rapiō, rapere, rapuī,
   ***raptum* snatch, seize**
rēgīna, -ae f. queen
rem thing, event
saevus, -a, -um savage,
   cruel
scūtum, -ī n. shield
serpens, serpentis f. snake,
   serpent
somnus, -ī m. sleep
***statim* immediately**
***tum* then**
vī "with strength"
vulnus, vulneris n. wound

POSTQUAM LĒGISTĪ

Answer these questions in English.

1. How does the conversation of Aelius and Licinia indicate that they are expectant parents? What does their conversation indicate about their relationship?
2. Why does Aelius prefer to compare his unborn son to Hercules rather than Perseus?
3. What do you think of Juno's behavior in the story about Hercules and the snakes? Does she act the way you would expect a god to act? What does this tell you about Roman gods?
4. What does the story of Hercules and the snakes suggest about Hercules as a hero?

Grammatica A

Superlative Adjectives and Adverbs

Regular Formation

Most Latin adjectives form **superlatives** by adding *-issimus, -a, -um* to the stem. This works for both 2-1-2 and 3rd declension adjectives:

ADJECTIVE	STEM	ENDING	EXAMPLE
laetus, -a, -um	laet-	-issimus, -a, -um	laetissimus, -a, -um
fortis, -e	fort-	-issimus, -a, -um	fortissimus, -a, -um

Exceptions

Any adjective with a masculine nominative singular ending in *-er* forms a superlative by adding *-rimus, -a, -um* **not to the stem** but directly to the masculine nominative singular form. This is true for both 2-1-2 and 3rd declension adjectives:

ADJECTIVE	MASCULINE NOMINATIVE SINGULAR	ENDING	EXAMPLE
miser, misera, miserum	miser	-rimus, -a, -um	miserrimus, -a, -um
pulcher, -chra, -chrum	pulcher	-rimus, -a, -um	pulcherrimus, -a, -um
ācer, ācris, ācre	ācer	-rimus, -a, -um	ācerrimus, -a, -um

Six adjectives ending in *-lis* form their superlatives by adding *-limus, -a, -um* to the stem:

ADJECTIVE	STEM	ENDING	EXAMPLE
facilis, -e	facil-	-limus, -a, -um	facillimus, -a, -um
difficilis, -e	difficil-	-limus, -a, -um	difficillimus, -a, -um
similis, -e	simil-	-limus, -a, -um	simillimus, -a, -um
dissimilis, -e	dissimil-	-limus, -a, -um	dissimillimus, -a, -um
gracilis, -e	gracil-	-limus, -a, -um	gracillimus, -a, -um
humilis, -e	humil-	-limus, -a, -um	humillimus, -a, -um

Other adjectives ending in *-lis* form their superlatives regularly, by adding *-issimus, -a, -um* to the stem:

$$\textit{crūdēlis, -e} \longrightarrow \textit{crūdēlissimus, -a, -um.}$$

Irregular Superlatives

Finally, here is a list of irregular superlative adjectives (along with their positive and comparative forms). They are marked in **bold**. All entail stem changes. You will see several of these for the first time in *Lectiō Secunda*. They are all *Verba Discenda*.

bonus, -a, -um	*melior, melius*	***optimus, -a, -um***	best
malus, -a, -um	*pēior, pēius*	***pessimus, -a, -um***	worst
magnus, -a, -um	*māior, maius*	***maximus, -a, -um***	greatest
multus, -a, -um	*plūrēs, plūra*	***plūrimus, -a, -um***	most
parvus, -a, -um	*minor, minus*	***minimus, -a, -um***	smallest
no positive	*prior, prius*	***prīmus, -a, -um***	first
superus, -a, -um	*superior, superius*	***suprēmus, -a, -um***	highest, final
		summus, -a, -um	highest, greatest

Using the Superlative

Quam is sometimes used with a superlative to mean "as _____ as possible"

quam plūrimī	as many as possible
quam celerrimē	as quickly as possible
quam facillimē	as easily as possible

You will see an example of this in the next *lectiō*.

EXERCEĀMUS!

20-2 **Comparatives and Superlatives**

Match the English word in column A with its Latin equivalent in column B.

	A		B
1.	greater	A.	celerrimus
2.	smaller	B.	difficillimus
3.	fastest	C.	facilior
4.	prettier	D.	intelligentior
5.	worst	E.	laetissimus
6.	better	F.	māior
7.	happiest	G.	maximus
8.	greatest	H.	melior
9.	best	I.	minor
10.	easier	J.	optimus
11.	most difficult	K.	pessimus
12.	more intelligent	L.	pulchrior

Lectiō Secunda

Antequam Legis

In *Lectiō Secunda* Aelius continues telling the story of Hercules to his wife. In the story, several years have passed since the events described in *Lectiō Prīma,* and Hercules is now married to his first wife. After finishing his story, Aelius suggests a name for his unborn child.

The Future Perfect Tense

As you read this story about Hercules, you are introduced to your final Latin tense, the future perfect. This is the third tense in the perfect system. The other two are the perfect and pluperfect.

Recognizing the Future Perfect

The name says it all. It is a tense that is in the future, but also has a "perfected" or "done" sense to it. In short, if two things are going to happen in the future, and one clearly happens first, then that one goes into the future perfect tense. Here is an example you will see in *Lectiō Secunda.*

> Sī nēmō mē **vīderit,** nēmō mē oppugnābit!
> If no one will have seen me, no one will attack me.

or, more colloquially,

> If no one sees me, no one will attack me.

Both parts of the sentence refer to the future, but one will clearly happen before the other occurs. That "done" one goes into the future perfect tense.

The literal translation of the future perfect is "will have," but this is rare in today's speech. Ask your teacher's preference in translating this tense.

Forming the Future Perfect

perfect stem (3rd PP minus the -ī)	+	-erō	-erimus
		-eris	-eritis
		-erit	-erint

Gemma

To "inform someone" in Latin is to "make them more certain" about it. *Tē certiōrem dē Marcō faciō* means "I inform you about Marcus." Look for this expression in *Lectiō Secunda*.

For now, when you see a future perfect, think "will have" and translate that thought into appropriate English. All future perfects in the *lectiō* are in ***bold italics***.

EXERCEĀMUS!

20-3   Recognizing Perfect, Pluperfect, and Future Perfect

As you read, make a line-by-line list of all the verbs marked in **bold** or ***bold italics***. The verbs in ***bold italics*** are future perfect. Those in **bold** are either perfect or pluperfect. The endings will help you tell the difference. Indicate the tense of each verb. Then translate the verb appropriately into English. Follow the models.

Line	Verb	Tense	Translation
→ 5	incidit	perfect	he fell into
→ 9	vīderit	future perfect	he will have seen

SCELUS HERCULIS

Aelius "Multōs post annōs," inquit, "mea cāra, Herculēs cum Megarā, uxōre suā, beātam vītam agēbat; sed paucōs post annōs Herculēs subitō in furōrem
5 **incidit** atque Megaram et līberōs suōs **occīdit**. Post breve tempus ad sānitātem **rediit**, et propter hoc scelus mox ex urbe **effūgit** et in silvās sē **recēpit**. "Sī nēmō mē ***vīderit***," inquit, "nēmō mē op-
10 pugnābit!'

"Herculēs tantum scelus expiāre cupiēbat. **Constituit** igitur ad ōrāculum Delphicum īre; hoc enim ōrāculum omnium suprēmum erat. Hīc, in templō
15 Apollinis, in summō monte sedēbat fēmina quaedam, nomine Pӯthia, quae consilium dabat eīs quī ad ōrāculum **vēnerant**.

Templum et Ōrāculum Apollinis Hodiē

"Herculēs 'Sī,' inquit, 'Pӯthia mē ***audīverit***, certē mihi auxilium dabit.'" Ubi Herculēs Pӯthiam certiōrem dē scelere
20 suō **fēcit**, Pӯthia prīmō tacēbat. Tandem tamen 'Sī ad urbem Tīryntha ***īveris***,' inquit, 'et omnia imperia Eurystheī rēgis ***fēceris***, iterum pūrus eris.' Herculēs, ubi haec **audīvit**, quam celerrimē ad urbem illam **contendit**, et Eurystheō rēgī sē in servitūtem **trādidit**.

"Herculēs, 'Pessimus,' inquit, 'hominum sum. Sed sī omnia quae mihi imperās facere ***potuerō***, scelus meum expiābō. Sī Minerva mē ***adiūverit***, omnia tua imperia facere poterō.'
25 "Duodecim annōs crūdēlissimō Eurystheō serviēbat, et duodecim labōrēs, quōs ille **imperāverat, confēcit**; hōc enim modō tantum scelus expiāre **potuit**. Dē hīs labōribus plūrima poetae Graecī atque Rōmānī **scrīpsērunt**."

Aelius **conclūsit:** "Itaque, Licinia, fīlius noster nōn Perseus novus erit, sed novus Herculēs! Herculēs māior hērōs quam Perseus erat et fīlius noster hērōs maximus erit! Nōmen eī igitur Maximus erit!"

🔊 VERBA ŪTENDA

Apollō, Apollinis m. Apollo,
  god of prophecy
**atque and, and also, and
  even, yet**
auxilium, -iī n.
  help, aid
beātus, -a, -um blessed,
  happy
certus, -a, -um certain
  certiōrem facere to
  inform
*conclūdō, conclūdere,
  conclūsī,* conclude,
  finish
conficiō, conficere, confēcī
  do, accomplish
consilium, -iī n. advice,
  plan
*constituō, constituere,
  constituī* decide
*contendō, contendere,
  contendī* make one's way
  toward
crūdēlis, crūdēle cruel
Delphicus, -a, -um Delphic,
  pertaining to Delphi
  (a shrine of Apollo)
duodecim twelve
effugiō, effugere, effūgī
  escape, flee
enim for

Eurystheus, Eurystheī m. Eurystheus, king of Tiryns
expiō (1) atone for
furor, -ōris m. fury, rage
Graecus, -a, -um Greek
Herculēs, Herculis m.
  Hercules
igitur therefore
imperium, -iī n. command,
  order
imperō (1) order
incidō, incidere, incidī meet,
  fall (into)
itaque therefore
līberī, -ōrum m. pl. children
Megara, -ae f. Megara, wife
  of Hercules
Minerva, -ae f. Minerva,
  goddess of wisdom
modus, -ī m. way,
  manner
mons, montis m. mountain
occīdō, occīdere, occīdī kill,
  slay
oppugnō (1) attack
ōrāculum, -ī n. oracle,
  divine pronouncement
pessimus, -a, -um worst
plūrimus, -a, -um most
prīmō at first
pūrus, -a, -um pure

Pȳthia, -ae f. Pythia,
  oracular priestess of
  Apollo at Delphi
*quīdam, quaedam,
  quoddam* "a certain"
recipiō, recipere, recēpī take
  back; *sē recipere* retreat
redeō, redīre, redīvī/rediī go
  back, return
sānitās, -tātis f. health,
  sanity
scelus, sceleris n. crime
serviō, servīre, servīvī serve
servitūs, -tūtis f. slavery,
  servitude
silva, -ae f. woods
**summus, -a, -um highest,
  greatest;** *summō monte*
  on the mountaintop
**suprēmus, -a, -um highest,
  final**
tamen nevertheless
tandem at last, at length
tantus, -a, -um so great
templum, -ī n. temple
Tīryntha (acc.) Tiryns, a
  Greek city in the Argolid
trādō, trādere, trādidī hand
  over
urbs, urbis f. city

POSTQUAM LĒGISTĪ

Answer these questions in both Latin and English if the question is followed by (L). Other-wise, just respond in English.

1. What does Hercules do while he is insane? (L)
2. After this where does he go first? Why?
3. Why does he eventually go to the Delphic oracle?
4. What does the oracle tell him? (L)
5. What happens after Hercules leaves Delphi?
6. How does Aelius conclude this tale?
7. What name does Aelius suggest for his son? Why?

Grammatica B

The Future Perfect Tense

With the addition of the future perfect, you now know all the tenses in Latin. This also completes the perfect system of the verbs.

PERFECT STEM = 3RD PRINCIPAL PART – "-ī"		
PERFECT	**PLUPERFECT**	**FUTURE PERFECT**
Perfect Stem +	Perfect Stem +	Perfect Stem +
-ī	*-eram*	*-erō*
-istī	*-erās*	*-eris*
-it	*-erat*	*-erit*
-imus	*-erāmus*	*-erimus*
-istis	*-erātis*	*-eritis*
-ērunt	*-erant*	*-erint*

Here is an overview of the perfect system of *vocō* with the translation of the future perfect forms.

PERFECT	PLUPERFECT	FUTURE PERFECT	FUTURE PERFECT TRANSLATION
vocāvī	vocāv**eram**	vocāv**erō**	I will have called
vocāvistī	vocāv**erās**	vocāv**eris**	you will have called
vocāvit	vocāv**erat**	vocāv**erit**	he/she/it will have called
vocāvimus	vocāv**erāmus**	vocāv**erimus**	we will have called
vocāvistis	vocāv**erātis**	vocāv**eritis**	you will have called
vocāv**ērunt**	vocāv**erant**	vocāv**erint**	they will have called

Notā Bene:

- The rules for forming the perfect system work for all verbs in all conjugations, even "irregular" verbs. Thus *sum, esse, fuī* → *fuī, fueram, fuerō*.

Future Perfect Tips

1. Be careful of your stems. Forms like *erō* (future) and *fuerō* (future perfect) can be confusing. The stems will guide you best. The *fu-* in *fuerō* tells you that this is part of the perfect system since it is based on the 3rd principal part. Therefore, the form has to be future perfect. Compare *poterō* versus *potuerō*.

2. Don't confuse the following endings:
   - *vēnērunt* perfect (they came, they have come)
   - *vēnerint* future perfect (they will have come)

3. You have probably figured out that the future perfect endings resemble the future of *sum*. But be careful! The 3rd plural is *-erint* not *-erunt*.

4. Also, as you read aloud, do not fall into the temptation to put the stress on the endings. You do not pronounce these forms

   clāmāverŌ, clāmāverIS, clāmāverIT, etc.

   Follow your normal rules for accent:

   clāmĀVerō, clāmĀVeris, clāmĀVerit, etc.

Using the Future Perfect Tense

The most important thing to remember about the future perfect tense is that it is used to show an action that "will have happened" before another action. Look at the two verbs in the following sentence from *Lectiō Secunda*:

Sī nēmō mē vīderit, nēmō mē oppugnābit!

Vīderit is future perfect, whereas *oppugnābit* is future. The future perfect is used to show that the "seeing" will have taken place before the "attacking."

Note that good English does not need to use the "have" in the future perfect. You can translate the sentence above as "If no one sees me, no one will attack me."

EXERCEĀMUS!

20-4 Tense Identification

For each of the following sentences from *Lectiō Secunda*, identify the tenses of the two verbs marked in **bold** and explain the relationship between the two actions. Follow the model.

→ *Sī nēmō mē vīderit, nēmō mē oppugnābit!*
  vīderit: future perfect   *oppugnābit*: future
  The future perfect is used to show that "seeing" would have to
  take place before "fighting."

1. Sī Pȳthia mē **audīverit**, certissimē mihi auxilium **dabit**.
2. Sī ad urbem Tīryntha **īveris**, iterum pūrus **eris**.
3. Sī omnia imperia Eurystheī rēgis **fēceris**, iterum pūrus **eris**.
4. Sī omnia quae mihi imperās facere **potuerō**, scelus meum **expiābō**.
5. Sī Minerva mē **adiuverit**, omnia tua imperia facere **poterō**.

More on Adverbs and Conjunctions

Many of the *Verba Discenda* in this chapter are indeclinable adverbs or conjunctions. They are your friends. Their spelling never changes. If you learn their meanings carefully, you can use them as translation aids. Here is a list of all the adverbs and conjunctions you have learned as *Verba Discenda* in either this chapter or earlier ones. They are grouped here thematically.

- **Connecting:** *atque* and, and yet, and even; *et* and; *et ... et* both ... and; *etiam* and also, even now; *-que* and; *-que ... -que* both ... *and*; *sīc* thus, in this way, yes; *sīcut* just as; *tam* so, so much (as)

- **Negative:** *nec* and not; *nec ... nec* neither, nor; *nōn* not

- **Contrasting:** *at* but, yet; *autem* however; *sed* but; *sōlum* only; *tamen* nevertheless

- **Causal:** *enim* for; *ergō* therefore; *itaque* therefore; *quia* since; *quod* because; *sī* if

- **Temporal:** *cotīdiē* daily; *crās* tomorrow; *diū* for a long time; *dum* while, as long as; *herī* yesterday; *hodiē* today; *iam* now, already; *iterum* again; *māne* early in the morning; *mox* soon; *numquam* never; *nunc* now; *ōlim* once, formerly; *priusquam* before; *saepe* often; *semper* always; *statim* immediately; *subitō* suddenly; *tandem* at last, at length; *tum* then; *tunc* then; *ubi* when

- **Locational:** *ubi* where

Mōrēs Rōmānī

Herculēs Rōmānus

Hercules is the Latin name of the hero the Greeks knew as Heracles. Actually, the hero and his myth are an amalgamation of Greek and Roman tales. Although the stories you read in this chapter deal with Hercules in Greece, there are many adventures of Hercules that take place in

Italy and even in Rome. In particular, ancient Romans told the story of Cacus and the cattle of Geryon. Hercules defeated Geryon, a three-bodied monster, in Spain. Driving the cattle back to Greece, the hero passed through the area where Rome would be founded and encountered another monster called Cacus. Stealing the cattle, Cacus brought them into his cave in the Aventine Hill. He led them in backward so that the tracks seemed to lead out of the cave, not into it. Eventually, Hercules heard his cattle mooing and tracked them to the cave, where he and Cacus wrestled to the death. Hercules, of course, won.

Here is an inscription from an altar dedicated to Hercules in late antiquity in Ostia: On the right is the full, unabbreviated text:

DEO
INVICTO HERCVLI
HOSTILIVS ANTIPATER
V P PRAEF ANN
CVRAT REI PVBLIC OST

Deō
Invictō Herculī
Hostilius Antipater
v(ir) p(erfectissimus) praef(ectus) ann(ōnae)
cūrāt(or) reī pūblic(ae) Ost(iensis)
(fēcit)

Herculēs Cācusque *ā Baccio Bandinelli (1525–1534) Florentiae*

Try reading the inscription as a single sentence.

> Hostīlius Antipater, vir perfectissimus, praefectus annōnae, (et) cūrātor reī publicae Ostiensis, (hoc) deō Invictō Herculī (fēcit).

🔊 VERBA ŪTENDA

annōna, -ae f. grain, the grain supply of Rome
cūrātor, -ōris m. caretaker, manager

invictus, -a, -um unconquered
Ostiensis, -se of Ostia, Ostian
perfectus, -a, -um perfect

praefectus, -ī m. director, supervisor
reī pūblicae of the republic

Latīna Hodierna

Herculēs Hodiē

While serving as ambassador to France during the Revolutionary War, Benjamin Franklin designed a medal to celebrate American independence. The obverse depicts the head of a woman representing the goddess Liberty, with the date 4 July 1776 below and the words *Lībertas Americāna* above. On the reverse baby Hercules is strangling the snakes while the goddess Minerva is fighting with a lion, along with the following Latin inscription:

> *nōn sine diīs animōsus infans*

This quote from Horace's *Odes* III.4.20 can be translated at least two ways: "a courageous infant is not without gods" and "an infant is not courageous without gods."

Hercules, of course, also appears in modern cinema and television, including Disney's 1997 film and the 2005 miniseries starring Paul Telfer as Hercules.

Nōn sine Diīs Animōsus Infans, Nomisma ā Benjamin Franklin

Orbis Terrārum Rōmānus

Herculēs Rōmae

Worship of the hero Hercules was an important part of the public religion of Rome. A round temple in his honor (depicted at right) stands in the *Forum Boārium* (Cattle Forum), an ancient meat and fish market on the Tiber River just west of the Circus Maximus. Nearby there was also the important *Herculis Invictī Āra Maxima* (Very Great Altar of Unconquered Hercules).

There were many temples or altars dedicated to this hero in Rome and throughout the empire. Another important temple of Hercules in Rome was known as the *Aedēs Herculis Mūsārum* (Temple of Hercules and the Muses), located near the Circus Flaminius near the Campus Martius. This temple was built by M. Fulvius Nobilior to celebrate his capture of the Greek city of Ambracia in 189 B.C. It contained statues of the nine Muses (goddesses of inspiration) and of Hercules playing the lyre. The coin at right probably depicts this statue of Hercules. Can you read the inscription on either side of the statue? Unfortunately, there are no visible signs of this temple in Rome today.

Templum Herculis in Forō Boāriō Hodiē

QUID PUTĀS?

1. Why do you think Aelius and Licinia prefer comparing their child to Hercules rather than to Perseus? Which hero do you prefer? Why?
2. Why do you think Hercules has appeared in so many different contexts in ancient Rome and in the modern world?
3. Which translation of the quote from Horace's *Odes* III.4.20 on Benjamin Franklin's Hercules coin do you prefer: "a courageous infant is not without gods" or "an infant is not courageous without gods"? Why?
4. Why do you think Benjamin Franklin chose to depict the infant Hercules on a coin celebrating America's recent independence?

Herculēs Mūsārum

Forum Boārium

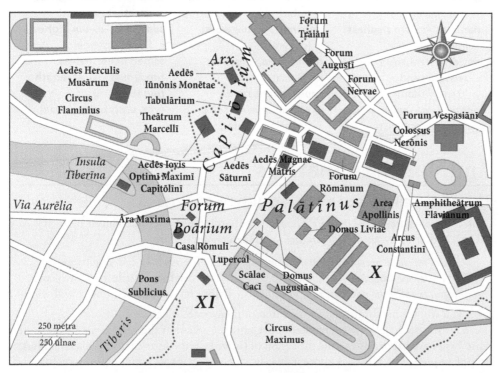

EXERCEĀMUS!

20-5 Scrībāmus

Respond to each of the following questions and supply an appropriate temporal adverb from the list. See how many other temporal adverbs you can use in your response to each question. You will have to change the verb's tense with adverbs like *crās* or *herī*. Follow the model.

Temporal Adverbs

cotīdiē; crās; diū; herī; hodiē; iam; iterum; māne; mox; numquam; nunc; ōlim; saepe; semper; statim; subitō; tum; tunc

→ Spectāsne lūdōs?   *Lūdōs numquam spectō.*   or   *Lūdōs crās spectābō.*

1. Lūdere vīs?   4. Bibisne aquam?
2. Legisne librōs?   5. Vidēsne canem?
3. Habitāsne in Ītaliā?   6. Vidēsne sīmiam?

20-6 Colloquāmur

Now practice asking and answering questions in Exercise 20-5 with other members of your class.

20-7 Verba Discenda

Regroup the *Verba Discenda* according to the following parts of speech: nouns, verbs, adjectives, adverbs, and conjunctions.

VERBA DISCENDA

at but, yet
atque and, and also, and even, and yet
autem however
clāmor, clāmōris m. shout [clamorous]
enim for
facilis, facile easy [facile]
factum, -ī n. deed [fact]
fāma, -ae f. fame, rumor, report [famous]

igitur therefore
itaque therefore
maximus, -a, -um greatest [maximize]
minimus, -a, -um smallest [minimal]
mittō, mittere, mīsī, missum send [transmission]
optimus, -a, -um best [optimal, optimist]

orbis, orbis m. circle, ring; *orbis terrārum* circle of the lands, i.e., the world [orbit]
pessimus, -a, -um worst [pessimist]
plūrimus, -a, -um most [plurality]
rapiō, rapere, rapuī, raptum snatch, seize [rapacious, raptor]

scelus, sceleris n. crime
statim immediately
summus, -a, -um highest, greatest [summit]
suprēmus, -a, -um highest, final [supreme]
tamen nevertheless
tandem at last, at length
tum then
urbs, urbis f. city [urban]

Angulus Grammaticus

The Future Perfect and Sequence of Tenses

Look for the future perfect tense especially in subordinate clauses introduced by *sī* (if), *cum* (when), and, more rarely, *antequam* (before) or *priusquam* (before).

Sī amīcī mē adiuvāverint, vincam!   If my friends help me, I will win!
Cum amīcī mē adiuvāverint, vincam!   When my friends help me, I will win!
Antequam amīcī mē adiuvāverint, vincam!   Before my friends help me, I will win!

Later you will see the future perfect used in more elaborate "if" clauses.

Can you see in all of the sentences above how the action of the verb in the future perfect tense "will have happened" before the action of the verb in the future tense? This is an illustration of **sequence of tenses**, a concept that is very important in Latin and to which we will return later.

Photo Credits

page 245 (top) Bob Cates Photo/Robert Cates; **page 246** Art Resource, N.Y.; **page 250** Photos.com; **page 254 (top)** Photos.com; **page 254 (bottom)** American Numismatic Society/American Numismatic Society of New York; **page 255 (top)** Giacomo Ciangottini/ Fotolia, LLC—Royalty Free; **page 255 (middle)** American Numismatic Society/American Numismatic Society of New York.

21

Speculum Aēneum

Lectiō Prīma

Antequam Legis

Aelius tells his wife more about the labors of Hercules, which he will engrave on a mirror for her. Aelius also promises to make for their child a *bulla,* or amulet that Roman children wore for good luck.

In this reading you have an opportunity to consolidate your knowledge of various kinds of pronouns and adjectives. They are marked in bold in the reading. You have seen many of these words before, and you will learn a few more in this chapter.

Pronouns and Adjective Consolidation

A number of these pronouns and adjectives belong to a special group of pronouns and adjectives we call UNUS NAUTA words. You already know some of them, including *hic, haec, hoc; ille, illa, illud; qui, quae, quod*; and more. Remember that they basically work like 2-1-2 adjectives that have special genitive and dative singulars.

CASE AND NUMBER	ENDING	EXAMPLES
genitive singular	-ius	*eius, huius, illīus, cuius*
dative singular	-ī	*eī, huic, illī, cuī*

Also watch in *Lectiō Prīma* for singular forms of this irregular 3rd declension noun: *vīs, vis* f. strength, power. These are marked in ***bold italics*** in the reading. More on this noun after you read!

Speculum Tuscum

GRAMMATICA

Personal and Reflexive Pronouns
Review of Possessive Adjectives
Irregular Adjectives and Pronouns:
   UNUS NAUTA Words
The Irregular Noun *Vīs*
Synopsis of All Active Tenses

MŌRĒS RŌMĀNĪ

Hospitium

LATĪNA HODIERNA

Hospitium and Hospitality

ORBIS TERRĀRUM RŌMĀNUS

Graecia

ANGULUS GRAMMATICUS

The Former and the Latter

> **LECTIŌNĒS:**
> **NOSTER HERCULĒS NOVUS**
> and
> **VĪS HERCULIS**
>
> Aelius continues the story of Hercules and offers to make his wife and unborn child some special gifts. Aelius and Licinia talk about the child who will soon be born and his future. The conversation then turns to more adventures of Hercules.

257

From *Disce! An Introductory Latin Course, volume 2*, First Edition. Francesco Bonavita. Copyright © 2011 by Pearson Education, Inc. Published by Pearson Prentice Hall. All rights reserved.

Nero cum Bullā

EXERCEĀMUS!

21-1 Personal and Reflexive Pronouns, Possessive Adjectives, and UNUS NAUTA Words

Scan the words marked in bold in *Lectiō Prīma* to find the Latin equivalent for each of the English words listed below. Give the line number of the Latin word. Then look at the grammatical context of the *lectiō* to give the GNC for each Latin word in your list. Use the *Verba Ūtenda* as a vocabulary aid. Watch out! Some words appear more than once. Follow the model.

English Word	Latin Word	Line	Gender	Number	Case
→ herself	*ipsa*	1	feminine	singular	nominative

1. this; 2. something; 3. my; 4. which; 5. you; 6. those; 7. alone; 8. certain; 9. himself; 10. the same; 11. that; 12. me; 13. our; 14. I

NOSTER HERCULĒS NOVUS

Licinia, verba marītī audiēns, **ipsa** quoque rīdet. "Ita," inquit, "**tū** vēra dīxistī! Parāre **nōs** fīliolō novō et **hunc** "novum Herculem" honōrāre dēbēmus. Nōmen **eī** Maximus erit. **Vim** Herculis habēbit. Aelī, potesne **aliquid** fabricāre, fortasse bullam **quae** labōrēs Herculis demonstrābit?
5 Tālis bulla fīliō **nostrō** donum bonum erit!"

Aelius "Cāra," inquit, "**Meus** amor **tuī** vērus est, sed **illōs** magnōs labōrēs Herculis nōn facile possum demonstrāre in **hāc** bullā parvā **quam** nostrō fīliō fabricābō. Sed **ego ipse tibi sōlī** speculum aēneum fabricābō, in **quō** Herculem et aprum Erymanthium efficiam. **Tū mea**
10 Alcmēna semper eris et **noster** fīlius **meus** Herculēs. Audī nunc dē **illō** labōre aprī Erymantheī **quem** in speculō pōnam:

"Olim, ut **quīdam** narrant, Eurystheus Herculem aprum **quendam, quī illō** tempore agrōs Erymanthiōs vastābat et incolās **huius** regiōnis magnopere terrēbat, capere iussit. Herculēs ergō in Arca-
15 diam, in **quā** regiōne agrī Erymanthiī erant, iter fēcit. Postquam in silvam paulum intrāvit, aprō **ipsī** occurrit. **Ille** autem simul atque Herculem vīdit, statim refūgit; et timōre perterritus in altam fossam **sē** prōiēcit. Hērōs igitur laqueum, **quem sē**cum attulerat, iniēcit, et summā cum difficultāte et magnā **vī** aprum ē fossā extraxit. Aper, quamquam
20 fortiter repugnābat, nūllō modō **sē** līberāre potuit. Herculēs nōn aprum in **agrīs** Erymanthiīs relīquit sed cum **eōdem** aprō ad rēgem Eurystheum rediit.

"Eurystheus perterritus, cum aprum ingentem vīdit, statim in urnam magnam insiluit et **sē** abdidit."
25 Licinia "Euge, mī marite!" inquit "Hic labor Maximō nostrō idōneus est—**id** speculum **quod** fabricābis **mihi** semper cārissimum erit!"

Herculēs et Aper

🔊 VERBA ŪTENDA

aēneus, -a, -um bronze

afferō, afferre, attulī bring to

Alcmēna Alcmena, Hercules' mother

aper, aprī m. boar

Arcadia, -ae f. Arcadia, a region in Greece

bulla, -ae f. bulla, a locket worn around a child's neck

dēmonstrō (1) show, depict

difficultās, difficultātis f. trouble, difficulty

efficiō, efficere, effēcī execute, render

Erymanthius, -a, -um Erymanthian

Erymanthos, -theī n. Erymanthus, a mountain in Greece

Euge! Wonderful!

extrahō, extrahere, extraxī draw out, drag out

fabricō (1) make

fīliolus, -ī m. little son (affectionate)

fossa, -ae f. ditch

hērōs, hērōos m. hero (note the Greek case endings)

honōrō (1) esteem, honor

īdem, eadem, idem the same

idōneus, -a, -um suitable

incola, -ae m./f. inhabitant

ingens, ingentis huge, great

iniciō, inicere, iniēcī throw in

insiliō, insilīre, insiluī/insilīvī leap into

iter facere to make a journey

laqueus, -ī m. snare, noose

līberō (1) free

magnopere greatly, especially

modō only, just now

nōs, nostrum/nostrī, nōbīs, nōs, nōbīs we, us

occurrō, occurrere, occucurrī, (+ dat.) encounter, run into

paulum a little, somewhat

perterritus, -a, -um very frightened

postquam after, since

prōiciō, prōicere, prōiēcī throw down

quamquam although

quīdam, quaedam, quoddam a certain (indefinite, as in "a certain person")

quisque, quaeque, quodque/quicque/ quidque each, every

redeō, redīre, redīvī/rediī, reditum come back, return

refugiō, refugīre, refūgī run away

regiō, regiōnis f. region, district

relinquō, relinquere, relīquī, relictum leave, leave behind

repugnō (1) fight back, resist

silva, -ae f. woods, forest

simul atque as soon as

speculum, -ī n. mirror

suī, sibi, sē, sē himself, herself, itself, themselves

tālis, tāle such, of such a kind, of such a sort

terreō, terrēre, terruī frighten, terrify

timor, timōris m. fear

tū, tuī, tibi, tē, tē you (sing.) yourself

urna, -ae f. large water jug

vastō (1) plunder, lay waste

vīs, vis f. strength, power, force; vīrēs, vīrium pl. strength, troops, forces

POSTQUAM LĒGISTĪ

1. Why does Licinia laugh at the beginning of this *lectiō*?
2. What name does Licinia give her child and why?
3. What scene does Aelius plan to engrave on the *bulla* for his son?
4. Why is it necessary for the Erymanthian boar to be captured?
5. How does Hercules capture it?
6. What humor do you notice in the story?

Grammatica A

Personal and Reflexive Pronouns

Personal Pronouns

These words refer to the "person" involved and you know them in English as "I, you, he, she, it, we, you, they." You have been using some of these forms for a while now, but, by way of consolidation, here are all the forms.

CASE	1ST SINGULAR I, ME	1ST PLURAL WE, US	2ND SINGULAR YOU	2ND PLURAL YOU ALL
Nominative	ego	nōs	tū	vōs
Genitive	meī	nostrum/ nostrī	tuī	vestrum/ vestrī
Dative	mihi	nōbīs	tibi	vōbīs
Accusative	mē	nōs	tē	vōs
Ablative	mē	nōbīs	tē	vōbīs

- Latin personal pronouns are not commonly found as the subject of verbs (as they are in English) unless they are used to show emphasis:

Quis hoc fēcit?	Who did this?
Fēcī.	I did it.
Ego fēcī.	*I* did it.

- The genitive of the 1st and 2nd person pronouns is used either as an objective or partitive genitive, but not to show possession.

	TYPE	USAGE
amor meī	objective	His **love of/for me** drove him to it.
timor nostrī	objective	**Fear of us** made them surrender.
pars tuī	partitive	**A part of you** wants to do this, another doesn't.
nēmō nostrum	partitive	**None of us** wants that!

- The preposition *cum* is attached to the end of the 1st and 2nd person pronouns:

  mēcum, tēcum, nōbiscum, vōbiscum

Reflexive Pronouns

You first met reflexive pronouns in Chapter 9, but in limited fashion. Here is the complete story:

- Reflexive pronouns refer back to the subject of the sentence, as in "Mary sees **herself** in the mirror" or "We liked hearing **ourselves** on the record."
- In Latin the reflexive and personal pronouns are identical in the 1st and 2nd person.

1st	*Mē laudat.* He praises **me**.	*Nōs laudat.* He praises **us**.
	Mē laudō. I praise **myself**.	*Nōs laudāmus.* We praise **ourselves**.
2nd	*Tē laudat.* He praises **you**.	*Vōs laudat.* He praises **you**.
	Tē laudās. You praise **yourself**.	*Vōs laudātis.* You praise **yourselves**.

- But the 3rd person uses the special forms *suī, sibi, sē, sē*.

  Sē laudat. He praises **himself**.

- As with the 1st and 2nd persons, the preposition *cum* is attached to the end of the 3rd person reflexive: *sēcum*.

Compare the uses of the 3rd person pronoun *is, ea, id* to the use of reflexive pronoun.

SUBJECT AND OBJECT ARE DIFFERENT PERSONS	SUBJECT AND OBJECT ARE THE SAME PERSON
Fēmina **eam** *laudat.* The woman praises **her.**	*Fēmina* **sē** *laudat.* The woman praises **herself.**
Vir **eum** *laudat.* The man praises **him.**	*Vir* **sē** *laudat.* The man praises **himself.**
Fēminae **eōs** *laudant.* The women praise **them.**	*Fēminae* **sē** *laudant.* The women praise **themselves.**
Virī **eās** *laudant.* The men praise **them.**	*Virī* **sē** *laudant.* The men praise **themselves.**

Review of Possessive Adjectives

- 1st and 2nd person personal pronouns (e.g., *tuī, vestrum*) are not normally used to express possession. Instead, Latin uses **personal adjectives**.

meus, -a, -um	my	*noster, -tra, -trum*	our
tuus, -a, -um	your	*vester, -tra, trum*	your
suus, -a -um	his own, her own, its own, their own		

These are all 2-1-2 adjectives.

- For the 3rd person (his, hers, its, their), Latin shows possession by using the genitive of *is, ea, id.*

- Latin uses the genitive of *is, ea, id* to show possession in the 3rd person (his, hers, its, theirs) when this person is not the subject of the sentence.

Domum eōrum videt.	He sees their house.
Domum suam videt.	He sees his (own) house.
Domum eius vident.	They see his house.
Domum suam vident.	They see their (own) house.

Irregular Adjectives and Pronouns: UNUS NAUTA Words

Latin is filled with a variety of small words that make a big difference. You have seen some of these before, but others here are new. We list them according to some categories grammarians like to use, but here is what you really need to know:

- All these words are declined like UNUS NAUTA words, meaning that they are 2-1-2 adjectives except that:

  genitive singular = *-ius*
  dative singular = *-ī*

- Many can act like either an adjective or a pronoun. Just look to see whether the word is modifying something or is working alone.

Intensives

Ipse, -a, -um emphasizes a person or thing.

Mē **ipsum** *laudō.*	I praise **myself.**
Ego **ipse** *id fēcī.*	I did it **myself.**

At first glance these translations do not seem "emphatic" enough. But in some parts of the country, they would be translated "I'm praising my own self!" or "I did it my own self!" In this regionalism, the emphasis is quite clear.

- *Ipse* can also be used to indicate gender where it otherwise might be unclear. What is the difference between these two sentences?

Mē ipsum laudō. I praise myself.

Mē ipsam laudō. I praise myself.

Demonstratives

These do what their name says—they "point out" (*dēmonstrāre*). Demonstratives include words like:

- *ille, illa, illud* (that man, that woman, that thing): *Videō illās.* I see those women.
- *hic, haec, hoc* (this man, this woman, this thing): *Videō hunc.* I see this man.
- *is, ea, id* is a demonstrative too, but less emphatic than *ille* or *hic: Ea venit.* The woman is coming.
- *īdem, eadem, idem* (the same): *Eaedem veniunt.* The same women are coming.
- *iste, ista, istud* (that one) has a derogatory overtone: *Istī hoc fēcērunt.* Those men did this.

Remember that **m + c = nc**, which explains forms like *hanc* and *hunc*.

Indefinites

Whereas demonstratives refer to specific people or things, indefinites do just the opposite. They imply uncertainty. Compare these uses of *quīdam, quaedam, quoddam* (a certain) both as pronoun and adjective:

Quaedam *navis advenit.* A certain ship is coming in.

Quaedam *venit.* A certain woman is coming. *or* Some woman is coming.

aliquis, aliquid	(someone, something)
Aliquis venit.	Someone is coming.
Aliqua venit.	Some lady is coming.
Aliquae puellae veniunt.	Some girls are coming.

Relative Pronouns

Quī, quae, quod (who, which) links a subordinate clause to an antecedent noun or pronoun. Its forms are used in sentences like the following:

Fēmina **quam** *amās alma est.*   The woman **whom** you love is kind.

Interrogatives

Interrogatives ask a question about a person or thing. The interrogative pronoun is *Quis?, Quid?* (Who? What?)

- Most of these forms look like the relative pronoun *qui, quae, quod:* **Cui** *pecūniam dedit?* To whom did he give the money?
- The only different forms are the nominative forms *quis, quid* and the accusative singular *quem*, which is feminine as well as masculine.

The forms of the interrogative adjective *quī, quae, quod* are identical to the relative pronoun, but these words ask a question and modify a noun. Compare:

Quid *in domō habēs?*	What do you have in the house? (interrogative pronoun)
Quod *animal in domō habēs?*	What animal do you have in the house? (interrogative adjective)

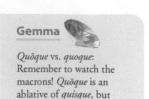

Gemma

Quōque vs. *quoque*: Remember to watch the macrons! *Quōque* is an ablative of *quisque*, but *quoque* means "also, too."

Other Irregular Adjectives and Pronouns

- *quisque, quidque:* each, every

> *Quisque librum habet.*   *Quaeque puella librum habet.*
> Each person has a book.   Each girl has a book.

- *īdem, eadem, idem:* the same

> *Eandem amāmus.*   *Eadem puella Cordum amat.*
> We love the same woman.   The same girl loves Cordus.

Notice how **m + d → nd**. Thus the expected form *"eamdem"* is really *eandem.* This explains forms like *eōrundem,* and *quendam.*

Notā Bene:

- *Hic* and *ille* are often used together to distinguish things close by or just mentioned from things further away or mentioned earlier:

> *Hic vir bonus est; ille nōn.*
> This man is good; that one is not.

- *Ille* also often indicates a change in subject:

> *Marcus Lūcium videt. Ille (= Lūcius) currit.*

- The neuter nominative/accusative singular of many of these words ends in *-d*: *id, illud, istud, quod,* and *quid.*
- Unlike most neuters, the nominative and accusative plurals of some of these words do NOT end in *-a*: *haec* (these things); *quae* (which); *quae* (what things?).

The Irregular Noun *Vīs*

VĪS, VIS F.		
	Singular	**Plural**
	Strength, Power	**Troops, Forces**
Nominative	vīs	vīrēs
Genitive	vis	vīrium
Dative	vī	vīribus
Accusative	vim	vīrēs
Ablative	vī	vīribus

The 3rd declension i-stem noun *vīs, vis* f. requires your attention for several reasons:

- Some forms are irregular in the singular.
- The plural, *vīrēs,* can still mean "force," but it also takes on the sense of military forces or "troops."
- The genitive singular form *vis* is almost never used.
- Be careful not to confuse the plural forms of *vīs* with forms of *vir, -ī* m. Thus, *virī* means "men," whereas *vīrēs* means "strength."

Here are the phrases from *Lectiō Prīma* that use some of these forms. How would you translate the words marked in ***bold italics***? What cases are these words in?

> ***Vim*** Herculis habēbit.
> Hērōs summā cum difficultāte et magnā ***vī*** aprum ē fossā extrāxit.

Watch for more appearances of this word in *Lectiō Secunda.*

EXERCEĀMUS!

21-2 Working with Pronouns

Substitute the words in parentheses for the word marked in **bold** in each of the following sentences. Then translate the new sentence you made. Be sure to show gender in your translation. Follow the model.

→ Licinia **Aelium** petit.   Licinia **hunc** petit.
(hunc)   Licinia is looking for **this man.**

1. Aelius **Liciniam** amat.
   (quendam)
   (eundem)
   (aliquōs)
   (illa)
   (hanc)

2. Licinia **Aelium** videt.
   (aliquid)
   (aliquōs)
   (eadem)
   (illās)
   (haec)
   (quandam)

3. **Omnēs** Augustum honōrāre dēbent.
   (Illī)
   (Istae)
   (Eaedem)
   (Aliquī)
   (Quīdam)

4. **Aelius** Augustum honōrāre dēbet.
   (Quisquis)
   (Aliqua)
   (Īdem)
   (Quīdam)
   (Aliquis)

Lectiō Secunda

Antequam Legis

This *lectiō*, which continues the story of Hercules, is designed to help you review all the verb tenses you have learned to date. Take the time to identify each verb fully and, if needed, review the rules for identifying Latin tenses. You will need this information very soon as you learn other forms.

EXERCEĀMUS!

21-3 Treasure Hunt for Verb Tenses

Gemma

A 3rd person form of *sum* can often be translated as "There is," "There are," and the like. Do this for *erat* in line 3.

Gemma

If *spēlunca, -ae* f. means "cave," what do you think a "spelunker" means in English?

Before you read *Lectiō Secunda,* find an example of each of the forms listed among the words marked in **bold** in the *lectiō.* Then translate each verb into English. Be careful to show person, number, and tense in your translation. Follow the model.

Verb Form	Line	Verb	Translation
→ imperfect, 3rd singular	3	habitābat	he was living

1. present, 3rd singular (find two)
2. perfect, 1st plural
3. perfect, 1st singular
4. future, 1st singular
5. future, 3rd plural

6. imperfect, 3rd plural (find two)
7. perfect, 3rd plural (find two)
8. pluperfect, 3rd singular
9. perfect, 2nd singular (find two)
10. perfect, 3rd singular (find two)

VĪS HERCULIS

"Cāra Licinia," Aelius **inquit**, "de eōdem labōre, quem iam **narrāvī**, haec alia etiam **audīvimus**:

"Herculēs, dum iter in Arcadiam **facit**, ad spēluncam dēvertit in quā centaurus quīdam, nomine Pholus, **habitābat**. Ille Herculem benignē

5 excēpit et cēnam parāvit. In spēluncā erat amphora magna plēna vīnō optimō.

Herculēs et Centaurus

"Hērōs postquam **cēnāverat**, aliquid vīnī **petīvit** et amphoram ā Pholō postulāvit. Pholus 'Hoc vīnum,' inquit, 'aliōrum centaurōrum est. Sī igitur hoc tibi **dabō**, centaurī mē **interficient**.' Herculēs tamen pōculum vīnī dē amphorā hausit.

10 "Simul atque amphoram aperuit, aliquī centaurī nōtum odōrem sēnsērunt et convēnērunt ad spēluncam.

"Ubi ad spēluncam **pervēnērunt**, magnopere īrātī **erant** quod Herculēs vīnum suum biberat. Tum magnae vīrēs centaurōrum arma sua rapuērunt et Pholum interficere **volēbant**.

"Herculēs ipse tamen in ōre spēluncae stetit et impetum vīrium fortissimē sustinēbat. Ibi multōs centaurōs sagittīs suīs **vulnerāvit**. (Hae sagittae eaedem erant quās ōlim sanguis venēnātus Hydrae imbuerat.) Omnēs aliōs cen-

15 taurōs, igitur, quī ad spēluncam **cucurrērunt**, statim necāvit.

"Postquam reliquae vīrēs fūgerant, Pholus ē spēluncā exiit. Quendam centaurum mortuum invēnit. Sagittam ē vulnere trāxit sed haec sagitta ē manibus eius cecidit, et pedem leviter vulnerāvit. Ille statim dolōrem gravem per omnia membra sēnsit, et post breve tempus vī venēnī mortuus iacuit."

"Tanta," fīniit Aelius, "erat vīs Herculis et tanta erit vīs fīliī nostrī."

20 "Bene dictum, Aelī!" inquit Licinia. "Tū fābulam bene **narrāvistī** et omnēs meōs timōrēs **āmōvistī**."

VERBA ŪTENDA

amphora, -ae f. amphora
aperiō, aperīre, aperuī open
Arcadia, -ae f. Arcadia, a region of Greece
arma, armōrum n. pl. arms, weapons
benignē kindly
cadō, cadere, cecidī, cāsum fall; be slain; end
cenō (1) dine
centaurus, -ī m. centaur, half-human and half-horse
dēvertō, dēvetere, dēvertī turn aside, stop to visit
dictum said
dolor, dolōris m. pain, grief
excipiō, excipere, excēpī receive, welcome
exeō, exīre, exīvī/exiī, go out
fābula, -ae f. story
hauriō, haurīre, hausī drink

hērōs, hēroos m. hero; note the Greek case endings
Hydra, -ae f. a many-headed serpent-like monster with poisonous blood
iaceō, iacēre, iacuī lie, lie still, lie dead
ibi there
īdem, eadem, idem the same
imbuō, imbuere, imbuī wet, soak
impetus, -ūs m. attack, assault
iter, itineris n. road, journey
leviter lightly
magnopere greatly, especially
manus, -ūs f. hand
membrum, -ī n. limb
mortuus, -a, -um dead
necō (1) kill, slay
nōs, nostrum/nostrī, nōbīs, nōs, nōbīs we, us

nōtus, -a, -um known, familiar
odor, odōris m. scent, odor
pēs, pedis m. foot
perveniō, pervenīre, pervēnī, perventum arrive at, reach
petō, petere, petīvī/petiī, petītum seek; look for; attack; run for political office
Pholus, -ī m. Pholus the centaur
pōculum, -ī n. cup
postquam after, since
postulō (1) ask for, demand
plēnus, -a, -um (+ abl.) full, full of
quīdam, quaedam, quoddam a certain (indefinite, as in "a certain person")
reliquus, -a, -um remaining

sagitta, -ae f. arrow
sanguis, sanguinis m. blood
sentiō, sentīre, sēnsī, sēnsum feel, hear, see, perceive
simul atque as soon as
spēlunca, -ae f. cave
sustineō, sustinēre, sustinuī, withstand
trahō, trahere, trāxī drag
tū, tuī, tibi, tē, tē you (sing.); yourself
venēnātus, -a, -um poisoned
venēnum, -ī n. poison
vīs, vis f. strength, power, force; pl. vīrēs, vīrium troops, forces, strength
vōs, vestrum/vestrī, vōbīs, vōs, vōbīs you (pl.); yourselves
vulnerō (1) wound
vulnus, vulneris n. wound

Amphorae

Centaurus

Herculēs et Hydra

POSTQUAM LĒGISTĪ

Answer the question in English, but then select the Latin words from the text that support your answer.

1. Describe the character of Pholus the Centaur.
2. Describe the character of Hercules in this story.
3. How is the wine special?
4. What draws the other centaurs to Pholus' cave?
5. Why are the centaurs angry at Hercules?
6. How does Pholus accidentally die?

Grammatica B

Synopsis of All Active Tenses

The word "synopsis" comes from Greek and means "overview." Here it refers to a certain kind of exercise where the student writes out forms of the verb in the same person and number in several tenses. It saves you from having to write out all six forms for each tense.

SYNOPSIS PRINCIPAL PARTS: VIDEŌ, VIDĒRE, VĪDĪ, VISUM PERSON AND NUMBER: 1ST PERSON PLURAL		
Tense	**Latin**	**English Translation**
Present	*vidēmus*	we see
Imperfect	*vidēbāmus*	we were seeing
Future	*vidēbimus*	we will see
Perfect	*vīdimus*	we saw
Pluperfect	*vīderāmus*	we had seen
Future Perfect	*vīderimus*	we will have seen

Before you try the next exercise, review the following "recipes" for forming the tenses. Then, using the synopsis as a guide, do Exercise 21-4.

Formulae for Forming the Active Tenses

USE PRESENT STEM (PS) OR SHORT PRESENT STEM (SPS) PS = 2nd principal part *-re* SPS = 1st principal part *-ō*	USE PERFECT ACTIVE STEM (PERF. ST.) Perf. St = 3rd principal part *-ī*

	Present						**Perfect**			
			ō	mus				ī	imus
1, 2	PS	+	s	tis		1, 2, 3, 4	Perf.St. +	istī	istis
			t	nt				it	ērunt

			ō	imus			**Pluperfect**		
3, 4	SPS	+	is	itis					
			it	unt				eram	erāmus
(**N.B.:** i + i = i; i.e. *capis*, not *capiis*.)						1, 2, 3, 4	Perf.St. +	erās	erātis
								erat	erant

	Imperfect						**Future Perfect**		
			bam	bāmus					
1, 2	PS	+	bās	bātis				erō	erimus
			bat	bant		1, 2, 3, 4	Perf.St. +	eris	eritis
			ēbam	ēbāmus				erit	erint
3, 4	SPS	+	ēbās	ēbātis					
			ēbat	ēbant					

	Future			
			bō	bimus
1, 2	PS	+	bis	bitis
			bit	bunt
			am	ēmus
3, 4	SPS	+	ēs	ētis
			et	ent

EXERCEĀMUS!

21-4 Making Synopses

Use the the synopsis of *videō* provided above as a guide to create synopses for the following verbs.

dō, dare, dedī, datum	1st singular
currō, currere, cucurrī, cursum	3rd plural
dūcō, dūcere, dūxī, ductum	2nd plural
audiō, audīre, audīvī, audītum	2nd singular

SYNOPSIS		
Principal Parts: **Person and Number:**		
Tense	**Latin**	**English Translation**
Present		
Imperfect		
Future		
Perfect		
Pluperfect		
Future Perfect		

Mōrēs Rōmānī

Hospitium

Romans listening to the story of Hercules and Pholus would have especially noticed the theme of *hospitium, iī* n. (guest friendship). This custom, widely practiced in the Mediterranean world, is based on courteous treatment of a stranger (*hospes, hospitis* m./f.). The concept was so ingrained that *hospes* is the Latin word not only for "stranger" but also for "guest" as well as "host." Pholus is a good host who treats his guest well, but Hercules is a poor guest who demands more than his host can give. The irony of the story is that the good host dies.

Watch for the appearance of a poorly behaved guest of Servilius at an important banquet later in the narrative.

Roman tradition is filled with stories about guest friendship. One of the best known is told by Ovid in his *Metamorphōsēs* (Book VIII). In this tale, Jupiter and Mercury come down to earth in disguise to see how they will be treated by mortals. A poor, elderly couple named Philemon and Baucis are the only humans who are good hosts. Though poor, they offer their guests all the food in their home. The gods reveal themselves and offer Philemon and Baucis their hearts' desire. Instead of asking for great riches or a prolonged life, the couple requests only that they die together. The gods grant their wish. When Philemon and Baucis die, they are turned into two trees whose trunks wind around each other.

Here is how Ovid describes the final moments of Philemon and his wife Baucis, just as the tree covers them over. The selection has been modified into prose to make it easier to read.

> Iamque dum frutex super vultūs geminōs crēscēbat et dum licuit, mūtua dicta reddēbant et "Valē, ō coniunx" dīxērunt simul, simul frutex ōra abdita tēxit.
>
> Ovid. *Metamorphōsēs* VIII.716–719

🔊 VERBA ŪTENDA

abditus, -a, -um hidden
coniunx, coniugis m./f. spouse
crēscō, crēscere, crēvī grow
dictum, -ī n. word
dum as long as

frutex, fruticis m. bush, shrub
geminus, -a, -um twin
licet, licēre, licuit (impersonal verb) it is permitted

mūtuus, -a, -um shared, mutual
ōs, ōris n. mouth; face
Philemōna acc. sing it.
reddēbant "they uttered in reply"

simul together, at the same time
tegō, tegere, tēxī, cover
vultus, -ūs m. face

Latīna Hodierna

Hospitium and Hospitality

You have probably already guessed that the English word "hospitality" is derived from *hospitium*. *Hospitium* could also mean "inn" and, through French, this led to the English words "host," "hostel," "hotel," "hospital," and "hospice," which are all places to take in guests or lodgers. The English word "hostage" is also derived from *hospes,* in the sense that "hostages" are the "guests" of their captor hosts.

Here is how *hospes* and *hospitium* have been transformed in some of the modern Romance languages:

	HOSPITAL	HOTEL	HOST	GUEST
Spanish	hospital	hotel	huésped	huésped
French	hôpital	hôtel	hôte	hôte
Italian	ospedale	hotel	ospite	ospite

Orbis Terrārum Rōmānus

Graecia

Hercules is the Greek national hero and this is exemplified by the fact that his journeys take him all over Greece. He was born in the city of Thebes, where his father Amphitryon was king and where, as an infant, he wrestled with the snakes sent by a jealous Juno. (You will also read about his conception and birth in this book.) Eurystheus was king of Mycenae, a city in the Argolid, and Hercules' first six labors all take place in the Peloponnesus. In this chapter you have read about two of these labors, the Erymanthian boar and the Hydra. In a later chapter you will read about two more, the Stymphalian birds and the Augean stables.

Graecia

The adventure of Hercules and Pholus takes place in Arcadia, a mountainous region of the Peloponnesus in Greece. The region's mountainous geography, suitable mostly for grazing animals like goats and sheep, results in the English word "Arcadian" (pastoral, bucolic). The region was also associated with the woodland god Pan, half-human and half-goat, who was very popular in Rome and Italy. The Latin equivalent of Pan is Faunus, like the bronze statue of a dancing Faun found in Pompeii. European painters sometimes created Arcadian landscapes entitled *Et in Arcadia Ego,* "And I too, in Arcadia." The source for this phrase is debated.

In 146 B.C., Greece came under Roman control and was organized in two provinces, Achaea in southern Greece, and Macedonia to the north.

QUID PUTĀS?

1. Compare the ancient custom of guest friendship to customs in your own family. How important are guests in your family? What are the expectations of your guests and of your family?
2. Do you think that Philemon and Baucis made the right request of their divine guests? Why or why not? Why is the form of their metamorphosis especially appropriate?
3. Why might *hospes* have come to mean both guest and host?
4. How has the meaning of the English word "hospital" changed from the meaning of its source, the Latin *hospitium*?

Faunus Saltāns

Faunus Saltāns Pompēiīs

Arcadia

EXERCEĀMUS!

21-5 Scrībāmus

This model sentence shows how *hic, haec, hoc* and *ille, illa, illud* are used to mean "this" and "that." Replace *sella* (chair) in this sentence with each of the following words. Follow the model.

Haec sella mea est; illa tua.

→ *liber* (book) *Hic liber meus est; ille tuus.*

1. *stilus* (pen or pencil)
2. *mensa* (table, desk)
3. *saccus* (wallet, purse)
4. *pecūnia* (money)
5. *amīcus* (friend)
6. *amīca* (friend)
7. *māter* (mother)
8. *pater* (father)

21-6 Colloquāmur

With a partner practice speaking the sentences you created in Exercise 21-5. Since *hic, haec, hoc* and *ille, illa, illud* are demonstrative words, be sure you point to or show the object you are talking about. In addition to the words used in the *Scrībāmus*, you can add the following:

crēta, -ae f. chalk
fenestra, -ae f. window
hōrologium, -ī n. clock
murus, -ī m. wall

21-7 Verba Discenda

Group the *Verba Discenda* in columns by parts of speech. List the first form of the word along with its English meaning. The number in parentheses tells you how many words to find in that part of speech. We have started this list for you.

Nouns (6)	Pronouns (4)	Verbs (9)	Adjectives (6)	Adverbs (1)	Conjunctions (2)
silva woods, forest	*suī* himself	*cadō* fall	*quīdam* certain		*postquam* after, since

🔊 VERBA DISCENDA

cadō, cadere, cecidī, cāsum fall; be slain; end [cadence]

commit [deposition]

dolor, dolōris m. pain, grief [dolorous]

iaceō, iacēre, iacuī lie, lie still, lie dead

ibi there

īdem, eadem, idem the same

iter, itineris n. road, journey [itinerary]

necō (1) kill, slay

nōs, nostrum/nostrī, nōbīs, nōs, nōbīs we, us [inter nos]

odor, odōris m. scent, odor [odorous]

perterritus, -a, -um very frightened

perveniō, pervenīre, pervēnī, perventum arrive at, reach

petō, petere, petīvī/petiī, petītum seek; look for; attack; run for political office [petition]

postquam after, since

quīdam, quaedam, quoddam a certain (indefinite, as in "a certain person")

quisque, quaeque, quodque/quicque/quidque each, every

redeō, redīre, redīvī/rediī, reditum come back, return

regiō, regiōnis f. region, district [regional]

relinquō, relinquere, relīquī, relictum leave, leave behind [relinquish, derelict]

reliquus, -a, -um remaining [reliquary]

sentiō, sentīre, sensī, sensum feel, hear, see, perceive [sentient, sensory]

silva, -ae f. woods, forest [sylvan, Pennsylvania]

simul atque as soon as

suī, sibi, sē, sē himself, herself, itself, themselves [per se]

tālis, tāle such, of such a kind, of such a sort

tū, tuī, tibi, tē, tē you (sing.) yourself

vīs, vis f. strength, power, force; *vīrēs, vīrium* pl. strength, troops, forces [vim]

vōs, vestrum/vestrī, vōbīs, vōs, vōbīs you (pl.); yourselves

Angulus Grammaticus

The Former and the Latter

As noted earlier, *hic* and *ille* are often used together to distinguish things close by, or just mentioned, from things further away, or mentioned earlier.

> *Marcum et Lūcium videō; hic vir bonus est; ille nōn.*
> I see Marcus and Lucius; this man (Lucius) is good; that one (Marcus) is not.

This sentence can also be translated into English in the following ways:
To show location:

I see Marcus and Lucius; this man here is good; that one over there is not.

To indicate order of reference (former/latter):

I see Marcus and Lucius; the latter [Lucius] is good; the former [Marcus] is not.

Notice that in English we generally say it the other way around. We would say, "I see Marcus and Lucius; the former [Marcus] is not good, the latter [Lucius] is.
Consider this Latin sentence where the difference is clear:

> *Habeō mālum et ōvum: hoc album est, ille rubeum.*
> I have an apple and an egg: the former is red, the latter white.

Whether showing location or order of reference, the word "this" means "closer" and "that" means "farther away." *Hic* and *ille* are paired in the same way in Latin and are used much more frequently than we use "the former" and "the latter" in English.

Photo Credits

Page 257 (bottom) William L. Urban(urban@monm.edu); **page 258 (top)** Dagli Orti/Picture Desk, Inc./Kobal Collection; **page 258 (bottom)** Danilo Ascione/Shutterstock; **page 262** Shutterstock; **page 265** Clipart.com; **page 266 (right)** Clipart.com; **page 266 (middle)** Clipart.com; **page 269** William L. Urban(urban@monm.edu); **page 270 (left)** Akarelias/Dreamstime LLC—Royalty Free; **page 270 (right)** Thomas J. Sienkewicz.

Harēna Pūrgātur

From *Disce! An Introductory Latin Course, volume 2*, First Edition. Francesco Bonavita. Copyright © 2011 by Pearson Education, Inc. Published by Pearson Prentice Hall. All rights reserved.

Gladiātōrēs Pugnantēs, Samnīs (ā sinistrā), rētiārius (ā dextrā), lanista (ā tergō)

GRAMMATICA
The Passive Voice
Ablative of Agent and Ablative of Means
The Imperfect Passive

MŌRĒS RŌMĀNĪ
Dē Gladiātōribus

LATĪNA HODIERNA
Semper Fidēlis

ORBIS TERRĀRUM RŌMĀNUS
Ītalia

ANGULUS GRAMMATICUS
Defective Verbs

LECTIŌNĒS:
PUGNA!
and
FINIS PUGNĀRUM
We witness the games and their aftermath.

22

Harēna Pūrgātur

Lectiō Prīma

Antequam Legis

As you read about the games that Lucius and Marcus are attending, watch out for verbs with a completely different set of endings. These endings indicate **passive voice**.

The Passive Voice

In introducing verbs to you, so far we have talked about **tense** (present, imperfect, perfect, etc.) and **mood** (indicative, infinitive, imperative, participle). It is time to talk about **voice**.

Voice is a term that grammarians use for a concept you know quite well, even if you do not know its name—**active** and **passive**.

Traditionally, a verb is described as **active** if the subject of the verb does the action. A **passive** verb is one where the subject receives the action of the verb.

Active	The bestiarius **wounds** the lion.
Passive	The lion **is wounded** by the bestiarius.

Many active verbs are made passive in English simply by adding **-ed** to the verb (= past participle of the verb) and by preceding it with an appropriate form of "be."

I	**am**	wound**ed**
you	**are**	robb**ed**
he	**is**	kill**ed**

But many other active English verbs form the passive differently.

we	**are**	**heard**
you	**are**	**seen**
they	**are**	**caught**

It is a good idea to make sure you can distinguish active and passive voice in English before you do it in Latin. The following exercise will help you do this.

EXERCEĀMUS!

22-1 Passive Practice

Convert each English sentence from the active voice to the passive voice. Follow the model.

→ The baseball breaks the windshield.
The windshield is broken by the baseball.

1. Bonnie and Clyde are robbing the bank.
2. They are shooting people with guns.
3. They steal bags of money.
4. They make their escape in that car!
5. A teller rings the alarm.
6. The sheriff catches them.
7. The judge puts them in prison.
8. He gives them each a sentence of forty years.

In Latin the present, imperfect, and future passive voice is formed with the following **passive endings**:

-r	-ris	-tur	-mur	-minī	-ntur
I am X-ed	you are X-ed	he/she/it is X-ed	we are X-ed	you (all) are X-ed	they are X-ed

Present passive infinitives end in *-ī* instead of *-e*; for example, *ferīrī* (to be hit) and *vincī* (to be conquered).

Watch for verbs with these endings marked in **bold** in *Lectiō Prīma*.

Ablative of Means and Ablative of Agent

Consider these sentences:

*Leō **gladiō** vulnerātur.*
The lion is wounded **with a sword**.
The lion is wounded **by a sword**.

*Leō **ā bestiāriō** vulnerātur.*
The lion is wounded **by the animal fighter**.

The thing by which something is done (the means or instrument) is indicated in Latin by the ablative without a preposition (*gladiō*) and is translated using "by" or "with." This construction is called the ablative of means. In a sentence with the verb in the passive voice, **the person by whom something is done** (the agent) is indicated in Latin by *ā* or *ab* + the ablative (*ā bestiāriō*). This is called the ablative of agent. Look for ablatives of agent and means marked in *italics* in *Lectiō Prīma*.

EXERCEĀMUS!

22-2 Cultural Awareness

As you read answer the following questions. Answer questions 1–8 in both Latin and English. Respond to question 9 in English only.

1. What is the signal for the games to begin?

2. How many *bestiāriī* are dressed like Hercules? How is one different from the others?

3. How many lions do these *bestiāriī* face? How do the spectators react?

4. What happens to the lions in this fight? What about the *bestiāriī*?

5. What kind of animals do the dwarves fight?

6. What happens in the arena during intermission? What do Marcus and Lucius do while this is happening?

7. What sort of contest occurs when they get back?

8. Which gladiator has the most victories?

9. What is your reaction to this sort of entertainment?

🔊 PUGNA!

Vēnātiō ā Marcō et Lūciō avidē **exspectātur**. Subitō sonitus tubārum **audītur** et sex bestiāriī, quī omnēs vestem Herculis gerunt—ūnus Oscus parvulus fustem ferēns, aliī hastās ferentēs—in harēnam intrant. Sex terga sua appōnunt et in circulō stant. Dum animālia ā *bestiāriīs* **exspectantur**, decem leōnēs ferōcissimī intrant et populī clāmant 5 iocantque.

"Tū! Osce," clāmat Lūcius, "minimus Herculēs in orbe terrārum es! Vōs omnēs ad mortem **dūciminī**!" Marcus "St!" inquit, "Nōlī crūdēlis esse! Praetereā, nōs ā *bestiāriīs* nōn **audīmur** quod vōcēs leōnum maximae sunt. Ecce! Leōnēs ad hominēs ruunt!"

Ūnus leō *hastā* **vulnerātur** et paulum recēdit. Mox duo aliī ā *bestiāriīs* **vulnerantur** 10 sed plūrēs leōnēs quam bestiāriī sunt et mox omnēs hī infortūnātī bestiāriī **necantur**.

Tunc multī hippopotamī et crocodīlī ferōcēs in harēnam **dūcuntur** et ā *nānīs nūdīs* **oppugnantur**. Intereā aliī nānī gregem gruum *parmīs* oppugnant.

Post multās aliās venātiōnēs, in quibus plūrima animālia plūrimīque hominēs **necantur**, harēna sanguine et corporibus plēna est. Dum harēna **purgātur**, Marcus et Lūcius aliquid cibī emunt.

15 Cum ad sedēs reveniunt, duo gregēs fēminārum inter sē ad missiōnem pugnant. Posteā gladiātōrēs ipsī, prīmus inter quōs est Probus, gladiātor plūrimārum palmārum, pugnant. Astacius, quī Probī amīcus est, quoque adest. Ambō de ludō Aemīliī sunt sed Probus murmillō et Astacius rētiārius est. Hodiē Astacius et Probus, hic adversus Thrācem et ille adversus rētiārium, pugnant. Probus, hic adversus Thrācem et ille adversus rētiārium, pugnant. **Vincī** ab illīs nōlunt. Vincere vōlunt!

20 Rētiārius Probō appropinquat et rēte, quod pedēs Probī capit, iacit. Cum Probus cadit, rētiārius tridentem iacit. Probus paene *tridente* **ferītur** sed effugit.

"Salvusne es?" clāmat Astacius. "**Vulnerārisne**, Probe?"

"Nōn **vulneror**!" respondet Probus. "Nullō modō *ab hōc inānī retiāriō* **ferīrī possum**! Sed tū, mī amīce, cavē! Thrāx ad tē ruit."

25 Diū **pugnātur** dōnec tandem missiō **dātur**. Neque Probus neque Astacius **necātur** et multī ā *Probō Astaciōque* **vincuntur**.

Ille fustem ferēns minimus Herculēs in orbe terrārum est!

🔊 VERBA ŪTENDA

ā, ab (+ abl. and passive verb) by
adversus (+ acc.) opposite to, against
alius...alius one...another
ambō both
appōnō, appōnere, apposuī put to (also see *terga sua appōnunt*)
avidē eagerly
bestiārius, -iī m. animal fighter
circulus, -ī m. circle
crocodīlus, -ī m. crocodile
crūdēlis, crūdele cruel
dōnec until
effugiō, effugere, effūgī escape, flee
feriō, ferīre, ferīvī strike, hit
fustis, fustis m. staff, club
grex, gregis m. flock; company, group
grus, gruis m./f. crane (a bird)
harēna, -ae f. sand; arena
hasta, -ae f. spear
hippopotamus, -ī m. hippopotamus
iaciō, iacere, iēcī, iactus throw

inānis, ināne poor, useless, vain
infortūnātus, -a, -um unlucky, unfortunate
intereā meanwhile
iocō (1) joke
ita so, thus; yes
medius, -a, -um midway, in the middle of, the middle of
missiō, missiōnis f. permission to cease fighting *ad missiōnem* "to a draw"
murmillō, murmillōnis m. mirmillo, a heavily armed gladiator
nānus, -ī m. dwarf
nūdus, -a, -um naked, nude; unarmed
oppugnō (1) attack
palma, -ae f. palm frond (of victory)
parma, -ae f. small shield
parvulus, -a, -um tiny, very small, little
paulum a little
plaudō, plaudere, plausī applaud
plēnus, -a, -um (+ abl.) full, full of

praetereā moreover
purgō (1) clean, cleanse
rēte, retis n. net
retiārius, -iī m. gladiatorial fighter with a net
recēdō, recēdere, recessī retire, withdraw
ruō, ruere, ruī, rutum rush, rush at; fall to ruin
sanguis, sanguinis m. blood
simul together, at the same time
sonitus, -ūs m. sound
St! Hush!
tergum, -ī n. back; *terga sua appōnunt* "they stand back to back"
Thrāx, Thrācis m. Thracian; a gladiator with lighter armor, including a helmet and greaves on both legs
tridens, tridentis m. trident
tuba, -ae f. trumpet
venātiō, -iōnis f. hunt
vestis, vestis f. garment, clothing
vulnerō (1) wound

Gemma

Did you notice the phrase *diū pugnātur*, in *Lectiō Prīma?* It is translated impersonally, literally, "it is fought for a long time." This means "the fight went on for a long time," or even "they fought for a long time."

POSTQUAM LĒGISTĪ

Gemma

Battles between Pygmies and cranes were a popular motif in Greco-Roman mythology and art.

Before you read the following *Grammatica*, go back through *Lectō Prīma* and find one passive form from each category. Follow the model.

Form	Line	Word	English Translation
→ 3rd person singular	1	*expectātur*	he/she/it is awaited
1st person singular			
2nd person singular			
1st person plural			
2nd person plural			
3rd person plural			
Infinitive			

Nanus et Grus

Grammatica A

The Passive Voice

Formation of the Passive

Basically, Latin merely substitutes the **passive personal endings** for the active ones. Study these charts and find the forms that have slight variations on this rule.

	1ST CONJUGATION		2ND CONJUGATION		3RD CONJUGATION	
	Active	Passive	Active	Passive	Active	Passive
Singular						
1st	voc**ō**	voco**r**	mone**ō**	moneo**r**	dūc**ō**	dūco**r**
2nd	voc**ās**	vocā**ris**	mon**ēs**	monē**ris**	dūc**is**	dūc**eris**
3rd	voc**at**	vocā**tur**	mone**t**	monē**tur**	dūc**it**	dūc**itur**
Plural						
1st	vocā**mus**	vocā**mur**	monē**mus**	monē**mur**	dūc**imus**	dūc**imur**
2nd	vocā**tis**	vocā**minī**	monē**tis**	monē**minī**	dūc**itis**	dūc**iminī**
3rd	voca**nt**	voca**ntur**	mone**nt**	monē**ntur**	dūc**unt**	dūc**untur**
Infinitive	voc**āre**	vocā**rī**	mon**ēre**	mon**ērī**	dūc**ere**	dūc**ī**

	3RD -IŌ CONJUGATION		4TH CONJUGATION	
	Active	Passive	Active	Passive
Singular				
1st	capi**ō**	capio**r**	audi**ō**	audio**r**
2nd	capi**s**	cap**eris**	aud**īs**	audī**ris**
3rd	capi**t**	capi**tur**	audi**t**	audī**tur**
Plural				
1st	capi**mus**	capi**mur**	audī**mus**	audī**mur**
2nd	capi**tis**	capi**minī**	audī**tis**	audī**minī**
3rd	capi**unt**	capi**untur**	audi**unt**	audi**untur**
Infinitive	cap**ere**	cap**ī**	aud**īre**	audī**rī**

Notā Bene:

- In the 3rd conjugation, the 2nd person singular changes its vowel from *-i* to *-e*. Note that it is *caperis*, not *capieris*.
- 3rd -iō and 4th conjugation verbs have identical endings in the present passive EXCEPT for the 2nd person singular. Compare *caperis* and *audīris*.
- The present passive infinitive is formed in the 1st, 2nd, and 4th conjugations by dropping the final *-e* on the present active infinitive and adding *-ī*; e.g., *amāre* (to love) becomes *amārī* (to be loved).
- The present passive infinitive of all 3rd conjugation verbs, including *-iō* verbs, is formed by dropping the *-ere* ending of the present active infinitive and adding *-ī*; for example, *mittere* (to send) becomes *mittī* (to be sent).

Formulae for Making Present Passives

1ST AND 2ND CONJUGATIONS USE PRESENT STEM (PS)			3RD AND 4TH CONJUGATIONS USE SHORT PRESENT STEM (SPS)		
PS = 2ND Principal Part— *-re*			SPS = 1ST Principal Part— *-ō*		
PS +	*or* *ris* *tur*	*mus* *minī* *ntur*	SPS +	*or* *ris* *tur*	*mus* *minī* *ntur*

Passive Facts

Transitive verbs: Only transitive verbs (i.e., verbs that take a direct object) can be passive. Notice how the direct object of a transitive verb becomes the subject of the passive verb:

<blockquote>I broke the vase.   vs.   The vase was broken by me.</blockquote>

Verbs that do not take a direct object rarely go into the passive. Such verbs are "be," "become," "happen," "go," etc.

    Videō **in the passive:** You would think that *vidētur* would mean "he is seen," but it more commonly means "he seems" or "he appears." Consider this short dialogue:

<blockquote>"Marce," Lūcius inquit, "maestus vidēris!"<br>"Maestus videor?" Marcus respondet, "Nōn maestus sum."
"Chīrōn," Lūcius rogat, "Nōnne Marcus maestus vidētur?"</blockquote>

Ablative of Agent and Ablative of Means

Ablative of Agent

We indicate the performer of an action with a passive verb in English with the preposition **by**:

<blockquote>The lion is wounded by the animal fighter.</blockquote>

In Latin the performer of the action of a passive verb is indicated in a similar fashion: the **person by whom** something is done in the passive voice is in the ablative case with the preposition *ā* or *ab*. This construction, called an **ablative of agent**, is used for both people and animals. The result is a lot like English.

<blockquote>Thrāx ā rētiāriō vulnerātur.
The Thracian is wounded by the retiarius.</blockquote>

Ablative of means

If the action is performed **by means of a thing** (a tool or instrument), Latin uses an ablative without a preposition with either an active or passive verb.

Passive	*Thrāx tridente vulnerātur.* The Thracian is wounded **by a trident**.
Active	Rētiārius tridente Thracen vulnerat. The retiarius wounds the Thracian **with a trident**.

In both sentences *tridente* is an ablative of means.

Both the ablative of means and the ablative of agent can appear in the same sentence:

> Leō ā bestiāriō gladiō necātur.
> The lion is killed with a sword by the animal fighter.

EXERCEĀMUS!

22-3   ### Ablatives of Agent and Means

Look back to the passive sentences you created in English in Exercise 22-1. Underline the phrase indicating the performer of the action. (HINT: In English the phrase begins with "by.") Then indicate whether this phrase would be an ablative of agent or an ablative of means in Latin. Follow the model.

→ The windshield is broken *by the ball*. ablative of means

22-4   ### Ablative of Agent or Means?

Go back to *Lectiō Prīma* and find the ablative used with each of the passive verbs listed below. These ablative phrases are marked in *italics*. Indicate whether each ablative is an ablative of agent or an ablative of means. Then translate verb with the ablative. Follow the model.

Line	Passive Verb	Ablative	Agent or Means?	Translation
→ 1	expectātur	ā Marcō et Lūciō	agent	It is expected by Marcus and Lucius

1. 8 vulnerātur   3. 11 oppugnantur   5. 21 ferīrī

2. 8 vulnerantur   4. 19 ferītur

Lectiō Secunda

Antequam Legis

The games provided more than entertainment for the masses. Some scholars believe that after the games the bodies of the slain animals were butchered and distributed to the poor. And, as with any production, there was a good deal of "post-production" work to be done.

The Imperfect Passive

As you read, see if you can recognize the forms of the **imperfect passive verbs** that this reading introduces (they are in **bold**). If you remember your passive personal endings, they will be fairly easy to spot. Translate these imperfects as "were being X-ed;" for example, *necābantur* would be "they were being slain."

EXERCEĀMUS!

22-5   ### Imperfect Passives

All of the passive verbs marked in **bold** in *Lectiō Secunda* are either 3rd person singular or 3rd person plural imperfect passives. Find five singular verbs and five plural verbs and translate them into English. (Remember that -*tur* is singular and -*ntur* is plural.) Follow the models.

Line	Verb	Number	Translation
→ 1	pugnābātur	singular	it was being fought = there was fighting
1	necābantur	plural	they were being killed

Gemma

Note that *lībertīnus* is used as a noun, "a freedman" whereas *lībertus* is the form used in inscriptions with the genitive of the former owner.

Gemma

The *Puticuli* were an area outside the Esquiline Hill, where bodies were left in pits (*puteī*) to rot because no one would pay for their proper burial.

🔊 FINIS PUGNĀRUM

Multās hōrās **pugnābātur** et nōnnūllī gladiātōrēs **necābantur**. Lūcius ā fratre Marcō domum **dūcēbātur** et aliī Rōmānī quoque
5 domum ambulābant. In mediā harēnā multum ā servīs **agēbātur**. Harēna, sanguinibus et corporibus plēna, **pūrgābātur** et corpora animālium **trahēbantur** ad
10 locum in quō corpora **secābantur** et carō populīs **dabātur**.

Potesne Astacium rētiārium invenīre?

Hīc sanguis permaximus novā harēnā **operiēbātur**. Leviora vulnera aliōrum gladiātōrum **cūrābantur** in harēnā, sed aliī, quī gravissima vulnera habēbant, ad medicum **portābantur**. Gladiātōrēs mortuī ad lanistam, quī eōs sepelīre dēbēbat, ā servīs **portābantur**.

In aliō locō Probus et Astacius de pugnīs dīcēbant. Probus Germānicus est, Astacius Umbricus. "Hodiē fortūnātī
15 erāmus, mī Probe. Sacrāmentum iurāvimus—ūrī, vincīrī, verberārī, ferrōque necārī—tamen vīvimus."

"Ita, rēctē dīxistī," respondit Probus. "Pugnāvimus bene et sine vulneribus gravibus. Sed aliī infortūnātī quoque bene pugnāvērunt et illī nunc mortuī sunt."

Dum talia dīcunt, spectābant illōs mortuōs quī ā servīs lentē **ferēbantur** ad plaustra. Inter quōs mortuōs cadāver parvulum bestiāriī, adhūc fustem Herculis gerentis, **spectābātur**. Hic bestiārius Oscus, Celsus nōmine, ab amīcīs
20 Probō et Astaciō **lūgēbātur**. Oscus amīcus semper fidēlis fuerat.

Haec plaustra nōn omnēs gladiātōrēs mortuōs portābant sed solum illōs malefactōrēs et egēnōs quī in harēnā mortuī erant. Illī mortuī quī līberī aut libertīnī erant, ad familiās suās **remittēbantur**. Malefactōrēs, quī multa crīmina ēgerant, ad locum quī "Puticulī" **nōminābātur**, **afferēbantur**.

In hōc locō egēnī, malefactōrēs et aliī quī nūllīus mōmentī erant semper **portābantur** et in puteōs **iaciēbantur**.

🔊 VERBA ŪTENDA

afferō, afferre, attulī carry toward

cadāver, cadāveris n. corpse, dead body

carō, carnis f. flesh; meat

crīmen, crīminis n. crime

egēnus, -a, -um in need of, in want of, destitute

ferrum, -ī n. iron; sword

fortūnātus, -a, -um lucky, fortunate

fustis, fustis m. staff, club, stick

gerō, gerere, gessī, gestum bear, carry

harēna, -ae f. sand; arena

iaciō, iacere, iēcī, iactum throw

infortūnātus, -a, -um unlucky, unfortunate

ita so, thus; yes

iurō (1) swear

lanista, -ae m. trainer, manager of a gladiatorial troop

lentē slowly

libertīnus, -ī m. freedman

lūgeō, lūgēre, lūxī mourn, lament

malefactor, -ōris m. criminal

medicus, -ī m. doctor, physician

medius, -a, -um midway, in the middle of, the middle of

momentum, -ī n. importance

mortuus, -a, -um dead

nominō (1) name

operiō, operīre, operuī cover

Oscus, -a, -um Oscan

parvulus, -a, -um tiny, very small, little

permaximus, -a, -um very much

plaustrum, -ī n. cart, wagon

plēnus, -a, -um (+ abl.) full, full of

pugna, -ae f. fight

pūrgō (1) clean, cleanse

puteus, puteī m. pit, well

Puticulī, -ōrum m. pl. an area outside the

Esquiline Hill used for mass burials

sacrāmentum, -ī n. oath

sanguis, sanguinis m. blood

secō (1) cut

sepeliō, sepelīre, sepelīvī/sepeliī bury

trahō, trahere, trāxī, tractum drag, haul, draw, remove

ūrō, ūrere, ussī burn

verberō (1) assail, flog, batter

vinciō, vincīre, vinxī tie up, bind

vulnus, vulneris n. wound

POSTQUAM LĒGISTĪ

Try to answer these questions in both Latin and English. The Latin part of your answer can be just a few key words. Full sentences are not necessary.

→ How long did the fighting in the arena last?

        multās hōrās   The fighting lasted for many hours.

1. Where did Lucius and Marcus go after the games?
2. Where were the bodies of the dead animals taken?
3. Where did the wounded gladiators go?
4. Who had to bury the dead gladiators?
5. What were Probus and Astacius talking about?
6. What did Probus and Astacius watch while they were talking?
7. By whom were the dead put on wagons?
8. Where were the bodies of the freeborn or freedmen brought?
9. Where were bodies of the dead criminals brought?

Grammatica B

The Imperfect Passive

Formation of the Imperfect Passive

Did you recognize the new tense of the passive as imperfect? If you remember that the imperfect tense is formed by added *-ba-* between the verb stem and the personal ending, you should have little difficulty with imperfect passive verbs. Compare these two forms:

        *portā**bā**t*   he was carrying
        *portā**bā**tur*   he was being carried

Formulae for Making Imperfect Passives

1ST AND 2ND CONJUGATIONS USE PRESENT STEM (PS)			3RD AND 4TH CONJUGATIONS USE SHORT PRESENT STEM (SPS)		
PS= 2ND Principal part— *-re*			SPS = 1ST Principal Part— *-ō*		
PS +	*bar* *bāris* *bātur*	*bāmur* *bāminī* *bantur*	SPS +	*ēbar* *ēbāris* *ēbātur*	*ēbāmur* *ēbāminī* *ēbantur*

Notā Bene:

- Note that there is a macron over the *-ā-* in the 3rd person singular. Otherwise the macrons appear in the same positions as the active forms.

EXERCEĀMUS!

22-6 From Imperfect Active to Passive

Change each of the following imperfect active verbs to passive. Follow the model.

→ pugnābant: pugnābantur

1. pūrgābant	4. trahēbatis	7. audiēbāmus	10. pugnābāmus
2. nōminābam	5. vulnerābat	8. vōcābātis	
3. iaciēbāmus	6. dūcēbat	9. capiēbam	

Mōrēs Rōmānī

Dē Gladiātōribus

After the games the gladiator Astacius reminds his colleague Probus of the powerful oath they had sworn when they became gladiators. This oath is based on one sworn by several characters comparing themselves to "real gladiators" in Petronius' *Satyricon* (117). Use the *Verba Ūtenda* to translate it:

> In verba Eumolpī sacrāmentum iurāvimus: ūrī, vincīrī, verberārī, ferrōque necārī, … tamquam lēgitimī gladiātōrēs dominō corpora animāsque religiōsissimē addicimus.

Sacrāmentum is the word Romans used for the oath sworn by new enlistees in the Roman army. Use of this word for gladiators emphasizes the strong military associations of the gladiators who lived in a highly regimented, military environment. This oath was only sworn by gladiators who were not slaves.

Romans had a fondness for battles between unusual gladiators such as dwarves and, later in the Empire, women. We have taken the liberty of inserting some female gladiators into this story set earlier, in the time of Augustus.

Gladiators lived in a *lūdus*, in what would best be described as a military camp. There were many such *lūdī* throughout Italy and even in Rome in the early empire. The most famous of these *lūdī* is probably the *Lūdus Magnus*, which was built in Rome long after our story and was located next to the Flavian Amphitheater (completed in 80 A.D. and known better today as the Colosseum).

The *Lūdus Magnus* was a square building with a practice space modeled on that of the Colosseum. Around the perimeter of the arena were storage and training rooms, as well as bedrooms for the *familia* (troop) of gladiators and their trainers (*lanistae*). An underground passageway led from the *Lūdus Magnus* into the Flavian Amphitheater.

Tombstone inscriptions suggest that, despite their military lifestyle and a law prohibiting gladiators to marry, gladiators often had women they called their wives (*coniugēs*) and children. Consider, for example, this funerary inscription of a *murmillō* named Probus who was the inspiration for the Probus you met in the narrative. This Probus died in Spain in the first or second century A.D. His name (*probus, -a, -um* "good, clever, honest") may have been a stage name, similar to those adopted by American professional wrestlers.

Probus Murmillō (Corpus Inscriptiōnum Latinārum, II2/7, 363)

TRANSCRIPTION OF INSCRIPTION	EXPANDED TEXT
MVR.>R	Mur(millō) (contrā) r(etiārium)
PROBUS	Probus
PAVIL.LXXXXIX	P(ublī) A(urēliī) Vī(tālis) l(ībertus) LXXXXIX (victōriārum)
NATIONE.GERMA	natiōnē Germā(nicus)
H.S.E.S.T.T.L	h(īc) s(itus) e(st). S(it) t(erra) t(ibi) l(evis)
VOLVMNIA.SPERA	Volumnia Sperā(ta)
CONIVCI.PIO	coniugī piō
MERENTI	merentī (fēcit).
P. VOLVMNIVS	P(ublius) Volumnius
VITALIS.PATRI.PIO	Vitālis patrī piō (fēcit)
S.T.T.L.	S(it) t(erra) t(ibi) l(evis)

Gemma

LXXXXIX victōriārum: The late letter forms of this inscription make the Roman numerals a bit deceptive, but it seems Probus died one short of reaching an even hundred victories.

The inscription may still seem a bit tricky to read with all those parentheses. See if it makes more sense to you this way. Notice how the tombstone speaks directly to the deceased (*tibi*)! Probus was a freedman and had a wife and child who put up this monument to him.

> Probus, murmillō contrā rētiārium, Publī Aureliī Vītālis lībertus,
> LXXXXIX victōriārum, natiōnē Germānicus, hīc situs est.
>
> Sit terra tibi levis.
> Volumnia Sperāta coniugī piō merentī fēcit.
> Publius Volumnius Vitālis patrī piō fēcit.
> Sit terra tibi lēvis.

🔊 VERBA ŪTENDA

addīcō, addīcere, addīxī consecrate
anima, -ae f. breath, soul, life
contrā (+ acc.) opposite, against
Eumolpus, ī m. Eumolpus, a character in the *Satyricon*
ferrum, -ī n. iron, sword
iurō (1) swear

LXXXXIX victōriārum "of 99 victories"
lēgitimus, -a, -um real, lawful, right
levis, leve light
mereō, merēre deserve
murmillō, murmillōnis m. murmillo, a heavily armed gladiator

necō (1) kill
natiōne "by nationality"
pius, pia, pium pious, devout
religiōsissimē most piously
sacrāmentum, -ī n. oath, sacred obligation (especially one sworn by soldiers)
sit "may (the earth)"

situs, sita, situm located, buried
tamquam just as, just like
ūrō, ūrere, ussī burn
verberō (1) lash, scourge, beat
vinciō, vincīre, vinxī tie up, fetter
victōria, -ae f. victory

Latīna Hodierna

Semper Fidēlis

Semper Fidēlis

Did you notice *Semper Fidēlis*, the Latin motto of the United States Marine Corps, in *Lectiō Secunda*? This motto is quite well known, but many other military organizations also bear Latin mottoes. Here are just a few:

ORGANIZATION	LATIN MOTTO	COMMON LATIN TRANSLATION
U.S. Marine Corps	*Semper Fidēlis*	Always Faithful
U.S. Coast Guard	*Semper Parātus*	Always Prepared
U.S. Air Force Security Force	*Dēfensor Fortis*	Defender of the Force
U.S. Navy (unofficial)	*Non sibi sed patriae*	Not for self but for country
U.S Naval Academy	*Ex scientiā trīdens*	From knowledge, sea power
U.S. Air Force Special Tactics Combat Controllers	*Prīmus eō*	First there
The Royal Canadian Infantry	*Dūcimus*	We lead
Royal Air Force	*Per ardua ad astra*	Through difficulties to the stars
Canadian Air Force	*Sīc itur ad astra*	Such is the pathway to the stars

Orbis Terrārum Rōmānus

Ītalia

Many different peoples inhabited ancient Italy in its earliest days, including Greeks, Etruscans, Messapians, Ligurians, and the Italic peoples of central and southern Italy.

Ancient Italy was a cultural and linguistic melting pot, and the unification of the Italian peninsula under Roman rule, culture, and language took centuries.

The Italic peoples (including the Latins) spoke linguistically related languages now classified as ancient Italic or Sabellic languages, including Latin, Oscan, and Umbrian. Much of central and southern Italy was inhabited by these non-Latin-speaking Italic peoples. By the Augustan period, both the Oscan and Umbrian languages were dying out and being replaced by Latin. Celsus, the short retiarius dressed like Hercules who dies in the amphitheater, is Oscan. His friend Astacius is Umbrian. Plautus, one of the earliest authors of Roman comedy, was Oscan.

Samnium and Umbria were two of the eleven administrative regions of Augustan Italy. Umbria is also one of the twenty regions of modern Italy. Other Oscan-speaking regions were Picenum (modern Marche) and Apulia (modern Puglia).

The modern Italian city of Benevento (ancient *Beneventum*) was originally Oscan, and Assisi (ancient *Assisium*) was Umbrian.

Beneventum Hodiē

Ītalicī

Ītalia Antīqua

Templum Assīnī Hodiē

QUID PUTĀS?

1. In what contexts might Americans be asked to swear an oath similar to the one sworn by Roman gladiators? How are these oaths similar or different?
2. How does the information on the tombstone of the mirmillo Probus compare to the information on modern tombstones of Americans who are also in the entertainment industry? Use the Internet to find some examples.
3. Summarize the private life of gladiators like Probus. Where did they live? Is there evidence of a family life?
4. Why do you think it took so long for the Romans to incorporate the Italian peoples into their empire? Why was there such resistance to Roman rule?
5. Use the ancient and modern maps of Italy to identify the regions of Italy that still bear essentially the same names used by the Romans. HINT: There are six, not including Sicily, which was not included in "Italy" by the Romans.

EXERCEĀMUS!

22-7 Colloquāmur

Read this dialogue aloud with another member of your class. Take turns with the roles, each person inserting the missing verb from the *Thesaurus Verbōrum* that makes the most sense.

Thesaurus Verbōrum

cavē	ferīris	sum
es	irruit	vulnerārisne
ferīrī	vulnerōr	

Astacius: _____, Probe?
Probus: Nōn _____, Astacī!
Astacius: Salvusne _____?
Probus: Salvus _____.
Astacius: _____, Probe?
Probus: Minimē, Astacī! Nōn ab hōc inānī retiāriō _____ possum!
Astacius: Sed mī amīce, cavē! Thrāx tē _____.
Probus: Et tū, mī amīce, _____!

22-8 Scrībamus

Now rewrite this dialogue as if someone is asking about Probus and Astacius in the 3rd person. Follow the model. See if you can add a bit more at the end.

→ Vulnerāturne Probus?

22-9 Verba Discenda

Find the *Verbum Discendum* from which each of the following English words is derived. Use the meaning of the Latin word to define the English word. If you are unfamiliar with the English word, look it up in the dictionary! Follow the model.

→ gestation: *gerō, gerere, gessī, gestum* bear, carry the act of carrying

1. arena	5. repugnant	9. mortuary
2. tractor	6. unfortunate	10. plenary
3. consanguineous	7. ferrous oxide	11. nomination
4. purgatory	8. intermediary	12. invulnerable

🔊 VERBA DISCENDA

egēnus, -a, -um in need of, in want of, destitute [indigent]
ferrum, -ī n. iron, sword [ferrous]
fortūnātus, -a, -um lucky, fortunate
gerō, gerere, gessī, gestum bear, carry [gestation]
harēna, -ae f. sand; arena

iaciō, iacere, iēcī, iactum throw [ejaculate]
infortūnātus, -a, -um unlucky, unfortunate
ita so, thus; yes
medius, -a, -um midway, in the middle of, the middle of [intermediary]
mortuus, -a, -um dead [mortuary]

nōminō (1) name [nominate]
plēnus, -a, -um (+ abl.) full, full of [plenary]
pugna, -ae f. fight [pugnacious]
pūrgō (1) clean, cleanse [purgative]
ruō, ruere, ruī, rutum rush, rush at; fall to ruin

sanguis, sanguinis m. blood [sanguinary, consanguineous]
tergum -ī n. back
trahō, trahere, trāxī, tractum drag, haul, draw, remove [tractor]
vulnerō (1) wound [vulnerable]
vulnus, vulneris n. wound

Angulus Grammaticus

Defective Verbs

In the *Angulus Grammaticus* to Chapter 11, we talked about verbs like **meminī** (I remember) and **ōdī** (I hate), which are perfect in form but are translated into English in the present tense.

Because these verbs lack present forms they are sometimes called defective verbs. Another verb that has only perfect forms is *coepī* (I begin). You can recognize such verbs in the dictionary because they have only two principal parts, both with perfect endings:

> *coepī, coepisse* begin
> *meminī, meminisse* remember
> *ōdī, ōdisse* hate

Other verbs are defective because they have no perfect forms. These include:

> *āiō* say
> *inquam* I say
> *feriō, ferīre* strike
> *quaesō, quaesere* ask for

English has some defective verbs, too. Some examples include:

- The verb "beware," which we only use in the present tense (we can't say "bewared").
- Modal verbs like "can/could," "may/might," and "will/would." We can say "I can" but not "I am canning" or "to can." So it is awkward for us to express the Latin infinitive *posse* in English with the verb "can." We can only say "to be able."
- The verb "used to" which is only used in the past, as in "I used to play the piano."
- The verbs "rumored" and "reputed," which are only used in the passive, as in "He is rumored to be out of the country."

Photo Credits

Page 272 (top) Photos.com; **page 272 (bottom)** Victor M. Martinez; **page 275** Jose Luis Trullo/Fotolia, LLC—Royalty Free; **page 279** Scala/Art Resource, N.Y.; **page 281** Courtesy Museo Arqueologico y Etnololico de Cordoba; **page 282** Clipart.com; **page 283 (top)** © Spectrum Colour Library/Heritage—Images/ImageState Media Partners Limited; **page 283 (bottom)** Michael Avory/Shutterstock.

Consilia

From *Disce! An Introductory Latin Course, volume 2*, First Edition. Francesco Bonavita. Copyright © 2011 by Pearson Education, Inc. Published by Pearson Prentice Hall. All rights reserved.

23

Consilia

Lectiō Prīma

Antequam Legis

Licinia's baby will be born soon. In *Lectiō Prīma*, Licinia talks with her husband, Aelius, and her mother, Valeria, about how the baby's birth will change their lives. As you read about their hopes and worries, watch how Latin expresses passive voice in the future tense.

In this *lectiō* you also hear about Hephaestus, Aelius' lame slave, who works in Aelius' blacksmith shop. As is the case of many slaves, Hephaestus spends the night locked into the shop where he works. Unlike many others, Hephaestus was not chained to the wall at night, as Aelius trusted him. The slave Hephaestus shares his name with the lame blacksmith god of the Greeks (known as Vulcan to the Romans). The god Hephaestus made Zeus' thunderbolts, and according to some traditions, his workshop was beneath Mt. Aetna, a volcano on Sicily. In the drawing at the top of pg. 287, based on a painting by the 17th-century Spanish artist Velasquez, Mercury, the Roman messenger god, is visiting the forge of Vulcan.

The Future Passive

Now that you have seen how present and imperfect passive verbs are formed in Latin, you can easily recognize the future passive. Just look for the passive instead of active endings at the end of the future forms. All future passive verbs are marked in **bold** in *Lectiō Prīma*.

Nōtā Bene: Remember to add "will be" when you translate the future passive into English, as in "will be captured" or "will be done."

EXERCEĀMUS!

23-1 **Comprehension Questions**

Before you read *Lectiō Prīma*, scan the text and try to answer these questions. Answer them in both Latin and English.

1. In lines 1–2, why does Licinia's family need to make lots of plans?
2. In lines 1–4, what does Licinia's family need to do to avoid difficulties?

GRAMMATICA
The Future Passive
The Irregular Verb *Ferō*
Counting Like a Roman

MŌRĒS RŌMĀNĪ
Epistulae Rōmānae

LATĪNA HODIERNA
Numerī Rōmānī

ORBIS TERRĀRUM RŌMĀNUS
Britannia

ANGULUS GRAMMATICUS
The Roman Calendar

LECTIŌNĒS:
IN INSULĀ VALERIAE
and
EPISTULA Ē CASTRĪS

Valeria and her family discuss the coming birth of a child to Licinia and Aelius and the changes it will cause in their lives. Then they receive a letter from Valeria's son, Licinius, who is serving in the army on the German border under Tiberius, the future emperor.

Milites Labōrantēs

3. To whom is Aelius speaking in lines 5–7? What does he call this person?

4. Why does Licinia tell her mother not to worry in lines 8–9?

5. Why does Plotia begin to cry in line 10–11?

6. What plan of Aelius do we hear about in lines 14–16?

7. What does everyone do after Aelius finishes speaking in line 17?

Fornāx Vulcānī *ā*
Velasquez (1599–1660)

IN INSULĀ VALERIAE

Sērō est et familia Valeriae sedet et colloquium inter sē habet. Familia multa consilia facere dēbet quod mox, in hāc ipsā mense, infans, quem Licinia gerit, **pariētur**.

Valeria "Aelī et Licinia," inquit, "Vōs moneō—mox plūs pecūniae invenīre dēbēbimus. Sī plūs pecūniae nōn **inveniētur**, difficultātēs habēbimus." Aspicit
5 Aelius ad ventrem Liciniae et, tangēns ventrem, infantī futūrō dīrectē dīcit: "Certē, dulcissime, ā mātre **nūtriēris** et ā nōbīs omnibus **amāberis**. Sed vērum est—infantem novum habēre pretiōsum est."

Licinia "Māter," inquit, "Nōlī timēre! Bene nōs monēs, sed negōtium Aeliī cotīdiē maius crescit et, dum domī cum infante maneō, paulum labōrāre poterō.
10 Ego et Aelius et Hephaestus omnēs dīligentius labōrāre **cōgēmur**."

Plōtia, māter Valeriae et avia Liciniae, lacrimāre incipit. "Vae mihi! Nam certē forīs **pulsābor** quod infans novus plūs quam ego **amābitur**. In viās sīcut canis **agar**! Et vōs omnēs magnopere improbī **vidēbiminī**."

Valeria suspīrāns mātrem leviter lēnit, "Mātercula, nūllō modō in viīs vīvere **cōgēris**. Sī tū in viīs vīvere **cōgēris**, nōs omnēs **cōgēmur**, nam ūna familia sumus!"

15 Aelius manum Plōtiae leviter tangit et "Avia," inquit, "Nōlī despērāre, nam consilium habeō! Ego et Hephaestus dīligentius quam aliī fabrī labōrābimus et mox, cum hominēs nova opera nostra vīderint, dēsīderiō illa opera emere **cōgentur**."

Omnēs rident et silentium tenent, sed quisque intrā sē dīcit, "Modo quid nōbīs **agētur**?"

Labōrābō dīligenter

VERBA ŪTENDA

aspiciō, aspicere, aspexī,
  aspectum **look at**
avia, -ae f. grandmother
canis, canis m./f. **dog**
certus, -a, -um **sure,**
  certain
cōgō, cōgere, coēgī,
  coactum **force**
colloquium, -iī n. talk,
  conversation
consilium, -iī n. **plan,**
  counsel
crescō, crescere grow,
  increase
cum when
dēsīderium, -iī n. desire,
  wish

desperō (1) despair of
difficultās, -tātis f. **trouble,**
  difficulty
dīligentius more carefully,
  more diligently
dīrectē directly
dulcis, -e **sweet**
faber, fabrī m.
  artisan, smith
forīs out of doors
improbus, -a, -um disloyal,
  shameless, morally un-
  sound
intrā (+ acc.) within
lēniō, lēnīre, lēnīvī/lēniī put
  at ease
levis, leve light, gentle

magnopere **much, greatly,**
  especially
maneō, manēre, mansī,
  mansum **stay, remain,**
  endure
manum hand
mātercula, -ae f. dear mother
mensis, mensis m. month
modo **but, only, just now**
moneō, -ēre, monuī,
  monitum **warn**
nam **for**
nūtriō, nūtrīre, nūtrīvī/nūtriī
  nurse, nourish, raise
opus, operis n. **work,**
  effort; structure, build-
  ing; (pl.) goods

pariō, parere, peperī bring
  forth, bear
paulum a little
pretiōsus, -a, -um valuable,
  expensive
pulsō (1) **strike, beat;**
  push, drive
sērō late, too late
silentium, -iī n. **stillness,**
  silence, tranquility; *silen-*
  tium tenēre to keep silent
suspīrō (1) sigh
tangō, tangere, tetigī touch
vae alas, woe
venter, ventris m. belly,
  abdomen
vidēbiminī you will seem

Gemma

In line 6 of *Lectiō Prīma* Aelius uses the word *dulcissime*. How would the meaning change if he had said *dulcissimē* instead? Remember: Macrons can make all the difference!

POSTQUAM LĒGISTĪ

1. Are the worries of Licinia and Aelius similar or dissimilar to those of expectant parents today?
2. What kinds of assistance are available to such families today but not to their ancient Roman counterparts?
3. Why do you think Plotia is so worried? Would a woman in her position and social class have the same concerns today?
4. How do members of her family try to make Plotia feel better?

Grammatica A

The Future Passive

The formulae for making future passives are the same ones you learned for future actives. Just use passive rather than active personal endings. Here is how it works:

1ST AND 2ND CONJUGATIONS USE PRESENT STEM (PS)			3RD AND 4TH CONJUGATIONS USE SHORT PRESENT STEM (SPS)		
Present Stem = 2nd Principal Part -*re*			**Short Present Stem = 1st Principal Part -*ō***		
PS +	*bor* *beris* *bitur*	*bimus* *biminī* *buntur*	SPS +	*ar* *ēris* *ētur*	*ēmus* *ēminī* *entur*
			Notā Bene: 3rd: i + i = i *caperis*, not *capieris* (3rd -*iō*) 4th: i + i = ī		

Now compare the future passive of *vocō* with the future passive of *dūcō*

PERSON	FUTURE PASSIVE OF *VOCŌ*	FUTURE PASSIVE OF *DŪCŌ*
	Singular	
1st	*vocābor* I will be called	*dūcar* I will be led
2nd	*vocāberis* you will be called	*dūcēris* you will be led
3rd	*vocābitur* he/she/it will be called	*dūcētur* he/she/it will be led
	Plural	
1st	*vocābimur* we will be called	*dūcēmur* we will be led
2nd	*vocābiminī* you (all) will be called	*dūcēminī* you (all) will be led
3rd	*vocābuntur* they will be called	*dūcentur* he/she/it will be led

Nōtā Bene:

- In the 1st and 2nd conjugations, the future passive ending in the 2nd person singular is -*beris*. You might expect -*biris* but the -*bi*- here becomes -*be*-; so *portāberis*.

23-2 Forming 2nd Conjugation Future Passives

Use your knowledge of the future active to translate each of the following future passive verbs, HINT: All these verbs appeared in *Lectiō Prīma.*

1. amābitur		6. cōgēmur	
2. cōgentur		7. agētur	
3. pariētur		8. pulsābor	
4. amāberis		9. cōgēris	
5. inveniētur		10. agar	

Lectiō Secunda

Antequam Legis

Letters and Numbers

In this day and age of e-mail and text messaging, it is important to stop and consider how important and difficult sending a letter was in antiquity. Although Roman roads were a marvel of engineering and ensured relatively fast travel times, it still could take weeks for letters to reach some parts of the Roman Empire.

In *Lectiō Secunda*, Valeria receives a rare letter from her son, Licinius, who is serving in the army under Tiberius near the German border. The future emperor Tiberius will use this campaign to earn a fine reputation as a general and will be awarded a triumph upon his return to Rome. You will witness this triumph later in the book.

We take the opportunity of this letter to formalize your knowledge of Latin numbers, so look out for some Roman numerals in this *lectiō*.

The Irregular Verb *Ferō*

Also look for forms of the irregular verb *ferō*, a very important verb meaning "carry," "bear" and a number of other things. *Ferō* has distinctly irregular principal parts: *ferō, ferre, tulī, lātum*. It is also an irregular 3rd conjugation verb in the present tense, but these forms use familiar personal endings. Watch for forms of *ferō*, marked in **bold**, in the *lectiō*, and see if you can identify where the verb is regular in the present system.

23-3 Recognizing Forms of *Ferō*

Before you read *Lectiō Secunda*, find the Latin forms of *ferō* for each of the following English verbs. Remember that all the forms of *ferō* are marked in **bold** in the *lectiō*. HINT: Pay attention to personal endings.

1. he carries	4. they carry	7. you carried
2. I carry	5. I carried	8. you (sing.) carry
3. we carry	6. you (all) carry	

🔊 EPISTULA Ē CASTRĪS

Dum familia inter sē dīcunt, aliquis portam pulsāns audītur. Aliquis portam pulsat—semel, bis, ter. Aelius ad portam festīnat et, portam aperiēns videt mīlitem fessum, quī epistulam **fert.**

Mīles "Avē!" inquit. "Nōnne invēnī domum Valeriae, cuius fīlius C. Licinius est? Quaerō hanc Valeriam."

5   "Valeriae domum invēnistī, amīce. Quae fortūna tē ad nōs **fert**?"

"Nōmen mihi est M. Vērus. Modo Rōmam ā Germāniā advēnī dē legiōne XVII. Bonum nuntium ab Germāniā **ferō**. Hanc epistulam Liciniī mēcum **tulī**."

Haec verba audiēns, Valeria laeta ad portam currit et epistulam grātissimē accipit. "Mille grātiās," inquit Valeria, "tibi agō quārē epistulam ad mē **tulistī**. Nōbīs optimum dōnum **fers**. Sitiensne es? Iēiūnusne es?"

10   "Alma es, sed missiōnem honestam mēcum quoque **ferō** et nunc stīpendiō meō in mātrimōnium uxōrem dūcere poterō. Plūs quam XL annōs nātus sum et magnopere quiētem cupiō! Valēte omnēs."

Postquam Vērus abiit, Valeria signum epistulae frangit et omnēs silentium tenent dum legit:

OSPD Licinius SVBEEV. Iam dūdum ad fīnēs Germānōrum sum, sed bellum in Germānōs gerere nōn iam parātī sumus. Multās difficultātēs et lābōrēs **ferimus**. Nunc castra fortissima pōnimus et viās novās struimus.

15   Cotīdiē, cum tempestās bona est, arborēs magnās in silvā secāmus et eās ad castra **ferimus**. Et cotīdiē centuriō clāmat: 'Estisne mīlitēs Rōmānī an nōn? Onus quod **fertis** leve est—levius pennā! Celerius! Fortius!' Et, cum centuriō clāmat, omnēs fortius onera sua **ferunt**. Herī pars viae novae vī flūminis **ferēbātur** sed hodiē pluit et nōn labōrāmus. Hoc centuriōnī displicet sed nōbīs maximē placet! Crās **ferēmur** ad viam et tunc magnus labor nōbīs erit!

Advēnitne infans quem Licinia **fert**? Estne puer aut puella?

20   Vīta dūra est sed quoque bona, nam labōrāre nōn mihi displicet. Mīles sum et dulce est prō patriā labōrāre et pugnāre! Mox in Germāniā pugnābitur! KAL IŪN.

Videt mīlitem quī epistolam fert

🔊 VERBA ŪTENDA

almus, -a, -um nourishing, kind, dear

an or

aperiō, aperīre open

arbor, arboris f. tree

bellum, -ī n. war; bellum gerere wage war

bis twice, two times

C. = Gaius

castra, -ōrum n. pl. camp

centuriō, -ōnis m. centurion (roughly like a sergeant today)

cum when

difficultās, -ātis f. trouble, difficulty

displicet impersonal (+ dat.) "it is displeasing"

dōnum, -ī n. gift

dūdum just now, a little while ago

dulcis, dulce sweet

dūrus, -a, -um hard, rough

epistula, -ae f. letter

ferēbātur it was carried away

ferēmur we will proceed, we will go (literally, "we will be carried")

ferō, ferre, tulī, lātum bear, carry

fīnēs, fīnium m. pl. country, territory

flūmen, flūminis n. river

frangō, frangere, frēgī break

gener, generī m. son-in-law

grātus, -a, -um pleasing, thankful

honestus, -a, -um honorable

in Germānōs (remember that *in* + acc. means "into, against")

KAL IŪN "on the June Kalends," i.e., June 1

legiōne XVII = legiōne decimā septimā = the 17th legion

levis, leve light, gentle

līberī, -ōrum m. pl. children

XL = 40

M. = Marcus

magnopere much, greatly, especially

mātrimōnium, -iī n. matrimony

mīles, mīlitis m. soldier

mille 1,000

missiō, -ōnis f. discharge (military); *missiōnem honestam* "an honorable discharge"

modo only, just now

nam for

onus, oneris n. load, burden

opus, operis n. work, effort; structure, building; (pl.) goods

patria, -ae f. country, fatherland

penna, -ae f. feather, wing

pluit (impersonal) "it is raining"

porta, -ae f. door, gate

pulsō (1), strike, beat; push, drive

pugnābitur "there will be fighting"

quārē for

quiēs, quiētis f. quiet, calm, rest

Rōmam "to Rome"

secō, secāre, secuī cut, cut off, cut up

semel once, one time

signum, -ī n. seal

silentium, -iī n. stillness, silence, tranquility; *silentium tenēre* to keep silent

sitiens, sitientis thirsty

stīpendium, -iī n. pay

struō, struere, strūxī build, construct

ter three times

POSTQUAM LĒGISTĪ

Answer questions 1–6 in both Latin and English. Answer question 7 in English only.

1. What happens while the family is talking about their plans?
2. Who is M. Verus?
3. Why is Valeria happy in line 8?
4. Why does Verus leave so quickly?
5. How does Licinius spend most of his time in the army?
6. What is his attitude toward his work?
7. How does his work compare to the duties of a modern American soldier?

Gemma

Look for these abbreviations in Licinius' letter: OSPD = *Omnibus salūtem plūrimam dīcit.*
SVBEEV = *Sī valēs, bene est. Egō valeō.*

Grammatica B

The Irregular Verb *Ferō*

Ferō is irregular only in the present tense, where some vowels drop out. These irregular forms are marked in **bold** in the chart below. Note, however, that the regular personal endings are used with this verb. The present passive forms of *ferō* are made by changing the active personal endings to passive ones.

Gemma

Dulce est prō patriā labōrāre et pugnāre: Licinius is here echoing a famous lines from Horace's *Odes* (3.2): *dulce et decōrum est prō patriā morī.* (It is sweet and fitting to die for one's country.)

PERSON	PRESENT ACTIVE		PRESENT PASSIVE	
Singular				
1st	*ferō*	I bear, carry	*feror*	I am borne, carried
2nd	**fers**	you bear, carry	**ferris**	you are borne, carried
3rd	**fert**	he/she/it bears, carries	**fertur**	he/she/it is borne, carried
Plural				
1st	*ferimus*	we bear, carry	*ferimur*	we are borne, carried
2nd	**fertis**	you (all) bear, carry	*feriminī*	you (all) are borne, carried
3rd	*ferunt*	they bear, carry	*feruntur*	they are borne, carried
Infinitive				
	ferre	to bear, carry	**ferrī**	to be borne, carried
Imperative				
	Fer!	Bear! Carry!		
	Ferte!	Bear! Carry!		

Gemma

False etymologies can be misleading. You might think that a "Ferris" Wheel is one where "you are carried." But actually, it was invented for the 1893 Chicago World's Fair by an engineer named George W. G. Ferris.

Remember! "*Dīc, dūc, fac,* and *fer,* lack the *e* that ought to be there."
All the other forms of *ferō* are regular:

Imperfect	*ferēbam, ferēbās,* etc, and *ferēbar, ferēbāris,* etc.
Future	*feram, ferēs,* etc, and *ferar, ferēris,* etc.
Participle	*ferēns*

The perfect system (perfect, pluperfect, future perfect) is formed normally from the perfect stem *tul-.* Thus:

tulī	I have carried
tuleram	I had carried
tulerō	I shall have carried

Translating Ferō

When you find a form of *ferō* in a sentence, the first meanings you should try to use are either "bear" or "carry."

*Mīles epistulam **fert**.*	The soldier is carrying a letter.

Although this gives you the basic meaning, *ferō* can often be better translated with different English words, depending on context. All of the following examples come from *Lectiō Secunda*:

- carry away, dispel

*Heri pars viae novae vī flūminis **ferēbātur**.*	Yesterday part of the new road was carried away by the force of the river.

- go, proceed

*Crās **ferēmur** ad viam.*	Tomorrow we will proceed to the road. (Literally, this means "we will be carried")

- lead

*Omnēs viae Rōmam **ferunt**.*	All roads lead to Rome.

- endure

*Multās difficultātēs et labōrēs **ferimus**.*	We endure many hardships and labors.

- bring, report

*Rēs novās dē Germāniā **ferō**.*	I bring news from Germany.

These are just a few examples. So when you see *ferō* in a sentence, be ready to consider other possible translations besides "bear, carry." A good Latin dictionary often will list some of these possibilities for you.

Compounding Ferō

Ferō is frequently compounded. Note where assimilation of the consonants and change of meaning occur in the following forms:

Gemma

English words derived from *ferō* compounds can help you sort out this assimilation. For example: confer, collate; differ, dilate; refer, relate.

ad- + ferō = **afferō, afferre, attulī, allātum**	carry to, bring to
ab- + ferō = **auferō, auferre, abstulī, ablātum**	carry off, carry away
con- + ferō = **conferō, conferre, contulī, collātum**	carry together, compare
dis- + ferō = **differō, differre, distulī, dīlātum**	put off, delay
ex- + ferō = **efferō, efferre, extulī, ēlātum**	carry out, produce
in- + ferō = **inferō, inferre, intulī, illātum**	bring into, bring against, inflict
ob- + ferō = **offerō, offerre, obtulī, oblātum**	bring before, offer, present
re- + ferō = **referō, referre, rettulī, relātum**	carry back, tell

Watch for some of these compounds of *ferō* in upcoming *lectiōnēs*.

EXERCEĀMUS!

23-4 *Ferō*: **From Active to Passive**

Change each of the following active forms of *ferō* into the passive. Then translate the passive form into English. Follow the model.

→ ferō   *feror*   I am carried

1. fert	5. feram	9. ferimus
2. ferēmus	6. ferēbāmus	10. ferre
3. ferēbam	7. fers	
4. ferunt	8. fertis	

Counting Like a Roman

You have seen numbers and translated them without effort prior to this. This section puts all the information in one place for you. You just need to know a few words and remember a few rules.

Abacus Rōmānus

- A cardinal number is the regular number used for counting.
- An ordinal puts something in order or tells the rank of something, as in "fifth" or "twentieth."
- The basics of Roman numerals are:
  - **I** = 1 **V** = 5 **X** = 10 **L** = 50 **C** = 100 **D** = 500 **M** = 1,000
  - A smaller letter to the left of a larger letter means subtract. Thus **XC** = 90
  - A smaller letter to the right of a larger letter means add. Thus **CX** = 110
- These rules for Roman numerals were often broken by the Romans themselves, and the system was flexible.

	ROMAN NUMERAL	CARDINAL NUMBER			ORDINAL NUMBER	NOTES
1	I	M. ūnus ūnīus ūnī ūnum ūnō	F. ūna ūnīus ūnī ūnam ūnā	N. ūnum ūnīus ūnī ūnum ūnō	prīmus, -a, -um	
2	II	duo duōrum duōbus duōs duōbus	duae duārum duābus duās duābus	duo duōrum duōbus duo duōbus	secundus, -a, -um	These three cardinal numbers are declinable.
3	III	trēs trium tribus trēs tribus	trēs trium tribus trēs tribus	tria trium tribus tria tribus	tertius, -a, -um	
4	IIII or IV	quattuor			quartus, -a, -um	
5	V	quīnque			quintus, -a, -um	
6	VI	sex			sextus, -a, -um	
7	VII	septem			septimus, -a, -um	
8	VIII	octō			octāvus, -a, -um	
9	VIIII or IX	novem			nonus, -a, -um	
10	X	decem			decimus, -a, -um	
11	XI	undecim			undecimus, -a, -um	"one and ten"
12	XII	duodecim			duodecimus, -a, -um	"two and ten"
13	XIII	tredecim			tertius decimus, -a, -um	"three and ten"
14	XIIII or XIV	quattuordecim			quartus decimus, -a, -um	Notice how both parts of these compound ordinals have adjectival endings.
15	XV	quīndecim			quintus decimus, -a, -um	
16	XVI	sēdecim			sextus decimus, -a, -um	
17	XVII	septendecim			septimus decimus, -a, um	

(*continued on next page*)

18	XVIII	duodēvīgintī	duodēvicēnsimus, -a, -um	"two from twenty"
19	XVIIII or XIX	undēvīgintī	undēvicensimus, -a, -um	"one from twenty"
20	XX	vīgintī	vicēnsimus, -a, -um	
21	XXI	vīgintī ūnus	vicēnsimus prīmus, -a, -um	
22	XXII	vīgintī duō	vicēnsimus secundus, -a, -um	Just follow the pattern for higher numbers.
30	XXX	trīgintā	trīcēnsimus, -a, -um	
40	XL or XXXX	quadrāgintā	quadrāgēsimus, -a, -um	
50	L	quinquagintā	quinquāgēsimus, -a, -um	
60	LX	sexāgintā	sexāgēsimus, -a, -um	
70	LXX	septuāgintā	septuāgēsimus, -a, -um	
80	LXXX	octōgintā	octōgēsimus, -a, -um	
90	XC	nōnāgintā	nōnāgēsimus, -a, -um	
100	C	centum	centēsimus, -a, -um	
500	D	quingentī	quingentēsimus, -a, -um	
1000	M	mille	millēsimus, -a, -um	*Mille* is an indeclinable adjective: *cum mille hominibus* (with a thousand men).
2000	MM	duo mīlia mīlia mīlium mīlibus mīlia mīlibus	bīs millēsimus, -a, -um	*Milia* is a declinable noun used with a partitive genitive: *duo milia librōrum* (two thousand books). One form for all three genders.

Nōtā Bene:

- *Ūnus* only has singular forms. *Duo* and *trēs* only have plural forms.
- Remember that *ūnus* forms its genitive and dative singulars like *sōlus* or *nūllus* (i.e., *ūnīus* and *sōlīus*). As such it is an UNUS NAUTA word.
- All ordinals are declined as 2-1-2 adjectives.
- *Ambo, ambae, ambo* (both) is declined like *duo, duae, duo.*
- You can also count by the number of times something happens. In this case the cardinal number has become an adverb instead of an adjective: *semel* (one time, once); *bis* (two times, twice); *ter* (three times, thrice); *quater* (four times). Look back in *Lectiō Secunda* and find where some of these adverbs are used.

EXERCEĀMUS!

23-5 Counting in Latin

Rearrange the following numbers in numerical sequence from one to twenty.

decem; duo, duae, duo; vīgintī; duodecim; duodēvīgintī; novem; octō; quattuor; quattuordecim; quindecim; quīnque; sēdecim; septem; ūnus, ūna, ūnum; septendecim; sex; tredecim; trēs, trēs, tria; ūndecim; undēvīgintī

Mōrēs Rōmānī

Epistulae Rōmānae

Letter-writing was an important vehicle for communication in the Roman world. Portions of the correspondence of several famous Romans survive, especially the letters of Cicero from the 1st century B.C. and the letters of Pliny the Younger from the end of the 1st century A.D. Both Cicero and Pliny wrote personal letters to their families and more formal, business letters to their colleagues. Even some letters between Cicero and Julius Caesar survive. Wealthy Romans would typically dictate their letters to their personal scribes.

There was no governmental postal system, so letter-writers had to arrange for their own transport. If they were wealthy enough, they had their own runners to carry their letters. Otherwise, they tried to find someone going the right way, as Licinius did. Obviously, then, the delivery of such letters could take many days or even weeks and was quite unreliable.

Licinius' letter could have been written on a wax or wooden tablet. Either wax or wood was a much less expensive and durable writing material than the other alternative, papyrus.

Even if Licinius knew how to read and write, he probably would have hired a scribe (*scrība, -ae* m. secretary, clerk, scribe) to write his letter for him. The expense of writing materials and hiring a scribe encouraged the practice of abbreviating formulaic expressions like the following used by Licinius:

OSPD	*Omnibus salūtem plūrimam dīcit.*
SVBEEV	*Sī valēs, bene est. Egō valeō.*

SVBEEV was often further abbreviated to SVV or *Sī valēs, valeō.*

Let's take a look at an actual letter that has been uncovered at Vindolanda, a fort near Hadrian's Wall in England. Written on a wooden writing tablet, it was preserved due to the special climatic conditions that are found at Vindolanda. In this letter, Claudia Severa is inviting Sulpicia Lepidina, the wife of the garrison commander, to a birthday party in c. 100 A.D.

Claudia's letter is particularly interesting because we can tell from the handwriting that the scribe started the letter, then Claudia herself wrote a brief personal greeting, and then the scribe finished the letter. This letter is one of the earliest pieces of writing in Latin in a woman's hand. Unfortunately, we do not know whether Sulpicia accepted the invitation and came to visit.

At right is the actual wooden tablet which Claudia sent. Below you see a transcription of what is written on the tablet. [*Vacat*] indicates a lacuna, or missing part of the text. A slash indicates the end of a line. A letter in square brackets is missing in the fragmentary original and has been added by the editors. The part in **bold** was written by Severa.

Ita valeam, karissima, et havē

cl · seuerá · lepidinae [suae] / [salu]tem / jiijdusseptemb[res]sororaddie[m] sollemnemn[a]talemmeumrogo / libenter[f]aciásutuenias / adnosi[u]cundioremmihi [diem]jnteruentútuofacturásj / [*vacat*] / cerial[emtu]umsalutáaeliusmeus / etfiliol[u]ssalutant [*vacat*] / [*vacat*] **sperabotesoror / ualesoro[r]anima / meaitau[al]eam / karissimaethaue**

The handwritten letter is difficult to read without training. You can tell from the transcription that there are lots of words understood or missing and that there are no spaces between many of the words. Here is the letter in a more readable version.

Claudia Sevēra Lepidinac suae salūtem dīcit. III Idūs Septembrēs soror ad diem sollemnem nātālem meum rogō libenter faciās ut veniās ad nōs. Iucundiōrem mihi diem interventū tuō factūra sī…

Ceriālem tuum salūtā. Aelius meus et filiolus [eum] salūtant.

Spērābō tē, soror. Valē, soror, anima mea. Ita valeam, karissima, et havē

On the front of the tablet the scribe also wrote the following by way of an address:

Sulpiciae Lepidinae, Ceriālis Sevēra

🔊 VERBA ŪTENDA

III Īdūs Septembrēs "three days before the Ides of September" i.e., September 11th

Aelius Claudia's husband

anima, -ae f. soul, breath

Ceriālis Sulpicia's husband

faciās ut veniās "make that you come"

factūra (est) "you will make"

havē = avē Hail. Hi.

interventus, -ūs m. arrival, coming

iūcundus, -a, -um pleasing, pleasant

karissima note spelling of *carissima*

nātālis, nātāle birth

salūtem dīcit says *Salvē*, says hello, greets

sī . . . The rest of this sentence is missing from the letter.

soror "sister" may not mean sibling here, but a term of affection among friends

spērābō tē "I will hope for you," i.e., "I will expect you"

valeam may I flourish, may I be well

Latīna Hodierna

Numerī Rōmānī

Now look at some of the many English words derived from Latin numbers.

CARDINAL NUMBER	ENGLISH DERIVATIVE	ORDINAL NUMBER	ENGLISH DERIVATIVE
ūnus, -a, -um	**un**ique, **un**it, **un**iverse	**prīm**us, -a, -um	**prim**al, **prim**er, **prim**ary
duo, -ae, -o	**du**al, **du**et	**secund**us, -a, -um	**second**, **second**ary
trēs, -ēs, -ia	**tri**ennial, **tri**centennial	**tert**ius, -a, -um	**tert**iary, **ter**centenary
quattuor	**quat**rain	**quart**us, -a, -um	**quart**, **quart**et
quinque	**quinqu**ennial	**quint**us, -a, -um	**quint**et, **quint**uplet
sex		**sext**us, -a, -um	**sext**et, **sext**uplet
septem	**Septem**ber	**septim**us, -a, -um	**sept**et, **sept**uplet
octō	**Octo**ber	**octāv**us, -a, -um	**octav**e, **oct**uplet
novem	**Novem**ber, **nov**ena	nonus, -a, -um	
decem	**Decem**ber, **dec**ennial	**decim**us, -a, -um	**decim**ate, **deci**gram, **deci**liter, **deci**meter
sexāgintā	**sexagen**arian		
septuāgintā	**Septuagint**, **septuagen**arian		
octōgintā	**octogen**arian		
nōnāgintā	**nonagen**arian		
centum	**cent**ennial, **cent**ury, **centi**gram, **centi**liter, **centi**meter, **cent**urion		
mille	**mile**, **milli**gram, **milli**liter, **milli**meter		

A Note on Roman Numerals

Roman numerals are used instead of Arabic numbers in a number of contexts today:

- Lower-case Roman numerals are used for page numbering in the front matter of books.
- In outlining
- Upper-case Roman numerals are used (sometimes) for:

    I. Numbering book chapters
    II. Numbering kings and queens (Queen Elizabeth II)
    III. On cornerstones of buildings
    IV. Numbering Superbowls
    V. The hours on fancy watches

As you can see in the photo at right, the 80 entrances of the Flarian amphitheatre were all marked with numerals over the arches to facilitate the entry and exit of large numbers of people.

LIII super portam
Amphitheātrum Flāviānum

EXERCEĀMUS!

23-6 Roman Numerals

1. What was the number of the last Superbowl? What will be the number of the next one? Write them out in Roman numerals.

2. Write the current year in Roman numerals.

3. Write the year you were born in Roman numerals.

4. Write the number of this book chapter in Roman numerals.

Orbis Terrārum Rōmānus

Britannia

Claudia Severa's letter to Sulpicia was written in Britain about 100 years after the time of our story. During the reign of Augustus, Britain was not part of the Roman Empire. The island was not conquered until 43 A.D. under the reign of Claudius.

In 60–61 A.D. the British queen Boudicca led a major but unsuccessful revolt against the Romans. Following the suppression of Boudicca's revolt, Rome's rule was firmly established on the island for centuries. Romans gradually expanded their sphere of influence beyond what is now southeastern England into Wales and north toward Scotland. The Scottish tribes were never fully conquered by the Romans, who built walls across the island to control and monitor movement across the border. The first of these walls, perhaps called *Rigor Valī Aelī* (the line of Hadrian's frontier) and known today as Hadrian's Wall, was built of stone and turf after 122 A.D. This wall ran from Luguvalium (modern Carlisle) to Coria (modern Corbridge) and was defended by a series of forts, including Vindolanda, where Claudia Severa's letter was found. The Antonine Wall, a series of earthen walls on stone foundations stretching from what is now Clyde on the west coast to the Firth of Forth on the east, was built after 142 A.D., during the reign of the emperor Antoninus Pius, in an attempt to bring southern Scotland under Roman control. The Antonine Wall was abandoned by Antoninus Pius' successor, Marcus Aurelius, who established the northern boundary of the Roman province along Hadrian's Wall.

Britannia Rōmāna

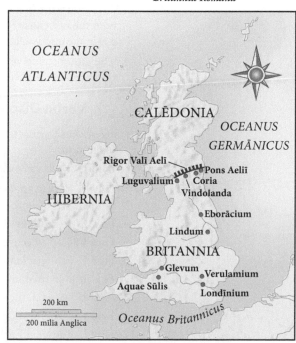

Rigor Valī Aelī

Boudicca cum filiābus Londīniī

Many major modern cities in England were originally Roman army camps or cities, including:

Londīnium (London)	Eborācium (York)
Verulamium (St. Albans)	·Lindum (Lincoln)
Glevum (Gloucester)	Aquae Sūlis (Bath)

Modern English city names ending in -chester come from the Latin *castra* and indicate that the site was a fort in Roman times: Chichester, Worcester, Gloucester, etc.

QUID PUTĀS?

1. Do you think Sulpicia Lepidina accepted Claudia Severa's invition to visit for her birthday? Why or why not?
2. Compare the way Claudia Severa invited Sulpicia to the way you might extend a similar invitation today. How are the technology and social customs different? How are they the same?
3. Explain to a friend what all these English words have in common and why: centennial, century, centigram, centiliter, centimeter, centurion. If you don't know the answer, look it up in an English dictionary.
4. In what other parts of the world have massive protective walls similar to Hadrian's Wall been built?

EXERCEĀMUS!

23-7 Scrībāmus

Using the letter from Claudia Severa to Sulpicia Lepidina as a model, write a letter in Latin to a relative or friend inviting them to your birthday party.

23-8 Colloquāmur

This game can be played in a number of variations:

1. Line up with a number of other students or sit in a circle. The *dux gregis* (the leader of the group) picks a number and says it aloud. The next person has to say aloud the next number in sequence.
2. The group sits in a circle and each person counts by twos or threes, having to come up with the right answer within five seconds. Say it correctly and you stay in the game. Make a mistake and you are out. Last person remaining is the winner.
3. The group counts off using ordinals. Ordinals have declinable forms, so remember to use the form that matches your gender.

23-9 Verba Discenda

Use the *Verba Discenda* to answer each of the following questions. Watch for Roman numerals in the questions.

1. Find **IV** *verba discenda* related to military life.
2. Find **V** *verba discenda* that are 2nd declension neuter nouns.
3. Find **III** words in the 3rd declension.
4. Find **I** i-stem noun of the 3rd declension.
5. Find **I** 2-1-2 adjective.
6. Find **II** two-termination adjectives of the 3rd declension.
7. Find **I** noun used only in the plural.
8. Find **II** nouns in the 1st declension.
9. Find **I** 1st conjugation verb, **I** 2nd conjugation verb, and **I** 3rd conjugation -*iō* verb.
10. Give **I** additional English derivative for **V** different *verba discenda*.

🔊 VERBA DISCENDA

aspiciō, aspicere, aspexī,
  aspectum **look at**
  [aspect]
bellum, -ī **n. war;** *bellum*
  gerere **wage war**
  [bellicose]
canis, canis **m./f. dog**
  [canine]
castra, -ōrum **n.**
  pl. camp
centuriō, -ōnis **m.**
  centurion
certus, -a, -um **sure,**
  certain [certitude]
cōgō, cōgere, coēgī,
  coactum **drive together,**
  force [cogent]
consilium, -iī **n. plan,**
  counsel, reason,
  judgment

difficultās, -ātis **f.**
  trouble, difficulty
dōnum, -ī **n. gift**
  [donation]
dulcis, dulce **sweet**
  [dulcet, dulcimer]
epistula, -ae **f. letter**
  [epistolary]
ferō, ferre, tulī, lātum
  bear, carry [refer,
  relate, confer, collate]
grātus, -a, -um
  pleasing, thankful
  [gratitude]
improbus, -a, -um
  disloyal, shameless,
  morally unsound
  [improbity]
levis, leve **light,**
  gentle [levity]

magnopere **much, greatly,**
  especially
maneō, manēre, mansī,
  mansum **stay, remain,**
  endure, await
mīles, mīlitis **m. soldier**
  [militant]
modo **only, just now, but**
nam **for**
opus, operis **n. work, ef-**
  fort; structure, build-
  ing; (pl.) goods
  [magnum opus,
  operate]
porta, -ae **f. door, gate**
  [portal]
pulsō **(1) strike, beat;**
  push, drive [pulsate]
silentium, -iī **n. stillness,**
  silence, tranquility

Angulus Grammaticus

The Roman Calendar

Although we are essentially still using the Roman calendar as revised by Julius Caesar and officially enacted on January 1, 45 B.C., you need to understand a few important differences and points of grammar in order to know how to read and to make calendar days in Latin.

First of all, the names of the Roman months will look quite familiar, although the forms Romans used to make calendar dates are all adjectives.

Iānuārius, -a, -um	*Māius, -a, -um*	*September, -bris, -bre*
Februārius, -a, -um	*Iūnius, -a, -um*	*Octōber, -bris, -bre*
Martius, -a, -um	*Iūlius, -a, -um*	*November, -bris, -bre*
Aprīlis, -e	*Augustus, -a, -um*	*December, -bris, -bre*

The original Roman calendar was lunar and only had ten months, beginning with *Martius* and ending with *December*. That is why *September* is named the seventh month, *Octōber* is the eighth month, etc. As various reforms tried to regularize this calendar, two months, *Iānuārius* and *Februārius*, were added at the beginning of the year. *Iānuārius* is appropriately named after Janus (*Iānus, -ī* m.), the two-faced Roman god of doorways, of entering and leaving. *Februārius* is related to *febris* and is the "Fever Month." After the death of Julius Caesar, *Quīnctīlis*, the fifth month, was renamed *Iūlius* in his honor. Later *Sextīlis*, the sixth month, was renamed *Augustus* in honor of the emperor.

In the Julian Calendar the number of days in each month is the same as in our modern calendar, but Romans used three fixed points in the month that dates are defined by:

Iānus

- **Kalends:** The first day of the month was called *Kalendae, -ārum* f. pl. and gives us our word "calendar."

- **Nones:** The second fixed day was the fifth day of the month and was called *Nōnae, -ārum* f. pl.

- **Ides:** The third fixed day was the thirteenth day of the month and was called *Īdūs, Īdus* f. pl.

> BUT … in March, May, July, and October the Nones fell on the seventh day and the Ides fell on the fifteenth. That is why the assassination of Julius Caesar in 44 B.C. took place *Īdibus Martiīs* (ID MAR) "on the Ides of March," i.e., (March 15th).

Here are some other dates following the same format:

Kalendiīs Iānuāriīs, "on the January Kalends"	KAL IAN	Jan. 1
Nonīs Iānuāriīs "on the January Nones"	NON IAN	Jan. 5
Īdibus Iānuāriīs "on the January Ides"	ID IAN	Jan. 13
Kalendiīs Maiīs, "on the May Kalends"	KAL MAI	May 1
Nonīs Maiīs "on the May Nones"	NON MAI	May 7
Īdibus Maiīs "on the May Ides"	ID MAI	May 15

The days before the Kalends, Nones, and Ides were introduced by *pridiē* (the day before) in this manner:

pridiē Kalendās Februāriās the day before the February Kalends	(*pridiē* + acc.) pri. KAL FEB	Jan. 31
pridiē Nonās Aprīlēs the day before the April Nones	pri. NON APR	Apr. 4
pridiē Īdūs Iūniās the day before the June Ides	pri. ID IUN	June 12

To refer to all other days of the month, Romans **counted ahead** to the next Kalends, Nones, or Ides. Here they used the formula *ante diem* "before the day" followed by a number and the words for the Kalends, Nones, or Ides, and the appropriate month in the accusative plural. **As they did this, they counted both the day they were counting from and the day they were counting to.** Thus:

> *ante diem III Kalendās Iūliās* three days before the July Kalends

- Kalends of July = July 1
- Three days before this, counting Roman style → July 1, June 30, June 29
- So, a.d. III KAL IUL = June 29

EXERCEĀMUS!

23-10   **The Roman Calendar**

Read these Roman dates in Latin, then convert them into our calendar format. Use the *Angulus Grammaticus* as your guide and remember to count like a Roman! You may well find a conversion engine online to help you, but try it the hard way first, and use the converters to check yourself.

1. ID DEC
2. a.d III NON OCT
3. a.d. IV ID IVL
4. a.d. X KAL OCT
5. NON MAI

6. pri KAL OCT
7. pri NON FEB
8. a.d. III KAL MAI
9. a.d. VIII KAL IAN
10. a.d. VII KAL APR

Photo Credits

Page 286 Victor M. Martinez; **page 287** Clipart.com; **page 293** Vanni/Art Resource, N.Y.; **page 295** Alison Rutherford/© The Vindolanda Trust; **page 297** Thomas J. Sienkewicz; **page 298 (top)** Dreamstime LLC—Royalty Free; **page 298 (bottom)** Photos.com; **page 299** Shutterstock.

24

In Theātrō

Lectiō Prīma

Antequam Legis

Going to the Theater

Romans had many opportunities to go to theatrical productions. In this chapter both families attend a revival of *Amphitruo*, a play by Plautus, one of Rome's comic playwrights. Plautus died in 184 B.C., but his plays were frequently performed after his death. The Roman theater was open to all classes, and the audiences were often rowdy. Even Mendax could have attended, as admission was free. But seats were often saved for the more influential Romans, and class-conscious Romans would know what section of the theater was reserved for their class. In *Lectiō Prīma* you will read about people arriving at the theater and their anticipation before the performance begins. Notice how Marcus summarizes for Lucius the plot of the play they are going to see. Such a plot summary, called an *argūmentum* (*-ī* n.), was often given by an actor at the beginning of the play. As you read this *lectiō*, watch out also for a special group of verbs called deponents.

Deponent Verbs

An extremely common class of Latin verbs is called **deponent**. Such verbs have passive forms but active meanings. To translate deponent verbs you only need to remember the dictum:

"Looks passive, isn't."

Regular passives and deponents are intermingled in *Lectiō Prīma*. To help you distinguish them, the deponents are in **bold** and the regular passives are in ***bold italics***. Remember to translate the deponents actively and the regular passives passively. Be careful of tenses as you read—watch especially for 3rd and 4th conjugation futures.

Persōna Rōmāna

GRAMMATICA
Deponent Verbs
"PUFFY" Verbs
The 4th and 5th Declensions

MŌRĒS RŌMĀNĪ
Theātra Rōmāna

LATĪNA HODIERNA
Rēs and *Diēs* in Modern Usage

ORBIS TERRĀRUM RŌMĀNUS
Geōgraphia Ītaliāna

ANGULUS GRAMMATICUS
Oh No, Not Semi-Deponents, Too!

> **LECTIŌNĒS:**
> **IN THEĀTRŌ**
> and
> **ALCMĒNA ET LICINIA PARIUNT**
>
> Both families attend a revival of a play of Plautus, and life imitates art.

301

From *Discē! An Introductory Latin Course, volume 2*, First Edition. Francesco Bonavita. Copyright © 2011 by Pearson Education, Inc. Published by Pearson Prentice Hall. All rights reserved.

EXERCEĀMUS!

24-1 Translating Deponent Verbs

Below is a list of some of the deponent verbs which appear in *Lectiō Prīma*. Since these are all new vocabulary words, we provide their meanings and conjugations. Use what you know already about Latin verbs to determine whether the tense of the verb is present or future. Then use the personal endings to translate the words. Remember to translate them ACTIVELY. Follow the model.

HINT: You do not even need to look at the *lectiō* to do this exercise, but you will find the *lectiō* a lot easier to understand if you do this exercise first.

	Line	Verb	Meaning	Conjugation	Tense	Translation
→	1	colloquuntur	speak together	3rd	present	they speak together
1.	1	ingrediuntur	enter	3rd		
2.	7	fruentur	enjoy	3rd		
3.	**9**	sequitur	follow	3rd		
4.	13	polliceor	promise	2nd		
5.	14	mentior	lie	4th		
6.	17	patitur	suffer	3rd *-iō*		
7.	18	prōgreditur	advance	3rd *-iō*		
8.	21	loquitur	speak	3rd		

🔊 IN THEĀTRŌ

· In theātrum multī spectātōrēs **ingrediuntur** et inter sē **colloquuntur** dum fābula Plautī, "Amphitruō" nomine, ab omnibus avidē *exspectātur*.

Novum theātrum Marcellī omnēs **intuentur** et valdē **admīrantur**. Patriciī sīcut Marcus et Lūcius et amīcī suī sēdēs in prīmīs gradibus theātrī, post
5 senātōrēs, tenent et ab hīs fābula melius *audiētur spectābitur*que. Aliī, sīcut Valeriae familia, in altissimīs sēdibus sedent. Sed omnēs—fēminae līberīque pauperēsque dīvitēsque—mox fābulā **fruentur**.

In theātrum Lūcius Marcum **sequitur** et frātrēs sedent cum amīcīs suīs. Multī iuvenēs inter sē **sermōcinantur** sed Marcus fēminam ūnam gracilem et
10 pulchram **intuētur** et cum eā dīcere **cōnātur**, sed Marcus ā Lūciō *turbātur*. "Quālis," rogat, "haec fābula est? Quid in fābulā *agētur*? Quid vidēbimus hodiē?" Marcus "Frātercule," inquit, "modo manēre dēbēs et mox omnia **intuēberis**. Tibi **polliceor**! Haec fābula optima est et multum rīdēbis! Nōn **mentior**. Nōnne Amphitruōnem scīs?"

15   Lūcius respondet: "Certē, Amphitruō pater Herculis est."

"Ita vērō! Et uxor eius Alcmēna, quae gravida est, domī remanet dum Amphitruō contrā hostēs bellum gerit. Mox infans **nascētur** et Alcmēna **patitur** quod vir suus domī nōn est. Tum Iuppiter, quī Alcmēnam vīderat et (ut semper) statim eam adamāvit, ad Alcmēnam **prōgreditur**. In formam Amphitruōnis Iuppiter sē mutat et cum Alcmēnā in Amphitruōnis lectō dormit. Sed, tunc Amphitruō vērus ā bellō revenit et uxōrem suam amāre sperat! Sed
20 Alcmēna fessa est et nōn ..."

In aliā parte theātrī, familia Valeriae quoque sedet et **loquitur**. Aelius "**Īrascor**," inquit, "quod uxor mea, tam gravida, tantōs gradūs ascendere dēbuit! Nōn aequum est! Decet nōbīs in gradibus inferiōribus nōn hīc in Alpibus aut Apennīnīs sedēre! Aliās sēdēs petere dēbēmus!"

Licinia rīdens, "Mī Aelī," inquit, "sede hīc! Initium fābulae iam adest."

Actor Rōmānus

🔊 VERBA ŪTENDA

adamō (1) love passionately
admīror, admīrārī admire
Alpēs, Alpium f. pl. Alps, the mountains of northern Italy
Apennīnī, -ōrum m. pl. Apennines, the mountains along the spine of Italy
ascendō, ascendere, ascendī, ascensum climb, ascend
colloquor, colloquī talk together, converse
cōnor, cōnārī, cōnātus sum try
decet, decēre, decuit (+ dat. +inf.) imp. it is fitting
dīves, dīvitis rich, talented

forma, -ae f. shape, form; beauty; ground plan
frāterculus, -ī m. little brother
fruor, fruī, fructus / fruitus sum (+ abl.) enjoy, profit by
gracilis, gracile thin, slender, scanty
gradus, -ūs m. step, pace, tier (of a theater)
gravidus, -a, -um pregnant
hostis, -is m. stranger, enemy; pl. "the enemy"
inferior, inferius lower
ingredior, ingredī, ingressus sum enter
initium, -iī n. beginning
intueor, intuērī gaze at
īrascor, īrascī be angry at

Iuppiter, Iovis m. Jupiter, king of the gods
līberī, -ōrum m. pl. children
loquor, loquī, locūtus sum speak, talk, say
mentior, mentīrī, mentītus sum lie, deceive
mī = vocative of *meus*
mutō (1) change
nascor, nascī be born
patior, patī, passus sum suffer, allow
patricius, -a, -um noble, patrician
pauper, pauperis poor
polliceor, pollicērī, pollicitus sum promise
prōgredior, prōgredī, prōgressus sum go to, move forward, proceed

quālis, quāle of what sort, of what kind
remaneō, remanēre, remansī remain, stay behind
senātor, senātōris m. senator
sequor, sequī, secutus sum follow
sermōcinor, sermōcinārī converse, talk, chat
situs, -a, -um located
spectātor, spectātōris m. spectator, observer
sperō (1) hope
tantus, -a, -um so great, so many
theātrum, -ī n. theater
turbō (1) disturb, disorder
ut as
vērō in truth, truly

POSTQUAM LĒGISTĪ

1. Describe the seating arrangements in the theater. Who sits where?
2. What does Marcus want to do while he waits for the play to begin?
3. What does Lucius want to do?
4. Briefly summarize the plot of the play.
5. What is Aelius angry about?

Grammatica A

Deponent Verbs

Look through the *Verba Ūtenda* and find all the deponent verbs marked in **bold**. They are easy to recognize with passive endings. Note that these deponent verbs have only three principal parts. Why? Because they (naturally) do not have the 3rd principal part, which is the perfect **active** form of regular verbs.

dīcō	*dīcere*	*dīxī*	*dictum*
I say	to say	I have said	(having been) said

loquor	*loquī*		*locūtus sum*
I say	to say		I have said

For now, you only have to worry about the first two principal parts. The 3rd principal part of deponents is a perfect passive form you have not yet learned. For now, this form will only be given for deponent verbs which are *Verba Discenda*. You will only see and use deponent verbs in the present and future tenses in this chapter. It is easy to recognize deponent verbs in the dictionary for the following reasons:

- All the endings are passive.
- They have only three principal parts.
- The 3rd principal part has two words, the second of which is *sum*. You will not see this *sum* in the dictionary with non-deponent verbs.

Gemma

Marcellus was the son of Augustus' sister, Octavia, and was a possible successor to Augustus. He died in 23 B.C., and Augustus had this theater built near the Tiber in his memory.

Deponents are formed just like the passives of regular verbs. The only difference is that they do not use active personal endings.

Now look at the present forms of these sample deponent verbs.

PRESENT DEPONENTS					
Person	**1st Conjugation** *cōnor* (try)	**2nd Conjugation** *polliceor* (promise)	**3rd Conjugation** *sequor* (follow)	**3rd-*iō* Conjugation** *patior* (suffer, allow)	**4th Conjugation** *mentior* (lie, deceive)
Singular					
1st	cōnor	polliceor	sequor	patior	mentior
2nd	cōnāris	pollicēris	sequeris	pateris	mentīris
3rd	cōnātur	pollicētur	sequitur	patitur	mentītur
Plural					
1st	cōnāmur	pollicēmur	sequimur	patimur	mentīmur
2nd	cōnāminī	pollicēminī	sequiminī	patiminī	mentiminī
3rd	cōnantur	pollicentur	sequuntur	patiuntur	mentiuntur

Unlike regular passive verbs, many deponent verbs are transitive and can take direct objects, like the words marked in bold in these sentences:

Novum theātrum Marcellī intuentur.   They look at the **new theater** of Marcellus.
Novum theātrum valdē admīrantur.   They admire very much the **new theater**.
Marcus fēminam intuētur.   Marcus looks at a **woman**.
Uxōrem suam amplectī sperat.   He hopes to embrace **his wife**.

Some deponent verbs are intransitive and thus do not take direct objects.

Iuvenēs inter sē sermōcinantur.   The youths chatted among themselves.
Ad Alcmēnam prōgreditur.   He goes to Alcmena.
Mox infans nascētur.   Soon the baby will be born.
In theātrum Marcus ingreditur.   Marcus enters the theater.

EXERCEĀMUS!

24-2 Deponent Verbs in the Future Tense

Now use your knowledge of future passive forms and the chart of present forms above to translate the following deponents in the future tense. Follow the model.

→ *cōnābor*   I will try

1. cōnābuntur
2. pollicēbitur
3. sequentur
4. patiēminī
5. mentiēris

6. cōnābimur
7. patientur
8. pollicēberis
9. mentiētur
10. sequēris

Look for more deponents in the future tense in *Lectiō Secunda*.

Lectiō Secunda

Antequam Legis

In *Lectiō Secunda* the play begins and the actor gives an *argūmentum,* or introduction, to the play. He explains not only the plot but also the role of the character he is playing. He uses the 2nd person plural to talk directly to the audience. His words are taken directly from the original *argūmentum* of Plautus' play.

Besides the excitement on stage, there is also some in the audience. Watch out in this *lectiō* for a special group of deponent verbs that take ablative rather than accusative objects. You will also learn about the last two declensions, the 4th and the 5th.

Ablatives with Certain Deponent Verbs

Five deponent verbs take ablative objects instead of accusative ones. You already saw one of these verbs in *Lectiō Prīma* in the phrase *mox fābulā fruentur* (Soon they will enjoy the story). The verb *fruentur* takes the ablative *fābulā* as its object. To help you spot these verbs in *Lectiō Secunda* we have marked them in ***bold italics***.

The 4th and 5th Declensions

In this *lectiō* you are also introduced to the last two declensions. You will find these endings relatively familiar, and you will be able to spot the declensions this way:

	HOW TO SPOT IT	EXAMPLES
4th Declension	*-u* in most of its endings	*manus, manūs, manuum,* etc.
5th Declension	*-e* in all of its endings	*rēs, reī, rērum, rēbus,* etc.

The 4th and 5th declension nouns are marked in **bold** in the *lectiō*. The case endings will not be a problem for you, as they are just variants of what you have already seen.

EXERCEĀMUS!

24-3 Finding Ablative Objects for Certain Deponent Verbs

Before you read *Lectiō Secunda*, scan it to find the ablative object(s) of the following deponent verbs. Then translate the verb with its object(s). Follow the model.

Line	Verb	Ablative Object(s)	Translation
→ 2	fruuntur (enjoy)	spectāculīs sonīsque	they enjoy the sights and sounds
1. 5	fruēminī (enjoy)		
2. 9	ūtitur (use)		
3. 12	fungar (perform)		
4. 22	potitur (possess)		
5. 23	fruitur (enjoy)		

ALCMĒNA ET LICINIA PARIUNT

Omnēs spectātōrēs, dīvitēs et pauperēs, nōbilēs et plēbēiī, spectāculīs sonīsque theātrī *fruuntur.* Subitō dominus actōrum prō spectātōribus stat et silentium poscit. "Amīcī," clāmat, "Mox fābulā
5 *fruēminī.* Sī vōbīs placeat, silentium tenēte! Nōlumus **sonitūs** infantium, sermōnum, **mōtuum**, aut rixārum audīre. Ecce! Incipimus!"

Tunc actor, **habitum speciemque** deī Mercuriī gerēns, intrat et, magnā vōce *ūtitur* et
10 prōnuntiat.

"Ego, Mercurius, Iovis **iussū** veniō. Ego *fungar* officiō meō et vōbīs argūmentum huius tragoediae ēloquar. Quid? Frontēs contraxistis quia 'tragoediam' dīxī? **Faciēs** maestae mihi displicent!
15 Nōlīte verērī! Deus sum et facile **rēs** commutābō. Sed, deīs in comoediā agere nōn decet. Quid faciam? **Rem** teneō! Nunc **rēs** mixta est et tragicomoediam habēbimus."

Actōrēs in comoediā Rōmānī

"Haec est Amphitruōnis domus, sed Amphitruō nōn adest; immō, in castrīs cum **exercitū** suō est. Sed alius
20 Amphitruō intus est!"

"Ille Amphitruō quī abest, vērus Amphitruō est. Hic Amphitruō, quī nunc in lectō Alcmēnae dormit, pater meus est—Iuppiter ipse, rex deōrum. Pater nunc et **speciē et habitū** Amphitruōnis *potitur* et uxōre Amphitruōnis vērī *fruitur.*"

Paulō post spectātōrēs Alcmēnam et Iovem haec dīcentēs audiunt:
25 Iuppiter: "Bene valē, Alcmēna. Mihi necesse est abhinc īre."

Alcmēna: "Nōn mihi placet. Quandō revertēris?"

Iuppiter: "**Fidem** habē, cāra uxor. Mox revertar! Hoc tibi polliceor!"

Et, paulō post, quid vident spectātōrēs? Illum vērum Amphitruōnem. A **portū domum** suum aggreditur. Alcmēna eum spectat et **manūs** ad **faciem** tollēns laetē exclāmat: "Revēnistī ad mē! Tam laeta sum! Sed nuper ē lectō
30 meō abiistī!"

Amphitruō, uxōris **manum** capiēns: "Quid dīcis?" inquit, "Ē lectō? Haec **rēs** mala mihi est! Ego mēnsēs multōs iam absum. Quid agitur?"

Omnēs spectātōrēs rīdent sed, in aliā parte theātrī, alīquī nōn rīdent. Licinia quoque patitur. In **genua** cadit, ventrem prehendēns et "Māter," inquit, "patior graviter et sīcut Alcmēna puerum mox pariam. Sed hodiē! Plūrēs **diēs**
35 mihi nōn sunt. Necesse est nōs simul dē **gradibus** descendere et subitō **domum** redīre."

Persōnae Rōmānae

🔊 VERBA ŪTENDA

abhinc from here

actor, actōris m. actor

aggredior, aggredī go to, approach

argūmentum -ī. n. plot

commutō (1) change

comoedia, -ae f. comedy

contrahō, contrahere, contrāxī draw together, gather

***diēs, diēī* m. day**

dēliciae, -ārum f. pl. delight, pleasures

dēscendō, dēscendere, descendī go down, descend

displiceō, displicēre, displicuī (+ dat.) displease

***dīvēs, dīvitis* rich, talented**

***domus, -ūs* f. house**

ēloquor, ēloquī, ēlocūtus sum speak out, declare

exclamō (1) cry out, exclaim

exercitus, -ūs m. army

***faciēs, -ēī* f. face, appearance, beauty**

fidēs, fideī f. faith, trust

frons, frontis f. forehead, brow

fungor, fungī, functus sum (+ abl.) perform, discharge

genu, -ūs n. knee

graviter severely

habitus, -ūs m. dress, clothing

immō rather

iussū "by order of" (+ gen.)

manus, -ūs f. hand

mensis, mensis m. month

***mentior, mentīrī, mentītus sum* lie, deceive**

mixtus, -a, -um mixed

mōtus, -ūs m. motion

nuper recently

officium, -iī n. task, duty, office

pariō, parere, peperī bring forth, give birth to

paulō post a little later, somewhat later

pauper, pauperis poor

plēbēius, -a, -um plebian, pertaining to the common people

portus, -ūs m. gate

***potior, potīrī, potītus sum* (+ abl. or gen.) take possession of, get, acquire**

prehendō, prehendere, prehendī take hold of, seize

prōnuntiō (1) proclaim, announce

quandō when

***rēs, reī* f. thing, matter, business, affair; reason**

rem teneō I have it!

revertor, revertī come back, return

rixa, -ae f. quarrel, brawl

sermō, sermōnis m. speech, talk

***simul* together, altogether, at the same time, all at once**

***sonitus, -ūs* m. sound**

spectāculum, -i n. spectacle, sight

***speciēs, speciēī* f. appearance, look, type**

tragicomoedia, -ae f. tragicomedy

tragoedia, -ae f. tragedy

***ūtor, ūtī, ūsus sum* (+ abl.) use, employ, enjoy, experience**

venter, ventris m. stomach, belly

***vereor, verērī, veritus sum* be afraid of, fear, show reverence to**

vōs you (acc. pl.)

POSTQUAM LĒGISTĪ

1. Who is the *dominus actōrum* and what does he tell the audience?
2. What role does the first actor play, and what does he tell the audience?
3. Why does Alcmena not want Jupiter-Amphitryon to leave?
4. What happens as soon as Jupiter-Amphitryon leaves the stage?
5. Why does the audience laugh when this happens?
6. Why is Licinia not laughing?
7. How do you think Licinia will get home?

Grammatica B

"Puffy" Verbs

There are five Latin deponent verbs that take ablative rather than accusative objects. These verbs are sometimes called "PUFFY" because of the following acronym:

    P*otior, potīrī, potītus sum* (+ abl. or gen.) take possession of, get, acquire

    Ū*tor, ūtī, ūsus sum* (+ abl.) use, employ, enjoy, experience

    F*ruor, fruī, fructus/fruitus sum* (+ abl.) enjoy, profit by

    F*ungor, fungī, functus sum* (+ abl.) perform, discharge

    V*escor, vescī* (+ abl.) take food, feed, devour (referring to animals, not people)

The last of these, *vescor*, rarely appears. The four other PUFFY verbs, however, are *Verba Discenda* in this chapter.

EXERCEĀMUS!

24-4 Distinguishing PUFFY Verbs from Regular Verbs

Choose the correct case of each word marked in **bold** to be the object of the verb. Remember to choose the ablative for PUFFY verbs and accusative for all other verbs. Then translate the verb and its object into English. Follow the model.

→ **Spectāculīs / Spectācula** theātrī fruuntur.

       Spectāculīs theātrī fruuntur.   They enjoy the sights of the theater.

1. Actor **magnā vōce / magnam vōcem** ūtitur.
2. Licinia **ventre / ventrem** amplectitur.
3. Iuppiter **Alcmēnā / Alcmēnam** intuitur.
4. Ego **officiō meō / officium meum** fungor.
5. Rēx deōrum **habitū / habitum** Amphitruōnis potitur.
6. Amphitruō **uxōre / uxōrem** admīrātur.
7. Iuppiter **dēliciīs / dēlicia** Amphitruōnis vērī fruitur.
8. Mox **fābulā / fābulam** fruentur.
9. Amphitruō vērus **portū / portum** aggreditur.
10. **Sīmiā / Sīmiam** sequuntur.
11. Familia Servīliī **multīs servīs / multōs servōs** potītur.

The 4ᵗʰ and 5ᵗʰ Declensions

Did you have any trouble translating the 4ᵗʰ and 5ᵗʰ declension nouns marked in **bold** in *Lectiō Secunda*? Here are the declension patterns.

The 4ᵗʰ Declension

	MASCULINE/FEMININE		**NEUTER**	
	Singular			
Nominative	man**us** (f.)	**-us**	gen**ū** (n.)	**-ū**
Genitive	man**ūs**	**-ūs**	gen**ūs**	**-ūs**
Dative	man**uī**	**-uī**	gen**ū**	**-ū**
Accusative	man**um**	**-um**	gen**ū**	**-ū**
Ablative	man**ū**	**-ū**	gen**ū**	**-ū**
Vocative	man**us**	**-us**	gen**ū**	**-ū**
	Plural			
Nominative	man**ūs**	**-ūs**	gen**ua**	**-ua**
Genitive	man**uum**	**-uum**	gen**uum**	**-uum**
Dative	man**ibus**	**-ibus**	gen**ibus**	**-ibus**
Accusative	man**ūs**	**-ūs**	gen**ua**	**-ua**
Ablative	man**ibus**	**-ibus**	gen**ibus**	**-ibus**
Vocative	man**ūs**	**-ūs**	gen**ua**	**-ua**

The 5ᵗʰ Declension

MASCULINE/FEMININE			
Singular			
Nominative	rēs f. thing	diēs m. day	-ēs
Genitive	reī	diēī	-ēī
Dative	reī	diēī	-ēī
Accusative	rem	diem	-em
Ablative	rē	diē	-ē
Vocative	rēs	diēs	-ēs
Plural			
Nominative	rēs	diēs	-ēs
Genitive	rērum	diērum	-ērum
Dative	rēbus	diēbus	-ēbus
Accusative	rēs	diēs	-ēs
Ablative	rēbus	diēbus	-ēbus
Vocative	rēs	diēs	-ēs

Nōtā Bene:

- The 4ᵗʰ declension has the vowel "*u*" in all cases except the dative and ablative plurals, which are usually *-ibus* (but *-ubus* is also used).
- 4ᵗʰ declension neuters are notable for the dative singular (no *-i*). Other than that, they have normal 4ᵗʰ declension endings and follow the "neuter rule."
- The 5ᵗʰ declension is marked by the vowel *e* throughout. You can see that most of the endings are fairly familiar.
- Note that there is no macron over the *e* in the genitive and dative singular of *rēs*.
- There are no adjectives that use 4ᵗʰ or 5ᵗʰ declension endings.

EXERCEĀMUS!

24-5 4ᵗʰ and 5ᵗʰ Declension Nouns

Use the declension charts to identify the declension, case, and number of each of the following nouns. The number in parentheses indicates how many forms are possible (not including vocatives). Follow the model.

Noun	Declension	Case	Number
→ domū (1)	4ᵗʰ	ablative	singular

1. manum (1)
2. rē (1)
3. gradus (1)
4. gradūs (3)
5. faciēī (2)
6. sonituum (1)
7. diēbus (2)
8. speciēs (3)
9. sonituī (1)
10. rem (1)

Gemma

Dē Diē et Hodiē: You can remember that the Latin word *diēs* is masculine by thinking of the word *hodiē*, a contraction for *hōc diē*, "on this day." You can see from *hōc* that *diēs* is masculine. The Spanish *Buenos días*, a plural meaning "Good day," still retains the masculine gender (buenos, not buenas).

EXERCEĀMUS!

24-6 Five-Declension Review

Compare the endings of the five declensions by filling in the empty boxes on following chart. As you do this, try to spot the patterns that seem to hold true across the declensions.

DECLENSION	1ST	2ND	3RD	4TH	5TH
Singular					
Nominative	fēmina	amīcus	frāter	gradus	speciēs
Genitive					
Dative					
Accusative			frātrem		
Ablative	fēminā				
Plural					
Nominative					
Genitive				graduum	
Dative					
Accusative		amīcōs			
Ablative					speciēbus

Nōtā Bene:

- All masculine and feminine accusative singulars end in -*m*.
- In most declensions, the ablative singular is a long vowel, except in 3rd declension non–i-stems (e.g., *homine*).
- The genitive plural always ends in some form of -*um*.
- All masculine and feminine accusative plurals end in a long vowel followed by -*s*.
- Within a declension, the dative and ablative plurals are always the same.

Gender in the Declensions

Notice from the chart below that some genders predominate in a given declension.

DECLENSION	MOSTLY	BUT!	NEUTER?
1st	feminine	PAINS words are masculine	never
2nd	masculine	Trees are feminine	yes
3rd*	all 3 genders		yes
4th	mostly masculine	*domus* (fem.) *manus* (sometimes fem.)	yes
5th	feminine	*diēs* (masc.)	never

If you don't remember the PAINS words of the 1st declension or the feminine words for trees, review the *Angulus Grammaticus* in Chapter 12.

Amīcī Falsī

You have now learned all five declensions. In the beginning you may have wondered why it was so important to learn both the nominative and genitive forms of each word in addition to the meaning. Now you know! Without this crucial information, you cannot know what case and number a word is in, as different endings in different declensions can look exactly the same.

These look-alike endings are called *amīcī falsī* or "false friends." The **only** way you will be able to tell the case and number of a word (and thus its function in the sentence) is by knowing its declension. So, if you were to see the unfamiliar word like *obsidum*, its ending might suggest that it was:

- an accusative singular from either *obsidus, -ī* (2nd) or *obsidus, -ūs* (4th).

or

- the genitive plural of *obsidēs, -is* (3rd).

But the dictionary entry reads *obsēs, obsidis* m. hostage, and your choice is clear once you know both the declension and the stem.

Similarly, the ending of *frātrī* could be

- genitive singular or nominative plural of a word such as *fratrus, fratrī*

or

- dative singular from *frāter, frātris*.

The dictionary entry confirms that the form is dative singular.

Or consider the particularly tricky ending *-a*. Unless you know, for example, that *ancilla* is from *ancilla, ancillae* (1st f.) and *verba* is from *verbum, -ī,* (2nd n.), you will not be able to tell which is feminine singular nominative and which is neuter plural nominative/accusative.

Remember: "When it doubt, look it up!"

Mōrēs Rōmānī

Theātra Rōmāna

Theaters were found in most Roman cities throughout the empire. Whereas the Greeks used their theaters primarily for dramatic performances, the Romans did not hesitate to mix various forms of entertainment in the same place. Comedies, tragedies, mimes, musical performances, and even the occasional acrobatic or gladiatorial contest were put on in Roman theaters. In addition to the comedies of Plautus (Ti. Maccius Plautus, c. 254–185 B.C.), the Romans liked to watch the comedies of Terence (P. Terentius Afer, c.185–159 B.C.), as well as tragedies like those of M. Pacuvius (c. 220–130 B.C.) and L. Accius (170–c. 86 B.C.). Many such works were written, but today we have only 20 comedies of Plautus (including *Amphitruo*) and six of Terence. The plots of most of these comedies are set in Greece and deal with situations from earlier Greek comedies—sons getting the better of their fathers and smart slaves deceiving their masters. Plautus' *Amphitruo* is unusual with its mythological plot.

Until the Theater of Pompey was built, c. 55 B.C., Rome had no permanent theater buildings made of stone, and these entertainments were held in temporary structures or in open spaces like the Forum.

The Theater of Marcellus, in which the two families see the performance of Plautus' *Amphitruo,* was dedicated by Augustus in 12 B.C. This building is the best preserved theater from ancient Rome, even though it was heavily changed in the medieval period and its upper levels have been replaced by modern apartments. Inside there was seating in three tiers for approximately 10,000–14,000 people. The stage (*scaena*) probably included a curtain *vēlum*, which was dropped into a slot on the stage to start the show and not raised as it is today. Many Roman theaters were roofed over, but probably not the Theater of Marcellus, which may have had awnings (*vēla*) that could be drawn across the top to protect the audience from sun and rain, as in the Flavian Amphitheatre (the Colosseum).

Theātrum Marcellī Hodiē

©National Gallery, London/Art Resource, NY

Vergilius dē Marcellō Legit ā Angelica Kauffman (1741–1807)

The Theater of Marcellus was named after Augustus' nephew, Marcus Claudius Marcellus (42–23 B.C.). Since Augustus never had a son of his own, it was natural that he would look to the son of his sister Octavia as a possible successor. Marcellus was married to Augustus' daughter Julia in 25 B.C. His untimely death at the age of 20 was apparently quite a shock and disappointment to the emperor.

Now look at two passages in which Augustan authors mention Marcellus. We have simplified these poetic passages, mostly by changing the word order. But we have left some of the poetic phrasing, with some explanation.

Vergil describes Marcellus in *Aeneid* VI when the hero Aeneas journeys to the Underworld to see the ghost of his dead father Anchises. Anchises points out to his son all the great Romans of the future waiting to be born. Among them is Marcellus' ancestor and namesake, Marcus Claudius Marcellus (c. 268 B.C.–208 B.C.), a great general during the First Punic War. Use the *Verba Ūtenda* and note that all the words marked in **bold** refer to Marcellus. Can you find the deponent verb in these lines?

> Aspice ut **Marcellus insignis** spoliīs opīmīs ingreditur, et **victor** omnēs virōs superēminet!
>
> *Aeneid* VI.855–856

Gemma

Spolia Opīma was the plunder taken by a Roman general from an enemy general whom he has killed in hand-to-hand combat.

Notice how Vergil uses an imperative (*aspice*) to draw Aeneas' and your attention to Marcellus. The general is coming forward "conspicuous with his plunder" (*īnsignis spoliīs opīmīs*) and stands out (*superēminet*) as a victor over all men.

Vergil then writes the following lines about Augustus' nephew Marcellus, the general's descendent. Remember that the young man was dead when Vergil wrote the lines, but in the dramatic scene he is writing Marcellus is yet to be born. Be sure to use the notes and vocabulary that follow. Can you find one 4th declension and two 5th declension nouns in these lines?

> Nec puer quisquam dē gente Īliacā avōs Latīnōs in tantum spē tollet, nec Rōmula tellūs quondam ūllō alumnō sē tantum iactābit. Heu pietās, heu fidēs prisca, et heu dextera manus invicta bellō! … Heu, miserande puer, sī quā viā fāta aspera rumpās, tū Marcellus eris.
>
> *Aeneid* VI.875–879; 882–883

🔊 VERBA ŪTENDA

alumnus, -ī m. foster son
aspiciō, aspicere, aspexī look
avus, -ī m. ancestor
dextera manus right hand. (Marcellus' right hand was never conquered in war (*inuicta bellō*) because the boy had served in the army in Spain under Augustus in 25 B.C.
gens, gentis f. family, tribe
heu alas
iactō (1) boast

Īliacus, -a, -um Trojan (Augustus claimed Trojan descent through Aeneas.)
ingredior, ingredī, ingressus enter, go in
insignis, -e notable, famous
inuictus, -a, -um unconquered
miserandus, -a, -um pitiable
opīmus, -a, -um rich, plentiful

pietās, pietātis f. reverence, respect
priscus, -a, -um ancient
quā viā by any way
Rōmula tellūs = Rōma
Romulus, -a, -um of Romulus (the founder of Rome)
rumpō, rumpere, rūpī burst, break down
spēs, speī, f. hope, expectation
spolium, -iī n. spoil of war

steterat "had stood still" (If his years "stand still," what does that mean?)
superēmineō, superēminēre stand out over
tantum so much, to such a degree
tellūs, tellūris f. earth, land *ut* how
victor, victōris m. conqueror

By tradition, when Vergil recited these lines to Augustus and his family, Marcellus' mother Octavia fainted. This scene has been a popular theme for artists, including Angelica Kauffman (1741–1807), whose painting in the Hermitage Museum in St. Petersburg, Russia, is depicted at the top of this page. The phrase *Tū Marcellus eris* is written on the scroll Vergil is holding in this painting.

Latīna Hodierna

Rēs and *Diēs* in Modern Usage

Rēs and *diēs* are the two most common words of the 5ᵗʰ declension, and each has had quite an impact on our culture. In Latin *rēs* means basically "thing." The Latin term *rēs pūblica* literally means "the public thing, the public affair." The Romans used it to refer to their government, i.e., the "republic." *Rēs gestae* ("things done" or "deeds") refers especially to Augustus' auto-biography, *Rēs Gestae Dīvī Augustī* ("The Deeds of the Divine Augustus").

Rēs is especially common in modern legal parlance, where it has come to mean many different things. Consider these common legal terms:

res iudicāta	"A matter already adjudicated."
res ipsa loquitur	"The matter speaks for itself." Used in cases where the issue seems open and shut and is so obvious that little argument is needed.
res nova	"A new thing." Something not decided before.
res nullīus	"A thing of no one." "Nobody's thing." Referring to property that has no obvious owner.

Diēs appears in the expression *Carpe diem* ("Seize the day")—the motto of Epicurean philoso-phers—and in *Diēs Irae* ("Day of Wrath"), the title of a medieval Christian poem/song about the day of judgment. The modern uses of *diēs* include the following legal, financial, and med-ical terms (as well as a few others):

ad alium diem	"to another day," referring to the deferment of a meeting to another day
ad certum diem	"to a certain day," referring to the fixing of a meeting for a set day
ad diem	"to the day," referring to the day appointed
ante diem	"before the day," referring to the termination of a contract before the day fixed in the contract
per diem	"by day," referring especially to a daily spending allowance
post diem	"after the day," referring to after the due date
sine die	"without a day," referring to adjournment of a meeting without setting a day to reconvene. You will hear politicians pronouncing it "Sign day."
alternis diebus	"on alternate days," referring to taking a drug every other day
bis in die	"two times in a day," referring to taking a drug twice a day

Orbis Terrārum Rōmānus

Geōgraphia Ītaliāna

Did you notice Aelius' reference to the Alps and Apennine mountains in *Lectiō Prīma*? The geography of the Italian peninsula had a great impact on Rome's history, and average Romans like Aelius were well aware of basic features of their homeland. Here are some important facts about Italian geography:

- Since Italy is a peninsula (*paeninsula, -ae* f. i.e., "almost an island"), the sea (*mare, maris* n.) is never far away. Sea travel, albeit dangerous, was a fact of Roman life. The sea provided essential food for the Italian diet.

- Eventually the Romans came to call the Mediterranean Sea *Mare Nostrum* because their empire surrounded it, but the Romans also had separate names for the waters surrounding Italy. The two most important of these are: *(H)adriaticum Mare*, the Adriatic Sea, to the east of Italy, and, to the south, the *Ionium Mare*, the Ionic Sea sep-arating Italy from Greece. To the west was the *Mare Tyrrhēnicum* (Tyrrhenian Sea).

- The Apennine mountain range (*Apennīnī, -ōrum* m. pl.) runs along the entire spine of Italy and divides the peninsula in half. Travel across these mountains from east to west was extremely difficult. This mountain range is a major reason why it took the

Ītalia ē Caelō

Romans so long to consolidate their control over the peninsula. The Alps (*Alpēs, Alpium* f. pl.) provide a natural barrier to the north between Italy and the rest of Europe. Hannibal's daring march across the Alps during the Second Punic War therefore took Rome by surprise.

- The Po river (*Padus, -ī* m.), flowing through the northern part of the peninsula, created a very fertile agricultural region in the area the Romans called Cisalpine Gaul.
- Rome is located on the Tiber River (*Tiberis, Tiberis* m.) at the first ford, about seven miles from the sea. The salt beds at the mouth of the Tiber were probably an important resource in the growth of the city.
- Sardinia (*Sardinia*) and Sicily (*Sicilia*), the two large islands that are part of modern Italy, were not politically part of Italy at the time of Augustus. They were provinicial areas.

QUID PUTĀS?

1. Compare the untimely death of Marcellus to that of a modern American who might have been thought of as "next in line" to succeed to some important post.
2. How does a Roman theater like the Theater of Marcellus compare in size and design to a modern American theater? What do you think it would have been like to attend a performance in such a theater?
3. Why do you think modern lawyers continue to employ Latin terms?
4. Is any part of the United States somewhat like Italy in its geography?

EXERCEĀMUS!

24-7 Scrībāmus

Use the information in the *Orbis Terrārum Rōmānus* to complete the following short essay about the geography of Italy.

Rōma in Ītaliā est. Ītalia paeninsula est. Ad septentriōnēs (*north*) sunt montēs (1) _____. Ab oriente (*east*) est Mare (2) _____. Ad merīdiem (*south*) est Mare (3) _____. Ad occidentem (*west*) est Mare (4) _____. Per Italiam currunt montēs (5) _____. Per Rōmam fluit flūmen (*river*) (6) _____. Ad septentriōnēs fluit flūmen magnum (7) _____. Duo insulae magnae sunt (8) _____ et (9) _____.

24-8 Colloquāmur

The following skit has four speaking parts. You know most of the dialogue, so put your efforts into making the lines sound "real" and in adding the gestures that should go with the feelings the characters are experiencing.

Narrātor: Paulō post Mercurius abit sed Alcmēna et Iuppiter-Amphitruō haec dīcunt.
Iuppiter: Bene valē, Alcmēna. Mihi necesse est abhinc īre.
Alcmēna: Nōn mihi placet. Quandō revertēris?
Iuppiter: Fidem habē, cāra uxor. Mox revertar! Hoc tibi polliceor!
Narrātor: Et, paulō post, quid vident spectātōrēs? Illum Amphitruōnem vērum. Ā portū domum suum aggreditur. Alcmēna eum spectat et manūs ad faciem tollēns laetē exclāmat:
Alcmēna: Revēnistī ad mē! Tam laeta sum! Sed nuper ē lectō meō abiistī!
Narrātor: Tunc Amphitruō uxōris manum capiēns dīcit:
Amphitruō: Quid dīcis? Ē lectō? Haec rēs mala mihi est! Ego mensēs multōs iam absum. Quid agitur?

24-9 Verba Discenda

The words marked in **bold** in this short narrative are derived from *Verba Discenda* for this chapter. Identify these Latin words.

The **spectators** (1) only thought **it was decent** (2) to pay attention to the **sequel** (3). They were all in a rather **jovial** (4) mood as they watched the **gradual** (5) **progress** (6) of the talented lead actor, a rather **eloquent** (7) but **loquacious** (8) fellow, onto the stage. At a **uniform** (9) pace he **ascended** (10) the stage, took the instruction **manual** (11) from the table, turned to face the audience, and fell flat on his **face** (12).

🔊 VERBA DISCENDA

ascendō, ascendere, ascendī, ascensum climb, ascend [ascendant]

cōnor, cōnārī, cōnātus sum try

decet, decēre, decuit (+ dat. + inf.) imp. it is fitting

diēs, diēī m. day [per diem]

dīves, dīvitis rich, talented

domus, -ūs f. house [domicile]

ēloquor, ēloquī, ēlocūtus sum speak out, declare [eloquent]

faciēs, faciēī f. face, appearance, beauty [facial]

forma, -ae f. shape, form; beauty; ground plan [formation]

fruor, fruī, fructus/fruitus sum (+ abl.) enjoy, profit by

fungor, fungī, functus sum (+ abl.) perform, discharge [function]

gradus, -ūs m. step, pace, tier (of a theater) [gradation]

ingredior, ingredī, ingressus sum enter [ingress]

Iuppiter, Iovis m. Jupiter, king of the gods [jovial]

loquor, loquī, locūtus sum speak, talk, say [loquacious]

manus, -ūs f. hand [manumission]

mentior, mentīrī, mentītus sum lie, deceive

patior, patī, passus sum suffer, allow [patience, passion]

polliceor, pollicērī, pollicitus sum promise

potior, potīrī, potītus sum (+ abl. or gen.) take possession of, get, acquire

prōgredior, prōgredī, prōgressus sum go to, advance, march forward, proceed [progressive]

rēs, reī f. thing, matter, business, affair; reason

sequor, sequī, secūtus sum follow [sequence, consecutive]

simul together, altogether, at the same time, all at once [simultaneous]

sonitus, -ūs m. sound

speciēs, speciēī f. appearance, look, type [species]

spectātor, spectātōris m. spectator, observer

ūtor, ūtī, ūsus sum (+ abl.) use, employ, enjoy, experience

vereor, verērī, veritus sum be afraid of, fear, show reverence to

Angulus Grammaticus

Oh No, Not Semi-Deponents, Too!

Although deponent verbs are very common in Latin, the concept of a deponent verb is almost unique to the Latin language. Greek, both ancient and modern, is one of the few other languages with deponents. Knowing a little bit about Greek will make you feel a little better about Latin deponents, because Greek deponent verbs are even more complicated than Latin ones. Greek has not one kind of deponent, but two. In addition to passive verbs translated actively (like Latin), Greek also has another voice, called middle (in which the subject performs the action on or for himself or herself). Some of these middle verbs are translated actively. A good example is the Greek verb ἔρχομαι (*erchomai*, I come or I go), which is middle/passive in form but active in meaning.

Now that you recognize the special nature of deponent verbs, you can become a real grammar dilettante and learn about **semi-deponents**. Semi-deponents are a blend of active and deponent forms in the same verb. You will see this clearly in their principal parts. Here are four semi-deponent Latin verbs with the deponent forms marked in **bold**:

> *audeō, audēre,* **ausus sum** dare
> *fīdō, fīdere,* **fīsus sum** (+ dat.) trust in
> *gaudeō, gaudēre,* **gavīsus sum** rejoice
> *soleō, solēre,* **solitus sum** (+ inf.) be in the habit of, be accustomed to

So *audeō* means "I dare" whereas *ausus sum* means "I dared."

What is important is that you can learn to recognize and translate forms like *fīsus est* "he trusted in." Let the principal parts be your guide. The first two are obviously active. When the 3rd principal part is passive instead of active, you know it is deponent.

And you will soon learn about *fīō*, which is active in form but passive in meaning in the present, future, and imperfect. Just the opposite of a deponent verb!

Photo Credits

Page 301 (top) Photos.com; **page 301 (bottom)** Victor M. Martinez; **page 302** © CM Dixon/ Heritage—Images/ImageState Media Partners Limited; **page 306 (top)** Clipart.com; **page 306 (bottom)** Photos.com; **page 311** Victor M. Martinez; **page 312** © National Gallery, London/Art Resource, NY; **page 314** Provided by the SeaWiFS Project, NASA/Goddard Space Flight Center and Orbimage.

Parātūs Magnī

From *Disce! An Introductory Latin Course, volume 2*, First Edition. Francesco Bonavita. Copyright © 2011 by Pearson Education, Inc. Published by Pearson Prentice Hall. All rights reserved.

Sepulcrum Obstetrīcis Rōmānae

GRAMMATICA
The Imperfect Tense of Deponent Verbs
The Infinitives, Imperatives, and Present
  Participles of Deponent Verbs

MŌRĒS RŌMĀNĪ
Birthing in the Roman World

LATĪNA HODIERNA
Latin in the Maternity Ward

ORBIS TERRĀRUM RŌMĀNUS
Alexandrīa

ANGULUS GRAMMATICUS
Bending Language: Linguistic Limitations
  and Linguistic Flexibility

LECTIŌNĒS:
MĒDĒA OBSTETRIX
and
SERVĪLIĪ CONSILIA
Licinia's family seeks a midwife to assist
in the birth of her child, while Servilius
and his family prepare for a big dinner
with an impressive guest list.

25

Parātūs Magnī

Lectiō Prīma

Antequam Legis

In this chapter you meet Medea, the midwife who will help Licinia give birth. Most neighborhoods had such midwives, many of whom were former slaves. Medea's name is ironic, since Medea, a witch from Colchis, was famous in mythology for killing her children to get even with her husband, Jason, who had left her for a young princess. Our Medea is from Thrace, another land famous for witchcraft, and her former owners undoubtedly found the name amusing.

This reading also introduces the imperfect passive of regular and deponent verbs.

Imperfect Passives and Deponents

If you remember the telltale *-ba-* as the mark of the imperfect, you will have no trouble recognizing and translating the imperfect passive of regular and deponent verbs. Here are the first imperfect passives you will find in the reading:

nītē**bā**tur	she was straining
adiuvā**bā**tur	she was being helped

Can you tell from the translations which one of these verbs is deponent?

EXERCEĀMUS!

25-1 **Deponents in the Imperfect Tense**

As you read *Lectiō Prīma*, answer the following Latin questions in complete English sentences. Each question asks you to find the subject of a deponent verb in the imperfect tense. All these deponents are marked in **bold** in the reading. Follow the model.

→ Quis nītēbātur? (line 1)   Licinia was struggling.

1. Quī prōgrediēbantur? (line 2)
2. Quis prōgrediēbātur? (line 11)
3. Quis cōnābātur iuvāre? (lines 11)
4. Quī moriēbantur? (line 12)
5. Quis saccum intuēbātur? (line 18)
6. Quis instrūmentīs ūtēbātur? (line 19)
7. Quis lentē profiscēbātur? (line 18)
8. Quis Mēdēam sequēbātur? (line 18)
9. Quis precēs fervidās loquēbātur? (lines 18–19)

MĒDĒA OBSTETRIX

Licinia, quae iam in dolōre magnō erat et **nītēbātur,** adiuvābātur ē theātrō ā mātre virōque. Per viās Rōmae lentē **prōgrediēbantur** et mox insulae suae appropinquābant.

Valeria "Māter!" clāmāvit, "Nōs adiuvā. Mox Licinia pariet! Flāvia, de-
5 scende et aquam nōbīs fer. Aelī, ī celeriter et Mēdēam mihi arcesse! Eam fer ad auxilium nostrum."

Mēdēa obstetrix, quae Rōmam ā Thrāciā vēnerat, multōs annōs in Subūrā habitābat et multae fēminae gravidae Rōmānae multōs per annōs ab eā adiuvābantur. In Rōmā antiquā, praesertim fēminīs pauperibus, parere
10 perīculōsum erat. Saepe obstetrix per viās Rōmanās mediā nocte ad domicil-ia fēminārum gravidārum **prōgrediēbatur** et fortiter eās iuvāre **cōnābātur.** Sed gravida Rōmāna semper in perīculō erat et multae **moriēbantur.**

Aelius iānuās fortiter pulsāvit

Aelius cucurrit per viās et, cōnāns obstetrīcem invenīre, iānuam Mēdēae fortiter pulsāvit. "Mēdēa! Mēdēa! Cūr ad iānuam nōn aggrederis? Diēs partūs adest! Nisi mēcum vēneris, uxor mea multa patiētur."
15 Mēdēa "Salvē, Aelī!" inquit. "Perturbātus vidēris. Nōlī timēre. Omnia salva erunt. Nōlī cunctārī! Tē sequar et mox uxor tua infantem sānum et salvum pariet. Postquam infantem in brachiīs tenueris, laetior eris."

Mēdēa saccum parvum cēpit et Aeliō id dedit.

Aelius saccum **intuēbātur** et "Quid" rogāvit, "inest?"

"In saccō omnia—herbās, instrūmenta—quibus prō sānitāte uxōris tuae et infantis futurī ūtar, habeō. Mihi
20 crēde, mī Aelī, illīs in Thrāciā **ūtēbar** et nunc cotidiē eīsdem ūtor. Multae fēminae in Thrāciā iam ā Mēdēā **adiuvābantur** et hodiē ūna alia adiuvābitur."

Mēdēa "Mēne," inquit, "nunc quiētē sequēris? Festīnā! Et mox omnēs mīrāculum parvum mirābimur!"

Mēdēa, quae septuāgintā duo annōs nāta erat, lentē **proficiscēbātur.** Aelius eam **sequēbātur** et intrā sē precēs fervidās **loquēbātur.**

VERBA ŪTENDA

arcessō, arcessere, arcessīvī/ arcessī summon
auxilium, -iī n. help, aid; pl. auxiliary forces
crēdō, crēdere, crēdidī, crēditum (+ dat.) believe, trust
cunctor, cunctārī, cunctātus est tarry, linger, hesitate
descendō, descendere, descendī go down, descend
domicilium, -iī n. home
fervidus, -a, -um fervent
gravidus, -a, -um pregnant

iānua, -ae f. door
insum, inesse, infuī be in
instrūmentum, -ī n. tool, instrument
intrā (+ acc.) within
intueor, intuērī, intuitus sum look at, gaze at; consider
iuvō, iuvāre, iūvi, iūtum help
Mēdēa, -ae f. Medea, the midwife
mīrāculum, -ī n. miracle
mīror, mīrārī, mīrātus sum wonder at, admire
morior, morī die

nisi unless
nītor, nītī exert oneself, struggle, strain
obstetrix, obstetrīcis f. midwife
herba, -ae f. herb
pariō, parere, peperī, paritum/partum bring forth, give birth, bear, create
partus, -ūs m. childbirth
pauper, pauperis poor
perīculōsus, -a, -um dangerous
perturbātus very frightened
praesertim especially, particularly

prex, precis f. prayer
proficiscor, proficiscī depart
quiētus, -a, -um calm, quiet
salvus, -a, -um safe, well
sānitās, sānitātis f. health
sānus, -a, -um healthy
septuāgintā seventy
Subūra, -ae f. Subura, a district in Rome
Thrācia, -ae f. Thrace, a Roman province located in what is now part of Greece, Bulgaria, and Turkey

POSTQUAM LĒGISTĪ

Read back through *Lectiō Prīma* and identify the speaker of each of these statements.

1. "Māter! Nōs adiuvā. Mox Licinia pariet!"
2. "Mēdēa! Mēdēa! Cūr ad iānuam nōn aggrederis? Diēs partūs adest! Nisi mēcum vēneris, uxor mea multa patiētur."
3. "Postquam infantem tuum in brachiīs tenueris, laetior vidēberis."
4. "Quid in saccō tuō inest?"
5. "Illīs in Thrāciā ūtēbar et nunc cotidiē eīsdem ūtor."
6. "Mēnē nunc quiētē sequeris?"

Grammatica A

The Imperfect Tense of Deponent Verbs

The imperfect tense of deponents is formed exactly like regular imperfect passives, but remember to translate deponents like active verbs.

	PASSIVE		DEPONENT	
	Singular			
1st	adiuvābar	I was being helped	loquēbar	I was saying
2nd	adiuvābāris	you were being helped	loquēbāris	you were saying
3rd	adiuvābātur	he/she/it was being helped	loquēbātur	he/she/it was saying
	Plural			
1st	adiuvābāmur	we were being helped	loquēbāmur	we were saying
2nd	adiuvābāminī	you were being helped	loquēbāminī	you were saying
3rd	adiuvābantur	they were being helped	loquēbantur	they were saying

EXERCEĀMUS!

25-2 **Deponent or Passive?**

Translate each verb form marked in **bold** in a way that shows you know whether the verb is a deponent or a true passive. Follow the model.

→ Aelius et Valeria ad īnsulam suam **aggrēdiēbantur.**   (they) were approaching

1. Mēdēa ab Aeliō **adiuvābātur.**
2. Herbae et instrumenta Mēdēae in saccum **ponēbantur.**
3. Aelius Mēdēam per viās **sequēbātur.**
4. Fēminae Rōmānae in domibus suīs semper **pariēbantur.**
5. In Thrāciā semper **proficīscēbar** ad fēminās.
6. Mēdēa numquam adiuvāre **cunctābātur.**
7. Valeria in lectō **inveniēbātur.**

Lectiō Secunda

Antequam Legis

In *Lectiō Secunda* Servilius lays out his plans to win over Augustus' support when he runs for the office of praetor (*praetor, praetōris* m.). During the Roman Republic, the praetorship was second only to the consulship in importance. Praetors served as judges and administrators in Rome, in the military and in the provinces. Servilius is running for *praetor urbānus*, which would position him, in the traditional *cursūs honōrum*, or order of offices, to run for consul eventually. A praetor had *imperium*, or power, wore a special toga called the *toga praetexta*, sat in a special chair of honor (*sella curūlis*) in the basilica or law court, and was attended by six lictors in the administration of his office. In the coin depicted at right you can see the praetor M. Iunius Brutus, one of the leaders of the assassination of Julius Caesar, walking among lictors.

Magistrātus Rōmānus Lictōrēsque

To advance his political ambitions, Servilius plans to present a copy of a rare book to Maecenas, Augustus' "Minister of Culture." The book is the *Aetia* (*Causes*) written by Callimachus (c. 280–243 B.C.), a poet who also served as head of the Library at Alexandria in Egypt. Callimachus was very popular with the poets of the Augustan age, and the gift, Servilius hopes, will help win over the support of Augustus and Maecenas for Servilius' campaign to become praetor.

As you read, look at the way the infinitives, imperatives, and present participles of deponent verbs are formed.

The Infinitives, Imperatives, and Present Participles of Deponent Verbs

As you would expect, deponent infinitives are simply the present passive infinitive translated actively; for example, *cōnārī* (to try); *pollicērī* (to promise); *sequī* (to follow); *patī* (to allow); and *mentīrī* (to lie).

Deponent imperatives end in *-re* in the singular and *-minī* in the plural; for example, *Cōnāre!/Cōnāminī!* (Try!); *Pollicēre!/Pollicēminī!* (Promise!); *Sequere!/Sequiminī!* (Follow!); *Patere!/Patiminī!* (Allow! Let!); and *Mentīre!/Mentīminī!* (Lie!).

To form present participles, deponent verbs use the active endings you already know: *cōnāns* (trying); *pollicēns* (promising); *sequēns* (following); *patiēns* (suffering); and *mentiēns* (lying). This participle is an exception to the rule that deponent verbs use passive endings. Just translate the participle as you usually would, with **-ing**. So, in *Lectiō Prīma* you probably had no trouble translating the phrase ***cōnāns obstrīcem invenīre*** as "**trying** to find the midwife."

All deponent infinitives, imperatives, and present participles are marked in **bold** in *Lectiō Secunda*.

EXERCEĀMUS!

25-3 **Imperatives, Infinitives, and Present Active Participles of Deponent Verbs**

You will find a number of imperatives, infinitives, and present active participles of deponent verbs marked in **bold** in *Lectiō Secunda*. Before you read, make three columns on a sheet of paper. Then sort the forms into imperatives, infinitives, and participles. Follow the model.

Line	Imperatives	Infinitives	Participles
→ 2			colloquentēs

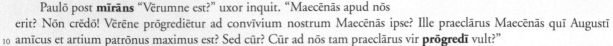

SERVĪLIĪ CONSILIA

In aliā parte urbis Servīlius et Caecilia Metella sedentēs in peristȳliō
domī et dē Servīliā **colloquentēs** inveniuntur. Perturbātī sunt quod fīlia
cāra sua tam infēlix est, sed quoque laetī sunt. Servīlius cum Caeciliā dē
epistulā, quae nūper ā Maecēnāte advēnit, colloquitur.

5   "Cāra," inquit, "**intuēre** hanc epistulam Maecēnātis!"
Caecilia, epistulam in manibus tollēns et magnā cum cārā signum
Maecēnātis **intuēns**, eam legit.

Servīlius et Caecilia sedentēs in peristȳliō

Paulō post **mīrāns** "Vērumne est?" uxor inquit. "Maecēnās apud nōs
erit? Nōn crēdō! Vērēne prōgrediētur ad convīvium nostrum Maecēnās ipse? Ille praeclārus Maecēnās quī Augustī
10 amīcus et artium patrōnus maximus est? Sed cūr? Cūr ad nōs tam praeclārus vir **prōgredī** vult?"
Servīlius "Nōlī **oblīviscī**," inquit, "cāra uxor, meī dōnī! Annō superiōre, cum ad Aegyptum iter faciēbam, librum quī in bibliothēcā Alexandrīnā fuerat, ēmī. Papȳrus magnī pretiī erat, et mox hic liber mē praetōrem faciet."
Caecilia: "Quōmodo rēs simplex tibi tam magnum auxilium feret?"
Servīlius: "Sed, mea uxor, **recordāre!** Hic liber nullō modō simplex, sed rarissimus est. Liber *Aetia* Callimachī
15 ōlim in Bibliothēcā Alexandrīnā erat sed nōn ab igne consumēbātur. Hoc librum invēnī et hoc est donum quod
Imperātōrī Augustō dare volō. *Aetia* Maecēnātī apud convīvium nostrum dabō et tunc Augustus mihi auxilium feret
cum praetōrem petam."
Caecilia quiēta est, multa dē convīviō futūrō **contemplāns**. "Mihi," intrā sē cōgitat, "cum servīs et coquō
colloquī necesse est. Omnēs hospitēs apud nōs **epulantēs** cibīs vinīsque praesertim optimīs fruuntur. Illīs apud mē
20 **epulantibus** cibīs et vinīs optimīs semper **fruī** decet!"
Caecilia ē sellā **oriēns**, ad sē Sicōnem, quī coquus Servīliōrum est, et Pardaliscam, quae "magistra ancillārum"
apud Servīliōs est, convocat. Caecilia "Sicō!" inquit "Pardalisca! Mē **sequiminī** ad culīnam! Nōlīte **cunctārī!**"
Coquus et ancilla, dominam suam per iānuam **sequentēs**, intrā sē cōgitant: "Quid nunc?"

VERBA ŪTENDA

Aegyptus, -ī f. Egypt, a
province of Rome
Aetia, -ōrum "The Causes,"
title of a book by
Callimachus, a famous
Greek poet who lived in
the 3rd century B.C.
Alexandrīnus, -a, -um
Alexandrian, pertaining
to the city in Egypt
annō superiōre "last year"
auxilium, -iī n. help, aid;
pl. auxiliary forces
bibliothēca, -ae f. library
**colloquor, colloquī,
collocūtus sum** talk
together, converse
*consūmō, consūmere,
consūmpsī* consume

convīvium, -iī n. feast,
banquet
convocō (1) call together
coquus, -ī m. cook
*crēdō, crēdere, crēdidī,
creditum* (+ dat.)
believe, trust
culīna, -ae f. kitchen
*cunctor, cunctārī, cunctātus
est* tarry, linger, hesitate
domina, -ae f. mistress (of
the house), the woman
in charge
epulor, epulārī feast
hospes, hospitis m. guest
iānua, -ae f. door
ignis, ignis m. fire
imperātor, -ōris m.
commander, ruler

infēlix, infēlicis unhappy
iter facere to make a journey
intrā (+ acc.) within
*intueor, intuērī, intuitus
sum* look at, gaze at;
consider
mīror, mīrārī, mīrātus sum
wonder at, admire
oblīviscor, oblīviscī (+ gen.)
forget
orior, orīrī rise
nūper recently, not
long ago
papȳrus, -ī f. papyrus
Pardalisca, -ae f. Pardalisca,
woman's name
patrōnus, -ī m. patron
paulō somewhat, by
a little

perditum esse "to be lost"
peristȳlium, -iī n. peristyle,
courtyard, colonnaded
garden
perturbātus, -a, -um
disturbed, confused
praesertim especially,
particularly
praetor, -ōris m. praetor,
judge
quiētus, -a, -um calm, quiet
recordor, recordārī remember
sella, -ae f. chair
Sicō, Sicōnis m. Sico, a man's
name
signum, -ī n. seal
simplex, simplicis simple,
naive
superiōre with *annō* "last"

POSTQUAM LĒGISTĪ

Aut Vērum Aut Falsum. Indicate whether each of the following statements based on *Lectiō Secunda* is true (*vērum*) or false (*falsum*). If you think the sentence is false, rewrite it to make it true. Don't simply add a negative word like *nōn*, but rewrite the sentence positively. Follow the model.

→ In hāc lectione Servīlius et Lūcius dē Lūciō colloquuntur.
  Falsum. In hāc lectione Servīlius et Lūcius dē Servīliā colloquuntur.

1. Epistula nūper ā Maecēnāte ad Servīlium advēnit.
2. Parentēs perturbātī quod fīlia cāra infēlix est.
3. Augustus ipse ad convīvium Servīliī prōgrediētur.
4. Maecēnās Servīliī amīcus et lūdōrum patrōnus maximus est.
5. Annō superiōre Servīlius iter ad Crētam faciēbat.
6. Maecēnās librum quī in Bibliothēcā Alexandrīnā fuerat, ēmit.
7. Hic liber cārus et rarissimus est.
8. Servīlius praetōrem petet.
9. Caecilia cum fīliīs et fīliae colloquī vult.
10. Pardalisca coqua est.
11. Servī Caeciliam ad culīnam sequuntur.

Papȳrus

Grammatica B

The Infinitives, Imperatives, and Present Participles of Deponent Verbs

Here are the infinitives of deponent verbs in *Lectiō Secunda*.

> *Cūr ad nōs tam praeclarus vir **prōgredī** vult?*
> Why does so famous a man want **to come** to our house?

> *Cum servīs et coquīs **colloquī** mihi necesse est.*
> It is necessary for me **to speak** with the slaves and the cooks.

> *Illīs cibīs et vīnīs optimīs **fruī** semper decet.*
> It is fitting for them **to enjoy** the best food and wines.

> *Nōlī **oblīviscī**!*
> Don't forget!

As long as you remember to translate these infinitive forms actively, you should have little difficulty understanding the infinitives of deponent verbs. You will, of course, also remember that the infinitive is the 2nd principle part of a deponent verb: for example *colloquor, **colloquī**, collocūtus sum.*

Three imperatives of deponent verbs appear in *Lectiō Secunda:*

***Recordāre**!*	Remember!
***Intuēre** hanc epistulam!*	Look at this letter!
*Mē **sequiminī**!*	Follow me!

You have not seen these passive imperative endings before because they are fairly rare with non-deponent verbs, but you could, for example, tell quiet speakers to speak up by saying *Audīre!/Audīminī!* (Be heard!). Deponent imperatives, however, are fairly common. The patterns are not difficult. The singular imperative ending is formed like a present active infinitive, by adding *-re* to the present stem in 1st and 2nd conjugations:

> *cōnā-* + *-re* → *Cōnāre!* Try!

and by adding *-re* to the short present stem in the 3rd and 4th conjugations:

> *mentī-* + *-re* → *Mentīre!* Lie!

The plural imperative ending is the same as the indicative. So, depending on context, the form *sequiminī* can mean either "you follow" or "Follow!" Negative imperatives for deponent verbs are formed by using the infinitive with *Nōlī/Nōlīte*: for example, *Nōlī pollicērī/Nōlīte pollicērī!* (Don't promise!).

Here are some of the deponent verbs used as present active participles in *Lectiō Secunda*.

*Servīlius et Caecilia Metella dē Servīliā **colloquentēs**.*
Servilius and Caecilia Metella **are speaking together** about Servilia.

*Caecilia ē sellā **oriēns** . . .*
Caecilia, **rising** from her chair . . .

*. . . multa dē convīviō futūrō **contemplāns** . . .*
. . . **contemplating** many things about the upcoming dinner . . .

*Coquus et ancilla dominam suam **sequentēs** intrā sē cogitant.*
Following their mistress, the cook and maid servant think to themselves.

These participles act exactly like others you have seen before. They become tricky only when you think too hard and say, "Wait a minute. Deponent verbs have passive endings." Since there is no present **passive** participle in Latin, Romans had to use the present **active** participle endings to make present participles for deponent verbs.

Here is a summary of deponent forms introduced in this reading:

	1ST CONJUGATION	2ND CONJUGATION	3RD CONJUGATION	3RD CONJUGATION - *IŌ*	4TH CONJUGATION
	Infinitive				
	cōnārī	pollicērī	sequī	patī	mentīrī
	Imperative				
singular	Cōnāre!	Pollicēre!	Sequere!	Patere!	Mentīre!
plural	Cōnāminī!	Pollicēminī!	Sequiminī!	Patiminī!	Mentīminī!
	Negative Imperative				
singular	Nōlī cōnārī!	Nōlī pollicērī!	Nōlī sequī!	Nōlī patī!	Nōlī mentīrī!
plural	Nōlīte cōnārī!	Nōlīte pollicērī!	Nōlīte sequī!	Nōlīte patī!	Nōlīte mentīrī!
	Present Participle				
	cōnāns	pollicēns	sequēns	patiēns	mentiēns

EXERCEĀMUS!

25-4 Imperatives of Deponent Verbs

Change the following negative imperatives to positive imperatives; i.e., instead of saying not to do something, say "Do it!" Then translate the command into English. Follow the model. HINT: Pay attention to singulars and plurals!

→ Nōlī mīrārī!   *Mīrāre!* Be amazed!

1. Nōlīte patī!
2. Nōlī loquī!
3. Nōlī mentīrī!
4. Nōlīte pollicērī!

5. Nōlīte meī dōnī oblīvīscī!
6. Nōlī hanc epistulam intuērī!
7. Nōlīte mē sequī!
8. Nōlī cunctārī!

25-5 **Present Participles of Deponent Verbs**

Choose the participle that agrees with each noun. Then translate the phrase. Follow the model.
HINT: Do not try to pick the participle until you are sure of the GNC of the noun!

→ vir (mīrantem; mīrantēs; mīrantī; mīrāns)

   vir mīrāns the man wondering or the wondering man

1. māter (loquentis; loquentēs; loquēns; loquentium)
2. Maecenātis (prōgredientis; prōgredientēs; prōgredientem; prōgrediente)
3. uxōrī (pollicente; pollicentibus; pollicentī; pollicēns)
4. servī (prōgredientēs; prōgredientium; prōgrediēns; prōgredientī)
5. Mēdēae (mīrante; mīrantibus; mīrantis; mīrāns)
6. Aeliō (loquēns; loquente; loquentēs; loquentis)
7. virōs (mentiēns; mentiente; mentientēs; mentientem)
8. mīrāculum (prōgrediēns; prōgredientium; prōgredientibus; prōgredientis)
9. ancillīs (pollicentis; pollicentibus; pollicēns; pollicente)
10. magister (loquentis; loquentēs; loquēns; loquentibus)

Mōrēs Rōmānī

Birthing in the Roman World

There were no maternity hospitals in ancient Rome, and childbirth was always difficult and dangerous for both mother and infant. Mortality rates were high, even in the upper classes. Cicero's daughter Tullia, for example, died at the age of 33 of complications related to childbirth.

Upper-class women may have had the services of both an *obstetrix* like Medea and a physician, but most women had to settle for the help of the *obstetrix* (if they could afford her services) as well as family and friends.

Ancient midwives were not schooled. Rather, they learned their craft as apprentices and from experience, taking much of their herbal knowledge from the sort of folk medicine recorded by Pliny the Elder (C. Plinius Secundus, 23 A.D.–August 24, 79 A.D.). Most midwives were probably freedwomen, but wealthy households could own slaves who served as midwives. The only surviving ancient medical treatise on childbirth is *Gynaecology*, written in Greek by the 2nd century A.D. physician Soranus.

Roman women gave birth in chairs like the one illustrated in the tombstone at the beginning of the chapter. The midwife sat or knelt in front of the pregnant woman, who was often attended by one or two other women as well.

We know something about Roman folk beliefs and practices regarding childbirth from the *Historia Nātūrālis* of Pliny the Elder. We do not recommend that you take any of these statements as true, but they do suggest ancient Roman attitudes toward a very important stage in human life. With a little help from the *Verba Ūtenda*, you should be able to read the following three slightly modified statements from Pliny.

> *Vulva [hyaenae] data in pōtū cum malī Pūnicī dulcis cortice mulierum vulvae prōdest.*
> HN 28.27.102

> *Partūs mulierum lacte suis cum mulsō adiuvantur.*
> HN 28.77.250

> *Penna vulturīna, subiecta pedibus, [fēminās] parturientēs adiuvat.*
> HN 30.44.130

In the following statement Pliny suggests that a woman pregnant with a male child (*marem ferentī*) has better color (*melior color*) and an easier labor (*facilior partus*). On what day does Pliny say she will feel a male child move in her womb?

> *melior color et facilior partus [fēminae] marem ferentī est; motus in uterō quadrāgensimō diē.*
> HN 7.6.41

🔊 **VERBA ŪTENDA**

cortex, corticis m./f. skin, bark, rind
ferentī "to a woman bearing"
hyaena, -ae f. hyena
lac, lactis n. milk
malus Pūnica, -i f. pomegranate (lit., "Punic apple")
mās, maris male
mōtus, mōtūs m. movement
mulier, mulieris f. woman
mulsum, -ī n. warm drink of honey and wine
parturiō, parturīre, parturīvī /parturiī be pregnant, be in labor, give birth
partus, partūs m. childbirth
pēs, pedis m. foot
penna, -ae f. feather
pōtus, -ūs m. drink
prōsum, prōdesse, prōfuī (+ dat.) be useful to
quadrāgensimus, -a, -um fortieth
sūs, suis m./f. pig, sow
subiecta "placed under"; refers to *penna*
uterus, -ī m. womb, belly
vulva, -ae f. womb
vulturīnus,-a, -um of a vulture

Instrūmenta Obstetrīcis Rōmānae

Latīna Hodierna

Latin in the Maternity Ward

LATIN WORD	MEANING	ENGLISH DERIVATIVE	MEANING
obstetrix, -trīcis f.	midwife	obstetrics obstetrician	
placenta, -ae f.	flat cake	placenta	mammalian organ which nurtures the fetus in the uterus; the afterbirth
umbilīcus, -ī m.	center, middle: a. the center of the world b. a decorative knob c. the cylinder around which a scroll was wrapped d. belly button	umbilicus	belly button
gravidus, -a, -um	pregnant	gravida nulligravida primigravida multigravida	a pregnant woman All of these words refer to a woman and her history of pregnancies. Can you see the difference among them?
forceps, forcipis f.	tongs, pincers	forceps	an obstetrical tool
fētus, -ūs m. *fētus, -a, -um*	birth, offspring, produce pregnant, fertile	fetus	an unborn child
puerpera, -ae f.	a woman in labor (related to *puer, -ī* m. boy, child)	puerperal puerperal fever	related to childbirth an infection following childbirth, often fatal well into the twentieth century
parturiō, parturīre, parturīvī/parturiī	be pregnant, be in labor, give birth to	parturient parturiency	bearing/about to bear a child
partus, -ūs m.	giving birth; fetus, offspring	postpartum	after birth, as in "post partum depression"
nātālis, nātāle	being born	prenatal	before birth
pariō, parere, peperī, paritum/partum	bring forth, bear	nullipara primipara multipara	a woman who has not borne a child bearing a firstborn bearing many children

Orbis Terrārum Rōmānus

Alexandrīa

The city of Alexandria in Egypt, where Servilius found his manuscript, was a major commercial and cultural center in the Greco-Roman world. Founded by Alexander the Great in 331 B.C., the city possessed one of the best harbors in the ancient Mediterranean. It became the capital of Egypt under the Ptolemies, who ruled Egypt after Alexander's death in 323 B.C. until 31 B.C. Following the Battle of Actium and the death of Cleopatra, Egypt came under the direct control of the Roman emperor. Egypt was so strategically important that Roman senators were forbidden to travel there without imperial permission. Servilius must have obtained such a dispensation, a sign of favor in Augustus' eyes.

The ancient city included a great palace and many temples, but it was best known for its Pharos, or lighthouse (one of the Seven Wonders of the Ancient World), and for the great *Mūsēum* (Museum) or Library of Alexandria, from which the manuscript of *Aetia* was obtained.

Very little of Greco-Roman Alexandria is visible today. The best known feature is the so-called "Pompey's Pillar," depicted at right, which actually has nothing to do with the Roman general who died near Alexandria in 48 B.C. This pillar was actually erected during the reign of the emperor Diocletian (c. 244–311). Also prominent are the remains of the Roman theater depicted on the following page.

The dimensions of the Pharos, built in the 3rd century B.C. under the Ptolemies, are uncertain, but the structure was so tall that its light was said to be visible more than 30 miles from land. The Pharos collapsed in an earthquake in the 14th century. Some remains of the lighthouse were found by underwater archaeologists in 1994.

The Library at Alexandria was the largest in the ancient world. Like the Pharos, it was built in the 3rd century B.C. The early librarians at Alexandria, including the Greek epic poet Apollonius of Rhodes, were great book collectors and brought to the library written works from all over the Mediterranean world.

In *Lectiō Secunda* Servilius refers to a fire at the Library during Julius Caesar's siege, but this fire was probably not responsible for the Library's demise. It is more likely that the institution disappeared gradually due to war and plunder over the course of several centuries.

A new Library of Alexandria, known as the Bibliotheca Alexandrina, opened in Egypt in 2003. A photograph of this new library appears on the next page.

"Columen Pompeii" Alexandrīnae

Pharos Alexandrīnae

Alexandrīa Antīqua

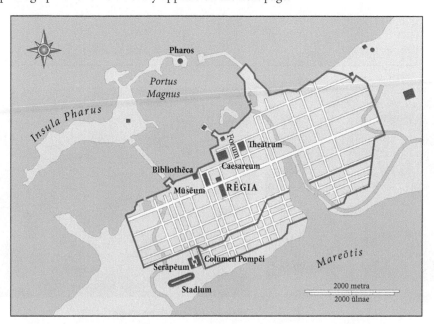

Aegyptus Rōmāna

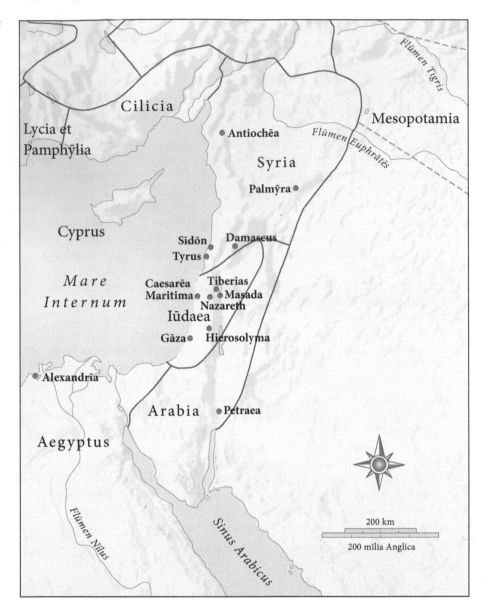

Theātrum Rōmānum Alexandrīnae

Bibliothēca Alexandrīna Hodiē

362

QUID PUTAS?

1. How do you think knowledge of pregnancy and birthing practices in the ancient Rome affected the lives of women?
2. Why do you think the same Latin word *umbilīcus* means "center of the world," "the rod in a book scroll," and "belly button"?
3. Pliny tells us how some Romans may have guessed the gender of unborn children. Have you heard of any similar techniques people used in the days before ultrasound?
4. To what modern city would you compare ancient Alexandria and why?

EXERCEĀMUS!

25-6 Scrībāmus

Rewrite the following section of *Lectiō Prīma* from Chapter 24 in the imperfect tense. Be careful, as not all verbs are deponent. Follow the model.

→ In theātrō multī spectātōrēs inter sē *colloquēbantur* . . .

> In theātrō multī spectātōrēs inter sē *colloquuntur* dum fābula Plautī, "Amphitruō" nomine, ab omnibus avidē *exspectātur*.
>
> Novum theātrum Marcellī omnēs *intuentur* et valdē *admīrantur*. Patriciī sīcut Marcus et Lūcius et amicī suī, sēdēs in primīs gradibus theātrī, post senatōrēs, *tenent*. Aliī, sīcut Valeriae familia, in altissimīs sēdibus *sedent*.
>
> In theātrum Marcus Lūciusque *ingrediuntur* et *sedent* cum amīcīs suīs. Multī iuvenēs inter sē *sermōcinantur* sed Marcus fēminam ūnam gracilem et pulchram *intuētur* et cum eā dīcere *cōnātur*.

25-7 Colloquāmur

Use the passage you rewrote in the imperfect tense in Exercise 25-6 to ask and answer questions with other members of your class. Follow the example.

→ **Quaestiō:** Quī in theātrō inter sē colloquēbantur?
   Responsum: Multī spectātōrēs in theātrō inter sē colloquēbantur.

25-8 Verba Discenda

Find the *Verbum Discendum* that best completes each of the following statements. Then translate the sentence into English. Follow the model.

→ Caecilia _____ domī Servīliī est.
   a. domina   b. culīna   c. auxilium   d. coquus
   a. domina: Caecilia is the mistress of Servilius' house.

1. Aelius _____ Mēdēae fortiter pulsāvit.
   a. culīnam   b. ianuam   c. sellam   d. convīvium

2. Servīlius et Caecilia dē Servīliā _____.
   a. crēdunt   b. cunctantur   c. colloquuntur   d. pariunt

3. Epistula _____ ā Maecēnāte ad Servīlium advēnit.
   a. praesertim   b. nūper   c. intrā   d. paulō

4. Maecēnās ipse ad _____ prōgrediētur.
   a. culīnam   b. ianuam   c. sellam   d. convīvium

5. Aelius _____ ā Mēdēā petit.
   a. dominam   b. culīnam   c. auxilium   d. coquum

6. Caecilia in _____ in peristȳliō sedet.
    a. culīnā   b. ianuā   c. sellā   d. convīviō

7. Licinia _____ est.
    a. perīculōsa   b. quiēta   c. coquus   d. gravida

8. Sicō _____ est.
    a. domina   b. culīna   c. auxilium   d. coquus

9. Magnā cum cārā Caecilia signum Maecēnātis _____.
    a. intuitur   b. colloquitur   c. cunctātur   d. paritur

10. Augustus _____ est.
    a. domina   b. culīna   c. imperātor   d. coquus

11. Coquī in _____ labōrant.
    a. culīna   b. ianuā   c. sellā   d. convīviō

12. In Rōmā antiquā, praesertim fēminīs pauperibus, parere _____ erat.
    a. perīculōsum   b. quiētum   c. coquum   d. salvum

13. Et mox omnēs mīrāculum parvum _____.
    a. colloquentur   b. parient   c. mīrābuntur   d. crēdent

🔊 VERBA DISCENDA

auxilium, -iī n. help, aid;
  pl. auxiliary forces
  [auxiliary]
colloquor, colloquī,
  collocūtus sum **talk**
  together, converse
  [colloquial]
convīvium, -iī n. **feast,**
  banquet [convivial]
coquus, -ī m. **cook**
crēdō, crēdere, crēdidī,
  crēditum **(+ dat.)**
  believe, trust [credible,
  creditor]

culīna, -ae f. **kitchen**
  [culinary]
cunctor, cunctārī,
  cunctātus est **tarry,**
  linger, hesitate
domina, -ae f. **mistress (of**
  the house), the woman
  in charge [dominatrix]
gravidus, -a, -um
  pregnant
  [multigravida]
iānua, -ae f. **door**
imperātor, -ōris m. **com-**
  mander, ruler [emperor]

intrā (+ acc.) **within**
  [intramural]
intueor, intuērī, intuitus
  sum **look at, gaze at;**
  consider [intuition]
iuvō, iuvāre,
  iūvī, iūtum **help**
mīror, mīrārī, mīrātus
  sum **wonder at,**
  admire
nūper **recently, not long**
  ago
pariō, parere, peperī,
  paritum/partum **bring**

forth, give birth, bear,
  create [postpartum]
paulō **somewhat, by a little**
pauper, pauperis **poor**
perīculōsus, -a, -um
  dangerous [perilous]
praesertim **especially,**
  particularly
quiētus, -a, -um **calm,**
  quiet [inquietude]
salvus, -a, -um **safe, well**
sānus, -a, -um **healthy**
  [sanity]
sella, -ae f. **chair**

Angulus Grammaticus

Bending Language: Linguistic Limitations and Linguistic Flexibility

Every language has its limitations and its little tricks around these limitations. The use of participles in Latin is a good example of this.

PARTICIPLE	ENGLISH	LATIN
present active participle	saying	dīcēns
present passive participle	being said	[lacking]
perfect active participle	having said	[lacking]
perfect passive participle	having been said	dictus

You will learn about the perfect passive participle in Latin in Chapter 26.

Now think about deponent verbs and look what happens.

LATIN	PARTICIPLE	TRANSLATION
loquēns	present active participle	saying
locūtus	perfect active participle	having said

Deponent verbs should have passive endings, but Latin has no present passive participle. So the choice was never to use a present participle of such verbs or to "bend the rules." Another twist is involved in the form *locūtus*. Though passive in form, it is translated actively, and this creates the perfect active participle that is lacking for non-deponent verbs.

Another example of linguistic flexibility and limitation appears by comparing the actions expressed by Latin and English verbs.

TYPE OF ACTION	ENGLISH	LATIN
Present Tense		
simple	I say	dīcō
continuous or progressive	I am saying	dīcō
emphatic	I do say	rē vērā dīcō
Future Tense		
simple	I will say	dīcam
continuous or progressive	I will be saying	dīcam
Past Tenses		
simple	I said	dīxī
continuous or progressive	I was saying	dīcēbam
present perfect	I have said	dīxī
perfect continuous	I have been saying	iam dīcō
past perfect	I had said	dīxeram

So an English speaker can make distinctions in the present and future tenses that a Latin speaker cannot, by showing the action is ongoing or progressive (I am saying) or by emphasizing the action (I do say). Latin speakers found other ways to express these ideas like *rē vērā dīcō* (I say indeed).

English has its limitations, too. We long ago abandoned 2nd person singular forms (thou seest) and only use the 2nd person plural "you," even if we are speaking to only one person. Imagine what a Roman would think of that!

Moreover, many languages, including Latin and English, cannot show gender in 1st and 2nd person personal pronouns. *Ego* (I), *tū* (you), *nōs* (we), and *vōs* (you) are used for both male and female genders. Arabic, for example, uses different forms of "you" for addressing males and females.

The main point, then, is to recognize that every language has its limitations, that some things can be easily expressed in one language but not in another. At the same time, all languages are flexible and find ways around their grammatical and linguistic limitations.

Photo Credits

Page 316 (top) Eric Lessing/Art Resource, N.Y.; **page 316 (bottom)** Marilyn Brusherd; **page 319** American Numismatic Association; **page 321** Clipart.com; **page 324** Courtesy of Claude Moore Health Sciences Library at University of Virginia; **page 325 (top)** Marilyn Brusherd; **page 326 (left)** Marilyn Brusherd; **page 326 (right)** Marilyn Brusherd.

Epulae Rēgum

From *Disce! An Introductory Latin Course, volume 2*, First Edition. Francesco Bonavita. Copyright © 2011 by Pearson Education, Inc. Published by Pearson Prentice Hall. All rights reserved.

Servī Labōrantēs in Epulīs

GRAMMATICA
Perfect Passive Participles
The 4th Principal Part
Ablative Absolutes
The Irregular Verb *Fīō*

MŌRĒS RŌMĀNĪ
Cibus Rōmānus

LATĪNA HODIERNA
Cornūcōpia

ORBIS TERRĀRUM RŌMĀNUS
Asia

ANGULUS GRAMMATICUS
Persons and Possession: Whose Money
    Bag Is It?

LECTIŌNĒS:
CONVĪVIUM
and
HOSPITĒS

This is the day of the big banquet at Servilius' house. The occasion marks his most serious attempt to date to rise in the ranks of the patricians.

26
Epulae Rēgum

Lectiō Prīma

Antequam Legis

The Banquet of a Lifetime

Many banquets like the one described in this chapter occurred in Augustan Rome. Augustus was very keen on making his new Rome the literary and cultural center of the Mediterranean. To do so he spared little time or money. Those who wanted to curry favor with the emperor often found it to their benefit to become patrons of poets, to hold readings, or to make contributions to the cultural cause. As you know from Chapter 25, the occasion for this banquet is Servilius' plan to give a copy of Callimachus' *Aetia* to Augustus. Though the emperor himself does not attend this banquet, the guest list includes a "Who's Who" of important people. You have read about several of these illustrious men already. Marcus Vipsanius Agrippa, the guest of honor, was advisor to his friend Augustus, the general who defeated Marc Antony and Cleopatra at Actium in 31 B.C., and later became the emperor's son-in-law. In 27 B.C. Agrippa built the original Pantheon, which was rebuilt, probably during the reign of the emperor Hadrian (117–138 A.D.). It is the later Pantheon, not Agrippa's, which is depicted in the photos below and on the next page. Gaius Maecenas, political advisor of Augustus and great patron of the arts in Rome, will receive Servilius' gift on behalf of the emperor. Asinius Pollio, another political advisor to the emperor and patron of the arts, built Rome's first public library. Quintus Horatius Flaccus (Horace), was a famous poet under Maecenas' patronage. Sextus Propertius and Publius Ovidius Naso (Ovid) were popular love poets of the period. Titus Livius (Livy) was the author of the monumental history of Rome called *Ab Urbe Conditā* (*From the Foundation of the City*). In creating this guest list we have taken some historical liberties. Although the date of our story is about 9 B.C., Agrippa had been dead for about three years. Horace will die in the next year, as will Maecenas.

   As you read about the banquet, you are introduced to a new participle, the **perfect passive participle**.

Pantheon Rōmae Hodiē

Gemma

Pantheon Rōmae Hodiē: Note the inscription on the façade.
M AGRIPPA COS TERTIUM FECIT
M(arcus) Agrippa Co(n)s(ul) tertium fēcit.
We know from ancient records that Agrippa was consul for the third time in 27 B.C.

Perfect Passive Participles

At long last you get to use the 4th principal part of a verb. It is called the perfect passive participle (P³). Here are its essential facts:

- P³ is a 2-1-2 adjective, so you already know all its endings. In fact, you have been translating perfect passive participles as simple adjectives for some time now.
- As both "perfect" and "passive" you can translate these literally as "having been X-ed," although translating without "having been" is sometimes preferable.

> Caecilia cibum **coctum** īnspectābat.
> Caecilia was inspecting the **having been cooked** food.

If this sounds a bit awkward to you, you can try translating this way:

> Caecilia was inspecting the **cooked** food.
> Caecilia was inspecting the food **that had been cooked**.

Look for this sentence in *Lectiō Prīma*.

EXERCEĀMUS!

26-1 Perfect Passive Participles

Perfect passive participles (P³s) are marked in **bold** in *Lectiō Prīma*. Before you read, make a line-by-line list of these words and translate them following the model.

→ line 10 *coctum*   (having been) **cooked**

🔊 CONVĪVIUM

Diēs convīviī adest et tōta domus Servīliī perturbātur. In
ūnā domūs parte Caecilia servīs imperat et in aliā parte
Sicō coquus quoque servīs in culīnam **convocātīs** imperat.

"Conservī," inquit, "hodiē diēs magna est. Sī hodiē
5 bene laborāverimus, fortasse aliquandō dominus noster
nōbīs lībertātem nostram dabit. Vidētis omnia **parāta**—
vīnum ā villā nostrā **portātum**, cibōs ad nōs trans mare
transportātōs. Nōbīs strēnuē laborāre et epulās rēgum
appōnere necesse est. Agedum! Laborēmus!"

Marcus et Lūcius et Servīlia colloquuntur.

10 Tōtam per illam diem servī ancillaeque strēnuē laborābant et Caecilia cibum ā Sicōne **coctum** saepe inspectābat.
Dēmum omnia **parāta** sunt et in mensīs stant. Servī **lavātī** et nova vestīmenta gerentēs hīc et illīc astant
hospitēs exspectantēs.

In aliā domūs parte, post iānuās **clausās**, Marcus, Lūcius et Servīlia dē hospitibus **invitātīs** inter sē colloquuntur.
Lūcius "Nōn," inquit, "aequum est! Cūr, Marce, tū cum hospitibus cēnāre potes, sed nōbīs hīc manēre necesse est?"
15 Marcus, "Frātercule, tacē!" inquit. "Hospitēs nihil dē puerīs cūrant. Maecēnās ipse venit, ille Augustī amīcus et
poētārum patrōnus. Quoque venit Gaius Asinius Polliō, alius patrōnus quī bibliothēcam Rōmae aedificāvit. Polliō
modo revēnit ab Asiā ubi urbēs magnās Troiam et Ephesum visitāvit. Maecēnās et Polliō papȳrum ā patre **emptam**
accipient et mox pater Augustī amīcus novissimus erit!"

"Huī! En Maecēnās?" Lūcius rogāvit. "Quis alius venit? Fortasse Augustus ipse adveniet?"
20 Marcus respondet: "Augustus nōn adveniet, sed Vipsānius Agrippa, multō ab Augustō **honorātus**, veniet et
optimī poētae et scriptōrēs Rōmanī advenient—poētae Propertius et Horātius et Ovidius aderunt et Līvius quī
scrībit dē rēbus **gestīs** maiōrum nostrōrum.

Marcus, sē ad Servīliam vertēns, "Soror," inquit, "Cordus tuus advenit hāc vespere sed iste Antōnius, cui tē pater
prōmīsit, quoque aderit."
25 Servīlia nihil dīcit. Nihil est quod dīcī potest!

🔊 VERBA ŪTENDA

aedificō (1) build, make
aequus, -a, -um fair
agedum Come! Well! All right!
aliquandō sometimes, at length, formerly, hereafter
ante in front, before, ahead; (+ acc.) before, in front of
appōnō, appōnere, apposuī, appositum serve, put to
Asia, -ae f. Asia, a Roman province in what is now Turkey
astō, astāre, astitī assist
bibliothēca, -ae f. library
claudō, claudere, clausī, clausum shut, close

conservus, -ī m. fellow slave
convocō (1) call together
coquō, coquere, coxī, coctum cook
dēmum finally, at length, at last
efficiō, efficere, effēcī, effectum execute
Ephesus, -i f. Ephesus, a city in the Roman province of Asia (modern Turkey)
epulae rēgum "a banquet fit for a king"
frāterculus, -ī m. little brother
ēn/ēm (in questions) really?
epulae, -ārum f. pl. food, dishes of food; banquet, feast
gestae from *gerō*; *rēs gestae* = "deeds"

honorō (1) honor
hospes, hospitis m. guest, host, stranger
huī! wow! (exclamation of astonishment or admiration)
imperō (1) (+ dat.) command, order, rule
invitō (1) invite
Laborēmus! "Let's get to work!"
lavō, lavāre, lāvī, lautum/ lavātum/lōtum wash
lībertās, -ātis f. freedom
multō much, by far, long
papȳrus, -ī f. papyrus
patrōnus, -ī m. patron
perturbō (1) disturb, trouble
posteā afterward, then

rēs gestae "deeds"
reveniō, revenīre, revēnī, reventum return
scriptor, -ōris m. writer
Sicō, Sicōnis m. Sico
strēnuē actively, vigorously
Troia, -ae f. Troy, a city in the Roman province of Asia (Modern Turkey)
transportō (1) carry, transport
vertō, vertere, vertī, versum turn, overturn
vesper, -eris m. evening
vestīmentum, -ī n. clothing
villa, -ae f. villa, country estate
visitō (1) visit

332

POSTQUAM LĒGISTĪ

Answer these questions in both Latin and English if the question is followed by (L). Otherwise, just respond in English.

1. What status does Sico seem to have in the house?
2. What do Marcus and Lucius talk about as the guests arrive? (L)
3. What do you learn about each of the following guests from Marcus: Agrippa, Pollio, and Maecenas? (L)
4. What news does Marcus tell his sister Servilia at the end of the conversation? (L)
5. If you were Servilia, how would you feel right now? Why?

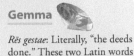

Gemma

Rēs gestae: Literally, "the deeds done." These two Latin words are best translated as "accomplishments."

Culīna Pompeiīs

Grammatica A

Perfect Passive Participles

Here are some of the perfect passive participles (P³) you saw in this *lectiō*. Compare your translations with these:

convocātīs	(having been) **called together**
emptam	(having been) **bought**
clausās	(having been) **closed**

Remember that participles are verbal adjectives. Therefore they have GNC's based on their antecedents. Here are these same participles used as adjectives.

*Haec **diēs perturbāta** est.*	This day is disturbed.
*Sicō **servīs convocātīs** dīcit.*	Sico speaks to the assembled slaves.
*Servīlius **papȳrum** in Aegyptō **emptam** habet.*	Servilius has a papyrus bought in Egypt.
*Puerī post **ianuās clausās** loquuntur.*	The children speak behind closed doors.

Note how the P³ is often translated into English by adding **-ed** to the English verb (disturb**ed**, assembl**ed**, clos**ed**). Some English verbs have "irregular" P³s like "bought" from "buy."

The 4ᵗʰ Principal Part

So far you have only used the first three principal parts of a Latin verb. P³ is the 4ᵗʰ principal part. Here are the four principal parts of the verb *coquō*, which is a *Verbum Discendum* in this chapter.

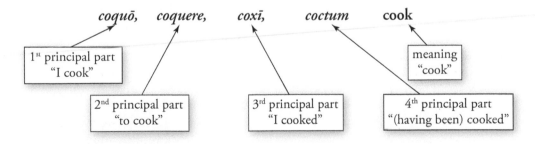

coquō,   coquere,   coxī,   coctum   cook

1ˢᵗ principal part "I cook"

2ⁿᵈ principal part "to cook"

3ʳᵈ principal part "I cooked"

4ᵗʰ principal part "(having been) cooked"

meaning "cook"

Notā Bene:

- Drop the *-um* from the 4ᵗʰ principal part to obtain the perfect passive stem of a verb: *coct-* from *coctum*.
- Then add *-us, -a, -um* to form the P³: *coctus, -a, -um*.

From now on, all four principal parts will be provided for verbs in the *Verba Ūtenda*.

EXERCEĀMUS!

26-2 Review of *Verba Discenda*

The 4ᵗʰ principal parts (P³) of some verbs you already know are listed in column A. Match them with the proper translation from column B.

	A		B
_____	1. vocātum	a.	asked
_____	2. creditum	b.	believed
_____	3. audītum	c.	captured
_____	4. bibitum	d.	drunk
_____	5. nōtum	e.	ended
_____	6. captum	f.	heard
_____	7. rogātum	g.	known
_____	8. lātum	h.	carried
_____	9. finītum	i.	run
_____	10. cursum	j.	called

Lectiō Secunda

Antequam Legis

Trīclīnia

Where would Servilius' banquet be held? The guests of honor eat in the *trīclīnium*, or formal dining room. As the word *trīclīnium* implies, three couches are set up in this room for the nine main diners. Other diners are served in the *peristȳlium*, where the formal presentation of the manuscript will be made.

It mattered greatly who sat where. Agrippa, as the most important man in the room, occupies the *locus consulāris* (consul's place) at the *lectus medius* (middle couch), the equivalent of our head table. With Agrippa on this couch are Maecenas and Pollio. On the couch to the right, called the *lectus summus* (highest couch) were the poets Propertius, Horace, and Ovid. On the couch to the left, called the *lectus īmus* (lowest couch) were Marcus, Livy, and Servilius, who as host, is called *cēnae pater*. A slave stood behind each diner, ready to assist, while other

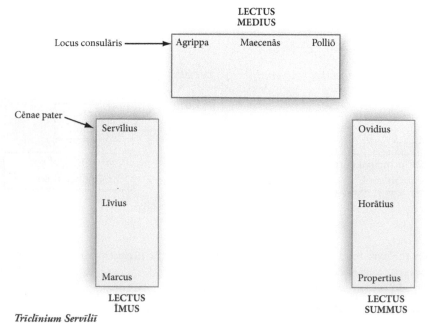

Trīclīnium Servīliī

slaves brought in the food and placed it on tables before each couch. Note that Caecilia did not eat in the room with the main guests.

The menu for this banquet is based one that found in the *Satyricon*, a 1st-century A.D. novel by Petronius. Servilius' banquet is not as lavish or pretentious as the one in the *Satyricon*, but contains several of the same dishes.

As you read about the banquet, watch for forms of the irregular verb *fīō*.

The Irregular Verb *Fīō*

Fīō, fīērī, factus sum is a "mixed" verb that has both active- and passive-looking forms. Forms of *fīō* in the next reading are in ***bold italics***.

You have to be creative in translating *fīō*. Be sure to try all its basic meanings: become, happen, be made, etc.

Multī laetī fīēbant.	Many were becoming happy.
Nōs omnēs mortuī fīēmus.	All of us will become/be rendered dead.
Clamor fīēbat.	An uproar occurred.

Lectiō Secunda also introduces you to a construction very common in Latin, but one of the most unusual for English speakers. It is called the **ablative absolute**.

Ablative Absolutes

Read this little paragraph in English:

When the food was prepared, Caecilia sighed in relief. **Because everything was fine**, she could get ready herself. Soon, **when the doors were opened**, the guests came in, hoping for a wonderful meal **since Servilius was the host**. **As the guests came in**, the children looked on from above.

Each of the English phrases marked in **bold** is a dependent (or subordinate) clause introduced by a conjunction like "when" or "after." In Latin, there is a shorthand way for doing the same thing. This is the **ablative absolute (AA)**, so named because virtually every word in it is in the ablative case.

There are two basic types of ablative absolute:

- A noun plus a participle
- A noun plus an adjective or another noun (with "being" understood)

ABLATIVE ABSOLUTE	LITERAL TRANSLATION	FREE TRANSLATION
Noun + Participle		
hospitibus ingressīs	"the guests having entered"	Once the guests had entered . . . After the guests entered . . .
hospitibus ingredientibus	"with the guests coming in"	As the guests come in . . . As the guests came in . . . (the tense depends on the general context)
Noun + Adjective or Noun		
omnibus bonīs	"everything being fine"	Because everything was fine . . . Since . . . Now that . . .
Servīliō hospite	"Servilius being host"	Because Servilius was the host . . . When . . . Because . . .

EXERCEĀMUS!

26-3 Identifying Tense and Translating Ablative Absolutes (AA)

Before you read *Lectiō Secunda,* make a line-by-line list of the ablative absolutes marked in **bold**. Indicate the tense of the participle. Then use the tense of the participle and the chart as guides to translate the ablative absolute literally. Watch out! One ablative absolute has no participle. When you find that one, don't translate it. Just say that it has no participle. Follow the model.

Line	Abl. Abs.	Tense of Participle	Literal Translation
→ 1	cibō parātō	perfect	the food having been prepared

 HOSPITĒS

Cibō parātō, Caecilia et fessa et laeta *fīēbat*. **Omnibus parātīs**, Caecilia ad sē ancillam, quae ornātrix sua erat, vocāvit et gradūs ascendērunt.

Mox **ianuīs apertīs,** hospitēs adveniēbant et dē fenestrā Lūcius et Servīlia omnia, quae intrā *fīēbant*, et omnēs, quī aderant, inspicere poterant.

5   Servīlius et Caecilia hospitēs in ātrium advenientēs salutābant et omnēs in trīclīnium ingrediēbantur.

Hospitibus plaudentibus, servī trīclīnium intrantēs lancēs maximās tulērunt. Servīlius, manūs plaudēns, clāmat: "Cēnēmus! Epulae *fīant*!"

Talibus dictīs, hospitēs valdē admīrābantur dum servī olīvas (albās et nigrās) et avēs assātās et, posteā, glīrēs melle ac papāvere sparsōs intulērunt. Aliī servī vīnum Falernum hospitibus offerunt et aliī immānem aprum et nōnnūllās speciēs piscium appōnunt. Omnēs hospitēs et aprō et piscibus avidē fruuntur—piscēs quī olim aut marī aut in piscīnīs Servīliī natābant, sed nunc in condīmentīs coctī, **garō appositō,** natant.

Dēmum, **ūvīs mālīsque ōvīsque nucibusque consumptīs**, Servīlius et hospitēs, peristȳliō appropinquantēs,
15   terribilem rixam audīvērunt.

Servīlius "Ei! Quid *fit*?" rogāvit. "Quis in domō meā talem rixam facit?"

Ecce, in mediō peristȳliō Iullus Antonius, quī nimis vīnī hauserat et ēbrius *fīēbat*, prō hospitibus stābat. **Corōnā** in capite suō **lapsante**, Iullus carmen dē infāmibus fēminīs cantābat.

Servīlius, īrātus "Iulle!" clāmāvit. "Mihi cantūs tuī displicent! Et ēbrius es! Discēde statim et nōlī domum meam
20   revertī! Vah! Apage!"

Aliīs hospitibus tristibus, Servīlius quoque tristis erat. "Dominī," inquit, "mihi istum ignāvum virum ignoscite, sī vōbīs placeat! Numquam iste sub tectum meum revertētur!"

Suprā, Servīlia dē fenestrā omnia dē Iullō intuēns et audiēns, rīdet et tunc, **Cordō** in peristȳlio **aspectātō**, suspīrat.

25   "Mī Corde," inquit, "Tōta tua sum! Aliquandō uxor tua nunc certē *fīam*!"

Epulae Rōmānae

POSTQUAM LĒGISTĪ

Gemma

Note that the Romans used *hospes* for both "guest" and "host."

1. What are some of the foods eaten at the banquet?
2. What does Iullus Antonius do at the end of the banquet, and how does Servilius react? How does his daughter Servilia react?
3. How does this banquet compare to formal dinners you and your family may have attended or hosted? Consider not only the menu but also the goals of the host.

🔊 VERBA ŪTENDA

ac and, and besides
admīror, admīrāri, admīrātus sum admire, wonder at
albus, -a, -um here: "unripe," i.e., green olives
aliquandō sometime, one day
apage! go! scram!
appōnō, appōnere, apposuī, appositum serve, put to
aspectō (1) gaze, look at
assō (1) roast
ātrium, -ī n. atrium, public greeting room of a Roman house
avidē eagerly
avis, avis f. bird
cantō (1) sing
cantus, -ūs m. song
caput, capitis n. head
cēnēmus! Let's dine!
condīmentum, -ī n. spice, seasoning
consūmō, consūmere, consumpsī, consumptum use up, eat, consume

coquō, coquere, coxī, coctum cook
corōna, -ae f. crown, garland
dēmum finally, at length, at last
displiceō, displicēre, displicuī, displicitum displease; displicet (impersonal) "it is displeasing"
discēdō, discēdere, discessī, discessum leave, depart
ei/hei ah! oh! (in fear or dismay)
epulae, -ārum f. pl. food, dishes of food; banquet, feast *Epulae fīant!* loosely: "Let the banquet begin!"
Falernum, -ī n. Falernian wine
fīō, fierī, factus sum be made, be done; happen, become
garum, -ī n. fish sauce
glīs, glīris m. dormouse (a great delicacy)

hauriō, haurīre, hausī, haustum drink, swallow
hospes, hospitis m. guest, host, stranger
ignāvus, -a, -um idle, cowardly
ignoscō (1) (+ dat.) pardon, forgive
immānis, immāne huge
infāmis, infāme disreputable
inferō, inferre, intulī, illātum bring, serve
inspiciō, inspicere, inspexī, inspectum look at, inspect
lanx, lancis f. dish, place
lapsō (1) slip
mel, mellis n. honey
natō (1) swim
niger, nigra, nigrum black
nimis too much
nux, nucis f. nut
olīva, -ae f. olive
ornātrix, ornātricis f. hair-dresser
papāver, papāveris n. poppy; poppyseed

peristȳlium, -iī n. peristyle, courtyard
piscīna, -ae fish pond
piscis, piscis m. fish
plaudō, plaudere, plausī, plausum clap, applaud
posteā afterward
Quid fit? What is going on? What's happening?
revertō, revertere, revertī turn back, return Also *revertōr, revertī, reversus sum* turn back, return
rixa, -ae f. loud quarrel, brawl
sī vōbīs placeat "Please"
spargō, spargere, sparsī, sparsum sprinkle
suprā (+ acc.) over, above
suspīrō (1) sigh
tectum, -ī n. roof, house
terribilis, terribile terrible
triclīnium, -iī n. triclinium, dining room
ūva, -ae f. grape
vah/vaha ah! oh! (in astonishment, joy, anger)

Grammatica B

Ablative Absolutes

An ablative absolute (AA) is a combination of words (participle, noun, pronoun, adjective) in the ablative case. As you saw earlier, these words are usually translated by an English subordinate clause beginning with "when," "since," "because," or "although." To put this another way, an ablative absolute describes an event that accompanies or is **subordinate** to the main action of the sentence.

Cibō parātō,   *Caecilia et fessa et laeta fīēbat.*

| Subordinate Clause | | Main action of sentence |

Relative Time

If a participle is part of the ablative absolute, note the following:

- Present active participle = same time as main verb
- Perfect passive participle = time before the main verb

Consider these examples:

Servīs intrantibus, omnēs plaudunt.
As the slaves enter, everyone applauds.

Gemma

corōnā lapsante: Note the ending on *lapsante*. In ablative absolutes, the present participle uses the alternate *-e* ending instead of the usual *-ī*.

Gemma

mihi istum ignāvum virum ignoscite: Notice how the verb *ignoscō* takes an accusative for the offense (*virum*) and a dative for the offender; i.e., in Latin you pardon someone (in the dative) for something (in the accusative.)

Here both the entering and applauding happen in the present.

Servīs intrantibus, omnēs plausērunt.
As the slaves entered, everyone applauded.

Here both the entering and the applauding happened in the past (because the main verb is in the perfect tense), and the present participle shows that the entering occurred at the same time as the applauding.

In the following sentences we know that the entering happens before the applauding because the participle is perfect:

Cibō consumptō, omnēs plaudunt. Now that the food has been eaten, everyone is applauding.
Cibō consumptō, omnēs plausērunt. After the food was eaten, everyone applauded.

So, before you translate an ablative absolute (AA), be sure to check the tense of the main verb.

Ablative Absolutes without Participles

Some AAs consist of two nouns or a noun and an adjective but no participle. Here is the one example from *Lectiō Secunda*:

aliīs hospitibus tristibus   Literal translation: the other guests **being** sad
Freer translation: because the other guests **were** sad

Note how "being" and "were" need to be added in the English translation, but are understood in Latin. So, when you find two nouns or a noun and an adjective in the ablative case, try translating them as an ablative absolute with the verb "to be" understood.

Notā Bene:

Latin does not have a perfect active participle to use in ablative absolutes. This means that, unlike English, it cannot say "Having seen him, I sighed." Instead, Latin would use a perfect passive participle:

Cordō aspectātō, Servīlia suspīrat. When Cordus was seen, Servilia sighed.

But, in English, we have a perfect active participle and can say: "Having seen Cordus, Servilia sighed."

EXERCEĀMUS!

26-4 Translating Ablative Absolutes

Translate each AA literally and then with a freer translation. Be sure to show the tense of the participle in your translation. If there is no participle, remember to understand "is" or "are." Follow the models.

→ gladiātōribus necātīs: Literal: the gladiators having been killed
Freer: after the gladiators were killed

→ gladiātōribus pugnantībus   Literal: the gladiators fighting . . .
Freer: since the gladiators are fighting

1. discipulō studente
2. discipulō doctō
3. discipulīs laetīs
4. discipulīs maestīs
5. magistrō docente
6. magistrīs doctīs
7. magistrā bonā
8. magistrō malō
9. Lūciō et Servīliā colloquentibus
10. cibō devorātō
11. vīnīs ad mensās trānsportātīs
12. hospite plaudente

The Irregular Verb *Fīō*

Latin also has another irregular verb that has active forms with passive meanings in the present, imperfect, and future. In that regard, it is sort of a "reverse deponent" in that it "looks active, but isn't."

fīō, fierī, factus sum be made, become, happen

So *fīō* means "I am made, I become," whereas *factus sum* means "I was made, I became." Note that *fīō* is used as the passive of *faciō, facere, fēcī, factus* make, do, become. *Fīō* is a *Verbum Discendum* in this chapter.

The irregular forms of *fīō* are all in the present tense:

fīō	I am made, become	*[fīmus]*	we are made, become
fīs	you are made, become	*[fītis]*	you are made, become
fit	he/she/it is made, becomes	*fīunt*	they are made, become

Gemma

fīat: A 3rd person singular form of this word that you will learn later means "Let it happen" and becomes the English word "fiat."

Notā Bene:

- The forms in brackets are rarely found.
- Note the short *-i* in *fit* and *fierī*.
- In other tenses *fīō* takes fairly normal 3rd conjugation verb forms. Thus, *fīēbam, fīēbās*, etc. (imperfect), and *fīam, fīēs* (future).

EXERCEĀMUS!

26-5 **Translating *fīō***

Translate the following forms of *fīō* into English using the correct form and tense of "become."

1. fīunt	3. fīēmus	5. fit	7. factae sunt	9. fīs
2. fīēbās	4. factus es	6. fīēbāmus	8. fierī	10. factī erant

Mōrēs Rōmānī

Cibus Rōmānus

Many of the foods we eat today, including many foods associated with modern Italy, were not known to the Romans. The coffee bean was not discovered in Ethiopia until the 9th century A.D. Pasta and macaroni were not eaten in Italy until after Roman times. The eggplant came from Asia and was introduced to Europeans by Arabs after 1500 A.D. The importation of tea into Europe from China and India did not begin until the 17th century.

Many other "Italian" foods were not known to the ancients. These foods include tomatoes, chocolate, zucchini, and many kinds of beans, including kidney, lima, butter, pole, snap, and string.

What, then, did the Romans eat and drink? Some of their staples included wheat, lentils, barley, olives, broad beans, fruit, nuts, melons, milk, cheese, eggs, wine, and, if they could afford it, all sorts of meat, fowl, and seafood.

Cibus Rōmānus

In order to illustrate how Romans prepared some of these foods, we offer you some recipes from an ancient cookbook entitled *Dē Rē Coquīnāriā* (*On Cooking*) attributed to a Caelius Apicius, who is otherwise unknown. (We do not even know when he lived.) This collection of approximately 500 gourmet recipes is divided into ten books organized according to types of food with Greek names like *Sarcoptes* ("Meats"), *Cepuros* ("Garden Vegetables"), *Aeropetes* ("Birds"), *Tetrapus* ("Quadrupeds"), and *Thalassa* ("Sea Creatures"). Many of these recipes included expensive and exotic ingredients like flamingo, which were not available to the average Roman, but the following recipes from book three on *Cepuros* could have been made in a typical Roman kitchen.

Also notice how the future tense (and, occasionally, the present) is used instead of imperatives to give directions:

faciēs	make (you will make)	*coquēs*	cook, fry, boil	*ligābis*	tie, bind
concīdēs	chop together	*eximēs*	remove	*mittēs*	put
		inferēs	serve		

Porrōs mātūrōs fīerī

Pugnum salis, aquam et oleum mixtum faciēs et ibi coquēs et eximēs. Cum oleō, liquāmine, merō et inferēs.

To make mature leeks.

You will make a mixture of a pinch of salt, water, and oil. And then you will cook it and remove it (from the heat). You will serve it with pure wine (sauce?).

Now try translating these actual recipes, using the words above and the *Verba Ūtenda*.

Aliter porrōs

Opertōs foliīs cōliculōrum et in prunīs coquēs ut sūprā et inferēs.

Aliter porrōs

In aquā coctōs ut suprā et inferēs.

Bētas

Concīdes porrum, coriandrum, cumīnum, ūvam passam, farīnam et omnia in medullam mittēs. Ligābis et ita īnferēs ex liquāmine, oleō et acētō.

Aliter bētās ēlixās

Ex sināpi, oleō modicō et acētō bene inferuntur.

Carōtae seu pastinācae

Carōtae frictae oenogarō inferuntur.

Aliter carōtās

Sale, oleō pūrō et acētō.

All the words preceded by + in the following *Verba Ūtenda* are ingredients in the recipes.

🔊 VERBA ŪTENDA

+ *acētum, -ī* n. vinegar
aliter in another way
+ *aqua, -ae* f. water
bene "nicely"
+ *bēta, -ae* f. beet
+ *carōta, -ae* f. carrot
concīdō, concīdere, concīdi, concīsum cut, chop up
coquō, coquere, coxī, coctum cook, boil, bake, fry
+ *coriandrum, -ī* n. coriander
+ *cumīnum, -ī* n. cumin
+ *cōliculus, -ī = cauliculus, -ī* m. small cabbage, cabbage sprout

eximō, eximere, exēmī, exemptum take out, remove
ēlixus, -a, -um boiled
folia, -ae f. leaf
fricō, fricere, fricuī, frictum rub, rub down
+ *garum, -ī* n. fish sauce
inferō, inferre, intulī, illātum translate here as "carry in" or "serve"
+ *liquāmen, liquāminis* n. liquid, especially fish sauce
+ *mātūrus, -a, -um* mature, of good size

merum, -ī n. pure (unmixed) wine
medulla, -ae f. marrow
misceō, miscēre, miscuī, mixtum to unite, blend, mix
modicus, -a, -um a moderate amount of
operiō, operīre, operuī, opertum cover
+ *oenogarum, -ī* n. a sauce made of garum and wine
+ *oleum, -ī* n. oil

passus, -a, -um spread out, dried
+ *pastināca, -ae* f. parsnip
+ *porrus, -ī* m. leek
+ *prūnum, -ī* n. plum
pugnum, -ī n. a pinch
pūrus, -a, -um pure, plain
+ *sāl, salis* m./n. salt
+ *sināpī* (indeclinable) n. mustard
ut as
+ *ūva, -ae* f. grape; *ūva passa* dried grape, raisin

Cornūcōpia Antīqua

Latīna Hodierna

Cornūcōpia

Americans associate the cornucopia (literally, "horn of plenty") with Thanksgiving. It is actually an ancient symbol used to suggest prosperity. Since the cornucopia is traditionally filled with fruits and vegetables, let's consider how the common names for many vegetables in English and the Romance languages, as well as many scientific names for these plants, are based on Latin words. A blank box indicates that the word for the item in that language is not clearly derived from the Latin.

SCIENTIFIC TERM	LATIN WORD	ENGLISH MEANING	ENGLISH DERIVATIVE	FRENCH	ITALIAN	SPANISH
Beta vulgaris	bēta	beet	beet	bette (chard) betterave (beet)	barbabieltola (beet) bietola (chard)	
Prunus cerasus (sour cherry)	cerasus	cherry	cherry	cerise	ciliegia	cereza
Cucurbitaceae	cucurbita	cucumber cucurbit	cucumber	concombre		
Malus domestica (domestic apple tree)	mālum	apple			mela	
Prunus persica	mālum Persicum (Persian apple)	peach	peach	pêche	pesca	melocoton (cotton apple)
Olea europaea	olīva	olive olivaceous	olive	olive	oliva	oliva
Pirus domestica (domestic pear tree)	pirum	pear	pear	poire	pera	pera
	pōmum	fruit	pomaceous pomade pomander	pomme (apple) pomme de terre (potato, i.e., earth apple)	pomodoro (tomato, i.e., golden apple)	
Prunus americana (wild plum tree)	prūnum	plum	prune	prune (plum) pruneau (prune)	prugna	
Vitis vinifera	ūva vītis	grape vine			uva	uva

Orbis Terrārum Rōmānus

Asia

In *Lectiō Prīma* Marcus mentions that Pollio had just returned to Rome from Asia. To the Romans, Asia (*Asia, -ae* f.) especially meant a province in what is now western Turkey, including important cities like Troy, Ephesus, and Pergamon. Troy, the site of the epic war between the Greeks and Trojans, was an important tourist location even in antiquity. Alexander the Great, for example, visited the city on his march east into Persia. The ancient Greek city of Ephesus was noted for the magnificent Temple of Artemis, one of the Seven Wonders of the Ancient World. Pergamon boasted a great Temple of Zeus (the remains of its altar are in the Pergamon Museum in Berlin) and an important library that rivaled the one in Alexandria.

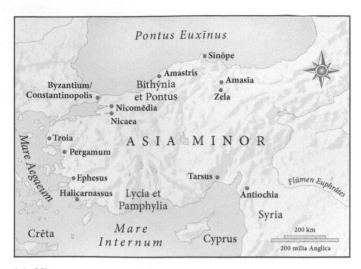

Asia Minor

Ephesus

Troia Rōmāna

Acropolis Pergamōnis et Theātrum Magnum

The territory, strategically located along major shipping routes in the Mediterranean, was bequeathed to Rome by its ally Attalus III of Pergamon and became a Roman province in 133 B.C. This wealthy region of ancient Greek cities suffered greatly from heavy taxation, corruption, and warfare in the Late Republic. Marc Antony even gave the library of Pergamon to Cleopatra as a gift.

Many important Romans spent time in the area. The poet Catullus made a pilgrimage to Troy, where his brother died. On his way to Egypt after the battle of Pharsalus in 48 B.C., Julius Caesar also visited the city, in order to honor the homeland of his mythic ancestor, Aeneas.

Augustus followed his adopted father to Troy and traveled widely in the province, which experienced an economic and cultural renaissance during the peace and properity of the Augustan age. The cities of Asia grew enormously in the early Empire. Widespread public building projects, including theaters, basilicas, baths, and other public facilities resulted in a highly urbanized and prosperous region.

Under Augustus, Troy was refounded as a Roman city, and remains of Roman buildings now lie adjacent to the ruins of the city recalled in Greek legend. During the imperial period Pergamon renewed its claim as a center of learning and culture. In the 2nd century A.D., the great Roman physician Galen was born here. The ancient Greek city of Ephesus also flourished in the empire and became an early center of Christianity.

QUID PUTĀS?

1. What modern foods would you miss most if you lived in ancient Rome?
2. Which of Apicius' recipes looks the most appealing to you? Why?
3. Compare the recipes of Apicius you read in *Mōrēs Rōmānī* with the menu for Servilius' banquet.
4. Did you notice the word "pomade" in the *Latīna Hodierna*? Do you know what it means? If you don't see the relationship between the English word "pomander" and the Latin *pomum* "fruit," look up the meaning and etymology of "pomander" in a good English dictionary.
5. List several historical and geographic reasons why the province of Asia was so important to Rome.

EXERCEĀMUS!

26-6 Scrībāmus: Composing Ablative Absolutes

Change the number in each of the following ablative absolute phrases; i.e., if the words are singular, make them plural; if they are plural, make them singular. Then translate each phrase. Follow the models.

→ *pomō ēsō* when the apple was eaten
pomīs ēsīs when the apples were eaten

1. cibō parātō
2. omnibus bonīs
3. ianuīs apertīs
4. hospitibus audientibus
5. ornātrice vocātā
6. carminibus cantātīs
7. papȳrīs emptīs
8. servō imperātō

26-7 Using *Fīō* and Ablative Absolutes

Combine AA phrases from column A and main clauses in column B to make five different sentences. Then translate these sentences into English. Follow the model.

→ Omnibus parātīs fīēbam laetus. *After everything was ready, I became happy.*

A	B
cibō parātō	fīēbam laetus/laeta
ianuīs apertīs	ūnus hospēs trīstis fīēbat
hospitibus plaudentibus	aeger/aegra (sick) fīēbat
corōnā lapsante	hospitēs īrātī fīēbant
Cordō aspectātō	Iullus ēbrius fīēbat
Servīs lavātīs	Lūcius iēiūnus fīēbat

26-8 Colloquāmur

This exercise is for pairs. One person says an ablative absolute from column A in Exercise 26-7 and then says the name of a character from the *lectiō*.

→ *Nucibus consumptīs Sicō*

The next person has to complete the thought with a brief statement about the person.

→ *laetus est.*

It may help to make up a list of verbs and adjectives to use before you begin.

26-9 Verba Discenda

Find the *Verbum Discendum* that best fits each statement.

1. 1st conjugation verb that takes a dative
2. A noun that has only plural forms
3. A deponent verb
4. Th opposite of *placet*
5. A 3rd declension i-stem noun
6. A 2nd conjugation verb
7. *Coxī* is the 3rd principal part of this word
8. A 2nd declension neuter noun

🔊 VERBA DISCENDA

admīror, admīrārī, admīrātus sum admire, wonder at [admiration]
aliquandō sometimes, at length, formerly, hereafter
appōnō, appōnere, apposuī, appositum serve, put to [apposition]
coquō, coquere, coxī, coctum cook [concoct]

dēmum finally, at length, at last
displiceō, displicēre, displicuī, displicitum displease; *displicet* (impersonal) "it is displeasing"
epulae, -ārum f. pl. food, dishes of food; banquet, feast
fīō, fierī, factus sum be made, be done; happen, become [fiat]

hospes, hospitis m. guest, host, stranger [hospitable]
imperō (1) (+ dat.) command, order, rule [imperial, imperious]
multō much, by far, long
patrōnus, -ī m. patron [patronize]
peristÿlium, -iī n. peristyle, courtyard

perturbō (1) disturb, trouble greatly [imperturbable]
piscis, piscis m. fish [piscine, Pisces]
plaudō, plaudere, plausī, plausum clap, applaud
strēnuē actively, vigorously [strenuous]
trīclīnium, -iī n. triclinium, dining room
vertō, vertere, vertī, versum turn, overturn [diversion]

Angulus Grammaticus

Persons and Possession: Whose Money Bag Is It?

In Chapter 21 you consolidated your knowledge of personal pronouns and possessive adjectives. You noted that possession is expressed by adjectives in the 1st and 2nd persons, and by either a pronoun or an adjective in the 3rd person (depending on the subject):

	POSSESSIVE ADJECTIVES VS. GENITIVE OF PERSONAL PRONOUNS			
	1st person (my, our, my own, our own)	2nd person (your, your own)	3rd person (his, her, its, their)	3rd person (his own, its own, their own)
Singular	meus, -a, -um	tuus, -a, -um	eius	suus, -a, -um
Plural	noster, nostra, nostrum	vester, vestra, vestrum	eōrum, eārum, eōrum	suus, -a, -um

Now let's consider this sentence from the *lectiō* in which Caecilia calls her hairdresser to help her get ready for the banquet:

Caecilia ad sē ancillam, quae ornātrix *sua* erat, vocāvit et gradūs ascendērunt.

The reflexive adjective *sua*, as you know, is used here to tell the reader that the *ornātrix* is Caecilia's hairdresser and not someone else's. Possessive adjectives would also be used in the 1st and 2nd person, as in *ornātrix mea* (my hairdresser), *ornātrix tua* (your hairdresser), *ornātrix nostra* (our hairdresser), and *ornātrix vestra* (your hairdresser).

Where Latin is much more precise than English is in the 3rd person, where we must distinguish *ornātrix sua*, "her own hairdresser," from *ornātrix eius* "her (someone else's) hairdresser." In order to understand the difference between *sua* and *eius* and to appreciate the precision of Latin and the ambiguity of English, consider the following sentence and try to imagine the scene in your mind (or even draw a picture):

He put **his** hand in **his** money bag.

How many people did you have involved in this scene?

- Only one? Then you understood the sentence to read "He put his own hand in his own money bag."
- But suppose scenario #2, in which "he" is a thief, and "He put his own hand in his (victim's) money bag.
- Or suppose scenario #3, in which there is actually a father and a son, and "He (the father) puts his (son's) hand in his (the father's) money bag" to get some candy?
- Or scenario #4, in which the father can put the son's hand in the son's money bag (where he hid the candy).

Are there any other possibilities you can now imagine for the original sentence? The point is that in Latin such ambiguity can be avoided:

- Scenario #1: *Is manum suam in saccō suō posuit.*
- Scenario #2: *Is manum suam in saccō eius posuit.*
- Scenario #3: *Is manum eius in saccō suō posuit.*
- Scenario #4: *Is manum eius in saccō eius posuit.*

Just remember that *suus, -a, -um* has to refer to the subject, and the rest is easy.

Photo Credits

Page 330 (top) Getty Images—Thinkstock; **page 330 (bottom)** Victor M. Martinez;
page 331 Victor M. Martinez; **page 333** Thomas J. Sienkewicz; **page 336** © CM Dixon/
Heritage—Images/ImageState Media Partners Limited; **page 339** Roman, (1st century AD)/
Museo Archeologico Nazionale, Naples, Italy/The Bridgeman Art Library; **page 340**
Victor M. Martinez; **page 342 (top)** Thomas J. Sienkewicz; **page 342 (middle)** Thomas J.
Sienkewicz; **page 342 (bottom)** Thomas J. Sienkewicz.

27

Duo Dōna

Augustus Prīmae Portae

Lectiō Prīma

Antequam Legis

The banquet marks a major turning point in the lives of the *Servīliī*. If his gift is well received, Servilius will surely have Augustus' support as he runs for praetor in the upcoming elections. Servilia, with Antonius in disgrace, has some hope of fulfilling her love interest in Cordus, while, for Marcus, this represents a sort of "coming out party" in front of Rome's most influential people. After the dinner is over, the entire crowd moves to the *peristȳlium* for the presentation of Servilius' gift to the emperor.

In this *lectiō* you also get a summary of the entire **perfect passive system**.

The Perfect Passive System

It may seem like a lot of work to look at the entire perfect passive system all at once, but it is not. Remember that the **perfect active system** was so called because it contained three tenses that shared the perfect stem—the perfect, pluperfect, and future perfect.

The passive system is similar, in that all three use the perfect passive participle (P^3) and a form of *sum* to form their passive tenses. Remember the perfect passive participle is the 4th principal part.

GRAMMATICA
The Perfect Passive System
The Perfect System of Deponent Verbs
The Verb *Videor*

MŌRĒS RŌMĀNĪ
Lux et Pater Patriae

LATĪNA HODIERNA
Pater Patriae Americānus

ORBIS TERRĀRUM RŌMĀNUS
Viae Rōmānae

ANGULUS GRAMMATICUS
Personal Pronouns in the Genitive Case

LECTIŌNĒS:
DŌNUM PRAECIPUUM
and
INFANS NOVUS

Servilius ceremoniously presents his gift for Augustus, and Licinia's baby is born.

TENSE	FORMATION	EXAMPLE	TRANSLATION
Perfect Passive	P^3 + **present** of *sum*	captus es vocāta est monitum est	you **have been** captured she **has been** called it **has been** advised
Pluperfect Passive	P^3 + **imperfect** of *sum*	audītae erāmus ductus erās capta erant	we **had been** heard you **had been** led they **had been** captured
Future Perfect Passive	P^3 + **future** of *sum*	vocātī eritis monitae erunt captum erit	you all **will have been** called they **will have been** warned it **will have been** captured

345

From *Disce! An Introductory Latin Course, volume 2*, First Edition. Francesco Bonavita. Copyright © 2011 by Pearson Education, Inc. Published by Pearson Prentice Hall. All rights reserved.

Note that these verb forms show gender as well as tense and number. So *captus est* means "he has been captured" and *capta est* means "she has been captured."

EXERCEĀMUS!

27-1 **Practicing the Perfect Passive System**

As you read *Lectiō Prīma*, be on the lookout for the forms in **bold**. These forms are passive. Your task is to find an example of the tenses asked for. Then translate the form you found. Be sure to include the line number. They do not necessarily appear in order. Follow the model.

	Passive Form to Find	Line	Form	Translation
→	perfect, 3rd pl. neuter	3	dicta sunt	they were said

1. perfect 3rd sing. neuter

2. perfect 3rd sing. fem.

3. perfect, 3rd pl. masc.

4. perfect, 2nd pl. masc.

5. pluperfect 3rd sing. fem.

6. pluperfect 3rd pl. neuter

7. future perfect 3rd sing. neuter

🔊 DŌNUM PRAECIPUUM

Iullō Antōniō ēbriō ē iānuīs domūs Servīliī expulsō, Servīlius īrātus et vexātus ad convīvium revēnit. Postquam omnēs hospitēs in peristȳlium **vocātī sunt**, ā Servīliō haec verba **dicta sunt**:

"Hospitēs praeclārī, mihi valdē placet quod vōs omnēs apud mē hāc nocte
5 **congregātī estis**. Nunc, Augustō duce, Rōma nostra—immō tōta Ītalia—post illōs annōs, in quibus multī nostrōrum patrum et fīliōrum **necātī sunt**, pācem et serēnitātem habet. Nōs omnēs—dīvitēs aut pauperī, cīvēs aut mīlitēs, in Urbe aut rurī, in Ītaliā aut in prōvinciīs habitantēs—Augustō nostrō, patrī patriae, grātiās maximās agere oportet. Ergō dōnum praecipuum Augustō ā mē **parātum est**.

10 "Nūper in Aegyptum itinere factō hoc libellum rārissimum ā mē **inventum est**. Haec papȳrus, quam nunc in manibus meīs teneō, omnēs versūs carminis Callimachī, *Aetia* nōmine, continet. Antīquissima est, ut opīnor, ē bibliothēcā Alexandrīnā, cuius pars, ut scītis, in bellō **combusta est**. Haec papȳrus (nesciō quōmodo) ex igne **servāta erat** et ā mē magnī pretiī **empta** et Rōmam
15 **transportāta est**. Hanc papȳrum ipsam Augustō nostrō dōnāre volō. Sī dōnum meum, quidquid est, ab Augustō **acceptum erit**, mihi et familiae meae bonum erit."

Hīs dictīs, sē ad Maecēnātemque Polliumque Servīlius vertēns, "Sī vōbīs placet," inquit, "hunc libellum dūcī nostrō ferte prō omnibus quae prō nōbīs fēcit!"

20 Papȳrus **recepta est** ā hīs vīrīs illūstribus. Attonitī atque pergrātī papȳrum statim legere incēpērunt. Paulō post Servīlius perlaetus rīsit et "Fortasse papȳrus iam satis **lecta est**," inquit, "Nunc bibāmus."

Postquam, omnibus volentibus, versūs paucī praeclārōrum poētārum **audītī sunt**.

Dēsuper, per fenestram, Servīlia et Lūcius omnia quae in peristȳliō **dicta et facta erant** audīvērunt et vīdērunt.

Lūcius sorōrem rīdentem vīdit et rogāvit: "Servīlia, cūr tam perlaeta es? Quā dē causā?"

25 Servīlia respondit: "Cūr laeta sum? Audī, Lūcī, audī. Hāc nocte omnia mīrābilissima quae **dicta sunt** audīre potuimus. A nōbīs carmina optima optimōrum poētārum **audīta sunt**. In nūllā aliā domō Rōmānā tam praeclārus conventus poētārum scrīptōrumque hodiē **inventus est**! Et Līvius ipse dē librō novō dē historiā Rōmānā lēgit! Et, ecce! Etiam nunc Cordum meum ē hāc fenestrā clārē vidēre possum!"

Dēsuper, per fenestram, Servīlia et Lūcius omnia quae in peristȳliō dicta et facta erant audīvērunt et vīdērunt.

🔊 VERBA ŪTENDA

attonitus, -a, -um
   astonished, amazed
audiāmus "Let's listen!"
bibāmus "Let's drink!"
***bibliothēca, -ae* f. library**
***cīvis, cīvis* m./f. citizen**
clārē clearly
combūrō, combūrere, com-
   bussī, combustus burn
congregō (1) gather
contineō, continēre, continuī,
   contentum contain
dōnō (1) present as a gift
***dux, ducis* m. leader**
***ēbrius, -a, -um* drunk**
expellō, expellere, expulī,
   expulsum throw out
immō rather, more precisely
libellum, -ī n. little book

Līvius, -iī m. Livy, the
   historian
nesciō, nescīre, nescīvī/
   nesciī, nescitum not
   know
opīnor, opīnārī, opīnātus
   sum think, believe
***papȳrus, -ī* f. papyrus**
***patria, -ae* f. country,**
   fatherland
***pax, pācis* f. peace**
pergrātus, -a, -um very
   agreeable
***perlaetus, -a, -um* very**
   happy
praecipuus, -a, -um
   special, particular
prōvincia, -ae f. province
***rārus, -a, -um* rare, thin**

recipiō, recipere, recēpī,
   receptum accept, receive
rurī "in the country;" note
   the lack of a preposition
satis enough
***scriptor, -ōris* m. writer**
serēnitās, -ātis f. cheerful
   tranquility
***servō* (1) save, protect; ob-**
   serve, pay attention to
***transportō* (1) carry**
   across, convey,
   transport
ut as
***versus, -ūs* m. verse, line of**
   poetry
videor, vidērī, vīsus sum
   seem, appear; be seen;
   vīsī sunt "they seemed"

POSTQUAM LEGISTĪ

1. Why does Servilius think that the reign of Augustus has been good for Rome?
2. How does Servilius say that the papyrus came from Egypt to Rome?
3. With what sort of entertainment does the dinner party end?
4. What does Servilia's reaction to the evening's activities tell us about her intellectual interests?
5. What does Servilia hope will happen to her personally as a result of the evening?

Grammatica A

The Perfect Passive System

Perfect passive verbs are formed by combining the perfect passive participle (P³) with forms of the verb *sum*.

Since the P³ is a 2-1-2 adjective, it must GNC with the subject. Thus:

- *Fēmina Servīlia vocāta est*
- *Vir Servīlius vocātus est.*
- *Animal canis vocātum est.*

Papȳrus

Now note how the forms change and how the tenses are translated:

Perfect Passive	
vocātus, -a, -um sum	I have been called, I was called
vocātus, -a, -um es	you have been called, you were called
vocātus, -a, -um est	he/she/it has been called
vocātī, -ae, -a sumus	we have been called
vocātī, -ae, -a estis	you have been called
vocātī, -ae, -a sunt	they have been called
Pluperfect Passive	
vocātus, -a, -um eram	I had been called
vocātus, -a, -um erās	you had been called
vocātus, -a, -um erat	he/she/it had been called
vocātī, -ae, -a erāmus	we had been called
vocātī, -ae, -a erātis	you had been called
vocātī, -ae, -a erant	they had been called
Future Perfect Passive	
vocātus, -a, -um erō	I will have been called
vocātus, -a, -um eris	you will have been called
vocātus, -a, -um erit	he/she/it will have been called
vocātī, -ae, -a erimus	we will have been called
vocātī, -ae, -a eritis	you will have been called
vocātī, -ae, -a erunt	they will have been called

The **perfect passive infinitive** of *vocō* is *vocātum esse* (to have been called). There are no pluperfect or future perfect passive infinitives.

EXERCEĀMUS!

27-2 Practicing the Perfect Passive System

Using the chart as a guide, translate the verbs into tenses of the perfect passive system as directed. The P³ is given in parentheses to help you. Follow the model. Watch out for gender and number.

→ he has been warned (*monitus, -a, -um*)   *monitus est*
    had been warned   *monitus erat*
    will have been warned   *monitus erit*

1. we (masc.) had been led (*ductus, -a, -um*)
    have been led

2. Valeria, you will have been seized (*captus, -a, -um*)
    had been seized

3. they (neuter) had been heard (*audītus, -a, -um*)
    have been heard

4. I (fem.) was loved (*amātus, -a, -um*)
    had been loved

5. it will have been given (*datus, -a, -um*)
      had been given

6. you (pl. masc.) have been prepared (*parātus, -a, -um*)
            will have been prepared

7. you (pl. fem.) had been sent (*missus*)
         were sent

8. they (neuter) had been carried across (*transportātus, -a, -um*)
         will have been carried across

Lectiō Secunda

Antequam Legis

In this *lectiō* Licinia's baby is born. As you read, note how Medea the midwife cuts the umbilical cord, cleans the infant, and puts it naked on the floor. Aelius then picks the infant up. This was a formal Roman custom requiring the *pater familiās*, in this case Aelius, either to pick up the child and acknowledge it as a member of the family or to leave it on the ground. If the newborn child were not picked up, it did not legally belong to the father and had no legal rights. Such a child could be given away, abandoned, or even sold into slavery. Do you think Aelius will accept this child as his own?

As you read, you will see deponent verbs in tenses of the perfect passive system. You will also learn how the passive forms of *videō* are used in Latin.

The Perfect System of Deponent Verbs

Do you remember the saying for deponent verbs: "Looks passive, isn't"? Well, that is all there is to it. Perfect deponents in the *lectiō* are marked in **bold**. When you see one, be sure to translate it actively.

The Verb *Videor*

The passive of *videō* is rather like a deponent. *Videor* should mean "I am seen, you are seen," etc. This meaning can occur occasionally, but the more common meaning of *videor, vidērī* is to "seem" or "appear." Thus: *Servīlia! Laeta vidēris!* = "Servilia, you seem happy." When it is used in the 3rd person singular with a dative and an infinitive, this verb can mean "it seems like a good idea" as in *mihi abīre vidēbātur*, "It seemed like a good idea for me to leave." All the forms of *videor* are marked in ***bold italics*** in the *lectiō*, but try translating a few more examples in the following exercise before you start reading.

EXERCEĀMUS!

27-3 **Translating Forms of *Videor***

All of the following phrases marked in ***bold italics*** in *Lectiō Secunda* use forms of *videor*. Match the phrase in column A with its translation in column B.

	A		B
_____	1. perlaeta vidēris	A.	He seems terrible.
_____	2. laeta videor	B.	I appear happy.
_____	3. laborāre vīsa est	C.	The mother seems healthy.
_____	4. puer sānus vīsus est	D.	She seemed to be laboring.
_____	5. terribilis vidētur	E.	You seem very happy.
_____	6. māter sāna vidētur	F.	It seems good for me to hear everything.
_____	7. omnia quiēta vīsa sunt	G.	Everything seemed quiet.
_____	8. mihi audīre omnia vidētur	H.	The boy seemed healthy.

🔊 INFANS NOVUS

In aliā parte urbis, in cellā squālidā in Subūrā, familia Valeriae anxiē nōn carmina sed infantem exspectābat. Licinia, in sellā sedēns, dolōre terribili **passa est**. Mēdēa, omnibus instrūmentīs et herbīs suīs ūtēns, Liciniae et infantī auxilium dare **conāta est**.

Multās post horās, vāgītus fortis infantis sānī atque fortis per insulam audītus est.
5 Infans puer est et sānus *vīsus est*. Umbilīcus amputātus est et infans ab obstetrīce
ablūtus est. Tunc, ut mōs māiōrum est, in terrā nūdus positus est et, brevī tempore sōlus
iacēns, fortiter clāmābat dōnec pater infantem in manibus sublevāvit.

Aelius laetus **locutus est**: "Mī filī, pater tuus sum et tū fīlius meus es. Egō
tē amābō et tuēbor. Nunc, mī filī, dormī in gremiō mātris."

10 Hīs dictīs, Aelius infantem Liciniae dedit et ā mātre infans novus
nūtrītus est. Valeria et Plōtia, dulce rīdentēs, nepōtem et pronepōtem
admirātae sunt et Plōtia **ēlocuta est**: "Licinia, nōn multō post, quia anus
sum, moriar—sed laeta moriar. Nunc quod hunc meum pronepōtem
vīdī, mors nōn tam terribilis *vidēbitur*. Et tū, pater Aelī, tū quoque
15 perlaetus *vidēris*!"

Licinia, quamquam fessa est, infantem suum accipit et eī mammam
offerēns eum lactāre **hortāta est**, hoc dulce et lēne carmen cantāns:

Lalla, lalla, lalla!

Ī, puer, aut dormī aut lactā.

20 Dēmum et māter et infans dormiēbant et omnia quiēta *vīsa sunt*. Nunc Mēdēae discēdere *vidēbātur*. Valeria
Mēdēam ad iānuam **secūta est** et ei nummōs dedit. Mēdēa exiēns **pollicita est**: "Sī febris Liciniam nōn cēperit, salva
erit. Partus facilis erat et māter sāna *vidētur*." Tunc addidit: "Sed, cavē febrem!" Talia dīcēns, Mēdēa domum **reversa
est**.

Mox silentium familiam fessam tenēbat et omnēs dormiēbant, Valeria Plōtiaque in ūnā cellā et Aelius Liciniaque
25 in aliā dormīvērunt. Flāvia, postquam omnia mundāvit, ut semper, prō iānuā cellae, in quā Aelius, Licinia et nunc
parvus infans dormiēbant, iacēbat.

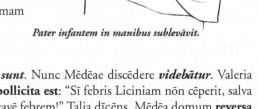

Pater infantem in manibus sublevāvit.

🔊 VERBA ŪTENDA

abluō, abluere, abluī,
ablūtum wash,
cleanse
amputō (1) cut off
anus, -ūs f. old woman
cantō (1) sing
caveō, cavēre, cāvī, cautum
beware
dōnec as long as, until
febris, febris f. fever
gremium, iī n. lap
herba, -ae f. herb
Ī imperative of *eo;* here,
"come now"

instrūmentum, -ī n. tool,
instrument
lactō (1) nurse
lalla exclamation; calming
sound
lēnis, lēne smooth, soft,
mild
mamma, -ae f. breast
mundō (1) clean
nepōs, nepōtis
m. grandson,
grandchild, descendant
nummus, -ī m. coin,
money

nūtriō, nūtrīre, nūtrīvī/nūtriī,
nūtrītum nurse, nourish
partus, -ūs m. child
birth
perlaetus, -a, -um very
happy
pronepōs, -nepōtis m.
great-grandson
quamquam
although, yet
squālidus, -a, -um dirty,
filthy
sublevō (1) lift, raise,
support

terribilis, terribile
frightening, terrible
tueor, tuērī, tuitus sum look
at, watch over
umbilīcus, -ī m. navel,
umbilical cord
ut as
vāgītus, -ūs m. cry, wail
videor, vidērī,
vīsus sum seem,
appear; be seen
vidētur (impersonal
+ inf.) it seems
good

POSTQUAM LEGISTĪ

1. Compare the description of childbirth in this reading to modern birthing customs and practices.
2. What does the midwife Medea do with the child after it is born? What does his father Aelius do? How does this compare to modern American practice?
3. Why does Plotia say she will now die happy?
4. What danger does Medea warn Aelius about as she leaves the house? Is this a concern today for women who have just given birth?

Gemma

Here are two other words where pronunciation, macrons, and declension endings matter: *anus, -ūs* f. old woman; *ānus, ānī* m. ring

Grammatica B

The Perfect System of Deponent Verbs

Now that you know about the 4th principal part of regular verbs, you can better understand why deponent verbs like *sequor* have only three principal parts. The form *secūtus sum* includes the perfect passive participle *secūtus* ("having been" followed) and means "I followed."
Here is how it works:

Gemma

The Latin lullaby is from the scholiast (a medieval commentator) to Persius' *Satires* 3.116.

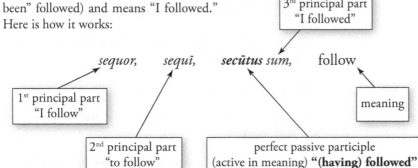

Deponent verbs form their perfect forms exactly as you would expect, by combining the P³ with the appropriate form of the verb *sum*. The only thing you have to remember is to translate this passive form in the active voice. Here is the perfect system of *cōnor* to use as a guide for all other deponent verbs.

CŌNOR, CŌNĀRĪ, CŌNĀTUS SUM			
Perfect Passive		**Pluperfect Passive**	
cōnātus, -a, -um sum	I have tried	cōnātus, -a, -um eram	I had tried
cōnātus, -a, -um es	you have tried	cōnātus, -a, -um erās	you had tried
cōnātus, -a, -um est	he/she/it has tried	cōnātus, -a, -um erat	he/she/it had tried
cōnātī, -ae, -a sumus	we have tried	cōnātī, -ae, -a erāmus	we had tried
cōnātī, -ae, -a estis	you have tried	cōnātī, -ae, -a erātis	you had tried
cōnātī, -ae, -a sunt	they have tried	cōnātī, -ae, -a erant	they had tried

Future Perfect Passive	
cōnātus, -a, -um erō	I will have tried
cōnātus, -a, -um eris	you will have tried
cōnātus, -a, -um erit	he/she/it will have tried
cōnātī, -ae, -a erimus	we will have tried
cōnātī, -ae, -a eritis	you will have tried
cōnātī, -ae, -a erunt	they will have tried

EXERCEĀMUS!

27-4 **Translating Perfect Deponents**

Which is the correct translation of the form? Remember, you have to know the 1ˢᵗ principal part of the verb in order to know if it is regular or deponent. When in doubt, use the *Verba Omnia*. Then be sure you have the right tense.

_____ 1. *cōnātus est*   a. he was tried; b. he tried; c. he had tried; d. he had been tried

_____ 2. *veritī erātis*   a. you were afraid; b. you had been afraid; c. you were feared; d. you had been feared

_____ 3. *secūta erō*   a. I will follow; b. I will have followed; c. I will be followed

_____ 4. *missae sumus*   a. we are sending; b. we have been sent; c. we sent

_____ 5. *datum erat*   a. it had been given; b. it gave; c. it had given; d. it was given

_____ 6. *arbitrātus erit*   a. he will have been thought; b. he will have thought; c. he is thought; d. he had been thought

_____ 7. *ausī sunt*   a. they were dared; b. they are daring; c. they will dare; d. they dared

_____ 8. *secutī sumus*   a. we followed; b. we have been followed; c. we had been followed; d. we will have followed

_____ 9. *ingressum erat*   a. it had been entered; b. it entered; c. it will enter; d. it had entered

_____10. *admirātus es*   a. you were admired; b. you are admired; c. you admired; d. you are admiring

The Verb *Videor*

As you saw in *Lectiō Secunda*, the passive forms of *videō* usually have the special meaning "seem" or "appear" in English. In a sense, then, *videor* is deponent because it has passive forms but an active meaning. Keep in mind, however, that *videor* can, at least occasionally, be translated passively as "I am seen." Here is a summary of uses of *videor*:

• With an adjective: *laetus vidētur* "He appears happy."

• With a complementary infinitive: *audīre vidētur* "He appears to be listening."

• With an infinitive and a person in the dative, the 3ʳᵈ person singular can mean "it seems good": *mihi audīre vidētur* "Listening seems like a good idea to me."

It all depends on context. The forms of *videor, vidērī, vīsus sum* offer no surprises. It is conjugated like any 2ⁿᵈ conjugation verb. Here are some selected forms of *videor* in the perfect passive system. Note the variety of possible translations for each form.

Perfect Passive	
vīsus, -a, -um sum	I (have) seemed, appeared I have been seen, was seen
vīsī, -ae, -a sumus	we (have) seemed, appeared we have been seen, were seen
Pluperfect Passive	
vīsus, -a, -um eram	I had seemed, appeared I had been seen
vīsī, -ae, -a erāmus	we had seemed, appeared we had been seen
Future Perfect Passive	
vīsus, -a, -um erō	I will have seemed, appeared I will have been seen
vīsī, -ae, -a erimus	we will have seemed, appeared we will have been seen

EXERCEĀMUS!

27-5 Translating Forms of *Videor*

Now use the chart to expand your knowledge of *videor* by translating each of the following forms at least three ways. Follow the model. Pay attention to tense signs!

→ vidēmur we seem; we appear; we are seen

1. vidēbantur	5. videor	9. vīsa erunt
2. vidēbor	6. vīsae erātis	10. vidēbuntur
3. vīsī sunt	7. vidētur	11. vidēris
4. vidēbāminī	8. vidēbēris	12. vidēbar

Mōrēs Rōmānī

Lux et Pater Patriae

Many of the guests invited to Servilius' *cēna* were members of tightly-knit literary group. Horace, for example, addressed Iullus Antonius at the beginning of his *Ode* V.4, and Vergil dedicated his fourth eclogue to Asinius Pollio. In his fifth satire Horace described a trip he took from Rome to Usu. Brundisium with Vergil and Maecenas. And, as Servilius does at the banquet, all these poets frequently sang the praises of Augustus himself.

Here is an example of such praise from Horace (*Odes* IV.5). The grammar and vocabulary are not difficult, but the poetic word order is, so here it is in a slightly less confusing form. As you read, you should know that the emperor had left the city to lead a military expedition in the Alps from 16 B.C. to 13 B.C. You should also remember that Horace is addressing the emperor directly in this poem, so look out for vocatives (marked in bold) and 2nd person singular verbs and imperatives (both in italics):

> **Orte** dīvīs bonīs, **optime custōs** gentis Rōmulae, *abes* iam nimium diū;
> Pollicitus reditum mātūrum sanctō conciliō, *redī.*
> **Dux bone**, *redde* lūcem patriae tuae;
> Enim ubi tuus vultus, instar vēris, populō affulsit, diēs gratior it et sōlēs melius nitent.

🔊 VERBA ŪTENDA

affulgeō, affulgēre, affulsī
(+ dat.) shine on,
smile on
concilium, -iī n. council
= Roman senate
custōs, custōdis m. guard

dīvus, -ī m. god = *deus*
dux, ducis m. leader
gens, gentis f. family, tribe
instar indecl. (+ gen.) like,
equal
lux, lūcis f. light

mātūrus, -a, -um timely, early
nimium too, excessively
niteō, -ēre to shine
orior, orīrī, ortus sum
rise, be born
reditus, -ūs m. return

Rōmulus, -a, -um of
Romulus = Roman
sōl, sōlis m. sun = day
vēr, vēris n. springtime
vultus, vultūs m. face

Augustus Pater Patriae

When Horace refers to Augustus in his ode as *lux patriae tuae*, he is alluding to one of the titles Octavian assumed after he became the emperor Augustus, *pater patriae* "father of the country." The same title had previously been bestowed not only on Cicero but also on Julius Caesar. A succession of Roman emperors following Augustus bore the title, which was often abbreviated "P.P." on coins. You can see the full title on the coin of Augustus depicted at left. Around the edge of the coin is written the following:

> ### *DĪV F PATER PATRIAE CAESAR AUGUSTUS*

Roman devotion to the rights belonging to the father, be it of the country or the *familia*, was a well-established part of the *mōs māiōrum*. Both Marcus and Servilia were raised on the *mōs māiōrum* and are aware of its obligations. For Servilia this means that she would have to accept the husband chosen for her by her father even if she liked Cordus better.

Latīna Hodierna

Pater Patriae Americānus

The Founding Fathers were often identified with the great leaders of ancient Rome. As the first president of the United States, George Washington, like Cicero, Julius Caesar, and Augustus before him, was called "Father of His Country." For this reason, Horatio Greenough depicted George Washington in a classical pose for a statue originally installed in the U.S. Capitol Rotunda in 1841 and now in the Smithsonian Museum of American History.

This Roman view of the country and its leaders as **pater**nalistic comes into English in words like **patri**ot, **patri**otism, and **patri**otic (showing respect for the fatherland), which are all derived from *patria, -ae* f.

Pater Patriae Americānus

Greenough represents George Washington handing his sheathed sword back to the country as he retires as general and returns to his farm in Mt. Vernon, Virginia. When he was later called back to be the first president of the United States, he was compared to the famous Roman Cincinnatus, who in 457 B.C. was called from his plow to serve as dictator in the Romans' war against their neighbors. After the war, like Washington, Cincinnatus put aside his power to return to his farm.

In honor of Washington and in order to preserve the ideals of the American Revolution, the Society of the Cincinnati was founded in 1783. In 1790, the city of Cincinnati, Ohio, was named in honor of this society.

Orbis Terrārum Rōmānus

Viae Rōmānae

The term *umbilīcus*, as you have seen, refers to the navel as well as to the umbilical cord. It is also surprising to find that Rome had an *umbilīcus*. The Romans built a network of excellent roads that allowed government officials and armies to move quickly throughout the empire.

With their precision, they measured their roads from the *Milliārium Aureum* (Golden Milemarker) established under Augustus. All the roads of Rome were said to start here, and the monument recorded the distance in miles to various cities in the Empire. In the reign of Septimius Severus (193–211 A.D.) or later, the monumental column called the *Umbilīcus Urbis Rōmae* was erected in the Roman Forum to mark the center of the city and of the empire and may have replaced the *Milliārium*.

One of these roads was the *Via Flaminia,* which ran north and west from Rome to the Adriatic Sea. The road was built by Gaius Flaminius in 220 B.C. Romans tended to name roads after their builders. Mile markers (*milliāria*) such as the one depicted at right usually marked distance along these roads.

Prima Porta, where the famous statue of Augustus shown at the beginning of this chapter was located, was an important stop on the Via Flaminia. At Prima Porta Augustus' wife, Livia had a country villa, known today as Villa Liviae. Besides the statue of Augustus, the most famous finds in the excavation of this villa were some garden frescoes now on display in the Palazzo Massimo in Rome.

Umbilīcus Urbis Rōmae

Milliārium Rōmānum

QUID PUTĀS?

1. In his ode, Horace addresses Augustus as the "best guardian of the Roman state" and "light of the fatherland." Would Americans address their presidents in this way? Why or why not?
2. Horace writes his ode as a request that the emperor return home quickly from a stay abroad. In what media besides a poem might Americans discuss the travels of their president today?
3. Many Americans did not like Horatio Greenough's statue of George Washington. What do you think their objections were? Could such a statue be created today for a modern president? Why or why not?
4. Do you think Americans today look upon their country and government as a parent? Why or why not? If so, is it more like a father or a mother?
5. Are there any modern equivalents of the Romans' *Milliārium Aureum* or the *Umbilīcus Rōmae*? Why is it so important to have a standard distance marker?
6. Why do you think this chapter is called *Duo Dōna*?

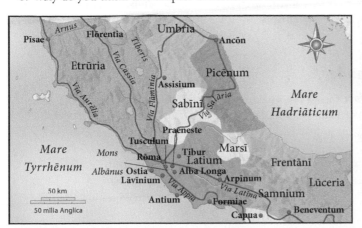

Rōma Umbilīcus Orbis Terrārum

Via Rōmāna in Hispaniā

EXERCEĀMUS!

27-6 Scrībāmus

The following passage is from Chapter 22. Change all the present passives to perfect passives.

> Ūnus leō hastā **vulnerātur** (1) et paulum recēdit. Mox duō aliī ā bestiāriīs **vulnerantur** (2) sed plūrēs leōnēs quam bestiāriī sunt et mox omnēs hī infortūnātī bestiāriī **necantur**.
>
> Tunc multī hippopotamī et crocodīlī ferōcēs in harēnam **dūcuntur** (3) et ā nānīs nūdīs **oppugnantur** (4). Intereā aliī nānī gregem gruum parmīs oppugnant.
>
> Post multās aliās venātiōnēs, in quibus plūrima animālia plūrimīque hominēs **necantur** (5), harēna sanguine et corporibus plēna est. Dum harēna **purgātur** (6), Marcus et Lūcius aliquid cibī emunt.

27-7 Colloquāmur

This speaking exercise requires groups of three. Using the adjectives from the *Verba Discenda*, follow these steps:

1. Student #1 makes up a question about Student #2. The sentence has to use *vidētur* and an adjective from the list below.

2. Student #2 makes a face or strikes a pose that is either what Student #1 said or its opposite. Thus, if Student #1 said that Student #2 looked happy, Student #2 could choose to look either happy or sad.

3. Student #3 then responds to the original question, saying that Student #2 does or does not look the way Student #1 suggested.

> → Classmate #1: Tristis Robertus **vidētur**?
> Classmate #2: smiles broadly
> Classmate #3: Nōn, Robertus non tristis sed laetus **vidētur**.

Ideally each group will have both male and female participants to allow for good GNCing practice. Students take turns being #1, #2, or #3.

tristis, triste	dormiēns	improbus, -a, -um
laetus, -a, -um	maestus, -a, -um	dulcis, -e
malus, -a, -um	fēlix, fēlicis	dīves, dīvitis
sānus, -a, -um	fortis, forte	mortuus, -a, -um
terribilis, terribile	territus, -a, -um	lēnis, lēne

27-8 Verba Discenda

Find the *Verbum Discendum* that is the source of each of the following words and phrases. Then use the meaning of the Latin word to define the English one. Follow the model.

→ Cantor: *Cantō*; one who sings

1. observatory
2. versify
3. anile
4. pacification
5. inscription
6. nepotism
7. incantation
8. inebriation
9. repatriate
10. lenient
11. civilization
12. rarify

🔊 VERBA DISCENDA

anus, -ūs f. old woman
[anile]

bibliothēca, -ae f. library

cantō (1) sing [incantation]

cīvis, cīvis m./f. citizen
[civility]

dōnec as long as, until

dux, ducis m. leader
[il Duce]

ēbrius, -a, -um drunk
[inebriation]

gremium, iī n. lap

instrūmentum, -ī n. tool,
instrument
[instrumentation]

lēnis, lēne smooth, soft,
mild [lenient]

nepōs, nepōtis m.
grandson, grandchild,
descendant [nepotism]

nummus, -ī m. coin, money

papȳrus, -ī f. papyrus

patria, -ae f. country,
fatherland [repatriate]

pax, pācis f. peace [pacify]

perlaetus, -a, -um very
happy

praecipuus, -a, -um
special, particular

quamquam although, yet

rārus, -a, -um rare; thin
[rarify]

scriptor, -ōris m. writer

servō (1) save, protect;
observe, pay attention
to [observation]

terribilis, terribile
frightening, terrible

transportō (1) carry
across, convey, trans-
port [transportation]

versus, -ūs m. verse, line of
poetry [versify]

videor, vidērī, vīsus sum
seem, appear;
be seen

vidētur impersonal
(+ inf.) it seems good

Angulus Grammaticus

Personal Pronouns in the Genitive Case

In Chapter 21 you consolidated your knowledge of Latin personal pronouns and noted that possession is expressed by adjectives in the 1st and 2nd persons and by either a pronoun or an adjective in the 3rd person (depending on the subject), as in *domus eius* (his/her house) but *domus mea* (my house). In the *Angulus Grammaticus* to Chapter 26 we talked more about using a 3rd person personal pronoun in the genitive case to express possession. This is unique to *eius, eōrum, eārum*.

The 1st and 2nd person pronouns (*meī, tuī, nostrum/nostrī, vestrum/vestrī*) can only be used as objective and partitive genitives (genitives of the whole). They cannot be used to express possession.

1. Use any form ending in *-ī* as an **objective genitive**:

> *memor meī* (mindful of me)
> *amor tuī* (love for you)
> *timor nostrī* (fear of us)
> *odium vestrī* (hatred for you)

2. Use *meī, tuī, nostrum*, and *vestrum* to express the **partitive genitive** (genitive of the whole):

> *pars meī* (part of me)
> *nēmō nostrum* (no one of us)

3. Use *nostrum* and *vestrum* instead of the possessive adjective when modified by *omnium*:

> *noster amor* (our love)
> *amor omnium nostrum* (the love of all of us)

Notā Bene: The phrases *noster amor* (our love) and *amor omnium nostrum* (the love of all of us) both mean that "we" are doing the loving. But compare *amor tuī* and *tuus amor*. In the former, "you" are being loved and in the latter "you" are doing the loving. Big difference! Perhaps *tuus amor tuī* (your love for yourself) will help you remember how this works.

Photo Credits

Page 345 (top) Photos.com; **page 345 (bottom)** Julia A. Sienkewicz; **page 346** Thomas J. Sienkewicz; **page 347** Ralf Juergen Kraft/ Shutterstock; **page 354 (top)** AKG—Images; **page 354 (bottom)** Julia A. Sienkewicz; **page 355 (top)** Victor M. Martinez; **page 355 (middle)** © Spectrum Colour Library/ Heritage—Images/ ImageState Media Partners Limited; **page 355 (bottom)** Quintanilla/ Shutterstock.

Labōrēs Herculis

From *Disce! An Introductory Latin Course, volume 2*, First Edition. Francesco Bonavita. Copyright © 2011 by Pearson Education, Inc. Published by Pearson Prentice Hall. All rights reserved.

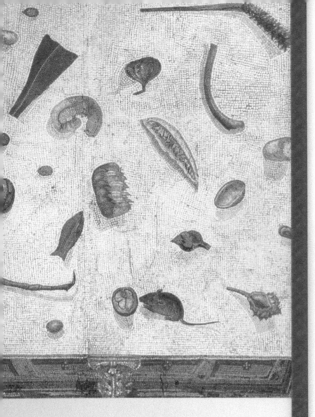

28

Labōrēs Herculis

Lectiō Prīma

Antequam Legis

An Augean Task

Xanthus and Rufus, two slaves, are cleaning up the Servilian peristyle after the big feast. Xanthus compares the enormity of this task to Hercules' sixth labor, the cleaning of the Augean stables in Elis, near Olympia. Rufus is German (his name means "reddish," referring to his hair) and Xanthus, whose name means "Blondie," is a Greek from Sicily.

Hercules, you may remember, went mad and killed his family. The Delphic oracle told him that he could atone for this by completing labors for King Eurystheus of Mycenae. In this labor he has to clean out, in a single day, an enormous pile of waste from the stables of King Augeas who lived in Elis, a city in the Peloponnesus area of Greece. He devised an ingenious way to do this, as you will see.

Passive Review

This chapter provides a review of all passive tenses. Remember that passives, deponents, and semi-deponents can look alike, so be sure what kind of verb you are dealing with before you translate.

Pavīmentum in Triclīniō
Heracleitus. "The Unswept Floor," mosaic variant of a 2nd-century BCE painting by Sosos of Pergamon. 2nd century CE. Musei Vaticani, Museo Gregoriano Profano, ex Lateranense, Rome. Studio Canali, Milano, Italy, NY

GRAMMATICA
Review of All Passive Tenses
Reflexive Verb Expressions
Review of Deponent Verbs: All Tenses

MŌRĒS RŌMĀNĪ
Deī Opificēs: Vulcānus et Minerva

LATĪNA HODIERNA
Scitisne?

ORBIS TERRĀRUM RŌMĀNUS
Aetna et Sicilia

ANGULUS GRAMMATICUS
More on Voice

LECTIŌNĒS:
OPERA SORDIDA
and
AVĒS UBĪQUE

Servants in the Servilian household clean up from the feast and compare their tasks with two labors of Hercules.

Review the following formulas for forming the passives:

PRESENT						
1, 2 Pr. St. +	or ris tur	mur minī ntur	3, 4 SPS +	or eris itur	imur iminī untur
				3rd: i + i = i *caperis*, not *capieris* (3rd -io) 4th: i + i = ī		
IMPERFECT						
1, 2 Pr. St. +	bar bāris bātur	bāmur bāminī bantur	3, 4 SPS +	ēbar ēbāris ēbātur	ēbāmur ēbāminī ēbantur
FUTURE						
1, 2 Pr. St. +	bor beris bitur	bimur biminī buntur	3, 4 SPS +	ar ēris ētur	ēmur ēminī entur
PERFECT						
1, 2, 3, 4	P^3 +		sum es est	sumus estis sunt	
PLUPERFECT						
1, 2, 3, 4	P^3 +		eram erās erat	erāmus erātis erant	
FUTURE PERFECT						
1, 2, 3, 4	P^3 +		erō eris erit	erimus eritis erunt	

Notā Bene:

- Pr. St. = present stem = 2nd principal part – -*re*
- SPS = Short Present Stem = 1st principal part – -*ō*
- P^3 = 4th principal part with -*us*, -*a*, -*um* endings. (Remember that it GNC's with the subject of the sentence.)

All regular passive verbs are marked in **bold** in *Lectiō Prīma*.

Reflexive Idioms

As you read this *lectiō*, watch for a number of verbal idioms that use the reflexive pronouns you learned earlier (especially *mē/nōs*, *tē/vōs*, and *sē*). These idioms are explained briefly in the *Verba Ūtenda* and in more detail after the *lectiō*.

EXERCEĀMUS!

28-1 Pre-Reading Exercise

Before you translate *Lectiō Prīma*, just scan it to get the gist, then try to answer the following questions. You will find you can then translate the *lectiō* more quickly.

1. Which rooms in Servilius' house particularly require cleaning after the banquet?

2. Why is the slave Rufus unfamiliar with the labors of Hercules?

3. Why was cleaning the Augean Stables such a difficult task?

4. Why was Eurystheus eager to give Hercules such a task?

5. In what way does Hercules clean out the stables?

6. What joke does Rufus make after the story is finished?

7. Find ten passive or deponent verbs marked in **bold** and translate them into English.

🔊 OPERA SORDIDA

In colle Vīminālī, apud Servīliōs, Servīlius et Caecilia bene dormiunt sed servī per domum labōrant. Aliī culīnam aliī trīclīnium purgant et multī in peristȳliō labōrant, sed omnēs fessī et ınfēlicēs fīunt. Rē vērā īrascuntur. Duo servī inter sē colloquuntur.

"Herculēs in Stabulō Augēō" *ā Francisco Zurbarán (1598–1664) picta.*

5 Rūfus: "Dī immortālēs!" clāmat, "Hoc peristȳlium sordidissimum est. Ecce! Cibus et pōcula ubīque! Sīc semper est—homō dīves, pavīmentum sordidum! Dominī epulantur et nōs servī squālōrem magnum purgāre **cōgimur**!"

Xanthus: "Tē gere placidē, amīce. Nōn solum ā servīs sed etiam ā
10 deō opus sordidum **agitur**. Mementō Herculis! Locus sordidissimus ab illō ōlim **purgātus est**!"

Rūfus: "Hercule! Dīc mihi dē hōc labōre! Ut scīs, Germānicus sum et paulum dē istīs tuīs fābulīs Graecīs sciō. Narrā! Tē narrante, tempus celerius fugiet!"

15 Xanthus: "Scisne nihil dē deīs nostrīs? Terribile est!"

Hīs dictīs, Xanthus narrāre incipit:

"Ōlim labor Herculis gravissimus ā rēge malō Eurystheō **impositus est**. Augēās quīdam, quī illō tempore regnum in Elide obtinēbat, tria mīlia bovum habēbat. Hī in stabulō ingentis magnitūdinis **inclūdēbantur**. Stabulum autem stercore ac squālōre **obsitum erat**, neque enim ad hoc tempus umquam **purgātum erat**. Hoc Herculēs intrā
20 spatium unīus diēī purgāre **iussus est**."

Eurystheus, "Nūllō modō," inquit, "tanta stabula ab ūnō virō in diē singulārī **purgārī** possunt! Tantus labor numquam et ab Hercule **conficiētur**."

Herculēs, etsī rēs erat difficilis, sē gessit bene et negōtium suscēpit. Prīmum magnō labōre et Minervā adiuvante, fossa XVIII pedum **ducta est**, per quam flūminis aqua dē montibus ad mūrum stabulī **perdūcēbātur**. Tum mūrō
25 ruptō, aqua in stabulum **immissa est**. Talī modō contrā opīniōnem omnium opus confēcit."

Fābulā narrātā, Xanthus "Intelligisne?" inquit. "Herculēs numquam dīxit 'Cur hoc agere **cōgor**?' Et nunc ille dīvus est!"

Rūfus, labōris dēsinēns, rīsit. "Manē hīc, Xanthe! Mox revertar! Mē flūmen magnum invenīre oportet! Tunc facilius hoc peristȳlium Augēum purgāre poterimus!" Tunc ad cisternam sē contulit.

🔊 VERBA ŪTENDA

bōs, bovis m./f. cow, bull, ox

cisterna, -ae f. cistern, well

collis, collis m. hill

conferō, conferre, contulī, collātum bring together, collect; sē conferre go (betake oneself); talk together

conficiō, conficere, confēcī confectum do, accomplish, complete

dēsinō, dēsinere, dēsīvī/ dēsīī, dēsitum (+ gen.) cease, desist (from)

Dī = deī

epulor, epulārī, epulātus sum feast, dine

et here: "even"

etsī although, even if

ferō: sē ferre go (betake oneself)

flūmen, flūminis n. river

fossa, -ae, f. ditch

gerō: sē gerere act, (conduct oneself)

Graecus, -a, -um Greek

Hercule By Hercules!

immittō, immittere, immīsī, immissum send to

immortālis, immortāle immortal

impōnō, impōnere, imposuī impositum (+ dat.) assign, impose upon

inclūdō, inclūdere, inclūsī, inclūsum enclose

infēlix, infēlicis unhappy, unfortunate

ingens, ingentis huge

īrascor, īrascī, īrātus sum be angry

iubeō, iubēre, iussī, iussum order

magnitūdō, -inis f. greatness

mementō! Remember!

mīlia thousands

Minerva, -ae f. Minerva, goddess of wisdom

mons, montis m. mountain

mūrus, -ī m. wall

neque and not; neque … neque neither … nor

obserō, obserere, obsēvī, obsitum cover

obtineō, obtinēre, obtinuī, obtentum hold, support

opīniō, -ōnis f. belief, opinion

paulum a little, somewhat

pavīmentum, -ī n. ground, floor

perdūcō, perdūcere, perdūxī, perductum lead through, conduct

pēs, pedis m. foot

prīmum first, at first

regnum, -ī n. kingdom

revertor, revertī, reversus sum turn back, return

rumpō, rumpere, rūpī, ruptum break, burst, break down

sciō, scīre, scīvī/sciī, scītum know, know about

singulāris, -e single

sordidus, -a, -um filthy

spatium, -iī n. space

squālor, squālōris m. filth

stabulum, -ī n. stable

stercus, stercoris n. dung, excrement

suscipiō, suscipere, suscēpī, susceptum accept

tantus, -a, -um so great

ubīque everywhere

umquam ever

ut as

POSTQUAM LĒGISTĪ

1. This *lectiō* describes the clean-up process after Servilius' banquet. Compare this task with the way such clean-ups occur today in your house, in a hotel room or after a catered banquet. Which of these clean-ups is most like the one in the *lectiō*? Why?

2. Use this *lectiō* to describe the relationship between master and slave in ancient Rome.

3. Explain the expression *homō dīves, pavīmentum sordidum*. In what way is this expression true in the story? In what way(s) might this expression still be true today?

4. Hercules had to clean the Augean Stables in a single day. Can you think of similar assignments from the world of fairy tales?

Grammatica A

Review of All Passive Tenses

The following chart contains all the passive forms of the 1st conjugation verb *vocō*:

1ST CONJUGATION						
Present System			**Perfect System**			
Singular						
Person	Present	Imperfect	Future	Perfect	Pluperfect	Future Perfect
1st	vocor	vocābar	vocābor	vocātus, -a, -um sum	vocātus, -a, -um eram	vocātus, -a, -um erō
2nd	vocāris	vocābāris	vocāberis	vocātus, -a, -um es	vocātus, -a, -um erās	vocātus, -a, -um eris
3rd	vocātur	vocābātur	vocābitur	vocātus, -a, -um est	vocātus, -a, -um erat	vocātus, -a, -um erit
Plural						
1st	vocāmur	vocābāmur	vocābimur	vocātī, -ae, -a sumus	vocātī, -ae, -a erāmus	vocātī, -ae, -a erimus
2nd	vocāminī	vocābāminī	vocābiminī	vocātī, -ae, -a estis	vocātī, -ae, -a erātis	vocātī, -ae, -a eritis
3rd	vocantur	vocābantur	vocābuntur	vocātī, -ae, -a sunt	vocātī, -ae, -a erant	vocātī, -ae, -a erunt

EXERCEĀMUS!

28-2 Passive Synopses

Write the same person and number of a verb (e.g., 1st plural) in the tenses indicated. This exercise, called a "synopsis," will help you practice the passive forms of verbs in many conjugations. We tell you the person and number to use. Gender is indicated by the subject supplied. Use the completed first synopsis as a model.

3RD PLURAL OF *VOCŌ* (1) "FĒMINAE"		
Tense	**Latin**	**English Translation**
Present	vocantur	they are called
Imperfect	vocābantur	they were being called
Future	vocābuntur	they will be called
Perfect	vocātae sunt	they have been called
Pluperfect	vocātae erant	they had been called
Future Perfect	vocātae erunt	they will have been called

2ND SINGULAR OF *MONEŌ, MONĒRE, MONUĪ, MONITUM* "MARCUS"		
Tense	**Latin**	**English Translation**
Present	monēris	you are warned
Imperfect		you were being warned
Future	monēberis	
Perfect		you have been warned
Pluperfect		
Future Perfect		you will have been warned

1ST PLURAL OF *DŪCŌ, DŪCERE, DŪXĪ, DUCTUM* "VALERIA ET LICINIA"		
Tense	Latin	English Translation
Present	dūcimur	we are led
Imperfect		
Future		we will be led
Perfect		
Pluperfect		we had been led
Future Perfect		

2ND PLURAL OF *AUDIŌ, AUDĪRE, AUDĪVĪ, AUDĪTUM* "XANTHUS ET RŪFUS"		
Tense	Latin	English Translation
Present		
Imperfect		
Future		
Perfect		
Pluperfect		
Future Perfect		

Reflexive Verb Expressions

As you review passive and deponent verbs in this chapter, this is a good opportunity to consider verbs in which the subject performs the action on himself or herself. These are called **reflexive verbs**. Some reflexive verbs are always used with reflexive pronouns as objects, and others can either have a noun or a reflexive pronoun for an object. Consider the verb *lavāre*:

- *Servī pōcula lavant.* The slaves wash the cups.
- *Marcus sē lavat.* Marcus washes up (washes himself).

Now consider these three reflexive verbs in the *lectiōnēs* in this chapter:

> *sē conferre* go (betake oneself)
> *sē ferre* go (betake oneself)
> *sē gerere* act (conduct oneself)

All three are based on verbs you already know (*ferō* and *gerō*) but have special meanings when used with reflexive pronouns. Such expressions are also called **idioms**. Notice how the reflexive pronoun can accompany all persons of the verb. Consider the expression: *sē ferre*:

mē ferō	I go (betake myself)
tē fers	you go
sē fert	he/she/it goes
nōs ferimus	we go
vōs fertis	you (all) go
sē ferunt	they go

While *mē ferō* literally means "I carry myself," this expression is not translated reflexively in English. We say simply, "I go." Now go back to *Lectiō Prīma* and find the reflexive expressions used there.

Lectiō Secunda

Antequam Legis

In this section Xanthus continues telling Rufus about the labors of Hercules. Here Xanthus describes the hero's encounter with the Stymphalian birds.

The Stymphalian Birds

In this labor Hercules must drive away the brass-beaked, man-eating birds that are devouring the inhabitants of a town called Stymphalus. He asks for help from Vulcan (Greek: Hephaestus), the blacksmith of the gods. You will remember that Aelius' slave is named Vulcanus.

Use this *lectiō* as an opportunity to consolidate what you have learned about deponent verbs.

Deponent Verb Review

Remember! "Looks passive, isn't." Just translate deponent verbs actively.
How can you tell a verb is deponent?

- **Principal parts** can help. If the 1ˢᵗ principal part ends in *-or*, it is deponent. If there are only three principal parts, the verb is probably deponent or semi-deponent.

- **Usage and context** can also help. For example, look at these two phrases from *Lectiō Prīma*:

Dominī **epulantur.**
Labor ā rēge **impositus est.**

You can tell at a glance that both *epulantur* and *impositus est* are passive in form, but consider their meanings and usage.

- The **ablative of agent** in *Labor ā rēge impositus est* shows you that the sentence is passive.

- Then there is common sense. Which translation makes more sense for *Dominī epulantur*. "The masters were dined upon" (passive meaning) or "The masters dined" (active meaning)?

So let context, usage, and common sense be your guides in identifying and translating deponent verbs.

EXERCEĀMUS!

28-3   Deponent or Regular Passive?

All verbs with passive endings in *Lectiō Secunda* are marked in **bold**. Some are deponents and some are regular passives. Use usage and context to find five deponent verbs and five regular passive verbs. Give the 1ˢᵗ principal part of each verb. Then translate the verb into English. Follow the model.

Line	Verb	1ˢᵗ PP	Type	Translation
1	verritur	verrō	regular passive	it is being swept
2	loquitur	loquor	deponent	he says

AVĒS UBĪQUE

In angulō peristȳliī pavīmentum ā Xanthō **verritur.** Subitō fortiter cachinnat et **loquitur:** "Rūfe, ecce! **Admirābār** ossa avium
ubīque in pavīmentō. In mentem fābula dē aliō Herculis labōre
vēnit. Audī."

5   Olim Eurystheus Herculī **allocūtus est.** "Labor sextus
tuus facillimus erit! Populī oppidum Stymphalum habitantēs
paucās avēs **verentur.** Tē hās avēs dispergere iubeō. Sī tē
gesseris bene et sī ad mē cum hīs avibus mortuīs **reversus eris,**
dīmidium labōrum tuōrum **conficiētur.** Tibi **polliceor.**" Post

Herculēs avēs Stymphalēs transfīgit.

10 paucōs diēs Herculēs ad oppidum Stymphalum **profectus est.** Hae avēs rostra aēnea habēbant et carne hominum
vescēbantur. Ille, postquam ad locum **aggressus est,** lacum **intuitus est;** in hōc autem lacū, quī nōn procul ab
oppidō erat, avēs habitābant. Sed avēs nōn facile **appropinquābantur;** lacus enim nōn ex aquā sed ē līmō cōnstitere
vīsus est. Herculēs igitur ad avēs neque pedibus neque nāviculā **aggredī** potuit.

       Herculēs "Quid," inquit, "faciam? Quōmodo illae avēs ā mē **capientur?** Avēs prīmum dē limō **agī** debent! Sed
15 quōmodo? Auxilium **requīritur!**"

       Tālibus **dictīs,** Herculēs ad Vulcānum sē contulit, et auxilium ab eō petīvit. Vulcānus (quī ā fabrīs maximē
colēbātur) crepundia quae ā deō ipsō ex aere **fabricāta erant** Herculī dedit. Herculēs ad lacum sē tulit et hīs
instrūmentīs **ūtēns** acrem crepitum fēcit. Statim avēs ē lacū perterritae **actae sunt.** Ille autem, dum āvolant, magnum numerum eārum sagittīs transfīxit et cum avibus mortuīs ad Eurystheum **reversus est.**"

20   Fābulā fīnītā, Rūfus **pollicitur:** "Hercule! sīcut hērōes Graecī, nōs ipsī hunc gregem maximum avium vincere
cōnābimur. Et nōbīs Vulcānus Minervaque ipsī auxilium dabunt. Ossa avium et alia scrūta relicta in focō
exūrāmus."

VERBA ŪTENDA

acer, acris, acre sharp
aēneus, -a, -um bronze
aes, aeris n. metal,
     especially copper or
     bronze
aggredior, aggredī, aggres-
     sus sum approach
angulus, -ī m. corner
***avis, avis* f. bird**
āvolō (1) fly away
cachinnō (1) laugh loudly
carō, carnis f. meat, flesh
colō, colere, coluī, cultum
     worship
conferō, conferre,
     contulī, collātum
     bring together,
     collect; *sē conferre*
     go (betake oneself);
     talk together

conficiō, conficere, confēcī
     ***confectum* do, accom-**
     plish, complete
consistō, consistere, constitī,
     constitum consist of
corpus, corporis n. body
crepitus, -ūs m. rattling
crepundia, -ōrum n. pl. rattle
dīmidium, -iī n. half
dispergō, dispergere, dispersī,
     dispersum scatter, disperse
exūrāmus "Let us burn"
***faber, fabrī* m. craftsman**
fabricō (1) make
***ferō: sē ferre* go (betake**
     oneself)
focus, -ī m. hearth
***gerō: sē gerere* act**
     (conduct oneself)
grex, gregis m. flock

iubeō, iubēre, iussī,
     ***iussum* order**
***lacus, -ūs* m. lake**
līmus, -ī m. mud, slime
nāvicula, -ae f. little boat
***neque* and not;** *neque ...*
     ***neque* neither ... nor**
numerus, -ī m. number
***oppidum, -ī* n. town**
***os, ossis* n. bone**
perferō, perferre, pertulī,
     perlātum convey
***prīmum* first, at first**
procul far, far away
proficiscor, proficiscī,
     ***profectus sum* set out,**
     depart
requīrō, requīrere, requīsīvī/
     requīsiī, requīsītum need,
     require

referō, referre, rettulī, relātum
     carry, bring back
revertor, revertī, reversus sum
     return
rostrum, -ī n. beak
***sagitta, -ae* f. arrow**
scrūta, -ōrum n. pl. trash
sextus, -a, -um sixth
Stymphalus, -ī m. Stymphalus,
     a Greek lake and town of
     the same name
transfīgō, transfīgere,
     transfīxī, transfīxum
     pierce through
***ubīque* everywhere**
ut as
verrō, verrere, verrī, versum
     sweep clean
vescor, vescī (+ abl.) take
     food, devour

POSTQUAM LĒGISTĪ

1. Why does Xanthus laugh while he is sweeping the floor of the peristyle?
2. What does Eurystheus promise Hercules?
3. What are the unusual characteristics of the Stymphalian birds?
4. What obstacle does Hercules face in dealing with these birds?
5. How does the god Vulcan help Hercules?
6. Who does Rufus suggest can help the servants in their task?

Grammatica B

Review of Deponent Verbs: All Tenses

The following chart provides all the forms of the 1st conjugation deponent verb *cōnor*.

	PRESENT SYSTEM			PERFECT SYSTEM		
				Singular		
Person	**Present**	**Imperfect**	**Future**	**Perfect**	**Pluperfect**	**Future Perfect**
1st	cōnor	cōnābar	cōnābor	cōnātus, -a, -um sum	cōnātus, -a, -um eram	cōnātus, -a, -um erō
2nd	cōnāris	cōnābāris	cōnāberis	cōnātus, -a, -um es	cōnātus, -a, -um erās	cōnātus, -a, -um eris
3rd	cōnātur	cōnābātur	cōnābitur	cōnātus, -a, -um est	cōnātus, -a, -um erat	cōnātus, -a, -um erit
				Plural		
1st	cōnāmur	cōnābāmur	cōnābimur	cōnātī, -ae, -a sumus	cōnātī, -ae, -a erāmus	cōnātī, -ae, -a erimus
2nd	cōnāminī	cōnābāminī	cōnābiminī	cōnātī, -ae, -a estis	cōnātī, -ae, -a erātis	cōnātī, -ae, -a eritis
3rd	cōnantur	cōnābantur	cōnābuntur	cōnātī, -ae, -a sunt	cōnātī, -ae, -a erant	cōnātī, -ae, -a erunt

EXERCEĀMUS!

28-4 Deponent Synopses

This exercise is exactly like 28-2. Remember that in some of the forms gender will be an issue! Fill in all the missing pieces.

3RD SINGULAR OF *CŌNOR, CŌNĀRĪ, CŌNĀTUS EST* "PUELLA"		
Tense	**Latin**	**English Translation**
Present	cōnātur	she tries
Imperfect	cōnābātur	
Future		she will try
Perfect	cōnāta est	
Pluperfect		she had tried
Future Perfect		

3RD PLURAL OF *POLLICEOR, POLLICĒRĪ, POLLICITUS SUM* "LICINIA ET VALERIA"

Tense	Latin	English Translation
Present	pollicentur	
Imperfect		
Future	pollicēbuntur	
Perfect		they have promised
Pluperfect		
Future Perfect		they will have promised

1ST PLURAL OF *SEQUOR, SEQUĪ, SECŪTUS SUM* "TŪ ET EGO"

Tense	Latin	English Translation
Present		we follow
Imperfect	sequēbāmur	
Future		
Perfect		we followed
Pluperfect		
Future Perfect		

2ND PLURAL OF *PRŌGREDIOR, PRŌGREDĪ, PRŌGRESSUS SUM* "PUERĪ"

Tense	Latin	English Translation
Present		
Imperfect		
Future		
Perfect		
Pluperfect		
Future Perfect		

Mōrēs Rōmānī

Deī Opificēs: Vulcānus et Minerva

Both gods who help Hercules in the labors narrated by Xanthus were patrons of arts and crafts. *Vulcānus, -ī* m. was the god of fire known to the Greeks as Hephaestus. *Minerva, -ae* f. was the goddess of arts and crafts known as Athena in Greece. Vulcan's forge was said to be in Mt. Aetna in Sicily. Here Vulcan made thunderbolts for Jupiter, the god of the sky, thunder, and lightning. Here Vulcan also made new armor for Aeneas at the request of Venus, the hero's mother. You can read about Aeneas' armor in Vergil's *Aeneid* 8. The Romans celebrated the feast of *Vulcānālia* on August 23. Vulcan was especially worshipped by craftsmen like Aelius. The "Steel City" of Birmingham, Alabama, celebrates Vulcan with a giant statue by Giuseppe Moretti (1857–1935), dedicated in 1904 and depicted at right.

Vulcānus Super Alabamam *statua aēnea ā Giuseppe Moretti (1857–1935)*

Minerva in Tennessee

Minerva was the goddess of wisdom, poets, actors, and physicians. Her most important temple was located on the Aventine Hill in Rome, but she was also worshipped along with Jupiter and Juno on the Capitoline Hill. A colossal statue of Minerva-Athena stands in the Parthenon in Nashville, Tennessee, a city which considers itself the "Athens of the South." Through her association with the Greek goddess Athena, Minerva was also associated with crafts, especially women's crafts like weaving. Ovid's tale of Minerva's competition with the mortal Arachne is told in his *Metamorphōsēs* VI:5–145. Here, Ovid describes how Minerva challenges Arachne to a weaving contest. The mortal woman works so well that, in the end, the goddess draws the contest to a close by transforming Arachne into the first spider. Here is how Ovid describes the transformation. Read the story in this simplified version with less poetic word order. All the words in bold are parts of Arachne's human body. Watch how they are changed into something else.

> **comae** dēflūxērunt, et cum comīs et **nārēs** et **aurēs** (dēflūxērunt),
> et **caput** fit minimum; quoque tōtō **corpore** parva est:
> **digitī** exīles in **latere** pro **crūribus** haerent;
> **venter** alia membra habet, dē quō tamen illa stāmen remittit
> et arānea tēlās antiquās exercet.

🔊 VERBA ŪTENDA

arānea, -ae f. spider	*exerceō, exercēre, exercuī,*	*nārēs, nārium* f. pl. nostrils
auris, auris f. ear	*exercitum* practice	*quīs = quibus* (poetic)
coma, comae f. hair	*exīlis, exīle* thin, small	*remittō, remittere, remīsī,*
crūs, crūris n. shin, leg	*haereō, haerēre, haesī,*	*remissum* send back
dēfluō, dēfluere, dēflūxī,	*haesum* cling to	*stāmen, stāminis* m. thread
dēflūxum	*latus, lateris* n. side	*tēla, -ae* f. loom, web
disappear	*membrum, -ī* n.	*venter, ventris* m. belly,
digitus, -ī m. finger	body part	abdomen

Latīna Hodierna

Scitisne?

Did you know that…

- The English word "volcano" is derived from *Vulcānus*? Why is this so?
- "Vulcanization" is a process named after the god? What is it and how did it get its name?
- Arachne gives her name to the scientific term for spiders? What is the name for the genus?
- A "ventriloquist" speaks (*loqu-*) from the stomach (*ventris*)? Is this true?
- A flower's stamen comes from the Latin word for "thread" (*stāmen*)? Why?
- Numbers are called "digits" because we count with our fingers (*digitī*)? Why then are we living in the digital age?
- The world's largest cast iron statue, representing Vulcan, can be found in Birmingham, Alabama?
- A replica of Phidias' statue of Athena was built to celebrate the 200th anniversary of Tennessee statehood and was placed in the Parthenon in Nashville in 1996?
- The largest active volcano in Europe is not Mt. Vesuvius but Mt. Etna in Sicily?
- The best preserved ancient Greek temples are in Sicily, not in Greece?

Orbis Terrārum Rōmānus

Aetna et Sicilia

Mt. Aetna (*Aetna, -ae* f. modern Mt. Etna), in Sicily (*Sicilia, -ae* f.), is the largest active volcano in Europe. The Romans considered it to be the forge of the god Vulcan.

Sicily first came under Roman control in 242 B.C. as a result of the First Punic War, which Rome fought against Carthage. Rome's first province, however, was not fully subdued until the end of the Second Punic War (218–201 B.C.). Sicily was an important agricultural center (especially for grain) for the Roman world, but the island continued to be a province of Rome (rather than part of Italy) until the end of the empire in the West.

During a siege of Syracuse in 212 B.C., Roman soldiers killed the Greek mathematician and inventor Archimedes (*Archimēdēs, -is* m.), who is said to have run out of his bath shouting "Eureka!" ("I found it!" in Greek) when he discovered the theory of water displacement. Archimedes is famous not just for sophisticated mathematical discoveries but also for such wonders as devices that could lift entire ships out of the water and set attacking ships on fire from afar. While a quaestor in Sicily, Cicero visited the tomb of Archimedes.

Many cities in Sicily were originally Greek and preserve impressive pre-Roman ruins, such as the temple depicted at right. The most important cities in Sicily during the Roman period were:

- *Syrācūsae, -ārum* f. pl. (modern Siracusa)
- *Agrigentum, -ī* n. (modern Agrigento)
- *Catana, -ae* f. (modern Catania)
- *Messāna, -ae* f. (modern Messina)

Eruptiō Aetnae

Agrigentum Hodiē

Sicilia et Ītalia

Archimedes dīcēns "Eurēka!" in labrō

QUID PUTĀS?

1. Why do you think the people of Birmingham, Alabama, chose a statue of the god Vulcan to overlook their city?
2. Why was Arachne's transformation into a spider both suitable and ironic?
3. What tombs or graves of famous people are visited in the United States? Why do you think people do this?
4. Why do you think Archimedes was killed by Roman soldiers during the Seige of Syracuse in 212 B.C.? Does this sort of thing happen in war today?
5. Make five more "Did You Know?" (*Scitisne?*) questions based on information you have learned about ancient Rome and Latin in this chapter.

EXERCEĀMUS!

28-5 Scrībāmus

Here is a simplified version of the story of Hercules and Pholus that you read in Chapter 21. Retell the story in the passive voice. Here is what you have to do.

- Marked in **bold** are all of the verbs you need to change from active to passive voice; e.g., **necāvit** would become **necātus est**.
- Marked in ***bold italics*** are the accusative objects of the active verbs you need to convert to the subjects of passive verbs; e.g., ***Pholum* necāvit** would become ***Pholus* necātus est**.
- Marked in *italics* are the subjects you need to turn into *ā/ab* + abl. to express the agent by whom the action of the passive verb is done; *Herculēs **Pholum** necāvit* becomes ***Pholus** ab Hercule* **necātus est**.

Follow the model.

Original

Herculēs, dum ***iter*** in Arcadiam **facit**, ad speluncam Pholī vēnit. *Pholus* (1) ***eum*** (2) benignē **excēpit** (3) et ***cēnam*** (4) **parāvit** (5). At *Herculēs* (6) ***vīnum*** (7) **postulāvit** (8). Sed *Pholus* (9) ***hoc vīnum*** (10) nōn **dedit** (11). "Sī ***hoc vīnum*** (12) **dederō**, (13) *centaurī* (14) ***mē*** (15) **interficient** (16)." *Herculēs* (17) tamen ***pōculum*** (18) vīnī dē amphorā **hausit**. (19).

Modified

→ Dum ***iter*** in Arcadiam **facitur** *ab Hercule*, vēnit ad speluncam Pholī.

28-6 Colloquāmur

Practice reading this dialogue between Rufus and Xanthus with a partner. Read with good intonation, as if these were lines from a play or a real conversation.

Rūfus: Dī immortālēs! Hoc peristȳlium sordidissimum est.
Zēthus: Sīc, verē! Ecce! Cibus et scrūta ubīque!
Rūfus: Sīc semper est—homō dīvēs, pavīmentum sordidum! Magistrī epulantur sed relinquunt squālōrem magnum quī semper ā servīs—ā nōbīs!—purgātur.
Zēthus: Nōn solum ā servīs, amīce, sed etiam ā deō opus sordidum agitur. Mementō Herculis! Locus sordidissimus ab illō ōlim purgātus est!
Rūfus: Dīc mihi dē hōc labōre! Ut scīs, Germānicus sum et paulum dē istīs tuīs fābulīs Graecīs sciō.
Zēthus: Narrābō! Mē narrante, tempus celerius fūgiet!

28-7 **Verba Discenda**

Find the *verbum discendum* that lies behind or is related to each word marked in **bold** in the following narrative. Look up the meaning of each English word if you have to.

As he walked through the museum, Dr. Osgood Littleworth, professor of **aviation** (1), was not pleased with the progress being made on the **mural** (2). Clearly, the date of completion the foreman had promised during their last **conference** (3) was a total **fabrication** (4). Angry, he ran outside, hopped on his bicycle, and **pedalled** (5) to the **prefabricated** (6) hut where the foreman had his office. The professor knew he would find the foreman there, eating donuts as usual, with **confectioner's** (7) sugar all over his shirt, and reading the paper. Well, he would just **interrupt** (8) him!

Dr. Littleworth should have been more attentive. He had forgotten about the **ubiquity** (9) of potholes in this area. His bicycle hit a **spacious** (10) pothole and he fell, fracturing his skull near the **sagittal** (11) crest. As he fell, it is reported, he uttered a **sordid** (12) word that must be expurgated here. Alas, the poor man died and his bones now reside in an **ossuary** (13) in the museum, next to the unfinished mural.

VERBA DISCENDA

avis, avis **f. bird** [avian, aviary]

conferō, conferre, contulī, collātum **bring together, collect;** *sē conferre* **go (betake oneself);** **talk together** [confer, collate]

conficiō, conficere, confēcī confectum **do, accomplish, complete** [confection]

faber, fabrī **m. craftsman** [fabricate]

ferō: sē ferre **go (betake oneself)**

gerō: sē gerere **act (conduct oneself)**

Hercule! **By Hercules!**

iubeō, iubēre, iussī, iussum **order**

lacus, -ūs **m. lake** [lacustrine]

mūrus, -ī **m. wall** [intramural]

neque **and not;** *neque... neque* **neither...nor**

oppidum, -ī **n. town**

os, ossis **n. bone** [ossify]

paulum **a little, somewhat**

pēs, pedis **m. foot** [pedestrian]

prīmum **first, at first**

proficiscor, proficiscī profectus sum **set out, depart**

rumpō, rumpere, rūpī, ruptum **break, burst, break down** [rupture]

sagitta, -ae **f. arrow** [Sagittarius]

sciō, scīre, scīvī/sciī, scītum **know, know about** [science]

sordidus, -a, -um **filthy** [sordid]

spatium, -iī **n. space** [spatial]

tantus, -a, -um **so great**

ubīque **everywhere** [ubiquitous]

umquam **ever**

Angulus Grammaticus

More on Voice

As you know already, **voice** indicates the relationship between the subject and the action of the verb. In active voice, the subject performs the action.

*Pater infantem ad uxōrem **gessit**.*   The father **carried** the infant to his wife.

In passive voice, the subject receives the action.

*Infans ā patre ad uxōrem **gessus est**.*   The infant **was carried** by his father to his wife.

Latin deponent verbs require attention because they use passive endings but have active meanings:

*Pater infantem gerēns ad uxōrem **profectus est**.*   The father, carrying the infant, **set off** to his wife.

In this chapter you saw these three Latin words in which the subject both performs and receives the action.

sē cōnferre go (betake oneself)
sē ferre go (betake oneself)
sē gerere act (conduct oneself)

As you have already seen, both Latin and English express reflexion by using **reflexive pronouns**.

*Pater **sē** cum dignitāte **gessit**.* The father **conducted himself** with dignity.

Such **reflexive** verbs are somewhat unusual in Latin but are very common in the modern Romance languages. Here are a few examples. Pay attention to where the reflexive appears in the modern verbs:

FRENCH	SPANISH	ITALIAN	LITERAL TRANSLATION	ENGLISH TRANSLATION
se marier	casarse	sposarsi	marry oneself (to)	marry, get married
s' habiller	vestirse	vestirsi	dress oneself	get dressed
s'appeler	llamarse	chiamarsi	call oneself	be called, be named, "My name is..."

Note that the best English translation for these reflexive verbs is usually active (get dressed) rather than the literal reflexive one (dress oneself).

As we pointed out in Chapter 24, ancient Greek had a separate voice, called the middle (between active and passive), to express actions done on oneself or in one's own interest. Occasionally, in Latin, a passive verb can be used reflexively. For example, *sē fert* and *fertur* can both mean "he goes." Here is an example from Caesar:

*Aliīque aliam in partem perterritī **ferēbantur**.*
And, terrified, some **were going off** in one direction, others in another.

Caesar *Dē Bellō Gallicō* 2.24

Note how the passive *ferēbantur* is translated like *sē ferēbant*, i.e., "they were going," even "they were rushing." Due to the influence of Greek on the Latin language, some Latin authors, like Vergil, occasionally used the passive voice as a **reflexive** (or Greek middle). Here are two examples from the *Aeneid*:

*Et formīdātus nautīs **aperitur** Apollo.*
And Apollo, dreaded by sailors, **shows himself**.

Vergil *Aeneid* 3.275

Note how the passive form *aperitur* is translated reflexively (shows himself) rather than passively (is shown).

*Hic torre **armātus** obustō.*
He having **armed himself** with a burnt stick.

Aeneid 7.506

Here the perfect passive participle *armātus*, used reflexively, is translated "having armed himself" rather than "having been armed."

But don't worry (yourself)! This middle use of the passive is mostly poetic and was not part of the everyday language of the Romans. You will not see such constructions until you move on to more advanced Latin readings, and, even then, you will not see them very often.

Photo Credits

Page 358 (top) Heracleitus. "The Unswept Floor," mosaic variant of a 2nd-century BCE painting by Sosos of Pergamon. 2nd century CE. Musei Vaticani, Museo Gregoriano Profano, ex Lateranense, Rome. Studio Canali, Milano, Italy; **page 358 (bottom)** Thomas J. Sienkewicz; **page 360** The Bridgeman Art Library International; **page 365** Marja—Kristina Akinsha/Shutterstock; **page 367** Darryl Vest/Shutterstock; **page 368** Thomas J. Sienkewicz; **page 369 (top)** Bastien Poux/Fotolia, LLC—Royalty Free; **page 369 (middle)** Jakub Pavlinec/Shutterstock; **page 369 (bottom)** © Ann Ronan Picture Library/Heritage—Images/ImageState Media Partners Limited.

29

Avus Cārus

Lectiō Prīma

Antequam Legis

Servīlius Avus

In this *lectiō* you meet Servilius' 82-year-old father, who lives with his son and his family. The elder Servilius is hard of hearing but enjoys being around his son and his grandchildren. Because of his hearing problem, he misunderstands many things he is told, and has to have things repeated to him by the slave who personally attends him.

Future Active Participles and Infinitives

This chapter introduces you to the final participle and infinitive you have to learn. It also provides an overview for both verb forms.

Participles

Latin has a **future active participle (FAP)** formed by adding *-ūrus, -a, -um* to the stem of the perfect passive participle:

> *vocāt-* + *-ūrus* = *vocātūrus* (being) about to call, going to call

Present active	*vocāns*	calling
Perfect passive (P³)	*vocātus, -a, -um*	(having been) called
Future active (FAP)	*vocātūrus, -a, -um*	(being) about to call

The FAP of *sum* is *futūrus, -a, -um* (about to be, going to be).

Infinitives

The future active infinitive = FAP + *esse*.

> *vocātūrum* + *esse* = *vocātūrum esse*   to be about to call

---

Pater familiās

GRAMMATICA
Participle Review and Consolidation
Infinitive Review and Consolidation
Indirect Statement
Relative not Real Time

MŌRĒS RŌMĀNĪ
Pater familiās

LATĪNA HODIERNA
Vēnātiō Verbōrum

ORBIS TERRĀRUM RŌMĀNUS
Urbs Rōma et Vigilēs

ANGULUS GRAMMATICUS
Archaisms

LECTIŌNĒS:
PATER ET FĪLIUS
and
AVUS ET NEPŌTĒS

Members of the Servilius family talk over last night's banquet with grandfather Servilius. A major topic, of course, is Servilia's arranged marriage to Iullus Antonius—or is it to be Cordus after all?

373

From *Disce! An Introductory Latin Course, volume 2*, First Edition. Francesco Bonavita. Copyright © 2011 by Pearson Education, Inc. Published by Pearson Prentice Hall. All rights reserved.

This now completes your list of infinitives.

Present active:	*vocāre*	to call
Present passive	*vocārī*	to be called
Perfect active	*vocāvisse*	to have called
Perfect passive	*vocātum esse*	to have been called
Future active	*vocātūrum esse*	to be about to call

The future active infinitive of *sum* is *futūrum esse* (to be about to be).

Watch in this *lectiō* for participles marked in ***bold italics*** and for infinitives marked in **bold**.

EXERCEĀMUS!

29-1 Recognizing Different Kinds of Participles and Infinitives

Gemma

M. Servīlius Sevērus: There are three men in this family with the same name. This was not uncommon in Roman families. Servilius could add the abbreviation M.f. (*Marcī fīlius*) after his name, but so could his own son.

As you read, find one example of each of the following kinds of Latin participles and infinitives. Then translate the word into English. Follow the model.

present active participle	present active infinitive
perfect passive participle	present passive infinitive
future active participle	perfect active infinitive
	perfect passive infinitive
	future active infinitive

Line	Latin Word	Type	Translation
→ 2	*esse*	present active infinitive	to be

🔊 PATER ET FĪLIUS

In Peristȳliō

Mane est et, ut solet, avus M. Servīlius Sevērus, in peristȳliō sedet. Ōlim senātor et pater familiās erat sed nunc avus benignus **esse** et in peristȳliō **sedēre** mavult. Surdus est et, cum avus adest, familia omnia **repetere** dēbet.

Servīlius, patrem ***sedentem vidēns***, intrat et "Avē, pater," inquit, "quid agis hodiē?"

5   Avus, manum post aurem ***ponēns***, rogat: "Quid? Quid dīxistī?"

Famulus, avum ut semper ***tuēns***, magnā vōce clāmat: "Dominus dīxit: 'Quid agis hodiē?!!!'"

Avus, "Bene," inquit, "hodiē! Bene! Sed, convīviō ***confectō***, quaestiōnēs habeō. Bonumne convīvium erat? Oportuit mē **adesse** et cum hospitibus **colloquī**, sed senēs quoque multum **dormīre** oportet! Sed, nōn mē **querī** decet—vīta, quamquam paene ***confecta***, bona est. Nōn mē vītam longam **vīxisse** paenitet et bonum est otium

10   **habēre**. Sed, dē convīviō dīcebāmus—eratne bonum?"

Servīlius: "Nōlī anxius **esse**, pater. Vidētur convīvium optimum **fuisse** et omnēs hospitēs ***exeuntēs*** laetī **esse** vidēbantur, praesertim Maecēnās Polliōque. Sed iste Iullus Antōnius ēbrius et valdē molestus fīēbat. Necesse erat eum, carmina ***cantūrum***, forās **ēiēcī**. Certum est istum nōn rursus hospitem meum **futūrum esse**!"

Avus: "Quid? Nōlī submissā vōce **ūtī**! Quid dīxistī?"

15   Famulus, "Iullus Antōnius," clāmat "ēbrius fīēbat!"

Avus: "Vae! Vērum est. Iullus dīcitur frequenter apud convīvia ēbrius atque molestus **factus esse**. Istō ad convīvium ***adventūrō***, pater cēnae semper cautus esse dēbet."

Servīlius, "Ita," inquit, "Vidētur nunc istum Servīliam nostram in mātrimōnium nōn **ductūrum esse**. Servīliā ***nuptūrā*** Caecilia laetissima est, sed nunc istum, nuptiīs ***ruptīs***, maesta est. Marītum fīliae Servīliae aptum **invenīrī**

20   necesse est. Quid, pater, dē Quīntō Naeviō Cordō intellegis?"

Avus "Familiam," inquit, "eius bene cognōvī. Adulēscēns probus et honestus vidētur et . . ."

Avō subitō fessō et dormītūrō, Servīlius nihil aliud rogat. "Pater," inquit, "nunc ad Forum **īre** dēbeō. Hāc nocte dē Cordō plūs loquēmur." Et, hīs ***dictīs***, abiit.

🔊 VERBA ŪTENDA

addō, addere, addidī, addi-
   tum add, say in addition
anxius, -a, -um uneasy,
   anxious
aptus, -a, -um suitable, fit
auris, auris f. ear
Avē! Greetings!
avus, -ī m. grandfather
cognoscō, cognoscere,
   cognōvī, cognitum
   learn, get to know,
   observe; (perfect)
   "know"
ēiciō, ēicere, ēiēcī, ēiectum
   throw out

famulus, -ī m. servant,
   attendant
forās outdoors, out
frequenter often, frequently
honestus, -a, -um worthy,
   decent, of high rank
mātrimōnium, -ī n.
   marriage, matrimony
molestus, -a, -um
   troublesome, tiresome
nūbō, nūbere, nupsī, nuptum
   marry
oculus, -ī m. eye
oportuit mē adesse "I ought
   to have been there"

ōtium, -ī n. leisure
paenitet, paenitēre, paeni-
   tuit (imp.) it gives reason for regret; ***mē***
   paenitet I am sorry
pater familiās, patris
   familiās m. **head**
   of the family
quasī as if, practically
queror, querī, questus sum
   complain
repetō, repetere, repetīvī/
   repetiī, repetītum repeat
senātor, -ōris m. **senator,**
   member of the senate

senātus, -ūs m. **senate**
senex, senis m. **old man**
soleō, solēre, solitus sum
   be accustomed (to)
submissus, -a, -um low (voice)
surdus, -a, -um deaf
tueor, tuērī, tuitus sum
   look at, watch over,
   look after, protect
vae! woe! alas!
vigil, vigilis m./f. **sentry,**
   guard; firefighter; pl.,
   fire brigade
vīvō, vīvere, vīxī, victum
   live

POSTQUAM LĒGISTĪ

Answer these questions in English (E) or Latin (L) as directed.

1. How is the life of Servilius' father different than it used to be when he was younger? (E)
2. Why didn't Servilius' father attend the banquet? (L)
3. What does Servilius tell his father about the banquet? (L)
4. What gossip has Servilius' father heard about Iullus Antonius? (L)
5. Do you think that Servilius' father approves of a possible match between Servilia and Cordus? Why or why not? (E)

Gemma

Because the Romans equated age with wisdom, there was a minimum age requirement for membership in the senate. So both *senātus* and *senātor* are derived from *senex*.

Grammatica A

Participle Review and Consolidation

The future active participle (FAP) is the last participial form you need to learn in Latin. Here is a list of all the Latin participles for the verb *audiō*:

Present active:	*audiēns*	hearing
Perfect passive:	*audītus, -a, -um*	(having been) heard
Future active:	*audītūrus, -a, -um*	about to hear, going to hear

Here are the participles for the deponent verb *cōnor*:

Present active:	*cōnāns*	trying
Perfect passive:	*cōnātus, -a, -um*	(having) tried
Future active:	*cōnātūrus, -a, -um*	about to try, going to try

Notā Bene:

- The present active participle is a 3rd declension adjective.
- The FAP and P³ are 2-1-2 adjectives.
- English has participles that Latin lacks:

    "being heard" (present passive)
    "having heard" (perfect active)

- As you might expect, the perfect passive participle of deponent verbs is translated actively.

- The present active and future active participles of deponent verbs are **exceptions** to the deponent rule. They are active in form and are translated actively.

As a **verbal adjective**, a participle has grammatical features of both an adjective and a verb.

As an **adjective**, a participle has gender, number, and case and GNCs with a noun or pronoun (either expressed or understood): *virīs audientibus* (the men listening); *fēminae audītae* (the women having been heard); *avus audītūrus* (grandfather about to hear).

As a **verb**, a participle has tense and voice and can take an object: *avus **verba** audītūrus* (grandfather about to hear the words).

The FAP adds another possibility to the ablative absolute. Consider the ablative absolutes in the following sentences.

Cordō dīcente, *Servīlia laeta est.*	When Cordus is speaking Servilia is happy.
Cordō vīsō, *Servīlia laeta est.*	Because Cordus was seen, Servilia is happy.
Cordō dictūrō, *Servīlia laeta est.*	When Cordus is about to speak, Servilia is happy.

EXERCEĀMUS!

29-2 Participle Review

In each of the following sentences identify the participle and the noun with which it GNC's. Give the tense and voice of the participle. Then translate the two words. Follow the model.

→ Avum in peristyliō sedentem vīdī.
   Avum sedentem (present active)   grandfather sitting

1. Avus sedēns in peristyliō multa dīxit.
2. Avus cum fīliō collocutus nunc dormit.
3. Avō habitante in fīliī dōmō, familia laeta est.
4. Servus avō in peristyliō sedentī cibum dat.
5. Dē avō fessō et dormītūrō servī anxiī erant.
6. Puerī avum dē conviviō audientem vīdērunt.
7. Avō dormiente famulus ē peristyliō currit.
8. Avō dormītūrō famulus ē peristyliō currit.
9. Cordō vīsō Servīlius nōn laetus est.
10. Servīlia, Cordum vīsūra, laeta est.

Infinitive Review and Consolidation

The future active infinitive is the last infinitive form you need to learn in Latin. Here is a list of all the Latin infinitives for the verb *dūcō*:

Present active	*dūcere*	to lead
Present passive	*dūcī*	to be led
Perfect active	*dūxisse*	to have led
Perfect passive	*ductum esse*	to have been led
Future active	*ductūrum esse*	to be about to lead

Here is a list of all the infinitives for the deponent verb *sequor*:

Present passive	*sequī*	to follow
Perfect passive	*secūtum esse*	to have followed
Future active	*secūtūrum esse*	to be about to follow

Notā Bene:

- Unlike regular verbs, deponent verbs have only one present and perfect infinitive.
- As you might expect, the present passive and perfect passive infinitives of deponents are translated actively, e.g, *cōnārī* (to try).
- Like the present and future active participles of deponent verbs (e.g., *cōnāns* or *cōnātūrus*), the future active infinitive is an **exception** to the deponent rule. It is an active form translated actively, e.g., *cōnātūrum esse* (to be about to try).

As a **verbal noun**, an infinitive has grammatical features of both nouns and verbs.
As a **noun**, an infinitive

- is neuter.

    Vivere bonum est.   It is good to be alive.

- can function as either the subject or object of a verb.

    Amāre bonum est.   To love is good.   (subjective infinitive)
    Volō amāre.   I wish to love.   (objective infinitive)

As a **verb**, an infinitive

- has voice and can be active or passive.

    *Vidētur **amāre**.* He seems to be in love.
    *Vidētur **amārī**.* He seems to be loved.

- has tense.

    ***Amāre** bonum est sed numquam **amāvisse** malum est.*
    To love is good but never to have loved is bad.

- can take a subject (usually in the accusative case).

    ***Tē** adesse volō.* I want **you** to be here.

- can take an object.

    *Vidētur **mē** amāre.* She seems to love **me**.

- can also **complement** or "complete" the action of another verb.

    Possum amāre. I can love.

EXERCEĀMUS!

29-3 Infinitive Review

Choose the answer that best translates the following infinitives.

1. sessūrum esse:	a. to sit	b. to be sat	c. to have sat	d. to be about to sit
2. collocūtum esse:	a. to talk	b. to have talked	c. to be talked	d. to be about to talk
3. factūrum esse:	a. to be done	b. to have been done	c. to be about to be done	d. to be about to do
4. invenīre:	a. to find	b. to be found	c. to have found	d. to be about to find
5. ductum esse:	a. to be led	b. to have led	c. to have been led	d. to be about to lead
6. futūrum esse:	a. to be	b. to have been	c. to be about to have been	d. to be about to be
7. potuisse:	a. to be able	b. to have been able	c. to be about to have been able	d. to be about to be able
8. tuērī:	a. to see	b. to be seen	c. to have seen	d. to have been seen
9. cognitum esse:	a. to know	b. to be known	c. to have known	d. to have been known
10. confectūrum esse:	a. to complete	b. to be completed	c. to have been completed	d. to be about to complete

Lectiō Secunda

Antequam Legis

At the time of our story, there was no public fire brigade in Rome despite the great danger and frequency of fires in the city. There were private fire companies, the most notorious of which, perhaps, had belonged to M. Licinius Crassus (c.115–51 B.C.), who was said to have acquired some of his great wealth by purchasing buildings as they burned and then having his private firefighters put out the blaze. Augustus did not establish public *cohortēs vigilum*, or fire brigades, until 6 A.D. The historical figure upon which Servilia's Cordus is based eventually became prefect of these *vigilēs*. Cordus' interest in fires, as well as his wealth, comes from his father's investment with Crassus in these "fire sales."

In *Lectiō Secunda*, the grandfather's deafness affects the grammar of the sentences as you enounter indirect statement.

Direct and Indirect Statement

These sentences are in direct statement, reporting the exact words of the speaker.

Kate said, "I will do this for you."
Kate said, "I did this for you."

Often, however, the words of a speaker are told to us by **indirect statement** as in these examples.

Kate said **that she would do this for you**.
Kate said **that she had done this for you**.

Now let's look at direct and indirect statements in Latin.

Direct Statement: *Servīlia dīxit, "Vīdī Cordum."*   Servīlia said, "I saw Cordus."
Indirect Statement: *Servīlia **dīxit sē Cordum vīdisse**.*   Servīlia said that she had seen Cordus.

In Latin, an indirect statement consists of:

- An introductory verb (also called a "head verb") (*dīxit*)
- An accusative subject + infinitive construction (*sē vīdisse*)

How do you translate this type of construction?

- The word "that" is optional to begin the indirect statement in English.

    a) Servilia said that . . . or b) Servilia said . . .

- Translate the infinitive as a regular verb.

    sē Cordum vīdisse. ⟶ she had seen Cordus

For now, these general examples will suffice:

Direct Statement: *Caesar venit.*   Caesar is coming.
Indirect Statements:
Sciō Caesarem venīre.   I know that Caesar is coming. (same time as main verb.)
Sciō Caesarem vēnisse.   I know that Caesar came. (time before)
Sciō Caesarem ventūrum esse.   I know that Caesar is going to come. (time after)
Scīvī Caesarem venīre.   I knew that Caesar was coming. (same time)
Scīvī Caesarem vēnisse.   I knew that Caesar had come. (time before)
Scīvī Caesarem ventūrum esse.   I knew that Caesar was going to come. (time after)

This is all you need to get started with indirect statements. To help you recognize them in *Lectiō Secunda*, we have marked the following words:

- The *verb* that introduces the indirect statement is in *italics*.
- The **infinitive construction** is in **bold**.
- The ***accusative*** subject of the infinitive is in ***bold italics***.

Servīlius *dīcit **sē** Iullum ēbrium **vīdisse**.*

EXERCEĀMUS!

Gemma

Macrons matter! What is the difference between *Avē* and *Ave*?

29-4 Relative Time in Indirect Statements

Before you begin, translate these indirect statements. Pay attention to the tenses of the main verb and of the infinitive. All the sentences refer to Servilia loving Cordus. Follow the model.

→ Servīlia dīcit sē Cordum amāre. Servilia says that she loves Cordus.

1. Servīlia dīxit sē Cordum amāre.
2. Servīlia dīcit sē nullum alium amāvisse.
3. Servīlia dīxit sē nullum alium amāvisse.
4. Servīlia dīcit sē Cordum semper amāvisse.
5. Servīlia dīcit sē Cordum semper amātūram esse.
6. Servīlia dīxit sē Cordum semper amātūram esse.

🔊 AVUS ET NEPŌTĒS

Avus manum post aurem ponit.

Postquam Servīlius exiit, nepōtēs in peristȳlium ruērunt.

Servīlia avum osculāvit et "Quid," inquit, "avus meus agit hodiē? Laeta avum meum videō!"

Avus: "Quid? Quid dīxit? Quid lātum est?"

Famulus, clāmāns in aurem: "Nihil lātum est! Servīlia *dīxit sē* 'laetam' avum suum **vidēre!**"

5 Servīlia: "*Sciō tē* cum patre dē Cordō **locūtum esse.** Paterne tibi *dīxit mē* Cordum **amāre?**"

Avus: "Quid? Dē corde meō dīcis? Cor meum, quamquam vetus, iam forte est. Fortasse moritūrus sum, sed nōn hodiē!"

Famulus, rīdēns, clāmat: "Servīlia nōn dē corde tuō sed dē adulescente Cordō dīcit. *Dīxit sē* Cordum **amāre** et **Cordum** bonum adulescentem **esse.**"

Avus: "Ita, Cordus bonus adulescens est. *Spērō tē* laetam **futūram esse.**

10 Lūcius quoque avum osculat et avus respondet: "Lūcī! Audīvī **sīmiam** ferōcem ā tē in Forō **captum esse.** Vērumne est?"

Lūcius: "Iam tibi *dīxī* nōn **mē,** sed **paedagōgum** sīmiam **cēpisse.** Iam tibi *dīxī* illum **sīmiam** nōn ferōcem sed sagācem **esse,** quod in ārā Dīvī Iūliī sēdit et sīc salvus erat!"

Avus: "Nōn, nōn, puer! Nōn licet tālia dīcere! Dīvus Iūlius nullus sīmia est. Hmmph! Nōlī nūgās dīcere!"

15 Famulus clāmat: "Nōn *dīxit* **Caesarem** sīmiam **esse!** *Dīxit* **sīmiam** in ārā Caesaris **sēdisse!** Āra! Āra!"

Avus respondet: "Ah, vērum est. Aura sub arbore bona est! Sed, tū, Marce. Quid tū, studiīs rhetoricīs confectīs, actūrus es?"

Marcus "Ave cāre," inquit, "*in animō habeō mē* in Graeciā rhetoricīs **studēre.** Sicut tū senātor fīam!"

Avus: "Quid? Quid dīxistī? 'Fīēsne vēnātor'? 'Vēnātor'? Sīmiās captūrus es? Nōn bene audīvī."

20 Marcus respondēre incipit, sed famulus, rīdēns, sē inclinat ad aurem avī et clāmat: "Marcus *dīxit sē* 'senātōrem,' nōn 'vēnatōrem,' **futūrum esse.** Domine, sitiens et fessus vidēris. Ecce! Pōtum bibe et, fortasse, paulisper resquiesce."

🔊 VERBA ŪTENDA

aestimō (1) consider
animus, -ī m. mind
arbor, arboris f. tree
aura, -ae f. breeze
auris, auris f. ear
avus, -ī m. grandfather
calidus, -a, -um warm
dīvus, -a, -um divine

famulus, -ī m. servant, attendant
gens, gentis f. family, tribe
in animō habēre "to have in mind, intend"
inclinō (1) bend, tilt
licet, licēre, licuit, licitum est (imp.) it is **permitted**

morlor, morī, mortuus sum die
nūgae, -ārum f. pl. trifle
osculō (1) kiss
paulisper for a little while
pōtus, -ūs m. (a) drink
quandō when
requiescō, requiescere requiēvī, requiētum rest

resideō, residēre, resēdī sit, remain in a place
sagāx, sagācis wise, sharp
sitiens, sitientis thirsty
sōl, sōlis, m. sun
tranquillus, -a, -um still, peaceful
vēnātor, -ōris m. hunter
vetus, veteris aged, old

POSTQUAM LĒGISTĪ

1. What does *Avus* hear when Servilia says, *"Laeta avum meum videō!"*?
2. What did Servilia know her father had been talking about to her grandfather?
3. Why does *Avus* say Cordus is a bit boring to talk to?
4. What reasons does *Avus* give Lucius to behave well in school?
5. What story did *Avus* hear about Lucius? What details did *Avus* get wrong?
6. What news does Marcus give his grandfather?

Grammatica B

Indirect Statement

As you saw in reading *Lectiō Secunda*, Latin marks an indirect statement much more clearly than English does. So, in line 2 Servilia speaks directly to her grandfather and says:

*Laeta avum meum **videō**.* Happily I see my grandfather.

Whereas in line 4 the *famulus* tells *Avus*:

*Servīlia dīxit sē 'laetam' avum suum **vidēre**!* Servilia said that she sees her grandfather happily.

Note the changes:

Direct		*Laeta avum meum **videō**.*
Indirect	*Servīlia dīxit*	*sē 'laetam' avum suum **vidēre**!*

- 1st person → 3rd person
- The implied *ego* → *sē*
- *laeta* → *laetam* because the subject of an infinitive (*sē*) is accusative.

Why an accusative subject? This all makes some sense if you think about this sentence:

"I saw Iullus drinking."

What did you see? You saw both Iullus and the act of drinking. So, in Latin, "Iullus" becomes an accusative "subject" and the "drinking" a verbal noun called the infinitive.

Vīdī Iullum bibere.

Eum vs. Sē

Consider this English sentence:

"Iullus knows that he is drunk."

In English, depending on context, the "he" could be Iullus or someone else. Latin has a way to avoid this confusion:

| *Iullus scit **sē** ēbrium esse.* | → | *sē* = same as subject |
| *Iullus scit **eum** ēbrium esse.* | → | *eum* = someone other than the subject |

Head Verbs

One way to know that an indirect statement is coming is to pay attention to the main verb of the sentence. Verbs of speaking, thinking, knowing, hearing, feeling, and the like are called "head verbs" and often introduce indirect statements. Here is a list of head verbs you have already seen as *Verba Discenda*:

dīcō	*spērō*	*monstrō*
respondeō	*intellegō*	*sentiō*
clāmō	*nārrō*	*loquor*
videō	*crēdō*	
audiō	*sciō*	

Do you remember what these verbs mean?

Now let's talk a little about word order in indirect statement. When the infinitive in an indirect discourse takes a direct object, two accusatives occur in a row, but the first is the subject and the second is the object. Compare:

Vīdī gladiātōrem leōnem interficere.
Vīdī leōnem gladiātōrem interficere.

In the first sentence the lion is dead, but not in the second one. So, in summary,

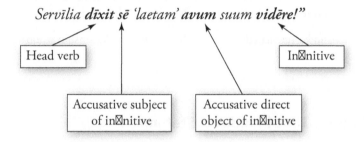

Relative not Real Time

When translating infinitives and participles, it is important to keep in mind that their tense indicates **relative time**, not real time. Remember this basic equation concerning participles and infinitives.

- The present tense of the infinitive or the participle shows **same time** as the main verb.
- The perfect tense shows **time before** the main verb.
- The future tense shows **time after** the main verb.

Consider the participles in these sentences.

Videō fēminam **canentem**.	I see the singing woman.
Vīdī fēminam **canentem**.	I saw the singing woman.
Vidēbō fēminam **canentem**.	I will see the singing woman.

The participle stays the same in each Latin sentence because as a present participle it shows that the singing is going on exactly at the same time as the seeing (no matter its tense).

Even in ablative absolutes, the tenses of the participles are relative rather than real. Here are some examples in which the main verb is in the past. Notice how the tense of the participle indicates when the action in the ablative absolute takes place relative to the action of the main verb.

Cordō dīcente, *Servīlia laeta erat.*	When Cordus was speaking Servilia was happy.
Cordō dictūrō, *Servīlia laeta erat.*	When Cordus was about to speak, Servilia was happy.
Cordō vīsō, *Servīlia laeta erat.*	Because Cordus was seen, Servilia was happy.

Now consider these sentences with infinitives.

Servīlia laeta **esse** *vidētur.*	Servilia seems to be happy.
Servīlia laeta **esse** *vidēbātur.*	Servilia seemed to be happy.
Servīlia laeta **esse** *vidēbitur.*	Servilia will seem to be happy.

In each case the present infinitive is indicating that, at the very time of the main verb, Servilia is happy.

Infinitives in indirect statement also show relative, not absolute, time. Compare these sentences:

SAME TIME	*Dīcit sē avum vidēre.*	She says she sees her grandfather.
	Dīxit sē avum vidēre.	She said that she was seeing/saw her grandfather.
TIME BEFORE	*Dīcit sē avum vīdisse.*	She says she saw her grandfather.
	Dīxit sē avum vīdisse.	She said that she had seen her grandfather.
TIME AFTER	*Dīcit sē avum vīsūram esse.*	She says she will see her grandfather.
	Dīxit sē avum vīsūram esse.	She said that she was going to see her grandfather.

The infinitive should be translated, therefore, based on the relationship it shows with the head verb that introduces it.

EXERCEĀMUS!

29-5 Relative Time in Indirect Statement

Indicate the tenses of both the main (head) verb and the infinitive in indirect statement in each of the following sentences. Then translate the sentence into English. Your translation can be a little loose, but be sure to show the time relationship between the head verb and the infinitive. Follow the model.

→ Marcus dīxit sē in Graeciā habitātūrum esse.

Main(head) verb	*dīxit*	perfect tense
Infinitive	*habitātūrum esse*	future tense

"Marcus said that he would live/was going to live in Greece."

1. Marcus dīcit sē in Graeciā habitāre.
2. Marcus dīxit sē in Graeciā habitāre.
3. Marcus dīcit sē in Graeciā habitātūrum esse.
4. Marcus dīcit sē in Graeciā habitāvisse.
5. Marcus dīxit sē in Graeciā habitāvisse.
6. Marcus dīcet sē in Graeciā habitāvisse.
7. Audiō sīmiam in forō captum esse.
8. Audiō sīmiam in forō capī.
9. Audiō tē sīmiam in forō captūrum esse.

Mōrēs Rōmānī

Pater familiās

Do you remember from Chapter 16 that the Latin word *familia* refers not only to a biological family, but to a legal one? To a Roman, *familia* technically and legally meant all those individuals under the *potestās* (legal control) of the *pater familiās*, or head of the family, including servants and slaves that belonged to the household. In fact, very often when you see the word *familia* in Latin you should try translating it first as "my household" rather than "my family" (as we understand it).

The individuals in the *familia* included one's own children as well as the children of one's son and grandson. Under certain circumstances a wife was also under the legal control of her husband or her father- or grandfather-in-law.

This legal control was called *patria potestās*. The word *potestās* is important here. It refers to the kind of absolute legal authority held by the head of a Roman family. In other words, a *pater familiās* had the same total power over his children and relatives that he held over his slaves. This was considered to be a power of life and death. Originally a *pater familiās* could even sell his children into slavery or kill them with legal impunity, but this was certainly no longer the case by the time of Augustus. Nevertheless, even under Augustus, anyone who was not *pater familiās* had no individual legal rights separate from the *pater familiās*; that is, they could acquire property, but it came under the control of the *pater familiās*; they could marry and divorce, but only with the consent of the *pater familiās*.

It was possible for a *pater familiās* to cede some of this authority to his son. This was called, legally, *maxima* or *media capitis dīminūtiō* (maximum or partial decrease of rights). This is what Servilius' father has done. Because of his advanced age, *Avus* has passed *patria potestās* over to his son Servilius, who is now *pater familiās*. If he had not done this, Servilius, Servilia, Marcus, and Lucius would all still be under the legal authority of *Avus*.

Here is how the power of *pater familiās* is described in the *Institūtiōnēs* I.IX of the emperor Justinian (527–565 A.D.), which is the most comprehensive Roman law code surviving today. This selection is from Book 1, Section 9, and is only slightly simplified. Notice how the law is written in the 1st person plural and addresses individual male citizens in the 2nd person singular.

Iustiniānus Imperātor

Dē Patriā Potestāte

In potestāte nostrā sunt līberī nostrī, quōs ex iustīs nuptiīs
prōcreāverimus. Nūptiae autem sīve mātrimōnium est virī et mulieris
coniunctiō, indīviduam consuētudinem vītae continēns. Iūs autem
potestātis quod in līberōs habēmus proprium est cīvium Rōmānōrum:
5   nullī enim aliī sunt hominēs quī tālem in līberōs habent potestātem
quālem nōs habēmus. [Is] quī igitur ex tē et uxōre tuā nascitur,
in tuā potestāte est: item [is] quī ex fīliō tuō et uxōre eius nascitur, id est
nepōs tuus et neptis, aequē in tuā sunt potestāte, et pronepōs et
proneptis et deinceps cēterī. [Is] quī tamen ex fīliā tuā nascitur, in tuā
10   potestāte nōn est, sed in [potestāte] patris eius.

> **Gemma**
>
> Look at the use of *id est* in line 7. This phrase is carried over into English in the abbreviation "i.e." (that is = *id est*).

🔊 VERBA ŪTENDA

coniunctiō, -iōnis f. joining together, union
consuētudinō, -inis f. companionship
contineō, continēre, continuī, contentum contain, hold
deinceps in succession
id est "that is"
indīviduus, -a, -um indivisible
item similarly

iūs, iūris n. law
iustus, -a, -um legal
līberī, -ōrum m. pl. children
mātrimōnium, -iī n. marriage, matrimony
nascor, nascī, nātus sum be born
neptis, neptis f. granddaughter
nuptiae, -ārum f. pl. marriage

potestās, -tātis f. power, authority
prōcreō (1) procreate, create
pronepōs, -pōtis m. great-grandson
proneptis, -neptis f. great-granddaughter
quālis, quāle See *tālis*.
sīve or
tālis, -e . . . quālis, -e of such a sort . . . as

Latīna Hodierna

Vēnātiō Verbōrum

In this word hunt, all of the English words marked in bold are based on Latin words you have seen as *Verba Discenda*. Identify these Latin words and use them to define the English words. If you do not know the meaning of these English words or do not recognize the Latin word on which they are based, look up the English word in a good college dictionary.

1. **Potatory** immoderation may lead to **inebriation**.
2. The **illicitness** of his behavior and his **fraternization** with **fugitives** led to his incarceration.
3. The stereotype of **anile** behavior is **loquaciousness**.
4. **Intramural** sports can be more **competitive** than **intermural** activities.
5. The original **ossuary** was full, and the cemetery attendants had to find an **alternative depository**.
6. **Lacustrine** creatures tend to be amphibian.
7. The classroom seemed more like a **scriptorium** as the students took the exam.
8. The politician was not re-elected due to serious charges of **nepotism**.

Orbis Terrārum Rōmānus

Urbs Rōma et Vigilēs

In 6 A.D. Augustus used a tax on slaves to establish and fund the *vigilēs urbānī* to serve as a fire brigade within the city of Rome. A cohort of about 500 men, commanded by a tribune, patrolled 2 of the 14 administrative regions of the city indicated on the map below. Each cohort consisted of 7 centuries of 70–80 men, usually *lībertīnī* led by a military centurion. These cohorts lived in barracks scattered stragetically throughout the city and patrolled the city from substations by night. All of the cohorts were overseen by the *praefectus vigilum* (of equestrian rank).

There was little elaborate equipment. Instead the *vigilēs* used blankets, buckets of water, sand, etc., to put out the fires. They also had ladders, ropes, and tools to tear down burning buildings and rescue people caught in fires. Like modern firefighters, the *vigilēs* were helmeted but carried no weapons.

The city of Ostia provides important evidence for the organization and lives of *vigilēs*, with a well-preserved barracks that was a model of efficiency. This rectangular, multi-storied building consisted of a series of small rooms built around a central courtyard. The *vigilēs* lived and stored their gear in these small rooms, most of which open onto the central courtyard.

Vigilēs Ostiensēs

Regiōnēs Urbī

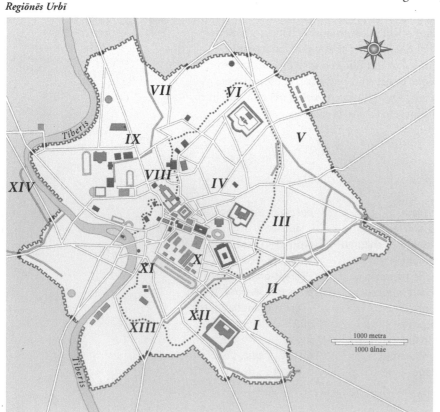

The size of the building, its prominent location, and its decoration with mosaics all point to the central role that the *vigilēs* played in the life of ancient Ostia. The building included an imperial shrine with the dedication to Marcus Aurelius depicted below. Notice how, in the transcription, all the words marked in **bold** are dative, referring to Marcus Aurelius, who is honored as the son, the grandson, the great grandson, and the great-great grandson of emperors. With the help of this bolding you should be able to understand this inscription without a *Verba Ūtenda*.

M. AVRELIO CAESARI
IMP(eratoris) CAESARIS T. AELI HADRIANI
ANTONINI AVGVSTI PII **FILIO**
DIVI HADRIANI **NEPOTI** DIVI TRAIANI
PRONEPOTI DIVI NERVAE **ABNEP(oti)CO(n)S(uli)**
OPTIMO AC PIISSIMO

M. Aureliō Caesarī

QUID PUTĀS?

1. How does the legal definition of marriage found in the Justinian Law code compare to the legal definition in your state? What is your opinion of the Justinian definition?
2. How does the legal role of *pater familiās* compare to the way your own family is run? How does it compare to the role of the chief male in other countries?
3. Compare the barracks of the *vigilēs* at Ostia to a firehouse in a modern American city.

EXERCEĀMUS!

29-6 Look for the Head Verbs

Here is a list of *Verba Discenda*. Which ones, based upon their meanings, are probably head verbs? HINT: Remember that a head verb is a word of speaking, thinking, knowing, hearing, or feeling. Follow the models.

Verb	Meaning	Head Verb?
→ sciō	know	yes, head verb
→ vertō	turn	no, not a head verb

1. sentiō	5. dōnō	9. pulsō
2. loquor	6. ingredior	10. sequor
3. audiō	7. servō	11. plaudō
4. spērō	8. narrō	12. admīror

29-7 Scribāmus

Use each of the following words or expressions with **one** of the infinitives in the pool. You can use an infinitive only once, but you have more infinitives than you need. Then translate the sentence you made. Follow the model.

The Infinitive Pool
amāre / monēre / abīre / mittere / inspicere / revertere / ēloquī / emere / habitāre / imperāre / purgāre / sedēre / lacrimāre / mirārī / nārrāre / parcere / quiescere / prōfīciscī / salīre / recumbere / scrībere

→ Bonum est **quiescere**. "It is good to be quiet."

1. Videor	5. Audeō	9. Studeō
2. Licet	6. Dēsinō	10. Solet
3. Oportet	7. Discō	11. Decet
4. Volō	8. Mē paenitet	

29-8 Colloquāmur

With two partners, practice speaking this dialogue out loud. There are three parts: *Avus,*
Famulus, and *Servīlia.* Words have been left out. Try to supply them without looking,
but they are in the *Thēsaurus Verbōrum* if you get stuck. Thesaurus words can be used more
than once.

Thēsaurus Verbōrum

adulescens	cor	puella
amāre	dīxit	stultus
aquam	esse	velle
audīre	fessus	vigilibus
avum	moritūrus	vīnum
canis	pōtum	

Servīlia: Avē, ave. Quid agis hodiē? Laeta _____ meum videō!

Avus: Quid? Nōn eam _____ possum! Quid lātum est?

Famulus: (clāmāns in aure avī) Nihil lātum est! Servīlia _____ sē "laetam"
_____ suum vidēre!

Servīlia: Sciō tē cum patre dē Cordō locutum esse. Pater tibi dīxit mē Cordum vehementer
_____! Vērum est! Cordus bonus _____ est.

Avus: Quid? Dē corde meō dīcis? _____ meum, quamquam vetus, iam forte est.
Fortasse _____ sum, sed nōn hodiē!

Famulus: (rīdēns et clāmāns) Servīlia nōn dē corde tuō sed dē adulescente Cordō dīcit. Dīxit
sē Cordum _____ et Cordum bonum adulescentem _____.

29-9 Thinking About the *Verba Discenda*

Use the *Verba Discenda* to translate the following phrases into English.

1. animī anxiī
2. arborēs vīventēs
3. oculī aurēsque senātūs
4. senātōribus honestīs

5. senex molestus
6. vigilibus tuentīs
7. Pater familiās mortuus est.
8. Avē, ave!

🔊 **VERBA DISCENDA**

animus, -ī m. mind
[animation]

anxius, -a, -um uneasy,
anxious [anxiety]

arbor, arboris f. tree

auris, auris f. ear [aural]

Avē! Greetings!

avus, -ī m. grandfather,
ancestor

cognoscō, cognoscere,
cognōvī, cognitum
learn, get to know,
observe; in perfect,
"know" [cognition]

dīvus, -a, -um divine
[divinity]

honestus, -a, -um worthy,
decent, of high rank

licet, licēre, licuit, licitum
est (imp.) it is
permitted

molestus, -a, -um
troublesome, tiresome
[molest]

morior, morī, mortuus sum
die [mortuary]

oculus, -ī m. eye
[ocular]

paenitet, paenitēre, paeni-
tuit (imp.) it gives reason for regret; *mē*
paenitet I am sorry

pater familiās, patris
familiās m. pater familias, head of the family

pōtus, -ūs m. (a) drink
[potable]

quandō when

senātor, -ōris m.
senator, member of the
senate

senātus, -ūs m. senate

senex, senis m. old man
[senile]

soleō, solēre, solitus sum
be accustomed (to)

tueor, tuērī, tuitus sum
look at, watch over,
look after, protect
[tutor]

vēnātor, -ōris m. hunter

vigil, vigilis m./f. sentry,
guard; firefighter; pl.,
fire brigade [vigilant]

vīvo, vīvere, vīxī, victum
live [vivacious]

Angulus Grammaticus

Archaisms

Did you wonder about the ending of *pater familiās*? The *-ās* in *familiās* is actually an archaic genitive singular, where you might expect *familiae*. The same form is preserved in phrases like *māter familiās*, *filius familiās*, and *filia familiās*. This is an example of archaism in language, i.e., a grammatical form or spelling that is no longer current.

For the words *dea* and *fīlia*, the archaic dative and ablative plurals, *deābus* and *fīliābus*, were sometimes used, especially to provide specifically feminine alternatives to the generic *deīs* and *fīliīs*. Other archaic forms include *honōs* and *colōs* instead of *honōr* and *colōr*.

Toward the end of the Republic, shortly before the time of our story, there were some significant sound/spelling shifts in Latin. For example,

> *antīquos, -a, -om* → *antīquus -a, -um*   *saevos, -a, -om* → *saevus, -a, -um*
> *reliquont* → *reliquunt*

In some Latin words *o* became *u*, as in

> *voltus* → *vultus*   *volt* → *vult*   *quom* → *cum*

And sometimes a *u* became an *i*:

> *optumus* → *optimus*   *lubet* → *libet*

You will find many of these early forms used in the plays of Terence and Plautus, and some of the characters in our narrative may well have held onto many of the older forms. But the later forms are more commonly accepted, and they are the ones you will generally find used in Latin books like this one.

The fact that Romans continued to use older forms like *pater familiās* even in later periods illustrates how important the word was to them and how linguistically conservative they were.

English speakers occasionally use archaic phrases for special effect, for example, "thee" and "thy" in prayers. Other archaisms in English include "naught" for "nothing," "albeit" for "although," and "ere" for "before."

Photo Credits

Page 373 Museo Capitolino, Rome/Art Resource, N.Y.;   **page 374** Leigh Anne Lane; **page 383** Clipart.com; **page 384** Thomas J. Sienkewicz; **page 385** Thomas J. Sienkewicz.

Rēs Agendae

From *Disce! An Introductory Latin Course, volume 2*, First Edition. Francesco Bonavita. Copyright © 2011 by Pearson Education, Inc. Published by Pearson Prentice Hall. All rights reserved.

30

Rēs Agendae

Caldārium

GRAMMATICA
The Gerund
The Double Dative
Gerundives
Future Passive Periphrastic and
    Dative of Agent

MŌRĒS RŌMĀNĪ
Thermae Rōmānae

LATĪNA HODIERNA
Memorandum

ORBIS TERRĀRUM RŌMĀNUS
Carthāgō

ANGULUS GRAMMATICUS
Periphrasis

LECTIŌNĒS:
IN THERMĪS
and
PARUM SPATIĪ

Ten months have passed. Servilius,
preparing to run for *praetor*, has a chat
with Cordus in the public baths. Meanwhile, the family of Valeria is finding
space tight at home.

Lectiō Prīma

Antequam Legis

A Few Months Later
in the Servilian Family . . .

Several months have passed since Servilius' party and his gift to Augustus.
As our story resumes, Cordus has been invited by Servilius to discuss his
future during a visit to the public baths, a place where a great deal of busi-
ness was conducted. Pay careful attention to the variety of things wealthy
Romans could do at a bath and compare it to today's health clubs and spas.
Also look for a new grammatical construction called the gerund.

The Gerund: "Noun-ing the Verb"

In English, a gerund is a verb with an **-ing** ending that is used as a noun.

> I learn Latin by **reading**!   *Linguam Latīnam **legendō** discō!*

Legendō is a gerund in Latin and is, like the infinitive, a neuter verbal
noun. For now, here is what you need to know:

- The gerund declines like *pōculum*.
- When you see one (in **bold**) translate it with an
  "-ing" on the end of the verb (e.g., "running")

Watch also for two special uses of the gerund that show **purpose**:

- In the **genitive case**, used with *causā* (on account of) or *grātiā* (for the sake of):

  *Lūcius ad lūdum **discendī causā** vēnit.*
  *Lūcius ad lūdum **discendī grātiā** vēnit.*

  Translate both sentences as "Lucius came to school **to learn (for the sake of learning)**."

- In the **accusative case**, with *ad*:

  *Advēnī **ad discendum**.*
  I have come **for learning/to learn**.

The Double Dative

Finally, as you read, watch for a construction called the **double dative**. Consider this sentence in which the datives are marked in **bold** in both the Latin sentence and its translations.

  *Spērō tē **mihi auxiliō** futūrum esse.*
  I hope you will be **to me for help**.
  I hope you will be **a help to me**.

Double datives are marked in *italics* in *Lectiō Prīma*.

EXERCEĀMUS!

30-1 **Gerunds**

As you read, take notice of the gerunds (marked in **bold**) in *Lectiō Prīma*. Identify the case of each gerund. (Keep in mind that all gerunds are neuter singular, 2nd declension, and have no nominative.) Then list them under the appropriate case heading. Follow the model.

→ Genitive   Dative   Accusative   Ablative
  exeundī (line 3)

Apodȳtērium

IN THERMĪS

Servīlius et Cordus, thermīs appropinquantēs, multa dē multīs
colloquēbantur. Balneās intrantēs prīmum in apodӯtērium
ingressī sunt **exuendī causā**. Tum, vestīmentīs dēpositīs in
apodӯtēriō apud servōs custōdēs, nūdī in tepidāriō sedēbant
5 **sūdandī causā**.

Cum satis calidī erant, in caldārium intrāvērunt. Dum hīc
manent, Servīlius "Corde," inquit, "tē vocāvī ad thermās **ad
loquendum**. Spērō tē *mihi auxiliō* fūtūrum esse. Ego praetūram
petītūrus, auxilium quam maximum in proximīs comitiīs habēre
10 dēbeō. Sciō tē et dīvitem et probum virum paucōrum hostium
esse, quī multa in Urbe āctūrus est, et tū *mihi auxiliō magnō* esse
potes. Praetereā, ut scīs, fīlia mea Servīlia, sēdecim annōs nāta,
mox virō nūptūra est et tē opīnor marītum optimum futūrum
esse. Sed iam saepe dē hīs rēbus dīximus. Quid in animō habēs?"

Servīlius et Cordus multa dē multīs colloquēbantur.

15 Cordus, sē aspergēns aquā frīgidā, "Servīlī," inquit, "intellegō
bene tē virum magnae auctōritātis in Urbe futūrum esse. Cognōvī fīlium tuum Marcum et Servīlia benigna vidētur.
Sī tibi aliquid auxiliī in comitiīs afferre potuerō, libenter tibi gener erō! Semper *tibi auxiliō* erō! Adsum **ad adiuvan-
dum**!"

"Optimē! Fīat! Sed nunc, hīc in caldāriō manēre mihi displicet. Redeāmus in tepidārium."

20 In tepidāriō virī duo dē multīs rēbus colloquēbantur—nōn sōlum dē comitiīs sed etiam dē Servīliā, dē rē
pūblicā, et dē Cordī futūrō.

Servīlius "Quōmodo," rogāvit, "mī Corde, *Rōmae beneficiō* esse vīs? Quās difficultātēs habēmus? Cupidus
audiendī sum."

Cordus statim respondit: "Ignēs! Ignēs quī in urbe semper fiunt semper futūrī sunt nisi quis aliquid faciet!
25 Dēbēmus vigilēs pūblicōs in urbe constituere. Volō urbem ab ignibus conservāre et sīc ūtilis et urbī et nostrō
imperātōrī Augustō esse. Fortasse Augustus adnuet coeptīs nostrīs. **Labōrandō** et **vigilandō** prō Rōmā ūtilis ac
fāmōsus fīam."

Servīlius adnuit et "Habēs," inquit, "rēctē. Ignēs semper *nōbīs perīculō* fuērunt. Sed ignēs hārum thermārum
quoque fortissimae sunt! Eāmus ad frīgidārium **refrīgerandī grātiā**, et posteā in bibliothecā plūs loquāmur quārē ibi
30 spatium plūs idōneum **loquendō** est."

Gemma

auxilium quam maximum =
as much help as possible. "As
much as possible" is the standard translation of *quam*
with a superlative.

Gemma

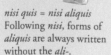

nisi quis = nisi aliquis
Following *nisi*, forms of
aliquis are always written
without the *ali-*.

POSTQUAM LĒGISTĪ

1. How many rooms do Servilius and Cordus
   visit in the bath complex? What is the name of
   each room, and what is each room used for?
2. What is Servilius' opinion of Cordus?
3. What propositions does Servilius put before
   Cordus?
4. How does Cordus respond, and what do you
   learn about Cordus' feelings for Servilia from
   his response? What is your reaction to this?
5. What are Cordus' plans for the future?

Annuit coeptīs

🔊 VERBA ŪTENDA

ac and, and besides

adnuō, adnuere, adnuī, adnūtum nod, nod assent

apodȳtērium, -iī n. dressing room

aspergō, aspergere, aspersī, aspersum sprinkle

auctōritās, -tātis f. authority, power

balneae, -ārum f. pl. bath

beneficium, -iī n. benefit

caldārium, -iī n. hot bath

calidus, -a, -um warm, hot

causa, -ae f. cause, reason; causā (+ gen.) on account of, because of

coepī, coepisse, coeptum begin (perfect in form, present in meaning)

combūrō, combūrere, combussī, combustum burn, burn up

comitia, -iōrum n. pl. elections

conservō (1) preserve, keep safe

constituō, constituere, constituī, constitūtum establish

cupidus, -a, -um (+ gen.) longing for, eager for

custōs, custōdis m./f. guard

eāmus "let's go"

exuō, exuere, exuī, exūtum strip, undress

fāmōsus, -a, -um famed, well-known

fīat "let it happen"

frīgidārium, -iī n. cold-water bath

gener, generī m. son-in-law

grātiā (+ gen.) for the sake of, for the purpose of

idōneus, -a, -um (+ dat.) suitable, fit

libenter willingly

loquāmur "let's talk"

nisi unless

nūdus, -a, -um naked, nude

nūbō, nūbere, nupsī, nuptum marry

occāsiō, -iōnis f. opportunity

opīnor, opīnārī, opīnātus sum think, believe

posteā afterward, then

praetereā besides

praetūra, -ae f. praetorship, judgeship

probus, -a, -um good, honest

proximus, -a, -um nearest, next

pūblicus, -a, -um public, common

quam + superlative = as . . . as possible

quārē because

redeāmus "let's return"

refrīgerō (1) make cool

rēs pūblica, reī pūblicae f. republic

satis enough, sufficient

sūdō (1) sweat, perspire

tepidārium, -iī n. warm bath

thermae, -ārum f. pl. public baths

ūtilis, ūtile useful

vestīmentum, -ī n. clothing

vigilō (1) keep watch

Gemma

Adnuet coeptīs: When Cordus uses this phrase he is referring to a line in Vergil's *Aeneid.* In *Lectiō Prīma* an alternative, more classical, spelling of this word is used: *adnuit.* The phrase is based upon Vergil's *Aeneid* IX.625:

Iuppiter omnipotens, audācibus adnue coeptīs

Omnipotent Jupiter, show approval on these daring undertakings.

Note how this is one of two Latin mottos on the second Great Seal of the United States on the dollar bill: *Annuit coeptīs,* "He has given his approval to (our) undertakings."

Gemma

Cordus is loosely based on a historical figure, Quintus Naevius Cordus Sutorius Macro. This Naevius was one of the earliest known prefects of the *vigilēs,* a group formed by Augustus to serve as a combination fire and police force for Rome. Macro, as he is known in the sources, went on, under Tiberius, to be head of the the praetorian guard, the force that protected the emperor. He lasted into the reign of Caligula, but was forced to commit suicide shortly thereafter. Our Cordus has a much brighter future ahead of him, as he will be appointed the first prefect of the *vigilēs.*

Grammatica A

The Gerund

In *Lectiō Prīma*, you saw how similar Latin and English gerunds are. Once you know that the Latin verbal suffix **-nd-** is equivalent to the English suffix **-ing**, you can easily translate most Latin gerunds. Note that:

- The gerund is 2nd declension, neuter singular.
- It is not used in the nominative, so there are only four endings to remember.

Here are examples of gerunds in each case from the reading:

Genitive	**exuendī** *causā*	for the sake of **undressing**
Dative	*idōneum* **loquendō**	suitable for **speaking**
Accusative	*ad* **loquendum**	for **talking/to talk**
Ablative	**labōrandō**	by **working**

Notā Bene:

- Watch the change in vowels from conjugation to conjugation. There are no surprises here:

1ˢᵗ conjugation:	*vocandī*	of calling
2ⁿᵈ conjugation:	*monendī*	of warning
3ʳᵈ conjugation:	*ducendī*	of leading
3ʳᵈ conjugation *-iō:*	*capiendī*	of seizing
4ᵗʰ conjugation:	*audiendī*	of hearing

- Deponent verbs form gerunds like regular verbs:

1ˢᵗ conjugation:	*cōnandī*	of trying
2ⁿᵈ conjugation:	*pollicendī*	of promising
3ʳᵈ conjugation:	*sequendī*	of following
3ʳᵈ conjugation *-iō:*	*patiendī*	of suffering
4ᵗʰ conjugation:	*mentiendī*	of lying

- There is no nominative form of the Latin gerund. Instead, Latin uses a subjective infinitive. English, however, can use a gerund as the subject of a sentence.

> **Learning** Latin is fun!
> *Linguam Latīnam **discere** iūcundum est!*

Gerunds of Purpose

- Gerunds in the **genitive case** with *causā* (on account of) or *grātiā* (for the sake of) show purpose.

> *Lūcius ad lūdum **discendī causā** vēnit.*
> Lucius came to school **to learn (for the sake of learning)**.

- Gerunds in the **accusative case** with *ad* also show purpose.

> *Advēnī **ad discendum**.*
> I have come **to learn (for learning)**.

Note: *Causā* and *grātiā* always follow the gerund, whereas *ad* precedes it.

EXERCEĀMUS!

30-2 Making Gerunds

Use the gerunds of *labōrō* in the following chart to form a gerund phrase in the case indicated for each of the following verbs. Then translate the gerund phrase. Follow the model.

Gen.	*labōrandī causā*	to **work**
Dat.	*idōneum **labōrandō***	suitable **for working**
Acc.	*ad **labōrandum***	to **work**
Abl.	***labōrandō***	by **working**
→ discō (gen.)	*discendī causā*	to learn

1. ambulō (dat.)	4. dūcō (gen.)	7. custōdiō (abl.)
2. respondeō (acc.)	5. ūtor (dat.)	8. moveō (gen.)
3. capiō (abl.)	6. lūdō (acc.)	9. opīnor (dat.)

The Double Dative

In *Lectiō Prīma*, Servilius said to Cordus:

Spērō tē mihi auxiliō futūrum esse!

Although this can be translated literally as

I hope you will be to me for help.

you can see how we are more likely to express this idea in English as "I hope you'll be of help to me."

Notā Bene:

- **Double datives** are most commonly used with a form of the verb *sum*.
- One of these datives refers to the person or thing concerned:

  *Tu es **mihi** maximō auxiliō!*

- The other refers to the role something serves:

  *Tu es mihi maximō **auxiliō**!*

Consider these other double datives:

Canere mihi voluptātī est.	Singing is a pleasure for me.
Hoc mālum tibi donō erit.	This apple will serve as a gift for you.
Cui bonō?	For whom is it (for) a good?
	(a legal term that asks who will benefit from a certain event or deed)

Gemma

Grammarians have various names for the parts of a double dative. The dative referring to the person can be called **dative of the person affected**, the **ethical dative**, or simply, **dative of reference**. The dative referring to the role something serves is called **dative of object for which** or **dative of purpose**.

Lectiō Secunda

Antequam Legis

A Few Months Later in the Valerian Family ...

Licinia's baby, Maximus, is now several months old. The infant was named nine days after his birth, at a special ceremony called the *Nōminālia*. This naming ceremony traditionally took place eight days after birth for females and nine for males. On this day, amid some festivity, Licinia's baby received the name Aelius Maximus A. f. (Aelius Maximus, son of Aelius). The newly named child wore a necklace of rattles called *crepundia* to scare away evil. It was also on this occasion that his *pater familiās* gave the child a *bulla*, a locket worn by male children until they came of age (between fourteen and seventeen at a toga ceremony) and by female children until they were married.

In *Lectiō Secunda* the family goes for a stroll in Rome and considers ways to deal with their over-crowded apartment. The mirror Aelius made for Licinia becomes an important topic of conversation.

As you read, watch how gerunds become gerundives.

From Gerunds to Gerundives

This is fairly simple, so don't be troubled! A gerundive is exactly like a gerund, and does everything a gerund does, but instead of being a verbal noun, it is a verbal adjective. Think of it this way:

A gerund**IVE** . . . is an adject**IVE**

This means that it will GNC with the noun it is joined to. What does this mean? Compare the following:

GERUND	GERUNDIVE
*Veniō **videndī causā**.* I am coming for the sake **of seeing**.	*Veniō **urbis videndae causā**.* I am coming for the sake **of seeing the city**.
*Vīcimus **oppugnandō**.* We won **by attacking**.	*Vīcimus **hostibus oppugnandis**.* We won **by attacking the enemy**.

For now, just translate these gerundives like gerunds (i.e., add **-ing** to the English verb) and you will be fine.

Gerundives can be used to express worthiness or obligation. For example, *servus laudandus* is "a slave worthy to be praised" or "a praiseworthy slave." Obligation is expressed by the gerundive + form of *sum* = "must be"

> *Imperātor Augustus **timendus** est.*   The emperor Augustus must be feared.

The person **by whom** the action must be done is in the **dative** case.

*Augustus **hostibus suīs** timendus est.*	Augustus must be feared	or	**His enemies** must fear Augustus.
	by his enemies.		

This use of the gerundive is called the **future passive periphrastic**.
All gerundive phrases are marked in **bold** in *Lectiō Secunda*.

EXERCEĀMUS!

30-3 Gerundives

As you read, make a line-by-line list of the gerundives marked in **bold**. Identify the word with which the gerundive GNCs. Then give the GNC of the gerundive. Follow the model.

Line	Gerundive	Word	Gender	Number	Case
→ 3	solvendae	difficultātis	feminine	singular	genitive

🔊 PARUM SPATIĪ

In aliā urbis parte Valeria, Aelius et Licinia per viās Sūbūrae ambulant. Ancilla Flāvia et avia Plōtia īnfantem cūrant dum parentēs novī et Valeria anxia inter sē colloquuntur **difficultātis suae solvendae causā**. Sōcratēs, clāmāns et garriēns, in umerīs Aeliī sedet. Sīmiīs magnopere āerem dulcem spīrāre placet.

Sōcratēs fortiter garrīre incipit.

5   Valeria, "**Aliquid**," inquit, "**nōbīs faciendum est**. Parum spatiī habēmus et sex hominēs habitāre in duōbus conclāvibus difficile est! Mox **plūs spatiī inveniendum est**, sed quōmodo? Plūrimōs hominēs sed minimam pecūniam habēmus."

Aelius, "Rēctē habēs," inquit. "Aut **familia nostra nova movenda est** aut **plūs pecūniae inveniendum est**! Ego et Hephaestus, **servus laudandus**, dīligenter labōrāmus sed **opus**
10   **novum nōbīs accipiendum est**. Opīnor **novās rēs** in officīnā meā **faciendās et vendendās esse**. Valeria, quid opīnāris? Aliquās rēs, quās in officīnā meā fabricābō, vendere in tabernā potes? Vīdistīne speculum quod Liciniae fabricāvī? Tāle vendere potes?"

Valeria "Profectō," inquit, "tālia vendere possum! **Speculum mīrandum** fabricāvistī! Sī tālia **plūra mīranda aut ūtilia**, fabricāveris, ea vendam!"

15   Respondet Aelius: "Bene, sed **exemplum** in tabernā **monstrandum est** et nihil promptum habēmus.

Licinia, quae adhūc nihil dīxit, "Accipe, māter," lacrimātūra inquit, "speculum meum ad monstrandum. Sed, tē obsecrō, **id** nullō modō **tibi vendendum est**. Speculum mihi cārum est quārē Aelius id mihi dōnō fabricāvit. Et quoque hās inaurēs meās, dōnum nūptiāle, accipe monstrandī causā, dōnec Aelius aliās inaurēs fabricāverit."

Valeria, "Nōlī tē perturbāre, Licinia. Hominēs tuās rēs spectābunt sed nōn ement. Sciō **speculum mihi custōdi-**
20   **endum esse et inaurēs prōtegendās esse**! Aelī, abī nunc et strēnuē labōrā **ad multās variāsque rēs fabricandās**!"

Subitō Sōcratēs, quī semper studiōsus familiae suae **dēfendendae** est, puerōs in viā lūdentēs vidēns, fortiter garrīre incipit et ex umerīs Aeliī **ad puerōs persequendōs** salīre vult.

Aelius, "Tacē," inquit, "sīmia! Sī nōn tacueris, aēneum **sīmiam vendendum** habēbimus!!"

Sōcratēs, timēns, **suī servandī grātiā** nihil dīcit et quiētus sedet. Ut dīcitur—"**Sīmiae videndī sed nōn audi-**
25   **endī sunt**!"

🔊 VERBA ŪTENDA

adhūc to this point, still, yet
aēneus, -a, -um bronze
āēr, āeris m. air
avia, -ae f. grandmother
causa, -ae f. cause, reason; causā (+ gen.) on account of, because of
conclāve, conclāvis n. room
custōdiō, custōdīre, custōdīvī/custōdiī, custōdītum watch, guard
dēfendō, dēfendere, dēfendī, dēfensum defend

dīligens, dīligentis **careful, diligent, frugal**
exemplum, -ī n. sample
fabricō **(1) forge, make, shape, build, construct**
garriō, garrīre, garrīvī/garriī, garrītum chatter
Hephaestus, -ī m. Hephaestus, the slave who works with Aelius in the blacksmith shop
inaurēs, inaurium m. pl. earrings

lūdō, lūdere, lūsī, lūsum **play, tease**
moveō, movēre, mōvī, mōtum **move, affect**
obsecrō (1) implore, beg
officīna, -ae f. workshop
parum too little, not enough
persequor, persequī, persecūtus sum pursue
profectō without question, undoubtedly
promptus, -a, -um ready

prōtegō, prōtegere, prōtexī, prōtectum protect
quārē **because, for**
solvō, solvere, solvī, solūtum loosen, unbind
speculum, -ī **n. mirror**
spīrō (1) breathe
studiōsus, -a, -um (+ gen.) eager (to)
umerus, -ī m. shoulder
varius, -a, -um **various, changeable, mixed**
vendō, vendere, vendidī, venditum **sell**

POSTQUAM LĒGISTĪ

1. Where is Socrates the monkey as this narrative begins?
2. What problem are Valeria, Aelius, and Licinia discussing?
3. What plan do they make to solve this problem?
4. How do modern couples tend to deal with the same issues?
5. How does Socrates misbehave at the end of the narrative?
6. What does Aelius threaten to do to Socrates for misbehaving?

Grammatica B

Gerundives

Latin gerunds and gerundives are usually easy to pick out because of the *-nd-* added before the ending. Remember that the gerund is a **verbal noun**, whereas the gerundive is a **verbal adjective**. Here are the main features of the gerundive:

- The **gerundive** is an adjective that uses the same endings as a 2-1-2 adjective.
- Like the **participle**, the **gerundive** is a kind of **verbal adjective**. Whereas the participle is simply descriptive, the gerundive expresses obligation or necessity.
- As a verbal adjective, the gerundive is also sometimes called a **future passive participle**, translated into English as "going to be [verbed], deserving to be [verbed]."

vir admirātus	perfect passive participle	an admired man
vir admirāns	present active participle	an admiring man
vir admirandus	gerundive	a man who ought to be admired an admirable man

Notā Bene: Gerundives are the **only** forms of deponent verbs that can have a passive meaning!

arbitrandus	worthy **to be** thought
recordandus	worthy **of being** remembered
loquendus	worthy **to be** spoken
ūtendus	worthy **of being** used

And here is an example from *Lectiō Prīma*:

> *Speculum **mīrandum** fabricāvistī.*
> You have made a mirror **worthy of being marvelled at**.

Future Passive Periphrastic and Dative of Agent

Gerundives in the nominative case with a form of *sum* are used to express **necessity**. Such phrases are called **future passive periphrastic** constructions. If you do not like that name, think of it as the "gerund of gottabe." The formal term is very descriptive:

- **Future** because the action hasn't happened yet.
- **Passive** because it is done to someone/something.
- **Periphrastic** because it needs a form of *sum*. (More on the term **periphrastic** in the *Angulus Grammaticus*.)

Consider this famous Latin phrase that uses a future passive periphrastic:

> *Carthāgo dēlenda est!*   Carthage must be destroyed.

Now here is the same phrase with the identity of the destroyer added:

> *Carthāgo **nōbīs** dēlenda est!*   Carthage must be destroyed **by us**.

Nota Bene:

- The *nōbīs* is called a **dative of agent** and is found only with the future passive periphrastic.
- If it helps to remember that it is a dative, not ablative, of agent, think of this literal translation—"To us there is something that must be done."
- You can always translate these phrases actively: "it must be done by us" = "we must do."

The title of this chapter is also a gerundive phrase. How would you now translate it?

EXERCEĀMUS!

30-4 Gerunds and Gerundives

Which gerund(ive) construction is the correct one for the underlined words? Do not let the translation fool you—they are all gerund(ive) constructions. Be careful of GNC when using gerundives!

1. <u>In order to make a new mirror</u>, Aelius worked harder.
   a. ad speculum novum fabricandam
   b. ad novī speculī fabricandī
   c. novī speculī fabricandī causā
   d. novum speculum fabricandum est

2. Aelius survives <u>by working</u> hard.
   a. labōrandum
   b. labōrandī
   c. labōrandō
   d. labōrāre

3. All the women in the neighborhood came <u>to see Maximus.</u>
   a. Maximum vidēre
   b. Maximī videndī gratiā
   c. Maximum videndum
   d. Maximus videndus est

4. Valeria, too, will work in the house <u>to get money.</u>
   a. pecūniam obtinēre
   b. pecūniae obtinendī causā
   c. ad pecūniam obtinendum
   d. ad pecūniam obtinendam

5. Socrates gets in trouble <u>by playing.</u>
   a. lūdendō
   b. lūdendī
   c. lūdendus
   d. lūdere

6. They were speaking together <u>to solve their difficulties</u>.
   a. difficultātum suārum solvendārum causā
   b. difficultātis suae solvendae causā
   c. difficultātēs suās solvendās causā
   d. difficultātum suōrum solvendōrum causā

30-5 Dative of Agent and the Future Passive Periphrastic

Find the dative of agent in each of the following future passive periphrastic constructions. Then translate each construction two ways (actively and passively). Follow the model.

→ Future Passive Periphrastic	Dative of Agent	Translations
Aliquid nōbīs faciendum est.	nōbīs	Passive: Something must be done by us. Active: We must do something.

1. Plūs spatiī familiae inveniendum est.
2. Familia nova mihi nōn videnda est.
3. Plūs pecūniae virō inveniendum erat.

4. Opus novum nōbīs accipiendum est.
5. Novae rēs Aeliō fabricandae sunt.

Mōrēs Rōmānī

Thermae Rōmānae

Public baths like the one visited by Servilius and Cordus were an important feature of Roman daily life. Very few Roman homes, even among the wealthy, had private bathing facilities in the first century B.C. Rather, both men and women would visit the public baths. Sometimes there were separate bath complexes for men and women, and sometimes they had separate hours in the same facility. Men and women never bathed together publicly.

A typical bath complex included the following parts:

- *apodȳtērium, -iī* **n.** undressing room
- *tepidārium, -iī* **n.** warm-water room
- *caldārium, -iī* **n.** hot-water or steam room
- *lābrum, -iī* **n.** basin with cool water in the *caldārium*
- *frīgidārium, -iī* **n.** cold-water room
- *palaestra, -ae* **f.** exercise space

- *bibliotheca, ae* **f.** library (occasionally)
- *piscīna, -ae* **f.** swimming pool (occasionally)
- *latrīna, -ae* **f.** public latrine, usually a row of benches with holes in the seats and flowing water underneath

Lābrum

Hypocauston Thermārum Stabiānārum Pompēiīs

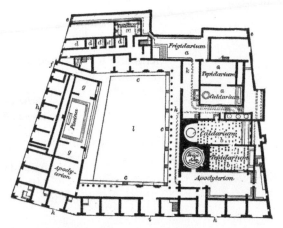

Forma Thermārum Stabiānārum Pompēiīs

An extensive aqueduct system was essential to these baths. Water from an aqueduct fed into a large reservoir and from there into the appropriate rooms. It was heated by means of a sophisticated heating system called a hypocaust, which took heat from the furnace and ran it under the raised floor of the rooms and in between its walls. Having gone through the rooms, the water often then passed through the latrines before flowing into the sewer.

These bath facilities were not just places to get cleansed. Massages and rub-downs using olive oil were also available. The baths were also important social meeting places. The conversation between Servilius and Cordus shows how serious business could also be conducted in the baths.

Latīna Hodierna

Memorandum

You may remember that you saw a future passive periphrastic phrase used by Chiron the schoolmaster in Chapter 6:

> Nunc est bibendum!

Chiron was quoting the first words of Horace's *Ode* I.37, a drinking song celebrating Octavian, the future Augustus, and his victory over Marc Antony and Cleopatra at the Battle of Actium in 31 B.C. Here is the first stanza of Horace's poem in simplified word order. See the *Verba Ūtenda* for help. Note that it actually contains two periphrastic constructions.

> Nunc bibendum est.
> nunc pede lībero tellūs pulsanda est;
> nunc Saliāribus dapibus ornāre pulvīnar deōrum tempus est,
> Ō sodāles.

Gemma

Notice how Horace repeats the word *nunc* three times. This is a poetic figure of speech called **anaphora**.

VERBA ŪTENDA

daps, dapis f. sacrificial feast, offering	*pulsō* (1) strike, beat; "strike the ground with feet," i.e., dance	(used for a religious statue)	*sodālis, sodālis* m. companion
līber, lībera, līberum free	*pulvīnar, -āris* m. cushioned couch	*Saliāris, -e* of the Salii (priests of Mars, god of war)	*tellūs, tellūris* f. earth, ground
ōrnō (1) decorate			

Gerundive forms should look familiar to you because we have been using them throughout the book as titles:

> *Verba Discenda* words that must be learned
> *Verba Ūtenda* words that must be used

Here are two gerundive names for girls:

> Amanda she who must be loved
> Miranda she who must be admired

A number of gerundives have been borrowed by English:

memorandum	something that must be remembered
referendum	something that must be carried back
addendum	something that must be added
corrigendum	something that must be corrected

Although some people (who do not know Latin) will make the plural of these words by adding a final -s (memorandums, referendums, etc.), these words traditionally use Latin neuter plural endings in English: memoranda, referenda, addenda, and corrigenda.

Note that English only uses the "plural" form of "agenda," and some other erstwhile gerunds have lost their endings:

legend	something that must be read
reverend	one that should be revered
tremendous	that which should be feared

Orbis Terrārum Rōmānus

Carthāgō

The great Punic city of Carthage, located in what is now Tunisia on Africa's northern coast, was Rome's bitter rival for control of the western Mediterranean. The two cities fought a series of three wars, known as the Punic Wars, which lasted from 264 B.C. to 146 B.C. The conflict did not end until Rome completely conquered Carthage and the city and its territory became the Roman province of *Āfrica*. During the imperial period, Carthage was an important commercial area, producing much grain and sending many wild beasts to circuses throughout the Roman Empire.

Cato the Elder (234–149 B.C.) was the sworn enemy of Carthage. It is said that when he spoke in the Senate, no matter the nature of the speech, he always worked in the phrase:

Carthāgō dēlenda est! Carthage must be destroyed!

Cato did this in the years following the Second Punic War (218–201 B.C.), which Rome almost lost to the Carthaginian general, Hannibal. Cato's point was that Rome would never be completely secure until it had destroyed its rival. Although several ancient authors, including Pliny the Elder and Plutarch, refer to Cato's practice, Cato's exact words are unknown today. An alternative ancient version survives in indirect statement:

Censeō Carthāginem dēlendam esse.

Thermae Rōmānae Carthāgine

Carthāgō Nova et Antīqua

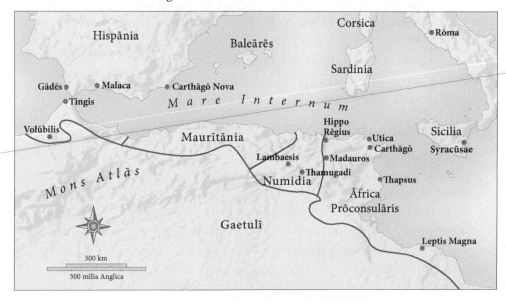

Carthāgō in Āfricā

QUID PUTĀS?

1. What does a Roman bath facility tell you about ancient Roman society?
2. What facilities in American society would serve social purposes similar to those of the ancient Roman baths?
3. What aspects of the ancient Roman bath facility would not be agreeable to Americans? What aspects might we like?
4. Horace's *Nunc est bibendum* ode is a drinking song about a major political event and naval battle. What poems or songs have been written to celebrate similar events in U.S. history?
5. Use the Latin word *referendum* to explain how a referendum works in the U.S. law.
6. Translate the two Latin mottoes on the Great Seal of the United States: *Annuit coeptīs* and *Novus Ordo S(a)eclōrum*. Then explain why you think these mottoes were chosen.
7. Look at the map of the Mediterranean in the endpapers of this book and explain how geography may have made a conflict between Rome and Carthage inevitable.

EXERCEĀMUS!

30-6 Scrībāmus

Rewrite the following passage, based on *Lectiō Secunda*, as indirect statement. Begin each sentence with *Flāvia dīcit*. Then change the main verb to an infinitive and make its subject accusative. Remember to use passive infinitives for the deponent verbs. Follow the model.

→ Valeria et Aelius et Licinia per viās Subūrae ambulant.
  Flāvia dīcit Valeriam et Aelium et Liciniam per viās Subūrae ambulāre.

1. Ancilla infantem cūrat.
2. Parentēs novī et Valeria anxia inter sē colloquuntur.
3. Sīmia, clāmāns et garriēns, in umerīs Aeliī sedet.
4. Puerī in viā lūdentēs ā sīmiā videntur.
5. Familia Valeriae paucum spatiī habet.
6. Sex hominēs in duōbus conclāvibus habitant.

30-7 Colloquāmur

Now use *Quis dīcit?* to introduce each of the indirect statements you made in Exercise 30-6. Take turns asking and answering these questions with a classmate. You can make up your own answers. Here is a pool of possible answers:

Flāvia dīcit / dīcō / nēmō dīcit / magister dīcit / dīcimus

→ Quis dīcit Valeriam et Aelium et Liciniam per viās Subūrae ambulāre?
  Dīcō Valeriam et Aelium et Liciniam per viās Subūrae ambulāre.

30-8 Thinking about the *Verba Discenda*

Use the *Verba Discenda* to answer the following questions.

1. Compare the meaning of *adhūc* with the meaning of *hūc*. One is temporal and the other spatial. Which is which?
2. If *avia* is grandmother, can you remember the word for grandfather?
3. Which principal part of *combūrō* provides English with derivatives? Give three derivatives.
4. Which *verbum discendum* is deponent? How can you tell?
5. What Latin verb is the origin of the noun *speculum*? What does this verb mean? Explain the relationship between the meanings of this verb and noun.

6. Use a *verbum discendum* to explain the English word "satisfaction."

7. Find the words in the following narrative that derive at least in part from the *verba discenda* below. List the English word and its Latin source. Follow the model.

→ custodian: custōs

The diligent school custodian moved slowly through the halls, speculating about who (or what) might have caused the internal combustion engine in his car to die so quickly. He opined that the culprit was young Mr. Sullivan, because the ludicrous story the young man had told was a mere fabric of various lies. He'd get to the bottom of the story and have the satisfaction of hearing the principal call the young man down to her office over the public address system!

🔊 VERBA DISCENDA

adhūc to this point, still, yet

aēneus, -a, -um bronze

avia, -ae f. grandmother

calidus, -a, -um warm, hot

causa, -ae f. cause, reason; **causā** (+ gen.) on account of, because of [causation]

combūrō, combūere, combussī, combustum burn, burn up [combustion]

custōdiō, custōdīre, custōdīvī/custōdiī,

custōdītum watch, guard [custody]

custōs, custōdis m./f. guard [custodian]

dīligens, dīligentis careful, diligent, frugal [diligence]

fabricō (1) forge, make, shape, build, construct [fabricate]

gener, generī m. son-in-law

grātiā (+ gen.) for the sake of; with a gerund(ive) = "for the purpose of"

lūdō, lūdere, lūsī, lūsum play, tease [ludicrous]

moveō, movēre, mōvī, mōtum move, affect [movable, motion]

nisi unless

opīnor, opīnārī, opīnātus sum think, believe [opinion, opine]

posteā afterward, then

probus, -a, -um good, honest [probity]

proximus, -a, -um nearest, next [proximate]

pūblicus, -a, -um public, common

quārē because, for

satis enough, sufficient [satisfactory]

speculum, -ī n. mirror

ūtilis, ūtile useful [utilitarian]

varius, -a, -um various, changeable, mixed [variegated]

vendō, vendere, vendidī, venditum sell [vendible]

Angulus Grammaticus

Periphrasis

The grammatical term "future passive periphrastic" sounds quite strange and intimidating in English, but we actually use periphrastic constructions all the time, probably more than Romans did. **Periphrasis** is a Greek word that means "speaking around," and its Latin equivalent, *circumlocūtiō*, gives us the English word "circumlocution."

You have seen at least one example previously. Remember that Latin uses *nōlī* or *nōlīte* + infinitive to create a negative command: *Nōlī tangere!* (Don't touch!). This is a periphrasis because it literally says, "Be unwilling to touch!"

Another example involves the FAP, future active participle. In English we have a tense with which to say things like, "I'm about to do this," or, in dialect, "She's fixing to leave." Such a tense does not exist in Latin but it can be said via periphrasis: *Id factūrus sum* or *Abitūra est*.

Seen another way, the whole perfect passive system in Latin is periphrastic, as it is in English:

Perfect	*vocātus sum*	I have been called
		Literally, "I am having been called"
Pluperfect	*vocātus eram*	I had been called
		Literally, "I was having been called"
Future Perfect	*vocātus erō*	I will have been called
		Literally, "I will be having been called"

So what is "periphrastic" about the **future passive periphrastic**? As you saw above, a form of *sum* needs to accompany the gerundive to create this expression: *Carthāgō delenda est!* Literally, this says "Carthage is having to be destroyed."

This construction is part of what is sometimes called the **periphrastic conjugation**, consisting of the future active participle or the gerundive with forms of *sum*:

TENSE	ACTIVE PERIPHRASTIC	PASSIVE PERIPHRASTIC
Present	*vocātūrus sum* I am about to call	*vocandus sum* I must be called
Imperfect	*vocātūrus eram* I was about to call	*vocandus eram* I had to be called
Future	*vocātūrus erō* I will be about to call	*vocandus erō* I will have to be called
Perfect	*vocātūrus fuī* I have been about to call	*vocandus fuī* I have had to be called
Pluperfect	*vocātūrus fueram* I had been about to call	*vocandus fueram* I had had to be called
Future Perfect	*vocātūrus fuerō* I will have been about to call	*vocandus fuerō* I will have had to be called

Photo Credits

Page 388 (top) Witchcraft/Fotolia, LLC—Royalty Free; **page 388 (bottom)** Thomas J. Sienkewicz; **page 389** Clipart.com; **page 390** PaulPaladin/Shutterstock; **page 397 (top)** Thomas J. Sienkewicz; **page 397 (bottom left)** Thomas J. Sienkewicz; **page 397 (bottom right)** Clipart.com; **page 399 (top)** Albo/Shutterstock; **page 399 (bottom)** Alexey Goosev/Shutterstock.

31

Fīat

Lectiō Prīma

Antequam Legis

This narrative takes place the morning after Servilius' conversation with Cordus in the baths. Servilius tells his wife that the wedding plans are fixed, and Caecilia decides to go shopping for possible wedding presents for her daughter. This scene illustrates the two-tiered organization of an upper-class Roman household as the slaves rush to prepare breakfast for the master and his family.

Are You in the Right Mood?

In this chapter, you will learn to recognize and use one more grammatical mood, the **subjunctive**. Whereas indicative verbs "indicate" an action that actually happens, and an imperative is an order or command, a subjunctive generally refers to an action that is not as "real" as an indicative verb. That is, the subjunctive (its name means something like "subordinate") indicates not so much fact as potential, possibility, or probability. It often helps to think of it this way: The subjunctive is the mood of "lesser reality."

In the *lectiō*, you will see the **present subjunctive** and some of its uses. You will learn names for these uses later, but for now just concentrate on recognizing subjunctives and how to translate them.

Recognizing Present Subjunctives

Present subjunctives are identical to present indicatives, except for a change in the vowel that links the ending to the stem.

You can remember the vowel changes between indicative and subjunctive with this time-honored acronym:

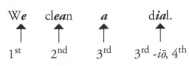

We clean a dial.

1st · 2nd · 3rd · 3rd -*iō*, 4th

We →	1st conjugation →	*a* and *o* change to *e*
clean →	2nd conjugation →	*e* changes to *ea*
a →	3rd (reg.) conjugation →	vowels change to *a*
dial →	3rd -*iō* and 4th conjugation →	vowels change to *ia*

From *Disce! An Introductory Latin Course, volume 2*, First Edition. Francesco Bonavita. Copyright © 2011 by Pearson Education, Inc. Published by Pearson Prentice Hall.
All rights reserved.

Domus L. Ceiī Secundī

GRAMMATICA
Mood Consolidation
Translating the Subjunctive
The Present Subjunctive
The Present Subjunctive of Irregular Verbs
The Independent Subjunctive
Purpose Clauses

MŌRĒS RŌMĀNĪ
Salūtātiō

LATĪNA HODIERNA
Latin in the Periodic Table
of the Elements

ORBIS TERRĀRUM RŌMĀNUS
Pompēiī et Vesuvius

ANGULUS GRAMMATICUS
More on the Independent Uses
of the Subjunctive

LECTIŌNĒS:
MĀNE
and
CAECILIA ET VALERIA

In this chapter Caecilia goes shopping to prepare for Servilia's wedding. The lives of our two families begin to intersect when Caecilia stops at Valeria's shop for a snack.

403

Now compare these subjunctive forms to their indicative equivalents:

CONJUGATION	MOOD	FORM	TRANSLATION
1st	Indicative	*Labōrāmus.*	We work.
	Subjunctive	***Labōrēmus!***	Let's work!
2nd	Indicative	*Vidēmus.*	We see.
	Subjunctive	***Videāmus!***	Let's see!
3rd	Indicative	*Loquimur.*	We are talking.
	Subjunctive	***Loquāmur!***	Let's talk!
3rd -*iō*	Indicative	*Facimus.*	We are doing.
	Subjunctive	***Faciāmus!***	Let's do!
4th	Indicative	*Dormit.*	She is sleeping.
	Subjunctive	***Dormiat!***	Let her sleep.

Translating Present Subjunctives

The subjunctive can be used independently or as part of a subordinate clause. All the subjunctives, marked in **bold** in *Lectiō Prīma*, are used independently. For now:

- If the verb is in the 3rd person, try "Let 'em" or "let him" or "let them." Thus: *inveniat* = Let him come in. *Fīat!* = Let it be done!
- If the verb is in the 1st person plural, try "Let's." Thus: *Eāmus!* = Let's go. *Bibāmus* = Let's drink.
- If the verb is anything else, choose what sounds best from the typical "subjunctive words": should, would, could, might, may.

EXERCEĀMUS!

31-1 **Subjunctives**

Which translation for the subjunctive (in **bold**) is best? Since these sentences are from your reading, this exercise will be of use to you as you read *Lectiō Prīma*.

1. Ientāculum **appōnātur.**   a. is served   b. will be served   c. let it be served
2. Nē **dormiāmus!**   a. let's not sleep   b. we have not slept   c. we are not sleeping
3. **Laborēmus!**   a. we are working   b. we work   c. let's work
4. Ligna in focō **impōnantur!**   a. they will be placed   b. let them be placed   c. they were placed
5. Fīcī **ferantur!**   a. they are brought   b. let them be brought   c. they will be brought
6. Pānis **pōnātur**   a. let it be laid out   b. it is laid out   c. it has been laid out
7. Quid **faciāmus?**   a. are we doing?   b. might we do?   c. did we do?
8. Dī mē **iuvent!**   a. may they help   b. they are helping   c. let's help
9. **Abeat!**   a. he will go away   b. let him go away   c. he goes away
10. Tranquillior **sit!**   a. He may be calmer   b. He will be calmer   c. He is calmer
11. Tranquillitās in culīnā **regnet!**   a. it reigns   b. let it reign   c. it will reign
12. **Fīat!**   a. it will be done   b. it is done   c. let it be done
13. Rēs aptae **fabricentur!**   a. let them be made   b. they will be made   c. let us make
14. **Nōlim** nostram fīliam nuptūrām esse sine rēbus optimīs pulcherrimīsque.   a. I do not wish   b. I wouldn't want   c. let's wish
15. "Servī meī," inquit, "cibum meum **edant!**"   a. they will eat   b. let's eat   c. let them eat

Gemma

Prōgrediendum est in lines 1-2 of *Lectiō Prīma* is an example of an impersonal use of the gerundive. *Forum* is the object of *ad*, not the subject of *prōgrediendum est*.

The expression is literally translated "there must be a going to the Forum by Servilius," but we would say "Servilius must go to the Forum."

MĀNE

Māne est sed iam diēs aestuōsus est. Mox ad Forum Servīliō progrediendum est
sed priusquam abit, clientēs suī recipiendī sunt prō ianuā domī. Rōmae cōtīdiē
māne quisque patrōnus clientēs suōs recipit et eīs aut pecūniam aut sportulam
dat. Post hanc "salūtātiōnem" patrōnus ad Forum ad rēs suās agendās abit.

Domina lectīcam suam ascendit.

5   Dum Servīlius et clientēs salūtātiōnem agunt, Caecilia expergiscitur, sē
lavat et ientāculum in peristȳliō exspectat. Ancillae cuidam imperat et "Ientāculum quam celerrimē **appōnātur**! Iēiūna
sum! Celerrimē!"

In culīnā Sicō ancillīs imperat et īrātus fit. "Anna! Pallas! Scybalē! Cur ientāculum nōn iam parātum est? Nē
dormiāmus. Celerius **laborēmus** omnēs! Ligna in focō **impōnantur**. Fīcī **ferantur**! Pānis in mensā **pōnātur**! Mel et
10   vīnum **effundantur**!"

Pallas "Sicō," inquit, "ubique quaesīvī sed nullum mel invenīre possum! Vēnitne herī mel dē apiāriīs?"

Sicō, dēspērāns, clāmat: "Quid **faciāmus**? Mel inveniendum est! Dī mē **iuvent**!" Tālibus clāmātīs, Sicō ē culīnā currit.

Scybalē Annam "Quō," rogat, "Sicō vādit?"

Anna respondet: "Sentiō coquum nostrum ad mel inveniendum abīre! Utinam aequiōris animī **sit**. **Abeat**! Postquam
15   reveniet, tranquillior **sit** et nē semper, sicut Vesuvius, ēruptūrus **sit**! Interim, tranquillitās in culīnā **regnet**!"

Caecilia, dum ientāculum exspectat, ad coniugem vocat. "Marce," inquit, "Quid dē Cordō herī accidit? Generne
noster fiet?"

"Ita, vērō," respondit Servīlius, "generum novum habēmus! Sed nunc mihi in Forō multae rēs agendae sunt. Quid
tū, cāra uxor, in animō hodiē agere habēs?"

20   "Volō quāsdam rēs inspectāre. Dōna fīliae nostrae nuptūrae apta invenienda sunt! Sī rēs aptās invēnerō, licetne eās
fabricārī?"

Servīlius "Ita, vērō," inquit, "**fīat**! Sī rēs aptās invēneris, **fabricentur**! **Nōlim** nostram fīliam nuptūram esse sine
rēbus optimīs pulcherrimīsque."

Tālibus dictīs, Servīlius abiit. Tunc, mele inventō, Sicō, cibum portāns, peristȳlium intrat. "Domina," inquit,
25   "tempus est ientāculī edendī. Ecce, mel novum habēmus!"

Caecilia, "Servī meī," inquit, "cibum meum **edant**! Nunc mihi abeundum est! Nullum tempus edendō habeō! **Eāmus**!"

Quam īrātus Sicō est! Sed coquus nihil dīcēns in culīnam abit. Sicō prūdentissimus servus est et numquam id
quod in mente habet dīcit. Quid aliud servī facere **possint**!? Interim domina celeriter domō abit et lectīcam suam
ascendit. Tunc statim ā servīs ad dōna fīliae emenda fertur.

VERBA ŪTENDA

aequus, -a, -um level, even
aestuōsus, -a, -um hot
apiārius, -iī m. beekeeper
aptus, -a, -um suitable, fit
cliens, clientis m. client
coniunx, coniugis m./f. spouse
despērō (1) despair
dī = deī m. nom. pl. "gods"
effundō, effundere, effūdī,
    effūsum pour out
ērumpō, ērumpere, ērūpī,
    ēruptum erupt
expergiscor, expergiscī,
    experrectus sum wake up
ficus, -ī f. fig

focus, -ī m. fireplace, hearth
ientāculum, -ī n. breakfast
impōnō, impōnere, imposuī,
    impositum put on
interim meanwhile
lavō, lavāre, lāvī, lautum/
    lavātum/lōtum wash
lignum, -ī n. wood, firewood
mel, mellis n. honey
mens, mentis f. mind
nē not, in order that
    not, lest
nūbō, nūbere, nupsī,
    nuptum marry
pānis, pānis m. bread

prūdens, prūdentis prudent
quisque, quaeque, quodque
    each
quō (to) where?
recipiō, recipere, recēpī,
    receptum accept, re-
    ceive, take back; *sē*
    recipere retreat (take
    oneself somewhere)
regnō (1) reign, hold
    power over
reveniō, revenīre, revēnī,
    reventum come back,
    return
Rōmae at/in Rome

salūtātiō, -ōnis f. greeting,
    formal morning visit by
    a client to a patron
Scybalē, -ēs f. a woman's name
    (Note Greek case endings.)
sportula, -ae f. gift of money
    or food from patron to
    client, lit., "little basket"
tranquillitās, -tātis f.
tranquillus, -a, -um calm,
    still calmness, stillness;
    fair weather
utinam (+ subj.) would that,
    how I wish that!
vādō (1) go, advance

POSTQUAM LĒGISTĪ

1. What obligation does Servilius have at home every morning before he goes to the Forum?
2. The cook Sico gets angry twice in this narrative. What are the two things that upset him?
3. Why does Sico leave the kitchen?
4. How does Anna feel the mood in the kitchen will be while Sico is absent?
5. Where does Caecilia wait for her breakfast? To whom does she talk to while she waits?
6. What news does Caecilia learn?
7. What does she decide to do as a result of this news?

Grammatica A

Mood Consolidation

As you know, every Latin verb form has tense, voice, and mood. There are three moods in Latin:

Mood	Examples	Characteristics
Indicative	amat, amābit, amāvit	fact
Imperative	Amā! Amāte! Nōlī amāre!	command, order
Subjunctive	amem, amēmus, ament	wish, possibility, polite command

Mood indicates the manner in which the action is expressed: as fact, as command, or as "less real" or subordinate. In addition to these three moods, you should also remember that verbs can become **verbals**:

Infinitive	amāre, amāvisse, amātum esse	verbal noun
Participle	amāns, amātus, amātūrus	verbal adjective
Gerund	amandī	verbal noun
Gerundive	amandus, -a, -um	verbal adjective

Translating the Subjunctive

There are no hard and fast rules as to how you should translate a Latin subjunctive into English. It all depends on context, but it may help you to study these examples to distinguish indicative, imperative, and subjunctive in English.

Indicative	**Subjunctive**
I praise my students.	I might praise my students.
Imperative	**Subjunctive**
Don't praise the lazy.	If you should praise the lazy . . .

However, there are many situations in which the subjunctive will have a very different meaning. You will learn these as you go along. It is useful to memorize these "subjunctive words" and use them when context seems to allow it: **should, would, could, might, may**.

The subjunctive mood is occasionally used as the main verb in the sentence. This is called an **independent** subjunctive. In this part of the chapter we introduce you to several uses of this kind of subjunctive. More frequently, subjunctive forms are found in dependent clauses, so called because they depend on and further elucidate the action of a main verb. In *Lectiō Secunda* you will see a **dependent** use of the subjunctive.

The Present Subjunctive

As you saw in *Lectiō Prīma*, the subjunctive forms of the verb use regular personal endings but distinctive connecting vowels. Compare here the present active indicative and present active subjunctive forms of all conjugations.

INDICATIVE				
1ˢᵗ Conjugation	**2ⁿᵈ Conjugation**	**3ʳᵈ Conjugation**	**3ʳᵈ Conjugation -iō**	**4ᵗʰ Conjugation**
vocō	moneō	dūcō	capiō	audiō
vocās	monēs	dūcis	capis	audīs
vocat	monet	dūcit	capit	audit
vocāmus	monēmus	dūcimus	capimus	audīmus
vocātis	monētis	dūcitis	capitis	audītis
vocant	monent	dūcunt	capiunt	audiunt

SUBJUNCTIVE				
1ˢᵗ Conjugation	**2ⁿᵈ Conjugation**	**3ʳᵈ Conjugation**	**3ʳᵈ Conjugation -iō**	**4ᵗʰ Conjugation**
vocem	moneam	dūcam	capiam	audiam
vocēs	moneās	dūcās	capiās	audiās
vocet	moneat	dūcat	capiat	audiat
vocēmus	moneāmus	dūcāmus	capiāmus	audiāmus
vocētis	moneātis	dūcātis	capiātis	audiātis
vocent	moneant	dūcant	capiant	audiant

Notā Bene:

- The 1ˢᵗ person singular active ending in the subjunctive is always *-m* instead of *-ō*.
- The connecting vowel in the present subjunctive follows the pattern in the sentence "We clean a dial."
- Passive verbs and deponents follow the same vowel pattern to create their present subjunctives.

Conjugation	Passive Indicative	Passive Subjunctive
1ˢᵗ	cōnor, cōnāris, etc.	cōner, cōnēris, etc.
2ⁿᵈ	vereor, verēris, etc.	verear, vereāris, etc.
3ʳᵈ	sequor, sequeris, etc.	sequar, sequāris, etc.
3ʳᵈ -io	ingredior, ingredieris, etc.	ingrediar, ingrediāris, etc.
4ᵗʰ	mentior, mentīris, etc.	mentiar, mentiāris, etc.

- **False Friends:** A handful of forms in the 3ʳᵈ and 4ᵗʰ conjugations are identical in the 1ˢᵗ person of the future indicative and the present subjunctive. Thus *dūcam* is either future indicative or present subjunctive. *Audiar* can be translated "I will be heard" or "Let me be heard." Don't worry too much about this. The form is usually clear in context.

The Present Subjunctive of Irregular Verbs

Latin verbs that are irregular in the present indicative are typically irregular in the present subjunctive as well. These forms require special attention.

SUM	POSSUM	EŌ	FĪŌ	VOLŌ	NŌLŌ	MĀLŌ
sim	possim	eam	fīam	velim	nōlim	mālim
sīs	possīs	eās	fīās	velīs	nōlīs	mālīs
sit	possit	eat	fīat	velit	nōlit	mālit
sīmus	possīmus	eāmus	fīāmus	velīmus	nōlīmus	mālīmus
sītis	possītis	eātis	fīātis	velītis	nōlītis	mālītis
sint	possint	eant	fīant	velint	nōlint	mālint

The Independent Subjunctive

In *Lectiō Prīma* all the subjunctives you saw were independent, i.e., they were used as main verbs in the sentence. Independent subjunctives fall into three groups:

- **Commands** Often called the **hortatory** (1st person) or **jussive** (3rd person) subjunctive

Eāmus!	Let's go!	*Nē dormiāmus!*	Let's not sleep!
Abeat!	Let him go away!	*Nē abeāt!*	Let him not go away!
Fīat!	Let it happen!	*Nē fīat!*	Let it not happen!
Tranquillior sit.	Let him be calmer.	*Nē tranquillior sit.*	Let him not be calmer.

- **Possibility or Wish**

Utinam aequiōris animī sit.	Would that he were of calmer mind.	*Nē aequiōris animī sit.*	Would that he were not of calmer mind.
Velim . . .	I would want	*Nōlim . . .*	I would not want
Tranquillior sit!	May he be calmer!	*Nē tranquillior sit.*	May he not be calmer!

- **Deliberation** (1st person only)

Quid faciam? What should/might I do?

Notā Bene:

- Independent subjunctives expressing commands, possibilities, or wishes use the negative *nē* instead of *nōn*.
- *Utinam* is optional: *Utinam aequiōris animī sit* and *Aequiōris animī sit* both mean "Would that he were of calmer mind."

Don't worry too much about distinguishing among commands, possibilities, wishes, and deliberation. Just keep these possibilities in mind, and see which one fits best in context.

EXERCEĀMUS!

31-2 **Translating Independent Subjunctives**

Here are some independent subjunctives. Translate each of them according to the samples in the previous section. Follow the model.

→ Audiāmus!   *Let's listen.*

1. Strēnuē cōnēmur!
2. Servī dūcantur!
3. Fīcī apponantur!
4. Prōgrediantur!
5. Quid aliud faciam?
6. Celerius currant!
7. Quid agāmus?
8. Utinem sedeat.
9. Nē abeant.

Gemma

Several independent Latin subjunctives have been borrowed by English. You have already seen *fiat* (Let it be done). A second, *imprimātur* (Let it be printed), is sometimes found in the front of religious books requiring permission from a church official to be published. Note that both *fiat* and *imprimātur* are usually used as nouns rather than verbs in English, as in "He ruled by fiat," or "The author was unable to obtain an imprimatur to publish the book." Then there is the common *Requiescat in pace* (Let him/her rest in peace), often abbreviated as R.I.P.

Lectiō Secunda

Antequam Legis

In *Lectiō Secunda* Valeria and Licinia meet Caecilia at the snack shop while Caecilia is out shopping in preparation for the upcoming wedding of Servilia and Cordus. Caecilia sees the mirror and earrings Aelius made and is so impressed with his craftsmanship that she suggests that Aelius meet her husband. This will lead to a formal patron-client relationship between the two families. Such alliances were a common type of interaction in the ancient Roman world.

Gemmae Rōmānae

Introduction to Purpose Clauses

You have learned that the subjunctive can be used independently, but verbs in this mood are more commonly found in clauses introduced by conjunctions. The first of these conjunctions is *ut*. You have aleady seen *ut* used with indicative verbs to mean "as" in phrases like *ut opīnor*, "as I think."

Now you meet *ut* + the subjunctive in what is called in Latin the **purpose clause**, which, as its name implies, shows the purpose of the subject's action. If the clause is negative, the formula is *nē* + the subjunctive.

For now, these pattern sentences will give you all you need to know to translate purpose clauses. Note the various translations of *ut* + subjunctive verb (in **bold**).

> *Veniō **ut** pōtum **emam**.*
>
> I come in order that I might buy a drink.
> I come so that I might buy a drink.
> I come (in order) to buy a drink.

> *Hominēs cibum habēre dēbent **nē moriantur**.*
>
> Humans must have food lest they die.
> Humans must have food so that they do not die.
> Humans must have food (in order) not to die.

Each sentence is translated three different ways so that you can see the wide range of options to express purpose in English.

EXERCEĀMUS!

31-3 Translating Purpose Clauses

As you read, list the purpose clauses and give the appropriate English translation. All of these purpose clauses in *Lectiō Secunda* are marked in **bold**. Follow the model.

Line	Purpose Clause	Translation
→ 10	Ut ... inveniam	in order to find

CAECILIA ET VALERIA

Caecilia, in lectīcā ā servīs lātā sedēns, dōnōrum Servīliae emendōrum causā ad multās tabernās multōrum fabricatōrum adīvit, sed nulla dōna idōnea vīdit. Alia dōna nōn satis pulchra sunt, alia nimium ostentātiōnis habent. Haec dōna turpia sunt, illa parum artis exhibent. Quid faciat?

5 Ubi dōna idōnea invenienda sunt?

Nunc quinta hora est—et Caecilia et illī servī lectīcam in umerīs lātīs portantēs iēiūnī sitientēsque sunt.

Caecilia servīs imperat: "Servī, sistite prope illam tabernam! Descendam **ut** pōtum cibumque **inveniam**. Aliquid edere pōtāreque

10 dēbeō **nē** fame sitīque **moriar**!"

Lectīcā in terrā depositā, Caecilia descendit et tabernae Valeriae appropinquat **ut** aliquid **pōtet**.

Caecilia Liciniam videt et "Salvē," inquit. "Maximē sitiō. Dā mihi vīnum, pānem, et mel. Sed, manē! Nōn vīnum, sed calidum volō, sī

15 tibi placeat!"

Licinia "Certē, domina," inquit. "Aliquid aliud vīs? Fortasse servī tuī quoque sitientēs sunt? Licetne eīs aquam dare?"

Caeciliā assentiente, Flāvia, **ut** aquam **arcessat** urnam portāns ad fontem abit. Valeria, quae infantem Maximum portat, Caeciliae appropinquat **ut** cum eā **sermōcinētur**.

20 Valeria, "Salvē," inquit, "Calidumne tibi placet? Vīnum Falernum est et hoc mel apiāriī optimī rusticī quī mel suum mihi sōlī vendit **ut** in tabernā meā calidum optimum **fiat**."

Caecilia, "Rectē habēs," inquit. "Hoc calidum est optimum quod pōtāvī et hodiē mihi vīnum necesse est! Sed, dīc mihi dē hōc speculō quod in mūrō videō.

Hoc speculum idem est quod Aelius Liciniae fabricāvit et Valeria, rīdēns, speculum dē mūrō tollit et Caeciliae,

25 **ut** illa id **inspectet**, dat. "Aelius," inquit, "gener meus hoc fabricāvit uxōrī et huic infantī suō quem vidēs. Quoque hās inaurēs fabricāvit."

Caecilia, "Ars magna in ambābus rēbus est. Hodiē frustrā multās horās circumiēns **ut** dōna nuptiālia fīliae **inveniam** nihil idōneum vīdī. Velim fīliae aliquid simile dare. Hic Aelius hās rēs argenteās quoque fabricāre potest?"

Valeria, "Potest," inquit, "sed argentum nōn habēmus. Egēnī sumus et pecūniam argentō Aelius nōn habet."

30 Caecilia: "Marītus meus vir dīves et senātor est et opīnor eum praetōrem mox futūrum esse. Aeliō ad marītum meum crās māne adveniendum est **ut** ab eō auxilium **petat**. Sī marītō placuerit, argentum Aelius habēbit et tum Aelius faber et cliens marītī et argentārius fīet. Consentīsne?"

"Consentiō, domina," respondet Valeria. "Gener meus ad senātōrem crās adveniet."

Dīc mihi dē hōc speculō.

Gemma

Watch for two versions of "please" in this reading. *Sī placet*, which you have seen before, is indicative and is a simple "please." *Sī placeat* is subjunctive and is more polite: "if it should be pleasing."

POSTQUAM LĒGISTĪ

1. How does Caecilia travel around the city?
2. Why doesn't she buy anything?
3. What does Caecilia order from the menu?
4. Why is Valeria's honey special?
5. What does Caecilia think about the mirror and earrings that Aelius made?
6. What does she suggest Aelius do in the morning?

🔊 VERBA ŪTENDA

alia ... alia "some ...
others"
ambō, ambae, ambō both
(of two); note the
irregular dat./abl. pl.,
ambābus
apiārius, -iī m. beekeeper
*arcessō, arcessere, arcessīvī/
arcessī, arcessītum* fetch
argentārius, -a, -um of
silver, pertaining to
silver
argenteus, -a, -um silvery,
of silver
argentum, -ī n. silver;
money
*assentior, assentīrī, assensus
sum* approve

*circumeō, circumīre,
circumīvī/circumiī,
circumitum* go around
*consentiō, consentīre,
consensī, consensum*
consent, agree
**descendō, descendere,
descendi, descensum
go down, descend**
*exhibeō, exhibēre, exhibuī,
exhibitum* show, exhibit
Falernus, -a, -um Falernian,
referring to a region in
Italy producing an
excellent wine
faber argentārius silversmith
famēs, famis f. hunger
fons, fontis m. spring, fountain

frustrā in vain
idōneus, -a, -um fit, suitable
inaurēs, inaurium m. pl.
earrings
lātus, -a, -um wide, broad
lectīca, -ae f. litter
*morior, morī, mortuus
sum* die
nōtus, -a, -um known
nuptiālis, nuptiāle nuptial,
for a wedding
ostentātiō, -ōnis f. display,
flashiness
parum little, too little,
not enough
pōtō (1) drink
praetor, -ōris m. praetor,
judge

quintus, -a, -um fifth
rusticus, -i m. peasant
**sermōcinor, sermōcinārī,
sermōcinātus sum
converse, talk, chat**
similis, simile like, similar to
sitiō, sitīre, sitīvī/sitīī be
thirsty
sitis, sitis f. thirst; *sitī* (Note
the alternative abl. sing.
i-stem ending.)
turpis, turpe ugly, foul,
loathsome
umerus, -ī m. shoulder
urna, -ae f. large water jar
ut in order that, so that;
how; as; when

Grammatica B

Purpose Clauses

Earlier you saw subjunctives used independently as the main verbs in the sentence. Subjunctives in purpose clauses are dependent. That is to say, they appear in subordinate clauses that depend on or hang from the main clause in the sentence. Consider this sentence:

> *Veniō **ut** pōtum **emam**.*

Veniō can stand alone as a sentence by itself. But *ut pōtum emam* cannot do this and is thus "dependent."

This, then, is the formula for a sentence with a purpose clause:

> main clause　　+　　*ut / nē*　　+　　verb in the subjunctive

> *Veniō **ut** pōtum **emam**.*　　I come in order that I buy a drink.
> *Veniō **nē** vīnum **bībās**.*　　I am coming so that you don't drink wine.

And remember: *ut* + the indicative = as, when

> ***Ut** tibi iam **dīxī**, calidum*　　As I already told you, we have
> *optimum habēmus!*　　the best warm wine drink!

The main verb must be in the present or future tense in order to use a present subjunctive.

Notā Bene: You now know four ways to express purpose in Latin.

- *ut* + subjunctive: *ut pōtum emam*
- gerund(ive) in the genitive + *causā: pōtī emendī causā*
- gerund(ive) in the genitive + *gratiā: pōtī emendī gratiā*
- *ad* + accusative gerund(ive): *ad pōtum emendum*

All of these phrases can be translated "to buy a drink."

> **Gemma**
>
> Another case in which the macron makes all the difference: *māne* "in the morning" versus *manē* "wait!"

EXERCEĀMUS!

31-4 **Purpose Clauses with *ut* + Subjunctive**

Change the following underlined gerund(ive) purpose phrases into purpose clauses using *ut* + subjunctive. Then translate the purpose clause into English at least two different ways. Follow the model.

→ Labōrō <u>familiae meae movendae causā</u>.   →   ut familiam meam moveam
in order that I move my family
to move my family

1. Caecilia <u>ad dōna invenienda</u> venit.
2. Valeria speculum in tabernā <u>ad id monstrandum</u> ponit.
3. Caecilia tabernae <u>calidī poscendī causā</u> appropinquat.
4. Licinia <u>ad aquam servīs dandam</u> venit.
5. Aelius ad senātōrem <u>auxiliī petendī gratiā</u> veniet.
6. Servīlius pecūniam Aeliō <u>ad argentum emendum</u> dabit.

Mōrēs Rōmānī

Salūtātiō

Before Servilius leaves for the Forum in the morning, he performs a daily task called the *salūtātiō, -iōnis* f. The *salūtātiō* is a formal greeting ceremony or morning call by a Roman client (*cliēns, clientis* m. client) at the house of his patron (*patrōnus, -ī* m.). The patron-client relationship formed the heart of Roman political and commercial enterprise. The wealthy and ambitious sought to have as many clients as possible. A Roman like Cicero would have boasted of hundreds. These clients were expected to come to the home of the patron every day to greet him. The homes of many wealthy Romans had benches along the outside wall of the house where clients could wait until the patron was ready to receive them in the atrium (*ātrium, -iī* n.), the formal greeting room. You can see one of these benches outside a house in Pompeii in the photograph at the beginning of this chapter.

The patron would strive to greet each client individually and ask about his family and situation. If the client needed help, this was the time to ask. Often, the patron might give his clients *sportula, -ae* f., little gifts of money or food. The *sportula* Servilius gave his clients that morning consisted of food left over from the big banquet. If private matters needed to be discussed, the patron might ask the client to step into the office or *tab(u)līnum, -ī* n., behind the atrium.

In return for these favors and patronage, clients were obligated to support their patron's commercial and political activities. If a patron were running for political office, clients would escort him as he campaigned. Clients were also expected to vote as the patron wished at the public assemblies and to campaign for him as well.

The system was complicated. Many clients of rich people had their own clients. The wealthiest and most powerful Romans were only patrons, not clients, and the poorest citizens, like Aelius, were lucky to have any patron at all.

In a famous poem Martial suggests that he left Rome for his native Spain because he did not enjoy the early morning salutation in his patron's atrium. Here is how he explains his position to a more ambitious fellow client, who obviously enjoys the custom more than Martial does. Martial does not like practicing law and would much rather sleep late and write poetry in Spain than get up early for a *salūtātiō* in Rome. As usual, we provide a simplified version.

Ō mātūtīne cliens, quī mihi es causa urbis reliquendae, sī sapiās, ātria
ambitiōsa colās. Ego nōn sum causidicus. Nec amārīs lītibus aptus sum.
Sed piger et senior comes Musārum sum. Ōtia somnusque, quae magna
Rōma mē negāvit, mē iuvant. Rōmam redibō sī et hīc in Hispaniā dormīre
nōn possum.

Epigrammata XII.68

🔊 VERBA ŪTENDA

amārus, -a, -um bitter
ambitiōsus, -a, -um
ambitious,
ostentatious
causidicus, -ī m. lawyer
colō, colere, coluī,
cultum pay court
to, haunt

comes, comitis m./f.
companion
et here; "even" or "also"
līs, lītis f. lawsuit
mātūtīnus, -a, -um of or
belonging to the early
morning
negō (1) deny

ōtium, -iī n. leisure
piger, pigra, pigrum low,
sluggish, lazy
Rōmam to Rome
sapiō, sapere, sapīvī/sapiī
show good sense
somnus, -ī m. sleep, rest

Latīna Hodierna

Latin in the Periodic Table of the Elements

In the readings you encountered *argentum*, the Latin word for silver. This leads us to the periodic
table of the elements. For centuries following the fall of the Roman Empire, Latin continued to be
the international language of communication among scientists. The periodic table of the elements
reflects the influence of Latin. Several elements use the actual Latin name for the element:

Abbreviation	Latin Name	English Name	English Derivatives
Au	*aurum, -ī* n.	gold	auriferous, aurous, aureate, aureole
Ag	*argentum, -ī* n.	silver	argent, argentiferous, Argentina
Pb	*plumbum, -ī* n.	lead	plumber, plumbiferous
Fe	*ferrum, -ī* n.	iron	ferric, ferrite, ferriferous

Au = Aurum

Some elements derive the names from Graeco-Roman mythology:

Ir	iridium	from *Īris -idis* f. goddess of the rainbow
Ur	uranium	a Latinized form of the Greek *Ouranos,* the first god of the sky, father of the Titans
Pm	promethium	from *Promētheus, Promētheī* m. Titan fire giver
Np	neptunium	from *Neptūnus, -ī* m. god of the sea
Pu	plutonium	from *Plūtō, -ōnis* m. god of the underworld
Ta	tantalium	from *Tantalus, -ī,* m. great sinner

Ag = Argentum

Many other elements were given Latinized names based on an important fact surrounding its
discovery. Here are just a few examples:

Sc	scandium	from Scandinavia
Am	americium	from America
Es	einsteinium	from Albert Einstein

All these elements are formed as 2nd declension neuter nouns.

Orbis Terrārum Rōmānus

Pompēiī et Vesuvius

At the time of our story in c. 9 B.C., Vesuvius had been quiet for more than 200 years, and the famous eruption of August 24, 79 A.D., was still 80 years in the future. So we used some poetic

license when we had Anna, in *Lectiō Prīma*, compare the unpredictable Sico to Vesuvius. At the base of this mountain lay the city of Pompeii, a small but prosperous town in southern Italy that would not be so well-known today if the eruption of 79 A.D. had not preserved the city under piles of volcanic ash. We know a lot more about everyday Roman life because of what was found in the excavation of Pompeii (as well as Herculaneum, her sister-city in destruction).

If you compare the photo of Vesuvius and Pompeii today at left with the ancient wall painting of Vesuvius below, you can see how much of the mountain fell on Pompeii in the eruption. Also notice Bacchus, the Roman god of wine, in the wall painting. Bacchus is wearing a bunch of grapes. Look closely at this picture and you will see that Vesuvius is covered with vineyards. The rich volcanic soil of the mountain was (and still is) excellent for agricultural use.

Vesuvius Nunc

Vesuvius Tunc

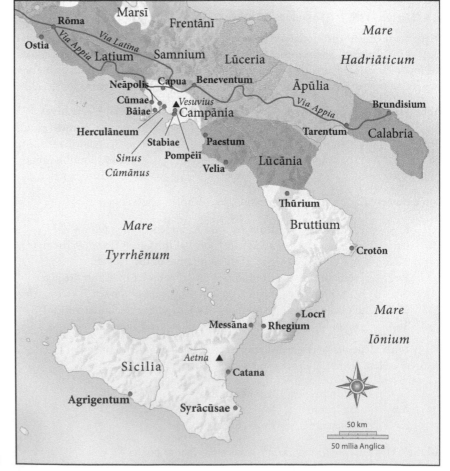

Pompēiī et Vesuvius in Campāniā

QUID PUTĀS?

1. Use the names of elements in the periodic table as guides to five new elements named after yourself or people you know or admire.
2. How does the Roman patron-client relationship compare to the way that politics and commerce are practiced in the United States today?
3. The patron-client relationship is an important element in the opening wedding scene of the movie *The Godfather*. Compare that relationship to one in ancient Roman practice.
4. Do you agree think that Martial had good reasons to leave Rome for Spain? What would you have done if you had been in his position? Why or why not?
5. Martial's comment that something might make him return to Rome hints at his real problem. What is it?

EXERCEĀMUS!

31-5 Scribāmus

Use the word pool to fill in the blanks with appropriate purpose clauses.
HINT: You will have to make the infinitives from the word pool subjunctive. Then translate your sentence. Follow the model.

multam pecūniam habēre	vīnum bibere	auxilium petere
laetus esse	fratrem vidēre	vītā fruī
difficultātem fugere	pōtum cibumque invenīre	dē infante audīre
bene edere	artem inspectāre	mel emere

→ Labōrō strenuē ut   *multam pecūniam habeam.*
  I work hard to have much money.

1. Epistulam scrībit ut
2. In Ītaliā habitāmus ut
3. Caecilia dē lectīcā dēscendit ut
4. Licinia Caeciliae speculum dat ut
5. Aelius ad Servīlium advenīre debet ut
6. Sicō abit ut

31-6 Colloquāmur

Now ask a classmate one of the following questions. Your classmate can use the sentences from Exercise 31-4 to reply. Follow the model.

→ Cūr strenuē labōrās?   *Labōrō strenuē ut multam pecuniam habeam.*

1. Cūr epistulam scrībit?
2. Cūr in Ītaliā habitātis?
3. Cūr Caecilia dē lecticā descendit?
4. Cūr Licinia Caeciliae speculum dat?
5. Cūr Aelius ad Servīlium advenīre debet?
6. Cūr Sicō abit?

31-7 Vēnātiō Verbōrum

Use the following hints to identify words in the *Verba Discenda*. A word can be used only once. Follow the model.

→ "Ineptitude" is a derivative of this word. *aptus*

1. *Bibō* is a synonym for this word.
2. This is an i-stem of the 3rd declension.
3. This word has irregular dative and ablative plurals.
4. This is a neuter hour of the 3rd declension.
5. This word is deponent.
6. This word is a metal.
7. *Calidus, -a, -um* is a synonym for this word.
8. This word refers to a Roman custom.
9. This word is used instead of *ut* in a negative purpose clause.
10. A calm person experiences this.
11. This word is a meal.
12. This word describes what you do to dirty dishes.
13. This word refers to the opposite of being hungry.
14. This word describes what Servilia will do soon.
15. This word is the antonym of *patrōnus*.
16. This word could describe a day with no wind.
17. This word is a 3rd conjugation *-iō* verb.

🔊 VERBA DISCENDA

aequus, -a, -um even, equal; fair; just; patient, calm [equitable]
aestuōsus, -a, -um hot
alius . . . alius one . . . another; pl. some . . . others
ambō, ambae, ambō both (of two); note the irregular dat./abl. pl., *ambōbus, -ābus* [ambidextrous]
aptus, -a, -um attached to, connected to; suitable, fit [aptitude]
argentārius, -a, -um of silver, pertaining to silver
argentum, -ī n. silver; money [Argentina]

cliens, clientis m. client
descendō, descendere, descendī, descensum go down, descend [descent]
ientāculum, -ī n. a light meal; breakfast; lunch
lātus, -a, -um wide, broad [latitude]
lavō, lavāre, lāvī, lautum/lavātum/lōtum wash [lavatory]
mel, mellis n. honey [mellifluous]
mens, mentis f. mind; reason; mental disposition [demented]

nē not, that not, in order that not, lest
nūbō, nūbere, nupsī, nuptum marry [nubile, nuptials]
pānis, pānis m. bread
pōtō (1) drink [potion]
recipiō, recipere, recēpī, receptum accept, receive, take back; *sē recipere* retreat (take oneself somewhere) [reciprocate, reception]
reveniō, revenīre, revēnī, reventum come back, return

salūtātiō, -ōnis f. greeting, formal morning visit by a client to a patron [salutation]
sermōcinor, sermōcinārī, sermōcinātus sum converse, talk, chat
sitiō, sitīre, sitīvī/sitiī be thirsty
tranquillitās, -tātis f. calmness, stillness; fair weather [tranquility]
tranquillus, -a, -um calm, still, peaceful [tranquil]
ut in order that, so that; how; as; when

Angulus Grammaticus

More on the Independent Uses of the Subjunctive

The independent uses of the subjunctive are sometimes divided into the following four categories:

Volitive (expressing a wish, from volō)

Eāmus!	Let's go!	*Nē eāmus!*	Let's not go!
Eat!	Let him go!	*Nē eat!*	Let him not go!

Notā Bene:

- Volitive subjunctives are the equivalent of mild imperatives, but in the 1st or 3rd person.
- The 1st person volitive is sometimes called **hortatory** (from *hortor*), because it urges "us" to do something. You can think of it as a "salad subjunctive" because it has "lettuce," in it, as in "Let us not go!"
- The 3rd person volitive is sometimes called **jussive** (from *iubeō*) because it is a polite order.
- Some grammar books do not use the term "hortatory" and classify forms like *Eāmus!* as jussives.
- The volitive subjunctive uses the negative *nē* instead of *nōn*.

Optative (wished for, from optō)

(Utinam) eāmus!	Would that we were going!
Utinam nē eāmus!	Would that we were not going!

Notā Bene:

- The optative subjunctive can be introduced by the word *utinam* (would that).
- The optative subjunctive uses the negative *nē* instead of *nōn*.
- *Eāmus* can equally be translated "Let's go!" or "Would that we were going!"

Potential (possible, from possum)

Velim ...	I would wish ...	*Nōn eam.*	I would not go.

Notā Bene:

- The potential subjunctive uses the negative *nōn*.

Deliberative (deliberating, from dēlīberō)

Quid faciam?	What should I do?	*Quid nōn faciam?*	What should I not do?

Notā Bene:

- The deliberative subjunctive uses the negative *nōn*.

Photo Credits

Page 403 Thomas J. Sienkewicz; **page 409** Clipart.com; **page 413 (top)** Clipart.com; **page 413 (bottom)** Clipart.com; **page 414 (top)** Leigh Anne Lane(llane@monm.edu); **page 414 (bottom)** © CM Dixon/Heritage—Images/ImageState Media Partners Limited.

Mementō Morī

From *Disce! An Introductory Latin Course, volume 2*, First Edition. Francesco Bonavita. Copyright © 2011 by Pearson Education, Inc. Published by Pearson Prentice Hall. All rights reserved.

32

Mementō Morī

Lectiō Prīma

Antequam Legis

Rome at Night

The city of Rome was noisy and dangerous, especially at night. There were no street lights and only the bravest or most desperate went out at night without protection. Wheeled traffic was prohibited in the city center in Rome during the day, so much of this commercial traffic took place at night. The noise from this traffic could be deafening and ancient Romans often complained about the racket. The night on which *Lectiō Prīma* takes place proves to be a fatal one for many inhabitants.

Result Clauses

Result clauses tell just that—a result. Consider these English result clauses:

> Marcus is **so** naughty *that his teachers don't like him.*
> Julia is **so** smart *that her teachers always love her.*

Note how the main clause contains a "so" word (marked in **bold**) followed by the result clause (marked in *italics*). Latin result clauses are very similar. The main clause contains a "so" word like *tam* followed by a result clause in the subjunctive. Here is how the same sentences would be written in Latin:

> Marcus **tam** imprōbus est *ut magistrī eum nōn ament.*
> Julia **tam** intellegens est *magistrae semper eam ament.*

We have marked the Latin result clauses in *Lectiō Prīma* in the same way that the result clauses were marked above:

- "so" word in **bold**
- result clause in *italics*

Simply translate these clauses "so . . . that . . ."

Mementō Morī

GRAMMATICA
Subordinate Clauses: Purpose and Result
The Imperfect Subjunctive
Forming the Imperfect Subjunctive
Why the Imperfect Subjunctive?
    Sequence of Tenses
Subjunctive Noun Clauses

MŌRĒS RŌMĀNĪ
Prōvinciae Rōmānae

LATĪNA HODIERNA
Latin Mottoes in the Modern World

ORBIS TERRĀRUM RŌMĀNUS
Bithynia-et-Pontus

ANGULUS GRAMMATICUS
Confusing Pairs: Latin Homonyms
    and Heteronyms

LECTIŌNĒS:
INCENDIUM!
and
EFFUGIUM!
The Servilius family deals with the death of their *avus.* Cordus' worst fears about fires are realized and Valeria's family is put into dire straits.

418

Here are the most common "so" words in Latin:

ita	so, thus; yes
tam	so, so much (as)
tantus, -a, -um	so great, so much
tot	so many

EXERCEĀMUS!

32-1 Practicing Result Clauses

Find the "so" word in each of the following Latin sentences. Then translate the sentence. Use the *Verba Ūtenda* following *Lectiō Prīma* for help with vocabulary.

→ Tam sērō est ut paucī in viīs Rōmae sint.   Tam: It is so late that few men are in the streets in Rome.

1. Servī tam molliter labōrant ut dominī bene dormiant

2. Avus tam aeger est ut familia Serviliī nōn dormīre possit.

3. Tot medicī adsunt ut domus plēna sit.

4. Rēs tantum perīcūlum habet ut familia deōs precētur.

32-2 Prereading for Content

Do this exercise before you try to translate the reading. For each question fill in the answer with the relevant Latin words from the reading. The line numbers indicate where you can find the answer. Follow the model.

→ Describe the streets of Rome at night. (lines 1–3) *desertae*

1. Who sleeps well this night? (lines 1–3)

2. Why isn't the Servilius family sleeping? (lines 4–7)

3. Who is Artorius? (lines 4–7)

4. What is Artorius' diagnosis? (lines 4–7)

5. What causes so much noise in Subura at night? (lines 8–10)

6. Why can't Licinia sleep? (lines 11–14)

7. Why can't Felix sleep? (lines 11–14)

8. Why does Mendax get drunk? (lines 11–14)

9. Why does Mendax push over the lamp? (lines 15–17)

10. What does Socrates do? (lines 18–21)

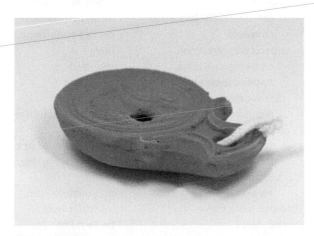

Lucerna Rōmāna

Mendax sicut mortuus dormit

🔊 INCENDIUM!

Sērō est et paucī in viīs Rōmae sunt. In Colle Vīmināli, prope domum Servīliōrum, viae dēsertae sunt et **tanta** est tranquillitās *ut omnēs dīvitēs in cubiculīs bene dormiant.* Servī molliter labōrant ut dominī bene dormiant. Familia Servīliī autem nōndum dormit quod avus aeger est. Multī medicī, inter quōs
5 quīdam Artōrius est, multa temptant ut avum sānent. Servīlius Artōrium ad sē vocat et eum rogat: "Quid dē patre meō?" Artōrius "Pater tuus" inquit, "**tam** aeger est *ut haec nox eī ultima sit.* Cum febrēs senēs tenent, rēs perīculōsa est. Nihil agendum, solum precandum est."

In Subūrā, autem, viae numquam omnīnō dēsertae sunt. **Tanta** est paupertās in Subūrā *ut hominēs interdiū noctūque semper cibum quaerant.* Noctū plaustra per viās urbis progrediuntur et **tantum** clāmōrem faciunt *ut multī*
10 *incolae insulārum frequenter nōn dormīre possint.*

In ūnā insulā Subūrae trēs nōn dormiunt. Infans Līciniae **tam** fortiter flet *ut Licinia expergiscātur* et nunc sedet, infantem nūtriēns. Mox, infante nūtrītō, fortasse Licinia iterum dormiet. Infrā Fēlix, Mendācis fēlēs, quoque, Mendācis stertendī causā, difficultātem dormiendī habet. Mendax hodiē **tantam** pecūniam ā transeuntibus habet *ut multum vīnum emere possit.* Vīnō consumptō, Mendax nunc sicut mortuus dormit et **tam** fortiter stertit *ut Fēlix nōn dormiat.*
15 Fēlix valdē īrātus est et primō ūnō pede faciem Mendācis tangit ut eum excitet et sonitum sistat. Mendax autem nōn expergiscitur! Fēlix īrātior fit et nunc faciem Mendācis ambōbus pedibus haud leniter pulsat! Mendax fēlem removēre cōnātur sed manus lucernam pulsat. Ignis lucernae pannōs, qui Mendācī lectō sunt, incendunt.

Fēlix ignem metuēns Mendācem iterum excitāre cōnātur sed ignis **tam** celeriter crescit *ut fēlī fugiendum sit.* Suprā, Licinia, quamvīs adhūc infantem Maximum nūtriēns, dormit. Sōcratēs, autem, quī in angulō dormit, fūmum
20 sentit et nunc fortiter clāmāre incipit. Subitō Licinia expergiscitur et fūmum sentiēns perterrita est. Perīculum adest! Ignis in insulīs Rōmae semper rēs gravissima est!

"Aelī!" clāmat. "Aelī! Expergiscere! Incendium!"

🔊 VERBA ŪTENDA

aeger, aegra, aegrum sick
angulus, -ī m. corner
Artorius, -iī m. Artorius, a man's name
collis, collis m. hill
consūmō, consūmere, consumpsī, consumptum consume
cresco, crescere, crēvī, crētum grow, arise, appear, increase
dēserō, dēserere, dēseruī, dēsertum desert
excitō (1) awaken, excite, raise
expergiscor, expergiscī, experrectus sum awake, wake up
febris, febris f. fever
fēlēs, fēlis f. cat

frequenter frequently
fūmus, -ī m. smoke
haud not, by no means
incendium, -iī n. fire, conflagration
incendō, incendere, incendī, incensum set fire to, inflame, burn
incola, -ae m./f. inhabitant
infrā below, underneath, under
interdiū by day
lucerna, -ae f. (oil) lamp
medicus, -ī m. physician, doctor
metuō, metuere, metuī, metūtum fear, be afraid of

molliter softly
mortuus, -a, -um dead
Nihil agendum, solum precandum est: Literally, "nothing must be done; there must only be praying." But we would say, "There is nothing to do except pray."
noctū at night
nōndum not yet
nūtriō, nūtrīre, nūtrīvī/ nūtriī, nutrītum nurse, nourish, raise
omnīnō utterly, altogether, completely
paupertās, -tātis f. poverty
plaustrum, -ī n. cart, wagon
precor, precārī, precātus sum pray

primō at first
quamvīs although
removeō, remōvēre, remōvī, remōtum remove
Rōmae at Rome
sānō (1) restore to health
sērō late
stertō, stertere, stertuī snore
suprā above; (+ acc.) over, on top of
tangō, tangere, tetigī, tactum touch; reach; affect; move; mention
temptō (1) feel; try; test
transeō, transīre, transīvī/ transiī, transitum go over, go across

POSTQUAM LĒGISTĪ

Respond to all the following statements or questions in English. Then answer those marked with (L) in Latin.

1. Describe the neighborhood on the Viminal hill at night. (L)
2. Describe the Subura at night. (L)
3. Why do you think there is such a difference between the two neighborhoods?
4. How did Mendax spend the day? (L)
5. How does the fire in the *insula* start? How is such a fire likely to start today?
6. Why do you think that the lower floors in a Roman *insula* were more expensive than higher floors? Is this still true today? Why or why not?

Gemma

The Artorius of this story is based on a real Artorius, a Greek physician and friend of Augustus early in his career. He died c.30 B.C.

Grammatica A

Subordinate Clauses: Purpose and Result

Both purpose and result clauses use *ut*, but they are different in meaning. Compare the relationship between the main and subordinate clauses in the following sentences:

Purpose

Indicative (or imperative) main verb + *ut* + **subjunctive subordinate** verb

> *Servī molliter **labōrant ut** omnēs dīvitēs in cubiculīs bene **dormiant**.*
> The servants work softly so that all the rich people might sleep well in their bedrooms.

Here the action of the main clause is performed with the intent or purpose that the action of the subordinate clause will happen. In this case Latin puts the main clause into the indicative mood, because this action actually happens. The verb of the subordinate clause is put into the subjunctive mood because this action is contingent on the action of the main verb. It is, if you will, "less real."

Result

Indicative main verb + "so" word + *ut* + **subjunctive subordinate** verb

> ***Tanta est** tranquillitās **ut** omnēs dīvitēs in cubiculīs bene **dormiant**.*
> There is such great tranquility that all the rich people sleep well in their bedrooms.

Here the action of the main clause leads to or results in the action of the subordinate clause. Latin puts the verb in the main clause into the indicative mood because this action is quite real, but puts the verb of the subordinate clause into the subjunctive mood, because this action is contingent on the main verb.

Compare the formulas for the two clauses:

Purpose: *ut/nē* + subjunctive

Servī molliter labōrant **ut** omnēs dīvitēs in cubiculīs bene **dormiant**.
Servī molliter labōrant **nē** omnēs dīvitēs in cubiculīs male **dormiant**.

Result: "so" word (*tantus, tam*) + *ut/ut nōn, ut nēmo,* etc. + subjunctive

Servī **tam** molliter labōrant **ut** omnēs dīvitēs in cubiculīs bene **dormiant**.
Servī **tam** molliter labōrant **ut** dīvitēs eōs **nōn audiant**.
Servī **tam** fortiter clāmant **ut nūllī** dīvitēs in cubiculīs **vigilent**.

Notā Bene: The negative forms of each clause can easily be distinguished. Negative purpose clauses are introduced by *nē* whereas negative result clauses are introduced by *ut + nōn* (or *ut +* other negatives like *nēmō, nūllus,* etc.).

> Tantus est clāmor ut omnēs dīvitēs in cubiculōsuō nōn bene dormiant.
> Tantus est clāmor ut nūllus dīvēs in cubiculō suō bene dormiat.
> Tantus est clāmor ut nēmō in cubiculō suō dormiat.

EXERCEĀMUS!

32-3 Distinguishing Purpose and Result Clauses

The subordinate clauses in the following sentences are marked in bold. Identify each as purpose or result. Follow the model.

result ⟶ Tanta est tranquillitās **ut omnēs dīvitēs in cubiculīs suīs bene dormiant.**

1. Servī molliter labōrant **ut omnēs dīvitēs in cubiculīs bene dormiant.**
2. Pauperēs in Subūrō noctū nōn dormiunt **ut cibum quaerant.**
3. Tanta est paupertās in Subūra **ut hominēs interdiū noctūque semper cibum quaerant.**
4. Fēlēs celeriter currit **ut incendium fugiat.**
5. Ignis tam celeriter crescit **ut fēlī fugiendum sit.**
6. Fēlī fugiendum est **nē igne moriātur.**
7. Fēlēs tam celeriter currit **ut nōn igne necētur.**
8. Pater tuus tam aeger est **ut haec nox eī ultima sit.**

Lectiō Secunda

Antequam Legis

Larēs

Pietās

As Valeria's family struggles to escape from the fire, watch for a literary allusion to a famous scene in Vergil's *Aeneid,* when the Trojan hero Aeneas escapes from his doomed city at the end of the Trojan War. He carries his father Anchises on his shoulder and has his son Ascanius (Iulus) at his side. Anchises holds in his hands the *Larēs* or household gods of the family. Even the poorest family, like that of Valeria, would have its own household gods for protection. The *Larēs* of Valeria's family have a major challenge on this particular night.

Notā Bene: If you look carefully in *Lectiō Secunda,* you will also find the mottoes of several U.S. states.

Faciō ut . . . (Subjunctive Noun Clauses)

Also watch out in this reading for forms of *faciō* followed by *ut / nē* and the subjunctive ("see to it that"). These clauses are marked in ***bold italics*** in *Lectiō Secunda.*

The Imperfect Subjunctive

In this reading you are introduced to the imperfect subjunctive, which is very easy to recognize and form:

present active infinitive + personal endings ⟶ imperfect subjunctive

Active

clamāre + m ⟶ clamārem
vidēre + s ⟶ vidērēs

Passive

capere + tur ⟶ caperētur
audīre + mur ⟶ audīrēmur

Deponent

cōnāre + minī ⟶ conārēmini
sequere + ntur ⟶ sequerentur

Nota Bene: Deponent verbs do not really have a present active infinitive, but one is "invented" in order to make the imperfect subjunctive.

Look for imperfect subjunctives in *Lectiō Secunda* marked in **bold**. For now, just translate them as you would present subjunctives, i.e., with a "subjunctive" word like "should, would, could, might, may" or as part of a purpose or result clause.

EXERCEĀMUS!

32-4 *Faciō ut...*

Each of the following sentences contains a form of *faciō* + *ut*. Translate each sentence using an appropriate variation on "I see to it that. . ." Use the *Verba Ūtenda* following *Lectiō Secunda* for help with vocabulary.

1. Facit ut bene agant.

2. Fac ut familia bene agat.

3. Facite nē sīmia ā tabernā currat.

4. Facient ut novam vītam incipiant.

5. Faciēmus ut incendium exstinguātur.

6. Fac nē omnēs in incendiō pereant.

32-5 **Reading Questions**

As you read, find the Latin words that answer these questions. Partial sentences are fine.

1. How does Valeria's family try to protect themselves from smoke and flames as they escape from the burning building?

2. What item(s) does each family member carry out of the building: Aelius, Licinia, Valeria, Flavia?

3. Which family member takes the lead in getting the family to safety?

4. How much damage does this fire cause?

5. To whom does Licinia attribute the family's safety? Why?

6. What addition does the family gain as a result of this fire?

7. What plan does Valeria propose for getting the family through the night?

EFFUGIUM!

Vōce Liciniae audītō, Aelius statim experrectus et cucurrit ad uxōrem ut dē nātūrā difficultātis sē certiōrem **faceret** et uxōrem **adiuvāret**.

Aelius tōtam familiam excitāvit et vōce fortissimā eīs imperāvit: "Valeria, tū et Flāvia pannōs invenīte et ***facite ut*** illī pannī super ōra omnium *sint*! Celeriter! Licinia, tū ***fac ut***
5 pannōs madefactōs super totum corpus Maximī ***ponās***! Ego Plōtiam Larēsque arcessam! Et Valeria, ***fac nē*** pecūniam familiae *amissās*!"

Per fūmum Aelius Plōtiam petīvit et anum umerīs posuit ut eam ad salūtem **ferret**.   *Aelius anum et Larēs portat.*
"Valeria," inquit. "***Fac ut*** tōta familia mē *sequātur*!"

"Dīrigō," Aelius clāmāvit et, Aeliō dūce, familia scālās timidē descendit. Aelius Plōtiam atque Larēs portāvit et
10 ***fēcit ut*** Valeria familiae pecūniam ***portāret***, Licinia infantem Maximum, et Flāvia Sōcratem. Āēr in insulā incendentī tam calidus erat ut familia vix spīrāre **posset**. Tandem ad salūtem in viīs pervēnērunt et āera pūriōrem spīrāre incipiēbant.

In viā multī accurrēbant ut familiās **iuvārent** et fortasse incendium **exstinguerent**. Sed tantus erat aestus incendiī ut adiuvantēs nihil efficere **possent** et mox nōn sōlum haec insula sed etiam duae aliae combustae sunt. Tam
15 celeriter ignis per insulam extendit ut sēdecim, inter quōs Mendāx, **perīrent**.

Paulō post, sedēns fessa in viā, familia Valeriae diū nihil dīxit. Quid dīcendum erat? Dēnique Valeria "Vōs cōnsōlēminī!" inquit. "Saltem neque mortuī neque vulnerātī sumus. Sīmia profectō servātor noster est! ***Facite ut*** vōs ***cōnsōlēminī nē***que *timeātis*. Dum spīrāmus, spērāmus!"

Valeriā haec dīcente, Fēlīx, nunc fūmōsus et leniter ustus, familiae appropinquāvit et sē in crūre Liciniae
20 fricābat. Licinia, fēlem intuēns, eum mulsit et "Vīvis!" inquit. "Nōmen aptum habēs, fēlēs—vērē 'fēlīx' es. Opīnor tē nōbīs ōminī bonō esse! Dīs gratiam habeāmus!"

Tunc Valeria, cuius nātūra fortissima est, stetit et pronuntiāvit: "Aelī, Licinia! Nōn hīc in viā nunc manēre possumus! Multa agenda sunt! Surgite omnēs! Viam inveniēmus! Lābor omnia vincit. Hāc nocte in tabernā et in officīnā Aeliī dormiēmus et crās ***faciēmus ut*** novam vītam ***incipiāmus***. Fortasse ōlim et haec meminisse nōs iuvābit!"
25 Tālia dīcēns et Fēlīcem tollēns, Valeria Liciniam et Maximum ad tabernam, Aelius Plōtiam Flāviamque cum sīmiā ad officīnam dūxit.

VERBA ŪTENDA

accurrō, accurrere, accurrī/ accucurrī, accursum run, hasten to

āēr, āeris m. air, atmosphere; **Greek acc. sing., āera**

aestus, -ūs m. heat

arcessō, arcessere, arcessīvī/arcessī, arcessītum fetch; call for; summon; procure

certiōrem facere make more certain, inform; with sē, make oneself more certain, to learn about

cōnsōlor, cōnsōlārī, cōnsōlātus sum console

crūs, crūris n. leg, shin

dēnique finally, at last; in fact

dīrigō, dīrigere, dīrexī, dīrēctum direct, guide

efficiō, efficere, effēcī, effectum execute, accomplish, do

excitō (1) awaken, excite, raise

exstinguō, exstinguere, exstinxī, exstinctum extinguish

extendō, extendere, extendī, extentum / extensum stretch out, extend

fēlēs, fēlis f. cat

fricō, fricāre, fricuī, frictum rub

fūmōsus, -a, -um smokey

fūmus, -ī m. smoke

Lār, Laris m. household god

madefaciō, madefacere, madefēcī, madefactum make moist, soak

meminī, meminisse remember; Mementō! (imp.) Remember!

mortuus, -a, -um dead

mulceō, mulcēre, mulsī, mulsum stroke, pet

nātūra, -ae f. nature, character

officīna, -ae f. workshop

ōmen, ōminis n. sign, omen

pannus, -ī m. cloth, garment, rag

pereō, perīre, perīvī/ periī, peritum perish, vanish

profectō without question, undoubtedly

prōnuntiō (1) proclaim, announce, say, recite, report

pūrus, -a, -um pure, plain

saltem at least

salūs, salūtis f. health, safety

scālae, -ārum f. pl. stairs, staircase

servātor, -tōris n. savior

spīrō (1) breathe

surgō, surgere, surrexī, surrectum get up, rise up

timidē timidly

ūrō, ūrere, ussī, ustum burn

vix scarcely, hardly

POSTQUAM LĒGISTĪ

1. How does Aelius' advice about the rags compare with what modern fire fighters would recommend?
2. What does the list of things the family saves suggest about what is important to them? What would you take under a similar situation? What would your parents take? Think about what victims of hurricanes or tornados search for in the rubble.
3. What factors do you think helped the fire spread so quickly?
4. Looking ahead, what do you think will happen to Mendax's body?

Grammatica B

Forming the Imperfect Subjunctive

As you can see, the imperfect subjunctive is easy to recognize by the active or passive personal endings added directly to the present active infinitive. The only trick is to pay attention to macrons. Here is the full conjugation of *vocō* in the imperfect subjunctive:

PERSON	ACTIVE	PASSIVE
Singular		
1st	vocārem	vocārer
2nd	vocārēs	vocārēris (or vocārēre)
3rd	vocāret	vocārētur
Plural		
1st	vocārēmus	vocārēmur
2nd	vocārētis	vocārēminī
3rd	vocārent	vocārentur

Deponents act the same way, but they "invent" a present active infinitive on which to put their passive endings.

sequerer	sequerēmur
sequerēris	sequerēminī
sequerētur	sequerentur

Notā Bene: The macrons of the imperfect subjunctive are not hard if you remember two rules.

- Vowels long in the infinitive are long in the imperfect subjunctive. So, for *vocāre*, the -*ā*- is long throughout the imperfect subjunctive.
- The final -*e*- of the present active infinitive becomes long, regardless of conjugation, in the 2nd person singular (active and passive), in the 3rd person singular passive, and in the 1st and 2nd person plural (active and passive).
- Pronouncing the forms out loud is the best way to remember the vowel pattern.

Based on these rules, you can easily form the imperfect subjunctive of any verb, no matter the conjugation. Even irregular verbs follow the regular pattern:

> *essem, essēs, esset,* etc. (*sum*)
> *possem, possēs, posset,* etc. (*possum*)
> *vellem, vellēs, vellet,* etc. (*volō*)
> *nōllem, nōllēs, nōllet,* etc. (*nōlō*)
> *māllem, māllēs, māllet,* etc. (*mālō*)
> *īrem, īrēs, īret,* etc. (*eō*)
> *fierem, fierēs, fieret,* etc. (*fīo*)

Gemma

insulā incendentī: Remember that when a present active participle acts like an adjective, the ablative singular often ends in -*ī*, not -*e*.

Gemma

Valeria's words of consolation are based upon Aeneas' advice to his men after they are shipwrecked in Vergil's *Aeneid* I.203: *forsan et haec ōlim meminisse iuvābit* (Perhaps someday it will be pleasing to remember even these things.)

Why the Imperfect Subjunctive? Sequence of Tenses

Why does Latin need an imperfect subjunctive? The answer lies in something grammarians call the **sequence of tenses**. What does this mean?

Your knowledge of the sequence of tenses will grow as you learn more subjunctive forms, but for now you only need to know that the tense of the **main** verb of the sentence determines the choice of the subjunctive tense that follows it in a subordinate clause.

The sequence follows a simple rule:

- If the main verb is **primary**, the subjunctive has to be **primary**.
- If the main verb is **secondary**, the subjunctive has to be **secondary**.

Which tenses are primary or secondary?

	PRIMARY AND SECONDARY TENSES	
	Indicative	**Subjunctive**
Primary	Present, Future, Future Perfect	Present
Secondary	Imperfect, Perfect, Pluperfect	Imperfect

Now compare these sentences. As you do, compare the tenses of the main and subordinate verbs.

	PRIMARY SEQUENCE	SECONDARY SEQUENCE
Purpose	Omnēs celeriter **currunt** ut incendium **fugiant**.	Omnēs celeriter **cucurrērunt** ut incendium **fugerent**.
Result	Incendium tam forte **est** ut omnēs **fugiant**.	Incendium tam forte **erat** ut omnēs **fugerent**.

Subjunctive Noun Clauses

In *Lectiō Secunda* you saw several examples of *ut* + subjunctive following a form of *faciō,* such as:

Facite ut vōs consōlēminī!	See to it that you console yourselves.
Facite nē timēatis!	See to it that you fear not.

These subjunctive clauses function as the objects of the verb: Aelius can make a mirror or can "make it that" something happens. For this reason this kind of subjunctive clause is called a **noun clause** rather than a purpose clause.

The formula for this use of the subjunctive is simple:

> verb of endeavoring or accomplishing   +   *ut / nē*   +   subjunctive
> *faciō* I see to it that
> *efficiō* I accomplish that
> *nītor* I endeavor that

Also note how these clauses follow the rules of sequence of tenses discussed earlier:

Primary Sequence
*Aelius **facit** ut Flāvia Sōcratem **portet**.*
Aelius sees to it that Flavia carries
   Socrates.

Secondary Sequence
*Aelius **fēcit** ut Flāvia Sōcratem **portāret**.*
Aelius saw to it that Flavia carried
   Socrates.

EXERCEĀMUS!

32-6   Using the Imperfect Subjunctive

Identify each sentence as primary or secondary sequence and translate it. Follow the model.

→ Fugiēbam nē ignis mē caperet.
Secondary. I was fleeing so that the fire would not get me.

1. Aelius omnēs duxit ut familia salūtem invenīret.
2. Mendax tam ēbrius est ut nōn expergiscātur.
3. Fēlēs tam fēlix est ut post ignem vīvat.
4. Aelius tam fortiter nōs duxit ut fugerēmus.
5. Deī facient ut familia Valeriae salva sit.
6. Labōrāre possumus ut domum nōvam habeāmus.
7. Labōrāre poterāmus nē iēiūnī essēmus.
8. Tū facere poterās nē ignis fieret.
9. Tam territus eram ut fugere vellem.

Mōrēs Rōmānī

Prōvinciae Rōmānae

Rome's first province was the island of Sicily, which became Roman territory at the end of the First Punic War in 241 B.C. Most provinces were acquired by conquest, but others came by bequest, like Bithynia, which became a Roman province in the will of its last king, Nicomedes IV in 74 B.C.

Originally, a province was managed by a governor (*prōpraetor, -ōris* m.) appointed by the senate. Becoming a governor was usually considered an important step in advancing one's political career. Julius Caesar, for example, conquered Gallia (France) while governor of *Gallia Cisalpīna* (northern Italy). Cicero was governor of Cilicia (modern Turkey).

In the imperial period, some provinces, especially ones in which large armies were stationed, were under direct control of the emperor, who sent a deputy (*lēgātus, -ī* m.) to represent him in the province. These were called imperial provinces. Senatorial provinces were still governed by propraetors appointed by the senate.

Here is a short list of some important provinces, their years of acquisition and status as imperial or senatorial provinces. Consult the endpaper map of the Roman Empire as you look at this list. The countries in parentheses are the approximate modern equivalents.

Sicilia (Sicily)	241 B.C.	Senatorial
Hispānia (Spain)	197 B.C.	Imperial
Macedonia (northern Greece)	148 B.C.	Senatorial
Āfrica (Tunisia)	146 B.C.	Senatorial
Āsia (western Turkey)	133 B.C.	Senatorial
Gallia Transalpīna or Narbonensis (southern France)	121 B.C.	Senatorial
Bithynia-et-Pontus	75/74 B.C.	Senatorial
Gallia (France)	59 B.C.	
Aquitānia		Imperial
Belgica		Imperial
Celtica		Imperial
Achaea (Greece)	27 B.C.	Senatorial
Britannia (England)	43 A.D.	Imperial

Egypt is not on this list because, technically, it was not a province. Rather, it was the personal property of the emperor.

Pliny served as governor of Bithynia-and-Pontus as *lēgātus Augustī prō praetōre consulārī potestāte ex senātūs cōnsultō missus*. Usually a *lēgātus Augustī prō praetore* (deputy of the Augustus in the place of a praetor) was sent to govern an imperial province, but *Bithynia-et-Pontus* was a senatorial province. That is why Pliny's title also included the phrase *ex senātūs cōnsultō missus* (sent by decree of the senate). He also governed with consular power (*consulārī potestāte*).

Latīna Hodierna

Latin Mottoes in the Modern World

Some states have Latin mottoes. In fact we incorporated versions of the following four into *Lectiō Secunda*:

Deō gratiam habeāmus	Kentucky
Dīrigō	Maine
Dum spīrāmus, spērāmus	South Carolina
Lābor omnia vincit	Oklahoma

Many other modern organizations have Latin mottoes, including these fire departments:

Ad serviendum dedicātus	Springfield, PA
Ut aliī vīvant	Buffalo, NY
Nōn sibi sed omnibus	Cottage Grove, MN
Semper parātus	Long Beach, CA
Vēnī, vīdī, vīcī	Douglas, MA
Vēritās ex cineribus	New York City, Bureau of Fire Investigation
Audāx et promptus	Metropolitan Fire and Emergency Services Board, Melbourne, Australia

Here is a small sample of Latin mottoes of colleges and universities:

Vēritās	Harvard University
In Hōc Signō Vincēs	College of the Holy Cross
Lūx	Monmouth College
Lūx et Vēritās	Yale University
Nūmen Lūmen	University of Wisconsin, Madison
Ense Petit Placidam Sub Libertāte Quiētem	University of Massachusetts, Amherst
Vēritās et Ūtilitās	Howard University
Quaecumque Sunt Vēra	Northwestern University
Deī Sub Numine Viget	Princeton University
Mens et Manus	Massachusetts Institute of Technology
In Lūmine Tuō Vidēbimus Lūmen	Columbia University

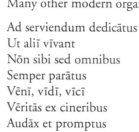
Dīrigō

VERBA ŪTENDA

cinis, cineris m./f. ash
dēdicō (1) dedicate
ensis, ensis m. sword
nūmen, nūminis n. divine presence; god
placidus, -a, -um peaceful
promptus, -a, -um ready
quiēs, quiētis f. rest, quiet, peace
vigeō, vigēre, viguī be strong, thrive

Sigillum Collēgiī Monmouthiensis

Sigillum Ūniversitātis Massachusettsiensis

Orbis Terrārum Rōmānus

Bithynia-et-Pontus

Pliny the Younger is one of our sources about how ancient fire brigades were organized. When he was governor of the province of *Bithynia-et-Pontus* from 109 through 111 A.D., Pliny had a correspondence with the emperor about the need to establish *vigilēs* in his province. This region, now part of northern Turkey, was first organized as a Roman senatorial province by Pompey the Great after 74 B.C. The area was settled by veterans of armies led by several generals or emperors, including Julius Caesar and Augustus.

The south coast of the Black Sea was a prosperous area during the Roman Empire and was dotted by Roman and/or Greek cities, including Amasia and Zela in Pontus, and Sinope, Nicaea, and Nicomedia in Bithynia. Nicomedia (modern Izmit) became a major imperial city under the emperor Diocletian (284–313 A.D.).

What follows is a simplified excerpt from a letter to Trajan in which Pliny describes a fire in the city of Nicomedia, tells the emperor about precautions he has taken, and asks the emperor's advice about setting up a public fire brigade in the city.

Plinius Trāiānō Imperātōrī,
Liber X. Epistula 33

Cum dīversam partem prōvinciae circumīrem, in Nīcomēdiā vastissimum incendium multās prīvātōrum domōs et, quamquam viā interiacente, duo pūblica opera (Gerusian et Īsēon) absumpsit. [Incendium] autem latius sparsum est prīmum violentiā ventī, deinde inertiā hominum quōs, satis constat, ut spectātōrēs tantī malī ōtiōsōs et immōbilēs perstitisse; et aliōquī in pūblicō nullus sīpō usquam, nulla hama, nullum dēnique instrūmentum ad incendia compescenda. Et, ut iam praecēpī, haec quidem parābuntur; tū, domine, dispice an putēs collēgium fabrōrum (dumtaxat hominum CL) instituendum esse . . .

Traiānus Imperātor

In his response, which survives in Pliny's correspondence (X.34), the emperor reminds Pliny about the dangers of setting up an official corporation of firefighters. Such organizations, the emperor warns, have sometimes become dangerous political organizations in Pliny's province and have disturbed the peace. Instead, Trajan advises Pliny instead to make available the equipment needed for fighting fires, but to encourage the inhabitants themselves to serve as volunteer firefighters when needed.

🔊 VERBA ŪTENDA

absūmō, absūmere, absumpsī absumptum ruin, lay waste
aliōquī besides
an whether
circumeō, circumīre, circumīvī /circumiī, circumitum go around
collēgium, -iī n. club, group
compescō, compescere, compescuī confine, restrain
constat See *satis*
cum when (introducing a subordinate clause with an imperfect subjunctive)

dispiciō, dispicere, dispexī, dispectum consider
dīversus, -a, -um different
dumtaxat only up to
faber, fabrī m. workman
gerūsia, -ae f. a council building for elders, senate house
hama, -ae f. fire bucket
interiaceō, -ēre, -ēcī, - actum/ectum lie between (The fire jumped the road.)
immōbilis, immōbile immovable, unmoving

inertia, -ae f. idleness
Īsēon, -ēī n. temple of the goddess Isis
opus, operis n. structure, building
ōtiōsus, -a, -um useless, unoccupied
praecipiō, praecipere, praecēpī, praeceptum order
perstō, perstāre, perstitī, perstātum stand around
prīvātōrum, of private (citizens)

pūblicus, -a, -um; in pūblicō in public, readily at hand
quidem certainly
satis constat "it is generally agreed (that)"
sīp(h)ō, -ōnis m. water hose
spargō, spargere, sparsī, sparsum spread, scatter
ut as
vastus, -a, -um huge
ventus, -ī m. wind
violentia, -ae f. force, violence

Bithynia-et-Pontus

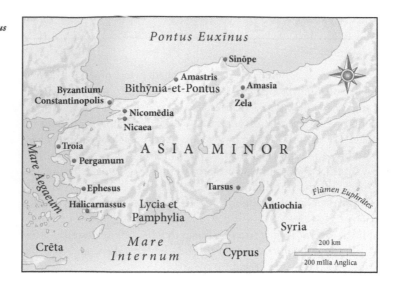

Theātrum Rōmānum Nicaeae

QUID PUTĀS?

1. Does your school, college, or university have a Latin motto? If so, find out what it means. Why you do you think this motto was chosen? If your school does not have a Latin motto, create one for it and explain why you consider this motto appropriate.
2. What is the motto of your state? If it is a Latin motto, translate it into English. If the motto is in English, try translating it into Latin.
3. Based upon his letter to Trajan, how would you evaluate Pliny's performance as governor of Bithynia?
4. Why do you think that the Romans developed a double system of government for their provinces? How efficient does this system sound?

EXERCEĀMUS!

32-7 Scrībāmus

Convert each sentence in primary sequence into a sentence in secondary sequence and then translate it. Follow the model.

→ Fugiō ne ignis mē inveniat.
   Fugiēbam ne ignis mē <u>invenīret</u>.
   I fled lest the fire get to me.

1. Aelius dūcit ut familia salūtem inveniat.
   Aelius dūxit ut familia salūtem _____.

2. Mendax tam ēbrius est ut nōn expergiscātur.
   Mendax tam ēbrius erat ut nōn _____.

3. Fēlēs tam fēlix est ut post ignem vīvat.
   Fēlēs tam fēlix erat ut post ignem _____.

4. Aelius tam fortiter nōs dūcit ut fugiamus.
   Aelius tam fortiter nōs duxit ut _____.

5. Deī faciunt ut familia Valeriae salva sit.
   Deī fēcērunt ut familia Valeriae salva _____.

6. Labōrāre possumus ut domum nōvam habeāmus.
   Labōrāre potuimus ut domum nōvam _____

7. Labōrāre poterimus nē iēiūnī sīmus.
   Labōrāre potuimus nē iēiūnī _____.

8. Tū facere potes nē ignis fīat.
   Tū facere poterās nē ignis _____.

9. Tam territus sum ut fugere volam.
   Tam territus sum ut fugere _____.

10. Tam ēbrius est ut nōn fugere possit.
    Tam ēbrius erat ut nōn fugere _____.

32-8 Colloquāmur

Use the first paragraph in *Lectiō Prīma* to answer the following questions in a complete Latin sentence. One student asks the question and another answers it. Follow the model.

→ Quī bene dormiunt in cubiculīs quod tanta est tranquillitās in viīs?
   Omnēs dīvitēs bene dormiunt.

1. Cur familia Servīliī nōn quiescit?
2. Quis avum aegrum adiuvāre nōn potest?
3. Quid nōmen est ūnī medicōrum?
4. Quem Servīlius ad sē vocat?
5. Quis aegrotissimus est?
6. Quem febris saevissima tenet?
7. Quid agendum est?

32-9 Verba Discenda

Identify the *Verbum Discendum* to which each of the following English words is linked. It need not be a direct derivation. Then use the meaning of the Latin word to define the English word. If you need help, use a dictionary. Follow the model.

→ aerodynamics: from *āēr*; "dynamics related to **air** or gases"

1. attempt
2. excitable
3. incendiary
4. incense
5. increase
6. infrared
7. inspiration
8. insurrection
9. memorabilia
10. remote
11. salutatory
12. supernatural
13. supraorbital
14. tactile
15. temptation
16. transitory

🔊 VERBA DISCENDA

āēr, āeris m. air, atmosphere; Greek acc. sing., **āera** [aerial]
arcessō, arcessere, arcessīvī/arcessī, arcessītum fetch; call for; summon; procure
collis, collis m. hill [colline]
crescō, crescere, crēvī, crētum grow, arise, appear, increase [crescent]
dēnique finally, at last; in fact
efficiō, efficere, effēcī, effectum execute, accomplish, do [efficient, effective]

excitō (1) awaken, excite, raise
expergiscor, expergiscī, experrectus sum awake, wake up
incendium, -ī n. fire, conflagration [incendiary]
incendō, incendere, incendī, incensum set fire to, inflame, burn [incensed]
infrā below, underneath, under [infrared]
meminī, meminisse remember; *Mementō!* (imp.) Remember! [memento]

nātūra, -ae f. nature, character [naturalistic]
nōndum not yet
omnīnō utterly, altogether, completely
pereō, perīre, perīvī/periī, peritum perish, vanish
prīmō at first
profectō without question, undoubtedly
removeō, removēre, remōvī, remōtum move back; remove [removable, remote]
salūs, salūtis f. health, safety [salutary]
spīrō (1) breathe [respirate]

suprā above; (+ acc.) over, on top of [suprarenal]
surgō, surgere, surrexī, surrectum get up, rise up [surge]
tangō, tangere, tetigī, tactum touch; reach; affect; move; mention [tangible, tactile]
temptō (1) feel; try; text [temptation]
transeō, transīre, transīvī/transiī, transitum go over, go across [transient, transitory]
vix scarcely, hardly

Angulus Grammaticus

Confusing Pairs: Latin Homonyms and Heteronymns

As you may remember from Chapter 14, words that are spelled and pronounced the same are often called **homonyms**. For example, in English, we have the "bark" of a dog and the "bark" of a tree. If words have the same spelling but different pronunciation and meaning, they are sometimes called **heteronyms.** For example, the word "row" can be used to "row" a "boat" and to have a "row" (argument). Or consider this sentence: "I refuse to pick up the refuse left behind after the party."

In Latin there are many examples of such confusing pairs that require special attention. Here are some confusing pairs you have seen earlier in this book. Keep in mind that Romans did not use macrons to distinguish long vowels in writing. They only "heard" the difference between these words:

anus	*ānus*	Which one means "old woman" and which means "ring"?
hic	*hīc*	Which means "here" and which "this fellow here"?
liber	*līber*	Which means "book" and which means "free"?
liberī	*līberī*	Which mean "children" and which means "free"?
malum	*mālum*	Which means "apple" and which means "bad"?

If you do not remember how the macrons change the meanings of these words, look them up in a dictionary.

Especially important in Latin are homonyms and heteronyms created by verb tense change. We have the problem in English as well. Consider the sentence "I read the book." Am I doing it now or did I already do it? Notice how English changes the pronunciation to indicate the tense change, rather like the difference between *venit* and *vēnit*. But some verbs are not as helpful.

Homonyms are especially common in 3rd conjugation verbs with the same stem in present and perfect active. Here are just a few examples. There are many more.

vertit	he turns or he turned
accendit	he climbs or he climbed
dēfendit	he defends or he defended

Some 3rd conjugation verbs have present and perfect stems that create **heteronyms**:

Present	Perfect
venit	vēnit
edit	ēdit
emit	ēmit
legit	lēgit
fugit	fūgit

There are several other confusing pairs in other parts of speech; for example, the dative singular of *lēx* (law) is *lēgī* and the present passive infinitive of *legō* (I read) is *legī*. Usually it is not difficult to distinquish such lookalike words in context, even when you don't have macrons to guide you:

Liber celeriter legī potest.	The book can be read quickly.
Cedō lēgī.	I yield to the law.

Finally, try to read this sentence with a triple play of heteronyms!

Eō eō *nē ab* **eō** *inveniar.*	I go there lest I be found by him.

Photo Credits

Page 418 Alfio Ferlito/Shutterstock; **page 419** Kiffka/Dreamstime LLC—Royalty Free; **page 422** American Numismatic Association; **page 428 (top)** U.S. Department of the Treasury; **page 428 (bottom left)** Monmouth College; **(bottom right)** University of Massachusetts Amherst; **page 429** Clipart.com; **page 430** Fotosearch.Com, LLC/Royalty Free.

33

Post Mortem

Lectiō Prīma

Antequam Legis

Lectiō Prīma takes place the morning after the fire. The family of Valeria meets at the *taberna* to discuss their situation. Their home is destroyed. Aelius' assistant Hephaestus is dead, and the shop severely damaged. Under these circumstances, Caecilia's suggestion that Aelius pay a visit to her husband, Servilius, becomes even more imperative.

Giving Commands

In this *lectiō* you encounter several more ways to express commands in Latin.

Indirect Commands

These clauses are commands or requests introduced by words like *imperō* (command), *hortor* (urge), and *orō* (pray) followed by *ut/nē* and the subjunctive.

Imperō ut sedēas.	I command that you sit.
	I command you to sit.
Hortor nē sedēas.	I urge you not to sit.

Iubeō / Vetō + *Infinitive*

Some Latin verbs of commanding use an objective infinitive to express the command.

Tē sedēre iubeō.	I order you to sit.
Tē sedēre vetō.	I forbid you to sit.

Cavē (te) nē + *Subjunctive*

The imperative of *caveō* (take care, beware) is used with *nē* + subjunctive to express a negative command.

Cavē nē sedēas!	Take care not to sit. / Don't sit.

Augustus Togātus

GRAMMATICA
Giving Commands in Latin
Indicative Temporal Clauses

MŌRĒS RŌMĀNĪ
Vestīmenta Rōmāna: Vestis Virum Facit

LATĪNA HODIERNA
Vested in English

ORBIS TERRĀRUM RŌMĀNUS
Via Appia

ANGULUS GRAMMATICUS
Command Performances

LECTIŌNĒS:
CONSILIA NOVA
and
FŪNERA

The family of Valeria deals with the aftermath of the fire while the family of Servilius mourns the death of *Avus*. The bodies of *Avus*, Mendax, and Hephaestus are prepared for burial.

From *Disce! An Introductory Latin Course, volume 2*, First Edition. Francesco Bonavita. Copyright © 2011 by Pearson Education, Inc. Published by Pearson Prentice Hall. All rights reserved.

Future Imperatives

Future imperatives are used in Latin to emphasize that an event will take place sometime in the future or that the event will occur repeatedly. Watch for these imperatives with the endings *-tō* in the singular and *-tōte* in the plural. Future imperatives are marked in ***bold italics*** in *Lectiō Prīma*.

Sedētō! Sit! Keep on sitting! *Sedētōte!* Sit! Keep on sitting (all of you)!

EXERCEĀMUS!

33-1 Classifying Commands

Make a line-by-line list of all the new command constructions in *Lectiō Prīma*. The verbs governing each construction are marked in **bold**. Classify each by type (indirect command, *iubeō/vetō* command, *cavē(te) nē* command, or future imperative). If the command includes an infinitive or a subjunctive, list this form as well. Follow the model.

Line	Command	Type	Infinitive or Subjunctive
→ 4	imperat	indirect command	expergiscātur / arcessat

🔊 CONSILIA NOVA

Posterō diē Valeria in tabernā suā experrecta est et longē hiāvit quārē nōn bene in pavīmentō sine lectō dormīverat. Nunc, sōle oriente, consilium cēperat et adventum Aeliī exspectābat. Liciniae appropinquat et, fīliam pede leniter fodicāns, eī **imperat** ut expergiscātur et aquam arcessat.

5 "Ego," inquit, "exibō ut panem emam. Licinia, tē **orō** ut ignem accendās. **Cavē** nē diūtius dormiās! Et, cum Aelius adveniet, **iubē** eum hīc manēre donec redībō."

Sērius, Aeliō adveniente et ientāculō confectō, familia dē futūrīs cogitābat dum Licinia infantem nūtrit. Valeria, "Quamdiū," inquit, "in tabernā aut in 10 officīnā habitāre possumus? Aliud domicilium nōbīs inveniendum est."

Aelius "Rēs," inquit, "gravior est quam opināris. Officīna igne graviter laesa et lapsūra stat et Hephaestus servus meus fūmō necātus est. Proximā nocte in officīnā dormīvī ut instrūmenta custōdīrem. Hodiē Flāviam et Plōtiam illīc manēre et omnia custōdīre **iussī**. **Vetuī** eās officīnam dēserere 15 hodiē. Sed mox mihi officīna in spatium tūtius movenda est. Quid faciāmus?"

Licinia ut semper infantem nūtrit

Valeria: "Omnēs mē audīte! Nōlīte dēspērāre! Spēm ***habētōte***! Rēs nōn tōta perdita est. Habēmus adhūc tabernam et pecūniam quam hūc dē insulā tulī. Et, mī Aelī, ***mementō*** uxōrem M. Servīliī Severī herī ad tabernam advēnisse et speculum ā tē fabricātum diū admīrātam esse. Plūrēs tālēs rēs—sed argenteās!—dēsīderābat. Cum eī dīxī nōs nullum argentum emere posse, illa **hortāta est** ut tū ad marītum eius advenīrēs et cliens eius fierēs. Sī cliens 20 eius fīēs pecūniam habēbis ad officīnam novam condendam et ad argentum emendum—posteā mox faber argentārius eris! Nunc ut ad Servīlium adveniās tibi **persuādēre** volō. **Moneō** nē occāsiōnem optimam abīre sinās. ***Estō*** bonae spēī! Fortūna fortēs iuvat!"

Aelius, "Certe," respondet, "hoc facere vēlim, sed togam nōn habeō et crēdō clientem togātum ad salūtātiōnem adīre dēbēre."

25 Licinia, pannōs infantis mūtāns, "Marīte," inquit, "togam ā fullōne in diem condūcere potes. **Fac** ut togam ab eō postulēs."

Aelius ad fullōnicam festīnāvit et **postulāvit** ut fullō eī togam in diem locāret. Pecūniā acceptā, fullō, strēnuē Aeliō **imperāns** nē togam amitteret aut eam laederet, vestem trādidit.

🔊 VERBA ŪTENDA

accendō, accendere, accendī, accensum light, burn
argenteus, -a, -um silver, of silver
caveō, cavēre, cāvī, cautum take care, beware of
condō, condere, condidī, conditum build, found
condūcō, condūcere, condūxī, conductum rent
dēserō, dēserere, dēseruī, dēsertum desert, abandon
dēspērō (1) despair (of)
domicilium, -iī n. home
fodicō (1) nudge, prod
fortūna, -ae f. fortune, chance, luck; wealth, prosperity

fullō, -ōnis m. launderer
fullōnica, -ae f. laundry
fūmus, -ī m. smoke
hiō (1) yawn
hortor, hortārī, hortātus sum urge
hūc here, to this place
in diem for a day
lābor, lābī, lapsus sum fall down
laedō, laedere, laesī, laesum hurt, damage
locō (1) contract for, rent
moneō, monēre, monuī, monitum warn, advise
mūtō (1) alter, change

nūtriō, nūtrīre, nūtrīvī/nūtriī, nūtrītum nourish, nurse
occāsiō, -iōnis f. opportunity
officīna, -ae f. workshop
orior, orīrī, ortus sum rise, get up, be born
ōrō (1) pray
pannus, -ī m. cloth, garment
pavīmentum, -ī n. floor, pavement
perditus, -a, -um ruined, lost
persuādeō, persuādēre, persuāsī, persuāsum (+ dat.) persuade
posterus, -a, -um following, next
postulō (1) ask for, beg, demand, require, request

praetereā besides, moreover
quamdiū how long
sinō, sinere, sīvī/siī, situm allow, permit
sōl, sōlis m. sun; day
spēs, speī, f. hope, expectation
toga, -ae f. toga
togātus, -a, -um dressed in a toga
trādō, trādere, trādidī, trāditum hand down, entrust, deliver
vestis, vestis f. clothing
vetō, vetāre, vetuī, vetitum forbid, prohibit

POSTQUAM LĒGISTĪ

Answer the following questions in English. Also answer in Latin if the question is followed by (L).

1. Why did Valeria not sleep well? (L)
2. How do Valeria's actions this morning indicate that she is the dominant member of her family?
3. Why does Aelius say the situation is worse than Valeria and Licinia imagine? (L)
4. What hope does Valeria offer to improve the family's circumstances? (L)
5. What is Licinia doing while talking to her husband and mother? (L)
6. Where can Aelius find a toga? (L)

Gemma

Fortūna fortēs iuvat.
Valeria is using a saying first found in Terence' *Phormio* (line 203). Vergil uses a slight variation: *Audentēs fortūna iuvat* (*Aeneid*, 10.284). The phrase has become the motto of many modern organizations.

Grammatica A

Giving Commands in Latin

You have already learned several ways to express commands in Latin:

Imperative	*Illīc manē!*	Stay there!	*Nōlī manēre illīc!*	Don't stay there!
Hortatory Subjunctive	*Illīc maneāmus!*	Let's stay there!	*Nē maneāmus illīc!*	Let's not stay there!
Subjunctive Noun Clause	*Fac ut maneās!*	See to it that you stay there!	*Fac nē maneās!*	See to it that you do not stay there!

Depending on the verb of commanding used, Latin can express commands in a number of other ways.

Indirect Command (ut / nē + subjunctive)

Most Latin verbs of commanding or ordering take a subjunctive construction called the **indirect command**.

Imperō ut maneās illīc.
I order you to stay there.

Imperō nē maneās illīc.
I order you not to stay there.

An indirect command looks a lot like a purpose clause. Both constructions use *ut* or *nē* and the subjunctive, but the verb of commanding is the hallmark of an indirect command.

Notā Bene:

- Formula: verb of commanding + *ut* or *nē* + subjunctive
- Be on the lookout for the case a given verb of commanding governs. When in doubt, check the dictionary entry.

> *Imperō **tibi** ut maneās illīc.*   I command you to stay there.
>   I command that you stay there.
> *Hortor **tē** ut maneās illīc.*   I urge you to stay there.

- The rules for sequence of tenses apply to indirect commands.

Primary sequence: *Imperō ut maneās illīc.*   I order you to stay there.
Secondary sequence: *Imperāvī ut manērēs illīc.*   I ordered you to stay there.

Here is a list of Latin verbs of command that are followed by an indirect command (*ut* or *nē* + subjunctive):

> *hortor, hortārī, hotātus sum* urge
> *imperō* (1) (+ dat.) command
> *moneō, monēre, monuī, monitum* warn, advise
> *ōrō* (1) pray
> *persuādeō, persuādēre, persuāsī, persuāsum* (+ dat.) persuade
> *petō, petere, petīvī/petiī, petītum* seek to, ask for, beg
> *postulō* (1) demand, require, request
> *quaerō, quaerere, quaesīvī/quaesiī, quaesītum* seek, request to
> *rogō* (1) ask to

All of these verbs are either already *Verba Discenda* or become *Verba Discenda* in this chapter.

Object Infinitive + Accusative

Remember the formula for an indirect statement in Latin:

head verb + infinitive with subject accusative

Direct Statement: *Illīc manēs.*   You stay there.
Indirect Statement: *Illīc tē manēre sciō.*   I know (that) you stay there.

Certain head verbs expressing commands work the same way. These include *iubeō* (order) and *vetō* (forbid):

Imperative: *Illīc manē!*   Stay there!
With *iubeō*:   *Illīc tē manēre iubeō.*   I order you to stay there.
With *vetō*:   *Illīc tē manēre vetō.*   I forbid you to stay there.

Cavē(te) + nē + Subjunctive

You have already seen how Latin can express commands with a subjunctive noun clause following the imperative of *faciō*:

> *Facite ut illīc maneātis.*   See to it that you stay there.

A negative command can be expressed by using *cavē(te)* + *nē* + subjunctive.

> *Cavēte nē illīc maneātis.*   Beware lest you stay there.
>   Take care not to stay there.

The Future Imperative

All imperatives technically refer to the present or immediate future time. If someone tells you to stand up, he or she intends for you do it after they have spoken. Latin has a special imperative that stresses the future nature of the act or that the action is one that should keep on going. For example, when a mother tells her children "Be good!" as they go off for a visit, she does not mean "just once." The endings for this future imperative are:

Singular	Plural
-tō	*-tōte*

Here is the future imperative of *sum*:

Singular	Plural
estō	*estōtē*

Notā Bene:

- A handful of verbs regularly use the future imperative instead of the regular present forms:

  Mementō meī!
  Habētōte spēm!
  Scītō parentēs tē amāre!
  Estōte bonī!

- There is a 3rd person future imperative, but it is rare.
- The negative of the future imperative is *nē*; e.g., *Nē estōte malī!* "Don't be bad. Don't misbehave!"

EXERCEĀMUS!

33-2 Commands

Determine whether each of the following verbs is likely to be followed by an infinitive with subject accusative or by *ut* + subjunctive. Then complete the sentence in Latin, telling the "you" addressed (either singular or plural) to "guard everything." Follow the models.

→ iubeō (vōs) *Iubeō vōs omnia custōdīre.*   I order you to guard everything.

→ imperō (tū) *Imperō tibi ut omnia custōdiās.*   I command you to guard everything.

1. vetō (tū)	4. rogō (vōs)	7. persuadeō (tū)
2. moneō (vōs)	5. petō (tū)	8. iubeō (tū)
3. ōrō (tū)	6. hortor (vōs)	9. imperō (vōs)

Lectiō Secunda

Antequam Legis

In this *lectiō* you read about the funerals following the night of the fire. Funeral rites in ancient Rome varied every bit as much as funerals do today. Bodies were both interred and cremated. After cremation, the ashes would probably be placed in a family tomb located outside the city walls. The city's poor received hasty burials, and the poorest or most despised were often simply dumped into public pits outside of the city gate on the Esquiline Hill. Such a common burial, or *fūnus plēbēium*, probably evoked little notice in ancient Rome, but, when a former senator like *Avus* passed away, a more public and elaborate display was called for. As much as he loved his father, Servilius also understood the political leverage a lavish public funeral could bring. You will also hear about the *imāginēs māiōrum* in this reading. These are the death masks of ancestors that adorned the walls of the atria of noble Roman houses. This tribute to ancestors demonstrated the importance of family among the patricians at all times, but especially at the time of a death.

Gemma

Watch in this *lectiō* for *domus* as a 4th declension noun. The Romans used this noun in either the 2nd or 4th declension: *domus, -ī* f. or *domus, -ūs* f.

Indicative Temporal Clauses

As you read *Lectiō Secunda,* also watch out for **indicative temporal clauses** introduced by conjunctions like *postquam* (after), *dum* (while), and *antequam* (before). All these conjunctions are marked in **bold** in the *lectiō.* You have seen most of these words before, but this is an opportunity to look at them as a group. In particular, pay attention to *cum,* which is not only a preposition (+ abl. meaning "with"), but also a temporal conjunction (when, whenever).

EXERCEĀMUS!

33-3 *Cum* **the Preposition vs.** *Cum* **the Conjunction**

Indicate whether the *cum* in each of the following sentences is a preposition or a conjunction. Then translate the sentence. The last five are based on sentences in the *lectiō.*

HINT: Look for an ablative with *cum* the preposition. Follow the model.

Gemma

Ollus Servīlius Quirīs lētō datus est!
This is an archaic and traditional formula for Roman funerals. *Ollus = ille, Quirīs* = "citizen," and *lētō* = "to death."

→ **Cum** avus mortuus est, fēminae flēbant.
  conjunction: *When the grandfather died, the women wept.*

1. Fēminae flent magnā **cum** clāmōre.
2. **Cum** Servīlia et māter flent, servī flent.
3. Sīmiae **cum** celeritāte cucurrērunt.
4. **Cum** sīmiae currunt, puerī rident.
5. Sīmiae mē**cum** currunt.
6. Parentēs cum servīs plōrāvērunt.
7. Cum avus mortuus est, familia plōrāvit.
8. Magnā cum dolōre oculōs parentis clausit.
9. Fēminae corpus cum cūrā lavērunt.
10. Cum plaustrum ad insulam vēnit, servī mortuōs in plaustrō deposuērunt.

🔊 FŪNERA

Cum Marcus Servīlius Avus mortuus est, tōta familia—parentēs et līberī cum servīs—plōrāvērunt. Corpus senis in terrā positum est et Servīlius, nōmen patris vocāns, magnā cum dolōre oculōs parentis cārī clausit. Fēminae domūs, quārum hoc opus est, corpus cum cūrā, lavērunt, et **dum** ululant, libitīnārius nummum sub linguā senis
5 posuit ut umbra senis pecūniam Charōnī, flūminis Stygis transeundī causā, dare posset. Tunc corpus, togā praetextā vestītum, in ātriō **ubi** imāginēs māiōrum in murō erant, positum est. In illō locō, māiōribus intuentibus, corpus avī in lectō fūnebrī iacuit.

Aelius corpus Hephaestī ad plaustrum ferēns

Priusquam corpus combūstum est et cinerēs in sepulcrō positī sunt, multa agenda erant. Servīlius libitīnāriō imperāvit ut, trēs post diēs, fūnus senātōrī idōneum ageret et eum ōrāvit nē
10 pecūniae parceret.

Simul ac Servīlius abiit, libitīnārius servīs imperāvit ut rāmus cupressī in foribus domī pōnātur et rogāvit ut tībīcinēs, cornicinēs, et praeficae invenīrentur. Fēcit ut per viās Rōmae nuntius clāmāret, "Ollus Servīlius Quirīs lētō datus est! Ollus Servīlius lētō datus est!"

Tālibus factīs Servīlius, nunc togam pullam gerēns, ad sē fīlium Marcum vocāvit. "Fīlī," inquit, "nōmen
15 Servīliōrum tibi tuendum est. **Cum** pompa fūnebris fīet, rogō ut tū in Forō ōrātiōnem fūnebrem habeās. Fac ut dē omnibus avī cārī honōribus dīcas et familiam laudēs."

In aliā urbis parte fūnera alia fīēbant. **Postquam** incendium exstinctum est, plaustrum sordidum, mūlīs tractum, per viās Subūrae lentē progrediēbātur. **Cum** plaustrum ad insulam combustam vēnit, servī mortuōs, inter quōs
20 erat Mendax, in plaustrō deposuērunt. Aelius ipse, corpus Hephaestī ferēns, ad plaustrum advēnit et nummō sub linguā servī fidēlis positō, cadāver in plaustrum posuit "Valē!" inquit cum maestitiā, "Valē, serve fidēlis! Dormītō bene. Ōrō ut dī tē benignē recipiant!"

Plaustrum ad collem Esquilīnum progrediēbātur et per Portam Esquilīnam ad Campōs Esquilīnōs iter fēcit. Paulō post, **ubi** plaustrum constitit, cadāvera in puteō ā servīs iacta sunt. Hīc, in perpetuum, nūllīs plōrantibus, Mendax Hephaestusque tandem dormient.

🔊 VERBA ŪTENDA

ac and, and besides; than
ātrium, -ī n. atrium, public greeting room of a Roman house
cadāver, cadāveris n. dead body, corpse
campus, -ī m. field
Charōn, Charōnīs m. Charon, the ferryman of the Underworld
cinis, cineris m. ashes
claudō, claudere, clausī, clausum shut, close
consistō, consistere, constitī, constitum stop, halt
cornicen, -cinis m. horn blower
cupressus, -ī f. cypress tree
cūra, -ae f. care
dī nom. pl. gods = *deī*
dolor, dolōris m. pain, grief
dum while, as long as; until

Esquilīnus, -a, -um Esquiline, one of the seven hills of Rome
exstinguō, exstinguere, exstinxī, exstinctum quench, extinguish
fidēlis, fidēle faithful, trustworthy
flūmen, -inis n. river
foris, foris f. door, gate
fūnebris, fūnebre funereal
fūnus, fūneris n. burial, funeral
imāgō, imāginis f. image, likeness
lētum, -ī n. death
līberī, -ōrum m. pl. children
libitīnārius, -ī m. undertaker
lingua, -ae f. tongue, speech
maestitia, -ae f. sadness, grief
mortuus, -a, -um dead

mūla, -ae f. mule
necessārius, -a, -um necessary, indispensable
nuntius, -ī n. messenger, news
occidō, occideren, occidī, occāsum set (of the sun)
Ollus archaic form of *ille*: that (man)
orātiōnem habēre give/ deliver a speech
perpetuus, -a, -um uninterrupted
plaustrum, -ī n. cart, wagon
plōrō (1) weep, cry
pompa, -ae f. ceremonial procession
praefica, -ae f. hired female mourner
praetextus, -a, -um bordered; *toga praetexta* a toga bordered with a purple stripe

pullus, -a, -um dingy, somber; *toga pulla* a dark gray toga worn in mourning
puteus, -ī m. pit
Quirīs, Quirītis m. archaic form of *civis* citizen
rāmus, -ī m. branch
requiesco, requiescere, requiēvī, requiētum rest
sepulcrum, -ī n. tomb
Styx, Stygis f. river Styx, river bordering the Underworld
tībīcen, -cinis m. piper
ululō (1) wail, weep
umbra, -ae f. shade, soul
ut (+ indicative) as
vestiō, vestīre, vestīvī/ vestiī, vestītum dress, clothe

POSTQUAM LĒGISTĪ

Answer the following questions in English. Also answer in Latin if the question is followed by (L).

1. What is the duty of each of the following after *avus* Servilius dies? His son? The women of the household? The *libitīnārius*? (L)
2. What instructions does the younger Servilius give the *libitīnārius*? What instructions does he give his son? (L)
3. What motivations do you think Servilius has for giving his father an extravagant funeral?
4. How does this funeral compare to modern funeral practices in the United States?
5. Describe how the bodies of Mendax and Hephaestus are disposed of. (L)
6. How does Aelius show his affection for his deceased slave? (L)

Charon Portitor Infernus

Grammatica B

Indicative Temporal Clauses

The following chart summarizes the use of indicative temporal clauses in Latin. Pay special attention to the tenses usesd with each conjunction.

CONJUNCTION	TENSE	USE	TRANSLATION
cum (temporal)	Any tense, although perfect and present are most common	Describes the actual time something occurred	when
cum (conditional or frequentative)	Any tense	Describes the situation	whenever
dum	Present	Describes simultaneous action	while
postquam, ubi, ut, simul ac/atque	Usually perfect	Tells the time when something happens	
antequam, priusquam	Present, perfect or future perfect	"Before" action	before

EXERCEĀMUS!

33-4 **Indicative Temporal Clauses**

All of the conjunctions marked in **bold** in *Lectiō Secunda* introduce indicative temporal clauses. Make a line-by-line list of these conjunctions. Then find the verbs they introduce and translate both conjunction and verb into English. Follow the model.

Line	Conjunction	Verb	Translation
→ 1	cum	mortuus est	when he died

Mōrēs Rōmānī

Vestīmenta Rōmāna: Vestis Virum Facit

The Romans were very dress conscious. Indeed, it was usually easy to determine the status and power of a Roman by the kind of clothing he or she wore. The basic garment for both men and women of all ranks and classes was a tunic (*tunica, -ae* f.) consisting of two rectangular pieces of cloth sewn together. Men wore tunics down to the knee. Women's tunics were longer. A wide purple stripe (*clāvus, -ī* m.) on a tunic indicated that the wearer was a senator. Equestrians had a narrower stripe. A victorious general celebrating a triumph would wear a *tunica palmāta*, i.e., a tunic embroidered with palm leaves.

The toga (*toga, -ae* f.) was worn only by male Roman citizens. Originally the toga was worn over a naked body, but by classical times it was usually worn over a tunic. A toga was not everyday attire. It was worn only on formal occasions.

Young boys and certain public officials wore a *toga praetexta*, which had a purple stripe at its edge. In a special ceremony a Roman boy put on an unstriped, off-white *toga cīvīlis* (also called *toga virīlis* or *toga pūra*) and entered the world of adult manhood at the age of sixteen. When running for office, a Roman would wear a special whitened toga called the *toga candida* (white toga), from which the English word "candidate" is derived. Finally, a Roman male mourning the loss of a family member would wear a dark colored toga called the *toga pulla* (dingy toga).

On their marriage day, Roman women would begin wearing a *stola*, a long rectangular cloak considered the female equivalent of a toga.

The procession of members of the Augustan family, depicted in the *Āra Pacis Augustae* (Altar of Augustan Peace) on the right, is important evidence of Roman clothing customs and their social significance. See also the photograph of Augustus wearing a toga at the beginning of this chapter.

Such fashion sense makes Aelius reluctant to visit Servilius without a toga. This garment is a mark of Aelius' status as a Roman citizen, but it is expensive enough that he does not own one.

The toga was commonly seen as a peacetime garment. So in *In Pisōnem* 30 Cicero says:

Āra Pacis Augustī

> cedant arma togae

i.e., let the military give way to civilian life, war to peace. (*Cedant arma togae* is today the motto of the State of Wyoming.)

Martial also uses the toga to praise his friend Fronto as a paragon of both military and civilian life, as he tells Fronto his prayer for a simple life. Note how Martial speaks of himself in the third person and refers to himself as Marcus.

> Ō Frontō, decus clārum mīlitiae togaeque,
> sī breviter vōtum tuī Marcī cognoscere vīs,
> hoc petit, esse suī nōn magnī ruris arātor,
> et ōtia sordida in parvīs rēbus amat.

Epigrams 1.55

Desiderius Erasmus (1466–1536), a Dutch humanist, summed it all up in his *Adagia* (*Adages*):

> Vestis virum facit. (III.i.60)

This adage is still heard in its English translation today.

Desiderius Erasmus Roterodamus (1466/1469–1536)

🔊 VERBA ŪTENDA

arātor, -ōris m. plower, farmer	*decus, decoris* n. glory	*vōtum, -ī* n. prayer

Latīna Hodierna

Vested in English

English has borrowed the Latin word for clothing (*vestis, vestis* f.) in a variety of words, including the following

di**vest**	**vest**
in**vest**	**vest**ee
in**vest**ment	**vest**ment
in**vest**iture	**vest**ry

Orbis Terrārum Rōmānus

Via Appia

The *Via Appia* is the main road from Rome south to Naples and east to Brundisium on the Adriatic. It was the first major road built by the Romans. Its construction began under the censor Appius Claudius Caecus in 312 B.C. The modern Via Appia runs parallel to the ancient road, which still exists. For hygienic and cultural reasons, burials inside the city walls were discouraged in Roman cities, and tombs were normally located just outside their walls. Wealthy families chose locations for their tombs that were very visible to travelers into and out of the city. Many such tombs were built along the Via Appia, where they can still be seen today. You should imagine the tomb of the *Servīliī* to be located here. Can you find it on the map below?

Two ancient tombs on the Via Appia are depicted on the next page. One of the largest tombs is the Tomb of Caecilia Metella, perhaps an ancestor of Servilius' wife. This Caecilia was daughter of Quintus Caecilius Metellus Creticus and the daughter-in-law of the triumvir Crassus. She died c. 80 B.C.

Via Appia

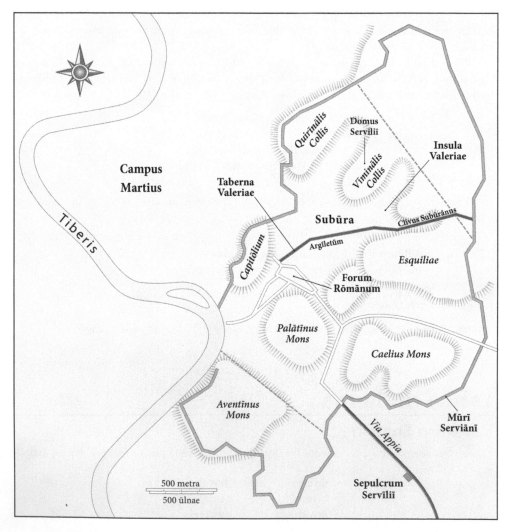

QUID PUTĀS?

1. Do you agree or disagree with Erasmus' adage *Vestis virum facit*? To what extent is this true today? By what classes or ages of people does it seem to be most believed?

2. Can you think of ways that clothing serves the same symbolic value in American society as the toga did in the Roman world? What would the American equivalent of a toga be?

3. How is the American view of togas different from Roman practice? Why do you think the difference is so great?

4. How do Roman attitudes toward clothing compare to modern American ones? Are there any kinds of clothes that indicate a person's rank or profession today? To what extent can the wealth and status of Americans be indicated by the clothes they wear?

5. Compare tombs on the Appian Way with modern American cemeteries. Think about things such as the cemetery's placement, the style and the location of monuments, and the need to make a social statement with the monument.

Via Appia Rōmā Brundisium

EXERCEĀMUS!

33-5 Scrībāmus

Retell these events in the present tense instead of the past. In order to do this, you need to change all the verbs marked in **bold** to the corresponding present tense form. Follow the model.

> Plaustrum sordidum, mūlīs tractum, per viās Subūrae lentē **progrediēbātur** (1). Cum plaustrum ad insulam combustam **vēnit** (2), servī mortuōs, inter quōs **erat** (3) Mendax, in plaustrō **deposuērunt** (4). Aelius quoque corpus Hephaestī ferēns ad plaustrum **advēnit** (5) et nummō sub linguā servī fidēlis positō, cadāver in plaustrum **posuit** (6).

> Plaustrum ad collem Esquilīnum **progrediēbātur** (7) et per Portam Esquilīnam ad Campōs Esquilīnōs iter **fēcit** (8). Paulō post, ubi plaustrum **constitit** (9), cadāvera in puteō ā servīs **iacta sunt** (10).

→ Plaustrum sordidum, mūlīs tractum, per viās Subūrae lentē **progreditur**.

Sepulchrum Viae Appiae

Sepulcrum Caeciliae Metellae

Sepulcrum Caeciliae Metellae

33-6 Colloquāmur

Use the verb *induō, induere, induī, indūtum* (put on) and the clothing vocabulary in the *Mōres Rōmānī* to describe Roman clothing to a classmate. Here is a sample sentence to get you started:

→ Et virī Rōmānī et fēminae Rōmānae tunicās induērunt sed virī solī togās induērunt.

33-7 Verba Discenda

Choose the *Verbum Discendum* that represents the **opposite** of the following definitions. Follow the model.

→ senior citizens: a. lingua b. *līberī* c. sōl d. atrium

1. die:	a. orior	b. sinō	c. trādō	d. moneō
2. one who gets a message:	a. atrium	b. sōl	c. flūmen	d. nuntius
3. let one do as one pleases:	a. vetō	b. hortor	c. orior	d. sinō
4. hold onto:	a. trādō	b. vetō	c. persuādeō	d. sinō
5. ask politely:	a. moneō	b. postulō	c. caveō	d. orior
6. despair:	a. flūmen	b. spēs	c. nuntius	d. vestis
7. be reckless:	a. caveō	b. sinō	c. postulō	d. trādō
8. forbid:	a. caveō	b. vetō	c. moneō	d. sinō
9. untrustworthy:	a. atrium	b. orō	c. fidēlis	d. fortūna
10. moon:	a. nuntius	b. ātrium	c. sōl	d. vestis

Gemma

veto: When presidents or governors "veto" bills, they are in effect, speaking Latin. What are they saying?

🔊 VERBA DISCENDA

ac and, and besides; than

ātrium, -iī n. atrium, public greeting room of a Roman house [atrial]

campus, -ī m. field

caveō, cavēre, cāvī, cautum take care, beware of [caution]

dum while, as long as; until

fidēlis, fidēle faithful, trustworthy [infidelity]

flūmen, -inis n. river [flume]

fortūna, -ae f. fortune, chance, luck; wealth, prosperity

hortor, hortārī, hortātus sum urge [exhort]

līberī, -ōrum m. pl. children

lingua, -ae f. tongue, speech [linguist]

moneō, monēre, monuī, monitum warn, advise [admonition]

nuntius, -iī m. messenger, news

orior, orīrī, ortus sum rise, get up, be born [orient]

ōrō (1) pray [oratory]

persuādeō, persuādēre, persuāsī, persuāsum (+ dat.) persuade [persuasive]

postulō (1) ask for, beg, demand, require, request [postulant]

sinō, sinere, sīvī/siī, situm allow, permit

sōl, sōlis m. sun; day [solar]

spēs, speī, f. hope, expectation

toga, -ae f. toga

togātus, -a, -um dressed in a toga

trādō, trādere, trādidī, trāditum hand down, entrust, deliver [trade, tradition]

vestiō, vestīre, vestīvī/vestiī, vestītum dress, clothe [invest]

vestis, vestis f. garments clothing [vestment]

vetō, vetāre, vetuī, vetitum forbid, prohibit

Angulus Grammaticus

Command Performances

Perhaps you are wondering why Latin needs both a present and a future imperative. The present imperative is used for a simple, immediate command, while the future imperative is especially used to refer to commands that are general rules or permanent laws, such as "Thou shall not steal." Here are some Latin examples:

- *Salūs populī suprēma lex estō.* (Let the welfare of the people be the supreme law.) This precept, the motto of the state of Missouri, is based on the following quote from Cicero's *Dē Lēgibus* 3.3.8: *Ollis salūs populī suprēma lex estō.* Note how Cicero modifies *salūs* with the archaic demonstrative *ollis* (= *illa*), which you saw in the traditional formula used to announce the death of Servilius Avus in *Lectiō Secunda*.

- *Boreā flante, nē arātō sēmen nē iacitō.* (When the north wind is blowing, do not plow or sow seed.) This is from Pliny's *Historiae Nātūrālēs* (xviii.334).

Latin also uses a future imperative with words or phrases that clearly refer to some point in the (distant) future, as in *crās labōrātō* or with a temporal clause clearly indicating future time, especially with the future perfect tense: *Cum bene dormīveris, labōrātō.* (When you will have slept well, work.)

Latin, like English, uses a number of adverbs to strengthen the force of a command. Here are some examples:

Note also the enclitic *dum*, used in classical Latin only with *age* or *agite*, as in *agedum* or *agitedum*, to mean "Come, then!"

Latin and English can both accompany imperatives, for the sake of politeness, with words like *amābō* (please), *obsecrō* (I beg), *quaesō* (I ask), and *sīs* (if you wish, from *sī vīs*). *Mē manē, amābō!* (Wait for me, please!)

The imperative expressions *fac ut, cūrā ut, cavē nē,* which you have already seen, are actually examples of imperative **periphrasis** or circumlocution; i.e., they represent a sort of round-about command: Instead of saying *Nōlī tangere!* (Don't touch!), you can beat around

modo (only)	*Modo manē!* (Only wait!)
statim (at once)	*Ī statim!* (Go at once!)
proinde (well, then)	*Proinde curre!* (Then run!)
sānē (certainly)	*Sānē sequere!* (Certainly follow!)

the bush, so to speak, and say *Cavē nē tangās!* (Beware lest you touch!). When do you think such a periphrasis would be preferable to a direct command?

Here are some other ways Latin (and English) can express commands:

- Sometimes a question can be an imperative: *Nōn dīcis?* (You aren't speaking?) or (Aren't you speaking?) (*Dīc!*).
- So can a simple future indicative: *Dīcēs!* (You **will** speak!).

Indirect commands, i.e., *ut/nē* + subjunctive are sometimes called **jussive noun clauses**. "Jussive" is derived from the PPP of *iubeō.*

Photo Credits

Page 433 (top) Getty Images/De Agostini Editore Picture Library; **page 433 (bottom)** Thomas J. Sienkewicz; **page 439** Photos.com; **page 441 (top)** Clipart.com; **page 441 (bottom)** Clipart.com; **page 443 (top)** Thomas J. Sienkewicz; **page 443 (bottom)** imagestalk/Shutterstock.

Patrōnus et Cliens

From *Disce! An Introductory Latin Course, volume 2*, First Edition. Francesco Bonavita. Copyright © 2011 by Pearson Education, Inc. Published by Pearson Prentice Hall. All rights reserved.

Officīna Fabrī

GRAMMATICA

Indirect Questions
The Perfect Subjunctive
Sequence of Tenses
The Pluperfect Subjunctive and
    Consolidation of Subjunctive Forms
Building the Sequence of Tenses
Consolidation of Interrogative Words
The Conjunction *Dum*

MŌRĒS RŌMĀNĪ

Commercium Rōmānum

ORBIS TERRĀRUM RŌMĀNUS

Germānia

LATĪNA HODIERNA

Latin Interrogatives in English

ANGULUS GRAMMATICUS

Macron or No Macron?

> **LECTIŌNĒS:**
> **SALŪTĀTIŌ**
> **and**
> **PATRŌNUS**
>
> Aelius attends the *salūtātio* at the house of Servilius. The city is filled with rumors of Tiberius' victory in Germany. Aelius pledges fealty and help in the election. The new patron and client exchange gifts.

446

34

Patrōnus et Cliens

Lectiō Prīma

Antequam Legis

In this *lectiō* Aelius anxiously prepares to attend the *salūtātiō* at the house of Servilius. He puts on his rented toga, and he and his family worry about an appropriate gift to bring Servilius and the appropriate procedure to greet his prospective patron.

As you read about Aelius' concerns, you will see a new use of the subjunctive called an **indirect question** and a new tense of the subjunctive (**perfect**) that is used in indirect questions.

Indirect Questions

In this *lectiō* you will encounter indirect questions. They are simply reported questions. Consider this:

Direct Question:	**How** can Hermes catch the monkey?
Indirect Question:	I know **how** Hermes can catch the monkey.

Latin uses the subjunctive in an indirect question.

Direct Question:	*Quōmodo Hermēs sīmiam capere **potest**?*
Indirect Question:	*Sciō **quōmodo** Hermēs sīmiam capere **possit**.*

The formula for an indirect question in Latin is:

main (head) verb + question word + subjunctive

As subjunctive subordinate clauses, indirect questions follow the sequence of tenses:

Primary Sequence:	*Sciō quōmodo Hermēs sīmiam capere* **possit**.
Secondary Sequence:	*Scīvī quōmodo Hermēs sīmiam capere* **posset**.

All the subjunctive verbs marked in **bold** in the *lectiō* are in indirect question constructions. As you read *Lectiō Prīma*, you will also see how another tense of the subjunctive, the perfect, is used in indirect questions.

The Perfect Subjunctive

How can you recognize these perfect subjunctive forms? Here are some tips:

- The **perfect active subjunctive** = perfect stem + *-erim, -eris, -erit*, etc.

vocāverim, vocāveris, vocāverit etc.	I called
habuerim, habueris, habuerit etc.	I had
potuerim, potueris, potuerit etc.	I was able to

- The **perfect passive subjunctive** = P^3 + present subjunctive of *sum*.

vocātus, -a, -um **sim**	*vocātī, -ae, -a* **sīmus**
vocātus, -a, -um **sīs**	*vocātī, -ae, -a* **sītis**
vocātus, -a, -um **sit**	*vocātī, -ae, -a* **sint**

The perfect subjunctive is used to show **time before** the main verb. Simply adjust your English accordingly.

Sciō quōmodo Hermēs sīmiam **cēperit**.
  I know how Hermes caught the monkey. (time before main verb)

Sciō quōmodo sīmia **captus sit**.
  I know how the monkey was caught. (time before main verb)

EXERCEĀMUS!

34-1 Recognizing Indirect Questions

As you read *Lectiō Prīma*, make a line-by-line list of all the subjunctive verbs marked in **bold**. These subjunctives are all in indirect question. Find the head verb and question word that introduce the indirect question. Then identify the tense of the subjunctive. Follow the model.

Line	Subjunctive	Head Verb	Question Word	Tense of Subjunctive
→ 3	dēs	scīs	quod	present

◀)) SALŪTĀTIŌ

Paucōs post diēs, ante ortum sōlis, Aelius surgit, et togam, quam ā fullōne
condūxit, induēns, sē praeparat ut salūtātiōnem apud Servīlium faciat.

Valeria, "Aelī," inquit, "scīsne quod dōnum Servīliō **dēs**?"

Respondet: "Nesciō aut quid **dem** aut quid **dīcam**! Dīc mihi quid
5 dīcere **dēbeam** et quid aliī antē mē **dīxerint**."

Valeria "Nesciō," inquit, "qualibus verbīs aliī **ūsī sint** sed hoc sciō—
urbānus estō! Plānē loquere et tōta rēs bona erit."

Aelius: "Sed quid dē dōnō? Incertus sum quale dōnum aliī **obtulerint**
aut quale **offeram**. Qualem opīniōnem tenēs?"

10 Valeria respondet: "Meministīne ānulum quod mihi duōs ante annōs
dedistī? Hoc patrōnō novō da et eī dīc tē alium meliōrem ac argenteum
fabricāre posse. Nunc, abī, et mementō—fortūna fortēs iuvat!!"

Aelius sōlus per viās obscūrās Subūrae ambulat facem in manū tenēns,
et ad domum Servīliī sōle oriente advenit. Longam ordinem clientium prō
15 foribus domūs stantium videt et sē in novissimō ordine pōnit.

Aelius iānitōrem Servīliī appropinquantem videt. Iānitor, togā Aeliī
vīsā, eī dīcit: "Salvē, cīvis. Cīvibus nōn in novissimō agmine standum est.
Mē sequere et dīc mihi cūr **vēnerīs**."

Aelius ianitōrī dīcit quid Servīliī uxor Valeriae **dīxerit** et **imperāverit**.

20 Iānitor "Manē hīc," inquit, et per forēs intrat.

Aelium, reditum iānitōris exspectantem, alius salūtat. "Nōnne nōvus
es? Trepidus vidēris. Ego, prīmum trepidus ad salūtātiōnem adveniēns,
nescīvī quid **agendum esset**, sed nunc sciō. Scīsne quid **agendum sit**?"

Aelius "Nihil," inquit, "sciō et ergō paulō trepidus sum. Dīc mihi vērē
25 quōmodo vōs omnēs salūtātiōnem **agātis**."

Ille: "Fac ut tranquillus sīs! Age sīcut agō. Sed, dīc mihi, audīvistīne dē Tiberiō?"

Aelius: "Nesciō. Quid audīvistī?"

Ille: "Ut scīs, Tiberius in Germāniā est. Sed scīsne quot Germānōs **vīcerit**? Herī audīvimus, magnō proeliō
factō, dūcēs Germānōrum sē Tiberiō tradidisse. Omnēs in urbe … sed ecce, forēs aperiunt."

Iānua

◀)) VERBA ŪTENDA

ac = atque and, and also,
and besides

ānulus, -ī m. ring

argenteus, -a, -um of
silver, silvery

*condūcō, condūcere,
condūxī, conductum* rent

fax, facis f. torch

foris, foris f. (pl. forēs, -um)
door, gate; *forīs* out of
doors, outside; abroad

Germānia, -ae f. Germany

Germānī, -ōrum pl. Germans,
the German people

iānitor, -ōris m. doorman,
porter

*induō, induere, induī,
indūtum* put on

**nesciō, nescīre,
nescīvī/nesciī,
nescītum** not know

obscūrus, -a, -um dark

officīna, -ae f. workshop

opīniō, -iōnis f. opinion,
belief; reputation

ordō, -inis m. row, line,
order; rank; class of
citizens

plānus, -a, -um plane, flat;
even; obvious; *plānē*
clearly

praeparō (1) prepare

proelium, -iī n. battle

qualis, quale? what kind
of? what sort of?

quot? (indeclin.) how
many?

Tiberius, -iī m. Tiberius,
stepson, son-in-law, and
successor of Augustus

trepidus, -a, -um alarmed,
anxious

urbānus, -a, -um polished,
refined; witty

POSTQUAM LĒGISTĪ

Answer all the following questions in English. Also answer in Latin if the question is followed by (L).

1. In what ways does Aelius prepare himself on the morning of the *salūtātiō*? How would someone prepare himself today for a similar interview?
2. What does Aelius hold in his hand while he walks through the streets? (L) Why?
3. What does he find at Servilius' house upon his arrival? (L)
4. Where does the *iānitor* bring him? (L) Why?
5. What news does Aelius hear while he is waiting? (L) Why might he and his family be especially interested in and concerned about this news?

Gemma

In novissimō ordine literally means "in the newest line," i.e., "at the end of the line." The idea is that it is the most recent thing to pass by. Where English uses an "of" phrase, Latin uses an adjective. Here is another example: *in summō monte* ("at the top of the mountain").

Grammatica A

Indirect Questions

Indirect questions are similar in structure to indirect statements, which you have already learned.

| Direct Statement: | *Ante ortum sōlis Aelius surgit.* | Aelius gets up before sunrise. |
| Indirect Statement: | *Sciō Aelium ante ortum sōlis surgere.* | I know Aelius gets up before sunrise. |

Here, in an indirect statement, the original verb becomes an infinitive (*surgit → surgere*) and the original subject becomes accusative (*Aelius → Aelium).*

Notice the parallels with indirect questions:

| Direct Question: | *Quandō Aelius surgit?* | When does Aelius get up? |
| Indirect Question: | *Sciō quandō Aelius surgat.* | I know when Aelius gets up. |

A direct question is an interrogative sentence and simply seeks information. We mark them in both English and Latin with question marks and with interrogative words like *quis* (who?), *quid* (what?), *ubi* (where?), *quandō* (when?), and *cūr* (why?).

However, when someone reports such a question, the resulting construction is called an **indirect question**. You can recognize an indirect question in both English and Latin because it begins with a head verb like *sciō* (know) followed by an interrogative word.

Here is the formula for an indirect question in Latin:

| main (head) verb | + | interrogative word | + | subjunctive |
| *sciō* | + | *quandō* | + | *surgat* |

Indirect questions follow the sequence of tenses:

| Primary Sequence: | *Sciō quid Aelius **facit**.* | I know what Aelius is doing. |
| Secondary Sequence: | *Scīvī quid Aelius **faceret**.* | I knew what Aelius was doing. |

In both of these sentences the "doing" and the "knowing" happen at approximately the same time, at what we call "near time" in this book.

To show an action that happens before the main verb, the tense of the subjunctive changes. Here is how this works in primary sequence:

| Primary Sequence: | *Sciō quid Aelius **fēcerit**.* | I know when Aelius got up. |

In this sentence the perfect subjunctive shows that this action happened before the action of *sciō*. For now, we will consider time before in primary sequence only. In the next *lectiō* we will consider time before in secondary sequence.

The Perfect Subjunctive

Here is the full paradigm of *capiō* in the perfect subjunctive.

PERFECT ACTIVE SUBJUNCTIVE	PERFECT PASSIVE SUBJUNCTIVE
cēperim	captus sim
cēperis	captus sīs
cēperit	captus sit
cēperimus	captī sīmus
cēperitis	captī sītis
cēperint	captī sint

perfect active subjunctive = perfect stem (3rd PP – *ī*) + *erim, eris, erit*, etc.
perfect passive subjunctive = P³ plus the present subjunctive of *sum*

Did you notice any similarities between perfect subjunctives and other verb forms you have learned? The perfect active subjunctive forms are very similar to the future perfect indicative.

PERFECT ACTIVE SUBJUNCTIVE	FUTURE PERFECT ACTIVE INDICATIVE
cēperim	cēperō
cēperis	**cēperis**
cēperit	cēperit
cēperimus	**cēperimus**
cēperitis	cēperitis
cēperint	**cēperint**

All the forms marked in bold are identical. But don't panic. Remember that perfect subjunctives in Latin are accompanied by word clues to warn you of their presence (in indirect questions, for example). In the *Angulus Grammaticus* to this chapter, you can read how some grammarians distinguish these forms.

Sequence of Tenses

Remember that the subjunctive does not show "real" time like indicative verbs do. When the subjunctive is used in a subordinate clause, it always shows time relative to the main verb of the sentence.

So far you have learned the present and imperfect subjunctive and know that each one shows a time that is near to the time of the main verb of the sentence—either same time as the main verb or time in the immediate future.

Purpose clause: *Ambulō ad amphitheātrum **ut** mūnera **videam**.*
*Ambulāvī ad amphiteātrum **ut** mūnera **vidērem**.*

In each of these sentences, the seeing is expected to happen immediately after the main verb of walking. Consider the same relationship in a result clause:

Result clause: *Sōcratēs tam celer est **ut** Hermēs eum capere **nōn possit**.*
*Sōcratēs tam celer erat **ut** Hermēs eum capere **nōn posset**.*

Here too the result (not being able to catch the monkey) is seen as either existing at the same time or shortly after the main verb of the sentence.

In order to express **time before the main verb**, Latin makes use of two other tenses of the subjunctive—the perfect (introduced here) and the pluperfect (introduced later in this chapter).

Of course, the option of **time after the main verb** also exists, and you can see this in indirect questions.

> I know what you are doing. (same time as or immediately after the main verb)
> I know what you did last summer. (time before main verb)
> I know what you are going to do next summer. (time after main verb)

Latin uses the subjunctive mood to accommodate all these options, and the tenses used follow what we call the **sequence of tenses**. See how the **perfect** subjunctive fits into this chart.

IF THE MAIN VERB IS . . .	USE THIS SUBJUNCTIVE TENSE	TO SHOW
Primary Sequence		
Present		near time
Future	present	
	perfect	time before
Future Perfect		
Secondary Sequence		
Imperfect		
Perfect	imperfect	near time
Pluperfect		

We will fill in more of this chart as you learn more forms of the subjunctive.

EXERCEĀMUS!

34-2 Changing Perfect Active Indicatives to Perfect Active Subjunctives

Change the following perfect active indicative forms to perfect active subjunctives, without changing person and number. Follow the model.

→ vocāvī   *vocāverim*

1. dūxistī
2. cēpērunt
3. fuistī
4. monuimus
5. fēcit
6. dīxī
7. vēnistis
8. spectāvērunt
9. voluit

Lectiō Secunda

Antequam Legis

In this *lectiō* Aelius meets Servilius, gives him his gift, and becomes his client. As you read about this meeting you will see the **pluperfect subjunctive** in use.

The Pluperfect Subjunctive

Like the perfect subjunctive, the **pluperfect subjunctive** shows **time before** the main verb. It is only used after main verbs that are in the secondary sequence. Compare:

> Sciō quid fēceris.   I know what you did. (primary)
> Scīvī quid fēcissēs.   I knew what you had done. (secondary)

Here is how you form the pluperfect subjunctive:

Active: perfect stem + *-issem, -issēs, -isset,* etc.
          fēcissem, fēcissēs, fēcisset, etc.

Passive: P³ + *-essem, -essēs, -esset,* etc.
          factus essem, factus essēs, factus esset, etc.
          Remember that the P³ GNCs.

EXERCEĀMUS!

34-3 **Pluperfect Subjunctive**

As you read, make a line-by-line list of the pluperfect subjunctive forms you see marked in **bold** in *Lectiō Secunda*. Identify the person, number, voice, and 1st principal part of each form. Then translate the word into English. Follow the model.

Line	Pluperfect	Person	Number	Voice	1st PP	English Meaning
→ 4	ēmissētis	2	pl.	active	emō	you bought

Interrogative Words

As you read *Lectiō, Secunda,* also look for interrogative words marked in ***bold italics***. We will review these words after you read.

The Conjunction *Dum*

Here is a new use of *dum*.

- *Dum* means "while" when used with the indicative, commonly with the present tense.
- *Dum* means "until" when used with the subjunctive and sometimes with the indicative.

As you read *Lectiō Secunda,* also look for uses of *dum* and decide whether you would translate them as "while" or "until."

🔊 PATRŌNUS

Foribus aperientibus, Servīlius clientēs suōs salūtāvit, ūnī sportulam aliī nummōs dans. Dē morbō uxōris alicuius rogāvit, dē negōtiō aliōrum.

"Dīcite mihi," inquit, "dē negōtiō vestrō. Trepidus eram postquam revēnistis et nemō mē certiōrem fēcit ***quot*** equōs **ēmissētis** et ***quantum*** lucrī dē illīs equīs **fēcissētis**."

5 Et alium interrogāvit ***quandō*** navēs ab Africā Ostiam **advēnissent** et ***quālēs*** mercēs ad Ītaliam **tulissent**. Nōnnullī clientēs dīxērunt sē mortis avī paenitēre et ūnus, haud venustus eques, Servīlium rogāvit ***quā dē causā*** avus **mortuus esset**.

Mox Servīlius Aeliō appropinquāvit et, manum eius tenēns, rogāvit ***quā dē causā*** **advēnisset**. Aelius, vōce tremente, "Domine," inquit, "fortasse iam intellegis ***cūr*** adsim. Paucōs ante diēs uxor tua ad tabernam Valeriae,

10 socrūs meae, advēnit, et ab eā postulāvit ut hūc advenīrem. Audīvī dē morte Servīliī avī et dum tempus idoneum esset, manēbam. Nōmen mihi M. Aelius est et faber sum. Domina Servīlia pauca ex operibus meīs, quae in tabernā Valeriae exposita erant, vīdit et ea illī placuērunt. Voluit mē alia, sed argentea, fabricāre, sed nōn potuī. Uxor tua mē ut ad salūtātiōnem tuam advenīrem hortāta est et nunc adsum."

Servīlius "Ita" inquit, "uxor mihi omnia haec narrāvit. Sed mihi nōn dīxit ***cūr*** rēs argenteās nōn **fabricāvissēs**."

15 Aelius "Domine" inquit, "pauper sum et argentum nōn habeō. Praetereā, recenter incendium officīnam meam et insulam in quā habitābāmus dēstrūxit. Paene omnia perdita sunt, sed mēcum hunc ānulum tulī. Dōnum tibi est."

Aelius Servīliō anulum dat.

Servīlius, ānulum recipiēns, dīxit: "Aelī, uxor mea, tuam artem admīrāns, mē imperāvit ut tē et familiam adiu-vārem. Et ars tua plāna est. Patrōnus tuus erō et cliens meus eris. Quid plūra? Intrā et manē in ātriō dum omnēs aliōs salūtō. Mox omnia necessāria habēbis—argentum, novam officīnam et novam insulam in quā familia tua habitāre

20 possit. Sērius disserēmus *quōmodo* mihi auxilium dare possīs."

Salūtātiōne confectā clientēs—aliī ad Forum, aliī ad patrōnum alium—abiērunt. Servīlius, revertēns intrā, multa cum Aeliō dē rēbus negōtiī fabrī disseruit. Antequam Aelius abiit, Servīlius et Aelius bene intellexērunt *quantum* lucrī Aelius Servīliō **prōmīsisset** et *quantam* pecūniam Servīlius Aeliō **pollicitus esset.**

Servīlius Aeliō abeuntī dīxit: "Fac ut officīnam novam celeriter inveniās, Aelī, et strēnuē labōrā! Pecūnia mea

25 quoque prō mē semper strēnuē labōrāre dēbet!"

🔊 VERBA ŪTENDA

Africa, -ae f. Africa, Roman province in modern Tunisia

antequam before

ānulus, -ī m. ring

argenteus, -a, -um of silver, silvery

destruō, destruere, destrūxī, destructum destroy

disserō, disserere, disseruī, dissertum discuss

eques, equitis m. horseman, knight; pl. cavalry; order of knights

equus, -ī m. horse

expōnō, expōnere, exposuī, expositum set out; exhibit

foris, foris (pl. forēs, -um) f. door, gate; forīs adv. out of doors, outside; abroad

interrogō (1) ask, question; examine

lucrum, -ī n. profit

merx, mercis f. a commodity; (pl.) goods, merchandise

morbus, -ī m. illness, sickness

navis, navis f. ship

necessārius, -a, -um **necessary, indispensible**

nummus, -ī m. coin, money

officīna, -ae f. workshop

ordō, -inis m. row, line, order; rank; class of citizens

Ostiam "to Ostia" (the port of Rome)

perditus, -a, -um ruined, lost

plānus, -a, -um plane, flat; even; obvious

praetereā besides, moreover

prōmittō, prōmittere, prōmīsī, prōmissum send forth; promise

quā dē causā? **for what reason? why?**

qualis, quale? **what kind of? what sort of?**

Quid plūra? "Why say more?"

quot? (indeclin.) **how many?**

recenter recently

socrus, -ūs f. mother-in-law

sportula, -ae f. little basket; gift of money or food from patron to client

tremō, tremere, tremuī tremble

trepidus, -a, -um nervous, anxious

venustus, -a, -um charming

POSTQUAM LĒGISTĪ

Answer all the following questions in English. Also answer in Latin if the question is followed by (L).

Nāvis Rōmāna

1. What does Servilius do and say as he greets his clients? (L)
2. How does Aelius' speech to Servilius suggest his deference to the great man and his fear of failure?
3. What part of Aelius' story did Servilius need more details about?
4. What evidence of Aelius' craftsmanship does Servilius have, and what is Servilius' opinion of Aelius' work? (L)
5. What does Servilius offer Aelius? (L)
6. What motivation does Servilius express for helping Aelius? (L)
7. Compare the way the Romans conduct business deals with modern American practices.

Grammatica B

The Pluperfect Subjunctive and Consolidation of Subjunctive Forms

With the addition of the pluperfect subjunctive forms, now you have seen all four subjunctive tenses. Here is the chart for *dūcō* with the new pluperfect subjunctive forms marked in **bold**:

PRESENT	IMPERFECT	PERFECT	PLUPERFECT
Active			
dūcam	dūcerem	dūxerim	**dūxissem**
dūcās	dūcerēs	dūxeris	**dūxissēs**
dūcat	dūceret	dūxerit	**dūxisset**
dūcāmus	dūcerēmus	dūxerimus	**dūxissēmus**
dūcātis	dūcerētis	dūxeritis	**dūxissētis**
dūcant	dūcerent	dūxerint	**dūxissent**
Passive			
dūcar	dūcerer	ductus sim	**ductus essem**
dūcāris	dūcerēris	ductus sīs	**ductus essēs**
dūcātur	dūcerētur	ductus sit	**ductus esset**
dūcāmur	dūcerēmur	ductī sīmus	**ductī essēmus**
dūcāminī	dūcerēminī	ductī sītis	**ductī essētis**
dūcantur	dūcerentur	ductī sint	**ductī essent**

Notā Bene:

- The vowel in the pluperfect active ending is always long in the 1st person plural and the 2nd person singular and plural.
- One easy way to remember the imperfect and pluperfect active subjunctives is to note that both forms are spelled like infinitives plus personal endings.

imperfect subjunctive	=	present active infinitive	+	personal endings
dūcerem	=	dūcere	+	m

pluperfect subjunctive	=	perfect active infinitive	+	personal endings
dūxissem	=	dūxisse	+	m

Building the Sequence of Tenses

The pluperfect subjunctive is used to indicate **time before a main verb in secondary sequence**. These four sentences illustrate the four possibilities you have learned so far.

Primary Sequence

Rogant cūr id faciat.   They ask why he is doing that.
    (present subjunctive, near time)

Rogant cūr id fēcerit.   They ask why he did that.
    (perfect subjunctive, time before)

Secondary Sequence

Rogāvērunt cūr id faceret.   They asked why he was doing that.
    (imperfect subjunctive, near time)

Rogāvērunt cūr id fēcisset.   They asked why he had done that.
    (pluperfect subjunctive, time before)

Now see how the **pluperfect** subjunctive fits into the chart for sequence of tenses:

IF THE MAIN VERB IS ...	USE THIS SUBJUNCTIVE TENSE	TO SHOW
Primary Sequence		
Present		near time
Future	present	
Future Perfect	perfect	time before
Secondary Sequence		
Imperfect		near time
Perfect	imperfect	
Pluperfect	**pluperfect**	time before

Consolidation of Interrogative Words

At the beginning of this chapter, we reminded you of interrogative words like *quis?, quid?, ubi?, quandō?,* and *cūr?* (who, what, where, when, and why). Here are several other interrogatives you saw marked in bold italics in *Lectiō Secunda*:

quantus, -a, -um?	how much?
qualis, quale?	what kind of? what sort of?
quā dē causā?	for what reason? why?
quōmodo?	how?
quot?	how many?

All of these words are now *Verba Discenda*. Now go back to *Lectiō Prīma* and see how many of these words you can find.

The Conjunction *Dum*

Earlier you learned that *dum* + indicative is translated "while." But *dum* can also be translated as "until" and can be used with either the indicative or the subjunctive. When it is used with the indicative, it is stating a **fact** that happened or will happen.

> *Manē hīc dum redibō.*   Wait here until I return.

When *dum* is used with the subjunctive, it is still translated as "until," but here it indicates that the anticipated event is more a possibility than a fact.

> *Manē hīc dum redeās.*   Wait here until I should return.

Here are two uses of *dum* from *Lectiō Secunda*:

> ... *dum tempus idoneum esset, manēbam*

> *Manē in ātriō dum omnēs aliōs salūtāverō.*

Which one indicates a fact and which one a possibility? How do you know?

EXERCEĀMUS!

34-4 Sequence of Tenses

In the following sentences, identify the subjunctive verb and its tense. Then indicate whether this verb shows same time or time before the main verb. Follow the model.

		Verb	**Tense**	**Time Sequence**
→	Scīsne quod dōnum Serviliō dēs?	*dēs*	present	near time

1. Nesciō quid dem.

2. Nesciō quid aliī clientēs Servīliō dederint.

3. Nescīvimus quid dīcerent!

4. Nescīvī qualibus verbīs aliī ūsī essent.

5. Incertus sum quale dōnum aliī obtulerint.

6. Rogāvit quā dē causā advēnissent.

Mōrēs Rōmānī

Commercium Rōmānum

Roman society was hierarchical and plutocratic. By the time of the Empire, the ancient division between patrician (aristocratic) and plebian families had broken down a bit. However, even in the Empire, citizens were grouped by census into six classes (*ordinēs*) according to wealth. The major public offices, such as the consulship, were only open to the wealthiest group or senatorial class, of which Servilius Severus was a member. Traditionally, the wealth of the senatorial class was based on large agricultural estates called *latifundia*, (*-ōrum* n. pl.). Members of this class were not allowed to participate directly in commercial activity.

The next wealthiest group were the knights (*equitēs, -um* m. pl.) who typically made their fortunes in a wide variety of business enterprises, including trade and manufacturing. Cordus is an *eques*. As part of our story on Cordus, we imagine that his father made money by helping Crassus, who used to go to fires and buy the houses at increasingly low prices as the fire progressed. Perhaps Cordus is trying to become more respectable by starting a fire brigade at Rome.

At the bottom of this social structure were citizens called *prōlētāriī*, who owned little or no property. Aelius and his family were of this class. This social structure, however, was very mobile. It was possible for a *prōlētārius* to rise quickly to the status of *eques* through the accumulation of great wealth.

Although men of Servilius' status could not, themselves, act as merchants or traders (*mercātōrēs*) or bankers (*argentāriī*), they could, as Servilius does, seek commercial profit indirectly, by working through freedmen, clients, or agents. A skilled craftsman like Aelius was a very attractive client for a patron like Servilius, because Aelius could make money for Servilius, as well as provide Servilius with valuable support in political elections.

There were great opportunities for financial gain (*lucrum, -ī* n.) in the export of Italian wines and olive oil and the importation of grain and slaves into Italy. The luxury trade items, such as silk and spices from the East and even amber from the Baltic, were also potentially lucrative. However, the danger of severe financial loss through shipwreck, theft, and natural disaster was also very real.

Mercury (*Mercurius, -iī* m.), the Roman god of messengers and commerce, is still depicted in that role today. The god appears wearing his trademark winged helmet and sandals on the facade of Grand Central Station in New York City. Mercury is flanked by Hercules and Minerva in a group sculpted by Jules-Felix Coutan (1848–1939).

Mercurius

Orbis Terrārum Rōmānus

Germānia

The Romans used the word *Germānia* to refer to a wide geographic area in north central Europe inhabited not only by German-speaking tribes but also by Celts and others. There were two Roman provinces called *Germānia* west of the Rhine river. *Germānia Inferior* consisted approximately of what is now Belgium and the Netherlands. *Germānia Superior* included modern Switzerland and the French province of Alsace. Under the Emperor Augustus, the Romans tried to push across the Rhine river. The successful expedition of Tiberius in 9–7 B.C. was one of these efforts. For a while, the Romans controlled territory as far east as the Elbe River.

Porta Rōmāna Augustae Trevirōrum

However, after Marcus Lollius' defeat at the hands of Germanic tribes in 17–16 and the disastrous loss in 9 B.C. of three legions under general Varus to the German leader Arminius in the Teutoburg Forest. Augustus settled the boundaries of the empire along the defendable lines of the Rhine and Danube rivers. Two of the most important cities in Roman Germany were *Colōnia Claudia Āra Agrippīnensium* (modern Cologne) and *Augusta Trevirōrum* (modern Trier).

Suetonius' account of Augustus' reaction to Varus' defeat in Germany is quite dramatic:

[23] Hāc nuntiātā excubiās per urbem indīxit, nē quis tumultus existeret. Vōvit et magnōs lūdōs Iovī Optimō Maximō. Adeō dēnique eum consternātum esse ferunt, ut per continuōs mensēs barbā capillōque summissō caput interdum foribus illīderet, vōciferāns: Quintilī Vare, legiōnēs redde!

Germānia

🔊 VERBA ŪTENDA

ac = *atque* and, and also, and besides

adeō so much, to such a degree

barba, -ae f. beard

capillus, -ī m. head hair

consternō (1) shock

continuus, -a, -um successive

excubiae, -ārum f. pl. guard, watch

existō, existere, extitī arise, appear

ferunt = *hominēs dīcunt*

foris, foris (pl. forēs, -um) f. door, gate; *forīs* adv. out of doors, outside; abroad

illīdō, illīdere, illīsī, illīsum strike against

imperium, -ī n. command, order, rule

indīcō, indīcere, indīxī, indictum proclaim

interdum occasionally

nuntiō (1) announce, report

quis = *aliquis*

reddō, reddere, reddidī, redditum give back

submittō, submittere, submīsī, submissum let grow

tumultus, -ī m. uproar, disturbance

vōciferor, vōciferārī, vōciferātus sum yell, cry out

voveō, vovēre, vōvī, vōtum vow

Arminius in Germāniā

Latīna Hodierna

Latin Interrogatives in English

Use the meaning of the following Latin interrogatives and verbs of asking to define their English derivatives. Consult an English dictionary if you need help.

quaerō, quaerere, quaesīvī/quaesiī, quaesītum	**quer**y, **quest**, **quest**ion, **quest**ionnaire
rogō (1)	ab**rog**ate, de**rog**ate, de**rog**atory, inter**rog**ative, pre**rog**ative, **rog**atory
quantus, -a, -um?	**quant**ity, **quant**ify, **quant**um **quant**itative
qualis, quale?	**quali**fy, **quali**fication, **quali**tative, **quali**ty
quid?	**quid**dity, **quid** prō quō
quot?	**quot**ient, **quot**a

QUID PUTĀS?

1. How do the attitudes of upper-class Romans toward commerce compare to those of upper-class Americans today? What modern American group compares to the upwardly-mobile *equitēs* in ancient Rome?
2. Are there any modern parallels to the Roman client-patron relationship?
3. Why do you think the Romans were so eager to advance into Germany? Why do you think they found this so difficult to do?
4. Can you give an example of a *quid prō quō*?
5. Describe Augustus' reaction to Varus' defect in Germany. What does this suggest about his leadership qualities?

EXERCEĀMUS!

34-5 Scrībāmus

Find the Latin words in *Lectiō Prīma* that best answer these Latin questions. Then answer the question in Latin. Follow the model.

→ Quandō Aelius surgit?
  ante ortum sōlis (line 1):
  Aelius ante ortum sōlis surgit.

1. Quid Aelius ā fullōne condūxit?
2. Quā dē causā Aelius sē praeparat?
3. Quale dōnum Aelius Valeriae dedit?
4. Ubi Aelius sōlus ambulat facem in manū tenēns?
5. Quandō Aelius ad domum Serviliī advenit?
6. Quid Aelius prō foribus domūs videt?
7. Quem appropinquantem Aelius videt?
8. Cūr iānitor Aelium civem esse scit?
9. Cui Aelius dīcit quid Serviliī uxor?
10. Quis trepidus vidētur?

34-6 **Colloquāmur**

Practice asking and answering in Latin the questions in Exercise 34-5.

34-7 **Vēnātiō Verbōrum Discendōrum**

Find the *Verbum Discendum* that best fits each of the following statements. HINT: Some statements have more than one answer, and a *Verbum Discendum* can be used more than once. Follow the model.

→ The opposite of *sciō*: *nesciō*

1. A 3ʳᵈ declension i-stem noun:

2. An indeclinable adjective:

3. An *eques* belongs to one of these ranks:

4. This Latin word comes to mean a maintenance person in a building in English:

5. A synonym for *iānua*:

6. A subordinate conjunction:

7. A 3ʳᵈ conjugation verb:

8. A 3ʳᵈ declension noun that is not i-stem:

9. A 4ᵗʰ conjugation verb:

10. An animal:

11. Refers to a metal:

12. This word refers to a place where crafts were made:

13. A synonym for *clārus, -a, -um*:

14. *Quaerō* is a synonym for this word:

15. A neuter noun of the\ second declension:

🔊 VERBA DISCENDA

antequam **before**

argenteus, -a, -um **of silver, silvery** [argenteous]

destruō, destruere, destrūxī, destructum **destroy** [destructive]

eques, equitis **m. horseman, knight; pl. cavalry; order of knights** [equestrian]

equus, -ī **m. horse** [equine]

foris, foris **f. (pl. forēs, -um) door, gate;** *forīs*

adv. out of doors, outside; abroad

iānitor, -ōris **m. doorman, porter** [janitorial]

interrogō **(1) ask, question; examine** [interrogation]

morbus, -ī **m. illness, sickness** [morbid]

navis, navis **f. ship** [naval]

necessarius, -a, -um **necessary, indispensible**

nesciō, nescīre, nescīvī/nesciī, nescītum **not know** [nescience]

officīna, -ae **f. workshop** [office]

opīniō, -iōnis **f. opinion, belief; reputation** [opinionated]

ordō, -inis **m. row, line, order; rank; class of citizens** [ordination]

plānus, -a, -um **plane, flat, even; obvious**

praetereā **besides, moreover**

proelium, -iī **n. battle**

prōmittō, prōmittere, prōmīsī, prōmissum

send forth; promise [promissary]

quā dē causā? **for what reason? why?**

qualis, quale? **what kind of? what sort of?** [quality]

quot? **(indeclin.) how many?** [quotient]

tremō, tremere, tremuī **tremble** [tremor]

Angulus Grammaticus

Macron or No Macron?

When we compared the perfect active subjunctive and future perfect active indicative forms earlier in this chapter, we did so this way:

PERFECT ACTIVE SUBJUNCTIVE	FUTURE PERFECT ACTIVE INDICATIVE
cēperim	cēperō
cēperis	**cēperis**
cēperit	cēperit
cēperimus	cēperimus
cēperitis	cēperitis
cēperint	cēperint

The situation, however, is actually a bit more complex. In some grammar books you will find that the 2nd person singular and plural, and the 1st person plural have a macron over the -*i* of the ending in the perfect subjunctive.

PERFECT ACTIVE SUBJUNCTIVE	FUTURE PERFECT ACTIVE INDICATIVE
cēperim	cēperō
cēperīs	cēperis
cēperit	cēperit
cēperīmus	cēperimus
cēperītis	cēperitis
cēperint	cēperint

This is because some Roman poets at various times used either a long or a short -*i* in these endings. It seems that there was confusion even at the time as to which was more corrrect. Such things are not uncommon, even today. Consider, for example, different American pronunciations of words like "aunt," "tomato," and "roof."

Photo Credits

Page 446 Getty Images/De Agostini Editore Picture Library; **page 448** Pierdelune/Dreamstime LLC—Royalty Free; **page 453** Clipart.com; **page 456** Stuart Monk/Fotolia, LLC—Royalty Free; **page 457 (top)** Bofotolux/Fotolia, LLC—Royalty Free; **page 457 (bottom)** Photos to Go.

Appendix

Forms

Nouns

	1ST DECLENSION		2ND DECLENSION				
Singular	**Fem.**	**Masc.**	**Masc.**	**Masc.**	**Masc.**	**Masc.**	**Neut.**
Nom.	fēmina	discipulus	vir	fīlius	magister	puer	vīnum
Gen.	fēminae	discipulī	virī	fīliī	magistrī	puerī	vīnī
Dat.	fēminae	discipulō	virō	fīliō	magistrō	puerō	vīnō
Acc.	fēminam	discipulum	virum	fīlium	magistrum	puerum	vīnum
Abl.	fēminā	discipulō	virō	fīliō	magistrō	puerō	vīnō
Voc.	fēmina	discipule	vir	fīlī	magister	puer	vīnum
Plural							
Nom.	fēminae	discipulī	virī	fīliī	magistrī	puerī	vīna
Gen.	fēminārum	discipulōrum	virōrum	fīliōrum	magistrōrum	puerōrum	vīnōrum
Dat.	fēminīs	discipulīs	virīs	fīliīs	magistrīs	puerīs	vīnīs
Acc.	fēminās	discipulōs	virōs	fīliōs	magistrōs	puerōs	vīna
Abl.	fēminīs	discipulīs	virīs	fīliīs	magistrīs	puerīs	vīnīs
Voc.	fēminae	discipulī	virī	fīliī	magistrī	puerī	vīna

	3RD DECLENSION			I-STEMS	
Singular	**Masc.**	**Fem.**	**Neut.**	**Masc./Fem.**	**Neut.**
Nom.	frāter	soror	nōmen	ignis	mare
Gen.	frātris	sorōris	nōminis	ignis	maris
Dat.	frātrī	sorōrī	nōminī	ignī	marī
Acc.	frātrem	sorōrem	nōmen	ignem	mare
Abl.	frātre	sorōre	nōmine	igne or ignī	marī
Voc.	frāter	soror	nōmen	ignis	mare
Plural					
Nom.	frātrēs	sorōrēs	nōmina	ignēs	maria
Gen.	frātrum	sorōrum	nōminum	ignium	marium
Dat.	frātribus	sorōribus	nōminibus	ignibus	maribus
Acc.	frātrēs	sorōrēs	nōmina	ignēs	maria
Abl.	frātribus	sorōribus	nōminibus	ignibus	maribus
Voc.	frātrēs	sorōrēs	nōmina	ignēs	maria

A1

From *Disce! An Introductory Latin Course, volume 2*, First Edition. Francesco Bonavita. Copyright © 2011 by Pearson Education, Inc. Published by Pearson Prentice Hall. All rights reserved.

4TH DECLENSION

Singular	Masc.	Fem.	Neut.
Nom.	lacus	manus	genū
Gen.	lacūs	manūs	genūs
Dat.	lacuī	manuī	genū
Acc.	lacum	manum	genū
Abl.	lacū	manū	genū
Voc.	lacus	manus	genū

Plural			
Nom.	lacūs	manūs	genua
Gen.	lacuum	manuum	genuum
Dat.	lacibus	manibus	genibus
Acc.	lacūs	manūs	genua
Abl.	lacū	manibus	genibus
Voc.	lacus	manūs	genua

5TH DECLENSION

Singular	Masc.	Fem.
Nom.	diēs	rēs
Gen.	diēī	reī
Dat.	diēī	reī
Acc.	diem	rem
Abl.	diē	rē
Voc.	diēs	rēs

Plural		
Nom.	diēs	rēs
Gen.	diērum	rērum
Dat.	diēbus	rēbus
Acc.	diēs	rēbus
Abl.	diēbus	rēs
Voc.	diēs	rēs

Irregular Noun *Vīs*

	Singular strength, power	Plural troops, forces
Nom.	vīs	vīrēs
Gen.	vis	vīrium
Dat.	vī	vīribus
Acc.	vim	vīrēs
Abl.	vī	vīribus

Adjectives

2-1-2 ADJECTIVES

	2ND DECLENSION	1ST DECLENSION	2ND DECLENSION
Singular	**Masc.**	**Fem.**	**Neut.**
Nom.	bonus	bona	bonum
Gen.	bonī	bonae	bonī
Dat.	bonō	bonae	bonō
Acc.	bonum	bonam	bonum
Abl.	bonō	bonā	bonō
Voc.	bone	bona	bonum
Plural			
Nom.	bonī	bonae	bona
Gen.	bonōrum	bonārum	bonōrum
Dat.	bonīs	bonīs	bonīs
Acc.	bonōs	bonās	bona
Abl.	bonīs	bonīs	bonīs
Voc.	bonī	bonae	bona

	2ND DECLENSION	1ST DECLENSION	2ND DECLENSION
Singular	**Masc.**	**Fem.**	**Neut.**
Nom.	pulcher	pulchra	pulchrum
Gen.	pulchrī	pulchrae	pulchrī
Dat.	pulchrō	pulchrae	pulchrō
Acc.	pulchrum	pulchram	pulchrum
Abl.	pulchrō	pulchrā	pulchrō
Voc.	pulcher	pulchra	pulchrum
Plural			
Nom.	pulchrī	pulchrae	pulchra
Gen.	pulchrōrum	pulchrārum	pulchrōrum
Dat.	pulchrīs	pulchrīs	pulchrīs
Acc.	pulchrōs	pulchrās	pulchra
Abl.	pulchrīs	pulchrīs	pulchrīs
Voc.	pulchrī	pulchrae	pulchra

3RD DECLENSION ADJECTIVES

3 Terminations

Singular	Masc.	Fem.	Neut.
Nom.	celer	celeris	celere
Gen.	celeris	celeris	celeris
Dat.	celerī	celerī	celerī
Acc.	celerem	celerem	celere
Abl.	celerī	celerī	celerī
Voc.	celer	celeris	celere

Plural			
Nom.	celerēs	celerēs	celeria
Gen.	celerium	celerium	celerium
Dat.	celeribus	celeribus	celeribus
Acc.	celerēs	celerēs	celeria
Abl.	celeribus	celeribus	celeribus
Voc.	celerēs	celerēs	celeria

2 Terminations

Singular	Masc./Fem.	Neut.
Nom.	fortis	forte
Gen.	fortis	fortis
Dat.	fortī	fortī
Acc.	fortem	forte
Abl.	fortī	fortī
Voc.	fortis	forte

Plural		
Nom.	fortēs	fortia
Gen.	fortium	fortium
Dat.	fortibus	fortibus
Acc.	fortēs	fortia
Abl.	fortibus	fortibus
Voc.	fortēs	fortia

1 Termination

Singular	Masc./Fem./Neut.
Nom.	fēlix
Gen.	fēlīcis
Dat.	fēlīcī
Acc.	fēlīcem (m./f.) fēlix (n.)
Abl.	fēlīcī
Voc.	fēlix

Plural	
Nom.	fēlīcēs (m./f.) fēlīcia (n.)
Gen.	fēlīcium
Dat.	fēlīcibus
Acc.	fēlīcēs (m./f.) fēlīcia (n.)
Abl.	fēlīcibus
Voc.	fēlīcēs (m./f.) fēlīcia (n.)

A4

Comparative Adjectives

Note: Comparatives are declined like 3rd declension regular (not i-stem) nouns.

Singular	Masc./Fem.	Neut.
Nom.	celerior	celerius
Gen.	celeriōris	celeriōris
Dat.	celeriōrī	celeriōrī
Acc.	celeriōrem	celerius
Abl.	celeriōre	celeriōre
Voc.	celerior	celerius
Plural		
Nom.	celeriōrēs	celeriōra
Gen.	celeriōrum	celeriōrum
Dat.	celeriōribus	celeriōribus
Acc.	celeriōrēs	celeriōra
Abl.	celeriōribus	celeriōribus
Voc.	celeriōrēs	celeriōra

Superlative Adjectives

REGULAR FORMATION

POSITIVE	SUPERLATIVE
laetus, -a, -um	laetissimus, -a, -um
fortis, -e	fortissimus, -a, -um
crūdēlis, -e	crūdēlissimus, -a, -um

IRREGULAR FORMATIONS

A. All adjectives ending in *-er* in the masculine nominative singular:

POSITIVE	SUPERLATIVE
miser, -era, -erum	miserrimus, -a, -um
pulcher, -chra, -chrum	pulcherrimus, -a, -um
celer, -is, -e	celerrimus, -a, -um

B. Some adjectives ending in -*lis* in the masculine nominative singular:

POSITIVE	SUPERLATIVE
facilis, -e	facillimus, -a, -um
difficilis, -e	difficillimus, -a, -um
similis, -e	simillimus, -a, -um
dissimilis, -e	dissimillimus, -a, -um
gracilis, -e	gracillimus, -a, -um
humilis, -e	humillimus, -a, -um

C. Irregular comparative and superlative adjectives:

POSITIVE	COMPARATIVE	SUPERLATIVE
bonus, -a, -um	melior, melius	optimus, -a,- um
malus, -a, -um	pēior, pēius	pessimus, -a, -um
magnus, -a, -um	māior, māius	maximus, -a, -um
multus, -a, -um	plūrēs, plūra	plūrimus, -a, -um
multī, -ae, -a	plūs (neuter form only)	plūrimī, -ae, -a
parvus, -a, -um	minor, minus	minimus, -a, -um
[no positive]	prior, prius	prīmus, -a, -um
superus, -a, -um	superior, superius	suprēmus, -a, -um
		summus, -a, -um

Personal / Reflexive Adjectives

PERSON	LATIN FORMS	TRANSLATION
Singular		
1st	meus, -a, -um	my
2nd	tuus, -a, -um	your
3rd	suus, -a, -um (reflexive)	his/her/its own
Plural		
1st	noster, -tra, -trum	our
2nd	vester, -tra, -trum	your
3rd	suus, -a, -um (reflexive)	their own

UNUS NAUTA Adjectives

Ullus, -a, -um any
Nūllus, -a, -um no, none
Ūnus, -a, -um one
Sōlus, -a, -um alone, only

Neuter, neutra, neutrum—neither
Alius, -a, -ud another, other
Uter, utra, utrum either, which (of two)
Tōtus, -a, -um whole, entire
Alter, altera, alterum the other (of two)

	MASC.	FEM.	NEUT.
Singular			
Nom.	sōlus	sōla	sōlum
Gen.	sōlīus	sōlīus	sōlīus
Dat.	sōlī	sōlī	sōlī
Acc.	sōlum	sōlam	sōlum
Abl.	sōlō	sōlā	sōlō
Plural			
Nom.	sōlī	sōlae	sōla
Gen.	sōlōrum	sōlārum	sōlōrum
Dat.	sōlīs	sōlīs	sōlīs
Acc.	sōlōs	sōlās	sōla
Abl.	sōlīs	sōlīs	sōlīs

Adverbs

REGULAR

	POSITIVE	COMPARATIVE	SUPERLATIVE
Based on 2-1-2 adjective	laetē	laetius	laetissimē
Based on 3rd declension adjective	fortiter	fortius	fortissimē

PARTIALLY IRREGULAR

	POSITIVE	COMPARATIVE	SUPERLATIVE
3rd declension adjectives ending in -er	celeriter	celerius	celerrimē
Other 3rd declension adjectives	fortiter	fortius	fortissimē

COMPLETELY IRREGULAR

bene	melius	optimē
male	pēius	pessimē
magnopere	magis	maximē
multum	plūs	plūrimum
parum	minus	minimē

Pronouns

	1ST PERSON	2ND PERSON	3RD PERSON		
Singular					
Nom.	ego	tū	is	ea	id
Gen.	meī	tuī	eius	eius	eius
Dat.	mihi	tibi	eī	eī	eī
Acc.	mē	tē	eum	eam	id
Abl.	mē	tē	eō	eā	eō
Plural					
Nom.	nōs	vōs	eī	eae	ea
Gen.	nostrī/nostrum	vestrī/vestrum	eōrum	eārum	eōrum
Dat.	nōbīs	vōbīs	eīs	eīs	eīs
Acc.	nōs	vōs	eōs	eās	ea
Abl.	nōbīs	vōbīs	eīs	eīs	eīs

RELATIVE PRONOUN AND INTERROGATIVE ADJECTIVE

	MASC.	FEM.	NEUT.
Singular			
Nom.	quī	quae	quod
Gen.	cuius	cuius	cuius
Dat.	cui	cui	cui
Acc.	quem	quam	quod
Abl.	quō	quā	quō
Plural			
Nom.	quī	quae	quae
Gen.	quōrum	quārum	quōrum
Dat.	quibus	quibus	quibus
Acc.	quōs	quās	quae
Abl.	quibus	quibus	quibus

INTERROGATIVE PRONOUN

	MASC./FEM.	NEUT.
Singular		
Nom.	quis	quid
Gen.	cuius	cuius
Dat.	cui	cui
Acc.	quem	quid
Abl.	quō	quō
Plural		
Nom.	quī	quae
Gen.	quōrum	quōrum
Dat.	quibus	quibus
Acc.	quōs	quae
Abl.	quibus	quibus

DEMONSTRATIVE: *hic haec hoc*

	MASC.	FEM.	NEUT.
Singular			
Nom.	hic	haec	hoc
Gen.	huius	huius	huius
Dat.	huic	huic	huic
Acc.	hunc	hanc	hoc
Abl.	hōc	hāc	hōc
Plural			
Nom.	hī	hae	haec
Gen.	hōrum	hārum	hōrum
Dat.	hīs	hīs	hīs
Acc.	hōs	hās	haec
Abl.	hīs	hīs	hīs

NUMBERS

Only the Latin words for the cardinal numbers 1, 2, 3 and 1000 are declinable:

	I			II			III			M
Nom.	ūnus	ūna	ūnum	duo	duae	duo	trēs	trēs	tria	mīlia
Gen.	ūnīus	ūnīus	ūnīus	duōrum	duārum	duōrum	trium	trium	trium	mīlium
Dat.	ūnī	ūnīus	ūnī	duōbus	duābus	duōbus	tribus	tribus	tribus	mīlibus
Acc.	ūnum	ūnam	ūnum	duōs	duās	duo	trēs	trēs	tria	mīlia
Abl.	ūnō	ūnā	ūnō	duōbus	duābus	duōbus	tribus	tribus	tribus	mīlibus

	ROMAN NUMERAL	CARDINAL NUMBER	ORDINAL NUMBER
1	I	ūnus, -a, -um	prīmus, -a, -um
2	II	duo, -ae, -o	secundus, -a, -um
3	III	trēs, -ēs, -ia	tertius, -a, -um
4	IIII or IV	quattuor	quartus, -a, -um
5	V	quinque	quintus, -a, -um
6	VI	sex	sextus, -a, -um
7	VII	septem	septimus, -a, -um
8	VIII	octō	octāvus, -a, -um
9	VIIII or IX	novem	nōnus, -a, -um
10	X	decem	decimus, -a, -um
11	XI	undecim	undecimus, -a, -um
12	XII	duodecim	duodecimus, -a, -um
13	XIII	tredecim	tertius decimus, -a, -um
14	XIIII or XIV	quattuordecim	quartus decimus, -a, -um
15	XV	quindecim	quintus decimus, -a, -um
16	XVI	sēdecim	sextus decimus, -a, -um
17	XVII	septendecim	septimus decimus, -a, -um
18	XVIII	duodēvīgintī	duodēvicēsimus, -a, -um
19	XVIIII or XIX	undēvīgintī	undevicensimus, -a, -um
20	XX	vīgintī	vicēsimus, -a, -um
21	XXI	vīgintī ūnus	vicēsimus, prīmus
22	XXII	vīgintī duo	vicēsimus, secundus
30	XXX	trīgintā	trīcēsimus, -a, -um
40	XL or XXXX	quadrāgintā	quadrāgēsimus, -a, -um
50	L	quīnquagintā	quīnquāgēsimus, -a, -um
60	LX	sexāgintā	sexāgēsimus, -a, -um
70	LXX	septuāgintā	sepuāgēsimus, -a, -um
80	LXXX	octōgintā	octōgēsimus, -a, -um
90	XC	nōnāgintā	nōnāgēsimus -a, -um
100	C	centum	centimus, -a, -um
500	D	quīngentī	quīngentēsimus, -a, -um
1000	M	mīlle mīlia	millēsimus, -a, -um

Regular Verbs

INDICATIVE MOOD

1ˢᵗ Conjugation   vocō, vocāre, vocāvī, vocātum

Active

PRESENT	IMPERFECT	FUTURE	PERFECT	PLUPERFECT	FUTURE PERFECT
vocō	vocābam	vocābō	vocāvī	vocāveram	vocāverō
vocās	vocābās	vocābis	vocāvistī	vocāverās	vocāveris
vocat	vocābat	vocābit	vocāvit	vocāverat	vocāverit
vocāmus	vocābāmus	vocābimus	vocāvimus	vocāverāmus	vocāverimus
vocātis	vocābātis	vocābitis	vocāvistis	vocāverātis	vocāveritis
vocant	vocābant	vocābunt	vocāvērunt	vocāverant	vocāverint

Passive

PRESENT	IMPERFECT	FUTURE	PERFECT (MASC.)	PLUPERFECT (FEM.)	FUTURE PERFECT (NEUT.)
vocor	vocābar	vocābor	vocātus sum	vocāta eram	vocātum erō
vocāris	vocābāris	vocāberis	vocātus es	vocāta erās	vocātum eris
vocātur	vocābātur	vocābitur	vocātus est	vocāta erat	vocātum erit
vocāmur	vocābāmur	vocābimur	vocātī sumus	vocātae erāmus	vocāta erimus
vocāminī	vocābāminī	vocābiminī	vocātī estis	vocātae erātis	vocāta eritis
vocantur	vocābantur	vocābuntur	vocātī sunt	vocātae erant	vocāta erunt

2nd Conjugation   moneō, monēre, monuī, monitum

Active

PRESENT	IMPERFECT	FUTURE	PERFECT	PLUPERFECT	FUTURE PERFECT
moneō	monēbam	monēbō	monuī	monueram	monuerō
monēs	monēbās	monēbis	monuistī	monuerās	monueris
monet	monēbat	monēbit	monuit	monuerat	monuerit
monēmus	monēbāmus	monēbimus	monuimus	monuerāmus	monuerimus
monētis	monēbātis	monēbitis	monuistis	monucrātis	monueritis
monent	monēbant	monēbunt	monuērunt	monuerant	monuerint

Passive

PRESENT	IMPERFECT	FUTURE	PERFECT (MASC.)	PLUPERFECT (FEM.)	FUTURE PERFECT (NEUT.)
moneor	monēbar	monēbor	monitus sum	monita eram	monitum erō
monēris	monēbāris	monēberis	monitus es	monita erās	monitum eris
monētur	monēbātur	monēbitur	monitus est	monita erat	monitum erit
monēmur	monēbāmur	monēbimur	monitī sumus	monitae erāmus	monita sumus
monēminī	monēbāminī	monēbiminī	monitī estis	monitae erātis	monita estis
monentur	monēbantur	monēbuntur	monitī sunt	monitae erant	monita sunt

3rd Conjugation Regular: scrībō, scrībere, scrīpsī, scriptum

Active

PRESENT	IMPERFECT	FUTURE	PERFECT	PLUPERFECT	FUTURE PERFECT
scrībō	scrībēbam	scrībam	scrīpsī	scrīpseram	scrīpserō
scrībis	scrībēbās	scrībēs	scrīpsistī	scrīpserās	scrīpseris
scrībit	scrībēbat	scrībet	scrīpsit	scrīpserat	scrīpserit
scrībimus	scrībēbamus	scrībēmus	scrīpsimus	scrīpserāmus	scrīpserimus
scrībitis	scrībēbātis	scrībētis	scrīpsistis	scrīpserātis	scrīpseritis
scrībunt	scrībēbant	scrībent	scrīpsērunt	scrīpserant	scrīpserint

Passive

PRESENT	IMPERFECT	FUTURE	PERFECT (MASC.)	PLUPERFECT (FEM.)	FUTURE PERFECT (NEUT.)
scrībor	scrībēbar	scrībor	scriptus sum	scripta eram	scriptum sum
scrīberis	scrībēbāris	scrībēris	scriptus es	scripta erās	scriptum es
scrībitur	scrībēbātur	scrībētur	scriptus est	scripta erat	scriptum est
scrībimur	scrībēbāmur	scrībēmur	scriptī sumus	scriptae erāmus	scripta sumus
scrībiminī	scrībēbāminī	scrībēminī	scriptī estis	scriptae erātis	scripta estis
scrībuntur	scrībēbantur	scrībentur	scriptī sunt	scriptae erant	scripta erunt

3rd Conjugation -iō: capiō, capere, cēpī, captum

Active

PRESENT	IMPERFECT	FUTURE	PERFECT	PLUPERFECT	FUTURE PERFECT
capiō	capiēbam	capiam	cēpī	cēperam	cēperō
capis	capiēbās	capiēs	cēpistī	cēperās	cēperis
capit	capiēbat	capiet	cēpit	cēperat	cēperit
capimus	capiēbāmus	capiēmus	cēpimus	cēperāmus	cēperimus
capitis	capiēbātis	capiētis	cēpistis	cēperātis	cēperitis
capiunt	capiēbant	capient	cēpērunt	cēperant	cēperint

Passive

PRESENT	IMPERFECT	FUTURE	PERFECT (MASC.)	PLUPERFECT (FEM.)	FUTURE PERFECT (NEUT.)
capior	capiēbar	capiar	captus sum	capta eram	captum erō
caperis	capiēbāris	capiēris	captus es	capta erās	captum eris
capitur	capiēbātur	capiētur	captus est	capta erat	captum erit
capimur	capiēbāmur	capiēmur	captī sumus	captae erāmus	capta erimus
capiminī	capiēbāminī	capiēminī	captī estis	captae erātis	capta eritis
capiuntur	capiēbantur	capientur	captī sunt	captae erant	capta erunt

4th Conjugation   audiō, audīre, audīvī, audītum

Active

PRESENT	IMPERFECT	FUTURE	PERFECT	PLUPERFECT	FUTURE PERFECT
audiō	audiēbam	audiam	audīvī	audīveram	audīverō
audīs	audiēbās	audiēs	audīvistī	audīverās	audīveris
audit	audiēbat	audiet	audīvit	audīverat	audīverit
audīmus	audiēbāmus	audiēmus	audīvimus	audīverāmus	audīverimus
audītis	audiēbātis	audiētis	audīvistis	audīverātis	audīveritis
audiunt	audiēbant	audient	audīvērunt	audīverant	audīverint

Passive

PRESENT	IMPERFECT	FUTURE	PERFECT (MASC.)	PLUPERFECT (FEM.)	FUTURE PERFECT (NEUT.)
audior	audiēbar	audiar	audītus sum	audīta eram	audītum erō
audīris	audiēbāris	audiēris	audītus es	audīta erās	audītum eris
audītur	audiēbātur	audiētur	audītus est	audīta erat	audītum erit
audīmur	audiēbāmur	audiēmur	audītī sumus	audītae erāmus	audīta erimus
audīminī	audiēbāminī	audiēminī	audītī estis	audītae erātis	audīta eritis
audiuntur	audiēbantur	audientur	audītī sunt	audītae erant	audīta erunt

SUBJUNCTIVE MOOD

1st Conjugation   vocō, vocāre, vocāvī, vocātum

Active

PRESENT	IMPERFECT	PERFECT	PLUPERFECT
vocem	vocārem	vocāverim	vocāvissem
vocēs	vocārēs	vocāveris	vocāvissēs
vocet	vocāret	vocāverit	vocāvisset
vocēmus	vocārēmus	vocāverimus	vocāvissēmus
vocētis	vocārētis	vocāveritis	vocāvissētis
vocent	vocārent	vocāverint	vocāvissent

Passive

PRESENT	IMPERFECT	PERFECT (MASC.)	PLUPERFECT (FEM.)
vocer	vocārer	vocātus sim	vocāta essem
vocēris	vocārēris	vocātus sīs	vocāta essēs
vocētur	vocārētur	vocātus sit	vocāta esset
vocēmur	vocārēmur	vocātī sīmus	vocātae essēmus
vocēminī	vocārēminī	vocātī sītis	vocātae essētis
vocentur	vocārentur	vocātī sint	vocātae essent

2nd Conjugation   moneō, monēre, monuī, monitum

Active

PRESENT	IMPERFECT	PERFECT	PLUPERFECT
moneam	monēre	monuerim	monuissem
moneās	monērēs	monueris	monuissēs
moneat	monēret	monuerit	monuisset
moneāmus	monērēmus	monuerimus	monuissēmus
moneātis	monērētis	monueritis	monuissētis
moneant	monērent	monuerint	monuissent

Passive

PRESENT	IMPERFECT	PERFECT (MASC.)	PLUPERFECT (FEM.)
monear	monērer	monitus sit	monita essem
moneāris	monērēris	monitus sīs	monita essēs
moneātur	monērētur	monitus sit	monita esset
moneāmur	monērēmur	monitī sīmus	monitae essēmus
moneāminī	monērēminī	monitī sītis	monitae essētis
moneantur	monērentur	monitī sint	monitae essēmus

3rd Conjugation Regular: scrībō, scrībere, scripsī, scriptum

Active

PRESENT	IMPERFECT	PERFECT	PLUPERFECT
scrībam	scrīberem	scripserim	scripsissem
scrībās	scrīberēris	scripseris	scripsissēs
scrībat	scrīberet	scripserit	scripsisset
scrībāmus	scrīberēmus	scripserimus	scripsissēmus
scrībātis	scrīberētis	scripseritis	scripsissētis
scrībantur	scrīberent	scripserint	scripsissent

Passive

PRESENT	IMPERFECT	PERFECT (MASC.)	PLUPERFECT (FEM.)
scrībar	scrīberer	scriptus sim	scripta essem
scrībāris	scrīberēris	scriptus sīs	scripta essēs
scrībātur	scrīberētur	scriptus sit	scripta esset
scrībāmur	scrīberēmur	scriptī sīmus	scriptae essēmus
scrībāminī	scrīberēminī	scriptī sītis	scriptae essētis
scrībantur	scrīberentur	scriptī sint	scriptae essent

3rd Conjugation -iō: capiō, capere, cēpī, captum

Active

PRESENT	IMPERFECT	PERFECT	PLUPERFECT
capiam	caperem	cēperim	cēpissem
capiās	caperēs	cēperis	cēpissēs
capiāt	caperet	cēperit	cēpisset
capiāmus	caperēmus	cēperimus	cēpissēmus
capiātis	caperētis	cēperitis	cēpissētis
capiant	caperent	cēperint	cēpissent

Passive

PRESENT	IMPERFECT	PERFECT (MASC.)	PLUPERFECT (FEM.)
capiar	caperer	captus sim	capta essem
capiāris	caperēris	captus sīs	capta essēs
capiātur	caperētur	captus sit	capta esset
capiāmur	caperēmur	captī sīmus	captae essēmus
capiāminī	caperēminī	captī sītis	captae essētis
capiantur	caperentur	captī sint	captae essent

4th Conjugation   audiō, audīre, audīvī, audītum

Active

PRESENT	IMPERFECT	PERFECT	PLUPERFECT
audiam	audīrem	audīverim	audīvissem
audiās	audīrēs	audīveris	audīvissēs
audiat	audīret	audīverit	audīvisset
audiāmus	audīrēmus	audīverimus	audīvissēmus
audiātis	audīrētis	audīveritis	audīvissētis
audiant	audirent	audīverint	audīvissent

Passive

PRESENT	IMPERFECT	PERFECT (MASC.)	PLUPERFECT (FEM.)
audiar	audīrer	audītus sim	audīta essem
audiāris	audīrēris	audītus sīs	audīta essēs
audiātur	audīrētur	audītus sit	audīta esset
audiāmur	audīrēmur	audītī sīmus	audītae essēmus
audiāminī	audīrēminī	audītī sītis	audītae essētis
audiantur	audīrentur	audītī sint	audītae essent

Infinitives

CONJUGATION	ACTIVE	PASSIVE
Present		
1st	vocāre	vocārī
2nd	monēre	monērī
3rd	scrībere	scrībī
3rd-iō	capere	capī
4th	audīre	audīrī
Perfect		
1st	vocāvisse	vocātus, -a, -um esse
2nd	monuisse	monitus, -a, -um esse
3rd	scripsisse	scriptus, -a, -um esse
3rd-iō	cēpisse	captus, -a, -um esse
4th	audīvisse	audītus, -a, -um esse
Future		
1st	vocātūrus, -a, -um esse	vocātum īrī
2nd	monitūrus, -a, -um esse	monitum īri
3rd	scriptūrus, -a, -um esse	scriptum īrī
3rd-iō	captūrus, -a, -um esse	captum īrī
4th	audītūrus, -a, -um esse	audītum īrī

Imperatives

CONJUGATION	ACTIVE		PASSIVE	
	Singular	Plural	Singular	Plural
Present				
1st	Vocā!	Vocāte!	Vocāre!	Vocāminī!
2nd	Monē!	Monēte!	Monēre!	Monēminī!
3rd	Cape!	Capite!	Capere!	Capiminī!
3rd-iō	Scrībe!	Scrībite!	Scrībere!	Scrībiminī!
4th	Audī!	Audīte!	Audīre!	Audīminī!
Future				
1st	Vocātō!	Vocātōte!		
2nd	Monētō!	Monētōte!		
3rd	Capitō!	Capitōte!		
3rd-iō	Scrībitō!	Scrībitōte!		
4th	Audītō!	Audītōte!		

Negative Imperative

CONJUGATION	SINGULAR	SINGULAR
1st	Nōlī vocāre!	Nōlīte vocāre!
2nd	Nōlī monēre!	Nōlīte monēre!
3rd	Nōlī scrībere!	Nōlīte scrībere!
3rd-iō	Nōlī capere!	Nōlīte capere!
4th	Nōlī audīre!	Nōlīte audīre!

Irregular Imperatives

	SING.	PL.
dīcō, dīcere	dīc	dīcite
dūcō, dūcere	dūc	dūcite
faciō, facere	fac	facite
ferō, ferre	fer	ferte

Participles

CONJUGATION	ACTIVE	PASSIVE
	Present	
1st	vocāns, -antis	
2nd	monēns, -entis	
3rd	scrībēns, -entis	
3rd-iō	capiēns, -ientis	
4th	audiēns, -ientis	
	Perfect	
1st		vocātus, -a, -um
2nd		monitus, -a, -um
3rd		scriptus, -a, -um
3rd-iō		captus, -a, -um
4th		audītus, -a, -um
	Future	
1st	vocatūrus, -a, -um	
2nd	monitūrus, -a, -um	
3rd	scriptūrus, -a, -um	
3rd-iō	captūrus, -a, -um	
4th	audītūrus, -a, -um	

GERUND(IVE)S

Gerund

Nom.	(vocāre)	(monēre)	(scrībere)	(capere)	(audīre)
Gen.	vocandī	monendī	scrībendī	capiendī	audiendī
Dat.	vocandō	monendō	scrībendō	capiendō	audiendō
Acc.	vocandum	monendum	scrībendum	capiendum	audiendum
Abl.	vocandō	monendō	scrībendō	capiendō	audiendō

Gerundive

vocandus, -a, -um	monendus, -a, -um	scrībendus, -a, -um	capiendus, -a, -um	audiendus, -a, -um

Supines

ACC.	ABL.
vocātum	vocātū
monitum	monitū
scriptum	scriptū
captum	captū
audītum	audītū

Deponent Verbs

Deponent verbs use passive endings but are active in meaning. Note the presence of a present active participle.

> **cōnor, cōnārī, cōnātus sum**
> **vereor, verērī, veritus sum**
> **sequor, sequī, secūtus sum**
> **patior, patī, passus sum**
> **potior, potīrī, potītus sum**

Indicative Mood

INDICATIVE

Present

cōnor	vereor	sequor	patior	potior
cōnāris	verēris	sequeris	pateris	potīris
cōnātur	verētur	sequitur	patitur	potītur
cōnāmur	verēmur	sequimur	patimur	potīmur
cōnāminī	verēminī	sequiminī	patiminī	potīminī
cōnantur	verentur	sequuntur	patiuntur	potiuntur

Imperfect

cōnābar	verēbar	sequēbar	patiēbar	potiēbar

Future

cōnābor	verēbor	sequar	patiar	potiar

Perfect

cōnātus sum	veritus sum	secūtus sum	passus sum	potītus sum

Pluperfect

cōnātus eram	veritus eram	secūtus eram	passus eram	potītus eram

Future Perfect

cōnātus erō	veritus erō	secūtus erō	passus erō	potītus erō

Subjunctive

Present

cōnar	verear	sequar	patiar	potiar

Imperfect

cōnārer	verērer	sequerer	paterer	potīrer

Perfect

cōnātus sim	veritus sim	secūtus sim	passus sim	potītus sim

Pluperfect

cōnātus essem	veritus essem	secūtus essem	passus essem	potītus essem

INFINITIVES

Present	cōnārī	verērī	sequī	patī	potīrī
Perfect	cōnātus esse	veritus esse	secūtus esse	passus esse	potītus esse
Future	cōnātūrus esse	veritūrus esse	secūtūrus esse	passūrus esse	potītūrus esse

IMPERATIVES

Singular	cōnāre	verēre	sequere	patere	potīre
Plural	cōnāminī	verēminī	sequiminī	patiminī	potīminī

Participles

Present Active	cōnāns	verēns	sequēns	patiēns	potiēns
Perfect Passive	cōnātus, -a, -um	veritus, -a, -um	secūtus, -a, -um	passus, -a, -um	potītus, -a, -um
Future Active	cōnātūrus, -a, -um	veritūrus, -a, -um	secūtūrus, -a, -um	passūrus, -a, -um	potītūrus -a, -um

Gerund(ive)s

GERUND

Nom.	(cōnārī)	(verērī)	(sequī)	(patī)	(potīrī)
Gen.	cōnandī	verendī	sequendī	patiendī	potiendī
Dat.	cōnandō	verendō	sequendō	patiendō	potiendō
Acc.	cōnandum	verendum	sequendum	patiendum	potiendum
Abl.	cōnandō	verendō	sequendō	patiendō	potiendō

Gerundive

cōnandus, -a, -um	verendus, -a, -um	sequendus, -a, -um	patiendus, -a, -um	potiendus, -a, -um

Supines

ACC.	ABL.
cōnātum	cōnātū
veritum	veritū
secūtum	secūtū
captum	captū
potītum	potītū

Irregular Verbs
sum, esse, fuī

Indicative

PRESENT	IMPERFECT	FUTURE	PERFECT	PLUPERFECT	FUTURE PERFECT
sum	eram	erō	fuī	fueram	fuerō
es	erās	eris	fuistī	fuerās	fueris
est	erat	erit	fuit	fuerat	fuerit
sumus	erāmus	erimus	fuimus	fuerāmus	fuerimus
estis	erātis	eritis	fuistis	fuerātis	fueritis
sunt	erant	erunt	fuērunt	fuerant	fuerint

Subjunctive

PRESENT	IMPERFECT	PERFECT	PLUPERFECT
sim	essem	fuerim	fuissem
sīs	essēs	fueris	fuissēs
sit	esset	fuerit	fuisset
sīmus	essēmus	fuerimus	fuissēmus
sītis	essētis	fueritis	fuisssētis
sint	essent	fuerint	fuissent

Infinitives

	ACTIVE
Present	esse
Perfect	fuisse
Future	futūrus, -a, -um esse

Imperatives

	SINGULAR	PLURAL
Present	Es!	Este!
Future	Estō!	Estōte!

Participle

Future	futūrus, -a, -um

possum, posse, potuī

Indicative

PRESENT	IMPERFECT	FUTURE	PERFECT	PLUPERFECT	FUTURE PERFECT
possum	poteram	poterō	potuī	potueram	potuerō
potes	poterās	poteris	potuistī	potuerās	potueris
potest	poterat	poterit	potuit	potuerat	potuerit
possumus	poterāmus	poterimus	potuimus	potuerāmus	potuerimus
potestis	poterātis	poteritis	potuistis	potuerātis	potueritis
possunt	poterant	poterunt	potuērunt	potuerant	potuerint

Subjunctive

PRESENT	IMPERFECT	PERFECT	PLUPERFECT
possim	possem	potuerim	potuissem
possīs	possēs	potueris	potuissēs
possit	posset	potuerit	potuisset
possīmus	possēmus	potuerimus	potuissēmus
possītis	possētis	potueritis	potuisssētis
possint	possent	potuerint	potuissent

Infinitives

	ACTIVE
Present	posse
Perfect	potuisse

Participle

Present	potēns

volō, velle, voluī

Indicative

PRESENT	IMPERFECT	FUTURE	PERFECT	PLUPERFECT	FUTURE PERFECT
volō	volēbam	volam	voluī	volueram	voluerō
vīs	volēbās	volēs	voluistī	voluerās	volueris
vult	volēbat	volet	voluit	voluerat	voluerit
volumus	volēbāmus	volēmus	voluimus	voluerāmus	voluerimus
vultis	volēbātis	volētis	voluistis	voluerātis	volueritis
volunt	volēbant	volent	voluērunt	voluerant	voluerint

Subjunctive

PRESENT	IMPERFECT	PERFECT	PLUPERFECT
velim	vellem	voluerim	voluissem
velīs	vellēs	volueris	voluissēs
velit	vellet	voluerit	voluisset
velīmus	vellēmus	voluerimus	voluissēmus
velītis	velētis	volueritis	voluissētis
velint	vellent	voluerint	voluissent

nōlō, nōlle, nōluī

Indicative

PRESENT	IMPERFECT	FUTURE	PERFECT	PLUPERFECT	FUTURE PERFECT
nōlō	nolēbam	nōlam	nōluī	nōlueram	nōluerō
nōn vīs	nolēbās	nōlēs	nōluistī	nōluerās	nōlueris
nōn vult	nolēbat	nōlet	nōluit	nōluerat	nōluerit
nōlumus	nolēbāmus	nōlēmus	nōluimus	nōluerāmus	nōluerimus
nōn vultis	nolēbātis	nōlētis	nōluistis	nōluerātis	nōlueritis
nōlunt	nolēbant	nōlent	nōluērunt	nōluerant	nōluerint

Subjunctive

PRESENT	IMPERFECT	PERFECT	PLUPERFECT
nōlim	nōllem	nōluerim	nōluissem
nōlīs	nōllēs	nōlueris	nōluissēs
nōlit	nōllet	nōluerit	nōluisset
nōlimus	nōllēmus	nōluerimus	nōluissēmus
nōlitis	nōlētis	nōlueritis	nōluissētis
nōlint	nōllent	nōluerint	nōluissent

mālō, mālle, māluī

Indicative

PRESENT	IMPERFECT	FUTURE	PERFECT	PLUPERFECT	FUTURE PERFECT
mālō	mālēbam	mālam	māluī	mālueram	māluerō
māvīs	mālēbās	mālēs	māluistī	māluerās	mālueris
māvult	mālēbat	mālet	māluit	māluerat	māluerit
mālumus	mālēbāmus	mālēmus	māluimus	māluerāmus	māluerimus
māvultis	mālēbātis	mālētis	māluistis	māluerātis	mālueritis
mālunt	mālēbant	mālent	māluērunt	māluerant	māluerint

Subjunctive

PRESENT	IMPERFECT	PERFECT	PLUPERFECT
mālim	māllem	maluerim	maluissem
mālīs	māllēs	malueris	maluissēs
mālit	māllet	maluerit	maluisset
mālimus	māllēmus	maluerimus	maluissēmus
mālitis	mālētis	malueritis	maluissētis
mālint	māllent	maluerint	maluissent

Infinitives

Present	velle	nōlle	mālle
Perfect	voluisse	nōluisse	māluisse

Imperatives (only nōlō)

	SINGULAR	PLURAL
Present	Nōlī!	Nōlīte!
Future	Nōlītō	Nōlītōte

Present Participle:

volēns	nōlēns	—

eō, īre, īvī / iī, itum
Indicative

PRESENT	IMPERFECT	FUTURE	PERFECT	PLUPERFECT	FUTURE PERFECT
eō	ībam	ībō	īvī	īveram	īverō
is	ībās	ībis	īvistī	īverās	īveris
it	ībat	ībit	īvit	īverat	īverit
īmus	ībāmus	ībimus	īvimus	īverāmus	īverimus
ītis	ībātis	ībitis	īvistis	īverātis	īveritis
eunt	ībant	ībunt	īvērunt	īverant	īverint

Subjunctive

PRESENT	IMPERFECT	PERFECT	PLUPERFECT
eam	īrem	īverim	īvissem
eās	īrēs	īveris	īvissēs
eat	īret	īverit	īvisset
eāmus	īrēmus	īverimus	īvissēmus
eātis	īrētis	īveritis	īvissētis
eant	īrent	īverint	īvissent

Infinitives

Present	īre
Perfect	īvisse
Future	itūrus, -a, -um esse

Imperatives (only nōlō)

	SINGULAR	PLURAL
Present	Ī!	Īte!
Future	Ītō	Ītōte

	PARTICIPLES	GERUND	GERUNDIVE
Present	iēns, euntis	eundum, -ī, etc.	eundus, -a, -um
Future	itūrus, -a, -um		
Perfect	itum (impers.)		

fīō, fierī, factus sum

Indicative

	PRESENT	IMPERFECT	FUTURE	PERFECT	PLUPERFECT	FUTURE PERFECT
fīō	[fīmus]	fīēbam	fīam	factus sum	factus eram	factus erō
fīs	[fītis]	etc.	etc.	etc.	etc.	etc.
fit	fīunt					

Subjunctive

PRESENT	IMPERFECT	PERFECT	PLUPERFECT
fīam	fierem	factus sim	factus essem

Infinitives

Present	fierī
Perfect	factus esse
Future	factūrus, -a,-um esse

Imperatives

SINGULAR	PLURAL
Fī!	Fīte!

PARTICIPLES		GERUND	GERUNDIVE
Future	factūrus, -a, -um	faciendī, -ō etc.	faciendus, -a, -um
Perfect	factus, -a, -um		

EDŌ, ESSE / EDERE "EAT"	
Present Indicative	
edō	edimus
ēs	ēstis
ēst	edunt

Verba Omnia

Modus Operandī: Words in bold are *Verba Discenda* through Chapter 40. Bracketed numbers indicate the chapter in which this word became a *Verbum Discendum*. Definitions of *Verba Discenda* aim for comprehensiveness. The definitions of other words are not necessarily comprehensive but rather focus on the meanings in the context of the narrative.

abl. = ablative
acc. = accusative
adj. = adjective
dat. = dative
conj. = conjunction
excl. = exclamation
esp. = especially
f. = feminine
imp. = impersonal
imper. = imperative

indecl. = indeclinable
interj. = interjection
interr. = interrogative
m. = masculine
n. = neuter
pl. = plural
prep. = preposition
subj. = subjunctive
v. = verb

A

ā, ab, abs (+ abl.) from, away from; by (with persons) [5]
abdō, abdere, abdidī, abditum hide, conceal [19]
abeō, abīre, abīvī/abiī, abitum go away [7]
abhinc from here; ago
abitus, -ūs m. departure
abluō, abluere, abluī, ablūtum wash, cleanse
absum, abesse, āfuī be absent [19]
abūtor, abūtī, abūsus sum (+ abl.) use up, waste
ac and, and besides; than [33]
acadēmia, -ae f. the academy
accēdō, accēdere, accessī, accessum agree, assent; approach; attack [38]
accendō, accendere, accendī, accensum light, burn
accidō, accidere, accidī, happen; fall at, fall near
accipiō, accipere, accēpī, acceptum accept, receive
accumbō, accumbere, accubuī, accubitum recline at table
accurrō, accurrere, accurrī/accucurrī, accursum run, hasten to
ācer, ācris, ācre sharp, violent, eager, swift [38]
acervus, -ī m. heap
acētum, -ī n. vinegar
acquiescō (1) quiet down, subside
Acrisius, -iī m. Acrisius (Perseus' grandfather)
ācriter sharply

Actiacus, -a, -um of Actium
Actium, Actiī n. Actium, site of Octavian's decisive battle with Marc Anthony and Cleopatra in 31 B.C.
actor, actōris m. actor
ad (+ acc.) to, toward, for [3, 5]
ad dextram to the right
ad lūnam by moonlight
ad sinistram to the left
adamō (1) fall in love, love passionately
addīcō, addīcere, addīxī, addictum consecrate
addō, addere, addidī, additum add, give; say in addition [40]
addūcō, addūcere, adduxī, adductum bring in, lead to
adeō so much, to such a degree
adeō, adīre, adīvī/adiī, aditum go to [7]
adeps, adipis m./f. fat
adhūc to this point, still, yet [30]
adiungō, adiungere, adiunxī, adiunctum join to, add to
adiūtor, -ōris m. helper
adiuvō, adiuvāre, adiūvī, adiūtum help [16]
adminiculum, -ī n. tool, support, aid
admīror, admīrārī, admīrātus sum admire, wonder at [26]
admoneō, admonēre, admonuī, admonitum warn strongly, admonish
adoleō, adolēre, adoluī, adultum burn
adoptō (1) adopt

A27

From *Disce! An Introductory Latin Course, volume 2*, First Edition. Francesco Bonavita. Copyright © 2011 by Pearson Education, Inc. Published by Pearson Prentice Hall. All rights reserved.

adsum, adesse, adfuī be near, be present; (+ dat.) be "there" for someone, be of assistance, help, aid [19]

adulescens, -entis m./f. youth [15]

advena, -ae m./f. foreigner, stranger

adveniō, advenīre, advēnī, adventum arrive at, come to [11]

adventus, -ūs m. arrival [39]

adversārius, -iī m. opponent, enemy

adversus (+ acc.) opposite to, against

adversus, -a, -um adverse, contrary

aedēs and *aedis, aedis* f. temple, house of a god

aedificium, -iī n. building [38]

aedificō (1) build, make

aedīlitās, -tātis f. aedilship, office of aedile (public works)

aedes, see *aedēs*

aeger, aegra, aegrum sick [37]

aegrescō, aegrescere grow sick

Aegyptus, -ī f. Egypt, a province of Rome

Aelius, -iī m. Aelius, a male name

aēneus, -a, -um bronze [30]

aequē fairly

aequinoctiālis, aequinoctiāle equinoctal, of the equinox

aequor, aequoris n. (level surface of the) sea

aequus, -a, -um even, equal; fair, just; patient, calm [31]

āēr, āeris m. air, atmosphere; Greek acc. sing., *āera* [32]

aes, aeris n. metal, especially copper or bronze

aestimō (1) value, estimate, consider [38]

aestuōsus, -a, -um hot [31]

aestus, -ūs m. heat

aetās, -tātis f. age, period of time

Aetia, -ōrum n. pl. "The Causes," title of a book by Callimachus

afferō, afferre, attulī, allātum bring to

afficiō, afficere, affēcī, affectum affect, move, influence

affinis, affine related by marriage

afflīgō, afflīgere, afflīxī, afflictum bother

affulgeō, affulgēre, affulsī (+ dat.) shine on, smile on; also spelled *adfulgeō,* etc.

Āfrica, -ae f. Africa, the Roman province of Africa (modern Tunisia)

Āfrus, -a, -um African

Agamemnōn, -nonis m. Agamemnon, king of Mycenae

age, agite come! well! all right! [36]

agedum come! well! all right!

ager, agrī m. field [14]

aggredior, aggredī, aggressus sum go to, approach

agitātor, -ōris m. driver, charioteer

agitātus, -a, -um shaken, disturbed, upset

agitō (1) agitate, disturb

agmen, agminis n. column of troops, battle line; troops, army; herd, flock; crowd [40]

agnoscō, agnoscere, agnōvī, agnōtum recognize, acknowledge

agō, agere, ēgī, actum act, do, lead, drive [4]

Agrippa, Agrippae m. Agrippa, Augustus' general and brother-in-law

Āh ha! ah!

aha ha! (in reproof, amusement, or denial)

ait, āiunt say (in present only)

albus, -a, -um white

Alcinous, -ī m. Alcinous, king of the Phaeacians and host of Odysseus

Alcmēna, -ae f. Alcmena, mother of Hercules

ālea, -ae f. die (singular of dice), dice-playing

Alexander, -ī m. Alexander (the Great), king of Macedonia

Alexandrēa, -ae f. Alexandria; *Alexandrēae* is locative "at Alexandria"

Alexandrēos, -ē, -on Alexandrian (Greek form of *Alexandrīnus*)

Alexandrīnus, -a, -um Alexandrian, pertaining to the city in Egypt

alibī elsewhere, in another place

aliōquī besides

aliquandō sometimes, at length, formerly, someday, hereafter [26]

aliquis, aliquid n. someone, something [18]

aliter otherwise, else, in another way [39]

aliunde elsewhere, from another person

alius, -a, -ud other, another [9]; *alius . . . alius* one . . . another; in pl. some . . . others [31]

allegō (1) deputize, commission, charge

alloquor, alloquī, allocūtus sum speak to, address

almus, -a, -um nourishing, kind, dear [18]

Alpēs, Alpium f. pl. Alps, the mountains of northern Italy

altē high

alter, altera, alterum the other (of two) [17]

altus, -a, -um high, deep [2]

alumnus, -ī m. foster son

alvus, -ī m. belly, stomach

amābilis, amābile lovable

amārus, -a, -um bitter

amātōrius, -a, -um loving, pertaining to love, amatory

ambitiō, -ōnis f. canvassing (for votes), political campaign [37]

ambitiōsus, -a, -um ambitious, ostentatious

ambō, ambae, ambō both (of two); (dat./abl. pl.) *ambōbus/ambābus* [31]

ambulō (1) walk [2]

Americānus, -a, -um American

amīca, -ae f. (female) friend, girlfriend [13]

amīcus, -ī m. friend [7]

āmittō, āmittere, āmīsī, āmissum lose, send away [9]

amō (1) love [13]

amor, amōris m. love [15]

āmoveō, āmovēre, āmōvī, āmōtum remove, move away

amphitheātrum, -ī n. amphitheater [17]

Amphitritē, -ēs f. Amphitrite, wife of Neptune.
   Note Greek case endings.

Amphitruō, -ōnis m. Amphitryon, husband of Alcmena

amphora, -ae f. amphora

amplector, amplectī, amplexus sum embrace, cherish

amputō (1) cut off

amulētum, -ī n. charm, amulet

an or, whether [39]

ancilla, -ae f. female servant [8]

angiportum, -ī m. alley

angulus, -ī m. corner

angustiae, -ārum f. pl. trouble, difficulty

angustus, -a, -um narrow

anīlitās, -tātis f. old age (of a woman)

anima, -ae f. breath, soul, life

***animadvertō, animadvertere, animadvertī,
   animadversum*** observe, remark, notice,
   understand [40]

animal, -ālis n. animal [17]

animus, -ī m. mind [29]

annō superiōre last year

annōna, -ae f. year's provision

annuō, annuere, annuī nod (in approval), agree with

annus, -ī m. year [12]

ante in front, before, ahead; (+ acc.) before, in front of

anteā previously

antehāc before this time, earlier

antequam before [34]

antiburschius, -iī m. someone who is anti-student,
   a student hater

antīquitās, -tātis f. antiquity

antīquus, -a, -um old, ancient [10]

Antōnius, -iī m. Antonius, Antony

ānulus, -ī m. ring

anus, -ūs f. old woman [27]

anxius, -a, -um uneasy, anxious [29]

apage go! scram!

aper, aprī m. boar

aperiō, aperīre, aperuī, apertum open; discover; show

apiārius, -iī m. beekeeper

apodȳtērium, -iī n. dressing room

Apollō, Apollinis m. Apollo, god of prophecy

Appennīnī, -ōrum m. pl. Appennines, the mountains
   along the spine of Italy

appetō, appetere, appetīvī/appetiī, appetītum seek,
   grasp for, grasp after

applaudō, applaudere, applausī, applausum applaud

*applicō, applicāre, applicāvī/applicuī,
   applicātum/applicitum* apply

appōnō, appōnere, apposuī, appositum serve,
   put to [26]

appropinquō (1) (+ dat.) approach, come near to [11]

aprīcus, -a, -um sunny

aptus, -a, -um attached to, connected to; suitable,
   fit [31]

apud (+ acc.) at the house of, with, at ____'s [16]

aqua, -ae f. water [2]

aquaeductus, -ūs m. aqueduct

āra, -ae f. altar [19]

arānea, -ae f. spider

arbitror, abitrārī, arbitrātus sum observe, perceive;
   think [37]

arbor, arboris f. tree [29]

arca, -ae f. chest

Arcadia, -ae f. Arcadia, a region in Greece

arcānus, -a, -um secret

arcessō, arcessere, arcessīvī/arcessī, arcessītum fetch;
   call for; summon; procure [32]

archierus, -ī m. chief priest

arcus, arcūs m. arch

ardeō, ardēre, arsī, arsum burn, glow

ardor, ardōris m. fire, flame

argentārius, -a, -um of silver, pertaining to silver [31];
   faber argentārius silversmith

argentārius, -iī, m. banker

argenteus, -a, -um of silver, silvery [34]

argentum, -ī n. silver; money [31]

Argī, Argōrum m. pl. Argos, a city in Greece

Argīlētum the Argiletum, (a street leading into
   the Roman Forum)

argūmentum -ī, n. plot, summary (of a play)

arguō, arguere, arguī, argūtum argue

arma, armōrum n. pl. arms, weapons

armō (1) arm [37]

ars, artis f. skill, art [16]

artifex, artificis m. artist, artisan, maker

Artorius, -iī m. Artorius, a male name

artus, -ūs m. limb

as, assis m. as, a small copper coin of minimal value

ascendō, ascendere, ascendī, ascensum climb,
   ascend [24]

Asia, -ae f. Asia, a Roman province in what is now Turkey

Asinius, -iī m. Asinius

asinus, -ī m. donkey

aspectō (1) gaze, look at

asper, aspera, asperum rough, harsh

aspergō, aspergere, aspersī, aspersum sprinkle

aspiciō, aspicere, aspexī, aspectum look at [23]

assentior, assentīrī, assensus sum approve

assequor, assequī, assecūtus sum pursue, gain

assō (1) roast

assuētus, -a, -um accustomed

astō, astāre, astitī stand (up); stand by, assist

astrologia, -ae f. astrology

astrologus, -ī m. astrologer

astūtus, -a, -um smart

***at* but, and yet [20]**

āter, ātra, ātrum black

Athēnae, Athēnārum f. pl. Athens, a city in Greece

***atque* and, and also, and even, yet [20]**

atquī yet

***ātrium, -iī* n. atrium, public greeting room**
of a Roman house [33]

atrōciter fiercely

attat Ah! (used to express surprise, fear, or a warning)

attendō, attendere, attendī, attentum listen carefully

attonitus, -a, -um astonished, amazed

auctōritās, -tātis f. authority, power

audācia , -ae f. daring

***audeō, audēre, ausus sum* dare [9]**

audiāmus "Let's listen!", subj.

***audiō, audīre, audīvī/audiī, audītum* hear, listen to [7]**

Augēās, Augēae m. Augeas, king of Elis in Greece

Augēus, -a, -um Augean, pertaining to King Augeas

augustus, -a, -um revered

Augustus, -ī m. "the revered one," a title of Octavius, the
emperor C. Julius Caesar Octavianus (63 B.C.–14 A.D.),
known as *Augustus* ("Revered")

aura, -ae f. breeze

aureolus, -a, -um golden

aureus, -a, -um golden

***auris, auris* f. ear [29]**

auscultō (1) listen

auspex, auspicis m. diviner, soothsayer

auspicium, -(i)ī n. sign, omen, auspices

***aut* or; *aut . . . aut* either . . . or [4]**

***autem* however [20]**

***auxilium, -iī* n. help, aid; pl. auxiliary forces [25]**

***Avē* Greetings! [29]**

aveō, avēre be eager

***avia, -ae* f. grandmother [30]**

avidē eagerly

avidus, -a, -um eager

***avis, avis* f. bird [28]**

āvolō (1) hasten away, fly away

***avus, -ī* m. grandfather, ancestor [29]**

B

Bacchus, -ī n. Bacchus, the god of wine;
also known as Liber

Baiae, Baiārum m. pl. Baiae, a resort town near
Naples, Italy

balneae, ārum f. pl. bath

barba, -ae f. beard

basilica, -ae, basilica, courthouse

beātus, -a, -um blessed, happy

***bellum, -ī* n. war; *bellum gerere* wage war [23]**

bellus, -a, -um handsome, pretty

***bene* well, nicely [4]**

***beneficium, -iī* n. kindness, benefit, favor [38]**

benevolens, benevolentis well-wishing, benevolent

benignē kindly

benignus, -a, -um kind, kind-hearted, bounteous

bestiārius, -iī m. animal fighter

bēta, -ae f. beet

***bibliothēca, -ae f.* library [27]**

bibliothēcē, -ēs f. library (the Greek equivalent
of *bibliothēca, -ae*)

***bibō, bibere, bibī* drink [2]**

biennium, -iī n. a two-year period

bīga, -ae f. two-horse chariot

***bis* twice, two times [36]**

***bonus, -a, -um* good [3]**

bōs, bovis m./f. cow, bull, ox

***brāc(c)hium, -iī* n. arm [14]**

brevī in a short time

***brevis, breve* short [18]**

Brundisium, -iī n. Brundisium, a city in Calabria

Brūtus, -ī m. Marcus Iunius Brutus (85–42 B.C.),
one of the leading assassins of Julius Caesar

būbō, būbōnis m. owl

bulla, -ae f. bulla, a locket worn around
a child's neck

C

cachinnātiō, -ōnis f. loud laughter

cachinnō (1) laugh loudly

cacūmen, cacūminis n. tree top

cadāver, cadāveris n. corpse, dead body

***cadō, cadere, cecidī, cāsum* fall (down); be slain;**
end [21]

Caecilia, -ae f. Caecilia, a female name

caelibāris, caelibāre unmarried

Caelius, -a, -um Caelian, pertaining to one
of the seven hills of Rome

caelum, -ī n. sky

Caesar, Caesaris m. Caesar

Calabria, -ae f. region in the heel of Italy

caldārium, -iī n. hot bath

calidum, -ī n. a hot drink

***calidus, -a, -um* warm, hot [30]**

Callimachus, -ī m. chief librarian at Alexandria
    and poet (c.280–243 B.C.)

calvus, -a, -um bald

calx, calcis f. goal, chalkline

Campānia, -ae f. Campania, region of southern
    Italy around Naples

***campus, -ī* m. field [33]**

candidātus, -ī m. candidate

candidus, -a, -um dazzling white; bright

***canis, canis* m./f. dog [23]**

***canō, canere, cecinī, cantum* sing, sing about [40]**

***cantō* (1) sing [27]**

cantus, -ūs m. song

cānus, -a, -um white-haired

capax, capācis spacious, roomy; "full of"

capillus, -ī m. hair

***capiō, capere, cēpī, captum* take, catch [3]**

Capitōlīnus, -a, -um Capitoline, pertaining
    to the Capitoline hill

Capitōlium, -iī n. the Capitoline hill, one of the seven
    hills of Rome

***captīvus, -ī* m. captive, prisoner [40]**

***caput, capitis* n. head; master [36]**

carcer, carceris m. prison; starting gate

***careō, carēre, caruī, caritum* (+ abl.) lack, be
    without, lose [36]**

cāritās, -ātis f. charity, generosity

***carmen, carminis* n. song, poem, poetry [17]**

carō, carnis f. flesh; meat

carōta, -ae f. carrot

carpō, carpere, carpsī, carptum seize, pluck, enjoy

***cārus, -a, -um* dear [13]**

Cassius, -iī m. C. Cassius Longinus (85–42 B.C.),
    one of the leading assassins of Julius Caesar

Castor, -oris m. Castor, the divine twin brother of Pollux,
    one of the Gemini

Castōrum of the Castors, i.e., Castor and Pollux

***castra, -ōrum* n. pl. camp [23]**

cāsus, -ūs m. event; misfortune

catēna, -ae f. chain, fetter

catulus, -ī m. puppy

caudex, caudicis m. piece of wood, as an oath "blockhead!"

***causa, -ae* f. cause, reason; *causā* (+ gen.) on account
    of, because of [30]**

causidicus, -ī m. lawyer

cautus, -a, -um cautious, careful

cavea, -ae f. cage

***caveō, cavēre, cāvī, cautum* take care, beware [33]**

***cēdō, cēdere, cessī, cessum* go, walk; (+ dat.) yield to,
    give way to; succeed; allow, grant [35]**

celeber, celebris, celebre frequent, famous

***celer, celeris, celere* fast, swift [15]**

celeriter quickly, swiftly

***cella, -ae* f. room [18]**

cēlō (1) hide

celsus, -a, -um high, lofty, tall

***cēna, -ae* f. dinner [12]**

***cēnō* (1) dine [12]**

censeō, censēre, censuī, censum be of the opinion

centaurus, -ī m. centaur, half-human and half-horse

***centum* indecl. one hundred [37]**

centuria, -ae f. century, i.e., a division of the Roman
    citizenry based on wealth; the two highest such
    centuries were the senators and the *equitēs* (knights)

***centuriō, -ōnis* m. centurion [23]**

Cephallenia, -ae f. Cephallenia (modern Kefalonia), an
    island on the west coast of Greece

***certāmen, certāminis* n. contest, race [35]**

certē certainly

certiōrem facere make more certain, inform; *sē certiōrem
    facere*, make oneself more certain, learn, learn about

certus, -a, -um sure, certain

cēterum besides, for the rest

Chaldaeus, -a, -um Chaldaean, an inhabitant of Mesopotamia

Charōn, Charōnis m. Charon, the ferryman
    of the Underworld

Chīrōn, -ōnis m. Chiron, a schoolmaster who shares his
    name with a centaur who taught various heroes.

***cibus, -ī* m. food [2]**

cicātrīcōsus, -a, -um scarred

cicātrix, cicātrīcis f. scar

cingō, cingere, cinxī, cinctum gird, put a belt around; tie

cingulum, -ī n. belt

cinis, cineris m./f. ash

circulus, -ī m. circle

***circum* (+ acc.) around [6]**

circumambulō (1) walk around

circumcingō, circumcingere, circumcinxī, circumcinctum
    gird around, surround

circumcurrō, circumcurrere run around

circumeō, circumīre, circumīvī/circumiī, circumitum
    go around

circumsiliō, circumsilīre leap around

circumspectō (1) look around

circumstō, circumstāre, circumstetī stand around, surround

circus, circī m. circle, circus; racetrack

cista, -ae f. chest, box

cisterna, -ae f. cistern, well

***cīvis, cīvis* m./f. citizen [27]**

cīvitās, -ātis f. citizenship, the state

clādēs, -is f. defeat

***clāmō* (1) shout, cry out [5]**

***clāmor, clāmōris* m. shout, cry, uproar [20]**

clāmōsus, -a, -um noisy

clārus, -a, -um clear, bright; loud, distinct; famous [36]

Claudius, -iī m. Claudius, *nōmen* of an old Roman family

claudō, claudere, clausī, clausum shut, close [38]

clēmentia, -ae f. mercy, clemency

Cleopatra, -ae f. Cleopatra, the last Ptolemaic ruler of Egypt

cliens, clientis m. client [31]

cloāca, -ae f. sewer

cōdex, cōdicis m. book

coepī, coepisse, coeptum begin

coetus, -ūs m. assembly, band

cōgitō (1) think, think about [10]

cognātus, -a, -um relative; kinsman

cognoscō, cognoscere, cognōvī, cognitum learn, get to know, observe; in the perfect: "know" [29]

cōgō, cōgere, coēgī, coactum drive together, force [23]

cōliculus, -ī = *cauliculus,-ī* m. small cabbage, cabbage sprout

collābor, collābī, collapsus sum fall in a faint, collapse [39]

collāre, collāris n. collar

collēgium, -iī n. club, group, corporation, association

collis, collis m. hill [32]

colloquium, -iī n. talk, conversation

colloquor, colloquī, collocūtus sum talk together, converse [25]

collum, -ī n. neck

colō, colere, coluī, cultum cultivate, take care of; honor, pay court to, worship

colōnia, -ae f. colony

color, -ōris m. color, complexion

columbārium, -iī n. a niche for a cinerary urn

coma, comae f. hair

combūrō, combūrere, combussī, combustum burn, burn up [30]

comes, comitis m./f. companion

comitia, -ōrum n. pl. elections

comitō (1) accompany, attend

comitor, comitārī, comitātus sum accompany, attend

commentāriolum, -ī n. small handbook, short essay

committō, committere, commīsī, commissum entrust

commodus, -a, -um pleasant, comfortable, convenient, suitable

commūnis, commūne common

commutō (1) change

comoedia, -ae f. comedy

compescō, compescere, compescuī confine, restrain

Compitālis, Compitāle of the crossroads

complector, complectī, complexus sum embrace

comprehendō, comprehendere, comprehendī, comprehensum seize, grasp, understand

compressus, -a, -um squeezed together, narrow

comprimō, comprimere, compressī, compressum press, squeeze together

computō (1) count up, calculate

concalescō, -ere, -uī to warm up

concēdō, concēdere, concessī, concessum (+ dat.) go way, yield, withdraw, allow, grant

concīdō, concīdere, concīdi, concīsum cut, chop up

concilium, -iī n. council = Roman senate

conclāve, conclāvis n. room

conclūdō, conclūdere, conclūsī, conclūsum conclude, finish

concordia, -ae f. concord, harmony

Concordia, -ae f. the goddess of Concord

concordō (1) be in agreement

condīmentum, -ī n. spice, seasoning

condō, condere, condidī, conditum build, found [40]

condūcō, condūcere, condūxī, conductum rent

conferō, conferre, contulī, collātum discuss, bring together, collect; *sē conferre* go (betake oneself), talk together [28]

conficiō, conficere, confēcī, confectum do, accomplish, complete [28]

confirmō (1) reassure, strengthen, confirm, encourage

congiārium, -iī n. largesse, gift

congregō (1) gather

coniciō, conicere, coniēcī, coniectum hurl, cast

coniunctiō, -iōnis f. joining together, union

coniungō, coniungere, coniunxī, coniunctus join, connect, ally

coniunx, coniugis m./f. spouse

cōnor, cōnārī, cōnātus sum try, undertake [24]

consacrō (1) dedicate, consecrate

conscendō, conscendere, conscendī, conscensum ascend; embark

conscrībō, conscrībere, conscripsī, conscriptum enlist

consentiō, consentīre, consensī, consensum consent, agree

consequor, consequī, consecūtus sum obtain, procure

conservō (1) preserve, keep safe [39]

conservus, -ī m. fellow slave

consīderō (1) consider, inspect

consilium, -iī n. plan, advice, counsel, reason, judgment [23]

consistō, consistere, constitī, constitum stop, halt; (+ *ā* or *ex* + abl.) consist of

consōbrīna, -ae f. female first cousin (on the mother's side)

consōlor, consōlārī, consōlātus sum console

conspiciō, conspicere, conspexī, conspectum catch sight of, see, look at, observe [9]

constat imp. "it is known (that)"; it is agreed

consternō (1) confuse, terrify, shock

constituō, constituere, constituī, constitūtum put, appoint, decide, establish *constō, constāre, constitī, constātum* **stand still; cost** [10]; *satis constat* it is agreed that, it is an established fact that

constringō, constringere, constrinxī, constrinctum bind fast; compress

construō, construere, construxī, constructum build

consuētūdō, -inis f. companionship

consul, consulis m. consul

consulāris, consulāre consular, of consular rank

consulātus, -ūs m. consulship

consūmō, consūmere, consumpsī, consumptum **use up, eat, consume** [38]

contemnō, contemnere, contempsī, contemptum scorn

contemplor, contemplarī, contemplātus est reflect on, contemplate

contendō, contendere, contendī, contentum make one's way toward

contentus, -a, -um content, satisfied

contineō, continēre, continuī, contentum **contain, hold** [40]

continuus, -a, -um successive

contrā (+ acc.) **against, opposite (to)** [19]

contractiō, -ōnis f. contraction

contrahō, contrahere, contraxī, contractum draw together, gather

conventus, -ūs m. gathering, assembly

convīvium, -iī n. **feast, banquet** [25]

convocō (1) call together

cōpiōsus, -a, -um plentiful

coquō, coquere, coxī, coctum **cook** [26]

coquus, -ī m. **cook** [25]

cor, cordis n. **heart** [17]

Corcyra, -ae f. Corcyra (modern Corfu), an island on the west coast of Greece.

Cordus, -ī m. Cordus, a male name

coriandrum, -ī n. coriander

Corinthiacus, -a, -um Corinthian, pertaining to Corinth

Corinthus, -ī f. Corinth, a city in southern Greece

Corinthus, -ī f. Corinth, a city in Greece

cornicen, -cinis m. horn blower

corōna, -ae f. crown, garland

corpus, corporis n. **body** [15]

corrumpō, corrumpere, corrūpī, corruptum spoil, destroy

cortex, corticis m./f. skin, bark, rind

cōtīdiē (cottīdiē) daily, every day

crās **tomorrow** [6]

crassus, -a, -um crass, less polite

crēbrō frequently

crēdō, crēdere, crēdidī, crēditum (+ dat.) **believe, trust** [25]

crepitus, -ūs m. rattling

crepundia, -ōrum n. pl. rattle

Crescens, -entis m. Crescens, a male name

crescō, crescere, crēvī, crētum **grow, arise, appear, increase** [32]

Crēta, -ae f. Crete, an island in the eastern Mediterranean

crīmen, crīminis n. crime

crīnis, crīnis m. hair

crocodīlus, -ī m. crocodile

crūdēlis, crūdēle harsh, cruel

cruentus. -a, -um bloody, gory

cruor, cruōris m. gore, blood

crūs, crūris n. leg, shin

cubiculum, -ī n. **bedroom** [12]

cubō (1) lie down (in bed) lie asleep, sleep

culīna, -ae f. **kitchen** [25]

culpa, -ae f. fault, blame

cultellus, -ī m. knife

cultūra, -ae f. agriculture

cum (+ abl.) **with** [6]

cum prīmum as soon as

cum **when** [15]

cumīnum, -ī n. cumin

cūnae, cunārum f. pl. cradle

cunctor, cunctārī, cunctātus sum **tarry, linger, hesitate** [25]

cupidus, -a, -um (+ gen.) **longing for, eager for, desirous** [39]

cupiō, cupere, cupīvī/cupiī, cupītum **wish, want to** [4]

cupressus, -ī f. cypress tree

cūr **why** [11]

cūra, ae f. worry, concern, care, anxiety

cūrātor, -ōris m. caretaker, manager

cūria, -ae f. curia, senate house

cūrō (1) **care for** [13]

currō, currere, cucurrī, cursum **run** [5]

currus, -ūs m. chariot

cursor, cursōris m. runner

cursum amittere to go off course

cursus, -ūs m. **course; voyage; journey; race; march; career** [35]

custōdiō, custōdīre, custōdīvī/custōdiī, custōdītum **watch, guard** [30]

custōs, custōdis m./f. **guard** [30]

D

Damascus, ī f. Damascus, city in Roman province of Syria

Danaē, Danaēs f. Danaë, mother of Perseus

daps, dapis f. sacrificial feast, offering

dē (+ abl.) **away from, down from; concerning, about** [7]

dea, -ae f. **goddess** [11]

dealbātor, -ōris m. whitewasher, someone charged with whitewashing walls either to cover up graffiti or to prepare the wall for new graffiti.

dealbō (1) whitewash

dēbellō (1) vanquish

dēbeō, dēbēre, dēbuī, dēbitum owe, ought, have to [7]

dēbilis, dēbile weak

decem ten [12]

dēcernō, dēcernere, dēcrēvī, dēcrētum judge, award

decet, decēre, decuit (+ dat. + inf.) imp. it is fitting [24]

dēcipiō, dēcipere, dēcēpī, dēceptum cheat

decōrus, -a, -um fitting, noble

dēdicō (1) dedicate, devote

dēdūcō, dēdūcere, dēdūxī, dēductum lead down, bring away; conduct, escort; *uxōrem dēdūcere* take a wife, marry [38]

dēductiō, -ōnis f. transportation

dēfendō, dēfendere, dēfendī, dēfensum defend [39]

dēfluō, dēfluere, dēfluxī, dēfluxus flow away; disappear

dēfungor, dēfungī, dēfunctus sum die

dehinc after this, next

deinceps in succession

deinde then

dēlectābilis, dēlectābile delicious

dēlectō (1) amuse, delight, charm [38]

dēleō, dēlēre, dēlēvī, dēlētum destroy, wipe out

dēlīberō (1) debate, deliberate

dēliciae, -ārum f. pl. delight, darling; pet

dēligō, dēligere, dēlēgī, dēlectum pick out, choose

Delphī, -ōrum m. pl. Delphi, a major oracular shrine of the god Apollo in Greece

Delphicus, -a, -um Delphic, pertaining to Delphi (a shrine of Apollo)

delphīnus, delphīnī m. dolphin

dēlūbrum, -ī n. temple, shrine

dēmānō (1) flow out, spread out

dēmittō, dēmittere, dēmīsī, dēmissum send down

demonstrō (1) point at, show, depict [40]

Dēmosthenēs, -is m. Demonsthenes, a famous Greek orator of the 4th century B.C.

dēmum finally, at length, at last [26]

dēnārius, -iī m. denarius, a silver coin

dēnique finally, at last, in fact [32]

dēplōrō (1) lament

dēpōnō, dēpōnere, dēposuī, dēpositum leave, lay down; commit; entrust, deposit

dēprecor, dēprecārī, dēprecātus sum beg pardon from

descendō, descendere, descendī, descensum go down, descend [31]

dēscrībō, dēscrībere, dēscripsī, dēscriptum describe, draw

dēserō, dēserere, dēseruī, dēsertum desert, abandon

dēsīderium, -iī n. desire, wish

dēsīderō (1) wish for

dēsinō, dēsinere, dēsīvī/dēsiī, dēsitum (+ gen.) cease, desist (from)

dēsistō, dēsistere, dēstitī, dēstitum stop, cease, desist

dēspērō (1) despair (of)

destruō, dēstruere, destruxī, destructum destroy [34]

dēsuper from above

dētergeō, dētergēre, dētersī, dētersum wipe away, rub clean

dētrīmentum, -ī n. loss, damage; defeat

deus, -ī m. god; *dī* (alternate nom. pl.) [14]

dēvertō, dēvertere, dēvertī, dēversum turn aside, stop to visit

dēvorō (1) devour, consume

dexter, dext(e)ra, dext(e)rum right *dext(e)ra (manus), -ae* f. right hand [38]

dī m. nom. pl. gods = *deī*

diabolus, -ī m. devil

Diāna, -ae f. Diana, goddess of the hunt and of the moon; the moon itself

dīcō, dīcere, dīxī, dictum say, tell [7]

dictum, -ī n. word

Dictys, -yos m. Dictys, brother of the king of Seriphos

diēs, diēī m. day [24]

differō, differre, distulī, dīlātum delay

difficilis, difficile hard, difficult [15]

difficultās, -tātis f. trouble, difficulty [23]

diffugiō, diffugere, diffūgī flee from

diffundō, diffundere, diffūdī, diffūsum pour forth, spread out

digitus, -ī m. finger [38]

dignitās, -tātis f. worthiness, merit; dignity; office; honor [35]

dignus, -a, -um worthy, deserving

dīligens, dīligentis careful, diligent, frugal [30]

dīligenter carefully

dīmidium, -iī n. half

dīmittō, dīmittere, dīmīsī, dīmissum let go, send out; dismiss; release; divorce [35]

Dioclēs, Dioclis m. Diocles, a male name

dīrectē directly

dīrectus, -a, -um straight, direct

dīrigō, dīrigere, direxī, dīrectum direct, guide

dīs dat./abl. pl. of *deus*

discēdō, discēdere, discessī, discessum leave, depart

discernō, discernere, discrēvī, discrētum separate, distinguish

disciplīna, -ae f. instruction, knowledge

discipula, -ae f. (female) student [2]

discipulus, -ī m. (male) student [2]

discō, discere, didicī learn [6]

disertus, -a, -um eloquent

dispergō, dispergere, dispersī, dispersum scatter, disperse

dispiciō, dispicere, dispexī, dispectum consider

displiceō, displicēre, displicuī, displicitum (+ dat.) displease; *displicet* imp. "it is displeasing" [26]

disputō (1) argue

disserō, disserere, disseruī, dissertum discuss

dissimilis, dissimile unlike [37]

diū for a long time [16]

diūtius (comparative of *diū*) for a bit longer

dīversus, -a, -um different, varied

dīvēs, dīvitis rich, talented [24]

dīvidō, dīvidere, dīvīsī, dīvīsum divide

dīvitiae, -ārum f. pl.wealth, riches

dīvus, -a, -um divine [29]

dīvus, -ī m. god = *deus*

dō, dare, dedī datum give [2]

doceō, docēre, docuī, doctum teach; show [35]

doctus, -a, -um learned

documentum, -ī n. instruction, warning

dolor, dolōris m. pain, grief [21]

dolōsus, -a, -um clever, crafty

domī at home

domicilium, -iī n. home

domina, -ae f. mistress (of the house), the woman in charge [25]

dominus, -ī m. master [18]

domus, -ī f. home, house; domum home, to a house [4]

domus, -ūs f. house [24]

dōnec as long as, until [27]

dōnum, -ī n. gift [23]

dormiō, dormīre, dormīvī/dormiī, dormītum sleep [12]

dorsum, -ī n. back

dōtālis, dōtāle dowry

Drusus, -ī m. Drusus, *cognōmen* in the Claudian *gens*; Tiberius and his descendants were members of this family

dubitō (1) doubt, hesitate [39]

dubius, -a, -um doubtful, uncertain [39]

dūcō, dūcere, duxī, ductum lead [4]

dūdum just now, a little while ago

dulcis, dulce sweet [23]

dulciter sweetly

dum while, as long as; until [33]

dummodo provided that, as long as

dumtaxat only up to, "only up to 150"

duo, duae, duo two [7]

duōbus two

duodecim twelve [12]

duodēvīgintī eighteen

dūrus, -a, -um hard, harsh, difficult

dux, ducis m. leader [27]

E

ē, ex (+ abl.) out of, from [5]

Eborācum, -ī n. Eboracum, city in Roman province of Britannia (modern York, England)

ēbrius, -a, -um drunk [27]

eburneus, -a, -um ivory

ecce Behold! Look! [11]

edax, edācis devouring

Edepol! By Pollux! [37]

ēditor, ēditōris m. organizer; *Ēditor ludōrum* public official in charge of the games

edō, ēsse/edere, ēdī, ēsum eat [7]

efficiō, efficere, effēcī, effectum execute, accomplish, do [32]

effrēnātus, -a, -um unbridled

effugiō, effugere, effūgī escape, flee

effugium, -iī n. flight, escape

effundō, effundere, effūdī, effūsum pour out

effūsē a lot

effūsus, -a, -um poured forth; widespread

ēgelidus, -a, -um warm

egēnus, -a, -um in need of, in want of, destitute [22]

ego I [7]

ēgredior, ēgredī, ēgressus sum march out, go out

ehem ha! aha! (in pleasant surprise)

ēheu alas! oh no! [16]

eho here you! hey! (often followed by *tū* or a vocative)

ei/hei ah! oh! (in fear or dismay)

ēia/hēia ah! ah ha! good! yes, indeed!; (+ *age*) quick! come on then!

ēiciō, ēicere, ēiēcī, ēiectum throw out

ēlāborō (1) take pains, exert oneself

elephans, elephantis m. elephant

ēlevō (1) raise up, lift up

ēligō, ēligere, ēlēgī, ēlectum pick out, choose

Elis, -idis f. Elis, a region in the Greek Peloponessus

ēlixus, -a, -um boiled

ēloquor ēloquī, ēlocūtus sum speak out, declare [24]

ēlūdō, ēlūdere, ēlūsī, ēlūsum mock, escape

Emerita Augusta, Emeritae Augustae, f. city in Roman Spain (modern Merida)

emō, emere, ēmī, emptum buy [18]

ēn/ēm (+ dat.) come on! (in commands); really? (in questions)

enim for [20]

ensis, ensis m. sword

eō, īre, īvī/iī, itum go [7]

Epaphrodītus, -ī m. Epaphroditus, a Greek name for a man

Ephesus, -ī f. Ephesus, city in the Roman province of Asia (modern Turkey)

epistula, -ae f. letter [23]

epulae, -ārum f. pl. food, dishes of food; banquet, feast [26]

epulor, epulārī, epulātus sum feast, dine

eques, equitis m. horseman, knight; pl. cavalry; order of knights [34]

equus, -ī m. horse [34]

ergō therefore [8]

ērigō, ērigere, ērexī, ērectum erect, raise

errō (1) wander

error, errōris m. mistake

ērubescō, ērubescere, ērubuī redden, blush

ērudītus, -a,-um skilled

ērumpō, ērumpere, ērūpī, ēruptum erupt

ēruptiō, -ōnis f. eruption

Erymanthius, -a, -um Erymanthian

Erymanthos, -theī n. Erymanthus, a mountain in Greece

Esquiliae, -ārum f. pl. the Esquiline hill, one of the seven hills of Rome

Esquilīnus, -a, -um Esquiline, one of the seven hills of Rome

est **is [1]**

ēsuriō, ēsurīre, ēsurītum be hungry

et **and [2]; also, even;** *et . . . et* **both . . . and [4]**

etiam **still; also, even, too, and also, even now [17]**

etsī although, even if

eu fine! great! (sometimes ironic)

euax hurray!

eugae/euge/eugepae **terrific! bravo! [36]**

Eumolpus, -ī m. Eumolpus, a character in the *Satyricon*

Eurystheus, -eī m. Eurystheus, king of Mycenae in Greece

ēveniō, ēvenīre, ēvēnī, ēventum **come about; happen [35]**

ēvītō (1) shun, avoid

ēvoluō, ēvoluere, ēvoluī, ēvolūtum unroll, unfold

exāminō (1) examine

excipiō, excipere, excēpī, exceptum receive, welcome

excitō **(1) awaken, excite, raise [32]**

exclāmō (1) cry out, explain

excubiae, -ārum f. pl. guard, watch

exemplar, exemplāris n. copy, model

exemplum, -ī **n. sample [40]**

exeō, exīre, exīvī/exiī, exitum go out

exerceō, exercēre, exercuī, exercitum **practice [40]**

exercitus, -ūs **m. army [38]**

exhibeō, exhibēre, exhibuī, exhibitum show, exhibit

exīlis, exīle thin, small

eximō, eximere, exēmī, exemptum take out, remove

existō, see *ex(s)istō*

exitiābilis, -e deadly, desctructive

exornō (1) adorn

exōticus, -a, -um strange, exotic, foreign

expallescō, expallescere, expalluī turn very pale

expellō, expellere, expulī, expulsum throw out

expergiscor, expergiscī, experrectus sum **awake, wake up [32]**

expiō (1) atone for

explicō (1) unfold, display; explain

explōrō (1) test, try

expōnō, expōnere, exposuī, expositum **set out; exhibit, explain [40]**

ex(s)istō, ex(s)istere, ex(s)titī arise, appear

exspectō **(1) await, wait for [16]**

exspīrō (1) breathe out

ex(s)tinguō, ex(s)tinguere ex(s)tinxī, ex(s)tinctum quench, extinguish

exsultō (1) exult in

extendō, extendere, extendī, extentum/extensum stretch out, extend

extimescō, extimescere, extimuī be alarmed, dread

extinguō see *ex(s)tinguō*

extrā **(+ acc.) beyond, outside of [40]**

extrahō, extrahere, extraxī, extractum draw out, drag out

extrēmus, -a, -um final, last; *extrēmās poenās habēre* die

exuō, exuere, exuī, exūtum strip, undress

exūrō, exūrere, exussī, exustum burn up

F

faber, fabrī **m. craftsman [28];** *faber argentārius* silversmith

Fabius, -iī m. Fabius, a Roman *praenōmen*

fabrica, -ae f. **workshop; art, craft [37]**

fabricō **(1) forge, make, shape, build, construct [30]**

fābula, -ae **f. story, play [9]**

faciēs, faciēī **f. face, appearance, beauty [24]**

facilis, facile **easy [20]**

faciliter easily

faciō, facere, fēcī, factum **make, do [6]**

factiō, -ōnis f. team

factum, -ī **n. deed [20]**

faenum, -ī n. hay

Falernum, -ī n. Farlernian wine

Falernus, -a, -um Falernian, referring to a region in Italy producing a particularly good kind of wine

fāma, -ae **f. fame, rumor, report [20]**

famēs, famis f. hunger

familia, -ae **f. family [4]**

fāmōsus, -a, -um famous, well known

famulus, -ī m. servant, attendant

farreus, -a, -um of grain, grain

fās (indecl.) n. right, law [40]

fatīgō (1) weary, tire

fātum, -ī n. fate, destiny

Faustus, -ī m. Faustus, a male name

faveō, favēre, fāvī, fautum (+ dat.) favor, support, cheer for

favor, -ōris m. favor, goodwill

fax, facis f. torch

febris, febris f. fever

fēlēs, fēlis f. cat

fēliciter luckily, with luck

fēlix, fēlīcis **lucky, fortunate [18]**

fēmina, -ae **f. woman [2]**

fenestra, -ae f. window

ferē nearly, almost, about; in general

feriō, ferīre strike, hit; kill, slay

ferō, ferre, tulī, lātum **bear, carry, lead** [23]; *sē ferre* go ("betake oneself")

ferox, ferōcis fierce, savage

ferrum, -ī n. iron, sword [22]

ferus, -a, -um wild, savage

fervidē heatedly, fervently

fervidus, -a, -um boiling, hot; fervent

Fescinnīnus, -a, um Fescinnine, pertaining to the Fescinnine verses sung at weddings

fessus, -a, -um tired [8]

festīnō (1) hasten [9]

festus, -a, -um festal, solemn, religious

Festus, -ī m. Festus, a man's name

fētidus, -a, -um filthy, foul smelling

fīcus, -ī f. fig; fig tree

fidēlis, fidēle faithful, trustworthy [33]

fidēs, fideī f. faith, trust; credibility

fidius see *medius*

fīgō, fīgere, fīxī, fīxum fasten in place

figūra, -ae f. shape, figure [10]

fīlia, -ae f. daughter [8]

fīliola, -ae f. dear daughter

fīliolus, -ī m. little son (affectionate)

fīlius, -ī m. son [4]

fingō, fingere, finxī, fictum shape, form, fashion

fīniō, fīnīre, fīnīvī/fīniī, fīnītum finish, end [8]

fīnis, fīnis m. end; pl. country, territory [14]

fīō, fierī, factus sum be made, be done; happen, become [26]

firmāmentum, -ī n. support

firmus, -a, -um firm, strong [36]

flagrans, flagrantis glowing, blazing, ardent

flamma, -ae f. flame

flammeum, -eī n. bridal veil

Flāvia, -ae f. Flavia, a female name

flectō, flectere, flexī, flexum turn, bend

fleō, flēre, flēvī, flētum weep, cry

flō (1) blow

floccus, -ī m. tuft of wool; *nōn floccī facere* to consider of no importance

flōrus, -a, -um bright, rich

Flōrus, -ī m. Florus, a male name

flōs, flōris m. flower, bloom

fluitō (1) flow, float

flūmen, -inis n. river [33]

focus, -ī m. fireplace, hearth

fodicō (1) nudge, prod; stab

folia, -ae f. leaf

fons, fontis m. spring, fountain

forās outdoors, out

foris, foris (commonly forēs, -ium pl.) f. door, gate; *forīs* out of doors, outside; abroad [34]

forma, -ae f. shape, form; beauty; ground plan [24]

formīdō (1) dread

formōsus, -a, -um beautiful, handsome, pretty [35]

forsitan perhaps

fortasse perhaps [11]

fortis, forte strong, brave, loud [15]

fortiter strongly, bravely, loudly

fortūna, -ae f. fortune, chance, luck; wealth, prosperity [33]

fortūnātus, -a, -um lucky, fortunate [22]

forum, -ī n. forum, city center [5]

fossa, -ae f. ditch

frangō, frangere, frēgī, fractum break; crush; conquer [36]

frāter, frātris m. brother [13]

frāterculus, -ī m. little brother [36]

fremō, fremere, fremuī, fremitum growl, groan

frequens, -entis frequent, usual

fricō, fricāre, fricuī, frictum rub, rub down

frīgidārium, -iī n. cold water bath

frīgidus, -a, -um cold

frons, frontis f. forehead, brow

fructus, -a, -um enjoyed

Fructus, -ī m. Fructus, a male first name

fruor, fruī, fructus/fruitus sum (+ abl.) enjoy, profit by [24]

frustrā in vain

frustum, -ī n. morsel, scrap

frutex, fruticis m. bush, shrub

fuga, -ae f. flight

fugiō, fugere, fūgī, fugitum flee, run away [12]

fugitīvus, -ī m. runaway, fugitive

fulgeō, fulgēre, fulsī shine, gleam

fulgur, -uris n. lightning

fullō, -ōnis m. fuller, launderer

fullōnica, -ae f. laundry

fūmōsus, -a, -um smokey

fūmus, -ī m. smoke

fundus, -ī m. farm

fūnebris, fūnebre funereal

fungor, fungī, functus sum (+ abl.) perform, discharge [24]

fūnis, fūnis m. cord, rope

fūnus, fūneris, n. burial, funeral [40]

furcifer, furciferī m. scoundel

furnus, -ī m. oven, bakehouse

fūror, -ōris m. fury, rage

furtīvē secretly

furtīvus, -a, -um secret

fūrunculus, -ī m. petty thief

fuscus, -a, -um dark

Fuscus, -ī m. Fuscus, a male name

fustis, fustis m. staff, club, stick

futūrum, -ī n. future [14]

G

Gāia, -ae f. Gaia, ceremonial name of a Roman bride

Gāius, -iī m. Gaius, ceremonial name of a Roman bridegroom

Gallia, -ae f. Gaul, the Roman province now known as France

gallīna, -ae f. hen

garriō, garrīre, garrīvī/garriī, garrītum chatter

garrulus,-a, -um chattering, blabbing

garum, -ī n. fish sauce

gaudeō, gaudēre, gavīsus sum rejoice, be glad [38]

gaudium, -iī n. joy

gelidus, -a, -um icy, cold

geminus, -a, -um twin

gemma, -ae f. gem

gemō, gemere, gemuī, gemitum moan, groan

gener, generī m. son-in-law [30]

geniālis, -e marriage; merry, festive

gens, gentis f. famly, tribe

genū, -ūs n. knee

genus, generis n. race, type

Germānī, -ōrum pl. Germans, the German people

Germānia, -ae f. Germany

Germānicus, -a, -um German

Germānicus, -ī m. Germanicus, the son-in-law of the emperor Tiberius

gerō, gerere, gessī, gestum bear, carry [22]; *bellum gerere* wage war [23]; *sē gerere* act, conduct oneself [28]

gerūsia, -ae f. a council building for elders, senate house

gestiō, gestīre, gestīvī/gestiī, gestītum exult

gladiātor, -ōris m. gladiator [17]

gladius, -iī m. sword [17]

glīs, glīris m. dormouse

glōria, -ae f. glory [40]

gracilis, gracile thin, slender, scanty

gradus, -ūs m. step, pace, tier (of a theater) [24]

Graecia, -ae f. Greece

Graecus, -a, -um Greek

grāmen, grāminis n. grass

grandis, grande great, old

grātiā (+ gen.) for the sake of, for the purpose of [30]

grātia, -ae f. grace, favor; (pl.) thanks; *grātiās agere* give thanks [19]

grātiōsus, -a, -um agreeable

grātulātiō, -ōnis f. congratulations

grātus, -a, -um pleasing, thankful [23]

gravidus, -a, -um pregnant [25]

gravis, grave heavy, serious, deep [15]

graviter severely

gremium, iī n. lap [27]

grex, gregis m. flock, herd (of animals); company, group (of people), troop (of actors)

grūs, gruis, m./f. crane (a bird)

gubernō (1) steer (a ship); govern

H

habeō, habēre, habuī, habitum have, hold [5]

habitō (1) live in, inhabit [12]

habitus, -ūs m. dress, clothing

haereō, haerēre, haesī, haesum cling to, stick

hahae hah!

Halicarnassus, -ī f. Halicarnassus, city in Roman province of Asia (modern Turkey)

hama, -ae f. fire bucket

harēna, -ae f. sand; arena [22]

hasta, -ae f. spear

haud not, by no means [16]

haudquāquam by no means

hauriō, haurīre, hausī, haustum drink, swallow, drain

Hephaestus, -ī m. Hephaestus, slave named after the blacksmith god

herba, -ae f. herb

Herculaneum, -eī n. Herculaneum, city destroyed by eruption of Vesuvius in 79 A.D.

Hercule by Hercules! [28]

Herculēs, Herculis m. Hercules, the Greek hero Heracles

hērēs, hērēdis m./f. heir, heiress

heri yesterday [19]

Hermēs, -ae m. Hermes, a slave named after the Greek messenger god

Hermēs, -ēs m. Hermes, the Greek messenger god

hērōs, hērōos m. hero

heu (often + acc.) oh! (in pain or dismay) [36]

heus say there! hey! you there! (to draw attention)

hic, haec, hoc this [19]

hīc here, in this place [10]

Hierosolyma, -ōrum n. pl. Jerusalem, city in Roman province of Judaea (modern Israel/Palestine)

hilaris, -e cheerful

hinc from here

hiō (1) yawn

hippopotamus, -ī m. hippopotamus

Hispānia, -ae f. Spain

Hispānus, -a, -um Spanish

historia, -ae f. history

hodiē today [4]

hodiernus, -a, -um today's, modern

holus, holeris n. vegetables

homō, hominis m./f. human being, person, man [13]

honestus, -a, -um worthy, decent, of high rank [29]

honor, -ōris m. honor, office, dignity

honōrō (1) esteem, honor

hōra, -ae f. hour, time [8]

Horātius, -iī m. Horace, a Roman poet

hōrologium, -iī n. clock
horrendus, -a, -um horrible, terrible
horribilis, horribile rough, terrible, horrible [37]
hortor, hortārī, hortātus sum urge [33]
hortus, -ī m. garden
hospes, hospitis m. guest, host, stranger [26]
hostis, hostis m./f. stranger, foreigner, enemy;
  (pl.) the enemy [14]
hūc here, to this place [36]
huī (exclamation of astonishment or admiration) wow!
humilis, humile low; humble
humus, -ī f. earth, soil
hyaena, -ae f. hyena
Hydra, -ae f. Hydra, a many-headed serpent-like monster
  with poisonous blood
Hymēn, only found in nom. m. Hymen, the god of
  marriage; also, the wedding song or the marriage itself
Hymenaeus, -ī m. Hymenaeus = Hymen
Hymettus, -ī m. Hymettus, a mountain near Athens,
  famous for its honey
hypocauston, -ī n. hypocaust; heating system for a bath

I

iaceō, iacēre, iacuī lie, lie still, lie dead [21]
iaciō, iacere, iēcī, iactum throw, hurl [22]
iactō (1) hurl, throw; boast
iam dūdum for a long time now
iam now, already [8]; *nōn iam* not any longer
iānitor, -ōris m. doorman, porter [34]
iānua, -ae f. door [25]
ibi there [21]
īdem, eadem, idem the same [21]
identidem again and again
idōneus, -a, -um (+ dat.) fit, suitable [36]
iēiūnus, -a, -um hungry [13]
ientāculum, -ī n. breakfast [31]
igitur therefore [20]
ignāvus, -a, -um idle, cowardly
ignis, ignis m. fire [14]
ignōminia, -ae f. dishonor
ignōrō (1) be ignorant of
ignōscō, ignōscere, ignōvī, ignōtum (+ dat.) forgive,
  grant pardon to
ignōtus, -a, -um unknown
Iliacus, -a, -um Trojan
ille, illa, illud he, she, it; they; that, those [17]
illīc there, over there [8]
illīdō, illīdere, illīsī, illīsum strike against
illūc to there [36]
illūminō (1) brighten
Illyria, -ae f. Illyria (modern Croatia)
Illyricum, -ī n. Illyricum, a Roman province in the Balkans

imāgō, -inis f. image, likeness; statue [40]
imbuō, imbuere, imbuī, imbūtum wet, soak
imitātiō, -ōnis f. imitation, copy
immānis, immāne huge, vast
immineō, imminēre (+ dat.) be on the watch for
immittō, immittere, immīsī, immissum send to
immō rather, more precisely
immōbilis, immōbile immovable, unmoving
immolō (1) offer as a sacrifice
immortālis, immortāle immortal
impatiens, impatientis impatient (of)
impediō, impedīre, impedīvī/impediī,
  impedītum hamper, hinder, impede [39]
imperātor, -ōris m. commander, general, ruler,
  emperor [25]
imperium, -iī n. command, order, rule, empire, supreme
  command
imperō (1) (+ dat.) command, order, rule [26]
impetrō (1) obtain by formal request or petition
impetus, -ūs m. attack, assault
impleō, implēre, implēvī, implētum fill
implōrō (1) plead, beg
impōnō, impōnere, imposuī, impositum
  (+ dat.) put on, put upon, assign, impose upon
improbus, -a, -um disloyal, shameless, morally
  unsound [23]
īmus, -a, -um inmost, deepest, bottommost
in (+ abl.) in, on, at [2]; (+ acc.) into, onto, against [5]
inānis, -e poor, useless, vain
inaurēs, inaurium m. pl. earrings
incautus, -a, -um uncautious, not careful
incendium, -iī n. fire, conflagration [32]
incendō, incendere, incendī, incensum set fire to, inflame,
  burn [32]
incertus, -a, -um uncertain [35]
incidō, incidere, incidī, incāsum fall (into); meet (with);
  occur, arise
incipiō, incipere, incēpī, inceptum begin [18]
incitō (1) incite; spur on
inclīnō (1) bend, tilt
inclūdō, inclūdere, inclūsī, inclūsum shut in, enclose
incognitus, -a, -um not known
incola, -ae m./f. inhabitant [38]
incolō, incolere, incoluī inhabit
incommodus, -a, -um disagreeable
incurrō, incurrere, incurrī/incucurrī run into
indecōrē sē gerere misbehave
indecoris, indecore shameful
indicō, indīcere, indīxi, indictum declare publicly
indīviduus, -a, -um indivisible
induō, induere, induī, indūtum put on
industria, -ae f. industry
industrius, -a, -um industrious, diligent

inertia, -ae f. idleness
infāmia, -ae f. dishonor
infāmis, infāme disreputable
infans, infantis m./f. infant [14]
infēlix, infēlīcis unhappy, unfortunate [36]
inferior, inferius lower
infernus, -a, -um infernal, pertaining to the underworld
inferō, inferre, intulī, illātum bring, serve
inferus, -a, -um below; *in inferōs locōs* into "the places below," i.e., hell
infortūnātus, -a, -um unlucky, unfortunate [22]
infrā below, underneath, under [32]
ingenium, -iī n. talent
ingens, ingentis huge, great
ingenuus, -a, -um freeborn
ingredior, ingredī, ingressus sum enter, go in [24]
inicio, inicere, iniēcī, iniectum throw in
inīquus, -a, -um unequal
initium, -iī n. beginning
inquīrō, inquīrere, inquīsīvī/inquīsiī, inquīsītum inquire
inquit, inquiunt say [2]
insānia, -ae f. madness, insanity
inscriptiō, -ōnis f. inscription, writing on stone
insequor, insequī, insecutus sum pursue
insignis, insigne conspicuous, famous, notable
insiliō, insilīre, insiluī leap into
inspectō (1) look closely at [19]
inspiciō, inspicere, inspexī, inspectum look (closely) at; inspect [10]
instar indecl. (+ gen.) equal
instrūmentum, -ī n. tool, instrument [27]
insula, -ae f. island, apartment block [9]
insum, inesse, infuī be in
intactus, -a, -um intact
intellegens, intellegentis smart, intelligent [15]
intellegō, intellegere, intellēxī, intellectum understand [13]
intendō, intendere, intendī, intentum stretch, direct
intentō (1) point (at), threaten
intentus, -a, -um intent, eager
inter (+ acc.) between, among [5]
intercēdō, intercēdere, intercessī, intercessum come between; interrupt
interdiū by day
interdum occasionally
intereā meanwhile [35]
interficiō, interficere, interfēcī, interfectum kill [14]
interiaceō, interiacēre, interiacuī lie between
interim meanwhile
interpellō (1) interrupt
interrogō (1) ask, question; examine [34]
intrā (+ acc.) within [25]
intrepidus, -a, -um fearless
intrō (1) enter [8]

introductiō, -ōnis f. introduction
intueor, intuērī, intuitus sum look at, gaze at, consider [25]
inūtilis, inūtile useless, profitless
inveniō, invenīre, invēnī, inventum find, discover [14]
invictus, -a, -um unconquered
invideō, invidēre, invīdī, invīsum (+ dat.) envy, hate, grudge; refuse [38]
invidiōsus, -a, -um arousing hatred or envy
invidus, -a, -um envious
invīsus, -a, -um hated
invītō (1) invite
iō a shout of religious emotion
iocor, iocārī, iocātus sum (1) joke
iocōsus, -a, -um funny
iocus, - ī m. joke
Iphiclēs, -eī m. Iphicles, Heracles' brother
Iphigenīa, -ae f. Iphigenia, daughter of Agamemnon
ipse, ipsa, ipsum he, she, it; they; himself, herself, itself, themselves (emphatic) [17]
īra, -ae, f. anger
īrācundē angrily
īrascor, īrascī, īrātus sum be angry at
īrātus, -a, -um angry [6]
irreparābilis, irreparābile irrecoverable, irreparable
irrīdeō, irrīdēre, irrīsī, irrīsum laugh at, mock [37]
irrīsor, -ōris m. mocker, "one who mocks"
irrītō (1) upset, annoy, aggravate
irrumpō, irrumpere, irrūpī, irruptum burst, break open
is, ea, id he, she, it; they [17]
Īsēon, -ī n. temple of the goddess Isis
iste, ista, istud that one of yours (derogatory) [17]
ita so, thus; yes [22]
Ītalia, -ae f. Italy
Ītalus, -a, -um Italian
itaque therefore [20]
item similarly, likewise [35]
iter, itineris n. road, journey [21]; *iter facere* to make a journey, to journey
iterō (1) repeat, do again
iterum again [4]
Ithaca, -ae f. Ithaca, island home of the Greek hero Ulysses, located in western Greece
iubeō, iubēre, iussī, iussum order [28]
iūcundus, -a, -um pleasant, agreeable [35]
Iūdaea, -ae f. Judaea, the Roman province in what is now approximately Israel
Iullus, -ī m. Jullus, Servilia's intended husband
iunctiō, -ōnis f. joining
iungō, iungere, iunxī, iunctum join [38]; *sē iungere* (+ dat.) to join oneself (with), to ally oneself (with)
Iūnō, Iūnōnis f. Juno, queen of the gods
Iuppiter, Iovis m. Jupiter, king of the gods [24]

iūrō (1) swear

iūs, iūris n. law

iussus, -ūs m. order, command (only used in abl.) "by order of"

iustus, -a, -um legal

***iuvenis, iuvenis* m./f. youth [15]**

iuventūs, -tūtis f. young men collectively, youth

***iuvō, iuvāre, iūvi, iūtum* help [25]**

iuxtā (+ acc.) near to

K

Kalendae, -ārum f. pl. kalends, the first day of the month

L

L. = Lūcius

***labor, lābī, lapsus sum* fall down [39]**

***labor, labōris* m. work, labor [16]**

labōriōsus, -a, -um working, laborious, tedious

***labōrō* (1) work [9]**

labrum, -ī n. basin; lip

Labyrinthus, -ī m. maze, labyrinth, especially the one in Crete in which the Minotaur was imprisoned

Lachesis, -is f. Lachesis, one of the three goddesses of Fate

Lacō, -ōnis m. Laconian, Spartan

lacrima, -ae f. tear

***lacrimō* (1) cry, shed tears [17]**

lactō (1) nurse

***lacus, -ūs* m. lake [28]**

laedō, laedere, laesī, laesum hurt, damage

laetitia, -ae f. happiness

laetor, laetārī, laetātus sum be happy, rejoice

***laetus, -a, -um* happy [3]**

lalla excl. calming sound

lāneus, -a, -um woolen

lanista, -ae m. trainer, manager of a gladiatorial troop

lanius, -iī m. butcher, butcher shop

lanx, lancis f. dish, place

lapsō (1) slip

laqueus, -ī m. snare, noose

Lar, Laris m. Lar, a household god

lateō, latēre, latuī hide

latericius, -a, -um brick, made of brick

lātifundium, -iī n. large country estate

lātrīna, -ae f. public toilet

latrō, latrōnis m. thief, robber

***lātus, -a, -um* wide, broad [31]**

latus, lateris n. side, ribs; *latus fodicō* poke in the ribs

laurea, -ae f. laurel wreath

laus, laudis f. praise

***lavō, lavāre, lāvī, lautum/lavātum/lōtum* wash [31]**

lectīca, -ae f. litter, a sedan chair

lectīcārius, -iī m. litter bearer

lectiō, -ōnis f. reading

***lectus, -ī* m. (dining) couch, bed [18]**

lēgātus, -ī m. lieutenant; legate

***legiō, legiōnis* f. legion, army [39]**

legitmus, -a, -um real, lawful, right

***legō, legere, lēgī, lectum* gather, choose; read [15]**

lēniō, lēnīre, lēnīvī/lēniī, lēnītum ease, put at ease; allay, mitigate

***lēnis, lēne* smooth, soft, mild, gentle [27]**

lēniter smoothly, softly, midly, gently

lentē slowly, calmly

lentus, -a, -um slow, calm; tough

leō, leōnis m. lion

lētum, -ī n. death

***levis, leve* light, gentle [23]**

levō (1) lift, lighten

libellum, -ī n. little book

***libens, libentis* cheerful [35]**

libenter freely, willingly

***līber, lībera, līberum* free [14]**

***liber, librī* m. book [14]**

***līberī, -ōrum* m. pl. children [33]**

***līberō* (1) (+ abl.) free, free from [36]**

***lībertās, -ātis* f. freedom, liberty [40]**

***lībertīnus, -ī* m. freedman (used as defining social status) [37]**

lībertus, -ī m. freedman (in relation to his master)

libet, libēre, libuit, libitum est (+ dat.) imp. it is pleasing (to someone)

libitīnārius, -iī m. undertaker

librārius, -iī m. bookseller, book copier

lībum, -ī n. special holiday cake or pancake

***licet, licēre, licuit* or *licitum est* imp. it is permitted [29]**

Licinia, -ae f. Licinia, a female name

Licinius, -iī m. Licinius, a male name

ligneus, -a, -um wooden

lignum, -ī m. wood, firewood

līmen, līminis n. threshold

līmus, -ī m. mud, slime

***lingua, -ae* f. tongue, speech [33]**

liquāmen, liquāminis n. liquid, especially fish sauce

liquor, -ōris m. fluid, liquid

līs, lītis f. lawsuit

littera, -ae f. letter of the alphabet

lītus, lītoris n. shore

Livius, -iī m. Livy, the historian

locō (1) put in place, contract for, rent

***locus, -ī* m. place [19]; also *locum, -ī* n.**

***longē* far off, far, a long distance, for a long time [11]**

longinquus, -a, -um far away, far off

***longus, -a, -um* long [19]**

loquēla, -ae f. speech, utterance

loquor, loquī, locūtus sum speak, talk, say [24]

lōtium, -ī n. urine

lubet = libet (+ dat.) imp. it is pleasing (to someone)

lūceō, lūcēre, luxī shine

lucerna, -ae f. (oil) lamp

lūcifer, lūcifera, lūciferum light-bearing (an epithet or nick-name for the goddess Diana); *Lūcifera Diana* "the light-bearer"

Lūcius, -iī m. Lucius, son of Servilius and Caecilia

lucrum, -ī n. profit

luctātor, luctātōris m. wrestler

lūdia, -ae f. a gladiator's girl

lūdō, lūdere, lūsī, lūsum play, tease [30]

lūdus -ī m. school, game [4]

lūgeō, lūgēre, luxī, luctum mourn, lament

lūgubris, lūgubre mourning

lūmen, lūminis n. light, torch

lupa, -ae f. wolf

lūteus, -a, -um yellow, saffron

lutum, -ī n. mud, dirt

lux, lūcis f. light

M

M. = Marcus

macellum, -ī n. (grocery) market, store

maculō (1) spot, stain, pollute

madefaciō, madefacere, madefēcī, madefactum make moist, soak

madidus, -a, -um moist, wet

Maecēnās, Maecēnātis m. G. Clinius Maecenas (70–8 B.C.), Augustus' close friend and advisor

maestitia, -ae f. sadness, grief

maestus, -a, -um sad, gloomy [18]

magis more, rather [16]

magister, -trī m. teacher (male), schoolmaster [2]

magistra, -ae f. teacher (female), schoolmistress [2]

magistrātus, -ūs m. office, magistracy; magistrate [37]

magnificus, -a, -um noble, elegant, magnificent

magnitūdō, -inis f. greatness

magnopere much, greatly, especially [23]

magnus, -a, -um large, great, loud [8]

magus, -ī m. magician

māiestās, -ātis f. majesty, authority

māior, māius older; m. pl. ancestors, elders [15]

male badly

malefactor, -ōris m. evil-doer, criminal

maleficus, -a, -um wicked, criminal, harmful

malleum, -ī n. hammer, mallet

mālō, mālle, māluī prefer [7]

mālum Pūnicum, -i f. pomegranate (lit., "Punic apple")

malus, -a, -um bad [6]

mamma, -ae f. breast

māne early in the morning [4]

maneō, manēre, mansī, mansum stay, remain, endure, await [23]

manifestus, -a, -um clear, evident

mansuētus, -a, -um gentle

manubiae, -ārum f. pl. general's share of an army's military plunder

manus, -ūs f. hand [24]

mappa, -ae f. table napkin; starting flag

Marcus, -ī m. Marcus, son of Servilius and Cornelia, brother of Lucius

mare, maris n. sea [14]

marītus, -ī m. husband [16]

marmor, -oris n. marble

marmoreus, -a, -um marble, made of marble

Mars, Martis m. Mars, god of war

Martius, -a, -um of Mars

mās, maris male

mastigia, -ae m. rascal, someone worthy of a whipping

māter, mātris f. mother [13]

matercula, -ae f. dear mother

māteria, -ae f. material

mātertera, -ae f. aunt, mother's sister

mātrimōnium, -iī n. marriage, matrimony [37]

mātrōna, -ae f. married woman

mātūrus, -a, -um timely, early

mātūtīnus, -a, -um of or belonging to the early morning

mausōlēum, ēī n. mausoleum, tomb

maximē, with *cum* especially

maximus, -a, -um greatest [20]

mē me [3]

Mēdēa, -ae f. Medea, the midwife

medicus, -ī m. doctor, physician

medius fidius/mediusfidius by the gods of truth! most certainly!

medius, -a, -um midway, in the middle (of), the middle of [22]

medulla, -ae f. marrow

Megara, -ae f. Megara, wife of Hercules

mehercle by Hercules! (as an oath to express strong feeling)

meī of me

mel, mellis n. honey [31]

melior, melius better [19]

membrum, -ī n. limb (arm or leg), body part; member

meminī, meminisse remember; *mementō, -tōte* (imper.) remember! [32]

memor, memoris mindful (of), remembering

memoria, -ae f. memory [37]

mendax, -dācis untruthful; *Mendax*, a beggar living in Valeria's *insula*

mendīcus, -a, -um beggar

mens, mentis f. mind; reason; mental disposition [31]

mensa, -ae f. table [16]

mensis, mensis m. month [14]

mentior, mentīrī, mentītus sum lie, deceive [24]

mercātor, -ōris trader, merchant

mercātōrius, -a, -um mercantile, commercial

Mercurius, -iī m. Mercury, the messenger god

mereō, merēre, meruī, meritum deserve

merīdiē at noon

merīdiēs, -ēī (f) midday, noon

merum, -ī n. pure (unmixed) wine

merx, mercis f. a commodity; (pl.) goods, merchandise

Mesopotamia, -ae f. Mesopotamia, the land between the Tigris and Euphrates rivers

mēta, -ae f. turning post

metuō, metuere, metuī, metūtum fear, be afraid of [39]

metus, -ūs m. fear [36]

meus, -a, -um my [5]

mī = mihi to me; my (vocative of *meus*)

mihi to me, my, [1]

mīles, -itis m. soldier [23]

mille indecl. thousand; *mīlia* n. pl. thousands

Minerva, -ae f. Minerva, Roman goddess of wisdom and crafts

minimus, -a, -um smallest [20]

minor, minus smaller [19]

Mīnōtaurus, -ī m. Minotaur, half-human, half-bull imprisoned in the Labyrinth

mīrābilis, mīrābile amazing, wondrous

mīrāculum, -ī n. miracle

mīror, mīrārī, mīrātus sum wonder at, admire [25]

mīrus, -a, -um astonishing, wonderful

misceō, miscēre, miscuī, mixtum unite, blend, mix, stir up

miser, misera, miserum wretched, miserable [35]

miserābilis, miserābile miserable

miserābiliter miserably

misereor, miserērī, miseritus sum pity; *mē miseret* it distresses me

miseria, -ae f. misery

misericordia, -ae f. pity

missiō, -ōnis f. discharge (military); permission (for gladiators) to cease fighting; *ad missiōnem* to a draw; *missiō honesta* an honorable discharge

mītis, mīte soft

mittō, mittere, mīsī, missum send [20]

modicum moderately

modicus, -a, -um a moderate amount of

modo only, just now, but [23]

modus, -ī m. way, manner

molae, -ārum f. pl. mill

molestus, -a, -um troublesome, tiresome [29]

mollis, molle soft

molliter softly

mōmentum, -ī n. importance, (important) moment; effort

moneō, monēre, monuī, monitum warn, advise [33]

monīle, -is n. necklace, collar

mons, montis m. mountain

monstrō (1) show, display, point out

monstrum, -ī n. monster

monumentum, -ī n. memorial, monument; tomb

morbus, -ī m. illness, sickness [34]

mordax, mordācis biting

mordeō, mordēre, momordī, morsum bite

morior, morī, mortuus sum die [29]

mors, -tis f. death

morsum, -ī. morsel

morsus, -ūs m. bite, nibble

mortuus, -a, -um dead [22]

mōs, mōris m. custom; (pl.) character [15]

mōtus, -ūs m. movement, motion

moveō, movēre, mōvī, mōtum, move, affect [30]

mox soon [9]

mūla, -ae f. mule

mulceō, mulcēre, mulsī, mulsum soothe, stroke, pet

mulier, mulieris f. woman, wife

mulsum, -ī n. warm drink of honey and wine

multitūdō, -inis f. great number, multitude

multō much, by far, long [26]

multum a lot, much [16]

multus, -a, -um much; (pl.) many [2]

mūlus, -ī m. mule

mundō (1) clean

mundus, -a, -um clean, refined, elegant

mundus, -ī m. world

mūnicipium, -iī n. town under Roman rule but governed by its own local laws

mūnus, -eris n. function, duty; gift; pl. games, public shows, spectacles [17]

murmillo, murmillōnis m. murmillo, a heavily armed gladiator

murmur, -uris n. whispering, murmur, growling

murmurō (1) mutter

mūrus, -ī m. wall [28]

mūs, mūris m. mouse

musca, -ae f. fly

musculus, -ī m. muscle

mūsicus, -ī m. musician

mussitō (1) mutter

mustāceus, -ī m. a grape-cake, a wedding cake baked with must on bay leaves

mūtō (1) alter, change

mūtus, -a, -um speechless, mute

mūtuus, -a, -um shared, mutual

N

Naevia, -ae f. Naevia, Servilia's friend.

Naevius, -iī m. Naevius, Naevius Cordus, object of Servilia's love *nam* for [23]

nānus, -ī m. dwarf

nārēs, -rium f. pl. nostrils

narrātiō, -ōnis f. narrative, story

narrō (1) say, tell [14]

nascor, nascī, nātus sum be born [37]

Nāsō, -ōnis m. Naso, Ovid's *cognomen*

nāsus, -ī m. nose

natiō, -ōnis f. nationality

natō (1) swim

nātū by birth

nātūra, -ae f. nature, character [32]

nātus, -a, -um born; *xx annōs nātus* = xx years old [12]

naufragium, -iī n. shipwreck, crash (of chariots), collision, wreck

nāvicula, -ae f. little boat

nāvigō (1) sail [36]

nāvis, nāvis f. ship [34]

nāvus, -a, -um active, industrious

-ne asks a yes/no question [4]

nē not, that not, in order that not, lest [31]

Neāpolis, f. Naples, a city in southern Italy

nec and not; *nec . . . nec* neither . . . nor [15]

necessārius, -a, -um necessary, indispensable [34]

necesse est (+ dat. + inf.) imp. it is necessary (to) [12]

necō (1) kill, slay [21]

negō (1) deny

negōtium, -iī n. business, task [8]

Nemausus, -ī f. Nemausus, a city in Roman Gaul (modern Nīmes)

nēmō, -inis m./f. nobody, no one [13]

nepōs, -ōtis m. grandson, grandchild, descendant [27]

neptis, -is f. granddaughter

Neptūnus, -ī m. Neptune, god of the sea

neque and not; *neque . . . neque* neither . . . nor [28]

nesciō, nescīre, nescīvī/nesciī, nescītum not know [34]

neuter, -tra, -trum neither [17]

nī unless

Nicopolis, -is f. Nicopolis, city in western Greece founded by Augustus after the battle of Actium in 31 B.C. ·*Nicopolin* Note Greek accusative ending.

niger, nigra, nigrum black

nihil nothing [3]

nihilōminus nevertheless [39]

Nīlōticus, -a, -um of the Nile (river)

nimbus, -ī m. cloud

nimis too much

nimium too, too much, excessively [16]

nisi unless [30]

niteō, nitēre, nituī shine, glitter

nitidus, -a, -um gleaming, shiny

nītor, nītī, nīsus/nixus sum lean on, rest on; endeavor, exert oneself, strain, struggle

nōbilis, nōbile noble [15]

noceō, nocēre, nocuī, nocitum (+ dat.) harm, hurt, injure, do injury to [12]

nocte for the night (abl.)

noctū at night

nocturnus, -a, -um nocturnal, of the night

nōdus, -ī m. knot

nōlō, nōlle, nōluī not want to, be unwilling [7]

nōmen, -inis n. name [1]

nōmenclātor, -ōris m. nomenclator, one who announces the names of people

nōminō (1) name [22]

nomisma, -atis n. coin

nōn iam not any longer

nōn not [3]

nōn sōlum . . . sed etiam not only . . . but also [18]

nōndum not yet [32]

nōnne asks a question expecting a yes answer [5]

nōnnullī, -ae, -a some, several [9]

nōnus, -a, -um ninth

nōs, nostrum/nostrī, nōbīs, nōs, nōbīs we, us [21]

noscō, -ere, nōvī, nōtum know, get to know [11]

noster, nostra, nostrum our [9]

nota, -ae f. sign, word

notō (1) mark, note; write down

nōtus, -a, -um known, familiar

novitās, -ātis f. newness, freshness

novus, -a, -um new [8]

nox, noctis f. night [14]

nūbēs, -is f. cloud

nūbō, nūbere, nupsī, nuptum marry [31]

nūdus, -a, -um naked, nude, unarmed

nūgae, -ārum f. pl. trifles, nonsense

nullus, -a, -um no, not any, none [17]

num asks a question expecting a no answer [5]

nūmen, nūminis n. divine presence; god

numerō (1) count, include

numerus, -ī m. number

nummus, -ī m. coin, money [27]

numquam never [17]

nunc now [3]

nuntiō (1) announce, report [37]

nuntius, -iī m. messenger; news [33]

nūper recently, not long ago [25]

nupta, -ae f. bride

nuptiae, -ārum f. pl. wedding, marriage

nuptiālis, -e nuptial, marriage for a wedding

nūtriō, nūtrīre, nūtrīvī/nutriī, nutrītum nurse, nourish, raise

nūtus, nūtūs m. nod

nux, nucis f. nut

O

ō oh! hey!

ob (+ prep.) in the direction of, towards

obeō, obīre, obīvī/obiī, obitum go away, die

obēsus, -a, -um fat

oblāta, -ōrum n. pl. "that which has been served"

oblīviscor, oblīviscī, oblītus sum (+ gen.) **forget [36]**

obscēnus, -a, -um obscene

obscūrō (1) darken, obscure, conceal

obscūrus, -a, um dark, shady; gloomy; uncertain [38]

obsecrō (1) implore, beg

obserō (1) block, obstruct

observō (1) pay attention (to)

obstetrix, obstetrīcis f. midwife

obtineō, obtinēre, obtinuī, obtentum hold, support, gain [9]

occāsiō, -ōnis f. opportunity, appropriate time

occīdō, occīdere, occīdī, occīsum kill, slay [39]

occlūdō, occlūdere, occlūsī, occlūsum shut, close

occupō (1) occupy, busy

occurrō, occurrere, occurrī/occucurrī, occursum (+ dat.) **encounter, run into [36]**

ocrea, -ae f. metal greave

Octāviānus, -ī m. Octavian

octāvus, -a, -um eighth

octō eight [12]

octōgintā eighty

oculus, -ī m. eye [23]

ōdēum, -ī n. odeum, a building for musical perforamances

ōdī, ōdisse hate

odor, odōris m. scent, odor [21]

Oedipus, -ī m. Oedipus, king of Thebes

oenogarum, -ī n. a sauce made of garum and wine

offerō, offerre, obtulī, oblātum (+ dat.) bring before, offer

officīna, -ae f. workshop [34]

officium, -iī n. task, duty

oleō, olēre, oluī smell, stink

oleum, -ī n. oil

ōlim once, formerly [19]

olīva, -ae f. olive

olla, -ae f. pot, jar; urn

Ollus archaic form of *ille* That (man)

ōmen, ōminis n. religious sign, omen

omnīnō utterly, altogether, completely [32]

omnis, omne each, every; (pl.) all [15]

onus, oneris n. load, burden

opera, -ae f. work, pain, labor [36]

operam dare (+ dat.) pay attention to

operiō, operīre, operuī, opertum cover

opīmus, -a, -um rich, plentiful

opīniō, -ōnis f. opinion, belief; reputation [34]

opīnor, opīnārī, opīnātus sum think, believe [30]

oportet, oportēre, oportuit (+ inf.) one ought [12]

oppidum, -ī n. town [28]

oppugnō (1) attack [39]

optimus, -a, -um best [20]

optō (1) wish [37]

opulentus, -a, -um rich, wealthy

opus, operis n. work, effort; structure, building; (pl.) **goods [23];** *opus est* (+ dat.) there is need for

ōrāculum, -ī n. oracle, divine pronouncement

ōrātiō, -ōnis f. speech [16]

ōrātiōnem habēre give/deliver a speech

ōrātor, -tōris m. speaker

orbis, -is m. circle, ring; *orbis terrārum* **circle of the lands, the world [20]**

ordinō (1) put in order

ordō, -inis m. row, line, order; rank; class of citizens [34]

oriens, orientis m. east

orīgō, -inis f. origin, beginning, source [38]

orior, orīrī, ortus sum rise, get up, be born [33]

ornāmentum, -ī n. decoration, mark of distinction

ornātrix, ornātrīcis f. hairdresser

ornātus, -a, -um decorated

ornō (1) adorn, decorate [35]

ōrō (1) pray [33]

ōs, ōris n. mouth, face [13]

os, ossis n. bone [28]

ōsculō (1) kiss

Oscus, -a, -um Oscan

ōsor, -ōris m. hater

ostendō, ostendere, ostendī, ostentum/ostensum show, display [38]

ostentātiō, -ōnis f. display, flashiness

Ostia, -ae f. Ostia, the harbor of Rome; *Ostiam* "to Ostia"

Ostiensis, -e pertaining to Ostia (Rome's port), "Ostian"

ōtiōsus, -a, -um useless, unoccupied

ōtium, -iī n. leisure

Ovidius, -iī m. Ovid

ovis, -is m./f. sheep

ōvum, -ī n. egg [10]

P

p. = pūblicus, -a -um

paedagōgus, -ī m. a slave assigned to a young boy, a tutor [5]

paene almost [18]

paeniteō, paenitēre, paenitui to cause dissatisfaction: **paenitet paenitēre, paenituit** imp., it gives reason for regret; *mē paenitet* I am sorry [29]

pāgus, -ī m. country district

Palātīnus, -a, -um Palatine, of the Palatine

Palātium, -iī n. the Palatine hill, one of the seven hills of Rome

palma, -ae f. palm frond (of victory)

Palmȳra, -ae f. Palmyra, city in Roman province of Syria

palpitō (1) beat, throb

palpō (1) stroke, caresss

pānis, -is m. bread [31]

Pannonius, -a, - um Pannonian, member of a Balkan tribe

pannus, -ī m. cloth, garment, rag

papāver, -eris n. poppy; poppy-seed

papȳrus, -ī f. papyrus [27]

pār, paris equal

pār, paris n. pair, couple

parātus, -a, -um prepared

parcō, parcere, pepercī/parcuī/parsī, parsūrus
   (+ dat.) spare, pardon, show mercy to [12]

Pardalisca, -ae f. Pardalisca, a female name

parens, parentis m./f. **parent [16]**

pariēs, parietis m. wall

pariō, parere, peperī, paritum/partum bring forth,
   give birth (to), bear, create [25]

parma, -ae f. small shield carried by a Thrax gladiator

parō (1) **prepare, make ready [12]**

pars, partis f. **part, piece [19]**

parturiō, parturīre, parturīvī/parturiī be pregnant,
   be in labor, give birth

partus, -ūs m. childbirth, birth

parum little, too little, not enough

parvulus, -a, -um very small, tiny, little

parvus, -a, -um small [10]

passer, -eris m. sparrow

passus, -a, -um spread out, dried

pastināca, -ae f. parsnip

pater familiās, patris familiās m. **pater familias**
   head of the family [29]

pater, patris m. **father [13]**

patiens, patientis patient

patientia, -ae f. patience

patior, patī, passus sum suffer, allow [24]

patria, -ae f. **country, fatherland [27]**

patricius, -a, -um noble, patrician

patrōnus, -ī m. **patron [26]**

patruus, -ī m. uncle (father's brother)

paucus, -a, -um few, little [9]

paulisper for a little while

paulō a little, somewhat, by a little [25]

paulō post a little later, somewhat later

paulum a little, somewhat [28]

pauper, pauperis poor [25]

paupertās, -ātis f. poverty

pavīmentum, -ī n. ground, floor, pavement

pax quiet! enough!

pax, pācis f. **peace [27]**

pectus, -oris n. breast, chest

pecūlium, -iī n. savings, private property

pecūnia, -ae f. **money [3]**

pēior, pēius worse [19]

pellō, pellere, pepulī, pulsum banish

Penātēs, -ium m. pl. Penates, household gods

penna, -ae f. feather, wing

per (+ acc.) through [5]

peragō, peragere, perēgī, peractum finish, complete

perditus, -a, -um ruined, lost

perdō, perdere, perdidī, perditum lose, destroy

perdūcō, perdūcere, perduxī, perductum conduct, bring
   through, lead through

peregrīnor, peregrīnārī, peregrīnātus sum travel, travel abroad

pereō, perīre, perīvī/periī, peritum perish, vanish [32]

perfectus, -a, -um perfect

perferō, perferre, pertulī, perlātum convey

pergō, pergere, perrexī, perrectum go ahead, advance,
   proceed [37]

pergrātus, -a, -um very agreeable

perīculōsus, -a, -um dangerous [25]

perīculum, -ī n. danger

peristȳlium, -iī n. **peristyle, courtyard, colonnaded**
   garden [26]

perītus, -a, -um experienced (in), skilled (in) + gen.

perlaetus, -a, -um very happy [27]

perlegō, perlegere, perlēgī, perlectum scan, survey

permaximus, -a, -um very great, very loud

permultus, -a, -um very many

perpetuus, -a, -um continuous, uninterrupted;
   in perpetuum forever

persequor, persequī, persecūtus sum pursue, chase [40]

Perseus, -eī m. Perseus, the Greek hero who decapitated
   Medusa

perstō, perstāre, perstitī, perstātum stand firm, stand around

persuādeō, persuādēre, persuāsī, persuāsum (+ dat.)
   persuade [33]

perterritus, -a, -um very frightened, terrified [21]

pertimescō, pertimescere, pertimuī become very scared

pertineō, pertinēre, pertinuī belong to

perturbātus, -a, -um disturbed, confused, very frightened

perturbō (1) **disturb, trouble greatly [26]**

pervehō, pervehere, pervexī, pervectum carry, bear

perveniō, pervenīre, pervēnī, perventum arrive at, reach [21]

pervigilō (1) be awake all night, "to be up all night"

pēs, pedis m. **foot [28]**

pessimus, -a, -um worst [20]

petītiō, -ōnis f. **candidacy, petition; lawsuit [37]**

petō, petere, petīvī/petiī, petītum seek; look for; attack;
   run for political office [21]

philosophia, -ae f. philosophy
philosophus, -ī m. philosospher
Pholus, -ī m. Pholus the centaur
pictor, -ōris m. painter, professional artist paid to write (political) graffiti on public wall
pictūra, -ae f. picture
Pieridēs, -um f. pl. the inhabitants of Pieria, i.e., the Muses
pietās, -ātis f. reverence, respect
piger, pigra, pigrum low, sluggish, lazy
piget imp. it displeases
pigmentum, -ī n. color, pigment
pila, -ae f. ball
pilleus, -eī m. felt cap worn by a freed slave
pingō, pingere, pinxī, pictum paint
pīpiō (1) chirp
pīrāta, -ae m. pirate
piscātor, -ōris m. fisherman
piscīna, -ae f. fishpond
piscis, -is m. fish [26]
pistor, -ōris m. miller
pistrīnum, -ī n. mill
pius, -a, -um pious, devout
placenta, -ae f. a flat cake (Roman cakes looked more like pancakes)
placeō, placēre, placuī, placitum (+ dat.) be pleasing to; esp. placet (+ inf.) imp. it is pleasing [12]
placidus, -a, -um calm, peaceful
plānē clearly
planta, -ae f. sole of the foot
plānus, -a, -um plane, flat; even; obvious [34]
Platō, -ōnis m. Plato, a Greek philosopher
plaudō, plaudere, plausī, plausum clap, applaud [26]
plaustrum, -ī n. cart, wagon
plausus, -ūs m. applause, recipient of applause
plēbēius, -a, -um plebian, pertaining to the common people
plēnus, -a, -um (+ abl.) full, full of [22]
plōrō (1) weep, cry
Plōtia, -ae f. Plotia, Valeria's mother
pluō, pluere, plūvī to rain; *pluit* imp. it is raining
plūrēs, plūra more (in number) [19]
plūrimus, -a, -um most [20]
plūs more (in amount) [19]
pōculum, -ī n. cup
poena, -ae f. punishment, penalty
poēta, -ae m. poet [14]
poliō, polīre, polīvī, polītum polish
polliceor, pollicērī, pollicitus sum promise [24]
Polliō, -ōnis m. Pollio, a wealthy patron of Vergil and advisor of Augustus
Pollux, -ūcis m. Pollux, divine twin brother of Castor, one of the Gemini
Polydectēs, -ae m. Polydectes, king of the island of Seriphus

pōmerium, -iī n. open space surrounding the walls of a Roman town
pompa, -ae f. ceremonial procession
Pompēiānus, -a, -um Pompeian
Pompēiī, -ōrum m. pl. Pompeii, city in Campania destroyed by eruption of Mt. Vesuvius in 79 A.D.
pōmum, -ī n. fruit, apple
pōne behind; (+ acc.) behind
pōnō, pōnere, posuī, positum put, place [4]
pontifex, -icis m. priest
populus, -ī m. people [4]
porrō and besides, further
porrus, -ī m. leek
porta, -ae f. door, gate [23]
portitor, -ōris m. ferryman
portō (1) carry [8]
portus, -ūs m. gate
poscō, poscere, poposcī ask for, demand, request [5]
possum, posse, potuī be able, can [7]
post (+ acc.) after, behind [5]
posteā afterward, then [30]
posterus, -a, -um following, next
postis, -is f. doorpost
postquam after, since [21]
postrēmō at last, finally
postrīdiē the next day [35]
postulō (1) ask for, beg, demand, require, request [33]
potens, potentis powerful [15]
potestās, -ātis f. power, authority
potior, potīrī, potītus sum (+ abl. or gen.) take possession of, get, acquire [24]
pōtō (1) drink [31]
pōtus, -ūs m. (a) drink [29]
praecipiō, praecipere, praecēpī, praeceptum order
praecipuus, -a, -um special, particular [27]
praeclārus, -a, -um very clear, famous, noble, excellent, beautiful [16]
praecox, praecocis naïve, premature
praefectus, -ī m. director, supervisor
praefica, -ae f. hired female mourner
praegredior, praegredī, praegressus sum go before, precede
praemium, -iī n. plunder; prize; reward; (pl.) discharge benefits [39]
Praeneste, -is n. Praeneste, a town in Latium
Praenestīnus, -a, -um of Praeneste, a town in in Latium
praeparō (1) prepare
praesentiō, praesentīre, praesensī, praesensum to perceive beforeheand
praesertim especially, particularly [25]
praeses, -idis m. guardian, warden
praesideō, praesidēre, praesēdī preside (over)

praestō, praestāre, praestitī, praestātum (+ dat.) be superior to; stand out from; surpass [10]

praeter (+ acc.) along, beyond; except [8]

praestereā besides, moreover [34]

praetereō, praeterīre, praeterīvī/praterīī, praeteritum go past; escape notice of; neglect [35]

praetextus, -a, -um bordered; *toga praetexta* a toga with a purple border

praetor, -ōris m. judge, praetor [35]

praetōriānus, -ī m. a man who has been praetor but has not yet become consul

praetrepidō (1) be nervous in ancitipation

praetūra, -ae f. praetorship, judgeship [36]

prandium, -ī n. noon meal, luncheon

prasinus, -a, -um green

precor, precārī, precātus sum pray

prehendō, prehendere, prehendī, prehensum take hold of, seize

prēlum, -ī n. wine- or oil-press

pretiōsus, -a, -um valuable, expensive

pretium, -iī m. price

prex, prēcis f. prayer

prīdiē on the day before [35]

prīmigenius, -a, -um original

prīmō at first [32]

prīmum first, at first [28]

prīmus, -a, -um first [18], *prīmum digitum* fingertip

princeps, -cipis m. head, leader, chief; title of Augustus and his imperial successors

prior, prius former [19]

priscus, -a, -um old, ancient

prius formerly, before, in the past

priusquam before [19]

prīvātus, -a, -um private (citizen)

prīvō (1), to deprive of

prīvignus, -ī m. stepson

prō (+ abl.) before, in front of, for, instead of [6]

proavus, -ī m. great-grandfather, remote ancestor

probus, -a, -um good, honest [30]

procax, procācis pushy, undisciplined

prōcēdō, prōcēdere, prōcessī, prōcessum proceed, advance [10]

prōcreō (1) procreate, create

procul far, far away, from far away [36]

prōcūrātor, -ōris m. administrator, procurator

prōdigus, -a, -um wasteful, extravagant

proelium, -iī n. battle [34]

profectō without question, undoubtedly [32]

professor, -ōris m. professor

proficiscor, proficiscī, profectus sum set out, depart [28]

prōgeniēs, -ēī f. family, children, progeny

prōgredior, prōgredī, prōgressus sum go to, advance, march forward, proceed [24]

prohibeō, prohibēre, prohibuī, prohibitum keep off; prevent; restrain; forbid [39]

prōiciō, prōicere, prōiēcī, prōiectum throw down

prōmittō, prōmittere, prōmīsī, prōmissum send forth; promise [34]

promptus, -a, -um ready

pronepōs, -ōtis m. great-grandson

proneptis, -is f. great-granddaughter

prōnuba, -ae f. matron-of-honor

prōnuntiō (1) proclaim, announce, say, recite, report

propāgō (1) increase, enlarge

prope (+ acc.) near [5]

prōpellō, prōpellere, prōpulī, prōpulsum drive, push forward

properō (1) hasten

Propertius, -iī m. Propertius, a Roman elegiac poet of the 1st century A.D.

propinquus, -a, -um neighboring, nearby

propitius, -a, -um favorable, propitious

proprius, -a, -um one's own, personal, unique

propter (+ acc.) on account of [9]

prōra, -ae f. prow

prorsus straight ahead; forward

proscaenium, -iī n. stage

prōsequor, prōsequī, prōsecūtus sum accompany, follow

prospectus, -ūs m. view

prōsum, prōdesse, prōfuī (+ dat.) benefit, profit, be useful to

prōtegō, prōtegere, prōtexī, prōtectum cover, protect

prōvincia, -ae f. province

prōvocō (1) challenge

proximus, -a, -um nearest, next [30]

prūdens, prūdentis foreseeing, prudent

prūnum, -ī n. plum

pūblicus, -a, -um public, common [30]

pudeō, pudēre, puduī, puditum be ashamed; *mē pudet* I am ashamed

pudor, -ōris m. shame, modesty, decency

puella, -ae f. girl [6]

puellāris, puellāre pertaining to a girl

puer, puerī m. boy [6]

pugna, -ae f. fight [22]

pugnō (1) fight [12]

pugnus, -ī m. fist

pulcher, pulchra, pulchrum pretty, handsome [13]

pullus, -a, -um dingy, somber; *toga pulla* a dark gray toga worn in mourning

pulsō (1) strike, beat; push, drive [23]; "strike the ground with feet," i.e., dance

pulvīnar, -āris m. cushioned couch (used for a religious statue)

pūmiliō, -ōnis m./f. dwarf

pūpa, -ae f. doll, girl

puppis, puppis f. stern (of a ship)

purgō (1) clean, cleanse [22]

pūrus, -a, -um pure, plain, without an iron tip

puteus, puteī m. well, pit

Puticulī, -ōrum m.pl. a nickname for a burial area outside the Esquiline hill

putō (1) think

Pȳthia, -ae f. Pythia, oracular priestess of Apollo at Delphi

Q

quā dē causā? **for what reason? why? [34]**

quā where, in so far as

quadrāgēsimus, -a, -um fortieth

quadrātus, -a, -um square

quadrīga, -ae f. pl. chariot with four horses

quaerō, quaerere, quaesivī/quaesiī, quaesītum **ask [18]**

quaestiō, -ōnis f. question

quaestūra, -ae **f. quaestorship [36]**

quālis, quāle? **what kind of? what sort of? [34];** see also *tālis*

quam **how! [13]**

quam **than [10]**

quamdiū for how long

quamquam **although, yet [27]**

quamvīs although

quandō **when [29]**

Quantī constat? How much does it cost?

quantus, -a, -um **how much, how many [10]**

quārē **for, because [30];** interr. in what way? how?; whereby; wherefore, why

quartus, -a, -um **fourth [38]**

quasi **as if, practically [37]**

quater **four times [36]**

quatiō, -ere, quassī, quassum shake, wave about

quattuor **four [10]**

-que **and;** *-que . . . -que* **both . . .** *and* **[4]**

queror, querī, questus sum complain

quī, quae, quod **who, which [18]**

quia **since, because [18]**

quid **what? [1]**

Quid agis? **How are you? How are you doing? [4]**

Quid fit? What is going on? What's happening?

Quid plūra? Why say more?

quīdam, quaedam, quoddam **certain (indefinite, as in "a certain person") [21]**

quidem certainly

quiēs, -ētis f. quiet, calm, rest, peace

quiescō, quiescere, quiēvī, quiētum **rest [14]**

quiētus, -a, -um **calm, quiet [25]**

quīlibet, quaelibet, quidlibet/quodlibet whoever, whatever

quīn **that not (with subj. "from X'ing"); indeed; why not? [39]**

Quinctilius, -iī m. Quinctilius, a male name

quindecim fifteen

quinquāgintā fifty

quinque **five [10]**

quintum for the fifth time

quintus, -a, -um fifth

Quirīnālis, -e Quirinal, pertaining to one of the seven hills of Rome

Quirīs, -ītis m. archaic form of *civis* citizen

quis = aliquis after *sī*

quis, quid **who? what? [6]**

quisque, quaeque, quodque/quicque/quidque **each, every [21]**

quisquis, quodquod/quicquid/quidquid **whoever, whatever [40]**

quīvīs, quaevīs, quidvīs anyone, anything

quō? where?

quod **because [3]**

quōmodo **how [17]**

quoque **also [8]**

quot? **indecl. how many? [34]**

quōusque how long

R

rādō, radere, rāsī, rasum scrape, scratch, shave, erase

rāmus, -ī m. branch

rapiō, rapere, rapuī, raptum **snatch, seize [20]**

rārō rarely, seldom

rārus, -a, -um **rare; thin [27]**

rāsilis, rāsile smooth, well-polished

ratiō, -ōnis f. account, transaction; *ratiōnem habēre* "to have a sense of"

recēdō, recēdere, recessī, recessum retire, withdraw

recens, recentis **recent [39]**

recenter **recently [37]**

recipiō, recipere, recēpī, receptum **accept, receive, take back;** *se recipere* **retreat (take oneself somewhere) [31]**

recordor, recordārī, recordātus sum remember

recreō (1) relax, restore

rectē straightly, correctly

rectus, -a, -um straight, correct

recumbō, recumbere, recubuī lie down, recline

reddō, reddere, reddidī, reditum give back

redeō, redīre, redīvī/rediī, reditum **come back, go back, return [21]**

redigō, redigere, redēgī, redactum drive back, restore

reditus, -ūs m. return

referō, referre, rettulī, relātum **carry, carry back, bring back [39]**

refrīgerō (1) make cool

refugiō, refugere, refūgī run away

rēgia, -ae f. palace

rēgīna, -ae f. queen

regiō, -ōnis f. region, district [21]

regnō (1) reign, hold power over

regnum, -ī n. kingdom [36]

regō, regere, rexī, rectum rule, govern [39]

regredior, regredī, regressus sum return

rēiciō, rēicere, rēiēcī, rēiectum throw

religiōsissimē most piously

religiōsus, -a, -um pious, devout

relinquō, relinquere, relīquī, relictum leave, leave behind [21]

reliquus, -a, -um remaining [21]

remaneō, remanēre, remansī remain, stay behind [40]

remittō, remittere, remīsī, remissum send back

removeō, removēre, removī, remōtum move back; remove [32]

repellō, repellere, reppulī, repulsum push back, repel, repulse [39]

repetō, repetere, repetīvī/repetiī, repetītum repeat

repleō, replēre, replēvī, replētum fill up, fill again

reportō (1) bring home

repōtia, -ōrum n. pl. celebration on the day following a festivity like a marriage

repugnō (1) fight back; resist

requiescō, requiesere, requiēvī, requiētum rest

requīrō, requīrere, requīsīvī/requīsiī, requīsītum seek, look for, search for

rēs gestae f. pl. deeds

rēs pūblica, reī pūblicae f. republic

rēs, reī f. thing, matter; business, affair; reason [24]

resideō, residēre, resēdī sit, remain in a place

respiciō, respicere, respexī, respectum take notice of, read (omens)

respīrō (1) breathe

respondeō, respondēre, respondī, responsum (+ dat.) reply, answer [3]

restituō, restituere, restituī, restitūtum replace, restore; give back [39]

restitūtus, -a, -um restored

rēte, rētis n. net

rētiārius, -iī m. gladiatorial fighter with a net

retineō, retinēre, retinuī, retentum hold fast, retain; cling to [37]

reveniō, revenīre, revēnī, reventum come back, return [31]

revertō, revertere, revertī come back, turn back, return; also *revertor, revertī, reversus sum* turn back, return

revocō (1) call back

rex, rēgis m. king [14]

rhētor, rhētoris teacher of rhetoric (public speaking) [16]

rhētorica, -ae f. rhetoric

rhētoricus, -a, -um rhetorical [16]

rīdeō, rīdere, rīsī, rīsum laugh [7]

rīdiculōsus, -a, -um laughable, riduculous

rigor, rigōris m. straight line; *Rigor Valī Aelī* Hadrian's Wall in Britain

rixa, -ae f. (loud) quarrel, violent quarrel, brawl

rōbustus, -a, -um strong

rogō (1) ask (for) [10]

Rōma, -ae f. Rome [11]

Rōmānus, -a, -um Roman [11]

Rōmulus, -a, -um of Romulus (the founder of Rome); Roman

rostra, -ōrum n. pl. speaker's platform

rostrum, -ī n. beak

rota, -ae f. wheel

ruber, rubra, rubrum red

Rūfus, -ī m. Rufus ("Red")

rumpō, rumpere, rūpī, ruptum break, burst, break down [28]

ruō, ruere, ruī rush, rush at; fall to ruin [22]

rursus again [16]

rūs, rūris n. country, country estate; abroad [36]; *rurī* "in the country" (note the lack of a prep.)

russātus, -a, -um red

rusticus, -a, -um rural, rustic

S

S.D. = salūtem dīcit

Sabīnus, -a, -um Sabine, pertaining to the Sabines, neighbors of Rome

saccus, -ī m. wallet, bag sack, pocket book [11]

sacer, sacra, sacrum sacred, holy

sacrāmentum, -ī n. oath, sacred obligation (especially one sworn by soldiers)

sacrificō (1) sacrifice

saeculum, -ī n. age, era

saepe often [6]

saevus, -a, -um raging, violent, savage, cruel, furious

sagax, sagācis wise, sharp

sagitta, -ae f. arrow [28]

sāl, salis m./n. salt

Saliāris, -e of the Salii (priests of Mars, god of war)

saliō, salīre, saliī/saluī, saltum leap, jump [11]

saltātor, -ōris m. dancer

saltem at least

salūs, -ūtis f. health, safety [32]

salūtātiō, -ōnis f. greeting, formal morning visit by a client to a patron [31]

salūtō (1) greet, say "Salvē!" [4]

Salvē/Salvēte! Hello. Hi. Be well! [3]

salvus, -a, -um safe, well [25]

sanguis, sanguinis m. blood [22]

sānitās, -ātis f. health, sanity

sānō (1) restore to health
sānus, -a, -um **healthy [25]**
sapiō, sapere, sapīvī/sapiī show good sense
satis **enough, sufficient [30]**
satura, -ae f. satire
scālae, -ārum f. pl. stairs, staircase
scalpō, scalpere, scalpsī, scalptum scratch
scelerātus, -a, -um wicked
scelus, -eris **n. crime [20]**
sciō, scīre, scīvī/sciī, scītum **know, know about [28]**
Scorpus, -ī m. Scorpus, a male name
scrība, -ae m. scribe, secretary
scrībō, scrībere, scripsī, scriptum **write [6]**
scriptor, -ōris m. writer [27]
scrūta, -ōrum n. pl. trash
scutum, -ī n. shield
Scybalē, -ēs f. Scybale, a female name
schola, -ae f. school, leisure
sē (see *suī*)
secō, secāre, secuī, sectum cut, cut off, cut up
secundus, -a, -um second; favorable
Secundus, -ī m. Secundus, a male name
sed **but [3]**
sēdecim **sixteen [8]**
sedeō, sedēre, sēdī, sessum **sit [5]**
sēdēs, -is f. seat, home, residence [14]
sēligō, sēligere, sēlēgī, sēlectum select, choose
sella, -ae f. chair [25]
semel once
semper **always [3]**
senātor, -ōris m. senator, member of the senate [29]
senātus, -ūs m. senate [29]
senectūs, -ūtis f. old age
senex, senis m. old man [29]
senex, senis old, aged
sensus, -ūs feeling
sententia, -ae f. proverb, saying
sentiō, sentīre, sensī, sensum **feel, hear, see, sense,**
  perceive [21]
sepeliō, sepelīre, sepelīvī/sepeliī, sepultum bury
septimum for the seventh time
septuāgintā indecl. seventy
sepulcrum, -ī n. tomb
sepultūra, -ae f. burial, grave
sequor, sequī, secūtus sum **follow [24]**
serēnitās, -ātis f. cheerful tranquility
sērius **later, too late, rather late [17]**
sermō, -ōnis m. speech, talk
sermōcinor, sermōcinārī, sermōcinātus sum **converse,**
  talk, chat [31]
sērō late, too late
serpens, serpentis f. snake, serpent

servātor, -ōris n. savior
Servīlia, -ae f. Servilia, daughter of Servilius
Servīliānus, -a, -um Servilian, of the Servilii
Servīlius, -iī m. Servilius, head of the *Servīliī*
serviō, servīre, servīvī/serviī, servītum serve, be a slave to
servitūs, -ūtis f. slavery, servitude
servō (1) **save, protect; observe, pay attention to [27]**
servus, -ī m. **slave, servant [7]**
Sevērus, -ī m. Severus, a male name
sex **six [10]**
sextus, -a, -um **sixth [37]**
Sextus, -ī m. Sextus, a male *praenōmen*
sī **if [7]**
sī placet **Please! lit., "if it pleases" [7]**
sī vōbīs placeat Please!
sīc **so, thus, in this way; yes [11]**
siccus, -a, -um dry
Sicō, Sicōnis m. Sico, a male name
sīcut **just as, like [7]**
significō (1) **mean [40]**
signō (1) mark, seal, stamp
signum, -ī n. **mark, token, sign, seal [38]**
silenter silently
silentium, -iī n. **stillness, silence, tranquility [23];**
  silentium tenēre to keep silent
silescō, silescere, silescuī grow quiet
silva, -ae f. **woods, forest [21]**
sīmia, -ae m./f. **monkey [5]**
similis, simile **similar, like to [37]**
simplex, simplicis simple, naïve
simul atque also **simul ac** **as soon as [21]**
simul **together, altogether, at the same time,**
  all at once [24]
Sinae, -ārum f. pl. China
sināpis, -is f. mustard
sine (+ abl.) **without [6]**
singulāris, singulāre single
singulātim one by one
singulī, -ae, -a individual, one to each (in a group);
  one by one; *singulō* one by one
sinister, -tra, -trum **left; sinistra (manus), -ae** f. **the left**
  hand [38]
sinō, sinere, sīvī/siī, situm **allow, permit [33]**
sīnus, -ūs m. lap; gulf
sīp(h)ō, -ōnis m. siphon, water hose
sistō, sistere, stetī/stitī, statum **stand still [8]**
sitiens, sitientis thirsty
sitiō, sitīre **be thirsty [31]**
sitis, -is f. thirst
situs, -a, -um located, buried
sīve or
soccus, -ī m. loose-fitting slipper

socer, soceris m. father-in-law

socius, -iī m. partner, companion [36]

Sōcratēs, -is m. 5th century B.C. Athenian philosopher

socrus, -ūs f. mother-in-law

sodālis, -is m. companion

sōl, sōlis m. sun; day [33]

sōlāciolum, -ī n. relief, comfort

sōlārium, -iī n. sundial

soleō, solēre, solitus sum be accustomed (to) [29]

solidum, -ī n. something firm, solid; "a substantial sum"

sollicitus, -a, -um uneasy, apprehensive, nervous, anxious that/lest [39]

sōlum only [3]

solum, -ī n. earth, soil

sōlus, -a, -um only, alone [6]

solvō, solvere, solvī, solūtum loosen, unbind; fulfil, perform; pay, deliver; *nāvem solvō* set sail [36]

sollicitō (1) upset, shake up

sollicitus, -a, -um uneasy, apprehensive, nervous, anxious that/lest

somniculōsus, -a, -um sleepy

somnus, -ī, m. sleep, rest; laziness

sonitus, -ūs m. sound [24]

sonus, -ī m. sound [6]

sordidus, -a, -um filthy [28]

soror, sorōris f. sister [13]

spargō, spargere, sparsī, sparsum spread, scatter, sprinkle

spatiōsus, -a, -um wide

spatium, -iī n. space [28]

speciālis, speciāle individual, particular, special

speciēs, -ēī f. appearance, look, type [24]

spectāculum, -ī n. sight, spectacle, game

spectātor, -ōris m. spectator, observer [24]

spectō (1) look at, watch [10]

speculum, -ī n. mirror [30]

spēlunca, -ae f. cave

spernō, spernere, sprēvī, sprētum reject, scorn, disregard

spērō (1) hope, hope for, look forward to [9]

spēs, speī f. hope, expectation [33]

spīna, -ae f. thorn; spine; center barrier of the circus

spiritus, -ūs m. soul

spīrō (1) breathe [32]

splendidus, -a, -um bright, shining, illustrious, splendid, shiny

spolium, -iī n. spoils (of war); *spolia opīma* spoils taken by one general from another in single combat

sponsa, -ae f. a woman engaged to be married

sponsiō, -ōnis f. bet, wager; *sponsiōnem facere* to make a bet

sportula, -ae f. little basket; gift of money or food from patron to client

squālidus, -a, -um dirty, filthy

squālor, squālōris m. filth

st shh! shush!

stabulum, -ī n. stable

stāmen, stāminis m. thread

statim immediately [20]

statūra, -ae f. stature

status, -ūs m. condition, position

stercus, -oris n. dung, excrement

sternō, sternere, strāvī, strātum spread out

stertō, stertere, stertuī snore

stilus, -ī m. stilus, pen

stīpendium, -iī n. tax, contribution, pay

stō, stāre, stetī, statum stand [5]

strangulō (1) choke, strangle

strēnuē actively, vigorously [26]

strēnuus, -a, -um active, vigorous, hard, strenuous

strepitus, -ūs m. noise

struō, struere, struxī, structum build, construct

studeō, studēre, studuī (+ dat.) devote one's self to, be eager for, study [12]

studiōsus, -a, -um (+ gen.) eager (to), devoted (to)

studium, -iī n. study, eagerness, zeal [6]

stultus, -a, -um stupid

stuprum, -ī n. dishonor, shame

Stygius, -a, -um Stygian, pertaining to the River Styx in the Underworld

Stymphālus, -ī m. Stymphalus, a Greek lake and town of the same name

Styx, Stygis f. river Styx, river bordering the Underworld

suāsōria, -ae f. persuasive speech

suāvis, suāve pleasant, agreeable, delightful

sub (+ abl.) under, from under; (+ acc.) under [6]

sūbiciō, sūbicere, sūbiēcī, sūbiectum throw from beneath, put under foot.

subitō suddenly [11]

sublevō (1) lift, raise, support, lighten, alleviate

submissus, -a, -um low (voice)

submittō, submittere, submīsī, submissum raise, rear; let grow; make subject to; *sē submittere* (+ dat.) to lower oneself to

subsīdō, subsīdere, subsēdī crouch

Subūra, -ae f. Subura, a neighborhood in Rome

succēdō, succēdere, successī, successum go below, go under; come to; succeed (to) [37]

sūdo (1) sweat, perspire

suffrāgātiō, -ōnis f. public espression of support

suī, sibi, sē, sē himself, herself, itself, themselves [21]

sum, esse, fuī be [2]

summittō, summittere, summīsī, summissum (with *sē* + dat.) lower oneself to

summus, -a, -um highest, greatest [20]

sumptuōsus, -a, -um expensive, costly

sunt (they) are [2]

super above; (+ acc. or abl.) over, on top of [10]

super left over

superbus, -a, -um proud, haughty [40]

superēmineō, superēminēre, stand out over

superficiēs, -ēī f. surface

superior, superius higher [19]

superō (1) surpass, conquer

supersum, superesse, superfuī be left over; survive; have strength (for) [35]

superus, -a, -um "above"; *in superōs (locōs)* = in heaven

suppetō, suppetere, suppetīvī/suppetiī, suppetītum be available for

suprā (+ acc.) over, above [32]

suprēmus, -a, -um highest, final [20]

surdus, -a, -um deaf

surgō, surgere, surrexī, surrectum get up, rise up [32]

sūs, suis m./f. pig, sow

suscipiō, suscipere, suscēpī, susceptum accept

suspendō, suspendere, suspendī, suspensum hang

suspīrium, -iī n. sigh, heartthrob

suspīrō (1) sigh

sustineō, sustinēre, sustinuī, sustentum hold up, support, withstand [37]

susurrō (1) whisper

suōpte = stronger form of *suō*

sūtor, -ōris m. cobbler, shoemaker

suus, -a, -um his/her/its/their own [9]

Syria, -ae f. Roman province located approximately where modern Syria is today

T

T. = *Titus*

taberna, -ae f. (snack) shop [2]

tabula, -ae f. counter, slate, tablet

tabulārium, -iī n. office

taceō, tacēre, tacuī, tacitum be quiet, be silent [13]

tacitus, -a, -um silent, secret

taeda, -ae f. pine-torch

taediōsus, -a, -um boring

taedit, taedēre, taesum est (+ gen.) or (+ inf.) imp. be tired (of), be sick (of)

taedium, -iī n. boredom, weariness; object of weariness, boring thing; *taedium habēre* to be bored

Talassiō, -ōnis m. Talasio! an ancient wedding cry

tālis, tāle such, of such a kind, of such a sort [21]; *tālis, -e . . . quālis, -e* of such a sort . . . as

tam so, so much (as) [11]

tamen nevertheless [20]

tamquam just as, just like

tandem at last, at length, finally [20]

tangō, tangere, tetigī, tactum touch; reach; affect; move; mention [32]

tantum so much, to such a degree

tantus, -a, -um so great, so much [28]

tardus, -a, -um late [39]

taurus, -ī m. bull

tectum, -ī n. roof, house

tegō, tegere, texī, tectum to protect, hide, conceal, cover

tēla, -ae f. loom, web

tellūs, tellūris f. earth, ground, land

tempestās, -ātis f. time, weather, season, storm [36]

tempestīvē on time

tempestīvus, -a, -um opportune, seasonable, timely

templum, -ī n. temple

temptō (1) feel; try; test [32]

tempus, -oris n. time, season [13]; forehead

teneō, tenēre, tenuī, tentum hold [6]

tener, -era, -erum soft, delicate

tenuis, tenue thin

tepidārium, -iī n. warm bath

tepor, -ōris m. warmth, heat

ter three times [36]

tergum, -ī n. back; *ā tergō* behind

terminō (1) conclude, end

terra, -ae f. land [8]

terreō, terrēre, terruī, territum frighten, terrify

terribilis, -e frightening, terrible [27]

terrificus, -a, -um terrifying

territus, -a, -um afraid, scared [14]

tertius, -a, -um third [38]

tessellātus, -a, -um mosaic

testor, testārī, testātus sum bear witness to, testify to

theātrum, -ī n. theater

Thēbae, Thēbārum f. pl. Thebes, a city in Greece

thermae, -ārum f. pl. public baths

Thracia, -ae f. Thrace, a Roman province located in what is now part of Greece, Bulgaria, and Turkey

Thrax, Thrācis m. Thracian; a gladiator with lighter armor, including a helmet and greaves on both legs

Tiberis, -is m. Tiber, the river running through Rome

Tiberius, -iī m. Tiberius, Augustus' stepson, adopted son, and successor

tibi your, to you [1]

tībīcen, -inis m. piper

timeō, timēre, timuī fear, be afraid [10]

timidē timidly

timidus, -a, -um afraid, timid

timor, timōris m. fear; object of fear

tintinnō (1) ring

Tīrō a male name, especially the slave and trusted scribe of Cicero

tīrō, -ōnis m. recruit

Tīryns, -nthos f. acc. *Tīryntha* f. a Greek city in the Argolid

Titus, -ī m. Titus, a male name

toga, -ae f. toga [33]

togātus, -a, -um dressed in a toga [33]

tolerō (1) bear, endure

tollō, tollere, sustulī, sublātum lift, raise [11]

tonō (1) thunder, make to resound

tonsor, -ōris m. barber

torpeō, torpēre, torpuī grow numb

torreō, torrēre, torruī, tostum bake

tortus, -a, -um twisted, crooked

torus, ī m. marriage bed

tot (indecl. adj.) so many [40]

tōtus, -a, -um whole, all, entire [17]

tractō (1) treat, handle

trādō, trādere, trādidī, trāditum hand down, entrust, deliver [33]

tragicomoedia, -ae f. tragicomedy

tragoedia, -ae f. tragedy

trahō, trahere, traxī, tractum drag, haul, draw, remove [22]

tranquillitās, -ātis f. calmness, stillness; fair weather [31]

tranquillus, -a, -um calm, still, peaceful [31]

trans (+ acc.) across [5]

transeō, transīre, transīvī/transiī, transitum go over, go across [32]

transfigō, transfigere, transfixī, transfixum pierce through

transportō (1) carry (across), convey, transport [27]

trecentī, -ae, -a three hundred

tremō, tremere, tremuī tremble [34]

tremulus, -a, um trembling

trepidus, -a, -um nervous, anxious

trēs, tria three [6]

tribūnicius, -a, -um m. belonging to a tribune

tribūnus, -ī m. tribune; *tribūnus militum* military tribune

tribūtim by tribes

trīclīnium, -iī n. triclinium, dining room [26]

tridens, tridentis m. trident

triennium, -iī n. a three-year period

trietēris, -idis f. triennial, unit of three years

trīgintā thirty

tristis, triste sad [15]

tristitia, -ae f. sadness

triumphālis, triumphāle triumphal

triumphātor, -ōris m. one who celebrates a triumph

triumphō (1) triumph, celebrate a triumph

triumphus, -ī m. triumph, triumphal procession, military triumph

trivium, triv(i)ī n. an intersection, a place where three roads meet

Trōia, -ae f. Troy, city in the Roman province of Asia (modern Turkey)

tropaeum, tropaeī m. trophy, victory monument

tū [3], tuī, tibi, tē, tē you (sing.) yourself [21]

tuba, -ae f. horn, trumpet [35]

tubicen, tubicenis m. trumpeter

tueor, tuērī, tuitus sum look at, watch over, look after, protect [29]

Tulliānum, -ī n. Tullianum, the state prison in Rome

tum then [20]

tumeō, tumēre swell

tumultus, -ī m. uproar, disturbance

tunc then [3]

tunica, -ae f. tunic

turba, -ae f. disorder, confusion; crowd [35]

turbō (1) disturb, disorder

turbō, turbinis m. whirlwind

turpis, turpe ugly, foul, loathsome [38]

Tuscus, -a, -um Etruscan

tūtus, -a, -um safe [14]

tuus, -a, -um your (sing.) [6]

Tyrius, -a, -um from Tyre; purple

Tyrus, -ī f. Tyre, city in Roman province of Syria (modern Lebanon)

U

ubi where; when [5]

ubīque everywhere

ūdus, -a, -um wet

Ulixēs, -is or *-ēī* m. Ulysses, the hero of Homer's *Odyssey*, known in Greek as Odysseus

ūllus, -a, -um any [17]

ulna, -ae f. yard (unit of measurement)

ulula, -ae f. screech owl

ululō (1) wail, weep

umbilīcus, -ī m. navel, belly button, center, umbilical cord

umbra, -ae f. shade, soul

umerus, -ī m. shoulder

umquam at any time, ever [28]

unda, -ae f. wave

unde from where

unguentārius, -iī m. perfume seller

ūnicus, -a, -um one and only, sole

ūnus, -a, -um one [7]

urbānus, -a, -um polished, refined; witty; of the city

urbs, -is f. city, esp. the city of Rome [20]

ūrīna, -ae f. urine

urna, -ae f. large water jar

ūrō, ūrere, ussī, ustum burn

usque as far as

ut in order that, so that; how; as; when [31]

uterus, -ī m. womb, belly

utilis, utile useful [30]

utinam if only! would that! [37]

ūtor, ūtī, ūsus sum (+ abl.) use, employ, enjoy, experience [24]

utrum whether

ūva, -ae f. grape; *ūva passa* dried grape, raisin

uxor, -ōris f. wife [18]

V

vādō, vādere go, advance, proceed

vae (often + dat.) woe! (in pain or dread) [36]

vāgītus, -ūs m. cry, wail

vagor, vagārī, vagātus sum wander

vah/vaha ah! oh! (in astonishment, joy, anger)

val(l)um, val(l)ī n. a line of palisades

valdē very (much), a lot [11]

valeō, valēre, valuī be strong, be well; *Valē/Valēte!* Farewell. Good-bye. Be well! [2, 3]

Valeria, -ae f. Valeria, owner of the snack shop

vāpulō (1) be beaten

varius, -a, -um various, changeable, mixed [30]

vastō (1) plunder, lay waste

vastus, -a, -um huge

Vatia, -ae f. Vatia, a Roman *nōmen*

Vaticānus, -ī m. Vatican, a hill on the right bank of the Tiber in Rome

vehemens, -entis violent, strong, intense, vehement

Vēiī, Vēiōrum m. pl. Veii, a very old Etruscan city north of Rome

vēlōciter quickly

velut just as, just like

vēnātiō, -ōnis f. hunt

vēnātor, -ōris m. hunter [29]

venditiō, -ōnis f. sale

venditor, -ōris m. merchant

vendō, vendere, vendidī, venditum sell [30]

venēnātus, -a, -um poisonous

venēnum, -ī n. poison

venetus, -a, -um blue

veniō, venīre, vēnī, ventum come [2]

venter, -tris m. belly, abdomen, womb

ventus, -ī m. wind [36]

Venus, -eris f. Venus, goddess of love

venustus, -a, -um charming, attractive

vēr, vēris n. springtime

verber, verberis n. lash, blow

verberō (1) assail, flog, batter, lash, scourge, beat

verbum, -ī n. word [11]

vērē truly [15]

verēcundus, -a, -um modest

vereor, verērī, veritus sum be afraid of, fear, show reverence to [24]

Vergilius, -iī m. Vergil, the poet

vēritās, -ātis f. truth

vērō indeed, in truth, truly

Vērōna, -ae f. Verona, a town in northern Italy

Vērōnensis, -ense Veronan, from Verona

verrō, verrere, versum sweep clean

versō (1) keep turning around, spin, whirl

versor, versārī come and go, frequent

versus, -ūs m. verse, line of poetry [27]

vertō, vertere, vertī, versum turn, overturn [26]

vērus, -a, -um true [15]

vescor, vescī (+ abl.) take food, feed devour

vesper, -eris m. evening

vesperascō, vesperascere, vesperāvī grow towards evening

Vesta, -ae f. Vesta, goddess of the hearth

vester, vestra, vestrum your (pl.) [6]

vestīmentum, -ī n. garment, clothing

vestiō, vestīre, vestīvī/vestiī, vestītum dress, clothe [33]

vestis, -is f. garments, clothing [33]

Vesuvius, -iī m. Vesuvius, volcanic mountain in Campania

vetō, vetāre, vetuī, vetitum forbid, prohibit [33]

vetus, -eris aged, old [39]

vexātus, -a, -um upset

vexillum, -ī n. standard, banner

vexō (1) agitate, harry, upset, disturb

via, -ae f. road, street, way [5]

Vibius, -iī m. Vibius, a male name

vīcennālis, -e made for a period of twenty years, 20th anniversary

vīcīnitās, -ātis f. neighborhood

vīcīnus, -ī m. neighbor

victor, -ōris m. victor, conqueror [35]

victōria, -ae f. victory [35]

victrix, -īcis f. female conquerer

videō, vidēre, vīdī, vīsum see, perceive [3]

videor, vidērī, vīsus sum seem, appear; be seen; *vidētur* (+ inf.) imp. it seems good [27]

vigeō, vigēre, viguī be strong, thrive

vigescō, vigescere become strong

vigil, -is m./f. sentry, guard; firefighter; (pl.) fire brigade [29]

vigilō (1) watch, keep watch; stay awake, stay awake all night; wake up

vīgintī twenty [12]

villa, -ae f. villa, country estate

Vīminālis, Vīmināle Viminal (hill in Rome), pertaining to the Viminal

Vīminālis, -is m. Viminal (hill), one of the seven hills of Rome

vinciō, vincīre, vinxī, vinctum tie up, fetter, bind

vincō, vincere, vīcī, victum conquer [12]
vīnum, -ī n. wine [3]
violentia, -ae f. force, violence
Vipsānius, -iī m. Vipsanius
vir, virī m. man [2]; husband
virga, -ae f. rod
virgō, -inis f. young girl
virītim, man by man, per person
vīs, vis f. strength, power, force; (pl.) *vīrēs, vīrium*
    strength, troops, forces [21]
vīscera, -um n. pl. internal organs, entrails
vīsitō (1) see frequently, visit
vīta, -ae f. life [13]
vitta, -ae f. ribbon
vīvo, vīvere, vīxī, victum live [29]
vīvus, -a, -um alive, living [35]
vix scarcely, hardly [32]
vōbīs dat./abl. you (all) [17]
vōcālis, vōcāle speaking, vocal
vōciferor, vōciferārī, vōciferātus sum yell, cry out
vocō (1) call [8]
Volcānus, -ī m. Vulcan, the god of fire and smiths
volō (1) fly; hasten [36]
volō, velle, voluī want to, be willing to [7]

vōs, vestrum/vestrī, vōbīs, vōs, vōbīs you (pl.);
    yourselves [21]
vōtum, -ī n. vow; votive offering
voveō, vovēre, vōvī, vōtum vow
vox, vōcis f. voice [15]
vulnerō (1) wound [22]
vulnus, -eris n. wound [22]
vult (s)he wants, wishes [5]
vulturīnus, -a, -um of a vulture
vultus, vultūs m. face; also spelled *voltus*
vulva, -ae f. womb

X

Xerxēs, Xerxis m. Xerxes, king of Persia

Z

Zakynthus, -ī f. Zakynthus, an island in
    western Greece
Zephyrus, -ī m. the West Wind, which brings
    mild weather
Zēthus, -ī, m. Zethus ("Westy"), a male name

Verba Discenda
English-Latin Glossary

English-Latin Lexicon: This English-Latin Lexicon is based on the *Verba Discenda* in Chapters 1–40. Numbers in brackets indicate the chapter in which the Latin word becomes a *verbum discendum*. Before you use a word in a Latin sentence, it is a good idea to check its entire meaning in the *Verba Omnia*.

abl. = ablative
acc. = accusative
adj. = adjective
dat. = dative
conj. = conjunction
esp. = especially
f. = feminine
inf. = infinitive

interj. = interjection
interr. = interrogative
m. = masculine
n. = neuter
pl. = plural
prep. = preposition
v. = verb

A

a lot *multum* [16]; *valdē* [11]
about *dē* (+ abl.) [7]
abroad *rūs, rūris* n. [36]
above *suprā* (+ acc.) [32]
abroad *forīs* adv. [34]
accept *recipiō, recipere, recēpī, receptum* [31]
accomplish *conficiō, conficere, confēcī, confectum* [28]; *efficiō, efficere, effēcī, effectum* [32]
acquire *potior, potīrī, potītus sum* (+ abl. or gen.) [24]
across *trans* (+ acc.) [5]
act *agō, agere, ēgī, actum* [4]
actively *strēnuē* [26]
add *addō, addere, addidī, additum* [40]
admire *admīror, admīrārī, admīrātus sum* [26]; *mīror, mīrārī, mīrātus sum* [25]
adorn *ōrnō* (1) [35]
advance *pergō, pergere, perrēxī, perrectum* [37]; *prōcēdō, prōcēdere, prōcessī, prōcessum* [10]; *prōgredior, prōgredī, prōgressus sum* [24]
advice *consilium, -iī* n. [23]
advise *moneō, monēre, monuī, monitum* [33]
affect *moveō, movēre, mōvī, mōtum; tangō, tangere, tetigī, tactum* [32]
affair *rēs, reī* f. [24]
afraid of (be) *metuō, metuere, metuī, metūtum* [39]
afraid *territus, -a, -um* [14]
after (conj.) *postquam* [30]

after (prep.) *post* (+ acc.) [5]
afterwards *posteā* [30]
again *iterum* [4]; *rursus* [16]
against *in* (+ acc.) [5]; *contrā* (+ acc.) [19]
aged *vetus, veteris* [39]
agree *accēdō, accēdere, accessī, accessum* [38]
agreeable *iūcundus, -a, -um* [35]
aid (n.) *auxilium, -iī* n. [25]
aid (v.) *adsum, adesse, adfuī* (+ dat.) [19]
air *āēr, āeris* m. [32]
alas! *ēheu* [16]
alive *vīvus, -a, -um* [35]
all at once *simul* [24]
all right! *age* [38]
all *omnēs, -ia* [15]; *tōtus, -a, -um* [17]
allow *cēdō, cēdere, cessī, cessum* (+ dat.) [35]; *patior, patī, passus sum* [24]; *sinō, sinere, sīvī/siī, situm* [33]
almost *paene* [18]
alone *sōlus, -a, -um* [6]
along *praeter* (+ acc.) [8]
already *iam* [8]
alright *salvus, -a, -um* [16] cf. "correct"
also *et* [4]; *etiam* [17]; *quoque* [8]
altar *āra, -ae* f. [19]
altogether *omnīnō* [32]; *simul* [24]
always *semper* [3]
am *sum* [2]
among *inter* (+ acc.) [5]
amphitheater *amphitheātrum, -ī* n. [17]

From *Disce! An Introductory Latin Course, volume 2*, First Edition. Francesco Bonavita. Copyright © 2011 by Pearson Education, Inc. Published by Pearson Prentice Hall. All rights reserved.

amuse *dēlectō* (1) [38]

ancestor *avus, -ī* m. [29]

ancestors *māiōrēs, māiōrum* m. pl. [15]

ancient *antīquus, -a, -um* [10]

and *ac* [33]; *et* [2]; *atque* [20]; *-que* [4]

and also *atque* [20]; *et* [2]; *etiam* [17]

and besides *ac* [33]

and even *atque* [20]

and not *nec* [15]; *neque* [28]

angry *īrātus, -a, -um* [6]

animal *animal, -ālis* n. [17]

announce *nuntiō* (1) [37]

another *alius, -a, -ud* [9]; another (of two) *alter, altera, alterum* [17]

answer *respondeō, respondēre, respondī, responsum* (+ dat.) [3]

anxious *anxius, -a, -um* [29]

anxious that/lest *sollicitus, -a, -um* [39]

any *ūllus, -a, -um* [17]

apartment block *insula, -ae* f. [9]

appear *crescō, crescere, crēvī, crētum* [32]; *videor, vidērī, vīsus sum* [27]

appearance *faciēs, faciēī* f. [24]; *speciēs, speciēī* f. [24]

applaud *plaudō, plaudere, plausī, plausum* [26]

apprehensive *sollicitus, -a, -um* [39]

approach *accēdō, accēdere, accessī, accessum* [38]; *appropinquō* (1) (+ dat.) [11]

are (they) *sunt* [2]

arena *harēna, -ae* f. [22]

arise *crescō, crescere, crēvī, crētum* [32]

arm (n.) *brāc(c)hium, -iī* n. [14]

arm (v.) *armō* (1) [37]

army *agmen, agminis* n. [40]; *exercitus, -ūs* m. [38]; *legiō, legiōnis* f. [39]

around *circum* (+ acc.) [6]

arrival *adventus, -ūs* m. [39]

arrive at *adveniō, advenīre, advēnī, adventum* [11]; *perveniō, pervenīre, pervēnī, perventum* [21]

arrow *sagitta, -ae* f. [28]

art *ars, artis* f. [16]; *fabrica, -ae* f. [37]

artisan *faber, fabrī* m. [28]

as if *quasī* [37]

as long as *dōnec* [27]; *dum* [10]; *ut* [31]

as soon as *simul ac* [21]; *simul atque* [21]

ascend *ascendō, ascendere, ascendī, ascensum* [24]

ask (for) *poscō, poscere, poposcī* [5]; *rogō* (1) [10]

ask *interrogō* (1) [34]; *quaerō, quaerere, quaesīvī/quaesiī, quaesītum* [18]

asking a question expecting a no answer *num* [5]

asking a question expecting a yes answer *nōnne* [5]

asking a simple question *-ne* [4]

assent *accēdō, accēdere, accessī, accessum* [38]

at *in* (+ abl.) [2, 5]

at _____ 's *apud* (+ acc.) [16]

at first *primō* [32], *prīmum* [28]

at last, *dēmum* [26]; *dēnique* [32]; tandem [20]

at length *aliquandō* [26]; *dēmum* [26]; *tandem* [20]

at the house of *apud* (+ acc.) [16]

at the same time *simul* [24]

atmosphere *āēr, āeris* m. [32]

atrium (public greeting room of a Roman house) *atrium, -iī* n. [33]

attached to *aptus, -a, -um* [31]

attack *accēdō, accēdere, accessī, accessum* [38]; *oppugnō* (1) [39]; *petō, petere, petīvī/petiī, petītum* [21]

auxiliary forces *auxilia, -iōrum* n. pl. [25]

await *exspectō* (1) [16]

awake, awaken *expergiscor, expergiscī, experrectus sum* [32]; *excitō* (1) [32]

away from *ā, ab, abs* (+ abl.) [5]; *dē* (+ abl.) [7]

B

bad *malus, -a, -um* [6]

bag *saccus, -ī* m. [11]

banquet *convīvium, -iī* n. [25]; *epulae, -ārum* f. pl. [26]

battle *proelium, -iī* n. [34]

battle line *agmen, agminis* n. [40]

be *sum, esse, fuī* [2]

be able *possum, posse, potuī* [7]

be absent *absum, abesse, āfuī* [19]

be accustomed (to) *soleō, solēre, solitus sum* [29]

be afraid of *vereor, verērī, veritus sum* [24]

be afraid *timeō, timēre, timuī* [10]

be born *nascor, nascī, nātus sum* [37]; *orior, orīrī, ortus sum* [29]

be done *fīō, fierī, factus sum* [26]

be eager for *studeō, studēre, studuī* (+ dat.) [12]

be glad *gaudeō, gaudēre, gavīsus sum* [38]

be made *fīō, fierī, factus sum* [26]

be near *adsum, adesse, adfuī* (+ dat.) [19]

be of assistance to *adsum, adesse, adfuī* (+ dat.) [19]

be pleasing to *placeō, placēre, placuī, placitum* (+ dat.); esp., it is pleasing *placet* (+ inf.) [12]

be present *adsum, adesse, adfuī* (+ dat.) [19]

be quiet, silent *taceō, tacēre, tacuī, tacitum* [13]

be slain *cadō, cadere, cecidi, cāsum* [21]

be strong *valeō, valēre, valuī, valitum* [3]

be superior to *praestō, praestāre, praestitī, praestitum/ praestātum* (+ dat.) [10]

be "there" for someone *adsum, adesse, adfuī* (+ dat.) [19]

be unwilling *nōlō, nolle, nōluī* [7]

be well *valeō, valēre, valuī, valitum* [3]

Be well! *Salvē/Salvēte!* [3]; *Valē/Valēte!* [2]

be willing to *volō, velle, voluī* [7]

be without *careō, carēre, caruī, caritum* + abl. [36]

bear *ferō, ferre, tulī, lātum* [23]; *gerō, gerere, gessī, gestum* [22];
pariō, parere, peperī, paritum/partum [25]

beat *pulsō* (1) beat [23]

beautiful *formōsus, -a, -um* [35]; *pulcher, -chra, -chrum* [13];
praeclārus, -a, -um [16]

beauty *faciēs, faciēī* f. [24]; *forma, -ae* f. [34]

because *quia* [18]; *quod* [3]

because of *causā* + gen. [30]

become *fīō, fierī, factus sum* [26]

bed *lectus, -ī* m. [18]

bedroom *cubiculum, -ī* n. [12]

before (conj.) *antequam* [34], *priusquam* [19]

before (prep.) *prō* (+ abl.) [6]

begin *incipiō, incipere, incēpī, inceptum* [18]

beginning *orīgō, orīginis* f. [38]

behind *post* (+ acc.) [5]

Behold! *Ecce!* [11]

belief *opīniō, -iōnis* f. [34]

believe *crēdō, crēdere, crēdidī, crēditum* (+ dat.) [25];
opīnor, opīnārī, opīnātus sum [30]

below *infrā* [32]

benefit *beneficium, -iī* n. [38]

be seen *videor, vidērī, vīsus sum* [27]

besides *praetereā* [34]

best *optimus, -a, -um* [20]

better *melior, melius* [19]

between *inter* (+ acc.) [5]

beware *caveō, cavēre, cāvī, cautum* [33]

beyond *extrā* (+ acc.) [40]; *praeter* (+ acc.) [8]

bird *avis, avis* f. [28]

blood *sanguis, sanguinis* f. [22]

body *corpus, corporis* n. [15]

bone *os, ossis* n. [28]

book *liber, librī* m. [14]

born *nātus, -a, -um* [12]

both (of two) *ambō, ambae, ambō* [31]

both . . . and *et . . . et* [4]; *-que . . . -que* [4]

boy *puer, puerī* m. [6]

brave *fortis, forte* [15]

bravo! *eugae/euge/eugepae* [36]

bread *pānis, pānis* m. [31]

break *frangō, frangere, frēgī, fractum* [36]

break down *rumpō, rumpere, rūpī, ruptum* [28]

breakfast *ientāculum, -ī* n. [31]

breathe *spīrō* (1) [32]

bright *clārus, -a, -um* [36]

bring away *dēdūcō, dēdūcere, dēdūxī, dēductum* [38]

bring back *referō, referre, rettulī, relātum* [39]

bring together *conferō, conferre, contulī, collātum* [28]

broad *lātus, -a, -um* [31]

bronze *aēneus, -a, -um* [30]

brother *frāter, frātris* m. [13]

build *condō, condere, condidī, conditum* [40];
fabricō (1) [37]

building *aedificium, -iī* n. [38]; *opus, operis* n. [23]

burial *fūnus, fūneris,* n. [40]

burn *incendō, incendere, incendī, incensum* [32]

burn, burn up *combūrō, combūrere, combussī,
combustum* [30]

burst *rumpō, rumpere, rūpī, ruptum* [28]

business *negōtium, -ī* n. [8]; *rēs, reī* f. [24]

but *at* [20]; *modo* [23]; *sed* [3]

but also *sed etiam* (with *nōn sōlum* . . . not only . . .) [18]

buy *emō, emere, ēmī, emptum* [18]

by (with persons) *ā, ab, abs* (+ abl.) [5]

by a little *paulō* [25]

by far *multō* [26]

By Hercules! *Hercule* [28]

by no means *haud* [16]

By Pollux! *Edepol!* [37]

C

call *vocō* (1) [8]

call for *arcessō, arcessere, arcessīvī/arcessī, arcessītum* [32]

calm *aequus, -a, -um* [31]; *lentus, -a, -um; quiētus,
-a, -um* [25]; *tranquillus, -a, -um* [31]

calmness *tranquillitās, -tātis* f. [31]

camp *castra, -ōrum* n. pl. [23]

campaign (political) *ambitiō, -iōnis* f. [37]

can *possum, posse, potuī* [7]

candidacy *petitiō, -iōnis* f. [37]

canvassing (for votes) *ambitiō, -iōnis* f. [37]

captive *captīvus, -ī* m. [40]

care for *cūrō* (1) [13]

career *cursus, -ūs* m. [35]

careful *dīligens, dīligentis* [30]

carpenter *faber, fabrī* m. [28]

carry *ferō, ferre, tulī, lātum* [23]; *gerō, gerere, gessī,
gestum* [22]; *portō* (1) [8]; *referō, referre, rettulī,
relātum* [39]

carry (across) *transportō* (1) [27]

cause *causa, -ae* f. [30]

cavalry *equitēs, equitum* m. pl. [34]

centurion *centuriō, -iōnis* m. [23]

certain (indefinite, as in "a certain person") *quīdam,
quaedam, quoddam* [21]

chair *sella, -ae* f. [25]

chance *fortūna, -ae* f. [33]

changeable *varius, -a, -um* [30]

character *mōrēs, mōrum* m. pl. [15]; *nātūra, -ae* f. [32]

charm *dēlectō* (1) [38]

chase *persequor, persequī, persecūtus sum* [40]

chat *sermōcinor, sermōcinārī, sermōcinātus sum* [31]

cheerful *libens, libentis* [35]

children *līberī, -ōrum* m. pl. [33]

choose *legō, legere, lēgī, lectum* [15]

circle *orbis, orbis* m. [20]

citizen *cīvis, cīvis* m./f. [27]

city, esp. the city of Rome *urbs, urbis* f. [20]

city center *forum, -ī* [5]

clap *plaudō, plaudere, plausī, plausum* [26]

class of citizens *ordō, -inis* m. [34]

clean, cleanse *purgō* (1) [22]

clear *clārus, -a, um* [36]

client *cliens, clientis* m. [31]

climb *ascendō, ascendere, ascendī, ascensum* [24]

cling to *retineō, retinēre. retinuī, retentum* [37]

close *claudō, claudere, clausī, clausum* [38]

clothe *vestiō, vestīre, vestīvī/vestiī, vestītum* [33]

clothing *vestis, vestis* f. [33]

coin *nummus, -ī* m. [27]

collapse *collābor, collābī, collapsus sum* [39]

collect *conferō, conferre, contulī, collātum* [28]

colonnaded garden *peristȳlium, -iī* n. [26]

column of troops *agmen, agminis* n. [40]

come *veniō, venīre, vēnī, ventum* [2]

come about *ēveniō, ēvenīre, ēvēnī, ēventum* [35]

come back *redeō, redīre, rediī, reditum* [21]; *reveniō, revenīre, revēnī, reventum* [31]

come near to *appropinquō* (1) (+ dat.) [11]

come to *accēdō, accēdere, accessī, accessum* [38]; *adveniō, advenīre, advēnī, adventum* [11]; *succēdō, succēdere, successī, successum* [37]

come! *age* [36]

command *imperō* (1) (+ dat.) [26]

commander *imperātor, -ōris* m. [25]

common *pūblicus, -a, -um* [30]

companion *socius, -iī* m. [36]

complete *conficiō, conficere, confēcī confectum* [28]

completely *omnīnō* [32]

conceal *abdō, abdere, abdidī, abditum* [19]

concerning *dē* (+ abl.) [7]

conduct *dēdūcō, dēdūcere, dēdūxī, dēductum* [38]

conflagration *incendium, -iī* n. [32]

confusion *turba, -ae* f. [35]

connected to *aptus, -a, -um* [31]

conquer *frangō, frangere, frēgī, fractum* [36]; *vincō, vincere, vīcī, victum* [12]

conqueror *victor, victōris* m. [35]

consider *aestimō* (1) [38]; *intueor, intuērī, intuitus sum* [25]

construct *fabricō* (1) [30]

consume *consūmō, consūmere, consumpsī, consumptum* [38]

contain *contineō, continēre, continuī, contentum* [40]

contest *certāmen, certāminis* n. [35]

converse *colloquor, colloquī, collocūtus sum* [25]; *sermōcinor, sermōcinārī, sermōcinātus sum* [31]

convey *transportō* (1) [27]

cook (n.) *coquus, -ī* m. [25]

cook (v.) *coquō, coquere, coxī, coctum* [26]

cost *constō, constāre, constitī, constātūrum* [10]

couch (dining) *lectus, -ī* m. [18]

counsel *consilium, -iī* n. [23]

country *fīnēs, fīnium* m. pl. [14]; *patria, -ae* f. [27]; *rūs, rūris* n. [36]

country estate *rūs, rūris* n. [36]

course *cursus, -ūs* m. [35]

courtyard *peristȳlium, -iī* n. [26]

craft *fabrica, -ae* f. [37]

craftsman *faber, fabrī* m. [28]

create *pariō, parere, peperī, paritum/partum* [25]

crime *scelus, sceleris* n. [20]

crowd *agmen, agminis* n. [40]; *turba, -ae* f. [35]

crush *frangō, frangere, frēgī, fractum* [36]

cry *lacrimō* (1) [17]

cry out *clāmō* (1) [5]

custom *mōs, mōris* m. [15]

D

dangerous *perīculōsus, a, -um* [25]

dare *audeō, audēre, ausus sum* [9]

dark *obscūrus, -a, -um* [38]

daughter *fīlia, -ae* f. [8]

day *diēs, diēī* m. [24]; *sōl, sōlis* m. [33]

day before *prīdiē* [35]

dead *mortuus, -a, -um* [22]

dear *almus, -a, -um* [18]; *cārus, -a, -um* [13]

deceive *mentior, mentīrī, mentītus sum* [24]

decent *honestus, -a, -um* [29]

decorate *ornō* (1) [35]

deed *factum, -ī* n. [20]

deep *altus, -a, -um* [2]; *gravis, grave* [15]

defend *dēfendō, dēfendere, dēfendī, dēfensum* [39]

declare *ēloquor, ēloquī, ēlocūtus sum* [24]

delight *dēlectō* (1) [38]

deliver *solvō, solvere, soluī, solūtum* [36]; *trādō, trādere, trādidī, trāditum* [33]

demand *poscō, poscere, poposcī* [5]; *postulō* (1) [33]

depart *proficiscor, proficiscī, profectus sum* [28]

depict *demonstrō* (1) [40]

descend *descendō, descendere, descendī, descensum* [31]

descendant *nepōs, nepōtis* m. [27]

desirous *cupidus, -a, -um* (+ gen.) [39]

destitute *egēnus, -a, -um* [22]

destroy *destruō, destruere, destruxī, destructum* [34]

devote one's self to *studeō, studēre, studuī* (+ dat.) [12]

die *morior, morī, mortuus sum* [29]

difficult *difficilis, difficile* [15]

difficulty *difficultās, -tātis* f. [23]

dignity *dignitās, -tātis* f. [35]

diligent *dīligens, dīligentis* [30]

dine *cēnō* (1) [12]

dining couch *lectus, -ī* m. [18]

dinner *cēna, -ae* f. [12]

discharge *fungor, fungī, functus sum* (+ abl.) [24]

discharge benefits (military) *praemia, -iōrum* n. pl. [39]

discover *inveniō, invenīre, invēnī, inventum* [14]

discuss *conferō, conferre, contulī, collātum* [28]

dishes of food *epulae, -ārum* f. pl. [26]

disloyal *improbus, -a, -um* [23]

dismiss *dīmittō, dīmittere, dīmīsī, dīmissum* [35]

disorder *turba, -ae* f. [35]

displease *displiceō, displicēre, displicuī, displicitum* [26]

distinct *clārus, -a, -um* [36]

district *regiō, regiōnis* f. [39]

disturb *perturbō* (1) [26]

divine *dīvus, -a, -um* [29]

divorce *dīmittō, dīmittere, dīmīsī, dīmissum* [35]

do *agō, agere, ēgī, actum* [4]; *conficiō, conficere, confēcī, confectum* [28]; *efficiō, efficere, effēcī, effectum* [32]; *faciō, facere, fēcī, factum* [6]

do injury to *noceō, nocēre, nocuī, nocitum* (+ dat.) [12]

dog *canis, canis* m./f. [23]

Don't! *Nōlī* + inf. (sing.)/ *Nōlīte* + inf. (pl.)

door *foris, foris* f. [34]; *iānua, -ae* f. [25]; *porta, -ae* f. [23]

doorman *iānitor, -ōris* m. [34]

doubt *dubitō* (1) [39]

doubtful *dubius, -a, -um* [39]

down from *dē* (+ abl.) [7]

drag *trahō, trahere, trāxī, tractus* [22]

dress *vestiō, vestīre, vestīvī/vestiī, vestītum* [33]

dressed in a toga *togātus, -a, -um* [33]

drink (n.) *pōtus, -ūs* m. [29]

drink (v.) *bibō, bibere, bibī* [2]; *pōtō* (1) [31]

drive *agō, agere, ēgī, actum* [4]; *pulsō* (1) [23]

drive together *cōgō, cōgere, coēgī, coactum* [23]

drunk *ēbrius, -a, -um* [27]

duty *mūnus, mūneris* n. [17]

E

each *omnis, omne* [15]; *quisque, quaeque, quodque/quicque/quidque* [21]

eager *ācer, ācris, ācre* [38]

eager for *cupidus, -a, -um* (+ gen.) [39]

eagerness *studium, -iī* n. [6]

ear *auris, auris* f. [29]

early in the morning *māne* [4]

easy *facilis, -e* [20]

eat *consūmō, consūmere, consumpsī, consumptum* [38]; *edō, ēsse/edere, ēdī, ēsum* [7]

effort *opus, operis* n. [23]

egg *ōvum, -ī* n. [10]

either . . . or *aut . . . aut* [4]

elders *māiōrēs, māiōrum* m. pl. [15]

else *aliter* [39]

emperor *imperātor, -ōris* m. [25]

employ *ūtor, ūtī, ūsus sum* (+ abl.) [24]

encounter *occurrō, occurrere, occurrī/occucurrī, occursum* (+ dat.) [36]

end (n.) *fīnis, fīnis* m. [14]

end (v.) *cadō, cadere, cecidi, cāsum* [21]; *fīniō, fīnīre, fīnīvī/fīniī, fīnītum* [8]

endure *maneō, manēre, mansī, mansum* [23]

enemy *hostis, hostis* m./f.; pl. the enemy *hostis, hostis* m./f. [14]

enjoy *fruor, fruī, fructus/fruitus sum* (+ abl.) [24]; *ūtor, ūtī, ūsus sum* (+ abl.) [24]

enough *satis* [30]

enter *ingredior, ingredī, ingressus sum* [24]; *intrō* (1) [8]

entire *tōtus, -a, -um* [17]

entrust *dēpōnō, dēpōnere, dēposuī, dēpositum; trādō, trādere, trādidī, trāditum* [33]

envy *invideō, invidēre, invīdī, invīsum* (+ dat.) [38]

equal *aequus, -a, -um* [31]

escape notice of *praetereō, praeterīre, praeterīvī/praterii, praeteritum* [35]

escort *dēdūcō, dēdūcere, dēdūxī, dēductum* [38]

especially *magnopere* [23]; *praesertim* [25]

estate *rūs, rūris* n. [36]

estimate *aestimō* (1) [38]

even *aequus, -a, -um* [31]; *plānus, -a, -um* [34]

even *et* [2]; *etiam* [17]

even now *etiam* [17]

every *omnis, omne* [15]; *quisque, quaeque, quodque/quicque/quidque* [21]

examine *interrogō* (1) [34]

excellent *praeclārus, -a, -um* [16]

except *praeter* (+ acc.) [8]

excessively *nimium* [16]

excite *excitō* (1) [32]

execute *efficiō, efficere, effēcī, effectum* [32]

exhibit *expōnō, expōnere, exposuī, expositum* [40]

expectation *spēs, speī,* f.

experience *ūtor, ūtī, ūsus sum* (+ abl.) [24]

explain *expōnō, expōnere, exposuī, expositum* [40]

eye *oculus, -ī* m. [23]

F

face *faciēs, faciēī* f. [24]; *ōs, ōris* n. [13]

fair *aequus, -a, -um* [31]

fair weather *tranquillitās, -tātis* f. [31]

faithful *fidēlis, fidēle* [33]

fall down *cadō, cadere, cecidī, cāsum* [21]; *lābor, lābī, lapsus sum* [39]

fall in a faint *collābor, collābī, collapsus sum* [39]

fall to ruin *ruō, ruere, ruī, rutum* [22]

fame *fāma, -ae* f. [20]

family *familia, -ae* f. [4]

famous *clārus, -a, -um* [36]; *praeclārus, -a, -um* [16]

far, far away *procul* [36]

far, far off *longē* [11]

Farewell! *Valē/Valēte!* [2]

fast *celer, celeris, celere* [15]

father *pater, patris* m. [13]

fatherland *patria, -ae* f. [27]

favor *beneficium, -iī* n. [38]; *grātia, -ae* f. [19]

fear (n.) *metus, -ūs* f. [36]

fear (v.) *metuō, metuere, metuī, metūtum* [39]; *timeō, timēre, timuī* [10]; *vereor, verērī, veritus sum* [24]

feast *convīvium, -iī* n. [25]; *epulae, -ārum* f. pl. [26]

feel *sentiō, sentīre, sēnsī, sēnsum* [21]; *temptō* (1) [32]

female servant *ancilla, -ae* f. [8]

fetch *arcessō, arcessere, arcessīvī/arcessī, arcessītum* [32]

few *paucī, -ae, -a* [9]

field *ager, agrī* m.[14]; *campus, -ī* m. [33]

fight (n.) *pugna, -ae* f. [22]

fight (v.) *pugnō* (1) [12]

figure *figūra, -ae* f. [10]

filthy *sordidus, -a, -um* [28]

final *suprēmus, -a, -um* [20]

finally *dēnique* [32]; *dēmum* [26]; *tandem* [20]

find *inveniō, invenīre, invēnī, inventum* [14]

finger *digitus, -ī* m. [38]

finish *fīniō, fīnīre, fīnīvī/fīniī, fīnītum* [8]

fire *ignis, ignis* m. [14]; *incendium, -iī* n. [32]

fire brigade *vigilēs, vigilum* m. pl. [29]

fire fighter *vigil, vigilis* m./f. [29]

firm *firmus, -a, -um* [36]

first (adj.) *prīmus, -a, -um* [18]

first(adv.) *prīmum* [28]

fish *piscis, piscis* m. [26]

fit *aptus, -a, -um* [31]; *idōneus, -a, -um* [36]

fitting (it is) *decet, decēre, decuit* (+ dat. + inf.) [24]

five *quinque* [10]

flat *plānus, -a, -um* [34]

flee *fugiō, fugere, fūgī, fugitum* [12]

flock *agmen, agminis* n. [40]

fly *volō* (1) [36]

follow *sequor, sequī, secūtus sum* [24]

food *cibus, -ī* m. [2]; *epulae, -ārum* f. pl. [26]

foot *pēs, pedis* m. [28]

for (conj.) *enim* [20]; *nam* [23]

for (prep.) *ad* (+ acc.) [2, 5]; *prō* (+ abl.) [6]

for a long time *diū* [16]; *longē* [11]

for a second time *iterum* [4]

for the purpose, for the sake of *grātiā* (+ gen.) [30]

for what reason? *quā dē causā?* [34]

forbid *prohibeō, prohibēre, prohibuī, prohibitum* [39]; *vetō, vetāre, vetuī, vetitum* [33]

force (n.) *vīs, vis* f. [21]; force (n.) *vīrēs, vīrium* f. pl. [21]

force (v.) *cōgō, cōgere, coēgī, coactum* [23]

forehead *tempus, temporis* n. [13]

foreigner *hostis, hostis* m./f. [14]

forest *silva, -ae* f. [21]

forge *fabricō* (1) [30]

forget *oblīvīscor, oblīvīscī, oblītus sum* [36]

form *forma, -ae* f. [34]

former *prior, prius* [19]

formerly *aliquandō* [26]; *ōlim* [19]

fortunate *felix, felicis* [18]; *fortūnātus, -a, -um* [22]

fortune *fortūna, -ae* f. [33]

forum *forum, -ī* [5]

foul *turpis, turpe* [38]

found *condō, condere, condidī, conditum* [40]

four *quattuor* [10]

four times *quater* [36]

free (adj.) *līber, lībera, līberum* [14]

free, free from (v.) *līberō* (1) (+ abl.) [36]

freedman *libertīnus, -ī* m. [37]

freedom *lībertās, -tātis* f. [40]

friend (female) *amīca, -ae* f. [13]

friend (male) *amīcus, -ī* m. [7]

frightening *terribilis, terribile* [27]

from *ā, ab, abs* (+ abl.) [5]; *ē, ex* (+ abl.) [5]

far away *procul* [36]

from under; *sub* (+ abl.) [6]

frugal *dīligens, dīligentis* [30]

fulfil *solvō, solvere, soluī, solūtum* [36]

full, full of *plēnus, -a, -um* [22]

function *mūnus, mūneris* n. [17]

funeral *fūnus, fūneris,* n. [40]

future *futūrum, -ī* n. [14]

G

gain *obtineō, obtinēre, obtinuī, obtentum* [9]

game *lūdus -ī,* m. [4]; public games *mūnera, mūnerum* n. pl. [17]

garden (colonnaded) *peristȳlium, -iī* n. [26]

garments *vestis, vestis* f. [33]

gate *foris, foris* f. [34]; *porta, -ae* f. [23]

gather *legō, legere, lēgī, lectum* [15]

gaze at *intueor, intuērī, intuitus sum* [25]

general *imperātor, -ōris* m. [25]

gentle *lēnis, lēne* [27]; *levis, leve* [23]

get *potior, potīri, potītus sum* (+ abl. or gen.) [24]

get to know *cognoscō, cognoscere, cognōvī, cognitum* [29]; *noscō, noscere, nōvī, nōtum* [11]

get up *orior, orīrī, ortus sum; surgō, surgere, surrēxī, surrectum* [32]

gift *dōnum, -ī* n. [23]; gift (public) *mūnus, mūneris* n. [17]

girl *puella, -ae* f. [6]

girlfriend *amīca, -ae* f. [13]

give *dō, dare, dedī, datum* [2]; *addō, addere, addidī, additum* [40]

give back *restituō, restituere, restituī, restitūtum* [39]

give birth (to) *pariō, parere, peperī, paritum/partum* [25]

give reason for regret *paenitet, paenitēre, paenituit* imp. [29]

give thanks *grātiās agere* [19]

give way to *cēdō, cēdere, cessī, cessum* (+ dat.) [35]

gladiator *gladiātor, -ōris* m. [17]

gloomy *maestus, -a, -um* [18]; *obscūrus, -a, -um* [38]

glory *glōria, -ae* f. [40]

go *accēdō, accēdere, accessī, accessum* [38]; *cēdō, cēdere, cessī, cessum* (+ dat.) [35]; *eō, īre, īvī/iī, itum* [7]; *prōgredior, prōgredī, prōgressus sum* [24]; go ("betake oneself") *sē conferre* [28]

go across *transeō, transīre, transīvī/transiī, transitum* [32]

go ahead *pergō, pergere, perrēxī, perrectum* [37]

go away *abeō, abīre, abīvī/abiī, abitum* [7]

go back *redeō, redīre, rediī, reditum* [21];

go below *succēdō, succēdere, successī, successum* [37]

go down *descendō, descendere, descendī, descensum* [31]

go in *ingredior, ingredī, ingressus sum* [24]

go over *transeō, transīre, transīvī/transiī, transitum* [32]

go past *praetereō, praeterīre, praeterīvī/prater+iī, praeteritum* [35]

go to *adeō, adīre, adīvī/adiī, aditum* [7]

go under *succēdō, succēdere, successī, successum* [37]

god *deus, -ī* m.; *dī* (alternate nom. pl.) [14]

goddess *dea, -ae* f. [11]

good *bonus, -a, -um* [3]; *probus, -a, -um* [30]

Good-bye! *Valē/Valēte!* [2]

goods *opera, operum* n. pl. [23]

govern *regō, regere, rēxī, rectum* [39]

grace *grātia, -ae* f. [19]

grandfather *avus, -ī* m. [29]

grandmother *ava, -ae* f. [30]

grandson, grandchild *nepōs, nepōtis* m. [27]

grant *cēdō, cēdere, cessī, cessum* (+ dat.) [35]

great *magnus, -a, -um* [8]

greater *māiōr, māiōris* [15]

greatest *maximus, -a, -um* [20]; *summus, -a, -um* [20]

greatly *magnopere* [23]

greet *salūtō* (1)

greeting (formal morning visit by a client to a patron) *salūtātiō, -ōnis* f. [31]

Greetings! *avē* [29]

grief *dolor, dolōris* m. [21]

ground plan *forma, -ae* f. [34]

grow *crescō, crescere, crēvī, crētum* [32]

grudge *invideō, invidēre, invīdī, invīsum* (+ dat.) [38]

guard (n.) *custōs, custōdis* m./f. [30]; *vigil, vigilis* m./f. [29]

guard (v.) *custōdiō, custōdīre, custōdīvī/custōdiī, custōditum* [30]

guest *hospes, hospitis* m. [26]

H

hamper *impediō, impedīre, impedīvī/impediī, impedītum* [39]

hand *manus, -ūs* f. [24]

hand down *trādō, trādere, trādidī, trāditum* [33]

handsome *formōsus, -a, -um* [35]; *pulcher, pulchra, pulchrum* [13]

happen *accidō, accidere, accidī; ēveniō, ēvenīre, ēvēnī, ēventum* [35]; *fīō, fierī, factus sum* [26]

happy *laetus, -a, -um* [3]

hard *difficilis, difficile* [15]

hardly *vix* [32]

harm *noceō, nocēre, nocuī, nocitum* (+ dat.) [12]

hasten *festīnō* (1) [9]; *volō* (1) [36]

hate *invideō, invidēre, invīdī, invīsum* (+ dat.) [38]

haughty *superbus, -a, -um* [40]

haul *trahō, trahere, trāxī, tractus* [22]

have *habeō, habēre, habuī, habitum* [5]

have strength (for) *supersum, superesse, superfuī* [35]

have to *dēbeō, dēbēre, dēbuī, dēbitum* [7]

he *ille, illīus* [17]; *is, eius, eī, eum, eō* [17]

he wants, he wishes *vult* [5]

head *caput, capitis* n. [36]

head of the family *pater familiās, patris familiās* m. [29]

health *salūs, salūtis* f. [32]

healthy *sānus, -a, -um* [25]

hear *audiō, audīre, audīvī/audiī, audītum* [7]; *sentiō, sentīre, sensī, sensum* [21]

heart *cor, cordis* n. [17]

heavy *gravis, grave* [15]

Hello! *Salvē/Salvēte!* [3]

help (n.) *auxilium, -iī* n. [25]

help (v.) *adiuvō, adiuvāre, adiūvī, adiūtum* [16]; *adsum, adesse, adfuī* (+ dat.) [19]; *iuvō, iuvāre, iūvī, iūtum* [25]

her own *suus, -a, -um* [9]

herd *agmen, agminis* n. [40]

here *hīc* [10]; (to) here *hūc* [36]

hereafter *aliquandō* [26]

herself *suī, sibi, sē, sē* [21]

herself (emphatic) *ipsa* [17]

hesitate *dubitō* (1) [39]

Hi! *Salvē/Salvēte!* [3]
hide *abdō, abdere, abdidī, abditum* [19]
high *altus, -a, -um* [2]
higher *superior, superius* [19]
highest *summus, -a, -um* [20]; *suprēmus, -a, -um* [20]
hill *collis, collis* m. [32]
himself *suī, sibi, sē, sē* [21]
himself (emphatic) *ipse* [17]
hinder *impediō, impedīre, impedīvī/impediī,*
    impedītum [39]
his own *suus, -a, -um* [9]
hold *contineō, continēre, continuī, contentum* [40];
    habeō, habēre, habuī, habitum [5]; *obtineō, obtinēre,*
    obtinuī, obtentum [9]; *teneō, tenēre, tenuī, tentum* [6]
hold fast *retineō, retinēre. retinuī, retentum* [37]
hold up *sustineō, sustinere, sustinuī, sustentum* [37]
home *domus, -ī* f. [24]; *sēdēs, sēdis* f. [14]
home, to a house *domum* [4]
honest *probus, -a, -um* [30]
honey *mel, mellis* n. [31]
honor *dignitās, -tātis* f. [35]
hope (n.) *spēs, spēī,* f. [33]
hope, hope for (v.) *spērō* (1) [9]
horn *tuba, -ae* f. [35]
horrible *horribilis, horribile* [37]
horse *equus, -ī* m. [34]
horseman *eques, equitis* m. [34]
host *hospes, hospitis* m. [26]
hot *aestuōsus, -a, -um* [31]; *calidus, -a, -um* [33]
hour *hōra, -ae* f. [8]
house *domus, -ī* f. [4]l; *domus, -ūs* f. [24]
how (conj.) *quōmodo* [17]
How are you? How are you doing? *Quid agis?* [4]
how many? *quot?* indecl. [34]
how many, how much *quantus, -a, -um* [10]
how (conj.) *quōmodo* [17]; *ut* [31]
how! (interj.) *quam* [13]
how? (interr.) *quārē* [30]
however *autem* [20]
human being *homō, hominis* m./f. [13]
hundred (one) *centum* indecl. [37]
hungry *iēiūnus, -a, -um* [13]
hunter *vēnātor, -ōris* m. [29]
hurl *iaciō, iacere, iēcī, iactus* [22]
hurt *noceō, nocēre, nocuī, nocitum* (+ dat.) [12]
husband *marītus, -ī* m. [16]

I

I *ego* [7]
I am sorry *mē paenitet* [29]
if *sī* [7]

if only! *utinam* [37]
illness *morbus, -ī* m. [34]
image *imāgō, -inis* f. [40]
immediately *statim* [20]
impede *impediō, impedīre, impedīvī/impediī,*
    impedītum [39]
in *in* (+ abl.) [2, 5]
in another way *aliter* [39]
in front of *prō* (+ abl.) [6]
in need of *egēnus, -a, -um* [22]
in order that *ut* [31]
in order that not *nē* [31]
in the middle (of) *medius, -a, um* [22]
in this place *hīc* [10]
in this way *sīc* [11]
in want of *egēnus, -a, -um* [22]
in what way? *quārē* [30]
increase *crescō, crescere, crēvī, crētum* [32]
indeed *quīn* [39]
indispensable *necessārius, -a, -um* [34]
infant *infans, infantis* m./f. [14]
inflame *incendō, incendere, incendī,*
    incēnsum [32]
inhabitant *incola, -ae* m./f. [38]
injure *noceō, nocēre, nocuī, nocitum* (+ dat.) [12]
inspect *inspiciō, inspicere, inspexī, inspectum* [10]
instrument *instrūmentum, -ī* n. [27]
intelligent *intellegens, intellegentis* [15]
into *in* (+ acc.) [5]
iron *ferrum, -ī* n. [22]
is *est* [1]
island *insula, -ae* f. [9]
it *id, eius* [17]; *illud, illīus* [17]
it is necessary (to) *necesse est* (+ inf.) [12]
it is pleasing to *placet* imp. + inf.
its own *suus, -a, -um* [9]
itself *suī, sibi, sē, sē* [21]
itself (emphatic) *ipsum* [17]

J

join *iungō, iungere, iunxī, iunctum* [38]
journey *cursus, -ūs* m. [35]
judge *praetor, praetōris* m. [35]
judgeship *praetūra, -ae* f. [36]
judgment *consilium, -ī* n. [23]
jump *saliō, salīre, saliī/saluī, saltum* [11]
Jupiter (king of the gods) *Iuppiter,*
    Iovis m. [24]
just *aequus, -a, -um* [31]
just as *sīcut* [7]
just now *modo* [23]

K

keep off *prohibeō, prohibēre, prohibuī, prohibitum* [39]
keep safe *conservō* (1) [39]
kill *interficiō, interficere, interfēcī, interfectum* [14]; *necō* (1) [21]; *occīdō, occīdere, occīdī, occīsum* [39]
kind *almus, -a, -um* [18]
kindness *beneficium, -iī* n. [38]
king *rex, rēgis* m. [14]
kingdom *regnum, -ī* n. [36]
kitchen *culīna, -ae* f. [25]
knight *eques, equitis* m. [34]
know *cognoscō, cognoscere, cognōvī, cognitum [29]; noscō, noscere, nōvī, nōtum* [11]
know, know about, know how to *sciō, scīre, scīvī/sciī, scītum* [28]

L

labor *labor, labōris* m. [16]; *opera, -ae* f. [36]
lack *careō, carēre, caruī, caritum* + abl. [36]
lake *lacus, -ūs* m. [28]
land *terra, -ae* f. [8]
lap *gremium, iī* n. [27]
large *magnus, -a, -um* [8]
late *tardus, -a, -um* [39]
later *sērius* [17]
laugh at *irrīdeō, irrīdēre, irrīsī, irrīsum* [37]
laugh *rīdeō, rīdere, rīsī, rīsum* [7]
law (it is) *fās* [40]
lawsuit *petitiō, -iōnis* f. [37]
lead down *dēdūcō, dēdūcere, dēdūxī, dēductum* [38]
lead *agō, agere, ēgī, actum* [4]; *dūcō, dūcere, dūxī, ductum* [4]; *ferō, ferre, tulī, latum* [23]
leader *dux, ducis* m. [27]
leap *saliō, salīre, saliī/saluī, saltum* [11]
learn *cognoscō, cognoscere, cognōvī, cognitum* [29]; *disco, discere, didicī* [6]
learn to know *noscō, noscere, nōvī, nōtum* [11]
leave *dēpōnō, dēpōnere, dēposui, dēpositum; relinquō, relinquere, relīquī, relictum* [21]
leave behind *relinquō, relinquere, relīquī, relictum* [21]
left *sinister, sinistra, sinistrum* [38]
left hand *sinistra (manus), -ae* f. [38]
left over (be) *supersum, superesse, superfuī* [35]
legion *legiō, legiōnis* f. [39]
lest *nē* [31]
let go *dīmittō, dīmittere, dīmīsī, dīmissum* [35]
letter *epistula, -ae* f. [23]
liberty *lībertās, -tātis* f. [40]
library *bibliothēca, -ae* f. [27]
lie *mentior, mentīrī, mentītus sum* [24]

lie, lie still, lie dead *iaceō, iacēre, iacuī* [21]
life *vīta, -ae* f. [13]
lift *tollō, tollere, sustulī, sublātum* [11]
light *levis, leve* [23]
like *sīcut* [7]
like to *similis, simile* [37]
likeness *imāgō, -inis* f. [40]
likewise *item* [35]
line *ordō, -inis* m. [34]
line of battle *agmen, agminis* n. [40]
line of poetry *versus, -ūs* m. [27]
linger *cunctor, cunctārī, cunctātus sum* [25]
little brother *frāterculus, -ī* m. [36]
little (adj.) *paucus, -a, -um* [9]
little (adv.) *paulō* [25]; a little *paulum* [28]
live *habitō* (1) [12]; *vīvo, vīvere, vīxī, victum* [29]
living *vīvus, -a, -um* [35]
loathsome *turpis, turpe* [38]
long (adj.) *longus, -a, -um* [19]
long (adv.) *multō* [2]
long distance *longē* [11]
longing for *cupidus, -a, -um* (+ gen.) [39]
look (n.) *speciēs, speciēī* f. [24]
look after *tueor, tuērī, tuitus sum* [29]
look at *aspiciō, aspicere, aspexī, aspectum* [24]; *conspiciō, conspicere, conspexī, conspectum* [9]; *intueor, intuērī, intuitus sum* [25]; *spectō* (1) [10]; *tueor, tuērī, tuitus sum* [29]
look closely at *inspectō* (1) [19]; *inspiciō, inspicere, inspexī, inspectum* [10]
look for *petō, petere, petīvī/petiī, petītum* [21]
look forward to *spērō* (1) [9]
Look! *Ecce!* [11]
loosen *solvō, solvere, soluī, solūtum* [36]
lord *dominus, -ī* m. [18]
lose *āmittō, āmittere, āmīsī, āmissum* [9]; *careō, carēre, caruī, caritum* + abl. [36]
loud *clārus, -a, -um* [36]; *fortis, forte* [15]; *magnus, -a, -um* [8]
love (n.) *amor, amōris* m. [15]
love (v.) *amō* (1) [13]
luck *fortūna, -ae* f. [33]
lucky *felix, felicis* [18]; *fortūnātus, -a, -um* [22]

M

magistracy, magistrate *magistrātus, -ūs* m. [37]
make *fabricō* (1) [30]; *faciō, facere, fēcī, factum* [6]
make ready *parō* (1) [12]
man *homō, hominis* m./f; *vir, virī* m. [2]
many *multī, -ae, -a* [2]
march (n.) *cursus, -ūs* m. [35]

march forward *prōgredior, prōgredī, prōgressus sum* [24]
mark *signum, -ī* n. [38]
marriage *matrimōnium, -iī* n. [37]
marry a husband *nūbo, nūbere, nupsī, nuptum* [31]
marry a wife *uxōrem dēdūcere* [38]
master *dominus, -ī* m. [18]; *caput, capitis* n. [36]
matrimony *matrimōnium, -iī* n. [37]
matter *rēs, reī* f. [24]
me *mē* (acc., abl.) [3]; *mihi* (dat.) [1]
mean *significō* (1) [40]
meanwhile *intereā* [35]
memory *memoria, -ae* f. [37]
mental disposition *mens, mentis* f. [31]
merit *dignitās, -tātis* f. [35]
messenger *nuntius, -iī* m. [33]
middle of, midway *medius, -a, -um* [22]
mild *lēnis, lēne* [27]
mind *animus, -ī* m.; *mens, mentis* f. [31]
mirror *speculum, -ī* n. [30]
miserable *miser, misera, miserum* [35]
mistress (of the house) *domina, -ae* f. [25]
mixed *varius, -a, -um* [30]
mock *irrīdeō, irrīdēre, irrīsī, irrīsum* [37]
money *argentum, -ī* n. [31]; *nummus, -ī* m. [27];
    pecunia, -ae f. [3]
monkey *sīmia, -ae* m./f. [5]
month *mensis, mensis* m. [14]
morally unsound *improbus, -a, -um* [23]
more *magis* [16]; (in amount) *plūs* [19];
    (in number) *plūres, plūra* [19]
moreover *praetereā* [34]
most *plūrimus, -a, -um* [20]
mother *māter, mātris* f. [13]
mouth *ōs, ōris* n. [13]
move *moveō, movēre, mōvī, mōtum* [30];
    tangō, tangere, tetigī, tactum [32]
move back *removeō, removēre, remōvī, remōtum* [32]
much (adj.) *multus, -a, -um* [2]
much (adv.) *magnopere* [23]; *multō* [26]; *multum* [16]
my *meus, -a, -um* [5]
my, to me *mihi* [1]

N

name (n.) *nōmen, nōminis* n. [1]
name (v.) *nōmīnō* (1) [22]
nature *nātūra, -ae* f. [32]
near *prope* (+ acc.) [5]
nearest *proximus, -a, -um* [30]
necessary *necessārius, -a, -um* [34]
neglect *praetereō, praeterīre, praeterīvī/praterii,*
    praeteritum [35]

neither . . . nor. . . *nec . . . nec . . .* [15];
    neque . . . neque . . . [28]
neither *neuter, neutra, neutrum* [17]
nervous *sollicitus, -a, -um* [39]
never *numquam* [17]
nevertheless *nihilōminus* [39]; *tamen* [20]
new *novus, -a, -um* [8]
news *nuntius, -iī* m. [33]
next day *postrīdiē* [35]
next *proximus, -a, -um* [30]
night *nox, noctis* f. [14]
no *nūllus, -a, -um* [17]
no one *nēmō, nēminis* m./f. [13]
noble *nōbilis, nōbile* [15]; *praeclārus, -a, -um* [16]
nobody *nēmō, nēminis* m./f. [13]
none, not any *nūllus, -a, -um* [17]
not *haud* [16]; *nōn* [3]; *haud* [16] *nē* [31]
not know *nesciō, nescīre, nescīvī/nesciī, nescītum* [34]
not long ago *nūper* [25]
not only . . . but also *nōn sōlum . . . sed etiam* [18]
not want to *nōlō, nolle, nōluī* [7]
not yet *nōndum* [32]
nothing *nihil* [3]
notice *animadvertō, animadvertere, animadvertī,*
    animadversum [40]
nourishing *almus, -a, -um* [18]
now *iam* [8]; *nunc* [3]

O

observe *animadvertō, animadvertere, animadvertī,*
    animadversum [40]; *arbitror, abitrārī, arbitrātus sum*
    [37]; *cognoscō, cognoscere, cognōvī, cognitum* [29];
    conspiciō, conspicere, conspexī, conspectum [9];
    servō (1) [27]
observer *spectātōr, spectātōris* m. [24]
obvious *plānus, -a, -um* [34]
odor *odor, odōris* m. [21]
of high rank *honestus, -a, -um* [29]
of such a kind, of such a sort *tālis, tāle* [21]
office *dignitās, -tātis* f. [35]; *magistrātus, -ūs* m. [37]
often *saepe* [6]
oh no! *ēheu!* [16]
oh! (in pain or dismay); *heu* (often + accusative) [36]
old *antiquus, -a, -um* [10]; *senex, senis; vetus,*
    veteris [39]
old man *senex, senis* m. [29]
old woman *anus, -ūs* f. [27]
older *māior, māiōris* (often with *nātū*) [15]
on *in* (+ abl.) [2, 5]
on account of *causā* (+ gen.) [30]; *propter* (+ acc.) [9]
on top of *super* (+ acc.) [10]

once *ōlim* [19]

one *ūnus, -a, -um* [7]

one hundred *centum* indecl. [37]

one ought, must *oportet, oportēre, oportuit*
  (+ acc. + inf.) [12]

one . . . another . . . *alius . . . alius . . .* [31]

only (adj.) *sōlus, -a, -um* [6]

only (adv.) *modo* [23]; *solum* [3]

opinion *opīniō, -iōnis* f. [34]

or *an* [39]; *aut* [4]

order (v.) *imperō* (1) (+ dat.) [26]; *iubeō, iubēre,*
  iussī, iussum [28]

order (n.) *ordō, -inis* m. [34]

order of knights *equitēs, equitum* m. pl. [34]

origin *orīgō, orīginis* f. [38]

other *alius, -a, -ud* [9]

otherwise *aliter* [39]

ought *dēbeō, dēbēre, dēbuī, dēbitum* [7]

our *noster, nostra, nostrum* [15]

out of *ē, ex* (+ abl.) [5]

out of doors, outside *forīs* adv. [34]

outside of *extrā* (+ acc.) [40]

over *super* (+ acc.) [10]; *suprā* (+ acc.) [32]

over there *illīc* [8]

overturn *vertō, vertere, vertī, versum* [26]

owe *dēbeō, dēbēre, dēbuī, dēbitum* [7]

P

pace *gradus, -ūs* m. [24]

pain *opera, -ae* f. [36]; *dolor, dolōris* m. [21]

papyrus *papyrus, -ī* f. [27]

pardon *parcō, parcere, pepercī/parsī/parcuī,*
  parsūrus (+ dat.) [12]

parent *parens, parentis* m./f. [16]

part *pars, partis* f. [19]

particular *praecipuus, -a, -um* [27]

particularly *praesertim* [25]

partner *socius, -iī* m. [36]

pater familias *pater familiās, patris familiās* m. [29]

patient *aequus, -a, -um* [31]

patron *patrōnus, -ī* m. [26]

pay *solvō, solvere, soluī, solūtum* [36]

pay attention to *servō* (1) [27]

peace *pax, pācis* f. [27]

peaceful *tranquillus, -a, -um* [31]

people *populus, -ī* m. [4]

perceive *arbitror, abitrārī, arbitrātus sum* [37];
  sentiō, sentīre, sensī, sensum [21]

perceive *videō, vidēre, vīdī, vīsum* [3]

perform *fungor, fungī, functus sum* (+ abl.) [24]; *solvō,*
  solvere, soluī, solūtum [36]

perhaps *fortasse* [11]

perish *pereō, perīre, perīvī/periī, peritum* [32]

peristyle *peristȳlium, -iī* n. [26]

permit *sinō, sinere, sīvī/siī, situm* [33]

permitted (it is) *licet, licēre, licuit, licitum* imp. [29]

person *homō, hominis* m./f. [13]

personal *proprius, -a, -um*

persuade *persuādeō, persuādēre, persuāsī, persuāsum*
  (+ dat.) [33]

petition *petitiō, -iōnis* f. [37]

piece *pars, partis* f. [19]

place (n.) *locus, -ī* m. [19]

place (v.) *pōnō, pōnere, posuī, positum* [4]

plan *consilium, -iī* n. [23]

plane *plānus, -a, -um* [34]

play (n.) *fābula, -ae* f. [9]

play (v.) *lūdō, lūdere, lūsī, lūsum* [30]

pleasant *iūcundus, -a, -um* [35]

please *placeō, placēre, placuit* (+ dat.) [12]

Please! *sī tibi placet/sī vobis placet* [7]

pleasing *grātus, -a, -um* [23]

plunder *praemium, -iī* n. [39]

pocketbook *saccus, -ī* m. [11]

poem *carmen, carminis* n. [17]

poet *poēta, -ae* m. [14]

point at *demonstrō* (1) [40]

political campaign *ambitiō, -iōnis* f. [37]

poor *pauper, pauperis* [25]

porter *iānitor, -ōris* m. [34]

power *vīs, vis* f. [21]

powerful *potens, potentis* [15]

practically *quasī* [37]

practice *exercereō, exercēre, exercuī, exercitum* [40]

praetor *praetor, praetōris* m. [35]

praetorship *praetūra, -ae* f. [36]

pray *ōrō* (1) [33]

prefer *mālō, malle, māluī* [7]

pregnant *gravidus, -a, -um* [25]

prepare *parō* (1) [12]

preserve *conservō* (1) [39]

pretty *formōsus, -a, -um* [35]; *pulcher, pulchra,*
  pulchrum [13]

prevent *prohibeō, prohibēre, prohibuī, prohibitum* [39]

prisoner *captīvus, -ī* m. [40]

prize *praemium, -iī* n. [39]

proceed *pergō, pergere, perrēxī, perrectum* [37];
  prōcedō, prōcēdere, prōcessī, prōcessum [10]; *prōgredior,*
  prōgredī, prōgressus sum [24]

procure *arcessō, arcessere, arcessīvī/arcessī,*
  arcessītum [32]

profit by *fruor, fruī, fructus/fruitus sum* (+ abl.) [24]

prohibit *vetō, vetāre, vetuī, vetitum* [33]

promise *polliceor, pollicērī, pollicitus sum* [24];
   prōmittō, prōmittere, prōmīsī, prōmissum [34]
prosperity *fortūna, -ae* f. [33]
protect *servō* (1) [27]
proud *superbus, -a, -um* [40]
public *pūblicus, -a, -um* [30]
public show *mūnus, mūneris* n. [17]
pursue *persequor, persequī, persecūtus sum* [40]
push *pulsō* (1) [23]
push back *repellō, repellere, reppulī, repulsum* [39]
put *pōnō, pōnere, posuī, positum* [4]
put to *appōnō, appōnere, apposuī, appositum* [26]

Q

quaestorship *quaestūra, -ae* f. [36]
question *interrogō* (1) [34]
quiet *quiētus, -a, -um* [25]

R

race *certāmen, certāminis* n. [35]; race *cursus, -ūs* m. [35]
raise *excitō* (1) [32]; *tollō, tollere, sustulī, sublātum* [11]
rare *rārus, -a, -um* [27]
rather *magis* [16]
rather late *sērius* [17]
reach *perveniō, pervenīre, pervēnī, perventum* [21];
   tangō, tangere, tetigī, tactum [32]
read *legō, legere, lēgī, lectum* [15]
reason *causa, -ae* f. [30]; *consilium, -iī* n. [23];
   mens, mentis f. [31]; *rēs, reī* f. [24]
receive *recipiō, recipere, recēpī, receptum* [31]
recent *recens, recentis* [39]
recently *nūper* [25]; *recenter* [37]
refuse *invideō, invidēre, invīdī, invīsum* (+ dat.) [38]
region *regiō, regiōnis* f. [39]
rejoice *gaudeō, gaudēre, gavīsus sum* [38]
release *dīmittō, dīmittere, dīmīsī, dīmissum* [35]
remain *maneō, manēre, mansī, mansum* [23];
   remaneō, remanēre, remansī [40]
remaining *reliquus, -a, -um* [21]
remark *animadvertō, animadvertere, animadvertī,*
   animadversum [40]
remember *meminī, meminisse* [32]
Remember! *Mementō* imper. [32]
remove *trahō, trahere, trāxī, tractus* [22]
remove back *removeō, remōvēre, remōvī, remōtum* [32]
repel *repellō, repellere, reppulī, repulsum* [39]
replace *restituō, restituere, restituī, restitūtum* [39]
reply *respondeō, respondēre, respondī, responsum* (+ dat.) [3]
report (n.) *fāma, -ae* f. [20]
report (v.) *nuntiō* (1) [37]

reputation *opīniō, -iōnis* f. [34]
request *poscō, poscere, poposcī* [5]; *postulō* (1) [33]
require *postulō* (1) [33]
residence *sēdēs, sēdis* f. [14]
rest *quiescō, quiescere, quiēvī, quiētum* [14]
restore *restituō, restituere, restituī, restitūtum* [39]
restrain *prohibeō, prohibēre, prohibuī, prohibitum* [39]
retain *retineō, retinēre, retinuī, retentum* [37]
retreat *sē recipere* [31]
return *redeō, redīre, rediī, reditum* [21]; *reveniō, revenīre,*
   revēnī, reventum [31]
reward *praemium, -iī* n. [39]
rhetorical *rhētoricus, -a, -um* [16]
rich *dīves, dīvitis* [24]
right (it is) *fās* [40]
right *dexter, dext(e)ra, dext(e)rum* [38]
right hand *dext(e)ra* (manus), *-ae* f. [38]
ring *orbis, orbis* m. [20]
rise *orior, orīrī, ortus sum* [33]
rise up *surgō, surgere, surrēxī, surrectum* [32]
river *flūmen, -inis* n. [33]
road *iter, itineris* n. [21]; *via, -ae* f. [5]
Roman *Rōmānus, -a, -um* [11]
Rome *Rōma, -ae* f. [11]
room *cella, -ae* f. [18]
rough *horribilis, horribile* [37]
row *ordō, -inis* m. [34]
rule *imperō* (1) (+ dat.) [26]; *regō, regere, rēxī, rectum* [39]
ruler *imperātor, -ōris* m. [25]
rumor *fāma, -ae* f. [20]
run *currō, currere, cucurrī, cursum* [5]
run for political office *petō, petere, petīvī/petiī,*
   petītum [21]
run towards *occurrō, occurrere, occurrī/occucurrī,*
   occursum (+ dat.) [36]
rush, rush at *ruō, ruere, ruī, rutum* [22]

S

sack *saccus, -ī* m. [11]
sad *maestus, -a, -um* [18]; *tristis, triste* [15]
safe *salvus, -a, -um* [16]; *tūtus, -a, -um* [14]
safety *salūs, salūtis* f. [32]
sail *nāvigō* (1) [36]
same *īdem, eadem, idem* [21]
sample *exemplum, -ī* n. [40]
sand *harēna, -ae* f. [22]
save *servō* (1) [27]
say *dīcō, dīcere, dīxī, dictum* [7]; *inquit, inquiunt* [2];
   loquor, loquī, locūtus sum [24]; *nārrō* (1) [14]
say hello, say "Salvē" *salūtō* (1) [4]
say in addition *addō, addere, addidī, additum* [40]

scarcely *vix* [32]

scared *territus, -a, -um* [14]

scent *odor, odōris* m. [21]

school *lūdus, -ī* m. [4]

schoolmaster *magister, -trī* m. [2]

schoolmistress *magistra, -ae* f. [2]

sea *mare, maris* n. [14]

seal *signum, -ī* n. [38]

season *tempestās, tempestātis* f. [36]; *tempus, temporis* n. [13]

seat *sēdēs, sēdis* f. [14]; *sella, -ae* f. [25]

see *conspiciō, conspicere, conspexī, conspectum* [9]; *sentiō, sentīre, sensī, sensum* [21]; *videō, vidēre, vīdī, vīsum* [3]

seek *petō, petere, petīvī/petiī, petītum* [21]

seem *videor, vidēri, vīsus sum* [27]

seem good, seem like a good idea *vidētur* imp. + inf. [27]

seize *rapiō, rapere, rapuī, raptum* [20]

sell *vendō, vendere, vendidī, venditum* [30]

senate *senātus, -ūs* m. [29]

senator *senātor, -ōris* m. [29]

send *mittō, mittere, mīsī, missum* [20]

send away *āmittō, āmittere, āmīsī, āmissum* [9]

send forth *prōmittō, prōmittere, prōmīsī, prōmissum* [34]

send out *dīmittō, dīmittere, dīmīsī, dīmissum* [35]

sense *sentiō, sentīre, sensī, sensum* [21]

sentry *vigil, vigilis* m./f. [29]

serious *gravis, grave* [15]

servant (female) *ancilla, -ae* f. [8]

servant (male) *servus, -ī* m. [7]

serve *appōnō, appōnere, apposuī, appositum* [26]

set fire to *incendō, incendere, incendī, incensum* [32]

set out *expōnō, expōnere, exposuī, expositum* [40]; *proficiscor, proficiscī, profectus sum* [28]

set sail *nāvem solvere* [36]

several *nōnnūllī, -ae, -a* [9]

shady *obscūrus, -a, -um* [38]

shameless *improbus, -a, -um* [23]

shape (n.) *figūra, -ae* f. [10]; *forma, -ae* f. [34]

shape (v.) *fabricō* (1) [30]

sharp *ācer, ācris, ācre* [38]

she *ea, eius* [17]; *illa, illīus* [17]

shed tears *lacrimō* (1) [17]

ship *nāvis, nāvis* f. [34]

shop *taberna, -ae* f. [2]

short *brevis, breve* [18]

shout (noun) *clāmor, clāmōris m.* [20]

shout (v.) *clāmō* (1) [5]

show *demonstrō* (1) [40]; *doceō, docēre, docuī, doctum* [35]; *monstrō* (1); *ostendō, ostendere, ostendī, ostentum/ostensum* [38]

show mercy to *parcō, parcere, pepercī/parsī/parcuī, parsūrus* (+ dat.) [12]

show reverence to *vereor, verērī, veritus sum* [24]

shut *claudō, claudere, clausī, clausum* [38]

sick *aeger, aegra, aegrum* [37]

sickness *morbus, -ī* m. [34]

sign *signum, -ī* n. [38]

silence *silentium, -iī* n. [23]

silver *argentum, -ī* n. [31]

silver, pertaining to silver *argentārius, -a, -um* [31]

silver, silvery *argenteus, -a, -um* [31]

similar *similis, simile* [37]

similarly *item* [35]

since *postquam* [30]; *quia* [18]

sing, *canō, canere, cecinī, cantum* [40]; *cantō* (1) [27]

sing about *canō, canere, cecinī, cantum* [40]

sister *soror, sorōris* f. [13]

sit *sedeō, sedēre, sēdī, sessum* [5]

six *sex* [10]

sixteen *sēdecim* [8]

sixth *sextus, -a, -um* [37]

skill *ars, artis* f. [16]

slave assigned to a young boy *paedagōgus, -ī* m. [5]

slave *servus, -ī* m. [7]

slay *necō* (1) [21]; *occīdō, occīdere, occīdī, occīsum* [39]

sleep *dormiō, dormīre, dormīvī/dormiī, dormītum* [12]

small *parvus, -a, -um* [10]

smaller *minor, minus* [19]

smallest *minimus, -a, -um* [20]

smith *faber, fabrī* m. [28]

smooth *lēnis, lēne* [27]

snack shop *taberna, -ae* f. [2]

snatch *rapiō, rapere, rapuī, raptum* [20]

so *ita* [22], *tam* [11]

so great *tantus, -a, -um* [28]

so many *tot* indeclinable adj. [40]

so much *tantus, -a, -um* [28]

so much (as) *tam* [11]

so that *ut* [31]

soft *lēnis, lēne* [27]

soldier *mīles, mīlitis* m. [23]

some *nōnnūllī, -ae, -a* [9]

some . . . others . . . . *aliī . . . aliī* [31]

someday *aliquandō* [26]

someone, something *aliquis, aliquid* n. [18]

sometimes *aliquandō* [26]

somewhat *paulō* [25]; *paulum* [28]

son *fīlius, -iī* m. [4]

song *carmen, carminis* n. [17]

son-in-law *gener, generī* m. [30]

soon *mox* [9]

sound *sonitus, -ūs* m. [24]

source *orīgō, originis* f. [38]

space *spatium, -iī* n. [28]

spare *parcō, parcere, pepercī/parsī/parcuī, parsūrus* (+ dat.) [12]

speak *loquor, loquī, locūtus sum* [24]

speak out *ēloquor ēloquī, ēlocūtus sum* [24]

special *praecipuus, -a, -um* [27]

spectator *spectātōr, spectātōris* m. [24]

speech *lingua, -ae* f. [33]; *ōrātiō, ōrātiōnis* f. [16]

stand *stō, stāre, stetī, statum* [5]

stand out from *praestō, praestāre, praestitī, praestitum/praestātum* (+ dat.) [10]

stand still *constō, constāre, constitī, constātum* [10]; *sistō, sistere, stetī/stitī, statum* [8]

statue *imāgō, -inis* f. [40]

stay *maneō, manēre, mansī, mansum* [23]

stay behind *remaneō, remanēre, remansī* [40]

step *gradus, -ūs* m. [24]

still (adj.) *tranquillus, -a, -um* [31]

still (adv.) *adhūc* [30]; *etiam* [17]

stillness *silentium, -iī* n. [23]; *tranquillitās, -tātis* f. [31]

storm *tempestās, tempestātis* f. [36]

story *fābula, -ae* f. [9]

stranger *hospes, hospitis* m. [26]; *hostis, hostis* m./f. [14]

street *via, -ae* f. [5]

strength *vīs, vis* f. [21]

strike *pulsō* (1) [23]

strong *firmus, -a, -um* [36]; *fortis, forte* [15]

structure *opus, operis* n. [23]

student (female) *discipula, -ae* f. [2]

student (male) *discipulus, -ī* m. [2]

study (n.) *studium, -iī* n. [6]

study (v.) *studeō, studēre, studuī* (+ dat.) [12]

succeed (to) *succēdō, succēdere, successī, successum* [37]; *cēdō, cēdere, cessī, cessum* (+ dat.) [35]

such *tālis, tāle* [21]

suddenly *subitō* [11]

suffer *patior, patī, passus sum* [24]

sufficient *satis* [30]

suitable *aptus, -a, -um* [31]; *idōneus, -a, -um* [36]

summon *arcessō, arcessere, arcessīvī/arcessī, arcessītum* [32]

sun *sōl, sōlis* m. [33]

support *obtineō, obtinēre, obtinuī, obtentum* [9]; *sustineō, sustinere, sustinuī, sustentum* [37]

surpass *praestō, praestāre, praestitī, praestātum* (+ dat.) [10]

survive *supersum, superesse, superfuī* [35]

sweet *dulcis, dulce* [23]

swift *ācer, ācris, ācre* [38]; *celer, celeris, celere* [15]

sword iron *ferrum, -ī* n. [22]; *gladius, -iī* m. [17]

T

table *mensa, -ae* f. [16]

take *capiō, capere, cēpī, captum* [3]

take a wife *uxōrem dēdūcere* [38]

take back *recipiō, recipere, recēpī, receptum* [31]

take care *caveō, cavēre, cāvī, cautum* [33]

take possession of *potior, potīri, potītus sum* (+ abl. or gen.) [24]

talented *dīves, dīvitis* [24]

talk *loquor, loquī, locūtus sum* [24]; *sermōcinor, sermōcinārī, sermōcinātus sum* [31]

talk together *colloquor, colloquī, collocūtus sum* [25]

tarry *cunctor, cunctārī, cunctātus sum* [25]

task *negōtium, -iī* n. [8]

teach *doceō, docēre, docuī, doctum* [35]

teacher (female) *magistra, -ae* f. [2]

teacher (male) *magister, -trī* m. [2]

teacher of rhetoric (public speaking) *rhētor, rhētoris* [16]

tease *lūdō, lūdere, lūsī, lūsum* [30]

tell *nārrō* (1) [14]

ten *decem* [12]

terrible *horribilis, horribile* [37]; *terribilis, terribile* [27]

terrific! *eugae/euge/eugepae* [36]

terrified *perterritus, -a, -um* [21]

territory *fīnēs, fīnium* m. pl. [14]

test *temptō* (1) [32]

than *ac* [33]; *quam* [10]

thankful *grātus, -a, -um* [23]

thanks *grātiae, -ārum* f. pl. [19]

that man *ille, illīus* [17]

that not (with subj. "from X'ing") *quīn* [39]

that not *nē* [31]

that one of yours *iste, ista, istud* (derogatory) [17]

that thing *illud, illīus* [17]

that woman *illa, illīus* [17]

their own *suus, -a, -um* [9]

themselves *suī, sibi, sē, sē* [21]

themselves (emphatic) *ipsī, ipsae, ipsa* [17]

then *posteā* [30]; *tum* [20]; *tunc* [3]

there *ibi* [21]; *illīc* [8]; (to) there *illūc* [36]

therefore *ergō* [8]; *igitur* [20]; *itaque* [20]

they *eī, eae, ea* [17]; *illī, illae, illa* [17]

thin *rārus, -a, -um* [27]

thing *rēs, reī* f. [24]

think *arbitror, abitrārī, arbitrātus sum* [37]; *cogitō* (1) [10]; *opīnōr, opīnārī, opīnātus sum* [30]

third *tertius, -a, -um* [38]

thirsty (be) *sitiō, sitīre, sitīvī/sitiī* [31]

this *hic, haec, hoc* [19]

those *illī, illae, illa* [17]

three times *ter* [36]

three *trēs, tria* [6]

through *per* (+ acc.) [5]

throw *iaciō, iacere, iēcī, iactus* [22]

thus *ita* [22]; *sīc* [11]

tier (of a theater) *gradus, -ūs* m. [24]

time *hōra, -ae* f. [8]; *tempestās, tempestātis* f. [36]; *tempus, temporis* n. [13]

tired *fessus, -a, -um* [8]

tiresome *molestus, -a, -um* [29]

to *ad* (+ acc.) [2, 5]

to me *mihi* [1]

to this place *hūc* [36]

to this point *adhūc* [30]

to you *tibi* [1]

today *hodiē* [4]

toga *toga, -ae* f. [33]

together *simul* [24]

token *signum, -ī* n. [38]

tomorrow *crās* [6]

tongue *lingua, -ae* f. [33]

too (also) *etiam* [17]

too late *sērius* [17]

too, too much *nimium* [16]

tool *instrūmentum, -ī* n. [27]

touch *tangō, tangere, tetigī, tactum* [32]

toward *ad* (+ acc.) [2, 5]

town *oppidum, -ī* n. [28]

tranquility *silentium, -iī* n. [23]

transport *transportō* (1) [27]

treasurer *quaestūra, -ae* f. [36]

tree *arbor, arboris* f. [29]

tremble *tremō, tremere, tremuī* [34]

triclinium *trīclīnium, -iī* n. [26]

troops *agmen, agminis* n. [40]; *vīrēs, vīrium* f. pl. [21]

trouble *difficultās, -tātis* f. [23]

trouble greatly *perturbō* (1) [26]

troublesome *molestus, -a, -um* [29]

true *vērus, -a, -um* [15]

truly *vērē* [15]

trumpet *tuba, -ae* f. [26]

trust *crēdō , crēdere, crēdidī, crēditum* (+ dat.) [25]

trustworthy *fidēlis, fidēle* [33]

try *cōnor, cōnārī, cōnātus est* [24]; *temptō* (1) [32]

turn *vertō, vertere, vertī, versum* [26]

tutor *paedagōgus, -ī* m. [5]

twelve *duodecim* [12]

twenty *vīgintī* [12]

twice *bis* [36]

two *duo, duae, duo* [7]

two times *bis* [36]

type *speciēs, speciēī* f. [24]

U

ugly *turpis, turpe* [38]

unbind *solvō, solvere, soluī, solūtum* [36]

uncertain *dubius, -a, -um* [39]; *incertus, -a, -um* [35]; *obscūrus, -a, -um* [38]

under (adj.) *sub* (+ abl.) [6]; *sub* (+ acc.) [6]

under (adv.) *infrā* [32]

underneath *infrā* [32]

understand *animadvertō, animadvertere, animadvertī, animadversum* [40]; *intellegō, intellegere, intellēxī, intellectum* [13]

undertake *cōnor, cōnārī, cōnātus est* [24]

undoubtedly *profectō* [32]

uneasy *anxius, -a, -um* [29]; *sollicitus, -a, -um* [39]

unfortunate *infēlix, -icis* [36]; *infortūnātus, -a, -um* [22]

unhappy *infēlix, -icis* [36]

unique *proprius, -a, -um*

unless *nisi* [30]

unlike *dissimilis, dissimile* [37]

unlucky *infortūnātus, -a, -um* [22]

until *dōnec* [27]; *dum*

urge *hortor, hortārī, hotātus sum* [33]

us *nōs, nōstrum/nōstrī, nōbīs, nōs, nōbīs* [21]

use *ūtor, ūtī, ūsus sum* (+ abl.) [24]

use up *consūmō, consūmere, consumpsī, consumptum* [38]

useful *utilis, utile* [30]

utterly *omnīnō* [32]

V

value *aestimō* (1) [38]

vanish *pereō, perīre, perīvī/periī, peritum* [32]

various *varius, -a, -um* [30]

verse *versus, -ūs* m. [27]

very (much) *valdē* [11]

very frightened *perterritus, -a, -um* [21]

very happy *perlaetus, -a, -um* [27]

victor *victor, victōris* m. [35]

victory *victōria, -ae* f. [35]

vigorously *strēnuē* [26]

violent *ācer, ācris, ācre* [38]

voice *vox, vōcis* f. [15]

voyage *cursus, -ūs* m. [35]

W

wage war *bellum gerere* [23]

wait for *exspectō* (1) [16]

wake up *expergiscor, expergiscī, experrectus sum* [32]

walk *ambulō* (1); *cēdō, cēdere, cessī, cessum* (+ dat.) [35]

wall *mūrus, -ī* m. [28]

wallet *saccus, -ī* m. [11]

want to *cupiō, cupere, cupīvī/cupiī, cupītum* [4]; *volō, velle, voluī* [7]

wants (he, she, it) *vult* [5]

war *bellum, -ī* n. [23]

warm *calidus, -a, -um* [33]

warn *moneō, monēre, monuī, monitum* [33]

wash *lavō, lavāre, lāvī, lautum/lavātum/lōtum* [31]

watch *custōdiō, custōdīre, custōdīvī/custōdiī, custōditum* [30]; *spectō* (1) [10]

watch over *tueor, tuērī, tuitus sum* [29]

water *aqua, -ae* f. [2]

way *via, -ae* f. [5]

we *nōs* [21]

wealth *fortūna, -ae* f. [33]

weather *tempestās, tempestātis* f. [36]

well (adj.) *salvus, -a, -um* [16]

well (adv.) *bene* [4]

well! *age* [36]

what? *quid* [1, 18]

whatever *quisquis, quodquod/quicquod/quidquid* [40]

what kind of? what sort of? *qualis, quale?* [34]

when *cum* [15]; *quandō* [29]; *ubi* [5]

where *ubi* [5]

whereby, wherefore *quārē* [30]

whether *an* [39]

which *quī, quae, quod* [18]

while *dum* [10]

who *quī, quae, quod* [18]

who? *quis* [1, 18]

whoever, whatever *quisquis, quodquod/quicquod/ quidquid* [40]

whole *tōtus, -a, -um* [17]

why *cūr* [11]; *quārē* [30]; *quā dē causā* [34]

why not? *quīn* [39]

wide *lātus, -a, -um* [31]

wife *uxor, uxōris* f. [18]

willing *libens, libentis*

wind *ventus, -ī* m. [36]

wine *vīnum, -ī* n. [3]

wish *cupiō, cupere, cupīvī/cupiī, cupitum* [4]; *optō* (1); *volō, velle, voluī* [7]

with *apud* (+ acc.) [16]; *cum* (+ abl.) [6]

within *intrā* (+ acc.) [25]

without *sine* (+ abl.) [6]

without question *profectō* [32]

withstand *sustineō, sustinere, sustinuī, sustentum* [37]

woe! (in pain or dread) *vae* (often + dative) [36]

woman *fēmina, -ae* f. [2]

woman in charge *domina, -ae* f. [25]

woman (old) *anus, -ūs* f.

wonder at *admīror, admīrārī, admīrātus sum* [26]; *mīror, mīrārī, mīrātus sum* [25]

woods *silva, -ae* f. [21]

word *verbum, -ī* n. [11]

work (n.) *labor, labōris* m.; *opera, -ae* f. [36]; *opus, operis* n. [23]

work (v.) *labōrō* (1) [9]

workman *faber, fabrī* m. [28]

workshop *fabrica, -ae* f. [37]; *officīna, -ae* f. [34]

world *orbis terrārum* [20]

worse *pēior, pēius* [19]

worst *pessimus, -a, -um* [20]

worthiness *dignitās, -tātis* f. [35]

worthy *honestus, -a, -um* [29]

would that! *utinam* [37]

wound *vulnerō* (1) [22]

wound *vulnus, vulneris* n. [22]

wretched *miser, misera, miserum* [35]

write *scrībō, scrībere, scripsī, scriptum* [6]

writer *scriptor, -ōris* m. [27]

Y

year *annus, -ī* m. [12]

years old *annōs nātus, -a, -um* [12]

yes *ita* [22]; *sīc* [11]

yesterday *heri* [19]

yet *adhūc* [30]; *at* [20]; *atque* [20] *quamquam*

yield to *cēdō, cēdere, cessī, cessum* (+ dat.) [35]

you (all) *vōs, vestrum, vōbīs, vōs, vōbīs* [21]

you (all) *vōbīs* (dat./abl.) [17]

you (sing.) *tū* [3]

your (sing.) *tuus, -a, -um* [6]; (pl.) *vester, vestra, vestrum* [6]

your *tibi* [1]

youth *adulescens, -entis* m./f. [15]; *iuvenis, iuvenis* m./f. [15]

Z

zeal *studium, -iī* n. [6]

Maps

From *Disce! An Introductory Latin Course, volume 2*, First Edition. Francesco Bonavita. Copyright © 2011 by Pearson Education, Inc. Published by Pearson Prentice Hall. All rights reserved.

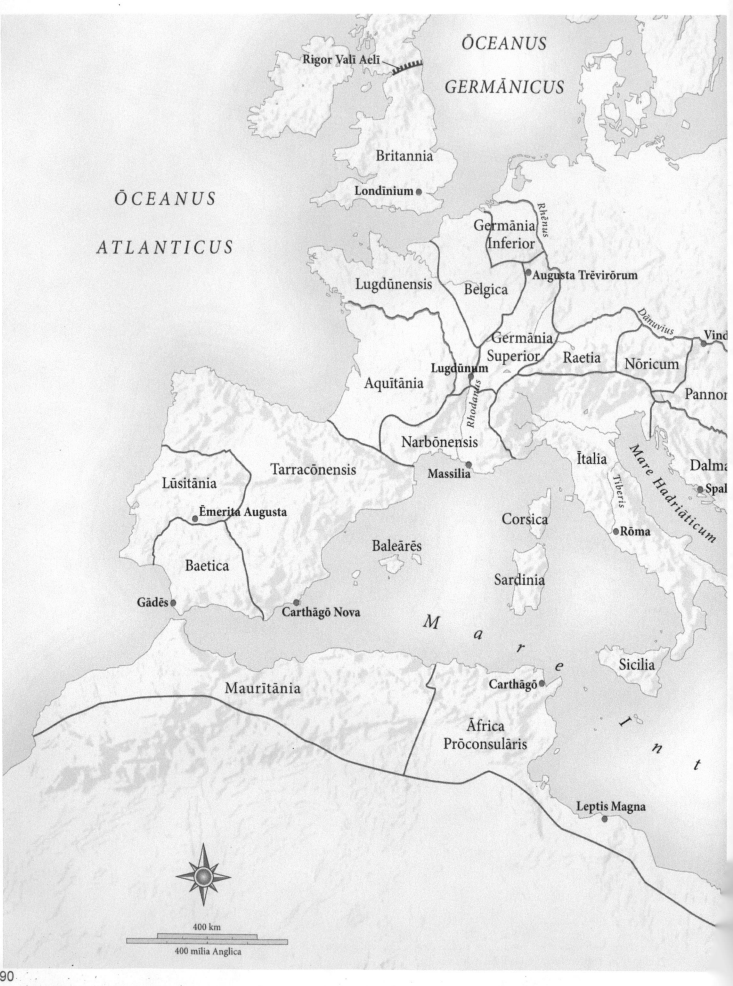

ŌCEANUS
GERMĀNICUS

Rigor Valī Aelī

ŌCEANUS

ATLANTICUS

Britannia

Londīnium •

Germānia
Inferior

Rhēnus

Lugdūnensis

Belgica

Augusta Trēvirōrum

Germānia
Superior

Dānuvius

Vind

Aquītānia

Lugdūnum

Raetia

Nōricum

Pannon

Narbōnensis

Ītalia

Dalma

Tarracōnensis

Massilia

Mare Hadriāticum

Spal

Lūsitānia

Ēmerita Augusta

Corsica

Tiberis

Baleārēs

Rōma

Baetica

Sardinia

Gādēs •

Carthāgō Nova

M
a
r
e

Maurītānia

Sicilia

Carthāgō

Āfrica
Prōconsulāris

I
n
t

Leptis Magna

400 km

400 mīlia Anglica

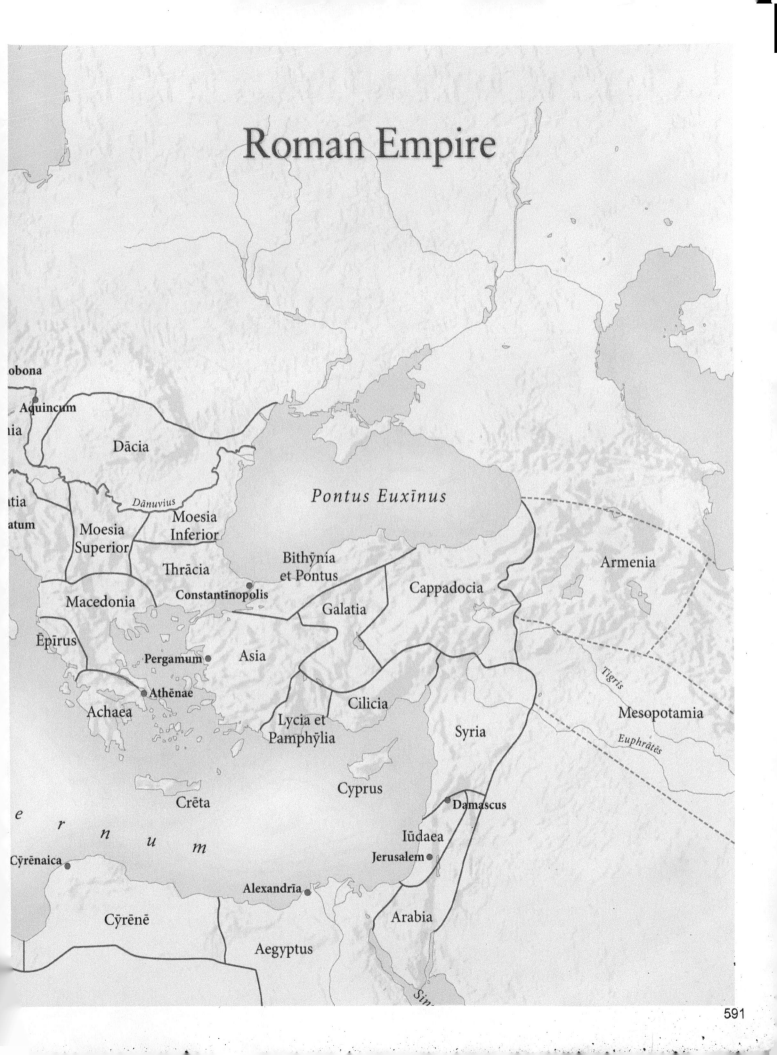

Roman Empire

obona

Aquincum

Dācia

Dānuvius

Moesia
Inferior

Moesia
Superior

Thrācia

Macedonia

Constantīnopolis

Ēpīrus

Pergamum

Asia

Athēnae

Achaea

Lycia et
Pamphȳlia

Bithȳnia
et Pontus

Galatia

Pontus Euxīnus

Cappadocia

Cilicia

Armenia

Tigris

Mesopotamia

Euphrātēs

Syria

Crēta

Cyprus

Damascus

Iūdaea

Jerusalem

e   r   n   u   m

Cȳrēnaica

Alexandrīa

Arabia

Cȳrēnē

Aegyptus

Sin

Imperial Rome

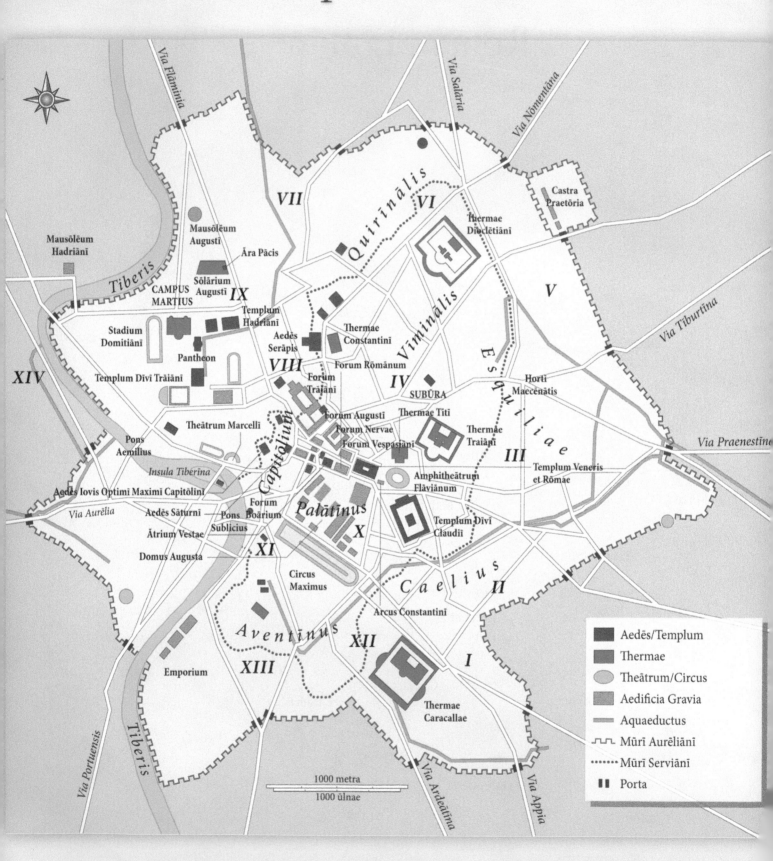

Ancient Italy

Mediolānum

Gallia
Cisalpīna

Venetia
Aquilēia

Vērōna

Padus

Liguria

A
p
p
e
n
n
ī
n
ī

Ravenna

Umbria

Pīsae

Etrūria

Tiberis

Ancōn

Picēnum

Sabīnī

Marsī

Frentānī

Rōma

Ostia

Latium

Lūceria

Samnium

Capua

Āpūlia

Neāpolis
Vesuvius

Brundisium

Campānia

Calabria

Lūcānia

Corsica

Mare
Hadriàticum

Dalmatia

Mare Tyrrhēnum

Sardinia

Bruttium

Crotōn

Mare
Internum

M
a
r
e
I
n
t
e
r
n
u
m

Sicilia

Aetna

Syrācūsae

100 km

100 mīlia Anglica

, 85

, 85, 115, 139, 197, 238, 281, 313, 445

, 183, 313

st conjugation verbs, 66, 70-71

-1-2 adjectives, 174, 177, 179, 189, 204, 208,
        235-236, 285, 289, 326, 419, 519
nd conjugation future, 217-218, 321
nd conjugation verbs, 65, 71
nd declension -er words, 187

rd conjugation future, 218-219, 222
rd conjugation verbs, 71, 98, 306, 482
rd declension adjectives, 202, 204-206, 208-209,
        212, 231, 273-274, 520, 523
rd declension adverbs, 202, 209
rd declension i-stem noun, 291, 381, 513
rd declension i-stems, 187, 191, 193, 198, 517
rd declension words, 191
rd person endings, 50

th conjugation future, 219
th conjugation verbs, 71, 94, 97-99, 218, 244, 306
th principal part, 66, 368-369, 371, 385, 391, 401

a, 21, 26, 33, 36, 40-41, 46, 53, 61, 64-66, 70, 75-76,
        80, 83, 86, 95, 100-101, 103, 108-109, 111,
        115, 117, 120, 122-125, 127, 130, 132,
        134-136, 138, 140, 175, 177, 179, 181, 185,
        188, 192, 195-196, 198-199, 203-204, 207,
        210, 213, 217, 221, 223-224, 227, 230,
        234-235, 238, 240, 243, 246, 248, 251, 253,
        271-274, 277, 280, 282, 287, 289, 291, 293,
        296, 299, 305, 309, 311-312, 315, 319, 322,
        325-326, 328, 331, 337, 341, 345-346, 353,
        356, 359-360, 364, 370-371, 375, 378, 382,
        387-391, 393-394, 396-397, 401, 403-404,
        407-408, 411, 413, 417, 419, 423, 427,
        430-431, 437, 444, 447, 453-454, 459,
        461, 464, 469-470, 474-475, 478-479, 487,
        491, 496, 501-502, 507, 509, 511-513,
        521-523, 526, 532-534, 536-537, 540-542,
        543-572, 573-588
ab, 64-65, 70, 78, 95-96, 103, 116, 120, 196, 210,
        218-219, 223, 226-227, 230, 233, 242, 286,
        303-305, 307-310, 314, 322, 324, 336, 340,
        348, 353-354, 356, 363, 368, 370, 386,
        389-390, 402, 404, 407-408, 412, 429, 436,
        440, 453, 458, 482, 486, 502, 506, 543,
        574-576, 578-579
abbreviations, 12, 22-23, 25, 68, 138, 323
abhinc from here, 341, 543
abit (he goes away), 96
ablative absolute (AA), 373, 375-376
        without participles, 376
ablative case, 63, 74-77, 86-87, 113, 129, 307, 373,
        375-376
ablative of accompaniment, 87
ablative of agent, 302-303, 307-308, 406
ablative of manner, 77, 87
ablative of means, 77, 87, 302-303, 307-308
ablative of time when, 113
ablative of time within which, 113
ablative phrases, 77, 86, 308
        without prepositions, 86
ablative plural, 76, 232
ac and, and besides, 543

accusative case, 30, 32, 36-37, 63, 65, 77, 113, 126,
        421, 435, 438
accusative endings, 30, 32
accusative of duration of time, 113
accusative of extent of time, 113
accusative of time, 113
Acrisius, 187-189, 196, 543
Actiacus, -a, -um of Actium, 543
active voice, 303, 391, 413
ad (+ acc.) to, toward, 543
Ad quem locum fugis? To what place are you fleeing?,
        248
ad sinistram to the left, 18, 543
Adagia (Adages), 493
adeps, adipis m./f. Fat, 543
adit (he goes to), 96
adjective, 10, 22, 32, 34, 54, 81, 87, 118, 122, 124,
        133, 177-180, 186, 189-190, 194-195,
        198-199, 202, 204-209, 212-213, 229, 233,
        235, 247, 271-274, 285, 289-290, 326, 330,
        369, 373, 375-376, 382, 387, 392, 396-397,
        419-420, 439, 441, 454, 475, 503, 513,
        523-524, 543, 573
adjectives, 10, 21, 32, 34, 36, 40, 119, 122-124, 128,
        129, 133, 136, 141, 174, 177, 179, 187,
        189-190, 198, 202, 204-206, 208-209,
        212-213, 229, 231-233, 235-236, 241, 245,
        247-248, 271-274, 282, 285-286, 289, 291,
        298, 326, 330-331, 343, 369, 371, 381-382,
        396-397, 419, 519-523
advena, -ae m./f. foreigner, stranger, 544
advenit, 22, 31-32, 64, 188, 190, 290, 370, 502, 512
adveniunt, 22, 31, 91, 94, 190
adveniunt come to, 31
adverbs, 202, 206, 209, 271-273, 279, 282, 298, 326,
        497, 523
adversus (+ acc.) opposite to, against, 544
adversus, -a, -um adverse, contrary, 544
-ae, 18, 21, 26, 31, 33, 36, 41, 46-47, 49, 53, 56, 61,
        64, 69-70, 75-76, 80, 83-84, 86, 95, 108-111,
        117, 120, 123, 125-127, 129-130, 132, 135,
        137-138, 140, 175, 179, 181-182, 184-185,
        188, 192, 195-196, 199, 203, 207, 210, 217,
        221, 223-224, 227, 230, 234, 243, 246-247,
        251, 253-254, 273, 277, 280, 282, 287,
        292-293, 298-299, 305, 309, 312, 315, 319,
        322, 327-328, 331, 337, 341, 347, 349, 353,
        356, 359-360, 364, 370, 375, 378-379,
        387-388, 390-391, 393-394, 397, 403-404,
        407-411, 413, 423, 437, 441, 443, 447, 453,
        459-460, 470, 474, 479, 481, 487, 491-492,
        496, 501-502, 507, 511, 513, 522, 526,
        543-572, 573-588
Aedēs Dīvī Iūliī, 67
aeger, aegra, aegrum sick, 544
Aelius, 2, 23, 122, 134, 226, 249-250, 271-273,
        275-277, 281, 285-287, 292-293, 318-320,
        322, 328, 336-337, 347, 353-354, 363,
        389-391, 406, 409, 439-442, 446, 457-458,
        460, 463, 473-477, 480, 485-487, 490-491,
        493, 495, 500, 502-503, 505-507, 510, 512,
        544
Aelius Maximus A. f. (Aelius Maximus, son of Aelius),
        439
aequa "fair things", 191
aes, aeris n. metal, especially copper or bronze, 544
age, agite come! well! all right!, 544
agmen, agminis n. column of troops, battle line, 544
alba "white things", 191
albus, -a, -um white, 544
Alighieri, Dante, 181
aliqua some (things), 130
aliquid some, 175, 237
aliquid something, 80, 91, 108, 135, 237
aliter in another way, 378
aliter otherwise, 91, 544
aliter otherwise, else, in another way, 544

alium another, 91
aliunde elsewhere, from another person, 544
alius another, 21
almus, -a, -um nourishing, kind, dear, 544
altus, -a, -um high, 544
-am, 33, 46, 76, 109, 132, 216, 218-219
ambulant, 19-21, 31, 36, 40, 45-46, 50, 91, 120, 122,
        124, 232, 440, 446
ambulant walk, 20
ambulat, 10, 13, 19, 40, 48-50, 75, 80, 82, 108, 112,
        122, 124, 203, 219, 502, 512
amor (love), 240
amphitheater, 184, 229, 234, 240, 311, 313, 545, 573
Amphitryon, 271, 297, 341, 545
amphora, -ae f. amphora, 545
an or, 322, 545
an whether, 217, 223, 479
ancilla maid servant, 18
Angulus Grammaticus, 1, 14, 17, 19, 26, 30, 41, 44,
        57, 60, 70, 74, 77, 86, 90, 96, 103, 107, 117,
        119, 128, 129, 133, 141, 174, 185, 187, 199,
        202, 213, 216, 228, 229, 240, 241, 254, 271,
        282, 285, 299, 302, 315, 318, 331-332, 335,
        344, 349, 352, 364, 368, 382, 385, 397, 400,
        413, 417, 431, 434, 442, 447, 451, 465, 468,
        482, 485, 497, 500, 504, 514
anima, -ae f. breath, soul, life, 545
annus (year), 240
ante in front, before, ahead; (+ acc.) before, in front of,
        545
antequam before, 507, 513, 545
antequam (before), 282, 490
Antequam Legis, 1, 17, 20, 30, 34, 44, 48, 60, 63, 74,
        79, 90, 94, 96, 107, 110, 119, 122, 129, 134,
        174, 177, 187, 191, 202, 206, 216, 220, 229,
        233, 241, 245, 271, 275, 285, 292, 302, 308,
        318, 321, 335, 339, 352, 355, 368, 372, 385,
        389, 400, 406, 417, 422, 434, 439, 451, 457,
        468, 472, 485, 489, 500, 505
Antonine Wall, 329
Antonius, Iullus, 220-221, 226, 230, 374, 393, 417-419
Antony, Marc, 211, 220, 368, 380, 444
anxius, -a, -um uneasy, anxious, 545
apage go! scram!, 545
apartment block, 123, 127, 556, 574
Apicius, Caelius, 377
apud familiam at home, 91
Apuleius, 239
aqua, -ae f. water, 545
aquam water, 20
Ara Pacis, 115
Arachne, 410, 412
arbor, arboris f. tree, 545
arbore tree, 108
arca, -ae f. chest, 545
Arcadia, -ae f. Arcadia, a region in Greece, 545
Arch of Titus, 11-12, 22-23
Argiletum, 24, 39, 64-65, 77, 126, 545
arma (pl.) arms, 125
Arminius, 511
Asia, -ae f. Asia, a Roman province in what is now
        Turkey, 545
Asia (Asia, -ae f.), 379
aspect, 17, 26-27, 241, 244, 331, 375
Assimilation, 141, 324
Astacius, 304, 309-311, 313-314
astrologus, 129, 134-135, 137, 188, 546
at = sed, 191
at but, and yet, 546
atque and, and also, and even, 546
Attalus III of Pergamon, 380
attonitus, -a, -um astonished, 546
attonitus, -a, -um astonished, amazed, 546
Augustan Italy, 313
Augustan monuments, 67
Augustus, 1, 4, 12, 23, 38-39, 55, 57, 66-68, 84, 115,
        133, 137-138, 184, 207, 211, 220, 222-223,

234, 238, 311, 329, 331, 337, 345-348, 355-357, 361, 364, 368, 370, 380, 385, 387, 393-395, 422, 427-428, 434, 436-437, 440, 444, 471, 478-479, 485, 493, 502, 511-512, 544, 546, 558, 560, 563-564, 569
aura, -ae f. breeze, 546
Aurelius, Marcus, 329, 429
aureus, -a, -um golden, 546
auris, auris f. ear, 546
auspex, auspicis m., 546
aut . . . aut either . . . or, 546
aut or; aut . . . aut either . . . or, 546
autem however, 188, 273, 279, 282, 546
Aventine Hill, 280, 410
avia, -ae f. grandmother, 546
avidus, -a, -um eager, 546
avis, avis f. bird, 546

B

banquets, 368
barba, -ae f. beard, 546
Basilica Aemilia, 39
Basilica Paulli, 39, 63
Battle of Actium, 68, 115, 361, 444, 560
be in labor, give birth, 562
bene "nicely", 378
bene well, 49, 56, 546
benevolens, benevolentis well-wishing, benevolent, 546
benignior kinder, 91
benignus, -a, -um kind, 546
bibit, 40, 49, 75, 95, 116
bibunt, 21, 31, 40, 49, 61, 91, 95-96
-bimus, 216, 218
-bis, 216, 218, 223
-bit, 216, 218
Bithynia-et-Pontus, 468, 477-480
-bitis, 216, 218
bona "good things", 191
book copier, 123, 557
Boudicca's revolt, 329
bracchia arms, 95
brevis, -e short brief, brevity, breviary, 238
Britannia, 318, 329, 477, 551
-bunt, 216, 218
butcher shop, 130, 557

C

Cacus, 280
cadunt fall, 36
Caecilia Metella Secunda, 3
Caesar, Julius, 23-24, 39, 64, 67, 100, 115, 126, 183, 209, 211, 223, 327, 331-332, 355, 361, 380, 394, 477, 479, 546-547
Calabria, -ae f. region in the heel of Italy, 546
calidum a hot drink, 21
calidus, -a, -um warm, hot, 437, 546
Callimachus, 355-356, 368, 544, 547
calvus, -a, -um bald, 547
calx, calcis f. goal, 547
Campus Martius (Field of Mars), 53, 115
candidus, -a, -um dazzling, 547
canis, canis dog, 68
capit, 25, 35-37, 39-40, 53, 61, 63, 80, 95, 98, 115-116, 126, 139, 196-197, 242, 245, 281, 304, 306, 455, 494, 528
"capital", 54
Capitoline Hill, 54-55, 115, 137, 139, 410, 547
Capitoline Museum in Rome, 196
Capitoline Triad, 139
capiunt, 40, 98, 188, 306, 455, 528
captives; tax farming redeem, redemption, 125
captus est, 386, 528
caput head, 75, 83
caput head (Martial means not only his head but his whole body), 83
Caracalla, 101
carcer, carceris m. prison; starting gate, 547
cardinal number, 325-326, 328, 526
care, anxiety, 549
carmen, carminis n. song, poem, 547
Carmina, 53, 114, 207, 230, 232, 386, 390, 418
Carthage, 238-239, 250, 411, 442, 445-446, 448
case endings, 32, 34, 132, 229, 287, 293, 339, 453, 545
case of a word, 32
Castor, -oris m. Castor, the divine twin brother of Pollux, one of the Gemini, 547

Catiline, 114, 210, 212, 223
Catullus, 174, 180-181, 183-184, 207-209, 230, 232-233, 237, 239, 380
cautus, -a, -um cautious, careful, 547
cavea, -ae f. cage, 547
celer a. clever, smart (an intelligent idea), 203
celer, celeris, celere swift, fast celerity, accelerate, decelerate, 238
celeriter quickly, 547
Celtica, 477
"CH", 6
Chaldaeus, -a, -um Chaldaean, an inhabitant of Mesopotamia, 547
Chiron, 3, 45, 74, 76-77, 81, 83-85, 90, 94, 96, 100, 116, 444, 547
Chiron, Lucius' magister (teacher), 74
cibum food, 18, 31, 49
circum (+ acc.) around, 80, 86, 547
circum (+ acc.) around [circumference], 86
Circus Flaminius, 115, 139, 197, 281
Circus Maximus, 54, 139, 197, 281
cista, -ae f. chest, box, 547
cisterna, -ae f. cistern, well, 547
cities, 85, 101-102, 119, 126, 138-139, 225-226, 239, 252, 330, 345, 379-380, 395, 411, 445, 479, 494, 511
Claudia's letter, 327
Claudius, Emperor, 251
Cleopatra, -ae f. Cleopatra, the last Ptolemaic ruler of Egypt, 548
cliens, clientis m. client, 548
clothing, 101, 124, 186, 305, 341, 370, 437, 487, 492-493, 495-496, 554, 571, 576
cenae pater, 372
coins, 11, 137, 139-140, 394
collis, collis m. hill, 548
Colosseum, 311, 345
coma, comae f. hair, 548
comes, comitis m./f. Companion, 548
comoedia, -ae f. comedy, 548
comparatives, 271, 275, 521
    forming, 275
    translating, 275
    using, 271
complementary infinitives, 90, 93
compound past tense, 110
compound verbs, 129, 133, 141
conditions, 327
coniunx, coniugis m./f. Spouse, 548
conjugations, 65, 90, 94, 96-97, 216, 218, 231, 243, 278, 306-307, 310, 320, 336, 357, 404, 455
conjunctions, 271, 279, 282, 298, 457, 490, 492
consonants, 5, 8-9, 65, 194, 324
constat see satis, 479
constitum consist of, 407
contentus, -a, -um content, satisfied, 549
continuus, -a, -um successive, 549
Cordus, 174-175, 178-179, 202-208, 210, 212, 216, 220-223, 291, 370, 376, 385, 394, 417, 419-420, 422-425, 430, 434, 436-437, 439, 443-444, 451, 457, 468, 510, 549, 559
Corinthiacus, -a, -um Corinthian, pertaining to Corinth, 549
cornicen, -cinis m. horn, 549
corpus, corporis n. body, 549
cortex, corticis m./f. skin, bark, rind, 549
Coutan, Jules-Felix, 510
crepundia, 407, 439, 549
cui to whom, 8, 196, 237
Cuius es? Whose (slave) are you?, 248
cum (+ abl.) with, 75, 86, 549
cum laude with praise, 84
cum (when), 282
cum when, 192, 203, 213, 319, 322, 479, 549
cum when (introducing a subordinate clause with an imperfect subjunctive), 479
cupidus, -a, -um (+ gen.) longing for, eager for, 549
cursum amittere to go off course, 549
cursum run [curriculum, cursor], 70

D

dabisne? will you give?, 61
Damascus, 11, 101-102, 135, 362, 549
dant, 22, 31, 34-36, 40
dat, 13, 21, 30-31, 40, 49, 116, 130, 133, 135, 207, 221, 223-224, 230, 234, 237, 240, 253, 287, 322, 337, 341, 349, 353, 356, 359, 364, 370, 375, 381, 394, 403, 420, 437-438, 453, 458-459, 463-464, 487-488, 496, 506,

517-521, 523-525, 534, 536, 543-545, 547-552, 555-558, 560-564, 566, 568, 571-572, 573-580, 582-588
dative case, 129, 132, 220, 440
dative singular, 132, 232-233, 235-236, 245, 248, 285, 289, 343, 345, 482
decem ten, 75, 108, 550
decet it is fitting, 217
declension nouns, 33, 47, 109, 126, 134, 174, 176-177, 179-180, 187, 189, 193, 208, 212, 339, 342-343, 346
    4th and 5th, 339, 342-343
declension vocatives, 107, 117
declensions, 30, 33-34, 76, 132, 136, 177, 206, 248, 335, 339, 342, 344-345
defective verbs, 302, 315
deinceps in succession, 427, 550
Delphicus, -a, -um Delphic, pertaining to Delphi (a shrine of Apollo), 550
demonstrative pronouns and adjectives, 229, 236
demonstratives, 236, 290
deponent imperatives, 355, 357
deponent infinitives, 355
deponent verbs, 335-339, 341, 349, 352, 354-355, 357-359, 365, 385, 389, 391, 400, 402, 405-406, 408, 413, 419-421, 438, 441, 446, 473, 534
derivatives, 10, 14, 17, 20, 140, 182, 188-189, 210, 213, 446, 461, 512
dictum said, 293
Dictys, -yos m. Dictys, brother of the king of Seriphos, 550
diem day, 114, 123
difficile hard, difficult, 203, 207, 213, 550
difficilis c. each, all (an omnibus tax bill), 203
difficilis, difficile not easy, harsh, difficult, 206
dignus, -a, -um worthy, deserving, 550
diphthongs, 7-8
direct object, 30, 32, 34-37, 81, 93, 95, 132-133, 198, 250, 307, 425
disposition, 123, 464, 558, 582
diurnus, -a, -um, daily, 115
doctus, -a, -um learned, 551
domina ma'am, 21, 75
domina mistress, 18, 31
Domna, Julia, 101
domum home, to a house, 551
double consonant rule, 194
double dative, 434-435, 439
duae two, 75
dulcis, dulce sweet, 206, 551
dulciter sweetly, 179, 551
dum as long as, 296
dum while, as long as, 279, 551
dummodo provided that, as long as, 551
dumtaxat only up to, 479, 551
duo two, 91, 95, 103, 551
duodecim twelve, 277, 551
dupondius bronze or copper, 137

E

ea them, 234
eam her, 45
eburneus, -a, -um ivory, 551
Ecce! Behold! Look!, 95, 130, 135
Ecce! Look!, 61, 581
Edepol! By Pollux!, 551
edit, 40, 95, 134, 304, 396, 482
education in ancient Rome, 84
edunt, 31, 40, 103, 130, 542
effectum execute, 370, 474, 481, 551
Egyptian obelisk, 115
enclitics, 44, 57
endure, await, 558
English derivatives of Latin words, 20
English infinitives, 79
English loan words, 1, 12
English verbs, 21, 70, 302, 321, 365, 371
English words derived from Latin numbers, 328
enim for, 188, 273, 277, 279, 282, 551
-ent, 216, 218-219, 231
eques, 506-507, 510, 513, 551, 580-581
-er, 46, 76, 132, 187, 189, 193, 198, 209, 235, 274, 521, 523
eram "I was", 192
erant were, 196
erit "he will be", 135
erit there will be, 120
Erymanthius, -a, -um Erymanthian, 552

Esquiline Hill, 308-309, 489, 552, 565
ess, 240
est, 4, 13-14, 17-18, 21-22, 26, 31-32, 34-38, 40,
    45-46, 49, 51-53, 55-56, 60-62, 64, 74-75,
    78-81, 83, 91-92, 95-96, 100, 103-104, 108,
    110, 116, 120, 122, 126, 134, 138, 175,
    177-179, 181, 185-186, 188, 192, 198, 203,
    207, 212, 217, 221-222, 226, 229-230, 233,
    242, 245-246, 253, 271-272, 286, 290-291,
    293, 298-299, 304, 309, 312, 319, 322-323,
    327-328, 336, 340, 348-349, 353, 356-357,
    359, 363-364, 370-371, 381, 385-392, 396,
    401-402, 404, 406-408, 410, 412-413, 418,
    420-421, 423, 427, 429-430, 436, 438-440,
    442-448, 452-453, 458, 468-472, 474,
    476-477, 479-481, 486, 490, 492, 502, 504,
    506-507, 527-529, 536, 542, 549, 552, 557,
    560-561, 569, 580, 587
Est! Est!! Est!!!, 52
Este! Be!, 80, 82
et, 216, 218-219
et and, 10, 18, 26, 49, 56, 279, 552
et even, 181
et here; "even" or "also", 461
euax! hurray!, 234
eugae! terrific! bravo!, 217
eugae/euge/eugepae terrific! bravo!, 552
Euge! Wonderful!, 287
eum him, 61, 175, 192
eunt they go, 80, 94
ex, 10, 61, 65, 70, 78, 121, 130, 135, 179, 226, 234,
    242, 276, 293, 296, 312, 324, 342, 378, 386,
    400, 407, 410, 415, 427, 440, 478, 506, 548,
    551-552, 573, 578-579, 583-584, 587
exiguus, -a, -um scanty, very small exiguous, exiguity,
    238

F
fabrica, -ae f. workshop, 552
facilis d. easy (a facile argument), 203
faciliter easily, 207, 209, 552
Falernian, 52, 375, 459, 552
familia, 1-3, 49, 56, 99, 108, 110, 117, 120-121, 182,
    217, 221, 242, 311, 319, 322, 336, 342, 363,
    389-390, 394, 417-420, 426-427, 429-431,
    439-440, 443, 446, 469-470, 473-474, 477,
    480-481, 486, 490, 507, 552, 562, 578
familia, -ae f. family, 552
farreus, -a, -um of grain, grain, 552
Faunus, 297-298
fax, facis f. torch, 552
febris, febris f. fever, 552
fessus, -a, -um tired, 553
fessus tired, 64, 91
festus, -a, -um festal, solemn, religious, 553
flagrans, flagrantis glowing, blazing, ardent, 553
flamma, -ae f. flame, 553
folia, -ae f. leaf, 553
fons, fontis m. spring, fountain, 553
forma, -ae f. shape, form, 553
fortasse perhaps, 91, 95, 120, 553
fortem strong, 123
fortis e. harsh (the cruel fact), 203
Forum Rōmānum, 25, 39, 53, 63, 115, 126, 139, 197,
    281, 494
fossa, -ae f. ditch, 553
frequenter frequently, 49, 470
frons, frontis f. forehead, brow, 553
frutex, fruticis m. bush, shrub, 553
fuge! avoid!, 224
Fugger, Johann, 52
fugiant "they should flee", 223
fuit was, 38
funeral rites, 489
fustis, fustis m. staff, club, 553
fustis, fustis m. staff, club, stick, 553
future imperatives, 486
future passive periphrastic constructions, 442-443
future passive verbs, 318, 321
future perfect tense, 271, 275, 278-279, 282, 497
future tense, 210, 216-218, 224, 227, 282, 318, 338,
    365, 377, 425-426, 459

G
Gaius, 2, 322, 368, 370, 395, 554
Gallia Cisalpīna, 183, 313
geminus, -a, -um twin, 554
gemma, -ae f. gem, 554

genitive case, 44, 46-47, 119, 121, 129, 131, 385, 397,
    435, 438
    endings, 44, 46, 129
genitive of description, 119-121, 128
genitive of the whole, 119-121, 397
genitive singular, 46, 69, 76, 81, 127, 132, 176, 193,
    205, 227, 232-233, 235-236, 285, 289, 291,
    345, 431
genitive with adjectives, 128
genitives, 45, 119-120, 128, 397
Germānia, 511
Germānia Inferior, 511
Germānia Superior, 511
gerund, 434-435, 437-439, 441-442, 447, 454,
    459-460, 534, 536, 541-542
    of purpose, 438-439
gerundives, 434, 439-442, 445
Geryon, 280
Gladiator, 6, 234, 240, 250, 304-305, 311-312, 554,
    558-559, 562, 569, 579
"GN", 6
GNC'ing and agreement, 206
go, walk; (+ dat.) yield, 547
Graecia, -ae f. Greece, 554
Graecus, -a, -um Greek, 554
grammatical gender, 136, 240
gravidus, -a, -um pregnant, 360, 554
gravis f. heavy, serious (a grave situation), 203
graviter severely, 341, 554

H
habent, 35-37, 40, 75, 219, 242, 245, 427, 458
habet, 36, 40, 46, 61-62, 75, 91, 100, 108, 177, 185,
    242, 246, 252, 291, 319, 371, 386, 410, 446,
    453, 458, 469-470
habet has, 36
hae these, 243
haec these (eggs), 130
haerent are connected with, 251
hahae hah!, 554
hama, -ae f. fire bucket, 554
haud by no means, 221, 227
haud not, by no means, 554
herba, -ae f. herb, 554
Herculaneum, 38, 462, 554
Hercule By Hercules!, 403, 554
Hercules' mother, 287
Hermes, 3, 44-45, 48-49, 60, 62-64, 67, 69, 74, 76, 81,
    90, 92, 102, 202, 500-501, 554
Hermitage Museum, 346
heteronyms, 468, 482
heu alas, 95, 346, 551
heu (often + acc.) oh! (in pain or dismay), 554
heus! hey! you there! (to draw attention), 175
Hic, 203, 272, 285-286, 290-291, 298-299, 304, 309,
    340, 356-357, 414, 458, 482, 525, 554, 586
hic this, 203
hoc this, 53, 192, 207, 554
holera vegetables (nominative and accusative plural),
    130
hominum of men, of people, 130
homonyms, 187, 199, 468, 482
homophones, 187, 199
honesta "decent things", 191
honestus, -a, -um honorable, 322
honestus, -a, -um worthy, decent, of high rank, 554
Horace, 53, 96, 114, 223, 280-281, 323, 368, 372,
    393-395, 444, 446, 554
horrendus, -a, -um horrible, terrible, 555
horribilis, horribile rough, terrible, horrible, 555
hospes, hospitis m./f., 296
hospitality, 285, 297
hospitium, 285, 296-297
"Hut of Romulus", 197
hyaena, -ae f. hyena, 555
hypocaust, 444, 555

I
-ia, 23, 193-194, 205, 254, 328, 526, 573
iacus, -a, -um Trojan (Augustus claimed Trojan
    descent through Aeneas.), 346
iam already, 83
iam now, already, 279, 555
ibi there, 192, 293, 299, 555
id it, 100
identidem again and again, 181, 555
idioms, 49, 401, 405
igitur therefore, 188, 273, 277, 282, 555

ignis, ignis m. fire, 555
III = three times, 138
Iliad, 181
Ille, 75, 181, 230, 234, 236, 240, 245-246, 248, 272,
    276, 285-286, 290-291, 293, 298-299, 304,
    340, 356, 370, 402, 407, 490-491, 502, 555,
    561, 579, 586
Illyria, -ae f. Illyria (modern Croatia), 555
Illyricum, 555
immolet "he should sacrifice", 223
impatiens, impatientis impatient, 555
imperatives, 17, 22, 37, 79, 81-82, 85, 90, 99, 107,
    352, 355, 357-358, 377, 394, 465, 486, 489,
    497, 532-533, 535, 537, 540-541
imperfect passive verbs, 308, 310, 318
imperfect subjunctive, 468, 473, 475-477, 479, 504,
    508
imperfect tense, 241, 243-244, 310, 352, 354, 363
    of regular verbs, 241
    of sum and possum, 241
impotens not being able, 254
impotentia state of not being able, 254
in diem for a day, 487
incognitus, -a, -um not known, 555
incola, -ae m./f. inhabitant, 555
indefinites, 290
independent subjunctives, 456
indicative mood, 82, 471, 526, 534
indicative temporal clauses, 485, 490, 492
indirect command, 486-488
indirect objects, 129, 132
indirect questions, 500-501, 503-505
    time after, 505
indirect statements, 422-424, 446, 503
    relative time, 423
industria, -ae f. diligence, hard work, 210
inertia, -ae f. idleness, 556
inferior, inferius lower, 556
infinitives, 79, 81, 90, 93, 104, 303, 352, 355, 357,
    388, 417-418, 420-421, 425-426, 429, 446,
    463, 508, 532, 535, 537-538, 540-541
inflection, 30, 41
ingens, ingentis huge, great, 556
inquit, 21, 26, 31, 40, 49, 61, 75, 80, 91, 95, 108, 130,
    134, 178, 192, 203, 207, 217, 221, 230, 234,
    242, 272, 276, 286, 293, 304, 307, 319, 322,
    336, 340, 353, 356, 370, 374, 386, 402, 407,
    418, 423, 436, 440, 452-453, 458, 470, 474,
    486, 490, 502, 506, 556, 584
inquiunt, 21, 26, 31, 40, 556, 584
inscriptions, 12-13, 308, 311
intellegens g. not easy, hard (a difficult task), 203
intellegens, intellegentis smart, intelligent, 556
intensives, 289
inter (+ acc.) between, among [intermediary], 70
interdum occasionally, 511, 556
interim meanwhile, 453, 556
interjection, 10, 107, 118, 227, 543, 573
interjections, 107
interrogative adjective, 290, 524
interrogative pronoun, 247, 290, 525
interrogative pronouns and adjectives, 247
interrogative words, 227, 500, 503, 506, 509
interrogatives, 241, 247-249, 290, 500, 509, 512
intransitive verb, 34-35
invictus, -a, -um unconquered, 556
invidus, -a, -um envious, 556
Iphicles, 271, 556
ipsam herself, 196
ipse, ipsa, ipsum he, she, it; they; himself, herself,
    itself, themselves (emphatic), 556
-ir, 46, 76, 132
irregular adjectives, 285, 289, 291
irregular noun, 285, 291, 518
irregular verb forms, 90
    in Latin and modern languages, 90
    possum, 90
irregular verbs, 70, 90, 92-93, 103-104, 216, 220, 222,
    226, 451, 456, 475, 536
is, 1-9, 12-14, 17-27, 30-41, 44-57, 60-69, 71, 74,
    76-79, 81-87, 90-94, 96-104, 107-118,
    119-128, 129-139, 141, 174-177, 179-182,
    184-186, 187-191, 193-198, 202, 204-206,
    208-211, 213, 216-220, 222-225, 227-228,
    229-238, 240, 241-245, 247-253, 271,
    273-282, 287-292, 294-297, 299, 302-308,
    310-315, 318-332, 335-339, 341, 343-349,
    352-355, 357-359, 361, 363-365, 368-373,
    375-379, 381-382, 385-389, 391-397, 400,

402-406, 408, 410-414, 417-425, 427-431, 434, 436-442, 444-448, 451-452, 454-460, 462-465, 468-471, 473, 475-482, 485, 487-491, 493-497, 500-501, 503-511, 513-514, 521, 524, 540, 544-545, 547-550, 552, 556-565, 567-571, 573-574, 578-581, 583-584
-issimus, 271-274
ista those, 130
i-stem ending, 459
i-stems, 187, 191, 193-194, 198, 344, 517
ita so, thus; yes, 469, 556
itaque therefore, 273, 277, 279, 282, 556
item similarly, likewise, 556
-ium, 193-194, 205, 553, 562
Iuppiter, Iovis m. Jupiter, king of the gods, 556
-ius, 109, 117-118, 233, 285, 289
iustus, -a, -um legal, 557

J

Jewish Wars, 11
Julian Calendar, 331
Jupiter, 54, 139, 187-190, 209, 271, 296, 337, 341, 349, 409-410, 437, 556, 580

K

karissima note spelling of carissima, 328
Kauffman, Angelica, 346

L

labor work, 120
lacrima, -ae f. tear, 557
laeta happy, 31
laetitia, -ae f. happiness, 557
laetus, -a, -um happy, 557
lalla exclamation; calming sound, 390
Lambaesis, 238-239, 445
lambentem licking, 196
land ut how, 346
lanista, -ae m. trainer, manager of a gladiatorial troop, 557
Lar, Laris m. Lar, a household god, 557
latericiam made of brick, 66
latifundia, 510
Latin language, 224, 349, 414
latus, lateris n. side, 557
laundry in Pompeii, 125
laurea, -ae f. laurel wreath, 557
laus, laudis f. praise, 557
leave behind, 287, 299, 566, 581
Lectio Secunda, 134
lectus medius (middle couch), 372
lectus summus (highest couch), 372
lentus, -a, -um slow, calm; tough, 557
Leptis, 238-239, 445
Lesbia, 180-181, 229-230, 237
letter-writing, 327
leviter lightly, 293
Lex Iulia, 225
libenter freely, willingly, 557
libenter willingly, 437
Library of Alexandria, 361
licet, 296, 423, 429-430, 557, 583
Licinia, 2-3, 17-18, 23, 30-31, 35-36, 40, 45, 49, 61, 75, 77, 86-87, 91, 109-111, 117, 119-124, 126-127, 129, 132, 134-135, 187, 226-227, 237, 242, 244, 248-250, 271-273, 276, 281, 285-287, 292-293, 318-320, 322, 335-336, 340-342, 352-354, 364, 385, 389-390, 405, 409, 439-441, 446, 457-458, 460, 463, 469-470, 473-474, 486-487, 557
Liciniae vir (Licinia's husband), 121
Licinia's taberna, 237
Licinius, 2, 17, 23, 250, 318, 321-323, 327, 422, 557
letter, 23, 318, 321-323, 327, 557
lingua, -ae f. tongue, 557
littera, -ae f. letter of the alphabet, 557
Lollius, Marcus, 511
longinquus, -a, -um far away, 557
longus, -a, -um long, 238, 557
longus, -a, -um long longitude, elongate, prolong, 238
loquimur we speak, 114
lucerna, -ae f. (oil) lamp, 558
Lucius, 3, 44-45, 74, 76, 81, 84, 87, 90, 92, 94, 99, 107-108, 175, 208, 216-218, 233, 235, 244, 250, 299, 302, 304, 308, 310, 335, 337, 371, 424, 427, 435, 438, 558
ludus, 45

Lusitania, 84
Lux et Pater Patriae, 385, 393

M

M. = Marcus, 322, 558
M. Aelius, 2, 23, 506, 544
maestitia, -ae f. sadness, grief, 558
maestus, -a, -um sad, gloomy, 558
magis more, 95, 221, 227, 558
magistra, -ae f. teacher (female), 558
Magna, 38, 64, 80, 87, 108, 110, 120, 134, 137, 188, 190-191, 194, 208, 234, 238-239, 272, 291, 293, 322, 356, 364, 370, 418, 445, 458, 461, 490
magna big, 38
magna "great things", 191
magnificus, -a, -um noble, elegant, magnificent, 558
magnopere greatly, 188, 287, 293
magnopere much, greatly, especially, 558
magnus, -a, -um large magnify, magnificent, 238
mala "bad things", 191
male facere to misbehave, 91
maleficus, -a, -um wicked, criminal, harmful, 558
malus, -a, -um bad, 199, 558
malus bad, 91
mamma, -ae f. breast, 558
mane in the morning, 83
manibus "with his hands", 273
manum hand, 175, 319
manumission of slaves, 90, 99, 102
mappa, -ae f. table napkin, 558
Marcus, 2-3, 23, 100, 124, 175, 191, 202-204, 206-208, 210-211, 216-218, 221, 223, 233-234, 242, 244, 250, 276, 291, 299, 302, 304, 307-308, 310, 322, 329, 335-338, 346, 363, 368, 370-372, 379, 385, 394, 396, 404-405, 423-424, 426-427, 429, 468, 490, 493, 511, 546, 558
marmoream made of marble, 66
Mars, Martis m. Mars, god of war, 558
Martial, 38, 40, 81, 83, 85, 126, 460, 463, 493
masculine nouns, 136
maternity ward, 352, 360
Mausoleum of Augustus, 115
Mausoleum of Halicarnassus, 68
maximus very great, 135
medius midway, 64
medulla, -ae f. marrow, 558
Megara, -ae f. Megara, wife of Hercules, 558
mehercle by Hercules! (as an oath to express strong feeling), 558
melius better, 108, 558
mens, mentis f. mind, 194, 558
mensa, -ae f. table, 558
merx, mercis f. a commodity; (pl.) goods, merchandise, 559
Mesopotamia, -ae f. Mesopotamia, the land between the Tigris and Euphrates rivers, 559
Metamorphoses, 114, 195, 239
meus, -a, -um my, 123, 289, 522, 559
midwives, 352, 359
mihi to me, 14, 181, 559
minor (the Younger), 23
minutia from a stem meaning "tiny", 115
miser, misera, miserum wretched, miserable, 559
miseria, -ae f. misery, 559
modern commerce, 119, 125
modicum moderately, 224, 559
modicus, -a, -um a moderate amount of, 559
molliter softly, 470, 559
mons, montis m. mountain, 194, 559
mood consolation, 451, 454
mortuus, -a, -um dead, 559
mox soon, 10, 64, 108, 120, 123, 127, 279, 559
Mt. Aetna (Aetna, -ae f. modern Mt. Etna), in Sicily (Sicilia, -ae f.), 411
mulier, mulieris f. woman, 559
mulier, mulieris f. woman, wife, 559
Mulsum, 52, 359, 474, 559
multa varia many different things, 120
mult(i)-, 213
multum a lot, 203, 217, 221, 227, 559
multum a lot, much, 559
multus, -a, -um much; (pl.) many, 559
mundus, -a, -um clean, 559
murmure with a murmur, growling (ablative), 83
-mus, 48, 50-51, 218
Mycenae, 223, 297, 400, 544, 552

N

Naevia, 178, 221-222, 225, 559
nam for, 64, 319, 322, 331, 560
-ne, 44, 48-49, 51-52, 56-57, 61-62, 212, 227, 560, 574
-ne asks a yes/no question, 49, 56, 560
nec and not; nec . . . nec . . . neither . . . nor . . ., 213
negative imperative, 81-82, 358, 533
neptis, neptis f. granddaughter, 182
neuter nouns, 129, 134-136, 177, 330, 461
Nicopolis, -is f. Nicopolis, city in western Greece, 560
niger, nigra, nigrum black, 560
nihil nothing, 31, 36, 41, 560
nihil nothing [nihilism], 41
nimis too much, 375, 560
nimium too much, 130, 217, 227
nimium too, too much, excessively, 560
nisi unless, 353, 437, 447, 560
nocturnal, of the night, 560
nocturnus, -a, -um, 560
nolle prosequi, 101
nolo contendere, 101-102
nominative case, 30, 32, 36-37, 117, 126, 442
nominative feminine singular, 205
nominative singular noun ends, 117
noster, nostra, nostrum our, 123, 560
nota, -ae f. sign, word, 560
noun, 10-11, 13, 30, 32, 34, 41, 46-47, 54, 63, 76, 81, 87, 94, 103, 117, 128, 134, 136, 176-180, 186, 187, 189-190, 193-194, 198-199, 205-208, 213, 227, 232, 240, 245, 247-248, 285, 290-291, 308, 326, 330, 343, 359, 373, 375-376, 381, 405, 420-421, 424, 434, 439, 441, 446, 454, 468, 472, 476, 487-488, 490, 497, 513, 518, 585
dictionary entry for, 47, 136
-nt, 17-20, 22, 48, 50-51, 90, 110, 136, 218, 231
num asks a question expecting a no answer, 61, 70, 560
numquam never, 80, 217, 230, 240, 279, 560
nunc now, 10, 36, 41, 120, 279, 560
nupta, -ae f. bride, 560
nux, nucis f. nut, 560

O

object of a verb, 421
objective genitive, 128, 397
objective infinitive, 421, 485
objects of the prepositions, 65
Octavia, 23, 68, 220, 337, 346
Odyssey, 181, 570
official in charge of the games, 551
Old English sentences, 41
olla, -ae f. pot, jar; urn, 561
Ollus archaic form of ille: that (man), 491
omne everything, 64
omnem all, 75
omnia everything, 123, 135
omnibus all, 130
omnis i. strong (fortitude), 203
omnis, omne each, every; pl. all [omnipotent], 213
onus, oneris n. load, burden, 561
opera, -ae f. work, pain, labor, 561
oportet (+ inf.) it is fitting that, 108
opposites, 229, 238
opulentus, -a, -um rich, wealthy, 561
opus est (+ dat.) there is need for, 561
opus, operis n. work, 561
opus, operis n. work, effort, 561
ordinal number, 325, 328, 526
Oscus, -a, -um Oscan, 561
ossa bones, 130
Ostia, 38, 60, 183, 211, 225, 241, 246-247, 251-252, 280, 313, 395, 411, 428-429, 462, 495, 507, 561
Ostiensis, -e pertaining to, 561
Ovid, 66, 114, 195, 224, 296, 368, 372, 410, 560-561

P

paene almost [peninsula], 253
PAINS words, 344
palma, -ae f. palm frond (of victory), 562
Palmyra, 101, 562
parisyllabic rule, 193
parma, -ae f. small shield, 562
participles, 229, 231-233, 352, 355, 357-359, 364, 368-369, 371, 376, 417-421, 425, 533, 53

541-542
as substantives, 232
perfect passive, 364, 368-369, 371, 376, 417-421, 536
relative time in, 232
-artum birth, 196
-arum (+ gen.) little, 111
-arum little, 120, 459, 562
-arum little, too little, not enough, 562
-arvae small, 120
-asserem sparrow, 123
-assive voice, 302-303, 306-307, 318, 412-414
endings, 302-303, 306, 318, 413
formulae for making present, 307
-assus, -a, -um spread out, dried, 562
-ater familias (father of the family), 182
-atiens, patientis patient, 562
-atientia, -ae f. patience, 562
-atrem father, 80
-atria, -ae f. country, 562
-atricius, -a, -um noble, patrician, 562
-auca a few, 80
-aucus, -a, -um few, little, 562
-aulisper for a little while, 80, 423, 562
-aulum a little, somewhat, 413, 562
-auper, pauperis poor, 562
Pellite! Banish! Drive away!, 53
Peloponnesus, 297, 400
-enna, -ae f. feather, wing, 562
-er (+ acc.) through, 64, 70, 562
-erditum esse "to be lost", 356
-erfect active subjunctive, 501, 504, 514
-erfect active system, 385
-erfect passive participle, 364-365, 368-369, 375-376, 385, 387, 391, 414, 417-419, 441
-erfect passive subjunctive, 501, 504
-erfect passive system, 385-389, 392, 447
-erfect subjunctive, 500-501, 503-505, 508, 514, 535
-erfect tense, 107, 110-112, 119, 191, 244, 271, 275, 278-279, 282, 376, 425-426, 497
-erfectus, -a, -um perfect, 562
-eriphrasis, 434, 447, 497
-eriphrastic conjugation, 448
-eriphrastic constructions, 442-444, 447
-erlaetus, -a, -um very happy, 562
-ermaximus, -a, -um very great, 562
-ermultus, -a, -um very many, 562
Perseus, 134-135, 187-190, 192, 195-196, 198, 202, 271-282, 543, 549, 562
-ersonal endings, 17, 21-22, 37, 44, 48, 50-51, 65, 78-79, 90, 92, 94, 97, 104, 110, 218, 220, 241, 306, 308, 320-321, 323, 336, 338, 455, 473, 475, 508
-ersonal pronouns, 50, 87, 104, 236, 287-289, 365, 382, 385, 397
-ersonal verbs, 37
-ersuasive speeches, 223
-erterritus, -a, -um very frightened, 562
-ets in stores, 60
Pharos, 361
-hilosophia, -ae f. philosophy, 563
-iger, pigra, pigrum low, sluggish, 563
-ila, -ae f. ball, 563
-illeus, 100, 563
-iscis, piscis fish, 68
-ius, -a, -um pious, 563
-lacenta, -ae f. a flat cake, 563
-lacet, 20-21, 49, 91, 95, 103, 130, 217, 322, 340, 348, 381, 386, 440, 458, 563, 567, 574, 580, 583
-lacet pleases, 20
-lacidus, -a, -um calm, 563
Plautus, 52, 100, 119, 181, 271, 313, 335, 339, 345, 431
Pliny the Elder, 52-53, 359, 445
-luperfect subjunctive, 500, 505-506, 508-509
-lural imperative, 81, 99, 358
-olitical office, 293, 299, 460, 562, 584
-ompa, -ae f. ceremonial procession, 563
Pompeii, 38, 125, 297, 460, 462, 563
Pompey the Great, 101, 479
-oscunt, 31, 40
-ositions, 310
-ositum put, 49, 56, 563
-ossessive adjectives, 123-124, 285-286, 289, 382
-ossum, 90-95, 103, 203, 207, 209, 220, 222, 234, 241, 244, 286, 304, 314, 386, 421, 430, 440, 453, 456, 461, 465, 475, 537, 563, 574-575
-ost (+ acc.) after, behind, 563

posterus, -a, -um following, next, 563
postquam after, 179, 188, 287, 293, 298-299, 563
postquam after, since, 298, 563
potens being able, 254
potens j. swift (an accelerant for fire), 203
potentia, -ae f. state of being able, 254
poterat he was able, 191
praecipuus, -a, -um special, particular, 563
praefica, -ae f. hired female mourner, 563
praesertim especially, 353, 356, 364, 563
praesertim especially, particularly, 353, 356, 364, 563
praeter (+ acc.) along, beyond; except, 117, 564
prandium lunch, 45
prasinus, -a, -um green, 564
predicate, 30, 34, 36-37
predicate nominative, 30, 34, 36-37
prepositional phrases, 63, 65, 77
prepositions, 60, 63, 65, 69, 74, 76-78, 86-87, 114, 127, 133
present participle, 229, 231, 233, 358, 365, 375-376, 425, 540
present participles of deponent verbs, 352, 355, 357, 359
present perfect, 295, 365, 482, 535
present subjunctives, 451-452, 455, 473
present system, 243, 321, 404, 408
present tense, 17-19, 26-27, 50, 96-97, 103, 110, 112, 116, 191, 216, 218, 231, 243-245, 315, 321, 323, 365, 377, 425, 495, 506
Prima Porta, 395
princeps, -cipis m. head, 564
principal parts (PP), 66
priscus, -a, -um old, ancient, 564
priusquam before, 80, 135, 279, 564
Probus, 304, 309-312, 314, 418, 437, 447, 564, 579-580
procul far, far away, 564
procul from far away, 207
promptus, -a, -um ready, 564
pronouns, 32, 34, 40, 50, 63, 87, 104, 177, 198, 229, 233, 236, 240, 241, 245, 247-248, 250, 285-292, 298, 365, 382, 385, 397, 401, 405, 414, 524
pronunciations, 5-6, 514
general rules, 5
Latin C, 6
Latin G, 6
vowels, 5-6
prope (+ acc.) near [propinquity], 70
prope near, 18
Propertius, Sextus, 368
proprius, -a, -um one's own, 564
propter (+ acc.) on account of [post hoc, propter hoc], 127
Ptolemies, 361
public baths, 434, 437, 443, 569
Publilius Syrus, 80, 91, 100-102
puella, -ae f. girl, 564
PUFFY verbs, 341-342
pugna, -ae f. fight, 564
pulchra pretty, 75
pullus, -a, -um dingy, 564
purpose clauses, 451, 457, 459-460, 463, 472

Q
quam, 4, 66, 95, 108, 134-135, 140, 174, 178-179, 185-186, 188, 202-203, 210, 230, 247, 249-250, 272-274, 276, 286, 290, 304, 319, 322, 386, 396, 402, 436-437, 453, 486, 502, 524, 554, 565, 580, 586
quam + superlative = as . . . as possible, 437
quam! how!, 179, 185
quam than, 95, 108, 135, 140, 565
quam which, 66
quamquam although, 287, 390, 397, 565
quamquam although, yet, 565
quattuor four, 95, 108, 130, 140, 565
quia since, because, 565
quid = aliquid some, 237
Quid agis? How are you?, 49, 565
Quid agit familia tua? How is your family doing?, 49
Quid fit? What is going on? What's happening?, 375, 565
quid what, 13-14, 224, 565
quidem certainly, 479, 565
quindecim fifteen, 565
quinque five [quinquennial], 140
Quintilian, 85
quintum for the fifth time, 565

quintus, -a, -um fifth, 565
Quirinal Hill, 55
quis = aliquis, 511, 565
Quis es? Who are you?, 248
quis, quid who? What?, 565
quis? who?, 75, 86
quisque, quaeque, quodque/quicque/quidque each, every, 565
quod a fact that, something which, 181
quod because, 31, 36, 41, 279, 565
quod that which, 100, 207
quoque also, 45, 49, 80, 108, 111, 117, 565
Q-words, 245

R
recens, recentis recent, 565
recenter recently, 507, 565
rectus, -a, -um straight, 550, 565
reflexive adjectives, 119, 122-124, 522
reflexive idioms, 401
reflexive pronoun, 289, 405
reflexive verbs, 405, 414
relative clause, 248
relative pronouns, 241, 245, 247-248, 250, 290
relative pronouns and adjectives, 241, 245
relative time, 232, 375, 423, 425-426
Remus, 54, 196-198
respondent, 34, 36, 40-41, 50
result clauses, 468-469, 471-472
rhetorical questions, 210
Rigor Valī Aelī, 329
Roman calendar, 318, 331-332
Roman Forum, 11, 17, 24, 54, 60, 64, 117, 395, 545
Roman Gods, 273
Roman laundry, 125
Roman numerals, 185, 312, 321, 325, 329-330
Roman provinces, 239, 511
Roman Syria, 101
Roman theaters, 345
Romulus, 54, 196-198, 346, 394, 566
Rostra, 39-40, 63-65, 78, 407, 566
rota, -ae f. wheel, 566
rēs, 238, 445
ruber, rubra, rubrum red, 566
Rufus, 217, 223, 400, 402, 406, 408, 412, 566
Rufus, Valgius, 217, 223
rursus again, 45, 95, 179, 217, 221, 227, 566

S
-s, 33, 48, 50-51, 71, 113, 177, 218, 344, 445
saccum, 49, 61-62, 64, 75, 78, 127, 226, 352-354
saepe often, 80, 86, 279, 566
sagax wise, 64
salūtō, salūtāre, salūtāvī, salūtātum greet, 66
saltem at least, 95, 474, 566
salutatorian, 24, 56
salvus, -a, -um safe, 566
salvus, -a, -um safe, well, 566
Samnium, 211, 225, 252, 313, 395, 411, 462, 495
sanguis, sanguinis m. blood, 566
satis enough, 95, 100, 387, 437, 447, 567
satura, -ae f. satire, 567
Satyricon, 53, 311-312, 373, 552
scholam school, 45
secunda that following first, 115
secundus, -a, -um second, 328, 567
sed but, 10, 31, 36, 41, 279, 567
seek, look for, 246, 566
sella, -ae f. chair, 567
semper always, 36, 41, 279, 567
Seneca, 53, 85, 125, 223
Seneca the Elder, 85, 223
Seneca the Younger, 53, 85
senex, senis m. old man, 567
sententia, -ae f. proverb, saying, 567
sententiae of Publilius Syrus, 100
septimum for the seventh time, 567
sequence of tenses, 271, 282, 468, 476, 488, 500-501, 503-505, 508-510
serpens, serpentis f. snake, serpent, 567
Servīlia, 425
sestertius metal alloy, 137
sex six [sextet], 140
Shakespeare's plays, 181
Short Present Stem (SPS), 97, 295, 307, 310, 320
siccus, -a, -um dry, 567
Sicily, 314, 318, 348, 400, 409-411, 477
Sidon, 101

significant, 22, 31, 100, 117, 242, 431
silenter silently, 135, 567
silva, -ae f. woods, 567
simple past tense, 110
simplex, simplicis simple, naïve, 567
simul atque as soon as, 179, 181, 192, 287, 293, 299
sine (+ abl.) without [sincere], 86
singular imperative, 81, 99, 357
sitiens, sitientis thirsty, 567
slavery, 90, 99-100, 102, 241, 250, 252, 277, 389, 427, 567
Sōlārium Augustī, 115
Smithsonian Museum of American History, 394
socer, soceris m. father-in-law, 568
somber; toga pulla a dark, 491, 564
soothe, stroke, 559
sordidus, -a, -um filthy, 568
soror sister, 108
Spanish, 38, 55, 60, 75, 85, 104, 115, 138, 195, 240, 251, 297, 318, 343, 379, 414, 554
Spanish cities, 85
Spartacus, 250, 252
splendidus, -a, -um bright, shining, illustrious, splendid, 568
St! Hush!, 305
st! shh! shush!, 120
statim immediately, 273, 279, 282, 568
stulte! stupid!, 120
Styx, Stygis f. river Styx, river bordering the Underworld, 568
subject of a verb, 30
subjective genitive, 128
subjunctives, 451-452, 455-456, 459, 465, 473, 501, 504-505, 508
 dependent, 459
 imperfect, 473, 504-505, 508
 independent uses of, 451, 465
 present, 451-452, 455-456, 459, 473, 501, 504-505, 508
submissus, -a, -um low (voice), 568
subordinate clauses, 282, 459, 468, 471-472, 501
substantives, 187, 190-191, 202, 206, 208, 232-233
Subura, 2, 119-120, 122, 126, 237, 244, 353, 469, 471, 568
summa cum laude, 87
sunt (they) are, 18, 21, 26, 568
super (+ acc.) over [supernatural], 140
superlatives, 271-275
 adjectives and adverbs, 271-273
 exceptions, 274
 irregular, 271-272, 274
 using, 271, 274
supines, 534, 536
surdus, -a, -um deaf, 569
suus, -a, -um his/her/its/their own, 569
syllables, 5, 8-9, 193
synopsis, 285, 294-296, 404
Syria, 11, 90, 100-102, 362, 380, 480, 549, 562, 569-570

T

-t, 17-20, 22, 48-51, 110, 176, 196, 209-210, 218, 224, 234, 557, 575, 577-578, 580-582, 586-588
T. = Titus, 569
taberna, 10, 17-27, 30, 32, 38, 40, 44-46, 49, 53, 60-65, 69, 75-78, 95, 107, 110, 116, 120-122, 126, 128, 195, 237, 440, 458, 460, 473-474, 485-486, 494, 506, 569, 585
tacitus, -a, -um silent, secret, 569
tacitus silently, 95
taeda, -ae f. pine-torch, 569
Ītalia, 297, 511
talia such, 120
tam . . . quam as . . . as . . ., 135
tam so, 83, 91, 279, 469, 569
tam so, so much (as), 279, 469, 569
tamen nevertheless, 188, 277, 279, 282, 569
tamquam just as, just like, 569
tandem at last, at length, 279, 569
tantum so much, to such a degree, 569
tantus, -a, -um so great, 469, 569
tardus, -a, -um slow tardy, tardiness, 238
Tarquin the Proud, 139
tax gatherer; savior redemptor, 125
Temple of Artemis, 379
Temple of Capitoline Jupiter, 54, 139
Temple of Jupiter Capitolinus, 54
Temple of Zeus, 379
tempora times, 114

tempus time, 111, 114
tentum hold, 75, 86, 569
tenuis mild, 196
tenuis thin (modifies flame), 179
ter three times, 322, 569
Terence, 100, 181, 345, 431, 487
terra the ground, 36
tertia third, 18
tertius a third (person), 120
"TH", 6
Thamugadi, 238-239, 445
Thapsus, 238-239, 445
Theater of Marcellus, 120, 338, 345-346, 348
Theater of Pompey, 115, 345
third principal part, 112
three termination adjective, 205
Tiber River, 53, 194, 196, 251, 281, 348
-tis, 48, 50-51, 218, 559
Titus, 11-12, 22-23, 138, 368, 569-570
toga, -ae f. toga, 570
toga candida, 492
toga praetexta, 355, 491-492, 564
toga pulla, 491, 493, 564
tomb of Cicero, 211
tot (indecl. adj.) so many, 570
tragicomoedia, -ae f. tragicomedy, 570
tragoedia, -ae f. tragedy, 570
Trajan, 85, 251, 479-480
trans (+ acc.) across [transfer], 70
trans Forum across the Forum, 65, 77
transitive verb, 32, 34-36, 307
transitive verbs, 34, 37, 307
tridens, tridentis m. trident, 570
tristia, 224
tristis k. unhappy, sad (Chopin's Valse Triste), 203
tristis, triste sad, 206, 570
-trix, 240
Trojan hero, 209, 472
tua your, 49
tuba, -ae f. horn, trumpet, 570
tum then, 237, 273, 279, 282, 570
tunc then, 31, 41, 64, 130, 279, 570
tunica, -ae f. tunic, 570
turpia "vile things", 191
tuus, -a, -um your, 123, 289, 522, 570
tuus, -a, -um your (sing.), 570
two termination adjective, 205
tyre, 570

U

ubi when, 36, 279
ulula, -ae f. screech owl, 570
-um, 21, 26, 33, 36, 40-41, 46, 53, 61, 64, 66, 70, 75-76, 80, 83, 86, 95, 100, 103, 108-109, 111, 115, 117, 120, 122-125, 127, 130, 132, 134-136, 138, 140, 175, 177, 179, 181, 185, 188, 192, 195-196, 198-199, 203-204, 207, 210, 213, 217, 221, 223-224, 227, 230, 234-235, 238, 240, 243, 246, 251, 253, 271-274, 277, 280, 282, 287, 289, 293, 296, 299, 305, 309, 311-312, 315, 319, 322, 325-326, 328, 331, 337, 341-342, 344, 346, 353, 356, 359-360, 364, 370-371, 375, 378, 382, 387-391, 393-394, 396-397, 401, 403-404, 407-408, 413, 417, 419, 423, 427, 430-431, 437, 441, 447, 453-454, 459, 461, 464, 469-470, 474, 478-479, 487, 491, 496, 501-502, 507, 509-513, 521-523, 526, 532-534, 536-537, 540-542, 543-572, 573-588
-um ending, 53, 134
umbra, -ae f. shade, soul, 570
Umbria, 183, 211, 225, 252, 313, 395
umquam at any time, ever, 570
umquam ever, 403, 413
unde from where, 192, 570
UNUS NAUTA forms, 235
UNUS NAUTA words, 236, 240, 285-286, 289
urbe city, 20-21
urbem city, 66
-us, 21, 33, 36, 46, 76, 109, 117, 132, 136, 187, 189, 235, 342, 371, 401
U.S. Capitol Rotunda, 394
ut as, 179, 196, 337, 378, 387, 390, 403, 407, 479
Utica, 238-239, 445
utrum whether, 571

V

vae woe! (in pain or dread), 230
vah/vaha ah! oh! (in astonishment, joy, anger), 571
valeam may I flourish, may I be well, 328
valedictorian, 24, 41
Valeria, 2, 17-18, 20-22, 24, 26, 30-31, 34-40, 44-46, 48-49, 60-61, 64, 69, 75, 77, 91, 94, 99-100, 107, 110, 117, 119-123, 126-128, 129-135, 183-184, 191, 226-227, 241-242, 244, 246-250, 252-253, 318-319, 321-323, 353-354, 388, 390, 405, 409, 434, 440-442, 446, 451, 457-458, 460, 468, 472-475, 485-487, 502, 558, 563, 571
Valeriae taberna (Valeria's shop), 121
varia various things, 120
varius, -a, -um various, changeable, 571
vastus, -a, -um huge, 571
vendit (she) sells, 18
venditor merchant, 130
vendunt, 18-19, 27
venetus, -a, -um blue, 571
venustus, -a, -um charming, 571
verb, 10, 13, 17-22, 26-27, 30, 32, 34-37, 40-41, 46, 48-51, 62, 65-66, 70-71, 74, 78-79, 81, 87, 90, 92-94, 96, 100-101, 103-104, 111-112, 116-117, 127, 132-134, 136, 139, 141, 186, 190, 199, 212, 216-219, 223-224, 228, 229, 231-233, 241-242, 244, 272, 276, 282, 292, 294, 296, 302-303, 305, 307-308, 310, 314-315, 318, 321, 323, 330, 336, 339, 342, 346, 349, 352, 354, 357, 368-369, 371, 373, 375-377, 381, 385-387, 389, 391-392, 400, 404-406, 408, 412-414, 417, 419-426, 429, 434, 439-440, 446, 451-452, 454-455, 457, 459, 464, 471, 475-476, 482, 487-488, 492, 496, 501-505, 508-510, 513, 543, 573
 ambulat, 10, 13, 19, 40, 48-50, 112, 219, 502
 compound, 96, 111, 133, 141
 English verb changes, 21
 intransitive, 32, 34-35, 37
 irregular, 70, 74, 78-79, 90, 92-94, 96, 103-104, 112, 216, 223, 244, 272, 318, 321, 323, 368, 371, 373, 376-377, 451, 459, 464, 475
 number of a, 18, 404
 present tense, 17-19, 26-27, 50, 96, 103, 112, 116, 216, 218, 231, 244, 315, 321, 323, 377, 425
 principal parts, 17-19, 65-66, 70-71, 90, 94, 141, 294, 296, 315, 321, 349, 371, 391, 406
 respondet, 10, 13, 21, 34, 40, 49-50, 242, 307, 336, 423, 440, 502
 to be, 13, 20, 37, 65, 74, 87, 92-93, 100-101, 103-104, 112, 133, 136, 139, 141, 199, 241, 303, 308, 315, 323, 342, 346, 373, 376, 389, 392, 417, 419-421, 425, 429, 440, 476
 transitive, 32, 34-37, 307
verb endings, 18, 20, 48, 219
 -nt, 18, 20, 48
 personal endings, 48
 -t, 18, 20, 48
verb tenses, 228, 292
verba words, 120
verbal adjective, 229, 420, 439, 441, 454
verbal adjectives, 231, 371
verbal noun, 81, 421, 424, 434, 439, 441, 454
verberibus with blows (ablative), 83
Vespasian, Emperor, 11-12, 138, 140
vesper, -eris m. evening, 571
vester, vestra, vestrum your, 123, 571
vester, vestra, vestrum your (pl.), 571
Vestis Virum Facit, 485, 492-493, 495
Vesuvius, 26, 52, 410-411, 451, 453, 462, 495, 554, 563, 571
Via Appia, 211, 225, 252, 297, 313, 395, 411, 462, 485, 494-495
vident, 19, 22, 31, 34, 37, 40-41, 108, 126-127, 289, 340, 348
videt, 19, 22, 31-32, 34-37, 40-41, 49, 61-62, 64, 75, 91, 95, 108, 116, 188, 191, 289, 291-292, 322, 458, 502, 512
Villa Liviae, 395
Viminal Hill, 44, 471
vine cultivation in Rome, 52
violentia, -ae f. force, violence, 572
virga, -ae f. rod, 572
vitium vice, 53
vitta, -ae f. ribbon, 572
vix scarcely, hardly, 572

vocabulary, 14, 31, 63, 70, 101, 115-116, 121, 125,
        133, 176, 184, 188, 202, 217, 238, 241, 254,
        286, 336, 346, 393, 469, 473, 496
vocative case, 107, 109, 117
vocative plurals, 109, 117
vocative singulars, 109
vowels, 1, 5-9, 19, 50, 65, 94, 97, 323, 438, 451, 455,
        475, 482
    long, 1, 6-7, 9, 50, 94, 475, 482
    pronunciations, 5-6
    short, 6-7, 9, 50, 94, 97
Vērōna, 183
vulva, -ae f. womb, 572

W

Washington, George, 12, 394-395
white; bright, 547
word order, 30, 34-35, 37, 41, 56, 81, 132, 135, 346,
        393, 410, 425, 444
word stress, 9, 44, 57
worn around a child's neck, 287, 546
W-words, 245

X

XL = 40, 322

Y

yes/no question in Latin, 51, 62

Z

Zethus, 572
Zeus, 195, 318, 379